Great Stay Guide

Australia

Great Stay Guide

Australia

 LITTLE HILLS PRESS

Text © Little Hills Press, February 2002
Photographs © Little Hills Press, 2002
or printed with permission - see Photo Credits

Maps by MAPgraphics © Little Hills Press, 2000

Editor: Mark Truman
Designers: Mark Truman and Michael Brown
Publisher: Charles Burfitt

Printed in Singapore

Australia
Great Stay Guide
ISBN 1 86315 111 7

Little Hills Press
Sydney, Australia
www.littlehills.com
info@littlehills.com

DISCLAIMER

Whilst all care has been taken by the publisher and authors to ensure that the information is accurate and up to date, the publisher does not take responsibility for the information published herein or the consequences of its use. The recommendations are those of the writing team, and as things get better or worse, with places closing and others opening, some elements in the book may be inaccurate when you arrive. Please inform us of any discrepancies so that we can update subsequent editions.

Contents

New South Wales (continued)

Australian Capital Territory

Victoria

Tasmania

South Australia

Western Australia

Northern Territory

Queensland

Index Section

Acknowledgements

A special thanks to the helpful staff at the following Tourism outlets for assisting with the production of this book:

Ballina Visitor Information, Byron Bay Visitor Information, Coffs Harbour-Tourism Holiday Coast, Eurobodalla Visitor Information, Great Lakes Visitor Centre, Newcastle Tourism, Port Macquarie Visitor Information, Port Stephens Visitor Information, Sapphire Coast Tourism, Shoalhaven Visitor Information, Wagga Wagga Visitor Information Centre,

Canberra Tourism and Events Corporation,

Tourism Victoria, Alpine Region Tourism, Ballarat Tourism, Bendigo Tourism, Bright Visitors Centre, City of Melbourne, Geelong Tourism, Lakes & Wilderness Tourism, Lorne and Surfcoast Visitor Information Centre, Mildura Rural City Council, Phillip Island Visitor Information, Warrnambool Visitor Information, Yarra Valley Regional Tourism Association,

Tourism Tasmania, Tasmania's South Regional Tourism Association,

South Australian Tourism Commission, Barossa Wine & Tourism Association, Renmark Paringa Visitors Centre, Whyalla Tourist Centre,

Western Australian Tourism Commission, Albany Visitor Centre and Travel Centre, Carnarvon Tourist Bureau, Derby Tourist Bureau, Esperance Tourism, Gascoyne Tourism Association, Great Southern Tourism Association, Kalgoorlie-Boulder Visitor Centre, Kimberley Tourism Association, Tourism South West,

Central Australian Tourism Association, Katherine Region Tourist Association, Wadlata Outback Centre,

Tourism Queensland, Brisbane Tourism, Airlie Tourist Information Centre, Capricorn Coast Tourist Organisation, Fraser Coast Tourism, Gold Coast Tourism, Mackay Tourism and Development Bureau, Mission Beach Visitor Information Centre, Mt Isa City Council, Sunshine Coast Tourism, Tourism Tropical North Queensland,

Bondi Beach

How to Use This Book

Symbols

Throughout the text you will find that symbols have been used to denote the information that follows, whether it be an admission price, opening time, phone number or web address. This will aid you in locating the specific details you desire more quickly.

Here is a list of the symbols used with an explanation of each:

- ✆   indicates a phone number
- ✪   indicates a price
- ☉   indicates opening times
- ◉   indicates a web site
- ✄   indicates an email address

Goods and Services Tax

The prices quoted in this book include Australia's 10% GST. It should also be kept in mind that many products are exempt from the tax, including basic food items.

Accommodation and Eating Out

The Accommodation and Eating Out sections contain by no means an exhaustive list of what Australia has to offer. We have tried to cater for a range of tastes and provide suggestions for your selection. They are designed to give you a basis for comparison and to act at the very least as a starting point for the planning of your holiday. All budgets from lavish to limited have been considered and included. With regard to eating out, remember that there are always cheaper meals available at fast food outlets and in the food courts of most shopping complexes; we have focused on listing only popular and recommendable restaurants. Again, the GST is excluded from any prices listed

Layout

The chapters of this book are laid out firstly by state, and then by region. The chapters work around Australia's states in a circle, beginning in New South Wales and ending in Queensland. You can access information on chosen locations easily, regardless of which direction you are heading, or what part of Australia you are covering.

From regional characteristics, how to get there, where to stay, and what to see, we have approached in detail every way a visitor might occupy his or her touring time, with the intention of helping to make the most of that limited time. The headings are clear for ease of use, and our comprehensive Index will assist you in locatating your area of interest.

Preface

Welcome to Australia.

You may be part of a family looking for a different place to enjoy that annual holiday, a couple seeking a secluded romantic retreat, an adventurous local with a sense of discovery, an independent traveller intent on trekking through the hot spots, or an overseas visitor keen to visit the famous and popular tourist drawcards. There is a part of Australia to meet every interest. This guide is intended to unlock the secrets and open up new possibilities.

An Australian journey might follow the ocean, taking in the Great Barrier Reef, Gold and Sunshine Coasts, and the beautiful beaches throughout the country. It could include tours inland, to experience the beauty of Australia's mighty rainforests and deserts. Along the way, there are also the cosmopolitan capitals and heritage-filled towns of each state.

Little Hills Press' *Australia* is designed to lead you through the best that this wonderful country has to offer.

Safe travelling. We hope your stay is memorable and enjoyable.

Australia: An Overview

Australia is an island continent in the South Pacific Ocean. It is the smallest continent and the largest island in the world with a coastline of 19,650km. Its nearest neighbours are New Zealand and Papua New Guinea, while East Timor and Indonesia are a little further away, off the north-western coast.

The country has an area of 7,682,300 square kilometres and is divided into six states - New South Wales, Queensland, Victoria, Tasmania, South Australia and Western Australia - and two territories - Northern Territory and Australian Capital Territory.

The capital of Australia is Canberra in the Australian Capital Territory (ACT). The capital cities of the states are as follows:

New South Wales - Sydney
Victoria - Melbourne
Queensland - Brisbane
Tasmania - Hobart
South Australia - Adelaide
Western Australia - Perth
Northern Territory - Darwin.

History

It was generally accepted that the continent was first settled by Aborigines around 20,000 years ago, until recent discoveries suggested that they may have arrived much earlier. They were Stone Age people, and as the country had virtually no indigenous plants that could be cultivated for crops, and no animals that could be domesticated, they neither grew nor bred their food, but survived by hunting and gathering. In the interior of the country, this necessitated a nomadic way of life, but in the coastal areas they led a more settled lifestyle because of readily available food from the sea.

Their diet consisted of animals, snakes, birds, birds' eggs, fish, insects, berries and fruits. Their main weapons were the spear and woomera (a sort of spear launcher) and the boomerang. In the hot weather, they didn't bother with clothes, but in the colder regions they wore cloaks of possum or kangaroo skin.

The Aborigines were a peaceful race, and were deeply religious. Their mythology described the creation and explained the reasons for most human behaviour. It was passed from generation to generation in stories, songs and dances, as they had no written language. The dances were called corroborees, and there was one for every special occasion from praying for rain, to mourning death or celebrating a successful hunt.

Aboriginal art was mostly linked with their religion, but sometimes it was only a form of self-expression and not meant to be permanent. Intricate bark paintings were often made for a corroboree, and when it was finished they were simply thrown away.

European Discovery

Many Europeans visited Australia from the early 1600s, but the honour of discovering the continent goes to Captain James Cook, who in the ship Endeavour sailed into Botany Bay on April 29, 1770. Two boats went ashore, and tradition says that the first man to set foot on the land was Isaac Smith.

Cook and his party continued sailing northward, naming bays, capes, mountains and islands as they went, and reached a small island off Cape York where they went ashore on August 22, and took possession of the whole eastern coast in the name of King George III. Cook called the land New South Wales, and the island Possession Island.

European Settlement

The American War of Independence in 1783 was directly responsible for the settlement of Australia, as Britain then had nowhere to send her convicted criminals. In 1779, Joseph Banks, who had sailed with Cook, suggested that New South Wales would be a good place for a penal settlement, but nothing was done about it. By 1786 the situation was critical; old ships that had been converted into prison hulks were bulging at the seams, and the government decided to act. New South Wales was proclaimed a Crown Colony and Captain Arthur Phillip, RN, was appointed its first governor with orders to establish a penal settlement at Botany Bay.

The First Fleet sailed from England on May 13, 1787, and comprised *HMS Sirius*, the armed tender Supply, three storeships and six transports, with food clothing and other supplies sufficient for two years. They carried 1,044 people, comprising 568 male and 191 female convicts with 13 children, 206 marines with 27 wives and 19 children, and 20 officials. The ships moored in Botany Bay, but found the area unsuitable for settlement because of a lack of fresh water.

After exploring further north, Philip found the entrance to a large harbour, and decided the best spot for the new settlement was in the area he called Sydney Cove. In the afternoon of January 26, 1788, he and a party of officers and marines raised the Union Jack on the foreshore, drank toasts, fired volleys, and gave three cheers. The rest of the fleet arrived later in the day, and work on the new settlement began in earnest the following morning.

Expansion

The infant colony was not without its problems. The soil, except for a small area around Sydney Cove, was found to be of inferior quality. The majority of the convicts were city people, and so had no experience in farming or agriculture. The government in Britain was very good at giving orders about what should be done, but not very good at understanding the colony's problems and giving assistance to implement solutions. They simply kept sending more convicts, putting more strain on supplies.

Nevertheless the settlement survived and grew. Intrepid explorers discovered new areas, and other settlements were established - Parramatta in 1788, Newcastle in 1803, Hobart in 1804, Brisbane in 1824, Perth in 1829, Melbourne in 1835, Adelaide in 1836, and so on.

The last convict ship to reach Australia arrived in Fremantle on January 9, 1868.

In the 1850s, the discovery of gold brought a huge influx of migrants from all over the world in search of their fortune. Australia's population increased from a little over 400,000 to more than a million in ten years.

Federation

The campaign to form a federation of the colonies began on October 24, 1889, with a speech by Sir Henry Parkes, known as the Father of Federation, at Tenterfield. The movement grew rapidly under his leadership, and there was a meeting of colonial leaders early in 1890 and a convention in March 1891 in Sydney. Parkes died in April, 1896, and the reins were taken over by Edmund Barton, barrister and statesman. A second convention was held at Adelaide in March 1897, and a third conference in January 1898, when a draft constitution was accepted. The next step was to hold referendums in the various colonies. The first, in 1898, was defeated. The second, in 1899, saw the five eastern colonies vote in favour of federation and Western Australia abstain.

Barton then headed a delegation to London, where various objections raised by the Colonial Office were overruled. Western Australia agreed to join in after receiving a promise that a transcontinental railway would be built to link Perth with the east coast. On July 9, 1900, Queen Victoria gave her assent to the act which would unite the six colonies into a Commonwealth.

The Commonwealth of Australia was proclaimed and the first Governor-General, the Earl of Hopetoun, was sworn in at a ceremony in Centennial Park, Sydney, on January 1, 1901. About 60,000 people were present. On May 9, in the Exhibition Hall, Melbourne, the Duke of York (later King George V) officially opened the first parliament. The first Prime Minister was Edmund Barton.

In 1910, competitive designs were invited for the federal capital, to be built on a site of 2356 sq km, about 240km south-west of Sydney. The competition was won by Walter Burley Griffin, and after much discussion, it was decided to call the capital Canberra, an Aboriginal name for 'meeting place'. The first Parliament House, which was always considered to be a temporary building, was opened by the Duke and Duchess of York (later King George VI and Queen Elizabeth) in 1927. The present Parliament House was opened by Queen Elizabeth II in 1988.

Australians fought in World Wars I and II, Korea and Vietnam. The nation has lost over 100,000 in war this century, and of these, 60,000 were casualties of the first World War.

The legal system, public service and government structure of Australia are English-based.

Population

During the 1950s and 1960s, people wishing to migrate from Europe and the United States were provided with assisted passage by the Australian government. However, it was not until the late 1960s that restricted entry to Australia from Asia was eased. In the last 40 years Australian society has undergone a tremendous change with now one in four people being a migrant or the child of a migrant.

Australia since the 1970s has become aware of its presence in South-east Asia. The countries of the region are starting to have more of an impact on Australian life. Many new migrants are Asian, and society reflects this blend of European and Asian cultures.

Approximately 85 per cent of the 18,783,600 inhabitants live in urban areas. The east coast of Australia is the most populous because of the fertile plain east of the Great Dividing Range of mountains. The major cities are the state capitals, and the most populous state is New South Wales with 6,173,000 people, followed by Victoria with 4,533,300 people.

The social environment is heavily influenced by the US media and movies. California has a lot in common with Australia's east coast.

Language

Australians speak English, although due to the many people from other countries that have come to live in the country, it is not unusual to hear conversations in other languages when travelling by public transport. Melbourne, for instance, has the second largest Greek population of any city in the world, surpassed only by Athens.

Like the English, Australians call 'gas' petrol and 'fries' chips; but you will find links to the US are perhaps stronger, with McDonalds, Pizza Hut and KFC firmly established in every suburb. There are a few words and phrases that are unique to Australia and in common usage, and dictionaries of Australian slang are available at local bookshops. Australians do say "G'Day", and if stressing authenticity or the truth of a statement, they might say that something is "fair dinkum" or "dinky-di".

There is not much difference between the accents of people from different states, although the pronunciation of particular words sometimes makes the distinction clear. For example, New South Welshmen say the place where a king lives is a 'carsel', but Victorians say it is a 'cassel'. People who live in the cities tend to speak much more quickly than those in isolated areas, and this becomes quite noticeable when travelling in the Outback.

Religion

The vast majority of Australians belong to the Christian Churches. There is only a slight margin between Roman Catholics and Anglicans, whose numbers hover around 26% each, reflecting the influence of migrating Irish and Italian Catholics, and the steady flow of English Anglicans into the country. All other religions and sects are present in Australia. Jews, Hindus and Buddhists are all represented strongly on account of the post World War II influx and other political developments since, which opened access to Australian shores. By and large there is peaceful coexistence, and the multicultural composition of society is typically celebrated and embraced.

Holidays

Christmas, New Year and Anzac Day (April 25) are the only holidays that are held at the same time throughout the country. Easter is a moveable feast that can fall in either March or April. Australia Day is accepted by all as January 26, but some states have their public holiday on the exact day, and others choose the closest Monday, so as to have a long weekend break.

The whole of Australia stops for five minutes on the first Tuesday in November for the running of the Melbourne Cup horse race, but only people living in Melbourne have the day off work.

In addition, school holidays are different in each state, although the long Christmas break is the most popular holiday time, and runs roughly from the end of the second week in December to the end of January.

It is a good idea to check with the Visitor Information Centres in the cities and towns before or upon arrival, as prices and availability of services will be affected on public holidays.

Overseas Visitors

Entry Regulations

All travellers to Australia need a valid passport, and visitors of all nationalities, except New Zealand, must obtain a visa before arrival. These are available at Australian Embassies, High Commissions and Consular offices listed in local telephone directories. No vaccinations are required.

Before you land you will be given immigration forms as well as Customs and Agriculture declarations. As a general rule you must declare all goods of plant or animal origin. Quarantine officers will inspect these items and return them to you if no disease or pest risk is involved. Even if they are not prohibited, some may need to be treated before being allowed entry.

Each incoming traveller over the age of 18 years is allowed duty free goods to the value of $400, plus 1125mL of liquor and 250g of tobacco products. These items must not be intended for commercial purposes and you must carry them with you through customs.

Exit Regulations

There is a Passenger Movement

Charge or Departure Tax of $30 for everyone over the age of 12 years, but this is generally prepaid with inclusion in the price of an airline ticket. People taking money out of the country, above the value of A$10,000 in Australian and/or foreign currency, must file a report with Customs. For more information on Customs or Quarantine Regulations, visit the following web sites:

👁www.aqis.gov.au for Quarantine
👁www.customs.gov.au for Customs

GST Refund

Overseas visitors qualify for a part refund of any GST they pay for items bought in Australia, if the total purchases made at any one business exceeds $300, and the purchases were made no more than 30 days before the date of departure. Present the goods, a tax invoice, your passport and a boarding pass at the TRS (Tax Refund Scheme) booth in the international airport you are leaving from. The items on which you are allowed to claim back GST are only the hand-held items you intend to carry with you onto the plane. Present your documents for verification and you will be given the refund to which you are entitled. If the total is less than $200 you can ask for the refund to be made in cash, otherwise it will be in the form of a mailed cheque or a credit arrangement. Foreign currency will also be accommodated in this transaction. Note that any general consumption purchases made within Australia (for example, hotel accommodation or meals) do not qualify for a refund claim.

Be aware that there is no GST imposed on duty-free items sold in duty-free stores.

For further details and enquiries, phone the Australian Customs Information Line on ✆1300 363 263.

Embassies

Nearly seventy countries have diplomatic representation in Canberra. Some missions are called Embassies, and others who represent countries belonging to the Commonwealth, are called High Commissions. There are also Consuls in the State capitals, and their addresses can be found in the local White Pages telephone directory. Following are the addresses of a few diplomatic missions in Canberra: The area code is (02).

New Zealand: Commonwealth Avenue, Canberra, ✆6270 4211.
👁www.passports.govt.nz
Canada: Commonwealth Avenue, Canberra, ✆6270 4000.
Britain: Commonwealth Avenue, Canberra, ✆6270 6666.
👁www.uk.emb.gov.au

USA: Moonah Place, Yarralumla, ☎6214 6600.
👁usembassy-australia.state.gov/embassy/
Singapore: Forster Crescent, Yarralumla, ☎6273 3944.
Japan: Empire Circuit, Yarralumla, ☎6273 3244.
👁www.japan.org.au

Money

The Australian Currency is decimal, with the dollar as the basic unit. Notes come in a colourful array of $100, $50, $20, $10 and $5 denominations, with minted coins for lesser amounts - gold $1 and $2 coins, and silver 50c, 20c, 10c and 5c.

Currency exchange facilities are available at international airports, and most banks and large hotels.

The Australian dollar tends to fluctuate quite frequently, but approximate rates of exchange at the time of writing, which really must be used as a guide only, are:

NZ$	=	A$0.82
CAN$	=	A$1.23
EURO	=	A$1.72
UK£	=	A$2.81
US$	=	A$1.96
S$	=	A$1.09
Baht	=	A$0.04

For the most accurate and up-to-date currency conversions, it is recommended that you use the simple and easy facility at 👁www. xe.com/ucc

Travellers cheques are one of the most convenient ways of carrying money when travelling, and these can be exchanged at any bank, large hotels, and in large department stores.

Automatic Teller Machines are another possibility. These machines are widely available in Australia, both in the cities and in country towns, and most are open 24 hours a day. Some banks allow access to overseas savings accounts via networks such as Cirrus and Plus, but it's best to check with your bank before departure to see if this is available in Australia.

If you are intending to stay for any great length of time, you might consider opening a local bank account. Different banks have different withdrawal limits, but it is generally about $1000 per day. All Australian banks operate this type of account.

General Information
Telephones

If you are calling any Sydney number from overseas, dial 61 for the country code and 2 for the area code, then the eight digit number. Area codes refer to states rather than districts. If calling from interstate, use the following prefix before any number you dial to:

New South Wales   - (02)
Australian Capital Territory - (02)
Victoria   - (03)
Tasmania   - (03)
Queensland   - (07)
South Australia   - (08)
Western Australia   - (08)
Northern Territory   - (08)

Public telephones are easy to find in the cities and suburbs on street corners, in hotels, shops, cafes, and so on. A local call costs 40c from a phone box, but may be dearer from the privately leased phones outside shops. Emergency calls are free.

For international calls, you can dial direct to nearly 20 countries from almost any hotel, home, office or public phone in Australia. Simply dial 0011 + country code + area code + local number. Country Direct is the easiest way of making international telephone card and reverse charge (collect) calls. Upon dialling your Country Direct number, you are immediately put in touch with your own country's operator who will then connect the call. To find out your country's number ©1800 801 800 (free call).

Newspapers

Morning and afternoon newspapers are available everywhere, with each state having their own press, as well as selling the national paper *The Australian*. There are also sev-eral local papers in city and suburban areas which have local news and advise on local events, such as *The Sydney Morning Herald* in Sydney and *The Age* in Melbourne.

Radio and Television

There is a national radio station and a national television channel, both of which are run by the Australian Broadcasting Commission (ABC). The capital cities have many AM and FM radio stations, and several free-to-air television channels. The television channels are: 2 (the national channel), 7 (commercial), 9 (commercial), 10 (commercial) and 0 (SBS, which is government sponsored and has mostly foreign language programs, with English sub-titles). Regional areas broadcast programs on these networks, so their may be slight differences in programming (eg. WIN (9) in Wollongong and Prime (7) in Newcastle). Cable television is also available.

Post

Australia has an efficient postal service, and postcards sent by airmail to overseas countries cost $1. To send a letter by Air Mail (weighing up to 50g) to the Asia Pacific Zone costs $1 and to the Rest of the World, $1.50.

Time Zones

Australia is divided into three time zones: Australian Eastern Standard Time, which covers Queensland, NSW, Victoria and Tasmania, is GMT plus 10 hours; Australian Central Standard Time, which covers South Australia and the Northern Territory, is GMT plus 9.5 hours; and Australian Western Standard Time, which covers Western Australia, is GMT plus 8 hours.

During summer, some of the states operate on daylight saving, putting their clocks ahead one hour on a designated Sunday morning in October, and back one hour on a Sunday in March. For NSW, Victoria and South Australia, it is the last Sunday in October and the first Sunday in March, but Tasmania remains on Summer Time until the end of March. Western Australia, Queensland and the Northern Territory do not have daylight saving, so at those times there are five different time zones in the country.

Credit Cards

American Express, Diners Club, Visa, Bank Card and MasterCard are widely accepted and usually signposted at participating retail outlets.

Electricity

Domestic electricity supply throughout Australia is 230-250 volts, AC 50 cycles. Standard three pin plugs are fitted to domestic appliances. 110v appliances, such as hairdryers and contact lens sterilisers, cannot be used without a transformer.

Videos

Australia uses the PAL system of videos. For the US market, tapes must be the NTSC system.

Internet General Information Sources

For general information on Australia, the best site to explore is 👁www.australia.com which is the official web page of the Australian Tourist Commission.

For phone numbers nationwide, go to:

👁www.whitepages.com.au
👁www.yellowpages.com.au
👁www.colourpages.com.au

Travel Information

How To Get There

To reach Australia from overseas, visitors must come either by air or sea. Information on arrivals is contained in the How To Get There sections of the various cities that accept international flights. Contact details for a number of major airlines is included in the Internet Information chapter at the back of the book, including web addresses which will allow you to access current schedules and fares.

Before booking a flight, it is best to shop around for any cheaper fares that may be available. Your travel agent will be able to advise. You may also be able to find a Package Tour that meets all your requirements. These save you money because the companies that organise them can obtain cheaper fares and accommodation prices, as they are booking for groups. Again, your travel agent is the best person to ask.

Accommodation

Australia has well-developed hotel and motel accommodation in cities, resorts and rural areas. A typical room is usually spotlessly clean and has air-conditioning, a private bathroom, tea and coffee making facilities, a telephone, television, and a small refrigerator. Note that some small hotels may not have a private bathroom for every room, and it is best to enquire when booking. Because of the climate, many hotels and motels have small outdoor swimming pools.

Although the rooms are often the same, there is a difference between a hotel and a motel in Australia. A hotel must have a public bar among its facilities; motels often provide a bar for paying guests and invited friends, although they are not obliged to do this. Most hotels and motels have a dining room or restaurant.

Premier class hotels include names familiar throughout the world - Hilton, Sheraton, Hyatt, Nikko, Holiday Inn, Intercontinental, Marriott, Ibis and Mercure, can all be found in Australia's major cities.

Motels have generally been developed to meet the needs of travelling motorists and are located in cities, towns and resorts, and along the major highways.

The majority of hotels and motels offer accommodation on a room-only basis, but some include one or more meals in their tariff. Enquire about any meals that might be automatically included in the room price and check whether you can pay just for the room, if this suits your travel schedule better. For example, there is no point paying for lunch if you plan on leaving before daybreak, or for a dinner if you know you won't reach your destination until late.

Youth Hostels in most parts of the country offer an inexpensive alternative for budget conscious travellers. Membership of the Youth Hostels Association is required, ©9261 1111. They have a compre-

hensive internet site showing all the hostel loctions at ☞www.yha.com.au and an email service at ✎yha@yhansw.org.au

Most towns and holiday resorts have caravan parks and camping grounds with shower and toilet facilities, at very reasonable rates. Caravan parks usually have some cabins or on-site vans available for overnight or longer stays. This is a comparatively inexpensive form of accommodation, but it usually means that you have to have your own bed linen, blankets and pillows.

Travelling Within Australia
By Air
The major interstate carrier is Qantas, ©13 1313. Virgin Blue, ©13 6789 and Ansett, ©13 1300 offer limited services. All three offer reduced fares and 'specials' from time to time, and it is best to find out what is available when you intend to travel.

At the time of printing, the airlines listed above are in the process of significant changes, so it is best to check with an AFTA travel agent, listed in the phone book, about regional flights at the time of your trip.

By Rail
Train travel is possible between Brisbane, Sydney and Melbourne,

and from Sydney to Canberra. Most towns in between are also linked, as well as those in popular outlying areas of each state. Rail Australia offers two rail passes that can only be purchased outside of Australia:

Austrail Flexipass - 8 (✪$550), 15 (✪$800), 22 (✪$110) or 29 (✪$1440) days travel in 6 months with unlimited stopovers, in economy class.

Austrail Pass - unlimited travel for 14 (✪$660), 21 (✪$860) or 30 (✪$1035) days consecutively anywhere in Australia, including metropolitan services, in economy class.

Passes that are available within Australia include:

East Coast Discovery Pass - travel one-way with unlimited stopovers in a six month period: Brisbane to Cairns (✪$160); Sydney to Brisbane/Gold Coast (✪$94); Sydney to Cairns (✪$248); Melbourne to Sydney (✪$176); Melbourne to Brisbane/Gold Coast (✪$176); Melbourne to Cairns (✪$228). Note that the above rates apply to travel in the opposite direction.

Countrylink Discovery Pass - unlimited use of Countrylink trains and connecting coaches for 14 (✪$165), 30 (✪$198), 90 (✪$220), or 180 (✪$330) days.

Queensland Road Rail Pass - unlimited use of Queensland Rail services (long-distance) and McCaffertys Coaches for any 10 days over a 60 day period (✪$286) or any 20 days over a 90 day period (✪$374).

To get the latest prices, visit the Rail Australia web site at 👁www.railaustralia.com.au/pass_rates.htm

By Bus

The major interstate coach companies are Greyhound Pioneer and McCafferty's. Tickets for both companies are now interchangeable. McCafferty's, ©13 1499, 👁www.mcaffertys.com.au

Aussie Passes: a pre-selected travel route along which you can stop off at designated points.

All Australian
Validity: 365 days
Cost: ✪$2100 full fare, ✪$1790 concession.

Aussie Highlights
Route: Melbourne - Sydney - Brisbane - Cairns - Uluru (Ayers Rock) - Adelaide - Canberra and many other outback, rural and coastal destinations in between.
Validity: 365 days
Cost: ✪$1255 full fare, ✪$1066 concession.

Sunseeker
Validity: 183 days
Cost: ✪$411 full fare, ✪$349 concession.

Best of the West
Validity: 365 days
Cost: ✪$1263 full fare, ✪$1074 concession.

Best of the East
Validity: 365 days
Cost: ✪$1026 full fare, ✪$872 concession.

Coast to Coast
Validity: 183 days
Cost: ✪$424 full fare, ✪$360 concession.

Western Explorer
Validity: 183 days
Cost: ✪$589 full fare, ✪$501 concession.

Reef & Rock
Validity: 183 days
Cost: ✪$596 full fare, ✪$507 concession.

Rock Track
Validity: 90 days
Cost: ✪$398 full fare, ✪$338 concession.

Outback & Reef
Validity: 183 days
Cost: ✪$726 full fare, ✪$617 concession.

An Aussie Kilometre Pass, valid for 12 months, allows you to 'bulk buy' the distance you think you will need to cover for your holiday, at a rate designed to increase your value for money with every kilometre purchased. Prices range from ✪$281 for 2000km to ✪$1077 for 10,000km to ✪$1975 for 20,000km.

By Road

Australians drive on the left-hand side of the road, and the speed limit in built-up areas is 50km/h or 60km/h, and on the open road up to 110km/h.

In an effort to cut the number of road fatalities, Australia has random breath testing which is carried out by police officers either from a standard police car or from what are known locally as 'booze buses'. The allowable blood alcohol level varies from state to state, but is generally around 0.05, or two standard drinks in the first hour and only one during every subsequent hour. But since body tolerance levels differ, it is best simply not to drink if you expect to drive soon after.

Eating Out

In every town and city in this guide we have included a selection of restaurants, and have stated whether they are licensed or unlicensed (BYO). Just to confuse everyone, some restaurants are both, so if you are unsure, check when reserving your table. Without going into the licensing laws of why this is so, here is a short explanation of how it will affect patrons.

A licensed restaurant has a wine list, and can provide beer, mixed drinks, ports, liqueurs, etc. Patrons are not allowed to provide their own drinks.

A BYO restaurant does not have a licence, so you Bring Your Own wine or beer or whatever. Glasses are provided, and a corkage fee (for opening the bottles!) may be charged, which is usually around $1.50 per bottle. The restaurant usually has a selection of soft drinks, mineral water and fruit juices.

A restaurant that is licensed and BYO can provide alcohol, but you have the choice of bringing your own wine (which works out cheaper), but you are not allowed to bring your own beer or mixed drinks.

Liquor stores in Australia are called 'bottle shops'. Many hotels have one, usually with its own street entrance, and there's one in every shopping centre.

Shopping

Toy kangaroos and koalas are high on everyone's shopping list, and are available everywhere. Everything Aboriginal is popular, and although it seems more appropriate to buy them in the Outback regions, they are available in the big cities in specialty shops.

Probably the most sought after articles, though, are opals. Australia produces more than 90% of the world's opals, and the three main areas where they are found are Lightning Ridge in western NSW, which produces the Black Opal; Quilpie, where the Queensland Boulder Opal originates; and Coober Pedy in South Australia, which has the White or Milk Opal.

When buying opals there are a few terms you should know:

Solid Opal - this is the most valuable, and good for investment purposes. The more colourful and complete, the greater its value.

Doublet - this is slices of opal glued together, and is of medium value. It has no investment value.

Triplet - this is slices of opal covered with quartz, perspex or glass, and is the least expensive. It has no investment value.

If your pocket can't stretch as far as a solid opal, but you still would like a piece of opal jewellery, remember that anything that is glued can come unstuck, and that condensation can form under perspex or glass. The less expensive types of opal are not suitable for rings, unless you are going to remember to take it off every time you wash your hands.

Beaches

Australian beaches are famous throughout the world, and they certainly live up to their reputation. All have white sandy shores, and rolling surf. Some offer better waves than others, and the bigger beaches are usually divided into sections for swimmers and for board riders.

The Surf Lifesaving Clubs which patrol the beaches during summer are often staffed by voluntary workers, young people who give up their weekends and holidays to keep a watchful eye out for others. They put up flags to show which part of the beach is safest for swimmers, and there are usually signs requesting people to swim between the flags. This is good advice - don't ignore it.

New South Wales

Sydney

Population over 3,900,000
Sydney is the capital city of the State of New South Wales, the birthplace of the Nation of Australia, and the largest city in the country.

It is located on the south-east coast of Australia, latitude 33' 53" south, longitude 151' 13" east, on the shores of Sydney Harbour, arguably the most beautiful harbour in the world. It is always busy with ferries, hydrofoils, charter cruisers and pleasure craft. Circular Quay, between the Harbour Bridge and the Opera House, is the ferry terminal, known locally simply as 'The Quay'. The area is always crowded with people arriving or departing on ferries, buskers competing for space, and culture buffs strolling towards the Opera House.

Australia's oldest city, Sydney began as a penal settlement clustered around what is now Circular Quay. The present city sprawls about 55km east-west from the Pacific Coast to the Great Dividing Range, and roughly 70km north-south.

The distance along the actual coastline, allowing for all the bays, is 350km, and in fact there are so many bays and beaches that even Sydneysiders who have lived here all their lives don't know every one by name, and probably haven't visited more than half of them. The ocean beaches have beautiful white sand and rolling surf.

Life in this cosmopolitan city is geared to outdoor activities, taking advantage of the long hours of sunshine and the moderate climate.

Climate

Sydney has a temperate climate, and the average temperatures are: January max 26C - min 19C; July max 17C - min 8C.

The Seasons are:

Summer - December through February

Autumn - March through May

Winter - June through August

Spring - September through November.

The average annual rainfall is 1216mm, with the heaviest falls in the period from February to July. Sydney does not experience snow and only rarely sleet, and quite often the temperature on a winter's day is higher than that of London or San Francisco in the middle of their summers.

Lightweight clothing is necessary for the summer months, and medium to heavy for the winter months. A raincoat, or at least an umbrella, should be included in your suitcase whatever the season.

How to Get There

By Air
Airlines in Australia

Sydney is the major gateway to Australia from overseas, and all overseas airlines servicing Australia fly into Kingsford-Smith International Airport.

Qantas, ✆13 13 13, is the major internal Australian airline, and there are a number of smaller ones servicing the country towns and some interstate destinations, such as Kendell Airlines and Hazelton, to name a few. Virgin Blue, ✆13 6789, are the latest carriers flying to major centres.

Airport Facilities

Kingsford-Smith is situated in the suburb of Mascot, 10km from the city centre. The Domestic Terminals are 3km to the east, and taxis and express buses connect them with the International Terminal. The large green and gold Airport Express bus runs every 10 minutes, 7 days a week and costs ✪$3 adults, $1.50 children and $7 for families.

The Airport Express also operate services between the Airport and City (route 300), Kings Cross (route 350), and Darling Harbour & Glebe (route 352), from all passenger terminals to Central Railway and return.

Bus Route 300 travels between the Airport and Circular Quay, stopping at specially-identified places along George Street, and in Eddy Avenue near Central Railway. Bus Route 350 travels between the Airport and Elizabeth Bay, passing through Kings Cross. Buses run every ten minutes to and from Central Railway Station and every twenty minutes to the city and

Kings Cross. No reservations are needed. Services run every day between, 6am and 11pm, ✆9667 3221 or ✆9667 0663. Fares are ✪$7 one way, $12 return, $4 for children under 12.

Other Sydney Buses routes that travel via the airport are Route 100 (Dee Why-Airport, every 30 minutes Mon-Fri), Route 305 (Railway Square-Airport, every 30 minutes Mon-Fri) and Route 400 (Bondi Junction-Airport-Burwood, every 20 minutes Mon-Fri, every 30 minutes Sat-Sun).

Major rental car companies have desks at the international and domestic terminals, but it is a good idea to book your car in advance - Hertz, ✆13 30 39; Avis, ✆13 6333; Budget, ✆13 27 27; Thrifty, ✆1300 367 227.

Taxis are readily available at the airport for transfer to the city, and the fare is at least ✪$25.

CityRail established a link between Sydney Airport and Central Station. It provides an efficient alternative method of transportation to the city. The line comprises four stops, running northwards from the International terminal to the Domestic terminal, then to Mascot and Green Square before joining the City Circle. Travelling southwards it connects with Wolli Creek. A single ticket to Central costs ✪$15 one-way from the domestic terminal and $20 from the international terminal. Trains operate at fifteen minute intervals between the four stations.

Sydney Airport has all the facilities expected of an international airport - money changing, information, hotel bookings, car hire, shops, cafes, bars, restrooms/showers.

International Airline Offices

Following is a selection of airline reservation and flight confirmation telephone numbers.

Qantas - ✆13 1313.
Ansett Airlines - ✆13 1300
Air New Zealand - ✆13 2476.
Canadian Airlines - ✆1300 655 767.
British Airways - ✆8904 8800.
Cathay Pacific - ✆13 1747.
Singapore Airlines - ✆13 1011.
United Airlines - ✆13 1777.

For further details of airline companies, refer to the *Internet Information* section at the back of the book.

By Bus

Following is a list of some of the bus companies that travel to/from Sydney and other cities and town in Australia. Many also offer day tours and package deals for touring the entire country.

Greyhound Pioneer - ✆13 2030 (see also *Internet Information*).
McCafferty's - ✆13 1499 (see also *Internet Information*).

AAT Kings - © 9666 3899.
Mylon Motorways - ©6056 3100.
Interline - ©9605 1811.
Firefly Express - ©9211 1644.
Murrays - ©13 22 59.

By Rail

The State Rail Authority's Countrylink branch, ©13 22 32, has XPT services between Sydney and Brisbane, Melbourne and Murwillumbah. The XPTs are fast, smooth and comfortable with air-conditioning, aircraft style seats and big panoramic windows.

There are overnight and daylight interstate services from/to Melbourne, frequent services to Canberra, an overnight service from/to Brisbane, and a motorail service from/to Murwillumbah with bus connection to the Gold Coast and Brisbane.

A **Countrylink East Coast Discovery Pass** may be a viable option if you plan to make rail your primary means of transport on your east coast holiday. This ticket offers travel one-way with unlimited stop-overs in a six month period from: ●Brisbane to Cairns ($160); Sydney to Brisbane/Gold Coast ($94); Sydney to Cairns ($248); Melbourne to Sydney ($94); Melbourne to Brisbane/Gold Coast ($176); Melbourne to Cairns ($330). Note that the above rates apply for travel in the opposite direction.

Other extended travel passes are available, and the website is ☜www.countrylink.nsw.gov.au

By Road

From *Melbourne*, via the Hume Highway (867km), via the Princes Highway (1032km).

From *Brisbane*, via the Pacific Highway (975km), or via the New England and Cunningham Highways (1008km).

From *Adelaide*, via the Sturt Highway (1427km), or via the Princes Highway (1936km).

From *Darwin*, via Tennant Creek, Mount Isa, Toowoomba, then New England Highway (4262km).

From *Perth*, via Great Eastern Highway, Eyre Highway, Sturt Highway and Hume Highway (3128km).

Visitor Information

The **Travellers Information Service** at the Airport can make accommodation bookings, and also has a telephone information service that operates seven days a week between ⏱8am and 6pm, ©9669 5111.

First stop in Sydney for all visitors should be the **Travel Centre of New South Wales**, 11-31 York Street, ©13 20 77. The office is ⏱open Mon-Fri 9am-5pm, and has numerous brochures, maps, etc, and a large and very helpful staff.

Pick up copies of all the current city information guides and you will have plenty of reading material, and good tips on what to see and where to go.

The AMP Sydney Tower Visitors Information and Booking Service is located at the top of the tower, ✆9229 7430. It is ⏰open seven days 9.30am-9.30pm (Sat till 11.30pm), and is a minefield of information for those people brave enough to take the lift to the top.

The *Sydney Convention and Visitors Bureau* has an information kiosk in Martin Place that is ⏰open Mon-Fri 9am- 5pm, ✆9235 2424.

The *Sydney Visitor Information Centre*, 106 George Street, The Rocks, is ⏰open seven days, 9am-5pm, ✆9255 1788. The website is 👁www.tourism.nsw.gov.au

There are three recommended websites that will give you additional information about Sydney's highlights, from obscure clubs and pubs to major attractions and current events.

👁www.sydneyvisitorcentre.com
👁sydney.citysearch.com.au
👁sydney.sidewalk.com.au
👁www.cityofsydney.nsw.gov.au

Independent Traveller Information

The *Youth Hostels Association Membership & Travel Centre* is at 422 Kent Street, ✆9261 1111.

For information and travel advice, there is a Backpacker Travel Centre in Shop P33, Imperial Arcade, Pitt Street Mall, ✆9231 3699.

The website for the Youth Hostels Association Australia is 👁www.

yha.com.au and their email is ✎ yha @nswyha.com.au

Accommodation

Sydney has a wide range of accommodation, from luxurious 5-star hotels such as the *ANA* and *Park Hyatt*, to small budget-priced establishments offering the basics. Something to keep in mind though: even if you opt for the lower-priced accommodation, you are still going to pay a significant amount for the quality you receive, as is common in major cities. Caravan parks, for example, are rare, and the closest you will find is in North Ryde, about half-an-hour's drive from the city centre. Simply put, if you wish to stay in the heart of Sydney you are going to have to pay for it - there are very few short-cuts.

If you are after something a little different, *Staying in Sydney* by Sam Lynch provides comprehensive details of those 'tucked-away' establishments in Sydney which offer a unique alternative to mainstream chains and well-known accommodation venues. Rates are listed and assessed by the author so that you have a good idea of the places with facilities, service-levels and an ambience to match their price tag. The information gives a valuable insight into this niche market.

Following is a selection of standard accommodation, with prices including the 10% GST, representing a double room per night, which should be used as a guide only. Establishments are listed initially by rating, and secondly from most expensive to least expensive (in terms of their base rate). Considering that prices increase frequently and without notice, listing hotels in this way will at least give you the best foundation for comparison.

The telephone area code is 02.

City Accommodation Hotels
5-Star

Even if you can't afford to stay in the places listed below, they *are* local icons in themselves, so if you find the time, have a quiet drink in the lounge or stroll through the foyer. The cocktail lounge of the *ANA* is recommended in particular for its panoramic views of Sydney from a stunning height; although here you will pay no less than $16 for a standard cocktail.

Park Hyatt Sydney, 7 Hickson Road, The Rocks, ✆9241 1234. 36 suites, 158 rooms, licensed restaurants (including the *harbourkitchen&bar*, Club Bar, rooftop heated swimming pool, spa, sauna, gym - ✪$600-5000.

Sir Stamford at Circular Quay, 93 Macquarie Street, ✆9252 4600. 13 suites, 106 rooms, licensed restaurants, cocktail lounge, heated swimming pool, sauna, gym - ✪$515-2000.

ANA Harbour Grand Hotel, 176 Cumberland Street, The Rocks, ✆9250 6000. 40 suites, 570 rooms, licensed restaurants, cocktail lounges, heated swimming pool, spa, sauna, gym - ✪$430-680.

Sheraton on the Park, 161 Elizabeth Street, ✆9286 6000. 48 suites, 558 rooms, licensed restaurants (*Botanica Brasserie* and *Gekko*), cocktail lounges, indoor heated swimming pool, sauna, gym - ✪$370-450.

Four Points Hotel Sheraton Sydney, 161 Sussex Street, ✆9299 1231. 47 suites, 645 rooms, licensed restaurants, cocktail bars, *Dundee Arms* pub, gym - ✪$315-340.

Hotel Inter-Continental Sydney, 117 Macquarie Street, ✆9696 9000. 29 suites, 498 rooms, licensed restaurants, cocktail lounges, heated swimming pool, sauna, gym - ✪$460-560.

Quay West Sydney, 98 Gloucester Street, ✆9240 6000. 132 suites, licensed restaurant, heated indoor pool, spa, sauna, gym - ✪$380-1650.

The Observatory Hotel

89-113 Kent Street, ✆9256 2222. 21 suites, 100 rooms, licensed restaurants, cocktail lounges, heated swimming pool, spa, sauna, gym - ✪$420-670.

"The Observatory is as good an example of a complete luxury hotel as can be found in Sydney. Located on the western edge of the Rocks area, the Observatory Hotel caters to every whim and caprice of its guests.

...The basement houses a fully equipped health centre including a pool with the most astonishing reproduction of the night sky. All the constellations are depicted by using optic fibres in its roof.

The Observatory is essentially an opulently luxurious hotel of the first order, every detail of which has been meticulously planned and cared for, without giving any impression of rigidity."

From *Staying in Sydney* by Sam Lynch

4-Star

The establishments below are centrally located and convenient for self-guided walking tours of the city.

All Seasons Premier Menzies Hotel Sydney, 14 Carrington Street, ✆9299 1000. 8 suites, 446 rooms, licensed restaurants, cocktail bars, heated indoor pool, spa, sauna, gym - ✪$200-350.

The Wentworth, 61 Phillip Street, ✆9230 0700. 29 suites, 384 rooms, licensed restaurants, cocktail lounges, gym, heated pool, sauna - ✪$300-720.

Sydney Hilton, 259 Pitt Street, ©9266 0610. 28 suites, 585 rooms, licensed restaurants, cocktail bars, heated swimming pool, spa, sauna, gym - ✪$260-400.

Old Sydney Holiday Inn, 55 George Street, The Rocks, ©9252 0524. 174 rooms, licensed restaurant, cocktail lounge, swimming pool, spa, sauna - ✪$255.

3-Star

The hotels listed below tend not to bear the frills and indulgences of the places mentioned above, but do provide you with good, clean accommodation, the occassional perk, and prices that are perhaps more reasonable for most travellers.

Harbour Rocks Hotel, 34-52 Harrington Street, The Rocks, ©9251 8944. 54 rooms, 1 unique suite, licensed restaurant, cocktail bar - ✪$220.

Sydney Vista Hotel, 7 York St, ©9274 1222. 120 units, 8 suites, pool - ✪$160-270.

Hyde Park Inn, 271 Elizabeth Street, ©9264 6001. 6 suites, 85 units, licensed restaurant (closed Sun), cocktail lounge - ✪$160.

Park Regis Hotel Sydney cnr Castlereagh & Park Streets, ©9267 6511. 120 units, 8 suites, swimming pool - ✪$170.

Castlereagh Inn, 169 Castlereagh Street, ©9284 1000. 2 suites, 83 rooms, licensed restaurants - ✪$145-170.

Lower Rating

The Lord Nelson Brewery Hotel, cnr Kent & Argyle Streets, The Rocks, ©9251 4044. 9 rooms (no private facilities), licensed restaurant - ✪$120-180 including breakfast.

The Wynyard Hotel, cnr Clarence and Erskine Streets, ©9299 1330. 14 rooms, restaurant open Mon-Fri - ✪$105.

The Mercantile Hotel

25 George Street, ©9247 3570. 19 rooms, 4 higher-standard rooms, spa bath - ✪$100-130.

"The Mercantile is an Irish theme pub that makes itself the centre of St Patrick's Day celebrations in Sydney and is generally a very popular night spot with tourists and locals alike. Being in the Rocks, the Mercantile is close to every amenity you could want, including shops, restaurants, the harbour, attractions and night life.

...Guests should be aware that the Mercantile's bar and night life and live entertainment all contribute to a delightfully rowdy atmosphere, so those seeking an early night with a book in bed should go elsewhere."

From *Staying in Sydney* by Sam Lynch

Y on the Park

5-11 Wentworth Avenue, ©9264 2451. 122 rooms - ✪$135.

"The Y has recently been totally refurbished and offers a broad range of accommodation from dorm to deluxe. The main benefit of staying at the Y for budget travellers is feeling safe. It is not a roach-filled dive near the beach, but a modern, clean, secure location that insists on civilised behaviour. Dorm rooms also feature single beds rather than bunk beds for extra comfort.

...Each floor offers large communal living areas including a TV lounge and mini-kitchen on each floor and there is a guest laundry. The Y is just across from Hyde Park, and is only 200 metres from Museum railway station. Public transport in the form of buses is also plentiful, but the central business district, shopping centres, museums, The Rocks and other attractions are all within walking distance as well.

...The Y represents good value, clean and secure accommodation in the heart of the city for travellers ranging from backpackers to business travellers, to families on holiday. Members of the YWCA get a 10% discount."

From *Staying in Sydney* by Sam Lynch

Serviced Apartments

The places below are recommended for those who wish to opt for the extra space of an apartment-style room, and prefer a sense of self-sufficiency, even though the rooms are serviced in a fashion similar to hotels.

High Rating

Saville 2 Bond Street, cnr George & Bond Streets, ☎9250 9555. 180 units, gym, heated pool, spa - ✪$245-1000.

The Waldorf Apartment Hotel, 57 Liverpool Street, ☎9261 5355. 60 units, swimming pool, spa, sauna - ✪$195-470.

Carrington Sydney City Centre Apartments, 57 York St, ☎9290 1577. 20 units - ✪$220-275.

The York Apartment Hotel, 5 York Street, ☎9210 5000. 134 units, 101 suites, licensed restaurant, heated swimming pool, spa, sauna - ✪$260-400 (suites $380-610).

The Stafford, 75 Harrington Street, The Rocks, ☎9251 6711. 40 units, 21 suites, swimming pool, spa, sauna, gym - ✪$240.

Metro Suites on King, 27-29 King St, ☎9290 9200. 17 units, pool - ✪$160-180.

Lower Rating

The Savoy Apartments, cnr King & Kent Streets, ☎9267 9211. 72 units - ✪$170.

Metro Suites on Sussex, Beehive Tower, 132 Sussex Street, ☎9290 9200. 32 units - ✪$135-185.

Inner-Suburban Accommodation

The suburbs listed here are within a 10km radius of the CBD. Staying in one of these adjacent areas will give you a feel for Sydney different

to what you would experience in its centre. The fringe suburbs have their own independent ambience - from beach life to night life - which may appeal to the visitor who has already seen it all and is searching for an alternative.

Bondi Beach (8km east of the city)
High Rating
Swiss-Grand Hotel Bondi Beach, cnr Campbell Parade & Beach Road, ✆9365 5666. 203 suites, licensed restaurant, heated swimming pool, spa, sauna, gym - ✪$230-720.
City Beach Motor Inn, 99 Curlewis Street, ✆9365 3100. 25 units, swimming pool - ✪$140-200.
Bondi Hotel, 178 Campbell Parade, ✆9130 3271. 50 rooms - ✪$95.
Lower Rating
Bondi Beachside Inn, 152 Campbell Parade, ✆9130 5311. 67 units, licensed restaurant - ✪$100-120.
Beach Road Hotel, 71 Beach Road, ✆9130 7247. 22 rooms, restaurant - ✪$90.
The Alice Motel, 30 Fletcher Street, ✆9130 5231. 31 units, swimming pool - ✪$100-120.

Coogee (8km east of the city)
High Rating
Crowne Plaza Coogee Beach, 242 Arden Street, ✆9315 7600. 207 rooms, licensed restaurant, heated swimming pool, gym, tennis - ✪$200-240.
Coogee Sands Apartments, 161 Dolphin Street, ✆9665 8588. 81 units - ✪$155-220.

Coogee Bay Boutique Hotel
9 Vicar St, ✆9665 0000. 52 rooms, *Selinas Night Club* - ✪$90-210.
"The Coogee Bay Boutique Hotel has been meticulously refurbished in contemporary mode and opened in 1998. Thoroughly modern, it is built with the business traveller in mind, and actively bids for the conference market. Business travellers will find special features such as in-room safes, private voice-mail, and modem connections for notebook computers cater to their special needs.

Decor is art deco styled, and rooms have a modern feel with shuttered balconies opening onto truly spectacular ocean views. Rooms are air conditioned and offer full kitchens and spa baths as options. ...The Coogee Bay Hotel is a well-known night spot and is very popular with the locals. It often hosts performers of international fame.

Coogee Bay Boutique Hotel offers a good alternative to the expensive city hotels with the added benefit of being pleasantly located at the beach. Business travellers won't miss any of the comforts or facilities that they would expect from larger hotels, are still reasonably close to the city, and stay in some luxury at a very reasonable price. Other travellers will appreciate the relaxed beach-side atmosphere which is less crowded than Bondi and not as remote as Manly."

From *Staying in Sydney* by Sam Lynch

Double Bay (4km east of the city)
High Rating
The Ritz-Carlton, 33 Cross Street, ℂ9362 4455. 15 suites, 140 rooms, licensed restaurant, swimming pool, gym - ✪$190-3000.
Savoy Double Bay Hotel, 41 Knox Street, ℂ9326 1411. 4 suites, 39 units - ✪$120-190.
Double Bay Bed & Breakfast, 63 Cross Street, ℂ9363 4776. 3 rooms - ✪$145-190.
Elizabeth Bay (3km east of the city)
High Rating
Sebel of Sydney, 23 Elizabeth Bay Road, ℂ9358 3244. 24 suites, 141 rooms, licensed restaurant, cocktail lounge, heated swimming pool, sauna, gym - ✪$280-340.
Gazebo Hotel, 2 Elizabeth Bay Road, ℂ9358 1999. 11 suites, 395 units, licensed restaurant, cocktail lounge, heated swimming pool, sauna - ✪$125-255.
Seventeen at Elizabeth Bay Boutique Apartments, 17 Elizabeth Bay Road, ℂ9358 8999. 35 units - ✪$180.

Madison's Central City Hotel
6-8 Ward Avenue, ℂ9357 1155. 8 suites, 39 rooms - ✪$110.
"Madison's is tucked away from Kings Cross by a matter of a couple of streets and is consequently only a few minutes walk from Kings Cross restaurants & clubs. This

modern, 5 storey hotel is designed around a central courtyard full of greenery that greets you as you enter. All the rooms face into this courtyard, which is open at the top.

...There are doors interconnecting adjacent rooms, so family groups can be accommodated. There are also some suite style rooms that have a small separate lounge area. There is no public space such as a large lobby area, lounge or restaurant in the hotel apart from the room on the top floor where complimentary breakfast is served each day. Madisons stands out in its area as being a comfortable base to operate from for anyone in Sydney for a short stay, whether on business or pleasure."

From *Staying in Sydney* by Sam Lynch

Lower Rating
Roslyn Gardens Motor Inn, 4 Roslyn Gardens, ✆9358 1944. 29 units - ✪$75-110.

Kings Cross (2km east of the city)
High Rating
Millenium Hotel Sydney, Top of William Street, ✆9356 1234. 390 rooms, licensed restaurants, swimming pool, gym - ✪$135 including breakfast.

The Crescent on Bayswater, 33 Bayswater Road, ✆9357 7266. 44 suites, 67 units, *Studebaker's Nightclub*, brasserie and bar, swimming pool, fitness centre - ✪$200 including breakfast.

The Crest Hotel, 111 Darlinghurst Road, ✆9358 2755. 226 rooms, licensed restaurant, cocktail bar, swimming pool, spa, sauna, gym - ✪$140 including breakfast.

Kingsview Motel, 30 Darlinghurst Road, ✆9358 5599. 67 units, unlicensed restaurant - ✪$75-110.

Lower Rating
Astoria Private Hotel, 9 Darlinghurst Road, ✆9356 3666. 30 rooms - ✪$95.

Cross Court Tourist Hotel, 203 Brougham Street, ✆9368 1822. 20 rooms, 2 suites - ✪$80.

North Sydney (4km north of the city)
High Rating
Rydges North Sydney, 54 McLaren Street, ✆9922 1311. 46 suites, 166 rooms, licensed restaurant, cocktail bar - ✪$160-200.

North Sydney Harbour View Hotel, 17 Blue Street, ✆9955 0499. 2 suites, 211 units, licensed restaurant, swimming pool - ✪$230.

Potts Point (3km east of the city)
High Rating
The Landmark Parkroyal Hotel, 81 Macleay Street, ✆9368 3000. 10 suites, 470 rooms, licensed restaurant, cocktail lounge, swimming pool - ✪$195.

The Grantham, 1 Grantham street, ✆9357 2377. 38 units, pool - ✪$120-180.

Macleay Serviced Apartments, 28

Macleay Street, ℂ9357 7755. 80 apartments, pool - ✪$110-150.

Simpsons of Potts Point
8 Challis Avenue, ℂ9356 2199. 14 rooms, ensuites - ✪$190.

The stately home which is now Simpsons was built as the residence of a prominent and wealthy parliamentarian in 1892. The current owners, Peter and Barbara Farris, have meticulously restored the building which gives the impression of being a vast and very beautifully decorated home, rather than a small hotel.

The House is elegant without giving an impression of its age ... A comfortably furnished drawing room at the front of the house, and a lovely conservatory at the rear where breakfast is served all help to give it an atmosphere that lovers of history and historic houses will appreciate greatly.

Rooms are generally very spacious and are likewise decorated and furnished beautifully ... All rooms are air-conditioned individually, as well as being equipped with ceiling fans, direct dial phones, mini-bar, and clock radio. Challis Avenue is a relatively quiet street several blocks away from the noise and lights of Kings Cross, and the house itself is drawn well back from the road, ensuring quiet.

Simpsons is located at Potts Point north of Kings Cross station in a street close to the harbourside. Potts Point being elevated well above the level of the harbour, strolling about in the leafy street rewards you with magnificent views of the city and harbour. Potts Point is also home to a good many restaurants, and multitudes of coffee shops."

From *Staying in Sydney* by Sam Lynch

Rushcutters Bay (3km east of the city)
High Rating
The Bayside Hotel, 85 New South Head Road, ℂ9327 8511. 99 rooms, licensed restaurant, cocktail lounge - ✪$140-160.

Budget Accommodation Caravan Parks
These tend to be in the outer suburbs, but are generally good value for money.

The Grand Pines Tourist Park Ramsgate Beach, 289 The Grand Parade, Sans Souci, ℂ2529 7329. (No pets allowed), 73 sites, unlicensed restaurant, barbecue - powered sites ✪$25-35 for two, park cabins $60-120 for two, on-site vans $50-60 for two.

Lakeside Caravan Park, Lake Park Road, Narrabeen, ℂ9913 7845. (No pets allowed), 368 sites, playground, barbecue - powered sites ✪$20-22 for two, park cabins $70-135.

Lane Cove River Caravan Park, Plassey Road, North Ryde, ©9888 9133. (No dogs or cats allowed), 216 sites, playground, pool - powered sites ✪$20 for two, park cabins $65-75 for two.

La Mancha Cara-Park, 901 Pacific Highway, Berowra, ©9456 1766. (No pets allowed), 196 sites, sauna, squash, pool, playground - powered sites ✪$20-22 for two, park cabins $64-69 for two.

YHA Hostels

The following Sydney hostels are listed with prices for a double room per night.

Central Station, 11 Rawson Place (corner Pitt Street), ©9281 9111 - ✪$35

Glebe Point, 262 Glebe Point Road, ©9692 8418 - ✪$27.

Collaroy Beach, 4 Collaroy Street, ©9981 1177 - ✪$26.

Pittwater, via Halls Wharf, Morning Bay via Church Point, (ferry from Church Point), ©9999 2196 - ✪$21.

Local Transport

Sydney has an efficient public transport system, with buses, ferries and trains covering the city and the suburban areas. For information on all public transport contact the Infoline, ©131 500, ✪6am-10pm, 7 days.

Train

The railway network is the backbone of the Sydney transit system and is operated by State Rail. There are ten route systems, each with a different colour code, and all services travel on part of the City Circle underground system.

The main station is *Central (Railway Square)*. All country trains begin their journey from here. All suburban trains pass through Central and Town Hall stations, and you can change at either to link up with the City Circle; to cross over the Harbour Bridge; or to board the train for Bondi Junction, which passes through Martin Place, Kings Cross and Edgecliff.

Central Station can be entered from Eddy Avenue, Elizabeth Street (best for suburban trains), or from the entrance road that runs off Pitt Street (best for country trains) to the left after crossing Hay Street if you are coming by car.

The stations in the City are:

Town Hall, Wynyard, Circular Quay, St James, Museum and Martin Place. These stations are all part of the underground network. The first five form the City Circle.

Wynyard Station has three entrances - one in George Street and two in York Street (one accessed from the transport interchange in Wynyard Park).

Town Hall Station has two entrances on each side of George Street.

St James Station has entrances in Elizabeth Street and Queens Square.

Museum Station has entrances on both sides of Liverpool Street and one in Elizabeth Street.

Martin Place Station is well sign-posted, as is **Circular Quay Station**. Tickets are purchased from a sales window before commencement of a journey, or you can use one of the machines on the city stations.

Bus

Details of the routes and schedules of Sydney Buses can be found by calling the Public Transport Infoline on ✆13 1500 or visiting the website at 👁www.sydneybuses.nsw.gov.au

Sydney Buses services radiate from the city, ferry wharves and railway stations, and connect the Sydney central business district with the suburbs.

Generally speaking, buses from the Eastern Suburbs terminate at either Central Railway or Circular Quay; those from the North-western and Western Suburbs terminate at York Street (near the Queen Victoria Building) or Circular Quay; and North Shore and Northern Suburbs bus routes end at Wynyard Park, near Wynyard Station, or outside the Queen Victoria Building.

Bus no. 888 runs between Wynyard Station, in George Street, and the Art Gallery of New South Wales in east Circular Quay every 10 minutes, Mon-Fri.

The Sydney Explorer Bus

The red Sydney Explorer bus is a great way to get around the city. It travels a 35km (21 miles) circuit to 22 different stops from 9am-5.25pm, beginning at Circular Quay, every day except Christmas Day. You can get on anywhere along the route where there is a distinctive Sydney Explorer bus stop sign. Passengers can get off at any stop, stay as long as they like, then pick up the next bus that arrives. The buses run every 20 minutes, and the fares are ✪$30 adults, $15 children under 16, $75 families.

If you miss the last Explorer bus, don't worry because your ticket is good on any State Transit bus running along the Explorer route until midnight.

1. Sydney Cove (Circular Quay)
2. Sydney Opera House
3. Royal Botanic Gardens/Museum of Sydney
4. State Library/The Mint
5. Mrs Macquarie's Chair
6. Art Gallery of NSW
7. Hard Rock Cafe
8. Kings Cross
9. Macleay Street
10. Elizabeth Bay House
11. Potts Point

Hyde Park

12. Woolloomooloo Bay
13. Wynyard Station/Martin Place
14. Queen Victoria Building/Sydney Tower/Planet Hollywood
15. Australian Museum
16. Central Station
17. Chinatown/Powerhouse Museum
18. Darling Harbour/National Maritime Museum
19. The Chinese Gardens/Powerhouse Museum
20. Sydney Aquarium
21. Campbell's Cove/Dawes Point
22. The Rocks Visitors Centre

Tickets can be purchased when boarding the bus, or beforehand from the NSW Travel Centre, 11-31 York Street; Australian Pacific Tours, 102 George Street, City; CountryLink Rail Travel Centres; 11 York Street, City; or from a local travel agent.

Bondi & Bay Explorer

Blue and white buses clearly marked Bondi & Bay Explorer operate on a 35km circular route from the city centre through the eastern harbour and bay-side areas.

They run at 30 minute intervals from 9am-4pm every day, departing from Circular Quay. The fares are ✪$30 adults, $15 children under 16, $75 families.

Bondi & Bay buses stop at the following destinations:

1. Circular Quay
2. Kings Cross
3. Top of the Cross
4. Rushcutters Bay
5. Double Bay
6. Rose Bay Ferry
7. Rose Bay Convent
8. Vaucluse Bay
9. Watsons Bay
10. The Gap Park
11. Bondi Beach
12. Bronte Beach
13. Coogee Beach
14. Royal Randwick Racecourse
15. SCG/Football Stadium/Paddington
16. Oxford Street
17. Hyde Park
18. Martin Place

If it suits your itinerary you can purchase twin tickets for both buses: ✪$50 adults, $25 children, $125 families.

Olympic Explorer

This service departs from the

Homebush Bay Visitors Centre between 9.20am and 5pm daily, at 10-15 minute intervals. This is the most efficient way to explore the sporting facilties, with ten stops along the route at which you can disembark, and join a later bus after viewing the attraction at your leisure. A ticket costs ✪$10 for adults and $5 for children, but the higher cost will come from making your way out to the Olympic site to take the tour. If you are in the city, the best choice is to take the RiverCat from Circular Quay and purchase an Olympic RiverCat Ticket for ✪$22 adults and $12 children - included in the price is access to the Olympic Explorer bus service.

Ferry

Providing undoubtedly the most scenic way to travel, Sydney's ferries and RiverCats ply the magnificent harbour.

Full information on routes and schedules can be obtained by phoning ✆131 500 or visiting the same site as for Sydney Buses (*see above*).

Ferry services operate daily, 6am-11pm, from Circular Quay up-harbour to Balmain, Long Nose Point, Hunters Hill and Greenwich.

Across-harbour ferries travel to Kirribilli, Neutral Bay, Cremorne, Mosman and Taronga Zoo. Ferries and hydrofoils also service Manly.

The wharves at Circular Quay are well sign-posted to indicate which area they service, but on weekends there are changes, and it is best to check before putting your ticket into the automatic turnstiles. Tickets can be purchased from machines on each wharf, or from the kiosk underneath the Circular Quay

Station. This kiosk also sells tickets to harbour cruises run by Sydney Ferries, which leave at 10am daily, 1pm Mon-Fri, Sat-Sun 1.30pm, and 8pm Mon-Sat; and river cruises which leave at 10am daily.

For information on times, connections and fares for all government and private bus, rail and ferry services in Sydney, contact the Infoline on ✆131 500 (daily 6am-10pm) - they can also advise on *Sydney Discovery Tours* tickets. Alternatively, visit the website listed above.

SydneyPass

If you are going to be in the city for at least a week, it will pay you to invest in a **SydneyPass**. It costs adults ✪$90 for 3 days, $120 for 5 days and $140 for 7 days. The Pass gives you unlimited use of the Sydney Explorer Bus, Manly Ferries, harbour cruises run by Urban Transit, and all jetcat, ferry and bus services. These passes are available from the Travel Centre of NSW and State Transit ticket offices displaying the SydneyPass sign.

The Monorail

The monorail system runs anticlockwise and has seven stations - Harbourside (Darling Harbour), Convention Centre, Haymarket, Garden Plaza, World Square (Liverpool Street), Galeries Victoria (Pitt Street, near Park Street) and City Centre (Pitt Street, near Market Street).

It is the best way to get from the city centre to Darling Harbour, and if you are travelling to the city by car you can park in Pyrmont behind the Darling Harbour complex and take the monorail into the city.

The fare for the monorail is ✪$3.50 for everybody 6 and over, whether you are going one stop or the complete circuit. You are not permitted to stay aboard for more than one circuit.

An unlimited travel **Supervoucher Day Pass** can be obtained if you plan to use the monorail several times to make your way around the city (it also contains discount coupons for nearby attractions). The ticket costs $8 per person (there is no adult/child distinction) and is valid until closing on the same day. The alternative is the **Supervoucher Family Pass**, which costs $24 for 2 adults and 2 children (or 1 adult and 3 children).

The monorail runs 7am-10pm Mon-Thu, Fri-Sat 7am-midnight and 8am-10pm on Sundays, ✆9552 2288 for further details. There is a website at 👁www.metromonorail.com.au

Sydney Light Rail

This tram service begins at Central Station and takes you through

Haymarket to Darling Harbour, up to Pyrmont, Star City, Fish Market, Wentworth Park, Glebe, Jubilee Park, Rozelle Bay and finally Lilyfield. It runs 24 hours a day and generally at 10 minute intervals. There are two zones for fares - Zone 1 (Central to Darling Harbour) and Zone 2 (Darling Harbour to Lilyfield). Fares per person are from ✪$2.50 to $4.80. Children are half fare. A ticket for unlimited weekly trips costs ✪$19 per person. This form of transport may prove useful as a quick and relatively cheap alternative for sightseeing. For further information, ✆9660 5288 or visit the web page at ✺www.metro lightrail.com.au

Taxi

Sydney is well served by taxis, and charges are set by the Department of Motor Transport. The main cab companies are:
Taxis Combined Services, ✆8332 8888;
RSL Cabs, ✆13 22 11;
Legion Cabs, ✆13 14 51;
ABC Taxis, ✆13 25 22;
Specially outfitted cabs for people in wheelchairs are available, and must be booked in advance.

Taxis may be hailed in the street, hired at a taxi rank, or arranged over the phone for a pick-up, though there will be an extra fee. This service has vastly improved in recent years.

Taxi ranks in the city include Central Station, Circular Quay, Park Street opposite the Town Hall, and outside all the major hotels.

If you hire a taxi in the city to take you over the bridge, ✪$3 will be added to the bill even though there is no toll for travel south to north. This extra fee is added because the taxi driver has to pay the toll to travel over the bridge when returning to the city, and may not get a fare going back that way. Be aware of this for other destinations whose routes involve toll roads.

If you are travelling to the airport from the northern side of the Harbour Bridge, it is safest to predict a $7 surcharge on your fare to cover all tolls and rates.

Water Taxi

Several companies operate on the harbour, including **Taxis Afloat**, ✆9955 3222; **Quay Water Taxis**, ✆9922 4252; and **Water Taxis**, ✆9755 4660. They will take you from one landing point to any other landing point on the harbour, and also offer scenic cruises.

Car

Renting a car is relatively cheap if you are travelling in a group, but driving in the city is not really recommended. The one-way streets take a bit of getting used to, and parking is a problem. Street parking is extremely hard to find, and the parking station fees add considerably to the cost of your day out. However, for travelling in the suburbs and outlying areas, a car is definitely the way to go.

Here are a few names of rental companies and their reservation phone numbers:

Avis, ☎13 63 33;

Budget, ☎13 27 27;

Hertz, ☎13 30 39;

Thrifty, ☎1300 367 227.

International and overseas drivers licences that are in English are accepted, and a deposit, or credit card details, are required before pick-up. Other car rental companies are found in the A-K Yellow Pages Telephone Directory.

The National Roads & Motorists Authority (NRMA) has reciprocal arrangements with overseas and interstate automobile associations. The head office is located at 151 Clarence Street, Sydney. The phone number for enquiries is ☎13 2132, and for road service, ☎13 1111.

Sydney Road Tolls

Both the Harbour Bridge (Bradfield Highway) and the Harbour Tunnel have a toll fee of ✪$3 for southbound cars. It should be mentioned that the Tunnel is not an alternative to the Bridge. It is for traffic heading for the airport and the eastern suburbs, and the Bridge is for traffic to the city and the Western Distributor.

The recently completed Eastern Distributor has cut travel time from the city to the airport dramatically, and for most tourists the ✪$3.50 toll (northbound) is worth paying to get to the hotel for a warm shower sooner.

If you are travelling out into the suburbs, the Motorways are the M4, (through mid-western Sydney out to Penrith) which costs ✪$2.20 both ways, and the M2 (to the Hills area in north mid-western Sydney) which will cost you ✪$3.30 east to west and ✪$1.70 from Seven Hills to Pennant Hills or $3.30 from Seven Hills right through to Lane Cove.

Eating Out

Sydney has a plethora of restaurants offering every type of cuisine imaginable. The harbour foreshores are liberally sprinkled with eating establishments, for there are not too many experiences that surpass, or for that matter match, a leisurely brunch on a sunny weekend with the harbour and all its craft as a backdrop.

Unfortunately, though, you often have to pay top prices for this indulgence. With so much competition, you would expect that prices would have to be kept to a minimum, but there are apparently

enough people to ensure that each restaurant is well-patronised, and indeed bookings are essential when a water view is offered.

Restaurants are classified as **Licensed** or **BYO**.

Licensed means that the establishment has a licence to sell alcohol. **BYO** means 'bring your own' wine, etc, because the restaurant does not have a liquor licence.

Some restaurants, although licensed, allow patrons to supply their own wine (not beer or spirits), which is usually less expensive than paying the mark-up on the wines that the restaurant is legally allowed to add. In this case a **corkage fee** may be added, which will be per bottle or per person, but the end result is usually still less expensive.

Alcohol can be purchased from the bottle department of a hotel, or from one of the many bottle shops that abound in every suburb.

It is reasonable to say that the price of a bottle of wine in one of these shops would be less than half the price of the same wine in a restaurant.

Following is a list of recommended restaurants, rated:

Expensive (main course ✪$23+), **Moderate** (main course ✪$15-$23)

Budget (main course under ✪$15). Not included here are the restaurants in the 5-star hotels, as everyone knows that they exist and are much the same the world over with regard to menus and prices.

Credit card abbreviations are:

Amex = American Express; BC = Bankcard; DC = Diners Club; MC = MasterCard; V = Visa.

One of Sydney's best, and most expensive, restaurants is **Forty One**, Level 41 Chifley Tower, Chifley Square, ©9221 2500. The view is magnificent, and complements rather than dominates the food. The cuisine is Modern Australian, and the presentation is first class. It is ☺open for lunch Mon-Fri and for dinner Mon-Sat 6-10.30pm.

Running a close second, though some might say that it is a dead heat, is *The Rockpool*, 107 George Street, The Rocks, ✆9252 1888. The cuisine here is also Modern Australian, the presentation is excellent, and the prices are commensurate. ☺Open for lunch Mon-Fri, dinner Mon-Sat.

Both the above are licensed and accept all credit cards.

At the other end of the scale is a Sydney landmark that has been around a very long time: *Harry's Cafe de Wheels*, Cowper Wharf Roadway, Woolloomooloo, ✆9357 3074. It is not a restaurant, not even a cafe, just a roadside stall - but everyone knows *Harry's*. Their delicious real Aussie meat pies, peas and more, are handed to you on a paper serviette. Eating a pie in this fashion requires complex synchronisation of hand and mouth - an ability with which most Sydneysiders are already born, or one they develop with rapid evolution at weekend football matches. So, when in Rome...

The City and The Rocks

Bilson's, Upper Level, Overseas Passenger Terminal, Circular Quay West, ✆9251 5600. Licensed, good harbour views, French/Australian cuisine, **expensive**, ☺open Sun-Fri noon-3pm and nightly 7pm-10pm, Amex, BC, DC, MC, V.

Doyle's at The Quay, Lower Level, Overseas Passenger Terminal, Circular Quay West, ✆9252 3400. Licensed, good harbour views, outside tables, seafood, **expensive**, ☺open Mon-Sun 11.30am-2.45pm and Mon-Sat 5.30pm-9.30pm, Sun 5.30-9pm, BC, DC, MC, V.

Bennelong, Sydney Opera House, Circular Quay, ✆9250 7548. Licensed, good harbour views, Modern Australian cuisine, **expensive**, ☺open Mon-Sat dinner from 5.30pm-11.30pm, Amex, BC, DC, MC, V.

Rossini Rosticceria, Shop W5, Circular Quay, ✆9247 8026. Licensed, good views, outside tables, Italian, cafeteria style, **budget**, ☺open daily 7pm-10.30am, 11am-4pm, 5-10.30pm, no credit cards accepted.

MCA Fish Cafe, Museum of Contemporary Art, Quayside, Circular Quay, ✆9241 4253. Licensed, good harbour views, outdoor tables, seafood, **moderate**, ☺open Mon-Fri 12pm-4pm, Sat-Sun 9am-4pm, Amex, BC, MC, V.

Imperial Peking Harbourside, 15 Circular Quay West, The Rocks, ✆9247 7073. Licensed, good views, outdoor tables, Chinese cuisine, **moderate**, ☺open daily noon-3pm,

Sun-Thurs 6pm-11pm and Fri-Sat 6pm-midnight, Amex, BC, DC, MC, V.

Sailors Thai, 106 George Street, The Rocks, ✆9251 2466. Licensed, Thai cuisine, **budget**, ☼open daily noon-2pm and 6pm-10am, Amex, BC, DC, MC, V.

The Summit, Level 47, Australia Square, 264 George Street, City, ✆9247 9777. Licensed, revolving restaurant, incredible views of the city its and outreaches, Modern Australian cuisine, **expensive**, ☼open daily 6pm-10pm and Sun-Fri noon-3pm, Amex, BC, DC, MC, V.

Casa Asturiana, 77 Liverpool Street, City, ✆9264 1010. Licensed, Mediterranean cuisine, **budget**, ☼open daily from 6pm and Tue-Fri noon-3pm, Amex, DC, MC, V.

Paragon Cafe, 1st Floor, Paragon Hotel, Circular Quay, ✆9241 3888. Licensed, Modern cuisine, **moderate**, ☼open Mon-Fri noon-3pm and Mon-Sat 6.30pm-10pm, Amex, BC, MC, V.

Merrony's, 2 Albert Street, Circular Quay, ✆9247 9323. Licensed, Australian/French, **moderate**, ☼open Mon-Fri noon-2.30pm, Mon-Sat 5.45pm-11pm, Amex, BC, DC, MC, V.

Caminetto, 13-17 Playfair Street, The Rocks, ✆9247 5787. Licensed, Italian cuisine, **moderate**, ☼open Fri-Sat 10am- midnight and Sun-Thu 10am-10pm, Amex, BC, DC, MC, V.

Phillip's Foote, 101 George Street, The Rocks, ✆9241 1485. Licensed (it is actually a pub), cook-your-own steaks, good salad bar, outdoor tables, **budget**, ☼open daily for lunch and dinner, Amex, BC, DC, MC, V.

Restaurant CBD, CBD Hotel, 75 York Street (cnr King Street), ✆9299 8911. Licensed, British/ Modern Australian, **moderate**, ☼open for lunch and dinner Mon-Fri, Amex, BC, DC, MC, V.

EJ's, 143 Macquarie Street, City (lower ground floor), ✆9247 8588. Licensed, cuisine includes a bit of everything from everywhere, **moderate**, ☼open for lunch only Mon-Fri noon-2.30pm, Amex, BC, DC, MC, V.

Capitan Torres, 73 Liverpool Street, City, ✆9264 5574. Licensed, Spanish fare, **moderate**, ☼open daily noon-3pm and 6pm-11pm, Amex, BC, DC, MC, V.

Botanic Gardens Restaurant, follow the signs once you are in the Gardens, ✆9241 2419. Licensed, good views, casual dining, outdoor tables, **moderate**, ☼open daily noon-2.15pm, Amex, BC, MC, V.

Dendy Bar & Bistro, 19 Martin Place, ✆9221 1243. Licensed, extensive menu, **budget**, ☼open daily 11am-midnight, Amex, BC, MC, V.

Zolie's Restaurant, 5 York Street, City, ✆9299 3276. European cuisine, **moderate**, ☼open Mon-Fri noon-3pm and nightly 6pm-10pm, Amex, BC, DC, MC, V.

Restaurant Suntory, 529 Kent Street, City, ☏9267 2900. Licensed, traditional Japanese cuisine, **expensive**, ☉open Mon-Fri noon-2pm, Mon-Sat 6.30pm-10pm and Sun 6pm-9pm, Amex, BC, DC, MC, V.

Papillon, 71 York Street, City, ☏9262 2624. Licensed, French cuisine, **expensive**, ☉open Mon-Fri noon-3pm and Tues-Fri 6pm-9pm, Amex, BC, DC, MC, V.

Don Quixote, 1 Albion Place, City, ☏9264 5903. Licensed, Spanish cuisine, **expensive**, ☉open Mon-Fri noon-3pm and Mon-Sat 6pm-11pm, Amex, BC, DC, MC, V.

Kamogawa, Corn Exchange Building, cnr Sussex & Market Streets, City, ☏9299 5533. Licensed, Japanese with teppan bar, traditional rooms and conventional dining area, **moderate to expensive** depending on locale, ☉open daily 6.30pm-10am, 6pm-10pm and Mon-Sat noon-3pm, karaoke bar Mon-Fri 8.30pm-1am, Amex, BC, DC, MC, V.

Amar's, 44 Bridge Street, City, ☏9247 9930. Licensed, Indian cuisine, **moderate**, ☉open Mon-Fri noon- 2.30pm and 5.30-10.30pm, Amex, BC, DC, MC, V.

Chinatown (Haymarket)

Golden Harbour, 31 Dixon Street, ☏9212 5987. Licensed & BYO (corkage fee per bottle), Cantonese, **budget**, ☉open Mon-Fri 10am-4.30pm, 5.30pm-11pm and Sat-Sun 9am-4.30pm, 5.30pm-1am, Amex, BC, DC, MC, V.

House of Guang Zhou, 76 Ultimo Road, ☏9281 2205. Licensed, Chinese, **budget**, ☉open Mon-Fri 11.30am-3pm, Sat-Sun noon-3pm and daily 5.30pm-2am, Amex, BC, DC, MC, V.

Golden Century Seafood Restaurant, 393-399 Sussex Street, Haymarket, ☏9212 3901. Licensed, popular venue, fresh seafood with Asian influence, **expensive**, ☉open daily noon-4am, Amex, BC, DC, MC, V.

Marigold, Levels 4 & 5, 683-689 George Street, ☏9281 3388. Licensed & BYO (corkage fee per person), Cantonese, **moderate**, ☉open daily 10am-3pm and 5.30pm-midnight, Amex, BC, DC, MC, V.

Malaya, 761 George Street, ☏9211 0946. Licensed, Malaysian cuisine, **budget**, ☉open daily noon-3pm, Mon-Sat 5-10pm and Sun 5-9pm, Amex, BC, DC, MC, V.

East Sydney

Beppi's, cnr Yurong & Stanley Streets, ☏9360 4558. Licensed, Italian cuisine, **expensive**, ☉open Mon-Fri noon-3pm and Mon-Sat 6pm-11.30pm, Amex, BC, DC, MC,

V.

Yutaka, 234 Crown Street, ✆9361 4804. Licensed & BYO (corkage fee per person), Japanese cuisine, **moderate**, ☺open Mon-Fri noon-2.15pm, Mon-Sat 6-10.45pm and Sun 6-10pm, Amex, BC. MC, V.

Tre Scalini, 174 Liverpool Street, ✆9331 4358. Licensed, Italian cuisine, **expensive**, ☺open Mon-Fri noon-2.30pm and Mon-Sat 6-10.30pm, Amex, BC, MC, V.

Ristorante Mario, 38 Yurong Street, ✆9331 4945. Licensed, Italian cuisine, **expensive**, ☺open Mon-Fri noon-3pm and Mon-Sat 6.30-11pm, BC, MC, V.

No Name, 2 Chapel Street, Darlinghurst, ✆9130 4898. BYO, Italian pasta and minestrone, **budget**, ☺open for lunch and dinner, no credit cards accepted. There are a few No Name restaurants around Sydney, but this is the original and most people think it is still the best.

Cruising Restaurants

Captain Cook Cruises, ✆9206 1111, have lunch and dinner options.

The *Luncheon Cruise* departs Circular Quay at 12.30pm, lasts one and a half hours and includes a Buffet Luncheon featuring Sydney rock oysters, Tasmanian trout, rare roast beef, ham, chicken, fresh salads, fruit platters and Australian cheeses - ✪$49 adult, $29 child.

The *Sunset Dinner Cruise* leaves from Wharf 6 Circular Quay at 5.15pm daily. The cruise offers a 2 course a la carte menu & wine or local beer. The cost is ✪$69 adult, $55 children. Reservations essential.

The John Cadman Dinner cruises every night of the year and departs Wharf 6 Circular Quay at 7.30pm. The a la carte menu is prepared by international chefs, and there is a selection of Australian and imported wines. Cost of the dinner cruise is ✪$97 adults, $55 children, and reservations are essential, ✆9206 6666.

Captain Cook Cruises also offer *Coffee* and *Explorer Cruises*.

Sail Venture Cruises have luncheon and dinner cruises on their Big Cats, with changing menus. The luncheon cruise departs Darling Harbour Aquarium Wharf at 12.15pm (returning at 2.25pm) and Campbells Cove, Circular Quay, at 12.35pm (returning at 2.05pm) - ✪$55 adult, $28 child.

The dinner cruise departs Darling Harbour at 7pm (returning at 10.10pm) and Campbells Cove at 7.30pm (returning at 9.45pm) - ✪$105 adult, $55 children.

For reservations and enquiries, ✆9262 3595.

Matilda Cruises serve lunch on their two-hour harbour cruises, which leave Darling Harbour Aquarium Wharf at 11.30am and

1.30pm, Campbells Cove Circular Quay at 11.45am and 1.45pm, and Taronga Zoo at 12.45pm and 2.45pm. The cruises cost ✪$56 adult, $28 children, and an Aussie BBQ lunch cooked on board. Reservations are necessary, ✆9264 7377.

Bounty Cruises have lunch and dinner cruises aboard the tall ship *Bounty*, and they always guarantee that part of the cruise will be under sail. The cruises leave from Campbells Cove Wharf, where you can also inspect the *Bounty* which is a replica of the one that Captain Bligh sailed on and was built for the movie *Mutiny on The Bounty*. The lunch cruise departs every day at 12.30pm, and costs ✪$65 on weekdays and $95 on weekends. The dinner cruise begins at 7pm and costs ✪$99 for adults. Both cruises offer buffet-style meals. For reservations, ✆9247 1789.

Don't think for one moment that the above lists all the restaurants in Sydney. It is little more than the tip of the iceberg. Often you will find restaurants that we have not listed in the same street as the ones included above. Our list gives you somewhere to start and an idea of what is on offer.

On weekends, it is a wise idea to phone ahead and book a table.

In case you are wondering about the availability of a Big Mac, be re-assured that there are 14 *McDonald's* in the city. *Pizza Hut* has two city branches; and *KFC* has one in the city and one at Darling Harbour.

Entertainment

As mentioned in the Introduction chapter, the Friday edition of *The Sydney Morning Herald* has 'Metro', and the Thursday edition of the *Daily Telegraph* has '7 Days' which list what's on at all of Sydney's night spots.

It would be lengthy and boring to list all the venues in the city and suburbs, so we took a survey amongst a group of Sydney ragers and the following are their favourites.

Night Clubs
City
Harbourside Brasserie, Pier One, Millers Point, ✆9252 3000. It has two cocktail bars and commands sweeping views of Sydney Harbour.
Paragon Hotel, 1 Macquarie Place, ✆9241 3522. Open ⊕Mon-Thu 9.30am-1am, Fri-Sat, 9.30-5am, Sun 12pm-10pm.
Orient Hotel, cnr Argyle & George Streets, ✆9251 1255. Open ⊕7 days 10am-3am (live bands every night of the week). Nightclub and live bands set out over three floors. Plenty of space. Tourist spot, very popular.

Retro Bar, 20 Sussex Street, City, ✆9212 4868. Open ⏰Thursday to Saturday 6pm-5am. Popular for those who wish to re-live the eighties, or are still there.

Riche, Hilton International Hotel, 259 Pitt Street, ✆9266 0610. Open ⏰Wed 9pm-2am, Fri-Sat 9pm-2am.

Bar Luna, Jackson's on George, 176 George Street, ✆9247 9334. Open ⏰Tues-Sun, afternoon or evening until early the following morning (restaurant service ceases 9.30pm). Very popular. The beer flows freely here.

Riva, Sheraton On The Park, 130 Castlereagh Street, City, ✆9286 6666. Open ⏰10pm to late Wednesday to Saturday. Excellent atmosphere for middle-aged crowds.

Darling Harbour/Pyrmont

The Cave, Star City, Pirrama Road, Pyrmont, ✆9566 4755. Open ⏰9.00pm to late (24 hour licence) 7 days a week. If you're tired of losing money in the Casino nearby, this is a good place to go to forget about it - provided you can still afford the cover charge.

Kings Cross

Round Midnight, 2 Roslyn Street, ✆9356 4045. Open ⏰Tue-Thu and Sun 8am-3pm, Fri-Sat 8am-5pm. Popular venue.

Sugareef, 20 Bayswater Road, Kings Cross, ✆9368 0763. Open ⏰9pm to 6am every day. Popular and often crowded.

Darlinghurst

Kinselas, 383 Bourke Street, Darling-hurst, ✆9331 3100. Open ⏰24 hours, 7 days. This building was once Kinsela's Funeral Parlour. You can find better.

The Cauldron, 207 Darlinghurst Road, ✆9331 1523. Open ⏰Tues-Sat 10am-3am. Very popular venue with the smart, well-dressed crowd, bookings advised.

North Shore

Greenwood Hotel, 36 Blue Street, North Sydney, ✆9964 9477. Open ⏰Monday to Saturday 11am to late. A very good club/bar with a nice atmosphere.

Metropole Hotel, 287-305 Military Road, Cremorne, ✆9909 8888. Open ⏰10pm until 5am(ish) Friday/ Saturday only. Very upmarket and popular.

Paddington

Fringe Bar, 106 Oxford Street, Paddington, ✆9360 3554. Open ⏰11.30am to midnight Monday to Thursday, 11.30am to 3am Friday to Saturday.

Bars & Bistros

City

Bridie O'Reilly's, corner Kent and Erskine Streets, ✆9279 3133. Open ⏰11am-midnight (Mon-Thurs), 11am-2am (Fri-Sat), 11am-10pm (Sun). Bistro. Light entertainment includes Irish bands.

Bridie O'Reilly's, cnr George and

Hay Streets, ©9212 2111. Open ⏰11am-midnight (Mon-Thurs), 11am-2am (Fri-Sat), 11am-10pm (Sun). Bistro. Light entertainment includes Irish bands.

Horizons Bar, ANA Hotel, 176 Cumberland Street, The Rocks, ©9250 6000. Open ⏰Mon-Thu noon-1am, Sat noon-2am, Sun noon-midnight. Light lunch noon-2pm.

Lucy's Tavern, 54 Castlereagh Street, ©9221 3908. Open ⏰Mon-Thurs 10.30am-10pm, Fri-Sat 10.30am-5am.

Marble Bar, Sydney Hilton Hotel, Pitt Street, ©9266 2000. Open ⏰Mon-Fri noon-11pm, Sat 3pm-2am. The Marble Bar was part of the Adams Hotel, dating from 1893, which was built by George Adams, founder of Tatts Lotto. When the Hotel was being refurbished by the new owners, the Italian Renaissance Marble Bar was dismantled stone by stone and rebuilt on the completion of the Hotel that stands today. Dressy and posh venue.

Customs House, Sydney Renaissance Hotel, 31 Alfred Street, ©9247 2285. Open ⏰Mon-Fri 11am-10pm (closed weekends). Lunch is served from noon-2pm, there is no dinner service. The bar is at the rear of the hotel and opens onto Macquarie Place Park where, in summer, a crowd of business movers and shakers spend their evenings. In operation since 1846, it has been said that should a bomb explode in this bar on any Friday evening, the Australian Stock Exchange would not open come Monday morning, not to mention the banking, legal and accounting professions.

Woolloomooloo Bay Hotel, 2 Bourke Street, ©9357 1177. Open ⏰Mon-Sat 10am-11pm, Sun 11pm-9pm, bistro lunch and dinner 12pm-9pm. The Woolloomooloo is a great place to spend a Sunday afternoon in summer. The patrons spill onto the pavement outside whilst the band is playing.

Darling Harbour

Craig Brewery Bar & Grill, Festival Market Place, Darling Harbour, ©9281 3926. Open ⏰Mon-Wed 10am-noon, Thurs-Sat 10am-3am. Dinner - cook your own steaks on the barbecue.

Pumphouse Restaurant & Bar, 17 Little Pier Street, Darling Harbour, ©8217 4100. Open ⏰Mon-Fri 11am-late, dinner till 9pm, nightclub and live bands. The pumphouse is known for the fabulous boutique beers available on tap.

East of the city

Kings Cross

Bourbon & Beefsteak, 24 Darlinghurst Road, Kings Cross, ©9358 1144. Open ⏰24 hours, 7 days a week, dinner 7.30-10.30pm

The Bourbon and Beefsteak is an institution. Nearly every Sydneysider has visited the Bourbon at least once.

Darlinghurst

Burdekin Hotel, 2 Oxford Street, ℄9331 3066. Open ☺11am-2pm, lunch & dinner 7.30-10.30pm.

Paddington

London Tavern & Restaurant, 85 Underwood Street, ℄9331 6192 (restaurant), 9331 3200. Open ☺Mon-Thurs 11am-11pm, Fri-Sat 10am-11:15pm. Pool Tables and card machines available.

Pubs

City

Lord Nelson Brewery Hotel, 19 Kent Street, ℄9251 4044. Open ☺7 days 11am-11pm. The Lord Nelson claims to be the oldest continually licensed hotel, and the only pub brewery in Sydney brewing natural ales.

Mercantile Hotel, 25 George Street, The Rocks, ℄9247 3570. Open ☺Mon-Thurs 10am-midnight, Fri-Sat 10am-1am. The Mercantile is frequented by Irish travellers and is known as the Irish Pub. It has an Irish flavour and St Patrick's Day, March 17 is a big day for the Mercantile. They even serve green beer!

The Hero of Waterloo Hotel, 81 Lower Fort Street, ℄9252 4553. Open ☺Mon-Sat 10am-11pm, Sun 10am-10pm. Bistro lunches and dinners available seven days. A museum downstairs shows a tunnel which runs down to the harbour. This pub is the oldest continuously trading pub in Sydney. Built in 1843.

Jazz Venues

The Basement, 29 Reiby Place, City, ℄9251 2797. Open ☺open nightly for dinner, Mon-Fri for lunch. Features modern local and international artists and serves contemporary Australian food. Excellent music and food. Guaranteed to have a good time. For jazz lovers.

Soup Plus, 383 George Street, City, ℄9299 7728. Open ☺Mon-Thu noon-midnight, Jazz 7:30-midnight; Fri-Sat noon-1am; Jazz 8pm-12.30am.

Strawberry Hills Hotel, 453 Elizabeth Street, Surry Hills, ℄9698 2997. Open ☺Mon-Thurs 11am-midnight. Fri-Sat 11am-12.30am. Sun noon-10.30pm.

The Classics

The Sydney Opera House is *the* venue in Sydney for opera, ballet, and performances by the Sydney Symphony Orchestra.

The newly refurbished Sydney Town Hall is also the scene of musical evenings. The 'Metro' has the information on programs, locations and times.

Theatres

Sydney has a vibrant theatre scene, and the local talent compares favourably with the rest of the world.

The large theatres have cocktail bars for pre-show or intermission drinks, and most of them have banned smoking in these areas, as well as in the auditoriums themselves. Some theatres have restaurants attached, where service is geared to getting patrons into the theatre on time.

Then there are the small theatre groups, and local dramatic and musical societies, whose performances are quite professional and you may see a star in the making. For example, **NIDA**, the National Institute of Dramatic Art (where Mel Gibson learnt his craft) presents plays at *The Parade Theatre* at 215 Anzac Parade, Kensington, ✆9697 7613, opposite the main entrance to the University of New South Wales. Prices vary according to the production but range from ✪$17 to $20, not much more than you pay to see Mel in a movie.

Half-tix

Speaking of prices, Sydney has a *Half-tix booth* in Darling Park, 201 Sussex Street, at the base of the IBM building, and it sells tickets to major venues at half price on the day of the performance.

It is ⊙open between 9am and 5pm Monday to Friday, and 10am-3pm Saturday. The phone number for selections and reservations is ✆9286 3310 and for the head office, ✆9966 1723. All major credit cards are accepted. They have a website at ☞www.halftix.com.au

Major Theatres

The Sydney Opera House has two theatres - the *Drama Theatre*, which seats 544, and the *Playhouse*, which seats 398. The Box Office is ⊙open Mon-Sat 9am-8.30pm, and charge telephone bookings may be made, ✆9250 7777. There are several eateries at the Opera House itself, or you can choose from those in the area of Circular Quay.

Her Majesty's Theatre, 107 Quay Street, ✆9212 3411, is close to Central Railway Station and within walking distance of the restaurants of Chinatown.

Capitol Theatre, 13 Campbell Street, Haymarket, ✆9320 5000 for recorded show information, or ✆9266 4800 for bookings. The theatre is in Haymarket, near Chinatown.

The Theatre Royal, MLC Centre, King Street, ℘9231 6111, is in the heart of the city.

The Ensemble Theatre, 78 McDougall Street, Milsons Point, ℘9224 8444, is situated in the Lower North Shore and has its own restaurant.

The Wharf Theatre, Pier 4, Hickson Road, Millers Point (The Rocks), ℘9250 1700, also has a restaurant, ℘9250 1761.

Belvoir Street Theatre, 25 Belvoir Street, Surry Hills, ℘9699 3444, doesn't have a restaurant, but does have a licensed bar offering light snacks before and after the show.

Seymour Theatre Centre, cnr Cleveland Street & City Road, Chippendale, ℘9531 7940, has three theatres - the *York*, *Everest* and *Downstairs*, and a very good restaurant, ℘9692 4138. There is also a coffee and snack bar in the upstairs foyer.

The Footbridge Theatre, Sydney University, Parramatta Road, Glebe, ℘9692 9955 or 9266 4800 (bookings), is actually in the grounds of Sydney University. It doesn't have a restaurant of its own, but there are plenty in nearby Glebe.

Small Theatres

Stables Theatre, 10 Nimrod Street, Kings Cross, ℘9361 3817.

Bay Street Theatre, 75 Bay Street, Glebe, ℘9692 0977.

New Theatre, 542 King Street, Newtown, ℘9519 3403.

Pilgrim Theatre, 262 Pitt Street, City, ℘9261 8981.

Enmore Theatre, 116 Enmore Road, Enmore, ℘9550 3666.

These small theatres may not have a current presentation when you are in town, and others not mentioned here may have something that you would be interested in seeing. Check 'Metro' for details. More live cinemas are found in the suburbs.

Rock Concerts

The main venue for these is the **Sydney Entertainment Centre**, near Chinatown, ℘1900 957 333 for recorded information or ℘9320 4200 for enquiries.

If the person or group is a big star, eg Michael Jackson, Billy Joel, Elton John, Madonna or U2, the promoters may opt to stage the concert at the Sydney Cricket Ground, even during the cricket season.

The Sydney Entertainment Centre is also used for ice shows, tennis tournaments, boxing matches, etc.

An increasingly popular venue for concerts and other large entertainment events is Olympic park in Homebush. These venues are now used for a variety of events, from big sporting matches, to the annual Royal Easter Show.

Cinemas

The main cinema area in the city is in George Street, between Park and

Liverpool Streets.

Here you will find:

Village Cinema City, 545 George Street, ✆9264 6701; **Hoyts Centre**, 505 George Street, ✆9273 7431; and **Greater Union**, 525 George Street, ✆9267 8666.

There are also many cinemas in the large suburban shopping areas. An independent cinema in the city is **Dendy**, 19 Martin Place, ✆9233 8558 and 261 King Street Newtown, ✆9550 5699.

As a general rule, Tuesday is half-price night at all cinemas, although some offer discounts on other nights.

Gambling Venues

Star City Casino, 80 Pyrmont Street, Ultimo, ✆9777 9000, is close to Darling Harbour, and can be reached by ferry and bus. There are the usual assortment of black-jack tables, roulette tables, and so on, and hundreds of poker machines where people queue up to lose their money 24 hours a day.

The complex contains a 352-room 5-star hotel, the Lyric Theatre seating 2000, a cabaret room seating 900, 14 restaurants, 12 bars, designer-name retail outlets, conference facilities, and 139 serviced apartments in the adjoining tower. It has its fair share of critics.

There are plenty of other places to go if you feel like a flutter. Firstly there are the **Clubs** - Leagues Clubs, RSL (Returned Servicemen's League) Clubs, Bowling Clubs, Worker's Clubs, Golf Clubs - which all have poker machines (that seem to offer better odds than those at the Casino), and most have keno.

Of course, it is not compulsory to play the pokies, and in fact, a lot of people don't - they go to the club to get a reasonably priced meal, and enjoy whatever entertainment is on offer. This varies from imported acts to cabaret shows with local talent, to movies, to chook raffles (yes, you do actually win a chook, or rather, a dead chicken).

Every suburb has one or more clubs, but if you are a first-time visitor to Sydney, I suggest that you stick to the suburban League Clubs. They are bigger, brighter, busier, and you can experience a good cross-section of Sydney life. Clubs are listed in the Yellow Pages Telephone Directory under *Clubs - Social and General*.

Although the clubs are there primarily for the use of members, visitors are always made welcome, as long as they are suitably dressed - no thongs, a collar with a shirt, and in the evening, long pants are preferred. Those dress rules are of course for men. Women must be 'decently' attired. Remember to sign the visitor's book in the foyer.

The clubs also have TAB facilities and SKY Channel television. This means that you can study the form guide in the comfort of a well-appointed club with a cold glass of whatever you fancy, place bets on your favourite horses, watch the race live, then collect your winnings (or tear up your ticket). Perhaps it should be mentioned that SKY Channel is only available to TAB agencies and licensed premises.

If you are not into the club scene you can, of course, place your bets at the local TAB agency, and they are in every suburb, but there is no atmosphere.

Alternatively you can venture outdoors and actually watch the horses, or dogs, go round at the track. Sydney's racetracks are very attractive, with good parking facilities, lots of grassed areas, plenty of bars, take-away food outlets, and restaurants, and the choice of investing your money on the Tote, or with a bookmaker. Children are welcome, and on a beautiful Sydney day it can be a great family day out.

The Horse-racing venues are:
Randwick Racecourse, Alison Road, Randwick, ©9663 8400.
Canterbury Racecourse, King Street, Canterbury, ©9930 4000.
Rosehill Gardens Racecourse, Grand Avenue (off James Ruse Drive), Rosehill, ©9930 4070.
Warwick Farm Racecourse, Hume Highway, Warwick Farm, ©9602 6199.

Races are held every Saturday and Wednesday at one of the above courses.

The first race is usually around 12.30, but during January and February the first race starts around 2.30pm. These are called *Twilight Meetings*, as the last race is around 6.30pm. The daily newspapers have details of race times, starters and jockeys, comprehensive form guides, TAB numbers and post positions.

Harness-racing venues are:
Harold Park Paceway, Ross Street, Glebe, ©9660 3688. Meetings are held on Tuesday and Friday nights, and first race is 7pm.
Bankstown City Paceway, 178 Eldridge Road, Bankstown, ©9708 4111. Meetings are held on Monday nights, and first race is 7pm.
Fairfield Paceway, Fairfield Showground, ©9604 4559. Meetings are not held on a regular basis, so either phone the club or look in the newspapers for forthcoming races.

Greyhound racing is held at **Wentworth Park**, Wentworth Park Road, Glebe, ©9660 6232. Meetings are held every Monday and Saturday nights and the first race is 7.30pm.

Shopping

The City
Sydney has a large shopping area

in the city, stretching from Park Street in the south to Hunter Street, with shops along George, Pitt, Castlereagh and Elizabeth Streets, which run south-north, and Market, King and Hunter Streets, which run roughly east-west. The section of Pitt Street between Market and King Streets is a pedestrian mall, with many arcades connecting it to both Castlereagh and George Streets. The closest railway stations to the shopping areas are Town Hall, Wynyard, St James and Martin Place.

If on the day you have set aside to shop, the heavens open and the rain pours down, remember it is possible to walk from Town Hall Station to the MLC Centre in Martin Place without venturing out of doors. It is rather a convoluted route, but there are signs pointing you in the right direction. Basically, from the station take the arcade under the Queen Victoria Building to Grace Bros, then from the first floor of Grace Bros take the overpass to Centrepoint, then travel across the Imperial Arcade, Glasshouse and Skygarden shopping centres to the King Street overpass, and, *voila*, you are in the MLC Centre. Of course, if the weather is warm and sunny, forget this option and stroll through the Mall.

Shops are normally ☉open Mon-Wed 9am-5.30pm, Thurs 9am-9pm, Fri 9am-6pm, Sat 9am-5pm, Sun 11am-4pm, but this is not a hard and fast rule. Some open earlier and close later, particularly on Sunday, and many suburban supermarkets are open until late at night six days a week, and until around 6pm on Sunday. The shops in the tourist areas are open every day, usually with extended hours.

Souvenirs

If you are only interested in buying souvenirs, such as cuddly koalas and kangaroos, T-shirts, etc, it is probably best to head for the tourist areas, such as The Rocks, Darling Harbour or Circular Quay.

Other 'typically Sydney' souvenirs are found in the range of goods at the Done Art & Design Shops at The Rocks, Darling Harbour, Queen Victoria Building and the departure level of the International Airport. Ken Done is a local artist who produces very colourful works of art featuring the harbour, the bridge, the opera house, koalas, kangaroos, etc. These paintings are reproduced on material and his wife, Judy, designs a spectacular range of sportswear, swimwear, homewares, bags, stationery - in fact, just about everything you can think of can be found in their shops.

Buying Opals

If you have your heart set on some opal jewellery, you should grab your passport and airline ticket and head for a duty free store, or a jewellery shop that has a 'Tax Free for Overseas Visitors' sign in the window. In the case of opals, which are mined in Australia and set in jewellery locally, there is no duty, therefore in both establishments you would avoid the 10% GST.

Australia produces more than 90% of the world's opals, and the three main areas where they are found are Lightning Ridge in NSW which produces the Black Opal; Quilpie, where the Queensland Boulder Opal originates; and Coober Pedy in South Australia, which has the White or Milk Opal. When buying opals there are a few important terms you should know:
Solid Opal - this is the most valuable, and is good for investment purposes. The more colourful and complete, the greater its value.
Doublet - this is comprised of slices of opal glued together, and is of medium value. It has no investment value.
Triplet - slices of opal covered with quartz, perspex or glass. This is the least expensive with no investment value.

If your pocket can't stretch as far as a solid opal, but you still would like a piece of opal jewellery, remember that anything that is glued can come unstuck, and that condensation can form under perspex or glass. The less expensive types of opal are not suitable for rings, unless you are going to remember to take them off every time you wash your hands.

Department Stores
David Jones
David Jones has two stores in the city - one bounded by Elizabeth, Market and Castlereagh Streets, the other diagonally opposite on the corner of Market and Castlereagh Streets. The Elizabeth Street store is devoted mainly to ladies' wear, except for the Lower Ground Floor (haberdashery, books, records, CDs, pharmacy, confectionery, wool, fabrics and restaurant); the 5th Floor (toys, children's wear and sporting goods) and the 6th Floor (manchester).

The Market Street store is known as the men's store, but it also has the Food Hall on the lower ground floor, and stocks travel goods, and small and large electrical appliances and furniture. Both stores have the same phone number: ℂ9266 5544.

David Jones was considered to be one of the most beautiful stores in the world, and was designed by the same person who later designed the refurbishment of Harrods in London, and there are similarities.

David Jones stores are ⊕open Mon-Fri 9am-5.30pm (Thurs to 9pm), Sat 9am-4pm, Sun 11am-5pm, and all major credit cards are accepted.

The Sydney Opera House

Grace Bros

Situated on the corner of George and Market Streets, Grace Bros is more of a family store and sells literally everything under one roof. It has seven floors of shopping and is ☉open Mon-Wed 9.30am-6pm, Thurs 9am-9pm, Fri 9.30am-6.00pm, Sat 9am-6pm, Sun 11am-5pm, ✆9238 9111.

Argyle Stores

Sydney's newest department store is situated in The Rocks. For more information see The Rocks section in the *City Sights* chapter.

City Shopping Centres
Town Hall Arcade

Situated underground in the Town Hall Station, there are two arcades of specialty shops. The shorter of the two from the station leads to Bathurst Street, near Kent Street, and the other continues under the Queen Victoria Building to Grace Bros.

The Queen Victoria Building

The QVB was built in 1898 in the Byzantine style, and originally housed the city markets. Bounded by George, Market, York and Druitt Streets, its prosperity was short-lived, and it fell into disrepair. At one stage it was used as part offices and part Municipal Library, and the partitions that succeeded in making the building into a rabbit warren were actually nailed onto the beautiful tiled floors. Both the inside and outside of the building

were decidedly tacky, and in 1959 there was much debate about demolishing the entire structure and building another shrine to modern architecture. Fortunately, common sense prevailed and the wreckers were not allowed to move in, but it was not until 1982 that a 99-year lease was granted and over $75 million invested to restore the building to its original state.

It is a magnificent building, and Pierre Cardin, on a visit to Sydney, christened it 'the most beautiful shopping centre in the world'. But, it is not only a shopping centre, there are a lot of things to see, all with a royal theme, in keeping with the name of the building. It even has replicas of the Crown Jewels on the top level.

The Royal Automata Clock 'performs' on the hour between 9am and 9pm daily, and you need to get there early to see the moving Royal Pageant. (It is a good idea to keep a firm grip on your handbag and wallet while waiting in this crowd.)

The QVB is open seven days a week. Apart from the range of boutiques and specialty shops, there are several restaurants and cafes, both in the QVB and in the underground walkway to Grace Bros. These exclusive retail outlets are housed in a setting lavish enough to match the prices of their merchandise. However, stunning architecture, the imitation Crown Jewels, and various other monuments and displays ensure that a browse through the QVB does not have to involve shopping to be enjoyed.

Centrepoint

Known as 'the heart of the city', Centrepoint is located on Pitt Street Mall, beneath Sydney Tower, and connects Grace Bros with David Jones. It has over 170 shops on four levels, including hairdressers, beauticians, leather shops, jewellery and accessory outlets, boutiques, and several coffee shops and takeaways. The lifts for Sydney Tower are found on the elegant Gallery Level of Centrepoint.

The lower ground floor is the Centrepoint Tavern, a good spot for a quick lunch, or a happy-hour drink.

Centrepoint is open daily, but not all the shops are open outside normal shopping hours.

Imperial Arcade

The Imperial runs between the Pitt Street Mall and Castlereagh Street, and has 114 specialty shops on 3 levels. It is also connected to Centrepoint.

Glasshouse on The Mall

Located in the middle of the Pitt Street Mall, the Glasshouse has three floors of shopping, with the usual collection of boutiques.

Skygarden

A very up-market shopping experience, Skygarden has three levels of prestigious shops under a huge crystal dome. The mosaic entrance arch is made of thousands of Venetian glass tiles, and depicts the day and night theme of the complex. The top dining level is nothing to write home about.

Strand Arcade

The Strand opened in 1892 and is an *olde worlde* walk-through with mosaic tiled floor and Victorian architecture. It connects Pitt Street Mall with George Street and is ☺open Mon-Wed and Fri 9am-5.30pm, Thu 9am-9pm, Sat 9am-4pm and Sun 11am-4pm.

Mid City Centre

This centre connects Pitt Street Mall and George Street, and is between the Strand Arcade and Grace Bros, with an entrance from Grace Bros. It has four levels of shopping with over 40 fashion boutiques, more than 50 specialty shops, and first class restaurants and coffee shops.

MLC Centre

The MLC Centre has entrances from Martin Place, Castlereagh Street and King Street, and has fashion boutiques, coffee shops and restaurants, and the Theatre Royal. The outdoor cafes overlooking Martin Place are popular lunchtime places.

Royal Arcade

Located under the Sydney Hilton Hotel, the Royal Arcade is between Market and Park Streets, and connects Pitt and George Streets. It has a range of rather expensive shops, typical of those found in hotel arcades.

Piccadilly Arcade

The Piccadilly is near the Pitt Street Cinema Centre, and connects Pitt and Castlereagh Streets. It also has overhead walkway connections to the Sydney Hilton and Sheraton on the Park Hotels. This is another rather upmarket shopping experience.

At the other end of the shopping district, near Wynyard Station, there are a few more places waiting to be discovered.

Wynyard Arcade

Fairly recently renovated, this arcade is situated inside the station and has specialty shops of its own as well as access to Westpac Plaza and the Hunter Connection.

Chifley Plaza

Situated on Hunter, Elizabeth and Phillip Streets, Chifley Square is home to, among other not-so-well-known names, the local branch of *Tiffany's*.

If after visiting all of the above you are still in a shopping mood, return to the city centre and hop on the monorail for Darling Harbour.

Harbourside, Darling Harbour

After undergoing an extensive renovation upgrade, the Harbourside Festival Marketplace has a new look for its 200 shops from boutiques to souvenirs, sportswear to art, and restaurants, cafes and bars. It is a bazaar for overseas visitors rather than for Sydneysiders, and the refit was no doubt pitched at attracting the Olympic crowds.

Markets

The Rocks Market

Every Saturday and Sunday, at the end of George Street in The Rocks, a sail-like canopy transforms the area into a Portobello Road. It is not an exceptionally large market, but it has many interesting articles for sale, and the Victorian terraces, pubs and old warehouses that surround it contribute to a holiday atmosphere year round. Nearby there are plenty of cafes, outdoor food stalls and restaurants.

Paddy's Markets

There are two locations:

The original Paddy's is in Haymarket, on the corner of Hay & Thomas Streets, near Chinatown. It is open Fri-Sun 9am-4pm.

The other is on Parramatta Road, Flemington, and it is open Fri 10am-4.30pm and Sun 9am-4.30pm.

There are over 1000 stalls in each location selling fashion garments, footwear, jewellery, household and electrical goods, takeaway foods, fresh fruit and vegetables, poultry, seafood, and heaps and heaps of souvenirs. Paddy's is the biggest market in Australia, and for further information, phone the Hotline - ✆1300 361 589.

Paddington Bazaar

Located at the corner of Oxford and Newcombe Streets, Paddington, in the grounds of the Uniting Church, this bazaar is held on Saturdays 10am-4pm, ✆9331 2646. There are over 250 stalls offering all types of clothing, crafts, jewellery and food.

While you are in Paddington you could visit *Coo-ee Aboriginal Art*, 98 Oxford Street, ✆9332 1544. They have a large display of Aboriginal Art, and are agents for Tiwi Design fabrics.

Balmain Saturday Market

Held in the grounds of St Andrew's Congregational Church, corner Darling Street and Curtis Road, Balmain, every Saturday 8.30am-4pm, ✆0418 765 736 (mobile).

Glebe Markets

These are held in Glebe Public School, cnr Glebe Point Road & Derby Place, on Saturday 9.30am-4.30pm. Many people think this Market has a lot of atmosphere.

City Sights

It is not possible to see the sights of the city of Sydney in one day on a walking tour, even if you are super-fit. Apart from the distance, Sydney is not a flat city, and the hills would slow you down. By taking advantage of **The Sydney Explorer** bus (see *Local Transport*) you could catch a glimpse of everything, but you still wouldn't have time to appreciate what you saw. It is best to allot at least a few days for the city itself before you spread your wings to the outer attractions. So this guide is set out in areas, perhaps you should allow one day per area. Note that all museums are closed on Christmas Day and Good Friday.

The grid references shown below refer to the colour map of Sydney at the front of the book.

Circular Quay Area

Sydney Harbour Bridge   E11
Affectionately known to Sydneysiders as 'The Coathanger' the Sydney Harbour Bridge dominates the city skyline. It is 503m long, and was completed in 1932 after nine years of construction. It was built from either shore, and when the two halves met they were only 7.6cm (3 inches in the old measurements) out of alignment! The Bridge opened with a piece of drama. The dignitaries were lined

up, the Premier, Jack Lang, stepped forward to cut the ribbon, and up rode Captain de Groot on a noble steed. He slashed the ribbon with his sword, and all and sundry stood speechless, at least for a few seconds. The miscreant was apprehended, the ribbon was rejoined, and the ceremony continued.

In August, 1992, came the opening of the long-awaited harbour tunnel, which has lived up to its expectations in reducing peak hour traffic snarls on the bridge. You can't walk through the tunnel but you can walk over the bridge, and you can climb up the south-east pylon for some of the best harbour views. The pylon is ⊙open daily 10am-5pm and admission is around ✪$2 adult.

A recent enterprise which has proved extremely popular is offered by *BridgeClimb*, 5 Cumberland Street, The Rocks. Included in the three hour package is a safety briefing and a magnificent walk up and across the great steel span. From the top of the bridge, spectacular views of Sydney by day or night are the reward for making it to the top, ✆9252 0077 for tickets, ⊙7am-7pm, 7 days a week.

From the bridge there is a good view of Sydney's newest crossing, the Glebe Island Bridge with its many suspension cables. The bridge has improved the traffic flow into the city from the west.

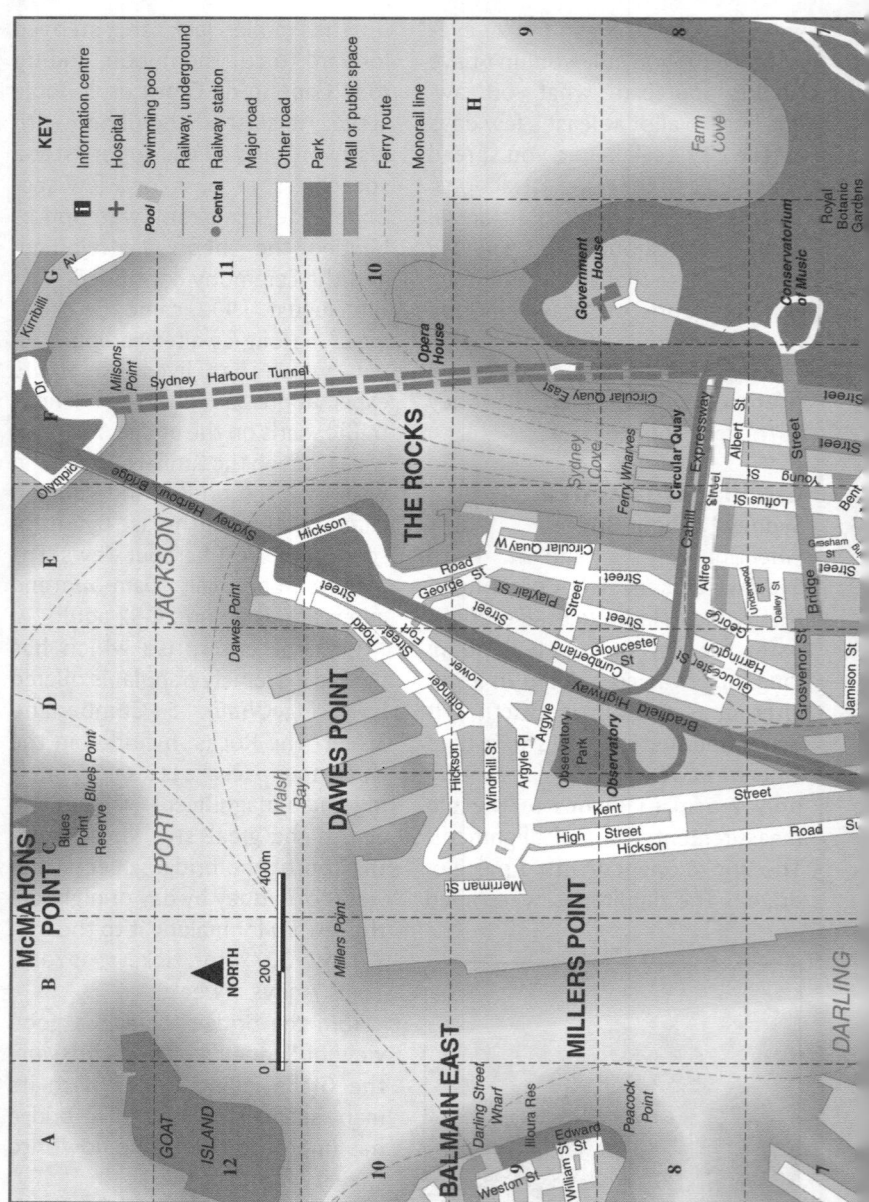

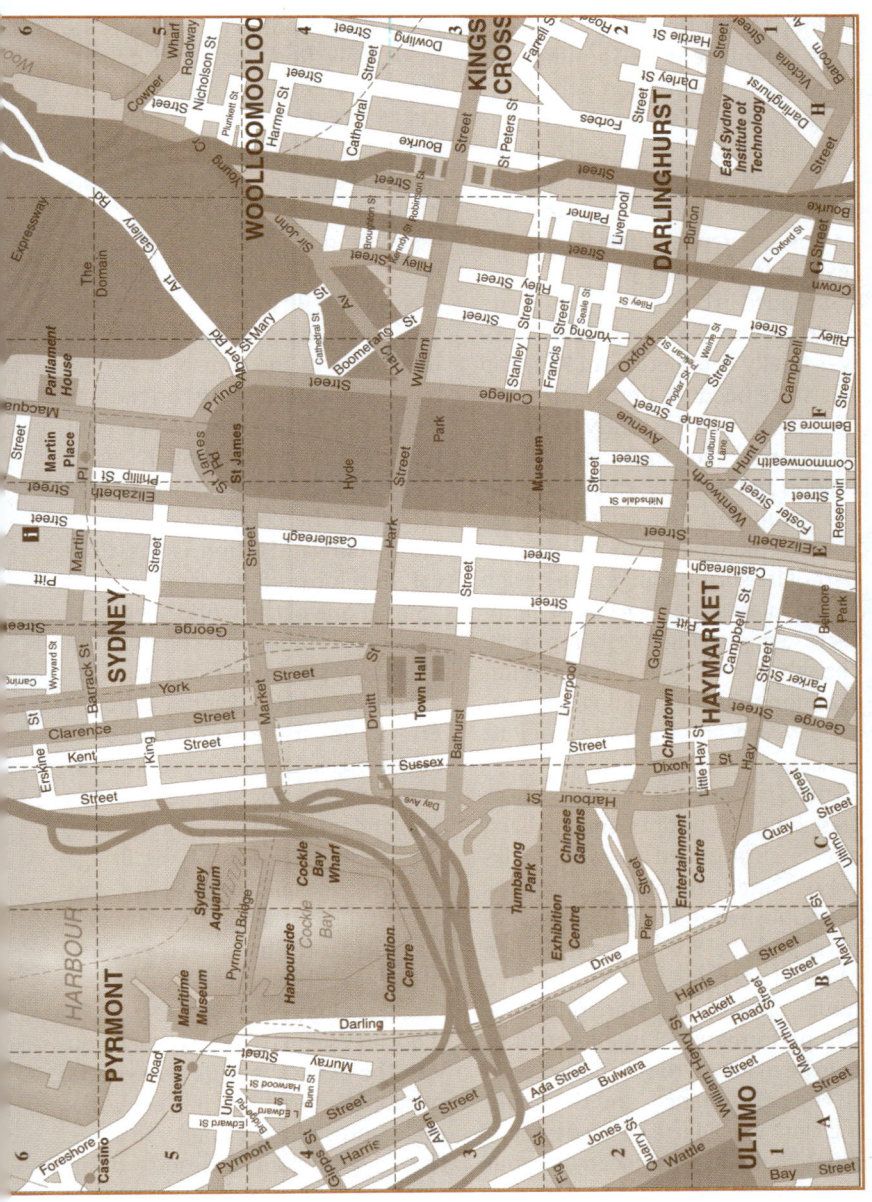

Sydney Opera House   G10

This magnificent performing arts complex is situated on Bennelong Point, which was named by Governor Phillip after an Aboriginal he befriended, taught English, and actually took back to England. This spot is apparently where Bennelong resided in his humpy.

Shrouded in controversy during its construction, Sydney Opera House was finally completed in 1973, and has since become almost the symbol of Australia. Instantly recognisable anywhere because of its unique architecture, this extraordinary building can only really be appreciated when acknowledged as part of its surroundings. The design encapsulates the concept of architecture mimicking its environment: the white sails give the vague impression that the building is a cluster of vessels on the waters of Port Jackson.

The Opera House has four theatres, four restaurants and six bars, and is surrounded by wide walkways. Details of current programs are published in the daily newspapers, and the Box Office is ☉open Mon-Sat 9am-8.30pm and two hours prior to the start of a Sunday performance. Phone bookings may be made up to seven days prior to the performance, and the booking clerk will advise when payment must be made, or you can use your credit card. Front of House tours are held ☉daily from 9am-4pm, departing every 30 minutes, and cost ✪$15 adults, $10 concession, ✆9250 7111. There are also tours on some Sundays that take visitors backstage and cost ✪$23 per person with no concessions (the tour is unsuitable for children under 12). The availability of the backstage tours depends on whether there are rehearsals in the house. It is best to contact *Guided Tours*, on the Saturday before you would like your tour, on the above number.

Bus no 438 travels down George Street to the concourse. Circular Quay Railway Station is the closest stop for train passengers.

Surely one of the world's greatest marine backdrops, the combination of Sydney's premier icons, the Opera House and the Sydney Harbour Bridge, must be appreciated at every angle. On any crystal morning, the white roof of the House is resplendent in the sunlight. Nearby, the impressive span of the Bridge arches over passing yachts and small cruisers carving their white trails across the harbour. The source of Sydney's beauty in a nutshell.

Circular Quay   F8

It doesn't seem to matter when you visit the Quay, there are always lots of people around, but it is on weekends and holidays that you have the added colour and noise of all the buskers. From men playing classical pieces on violins, to little kids belting it out on a range of brass instruments, to Aborigines and (non-Aborigines) playing didgeridoos and teaching people to perform kangaroo and emu dances - it's all captivating entertainment.

The Quay is the heart of the Sydney Ferry network. At any given time, at least one of these green-hulled vessels will be visible at the docks, either accepting passengers or waiting for them to disembark. They then make their way slowly to and from the middle harbour on routes that stretch north-east to Manly and west towards Parramatta River.

It is a real *mezcla* of people milling in anticipation of their ferry; people hurrying to catch their train at the railway station; some buying tickets for harbour cruises; some fishing in the doubtful water near Wharf 5; others, the well-dressed ones, beginning their walk around to the Opera House for a ballet or opera matinee.

A fairly recent and certainly controversial development has been established along the eastern promenade, stretching most of the way to the forefront of the Opera House. It is lined with up-market cafes, restaurants, shops and a movie cinema. The top levels are exclusive apartment residences.

This imposing complex was initally dubbed 'The Toaster' by protesters who demonstrated on the steps of the Opera House in December 1996, during its construction, hoping to preserve the aesthetic quality of this landmark area. You can judge for yourself the final result.

Circular Quay Railway Station, although not underground, is part of the City Circle, and the Cahill Expressway on top of the railway takes traffic from the Bridge to the Eastern Suburbs and Macquarie Street.

Justice & Police Museum   F8

This museum, at 9 Phillip Street, ✆9252 1144, is almost directly opposite Wharf 5, and if you look across you will see figures of 'burglars' apparently trying to break into the building on the corner. It is only ⏰open Sunday 10am-5pm, but is worth a visit if you are in the area, and interested in phrenology or medieval-style weaponry. The collection began with the Police Exhibition that was an exhibit at the Royal Easter Show for many years. It is now housed in a former police station and court house, and has displays of relics from police investigations and trials, as well as record sheets of some of Sydney's most notorious felons. Admission is ◆$7 adults, $4 children.

Museum of Sydney   F7

Situated on the corner of Phillip and Bridge Streets, on the site of First

Government House, this modern museum is ⊕open daily 10am-5pm and admission is ✪$7 adults, $4 children, $17 family, ✆9251 5988. It has an excellent cafe and a good bookshop, both of which can be visited without entering the museum. The bookshop specialises in architecture and design titles. There are also exhibits in the forecourt, and in the entrance foyer the foundations of Australia's first Government House are visible. Over the years there has been some controversy about the exhibits on show, and about the quotations of famous people that are on display throughout the galleries.

Museum of Contemporary Art (MCA)　　E8

The MCA is the Art Deco building on the waterfront around from Wharf 5. It formerly housed the Maritime Services Board and when the board moved to new premises, there was some talk of levelling this imposing structure. Then somebody realised that it would be the perfect place for the J.W. Power collection of contemporary art, which had been left to the University of Sydney many years before. Now the museum is run as a nonprofit company by a joint venture between Sydney University and the NSW Government. The museum's brochure proclaimed:

"This is a museum about the beautiful under our noses, the unusual, the weird and wacky in the visual, electronic, sound and tactile world we all live in."

And that just about sums it up! The museum is ⊕open daily 10am-5pm every day except Christmas. Admission is free. Entrance is from the Quay or from George Street. Volunteer-led guided tours are available for free, and curator-led tours cost $25 a head ad must be booked two weeks in advance. For details of current exhibitons phone ✆9252 4033 or the Infoline on ✆9241 5892.

The MCA Store in George Street has an incredible range of books, magazines, posters, etc, and the MCA Cafe next to the Quay entrance is worth a visit in itself. Why? It is managed by the people from the award-winning restaurant, Rockpool, which is nearby at 109 George Street, The Rocks.

Cadman's Cottage　　E9

Continuing along the waterfront, the cottage is situated in a reserve on the corner of Argyle Street. It is the oldest remaining house in Sydney, and was home to John Cadman, the last Government Coxswain.

The two-storey sandstone cottage was finished in early 1816, and its building was possibly supervised by Francis Greenway, the convict architect, who lived nearby. At that time the house stood two metres from the water, on a small sandy beach, and had a wharf on its northern side. Its present position resulted in the late 1840s when ten acres of land were reclaimed to form Circular Quay. The lack of recorded history, artefacts or detailed plans of the cottage has stopped the National Parks & Wildlife Service (NPWS) from restoring the building as an historical museum.

It is presently an information centre for Sydney Harbour National Park, ☏9247 5033, and has plenty of brochures on walks and trips in Sydney parks and those further afield. It is open seven days a week.

The waterside walk continues around the back of the Overseas Terminal. There is a new upmarket bar and restaurant here over two levels, with great views. Continue on to Campbell's Cove, which has many restaurants in converted storehouses, and the wharf from which the *Bounty* and other cruise ships depart. Nearby is the Park Hyatt Sydney Hotel.

The Rocks
E9-E10

The Rocks nestles on the western edge of Circular Quay, the initial point of colonial settlement. Preservation of the area's heritage was the subject of conflict during the 1970s, but eventually common

sense prevailed and the region has undergone restoration and improvement to become popular with both locals and tourists. The architecture transports the visitor to a previous era, and even products of modern consumerism attempt to blend in with the nostalgic theme.

The Sydney Visitor Centre   E9
Steps beside Cadman's Cottage lead up to George Street, and if you turn right at the top of the steps you will come to the old Sailors' Home which now houses The Rocks Visitor Centre, ☏9255 1788. The Centre is ⏰open daily 9am-5pm, and has a very good video presentation on the first floor, of the growth of Sydney from a small penal colony to a thriving modern city. They carry brochures and maps for tourist attractions all over Sydney.

George Street   E9-E10
Continuing along George Street, there are many old historic buildings and pubs, and on the weekends the Bridge end of the street is closed off and The Rocks Markets are held (see *Shopping* section).

In the building on the right hand side of the markets there are some interesting craft displays and shops.

Westpac Museum   E9
Retrace your steps along George Street, walk past the Old Sydney Parkroyal Hotel, then turn up Playfair Street. Here at no 6-8 is the

Westpac Museum, ©9763 5670, which traces the history of the bank from its beginnings in 1817 as the Bank of NSW, to the present day of technological banking. There are also temporary exhibitions featuring subjects as diverse as the Royal Flying Doctor Service and Antarctica. The museum is ⊙open Tues-Fri 10.30am-4pm, Sat-Mon 1-4pm and admission is free.

By the way, Playfair Street bends to the left, and straight ahead from the museum is Atherden Place, with four terrace houses. It is the shortest street in Sydney.

The Rocks Square   E9

The square is in the middle of Playfair Street (which is closed to traffic) and this area has many outdoor eateries, little shops, jazz or rock bands, and several lanes sprouting in all directions. Following Playfair Street to its end brings you to Argyle Street.

The Rocks Puppet Cottage   E8

The cottage is situated in Kendall Lane, and can be reached from George Street through a lane at no 77. It is ⊙open 10am-5pm Wed-Sun, ©9241 2902. There are hundreds of puppets on display, and shows are held at 11am, 12.30pm, 2pm and 3.30pm on weekends, and other days during school holidays. Admission is free, and the cottage is sponsored by the Sydney Cove Authority.

Susannah Place   D8

Situated at 58-64 Gloucester Street, Susannah Place, © 9241 1893, is a terrace of four brick houses that was built in 1844. It is now a museum of the lifestyle in the area from the 1840s until the turn of the century. Included is a shop that stocks the type of goods that would have been available then.

The Rocks Centre   E9

The centre is on the corner of Playfair & Argyle Streets and offers two floors of boutiques and eateries.

Argyle Stores   E9

The Rocks' newest addition is Argyle Stores, 18-24 Argyle Street, ©9251 4800, which has around 5000 square metres of upmarket shopping. Modelled along the lines of France's Galleries Lafeyette, the different departments are managed by individual operators, but blend to give the appearance of one entity.

The building was initially completed in 1828 using convict labour, and was the first Customs House in Australia. Over the years it has had several uses, and names, until in 1993 it was completely restored by the Sydney Cove Authority at a cost of around $9 million. In 1994 it was offered for lease as a department store, and back in October 1996 the Argyle opened its doors to customers.

A few doors up Argyle Street is

The Argyle Restaurant, which is ☺open daily 11.30am-3pm, 7.30-10.30pm, ✆9247 7782. This is a real Aussie theatre-restaurant, that serves good old fashioned tucker (food) with large helpings of fun and laughter.

Clocktower Square   E9

The square is the building on the corner of Argyle and Harrington Streets with the clocktower, and it contains several souvenir shops, a Japanese restaurant, and **The Rocks Opal Mine**, ✆9247 4974. Here you can not only buy tax-free opals, you can dig for them! There is a mine shaft elevator which really does seem to travel down to the depths of the earth, then the door opens and an old mine tunnel appears with 'miners' busy at work. It's good fun even if you are not interested in buying opals, and is ☺open seven days.

Millers Point   E11

Millers Point is the suburb on the opposite side of the Harbour Bridge (and the Bradfield Highway which crosses it) to The Rocks. It can be reached by following Hickson Road from the Park Hyatt Sydney Hotel around the base of the south-east pylon of the Bridge to Dawes Point; by following George Street to its end, then walking down steps to Hickson Road; or by continuing along Argyle Street and passing under the Bradfield Highway.

Holy Trinity (Garrison) Church D9

The Church is in Argyle Street. It was built in 1848 and is called the Garrison Church because it was compulsory for the soldiers of the 50th Regiment stationed at Dawes Point Battery to attend the morning service. There is a leaflet available for a small purchase fee at the rear of the church which details its complete history.

Argyle Place   D9

The little park just up the street, is Sydney's oldest village green.

Sydney Observatory   D8

The Observatory is on Watson Road, Observatory Hill, and can be reached by following Argyle Street, then walking up some steep steps. The Observatory, ✆9217 0485, has a regular program of exhibitions, films, talks and night viewings, and a hands-on exhibition. During the day it is ☺open Mon-Fri 2-5pm, Sat-Sun 10am-5pm and admission is ✪free. It is also ☺open nightly, except Wednesday, and has two programs in winter (6.15 and 8.15pm) and one in summer (8.15pm). Bookings are necessary for the night sessions, and charges are ✪$10 adults, $5 children, $25 family.

You may wonder about the ball on top of the building. It has been part of the synchronisation of time in Sydney since the building was erected in 1858. In the early days of the colony, a gun was fired at exactly 1pm from Dawes Point, and another from Fort Denison. These were for the ships in the harbour to check their chronometers. To enable the settlers in the colony to also check their time-pieces, the ball on the Observatory was hoisted by mechanical means to the top of the pole at approximately five minutes to one, then when the guns fired, the ball dropped back to the bottom. The ball still fulfils its function, but only on special occasions such as public holidays and during school holidays.

S.H. Ervin Gallery   D8

The Gallery is in the National Trust Centre, almost next door to the Observatory. The building was erected in 1815 as a military hospital, then for many years was home to one of Sydney's leading girls' high schools.

The Gallery has changing exhibitions, and for current programs and entry charges, ✆9258 0173.

The Royal Botanical Gardens & Macquarie Street

The Gardens are a popular lunchtime spot for city workers, and weekends see many family picnics. They are situated on the edge of Farm Cove, where the early colonists first tried to grow vegetables.

As you enter through the gate near the Opera House and climb the slight slope, the astonishing building to your right is **Government House**. It is the state's finest example of sophisticated Gothic Revival and took eight years to build, finally completed in 1845. Although the battlements, turrets and arches present it for all intents and purposes as a castle, defence was not one of the building's intended functions, and it was instead given over to the administration of colonial affairs. Surrounded by scenic gardens in one of the city's finest corners, it now acts as a pleasant welcoming venue for the Governor's official receptions. It is ◷open to the public Fri-Sun 10am-3pm, ✆9931 5222. The garden belonging to the House is ◷open every day 10am-4pm.

The building at the end of the driveway leading from Government House is the **Conservatorium of Music**, which was originally the Governor's stables.

Signposts point the way to **Mrs Macquarie's Chair**, a rock outcrop where the Governor's wife apparently sat to watch for ships arriving from England.

The small remote island you can see in the centre of the harbour is **Fort Denison**. For a short time it was regarded notoriously among early convicts as the most inescapable gaol of the colony and the destination of wayward miscreants. The nickname 'Pinchgut' evolved from the starvation men unlucky enough to spend time on the island experienced. Poorly treated and unfit to attempt a fleeing swim, these criminals were naturally inappreciative of their otherwise superb location. Feared and despised in those times, the fort is now a prime location commanding one of the best views of the city and harbour. It was built as part of Sydney's defences, and has come under the jurisdiction of the National Parks and Wildlife Service, as part of Sydney Harbour National Park.

Tours of Fort Denison leave from Wharf 6, Circular Quay, but must be booked in advance, ☎9247 5033 (NPWS at *Cadman's Cottage*). The tour costs ✪$16 for adults, $10 for children and concession and $40 for families.

Back on land, the footpath by the sea wall leads to the Visitors Centre and shop, a kiosk, and a restaurant; and signposts show the way to the herbarium, the pyramid glasshouse and other exhibits. There are two exits near the pyramid, one on to Macquarie Street, the other leads to the Art Gallery. The Royal Botanical Gardens are ⊙open daily 8am to sunset, ☎9231 8125.

Art Gallery of New South Wales   G5

The Art Gallery is in Art Gallery Road, in the Botanical Gardens, and faces The Domain. It is a spectacular building, housing a vast contemporary collection of Australian, European and Asian Art, and a fine collection of Aboriginal paintings and artefacts. The names of famous artists are set in stone on the front of the building, upon the tier just below the roof level. Two statues of mounted horseman grace the patches of lawn on either side of the entrance.

Many special exhibitions are held at the Gallery, and for recorded information on current exhibits, ☎9225 1744 or ☎9225 1790. Free guided tours of the Gallery are available - check at the information desk on your left as you walk into the gallery through the vestibule. There is no charge for admission to the Gallery and its permanent collection, but a fee is levied for special exhibitions.

There is a restaurant and a coffee shop, and the Gallery is ⊙open daily, 10am-5pm.

In this enriching environment, you can immerse yourself in culture and history before relaxing and reflecting among the flora of the Domain across the road or in the Botanical Gardens nearby.

The Domain　　　G5

The Domain is the large grassed area between the Art Gallery and the Public Library. It is a peaceful park setting for soap box orators on Sundays, and the venue for a number of Sydney's free summertime open-air concerts, such as *Opera In The Park* and *Symphony in the Park*.

State Library of
New South Wales　　　F6

The original, imposing building of the Library faces Shakespeare Place, on the corner of Macquarie Street. The new section has been built behind, but can also be accessed from Macquarie Street. The hushed ambience of the library envelops you upon entering.

The Library, commonly referred to as the Mitchell Library, contains the nation's finest collection of Australiana and an amazing wealth of historical records. The accumulation of this stored knowledge continues to grow with the obligation under law placed on all publishing houses to supply the library with a copy of each of their publications.

There is a magnificent reading room with wood panneling and tiered shelving, complete with matching stairs and narrow walkways. There is also an excellent Reference Library. The new wing contains the latest technology for reading and learning. The information desk has a self-guided tour sheet with information on every part of the library, and it is worth obtaining.

There is a restaurant and a bookshop, and the Library is ✆open Mon-Fri 9am-9pm, Sat 9am-5pm, Sun 11am-5pm, and admission is of course free, ✆9230 1414. The Library has changing exhibitions, usually of an historic nature, and information on current programs can be obtained by calling the above number.

Parliament House　　　F6

Situated in Macquarie Street, Parliament House has experienced several additions, removals, renovations and upgrades since its initial construction in 1816. It is a combination of styles - from Georgian to Victorian to contemporary - which have been carefully designed over the years to blend the variety and preserve the pleasant small scale of the building despite necessary expansions. The most recent challenge was the attachment of a twelve-storey office block to the existing framework, and its relative obscurity was accomplished by setting part of it underground, so that the new floors are only visible from the Domain at the rear rather than spoiling the Macquarie Street frontage.

The House is open to visitors, and they can even attend a session. Parliament generally sits from mid-February to early May, and from mid-September to early December, on Tues, Wed and Thurs. ☉For information on hours, ✆9230 2111.

The Mint   F5

The Mint is further south of Parliament House and next to Sydney Hospital (which was once a wing of Governor Macquarie's Rum Hospital). Built in 1816, it was the 1850s that earned the building its name for it was here that gold sovereigns were coined. Visitors can visit the Mint's former vaults, strike their own souvenir coin, and learn how raw gold was turned into bullion and currency. The Mint is ☉open daily 9am-5pm and admission is free, ✆9217 0311.

Hyde Park Barracks   F5

The Barracks is a Georgian building designed by convict architect Francis Greenway, and was intended for convict accommodation when it was built in 1819. It now houses an impressive collection which shows how the convicts spent their daily lives; where and how they slept, ate and worked. The Barracks also has the Greenway

Gallery, which has changing exhibitions of historical and cultural interest. The Barracks Cafe is in the original confinement cell area and has an imaginative menu, but it's a bit on the expensive side.

The Historic Houses Trust of New South Wales has control of the Barracks which is in Queens Square, adjacent to The Mint and northeast of Hyde Park itself. The museum ☉opens daily (except Christmas Day and Good Friday) 10am-5pm, ✆9223 8922. Admission is ✪$7 adults, $3 children, $17 family.

Francis Greenway also designed St James' Anglican Church on the other side of the street from the Barracks.

St Mary's Cathedral   F4

The Cathedral, on the corner of College Street and St Mary's Road, ✆9220 0400, is a magnificent example of revival Gothic architecture in Hawkesbury sandstone, outmatched in its style only by Government House.

Begun in 1866, after a fire destroyed the previous church, the workmen laid down their tools in 1928, standing back to admire the legacy of a 62-year project. The twin spires over the southern nave were added in early 2000, rectifying the unfinished look the exterior bore for seventy years.

Vaulted ceilings, intricate stat-

ues, period-piece gargoyles and crafted side altars make the church interior both beautiful and fascinating.

Perhaps the pinnacle of the labour is the outstanding stained-glass window features, depicting scenes from the life of the Blessed Virgin Mary, and the early days of the Catholic Church in Australia. Under the Cathedral is a crypt where the Catholic Archbishops of Sydney are interred, and there is also an exhibition on the background of the Cathedral and the plans for its future.

The Chapter Hall is the earliest building on the site. Built in Gothic Revival style between 1843 and 1845, it was to form part of a Benedictine Monastery planned to include the original cathedral. The monastery was never completed. The Chapter Hall was commissioned by John Bede Polding, the first Bishop of Sydney, and since its construction it has been used as a meeting hall, classics school and general purpose hall. It is classified by the National Trust.

Another attraction of the Cathedral is its world-famous choir which sings every Sunday at the 10.30am Mass.

Hyde Park   F5-F2

Opposite Hyde Park Barracks is Queen's Square with an imposing statue of Queen Victoria, and adjoining that is Hyde Park. Further south into the park is the impressive **Archibald Fountain.** Its fanning peacock-spray captures the attention of people strolling through the northern section of Hyde Park.

Hyde Park is bounded by Queen's Square, College Street, Liverpool Street and Elizabeth Street, with Park Street running through the centre, and changing its name to William Street as it crosses College Street. The western boundary of the park adjoins the hectic commerce-and-trade climate of Market and Elizabeth Streets while St Mary's Cathedral to the east encourages quiet contemplation and prayer.

At the Queen's Square end of the park there are entrances to the underground **St James Station** from Macquarie Street, Elizabeth Street (at the end of Market Street) and Queen's Square. At the Liverpool Street end of the park there are entrances to the underground **Museum Station** from Elizabeth Street (at the end of Bathurst Street) and near the corner of Elizabeth and Liverpool Streets.

The **Anzac War Memorial**, with the tomb of the Unknown Soldier and the Pool of Reflection, is in the southern section. Protruding from its lush surrounds, this enormous monument commemorates those Australians who gave their lives in wars - a significant proportion of the population each time. The poignant carvings on the Memorial pitch solemn order against the rage of battle, evoking a sense of reflection and an awareness of great loss. It is a remarkable feature with outstanding architecture that should be viewed.

The Australian Museum F3

The Museum is at 6 College Street, and is ☺open daily, except Christmas Day, 9.30am-5pm, ✆9230 6000. General admission to the museum is ◑$8 adult, $3 child (5-15), $19 family, but for special temporary exhibitions there may be an extra fee. There is no charge after 4pm each day. Phone the above number for all details of current attractions, special programs for children, information on guided tours and any other query you could possibly have.

The Australian Museum is recognised as one of the foremost museums of its type in the world. There is a bookshop and restaurant in the complex.

Parking

It is not really recommended that you take your car to the city if you intend to visit several places. Wherever you find a place to park, you will be walking quite a distance away from it, then have to retrace your steps to retrieve it. There is very limited long term street parking, and although there are parking stations in The Rocks area (behind the Regent Hotel), it could end up costing you more for the car than for your day out.

Another alternative is the council-run **Domain Parking Station**, which is entered from Sir John Young Crescent, east of St Mary's Cathedral. If a car is a necessity, ©9232 6165 for current opening times and daily charges and flat rates. Take note of the closing time because a fee exceeding $50 will be levied against you if you are forced to call the emergency number on the ticket and call someone out to open the station for you to retreive the car.

There is a moving underground footway from the parking station to the intersection of St Mary's Road, Prince Albert Road and College Street, in the front of the Cathedral. Privately-owned parking stations in other parts of the city are more expensive than the Domain.

City Centre

Pedestrians flock through city centre thoroughfares for many reasons. Most shop at the many lavish malls, plazas, arcades and complexes. Others hunt for a snack in an elegant food court, a fresh seafood meal by the waterside, or dinner with a view at one of the upper-floor restaurants in the middle of the CBD. Still more stroll on their way to relax with friends over coffee at a promenade cafe. And all enjoy the sights and sunshine of a remarkable city, drawn like moths to a flame.

Though this is principally a shopping area, here are a few sites worth visiting.

Martin Place   E6-F6

A traffic thoroughfare until 1973, Martin Place, or Martin Plaza as it is sometimes called, is a wide pedestrian mall that stretches for five blocks from George Street to Macquarie Street. At the George Street end near the GPO is the **Cenotaph**, where a Military Memorial Ceremony takes place on the last Thursday of the month at 12 30pm. On other Thursdays the Army Band plays near the monument. It is near the Cenotaph that Sydney's official Christmas Tree is erected (very tall and impressively decorated, it is disappointingly artificial nevertheless).

Between Pitt and Castlereagh Streets, near the *MLC Centre*, there is a sunken amphitheatre where free lunchtime entertainment is sometimes staged.

The entrance to Martin Place Railway Station is between Phillip and Macquarie Streets.

Sydney Tower   E5

Now burdened with the most overbearing advertisement visible, AMP Sydney Tower soars over 300m

above the city, and is the highest public building in the Southern Hemisphere. It is located above the Centrepoint Shopping Complex, bounded by Pitt, Market and Castlereagh Streets. From the Market Street foyer take the lift to the Podium Level, then board one of three double-decker lifts that will take you to the Observation Level (Level 4). Here there are high-powered binoculars, an illuminated display of Sydney Harbour's water traffic, a tourist booking and information service, audio and guided tours.

Level 3 has the highest coffee lounge in Australia; Level 2 has a self-service revolving restaurant; and Level 1 has an a-la-carte upmarket restaurant.

The Observation Level is ☺open daily 9am-10.30pm Sun-Fri and 9.30am-11pm on Saturday. A general tour is available, lasting between 30 and 45 minutes. The 76-floor ascension costs adults ✪$20, children $14, and $55 for a family, ✆9229 7444.

The Queen Victoria Building   D4

There is more information on this restored building in the *Shopping* chapter, but even if you aren't interested in shopping, you should call in and have a look. It is not just a shopping centre, it is a remarkable building, with style.

From the outside it gives a visually comparative insight into Sydney's architecture, which is an eclectic mix of old and new. The ostentatious towers, arches, angelic figureheads and pale green domes of the restored QVB contrast with the streamlined walls and dominant glass of the typical modern skyscrapers occupying the background. Yet somehow the clash pleasantly co-exists.

The QVB is located at 455 George Street, ✆9264 9209.

Sydney Town Hall   D3

Situated on the corner of George and Druitt Streets, the Town Hall was built between 1868 and 1889 in French Renaissance style. Its concert hall houses a pipe organ which ranks with the biggest and best in the world. The Sydney City Council administrative offices occupy the modern tower block at the rear of the building. The Town Hall was given a facelift in time for Sydney's Sesquicentenary in 1992 (prior to 1842, Sydney had not received city status).

The steps of Town Hall are often

crammed with people catching their breath, snacking on food, making a protest, selling something suspect or busking with limited talent. At night, the building's spires and recesses are aesthetically floodlit.

Centrepoint Touring Company conduct tours of the building when there are no functions taking place, ©8223 3815 for further information.

Town Hall Railway Station has entrances to the underground on both sides of George Street.

St Andrew's Cathedral   D3

The Cathedral has twin towers reminiscent of York Minster, and is the oldest cathedral in Australia. The foundation stone was laid on May 17, 1837 by Governor Bourke. Work stopped in 1842 due to lack of funds; a three year drought had caused the colony financial problems. The Cathedral was finally completed in 1868.

There was lot of drama during its construction, including a change of architects, and the complete reversal of the church's interior - the back door of which appeared on the original plans as opening onto George Street where the main entrace should have been. It is possible to buy a book detailing the history of this beautiful Cathedral. St Andrew's is just south of Town Hall.

Cinema District   D3

The next block on George Street, between Bathurst and Liverpool Streets, a large cinema complex jointly run by three different chains, a couple of McDonald's, a Pizza Hut, and other varieties of fast food outlet-. There are also arcade parlours, restaurants and coffee shops. In short, this is a very busy part of the city.

Chinatown   D2

Continue down George Street, turn right at Goulburn Street, and the first turn on the left will bring you to Chinatown, which has the usual amount of restaurants, delicatessens and herbalists.

From here it is a short walk to **Paddy's Markets**, the **Entertainment Centre** and the restored **Capitol Theatre**.

Darling Harbour

Darling Harbour is Sydney's newest area, and is nearly half the size of the Sydney Business District at 54ha (133 acres). It was originally a shipping and storage area for the Port of Sydney, but the advent of container ships sounded its death knoll and it became nothing more than an eyesore. After years of planning, wrangling amongst civic authorities, and the investment of millions of dollars, Darling Harbour is rapidly becoming the entertainment hub of Sydney. The Conference Centre, Exhibition Centre, Maritime Museum, Aquarium, IMAX Theatre, Chinese Gardens and Sega World can all be found here. A short distance away is the Entertainment Centre, the penultimate venue for concerts. In recent years, the Harbourside Festival Marketplace upgrade and construction of Cockle Bay Wharf has raised the profile of the location further.

On weekends families can be seen strolling along the walkways, picnicing on the grass and having a pleasant time.

There is always something on at Darling Harbour. Every weekend there is a program of entertainment, and almost every yearly festival or show has changed its venue to this central area - the Home Show, the Boat Show, Navy Week, Music Festivals, Book Fairs, Antique Fairs, and the list goes on.

For information on special events when you are in town, phone the Darling Harbour Infoline on, ©1902 260 568. Alternatively, you can visit the Darling Harbour Information Centre, situated between the IMAX Theatre and Sega World, or phone them directly on, ©9286 0111. Their web site is at ✆www. darlingharbour.com.au

How to Get There

By Monorail, the closest station to the Pitt Street Mall is near the corner of Pitt and Market Streets. There is a stop on both sides of Darling Harbour: Darling Park Station on the city side and Harbourside Station on the other. The monorail operates 7am-10pm Mon-Thu, Fri-Sat 7am-midnight and 8am-10pm on Sundays (see also under *Local Transport*).

By Light Rail, which runs from Central Station to Darling Harbour, in the middle of the circuit.

By Bus no 456 from Circular Quay via Town Hall to Darling Harbour, Mon-Fri 10am-2.30pm, Sat-Sun 11.30am-5pm, every 30 minutes.

By Sydney Ferries from Wharf 5 at Circular Quay to the Aquarium via Pyrmont Bay (Casino and Maritime Museum).

By Sydney Explorer Bus, which stops at Harbourside and the Chinese Gardens.

By Train, the nearest stations are Town Hall, from where you can walk down Market or Bathurst Streets then across Pyrmont Bridge; and Central Station, from where you can catch Bus 469, or take any bus travelling north along George Street and alight at Chinatown.

Parking

Although several thousand car parking spaces are available on the western side of Darling Harbour - off Quay Street, adjacent to the Sydney Entertainment Centre; off Murray Street behind Harbourside; off Darling Drive under the Sydney

Exhibition Centre; and off Sussex Street underneath Darling Park through to Cockle Bay Wharf - it is an expensive operation to park your car for a whole day, so the best advice is to leave the car at home, or at a railway station on the outskirts of the city.

Getting around Darling Harbour

Of course, you can walk from attraction to attraction, but if you have small children, or elderly people with you, there is the *The People Mover* train, a 20-minute ride operating between 10am and 5pm daily, which stops at all the major attractions in Darling Harbour. It costs adults ✪$3.50 and children $2.50.

Taxis

If you have overstayed your visit and missed all the public transport available, there is always the option of grabbing a cab.

Taxi Ranks are located at the Convention Centre entrance (rear of Harbourside off Darling Drive), in front of Sydney Entertainment Centre, and at all the hotels.

Darling Harbour Super Ticket

Several of the attractions at Darling Harbour have banded together to offer reductions in the form of the Darling Harbour Super Ticket, which can be purchased at any of the information booths at Darling Harbour, the Sydney Aquarium, the Monorail, the Chinese Garden, or at Matilda Cruises. The cost is ✪$45 adults, $30 children under 12, which may sound a bit expensive, but this is what you receive:

A two hour Matilda Harbour Cruise.

Entry to Sydney Aquarium.

Discount entry to IMAX theatre.

Discount entry to the Powerhouse Museum.

A ride on the Monorail.

A visit to the Chinese Gardens.

Lunch at the Shark Bite Restaurant at the Aquarium.

When you add all that, the ticket is definitely worth considering. Also, all sections of the ticket can be used on the one day, or you can use some sections on that day, and the rest are good for one month from the date of issue. The ticket also has a few optional extras, such as discount on the People Mover and on the bus fare to Homebush Bay.

Now that you know how to get there, how to get around, how to leave, and all about the Super Ticket, let's see what there is to see and do.

Cockle Bay Wharf   C4

Located on the city side of Darling Harbour, this is the area's latest development. Modern, innovative and precise architecture is a feature of the construction, complemented by the space-age IMAX Theatre hovering at its southern end.

Cockle Bay is worth visiting for its photogenic appeal alone, but there is much more.

During the lunch hour and in the evening, corporate types stream from their multi-windowed offices in Sussex Street, behind the wharf, to patronise the many cafes, bars and restaurants found along this trendy strip. At night, an influx of people eager to participate in the atmosphere ensures the area bustles with life. Both a nightclub and a pub can also be found along the promenade, and the restaurants are outstanding. It is definitely a recommended place to dine, and two excellent choices are *Coast*, ©9267 6700, and *Nick's*, ©9264 1212, if you don't mind lightening your wallet.

Sydney Aquarium   C5

The Aquarium is located rear the city end of Pyrmont Bridge, and is one of the largest and most spectacular in the world. The numerous tanks and tunnels allow the visitor to experience life on the ocean floor, surrounded by hundreds of different species of marine life. There are also displays of river systems, crocodiles, rocky shores, and the Great Barrier Reef. A touch pool allows you to get your hands onto some rough and spiky creatures.

The Aquarium is ©open daily 9.30am-9pm, and admission is ❍$22 adult, $10 child, $48 family (2 adults and up to 3 chil-dren), ©9262 2300. The *Shark Bite Restaurant* has plenty to tempt your taste buds while you are here.

Australian National Maritime Museum   B5

The museum, at the western end of Pyrmont Bridge, is dedicated to helping people understand and enjoy Australia's ongoing involvement with the sea. Among the craft moored at the museum are yachts, warships, tugboats, and a refugee boat.

Free guided tours of the Museum building are available at regular intervals throughout the day, and a booking must be made at the Information Counter on arrival. Audio tours are also available from the Information Counter - ❍$3 adults, $5 for 2 adults sharing, $2 children.

The museum has a program of changing exhibitions, and information can be obtained by phoning the recorded information line on, ©1900 962 002, or for general information, ©9298 3777. There is also a library, a kiosk on the waterfront, and a shop with a wide range of nautical gifts. The museum is ©open daily 9am-5pm (closes at 6pm in January), and minimum general admission is ❍$10 adult, $6 child, $25 family. There are extra charges for special exhibitions.

Harbourside   B4

Harbourside Darling Harbour is a

shopping centre with 200 shops that include 54 waterfront restaurants and food places. There are no department stores, and many of the shops sell for the tourist trade although there are branches of fashion outlets that seem to find their way into every shopping centre in Sydney.

Harbourside shops have ☺longer trading hours than in any other complex in the city - Mon-Sat 10am-9pm, Sun 10am-6pm - the restaurants, of course, stay open even longer.

Harris Street Motor Museum   A3

The building next to Harbourside is the **Convention Centre**, and for people that are interested in cars, motoring and associated memorabilia, their next stop should be the **Motor World Museum Gallery**, Level 1, 320 Harris Street, a short walk from the Convention Centre Monorail Station, ✆9552 3375. Here you will find a spectacular array of classic machines from the earliest to the latest, with lots of hands-on exhibits, in an historic old Woolstore building. The museum and carpark cover almost 4ha on two levels. It even has a place where you can 'park' the kids for a while under supervision. *The Cadillac Cafe* is available for roadside snacks, and the bookshop stocks everything ever written about cars, and some out-of-the-

ordinary souvenirs. The museum is ☺open Wed-Sun 10am-5pm, and admission is ✪$11 adults, $6 children, family $22, ✆9552 3375.

The Powerhouse Museum   B2

While you are in Harris Street, you continue in the direction away from the water until you arrive at Australia's largest museum, The Powerhouse Museum, on your left. Created from the shell of an old Sydney power station, the museum is alive with dynamic exhibitions, hands-on fun and special performances. There is so much to see that some people spend the whole day wandering through this incredible exhibition. Tours, talks, films, performances, demonstrations and workshops are continually in progress, and there is the *Ken Done Restaurant* (painted by, guess who?) and a kiosk when you need sustenance. As always, there is a souvenir/book shop, but this one offers some unusual merchandise. The Powerhouse Museum is ☺open daily 10am-5pm. Admission is ✪$8 adults, $2 children, under 5 free, $18 family, and the first Saturday of every month is free, ✆9217 0100.

Back at Darling Harbour proper, the **Exhibition Centre** is the next group of buildings, and information on current shows is available from the Infoline.

In front of the centre is **Tumbalong**

Park, and from there it is a short walk to the next attraction.

The Chinese Garden   C2

The Garden was specially designed by landscape architects from Guangdong Province, and is the largest and most elaborate outside China. It covers a full hectare, and has a two-storey pavilion above a system of lakes and waterfalls. It is a serene retreat from the mayhem of the waterfront.

The Garden is ⊙open daily 9.30am-5pm and admission is ✪$4.50 adults, $2 children.

Across Pier Street from the Chinese Garden is the **Sydney Entertainment Centre**. Chinatown is opposite the main entrance to the Centre, in Harbour Street.

From the Chinese Garden walk back towards the waterfront, and you will come to **Darling Walk**, opened in 1997. It covers 20,000 square metres of mainly restaurants, bars, clubs and shops.

Panasonic IMAX Theatre   C3

There is no way you could miss this building - it is the strangely-shaped monolith painted with yellow and black squares. The theatre has a 900m² movie screen, the largest size in the world, and seating for over 500 people. Programs have varied from documentaries on Antarctica and the Ocean to concerts, virtual roller-coaster rides and 3-dimensional cartoon features. Current showings are advertised in the daily newspapers on the same pages as the more conservative cinemas, or you can contact IMAX on ✆9281 3300. Admission is ✪$17.50 adults, $12.50 children, and $50 for a family pass.

The complex also contains the *Wockpool Noodle Bar*, ✆9211 9888.

Star City Casino   A5

An $867 million testament to the Aussie love affair with luck and misfortune, Star City coaxes punters inside with its glittering neon lights and extravagant surrounds. The exterior looks as if it has been airlifted to the site directly from Vegas; you will either be disgusted by its tackiness or impressed with

its dazzling lavishness. A mecca for the nocturnal, this enormous complex sprawls over almost three-and-a-half hectares and consists of a five star hotel, an apartment complex, a huge gaming room, the Lyric Theatre, the Showroom, 20 bars and restaurants, shops and a nightclub. If you are going to lose your money, you might find some comfort in doing it here in style - and knowing you are not alone.

The casino is at 80 Pyrmont Street, Pyrmont, a short stroll from Darling Harbour, and its doors are open 24 hours, © 9777 9000.

Sydney Jewish Museum

Over in Darlinghurst to the east, the Sydney Jewish Museum is worth the trip across town. It is the corner of Darlinghurst Road and Burton Street, south of Kings Cross Station, and is ⊙open Mon-Thurs 10am-4pm, Fri 10am-2pm, Sun 11am-5pm (closed Saturday and Jewish Holidays). Admission is ✪$7 adult, $5 child, $16 family, ©9360 7999.

The exhibits are spread over three floors with six mezzanine levels. The ground floor has a re-creation of George Street in the 1840s, showing the homes and businesses of some of the Jewish settlers. There are also displays of elements of contemporary Jewish rituals, with guides available to answer any questions, and information on some famous Jewish Australians. The mezzanines contain the permanent exhibition of The Holocaust, and survivor volunteers are present on each level to offer a rare insight into the displays. However, Catholics argue that the role of the Vatican during World War II is inaccurately recounted by the Museum, and that the aid which Pius XII gave to thousands of Jews at the time unfortunately goes unacknowledged.

The museum has a shop with a wide range of souvenirs, and on the lower ground floor the excellent *Cafe Macc* offers traditional European and Israeli cuisine at reasonable prices.

Sydney Beaches

Sydney's coastline stretches for approximately 65km, from Palm Beach in the north, to Cronulla in the south. Most Sydneysiders have their 'favourite' beach, which is not necessarily the closest to their homes. Some people grew up living near one beach, then moved as an adult to another, but you will usually find them returning to their original haunt. The people who live here have a connection with the ocean that develops from a very early age; sand between the toes and watery foam lapping at the ankles are not cliches but sensations simply indicative of a way of life.

Most of the ocean beaches are patrolled during the summer months on the weekends and during school holidays. The lifesavers, who know what they are doing, erect flags in the safest part of the beaches, and people are requested to make sure they swim between these flags. If they don't, and get into difficulties, the lifesavers are not going to let them drown, but under reasonable circumstances it should not come to this point.

If the beach is considered unsafe, perhaps because of a strong undertow or a very high tide, the lifesavers will close it and erect a sign warning people not to enter the water. Take notice of such signs and decide to spend the day somewhere else.

Board riders are given their own stretch of beach, so that they don't interfere with swimmers, and swimmers should keep out of designated board areas.

On weekends, Lifesavers n this country are not paid for the hours they spend on duty. They are willing volunteers who give freely of their time to keep our beaches safe.

Harbour beaches are not patrolled. It must not be assumed that the harbour is one giant swimming pool. There are several places where shark-nets have been strung across inlets, and these are the only places where you should venture into the water. You won't see one, but there are sharks in Sydney Harbour. It is generally believed that old sharks, unable to fend for themselves in the open sea, come into the harbour for easy feeding - and what could be easier than a human thrashing around? Of course, there are also sharks in the open ocean, but the surf patrols on these beaches keep a sharp lookout, and sound alarms if a shark is sighted. You may not have caught a wave all day, but if a shark alarm sounds it is incredible how quickly you can get yourself back on the beach.

Having said all that, there has not been a shark attack in Sydney since 1963, when two children were taken whilst swimming in Middle Harbour.

Ocean Beaches

Listed below are the beaches stretching from Palm Beach in the north to Bundeena in the south, with the closest main road, and the public transport that gives access. Also included is the following information for each venue:

Dressing Shed - usually will include showers and toilets.

Patrolled - in summer on weekends and during school holidays, ie from the first weekend in October to Easter the following year.

Pool - rock pool suitable for children.

Board - surf is suitable for board riders.

Surfers - surf is suitable for body surfers.

Usually beaches back onto a park or a reserve, and there are clear directions on the major roads indicating the way to the beach. Most beaches tend to have some topless sunbathers during the hottest parts of the day.

North of the Harbour

Palm Beach, off Barrenjoey Road, was once mainly frequented by the wealthy and yuppy set. It has now become very popular with British tourists because it is the setting for the TV series *Home and Away*. Dressing shed, patrolled, surfers and board, pool south end. About one-and-a-half hours drive from the city centre.

Bus no 190 from Wynyard.

Whale Beach, off Barrenjoey Road. Dressing shed, patrolled, surfers and board, pool south end.

Bus 190 from Wynyard, Bus 193 from Avalon (infrequent service).

Avalon Beach, off Barrenjoey Road. Dressing shed, patrolled, surfers and board, pool south end.

Bus 190 from Wynyard.

Bilgola Beach, off Barrenjoey Road. Dressing shed, patrolled, surfers and board.

Bus 190 from Wynyard.

Newport Beach, off Barrenjoey Road. Dressing shed, patrolled, surfers and board.

Bus 190 from Wynyard.

Bungan Beach, off Barrenjoey Road. Patrolled, board.

Bus 190 from Wynyard.

Mona Vale Beach, off Barrenjoey Road. Top end not patrolled (Bongin Bongin). Dressing shed, patrolled south end, surfers south end, board north end.

Bus 157 from Manly, Bus 184 from Wynyard (peak hour).

Warriewood Beach, off Pittwater Road. Dressing shed, patrolled surfers and board.

Bus 157 from Manly.

Turimetta Beach, off Pittwater Road. Not patrolled, board.

Buses 155 and 157 from Manly.

Narrabeen Beach, off Pittwater Road. Dressing shed, patrolled, surfers and board.

Buses 182 and 190 from Wynyard, Buses 155 and 157 from Manly.

Collaroy Beach, off Pittwater Road adjoining Narrabeen Beach. Dressing shed, patrolled, surfers and board, pool at southern end.

Buses 182 and 190 from Wynyard. Buses 155 and 157 from Manly.

Collaroy Basin, off Pittwater Road. Surfers, little swell.

Via Collaroy Beach.

Long Reef Beach, off Pittwater Road. Dressing shed, patrolled, surfers and board.

Bus 182 and 190 from Wynyard, Bus 155 and 157 from Manly.

Dee Why Beach, Howard Street, off Pittwater Road, adjoins Long Reef Beach. Dressing shed, patrolled, surfers and board, pool south end. Bus 178 and 180 from Queen Victoria Building, Bus 190, 182, 184 from Wynyard.

Curl Curl Beach, Oliver Road, off Pittwater Road. Dressing shed, patrolled, surfers and board, pool south end.

Bus 136 from Manly.

Freshwater (Harbord) Beach, Oliver Road, via Pittwater Road. Dressing shed, patrolled, surfers and board, pool north end.

Bus 139 from Manly.

Queenscliff Beach, off Pittwater Road. Dressing shed, patrolled, surfers and board, pool north end.

Bus 136 and 139 from Manly.

North Steyne Beach, off Pittwater Road, adjoins Queenscliff Beach. Dressing shed, patrolled, surfers and board.

See *Manly Beach* for travel information.

Manly Beach, off Pittwater Road, adjoins North Steyne Beach. Dressing shed, patrolled, surfers and board.

Bus 169 from Wynyard or Buses 143 and 144 from Chatswood, ferry from Circular Quay, JetCat from Circular Quay. Peak hour bus services available from Wynyard.

Shelly Beach, off Darley Road. Sheltered area with little swell, suitable for swimmers. Between Shelly Beach and Manly Beach there is a

pool at Fairy Bower.
Via Manly Beach.

South of the Harbour

Bondi Beach, via Bondi Road off Old South Head Road. Dressing shed, patrolled, surfers and board, sanctioned topless area south end, pool at south end.

Bus 380 and 389 from Circular Quay, 365 from Edgecliff.

An internationally famous beach, **Bondi** can attract more than 40,000 people on a sunny Sunday afternoon. Crowds filter through even the farthest reaches of the city to stake their claim to a golden patch of sand for a few hours. Inviting ocean temperatures and the safety provided by an elite surf life-saving team have made this coastal stretch extremely popular during the summer months.

The 1km strip of beach has a long history of development, since the local government authority gained control of it in 1881. By 1907 it was very popular with the neck-to-knee fraternity, although bathing time was limited to half an hour to avoid loitering. In 1928, the Bondi Beach Pavilion was built and then contained changing rooms for 1200 people, turkish baths, shops, a gymnasium and a ballroom. Today it is a community centre.

Surf life saving had its origins here and at nearby Bronte, with these clubs claiming to be the world's oldest. Surf Carnivals are often held at the beach, but the standard of the surf depends on the wind, and can range from enormous waves one day to a mill-pond the next. In the event that the swell is disappointing, there are plenty of cafes and restaurants to attend, or some casual street shopping to enjoy. Bondi has its own distinct lifestyle, and the pace slows as soon as you cross into its suburban boundary.

Tamarama Beach. Off Bronte Road. Dressing shed, surfers and board.

Bus 360 and 361 from Bondi Junction.

Bronte Beach, off Bronte Road. Squeezed between Tamarama and Clovelly it can experience some rough surf at times. Dressing shed, patrolled, surfers and board, pool south end.

Bus 378 from Railway Square.

Clovelly Beach, off Clovelly Road. Dressing shed, patrolled.

Bus 339 and 340 from Millers Point. Although Clovelly has a sandy foreshore, it is more like a swimming pool than a beach. Good for children.

Coogee Beach, off Coogee Bay Road. Dressing shed, patrolled, surfers and board, pool south end.

Bus 372 from Railway Square, Bus 373 from Circular Quay (Pitt Street).

Maroubra Beach, Fitzgerald Avenue, off Anzac Parade. Dressing

Above: Bondi Pavilion, Bondi Beach   Below: Coogee Beach

SYDNEY

KEY

- **i** Information centre
- **+** Hospital
- **Pool** Swimming pool
- Railway, underground
- **• Central** Railway station
- Major road
- Other road
- Park
- Mall or public space
- Ferry route
- Monorail line

PORT JACKSON

GOAT ISLAND

McMAHONS POINT

Blues Point Reserve

Blues Point

Milsons Point

Kirribilli Av

Olympic Dr

Sydney Harbour Bridge

Dawes Point

Walsh Bay

DAWES POINT

THE ROCKS

Hickson Road

Sydney Harbour Tunnel

Sydney Cove

Opera House

Government House

Royal Botanic

Conservatorium of Music

Farm Cove

Circular Quay East

Circular Quay

Ferry Wharves

Cahill Expressway

Circular Quay W

George St

Playfair St

Street

Street

Loftus St

Albert St

Young St

Alfred Street

Underwood St

Dalley St

Gresham St

Street

Bridge Street

George St

Harrington St

Gloucester St

Grosvenor St

Jamison St

Cumberland St

Gloucester St

Bradfield Highway

Lower Fort Street

Pottinger Street

Argyle Street

Windmill St

Argyle Pl

Observatory Park

Observatory

Kent Street

High Street

Hickson Road

Hickson Street

Merriman St

Millers Point

MILLERS POINT

Peacock Point

Edward St

William St

Weston St

Darling Street Wharf

Illoura Res

BALMAIN-EAST

NORTH

0 200 400m

A B C D E F G H

12 11 10 9 8 7

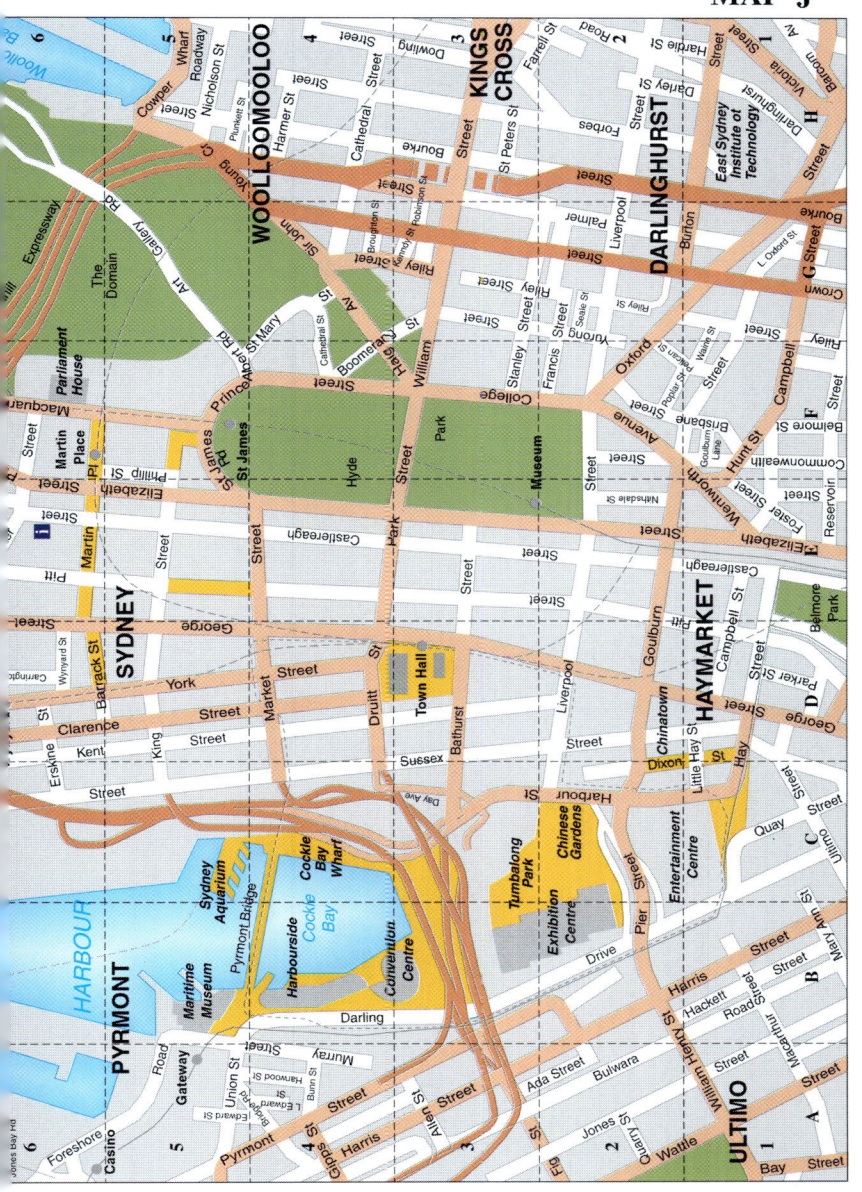

Above: Manly Beach   Below: Terrace housing in Paddington

shed, patrolled, surfers and board. Bus 395 from Railway Square, Bus 396 from Circular Quay.

Wanda Beach, off The Kingsway. Dressing shed, patrolled, surfers and board.

Catch a train to Cronulla and then make the short walk to beach.

Elouera Beach, adjoins Wanda Beach. Dressing shed, patrolled, surfers and board, pool south end. Train to Cronulla, walk to beach.

North Cronulla Beach, adjoins Wanda and Elouera Beaches, off The Kingsway. Dressing shed, patrolled, surfers and board, pool south end.

Train to Cronulla, walk to beach.

South Cronulla Beach, off The Kingsway. Dressing shed, patrolled, surfers and board, pool north end. Train to Cronulla, walk to beach.

Shelly Beach, off Cronulla Street. Dressing shed, patrolled, surfers and board, pool south end.

Train to Cronulla, walk to beach.

Harbour Beaches

There are hundreds of coves and bays around the harbour, but we are only including those that have shark-proof nets, changing facilities, takeaway food outlets, and picnic areas. Obviously the beaches on the harbour do not have waves.

Clifton Gardens, Chowder Bay. The bay is two bays north-east of Taronga Park Zoo, and not easy to get to by public transport.

Take Bus 228 from Milsons Point (Mon-Fri), Bus 247 from Wynyard/QVB to Taronga Zoo, alight at Thompson Street and follow the signs.

Balmoral, Hunter's Bay. This is quite a pretty beach and is divided into two by Rocky Point, a tree-covered outcrop. Balmoral is very popular and has takeaway food bars as well as coffee shops and an up-market restaurant. The rotunda on the beach is used for many shows on summer evenings, the 'Shakespeare on the Beach' programs in particular have a large following.

Bus 238 from Taronga Zoo, Bus 257 from Chatswood, or Bus 233 from Mosman Wharf.

Manly Cove, Manly. The swimming enclosure is adjacent to Manly Wharf, where the ferry from Circular Quay docks.

Travel by Ferry, or Bus 144 from Chatswood.

Nielsen Park, between Vaucluse Road and Greycliffe Avenue, Vaucluse, in the eastern suburbs. During the swimming season (October to April) a shark-proof net is erected at Shark Beach. Experience has shown that this net must be taken down during the colder months because it cannot withstand the winter storms and heavy seas. There are dressing sheds and showers for swimmers, and a kiosk

is situated opposite the beach.
Ferry from Circular Quay, Bus 325
from Circular Quay.

Botany Bay Beaches

Botany Bay was where Captain
James Cook landed, and where Captain Phillip was sent to begin the
new colony. Phillip, unable to find
a fresh water supply, sailed further
north to Sydney Harbour. Nowadays Botany Bay is a densely populated area, and if you arrived in
Sydney by air, you have already
spotted it; Kingsford Smith Airport
is situated on its shores.

The Bay also has its share of sharks,
so if you feel like a swim, stick to:
Brighton-le-Sands Baths, off
Grand Parade. It has wire netting
for protection, although the rest of
the Lady Robinson Beach is not
protected and is frequented by
swimmers. There are dressing
sheds. Bus 302-303 from Circular
Quay, Bus 478 from Rockdale.

Bundeena

South of Botany Bay is Port Hacking. Cronulla is on its northern side,
and Bundeena on the southern side
borders the Royal National Park.
Access is by ferry from Cronulla.

Surrounding Bundeena are
Hordens, Gunyah and Jobbons,
pleasant but small beaches which
have little swell and are suitable
only for swimming. They have no
safety nets and are not patrolled.

Inner-City Suburbs

As an introductory note, it is recommended that if you wish to explore the inner suburbs and
outlying regions of Sydney by car,
you should use a detailed Street Directory to find you way around. The
directions listed in the *How To Get
There* sections below are based on
that premise; they are street-specific and really require the aid of a
comprehensive map. Several Street
Directories are available from book
stores, newsagencies and information centres.

If you wish to explore a little further afield, the suburbs bounding
the city may be worth visiting.
Major city centres around the world
are becoming increasingly similar,
and the real distinctions can sometimes only be gleaned from the lifestyles exhibited on their perimeter,
where the homogenising effect of
commercialism is softened by the
first stages of urban sprawl. Surry
Hills, Paddington and Newtown are
examples offering their own
insights.

Terrace housing is a quaint and
common feature of inner-suburban
dwelling. Density of living in popular regions with close proximity to
the CBD means that town houses,
duplexes and apartments are basically the only form of accommodation on offer. Sometimes these

linked buildings stretch the distance of a whole street, separated in appearance only by exterior colours and the barest architectural trimmings. Those craving a big backyard head into the outer suburbs while inner-suburbanites tend to their flower pots on two-square-metre balconies, choosing the lifestyle instead. Although the frontal facade of these places is standard and often unimpressive, the interior is typically where owner's exert their effort, and they are often breathtaking. A pleasant stroll through these quiet, leafy backstreets can be worth the trip.

You can also make your way through the flurry of the main thoroughfares nearby. The consistency of building styles in the inner-city is an instantly noticeable trait. Commercial outlets are crammed into and against terraces that match the homes lining residential streets nearby. While there are a few shopping centres and several walk-through arcades, the space restrictions and advertising value mean that most retail businesses have main street fronts, and the majority of local shopping is done outside.

The inner-suburban people will most likely draw your interest. The clash of fashion, status and ideology within a small geographical radius is fascinating. Paddington east of Sydney is known for its concentrated gay community while Newtown to the city's south is the cultural centre of liberal alternative youths epitomising New Age living. A half-hour walk can take you between worlds.

NORTH
Although the Lower North Shore harbour front now contains some of the most valuable and exclusive real estate in Australia, it was originally the burial ground of the infant colony because it was considered to be far enough away to prevent the spread of disease.

How To Get There
Whatever form of transport is used, visitors must first cross the Sydney Harbour Bridge.

By Train
Trains from Central Station pass through Town Hall, Wynyard and Milsons Point to North Sydney. If you are on a train that is going to travel the City Circle, you must change trains at Town Hall or Wynyard for one on the Northern Line.

After North Sydney, the service continues through many suburban stations to Hornsby, where it may terminate, or link up with the main northern line to Newcastle, Dungog and Scone.

There is no rail service to the Lower North Shore suburbs, but buses from the city stop at North Sydney Station.

By Bus

Buses to the Lower North Shore begin in Carrington Street, at Wynyard Station. There are several to choose from, but there is a route map there, and a ticket machine. Some buses travel via North Sydney Station, while others take the Freeway and exit the Bridge on Military Road.

By Car

There are signs on all roads leading to the city that direct you to the Bridge or the Cahill Expressway. Once on the Bridge, Lane 1 has an exit for Lavender Bay, Milsons Point, and access under the Bridge to Kirribilli; Lanes 1 and 2 allow cars to exit to North Sydney, and Lane 2 also allows travel to the next exit for Crows Nest and Manly. To reach Military Road, and the suburb of Neutral Bay, follow the signs leading to Manly. Lane 4 also has an exit for Neutral Bay and Kirribilli, but this is not as easy to follow.

By Ferry

Ferries leave from Circular Quay Wharf 4 for the Lower North Shore suburbs. Buses meet the ferries to take passengers to the main street, Military Road.

Attractions

On the western side of the Bridge are the suburbs of **Milsons Point** and **Lavender Bay**. Milsons Point is home to North Sydney Olympic Pool, and the now inoperative Luna Park. Lavender Bay has harbourside parkland, from where you can get great photographs of the harbour.

The suburb of **North Sydney** rivals the Sydney CBD for skyscraping office blocks, and has a few large shopping areas, and numerous restaurants. North Sydney is really a mid-week place, as the service industry is geared for the office worker rather than the resident. This, of course, does not apply to a few good quality night venues.

On the eastern side of the Bridge lies **Kirribilli** and the stately mansions, *Admiralty House*, Sydney residence of the Governor-General, and *Kirribilli House*, Sydney residence of the Prime Minister. These two imposing buildings can be seen from the Harbour, and about twice a year they are opened for public inspection. Even if you are lucky enough to be in Sydney that particular weekend, think twice about going to view them for the queues of locals extend for blocks. By the way, Admiralty House is the one closest to the Bridge. Also in Kirribilli is the *Ensemble Theatre*.

Neutral Bay is the first suburb over the Bridge if you have used the Expressway, and the main street is lined with designer shops and restaurants. The side streets on the right hand side lead to the Harbour and open parklands, and there are many interesting old Federation homes. The side streets on the left lead to the suburb of **Cammeray**, and Long Bay, part of Middle Harbour.

Military Road, still with door-to-door shops and restaurants, continues through the **Cremorne Junction** to **Spit Junction**, where Spit Road branches off towards **Manly**, and Military Road continues on its way to **Mosman**, where the biggest attraction has to be Taronga Zoo. There is a lovely walk along the foreshores of the Harbour between Cremorne Point Wharf and Mosman Bay Wharf.

Taronga Park Zoo

The Zoo, ✆9969 2777, has Australia's best collection of native and exotic animals. Its main entrance (for car and bus access) is on Bradley's Head Road, but it is only a pleasant 12 minute ferry ride from Wharf 4 Circular Quay (leaving every half hour). Admission prices are ✪$21 adults, $15 children and $55 for families.

Taronga has Australia's best collection of native and exotic animals, and also offers some of the finest views of the city, particularly from near the giraffe enclosure. There are seal shows, a rainforest aviary, a nocturnal house, all the usual animals, and Friendship Farm, where children can pat baby animals.

Throughout the park there are plenty of food outlets, and there is also a licensed restaurant.

Probably the best way to explore the exhibits is to take the air cable from the lower wharf to the main entrance at the top of the hill and work your way down to catch the ferry back at the end of your journey. Of course, if you use the main entrance to begin with, walk at your leisure to the bottom of the zoo and remember to catch the air cable back in order to save your legs.

A *ZooPass* ticket is available from the ticket office at Circular Quay, and it costs ✪$28 adult, $14 child, with no combination ticket for a family. The pass includes the ferry to the Zoo, a bus up to the main entrance, and the admission fee.

Taronga is ☺open every day, including Christmas Day, 9am-5pm, ✆9969 2777.

From Mosman, it is also a short drive, or bus ride, to **Balmoral Beach**. If you head back to Spit Junction, and turn right down Spit

Road, you will come to The Spit, the entry to Middle Harbour and the famous, or infamous, Spit Bridge, which opens to allow tall-masted boats to pass through into Middle Harbour, where they moor. There are set times for the opening of the bridge, but for the unwary driver it seems to be a very time-consuming occasion. On the other hand, for people on harbour cruises, it is fascinating to see the giant piece of the bridge lift skyward.

Once through The Spit, the road goes up a sweeping hill, then a right turn leads through the suburb of **Balgowlah** to popular **Manly**.

Manly
The *Manly Visitor Information Centre*, ✆9977 1088, is at North Steyne, on the beach opposite the Steyne Hotel. There are two websites to visit for this locality: ☞www.pcn.com.au and the official website of Manly Council, which is ☞www.manly.nsw.gov.au with an email address at ✉vic@manly.nsw.gov.au

Probably the most popular attraction at Manly is **Oceanworld**, West Esplanade, ✆9949 2644. You have three options for getting close to the sea creatures: viewing them through the safety of glass, handling them in touch pools or - for the fearless - rubbing skin against scale with the sharks in the diving tank. Seals perform at 11.45am and 2pm. Oceanworld is open ◷10am-5.30pm and entry fees are ✪$16 adults, $8 children.

EAST
Travelling to the inner eastern suburbs may seem that you have never left the city. The reason for this is that you really haven't. It is just that most of the streets have changed their names.

How To Get There
By Train
The Eastern Suburbs line runs to Kings Cross, Edgecliff and Bondi Junction.
By Bus
Buses to the eastern suburbs leave from Circular Quay and Railway Square.
By Car
Drive up William Street from the Australian Museum. At the top of the street, turn left into Darlinghurst Road to tour Kings Cross, or continue straight ahead for New South Head Road.

To get to Paddington, follow Oxford Street from Hyde Park.
By Ferry
Ferries travel from Circular Quay Wharf 4 to Double Bay, Rose Bay and Watsons Bay.
Attractions
The first suburb on this trip is **Kings Cross**, probably one of the best-known Sydney areas. The

Cross is sleazy, of that there is no doubt, with its strip joints, sex shops and ladies of the night. But, if you drive through during the day mid-week, it may seem like any other suburb. It is when the sun drops that it comes into its own. There are some excellent restaurants and night spots, and there are some places where you have to be brave to enter. It is not the type of place where you talk to strangers, and believe me, there are some strange people walking the streets. Nevertheless, there are people who would think they had not seen Sydney if they hadn't been to the Cross. It is a haven for backpackers because of the number of cheap hostels, and it is certainly a central area, but it is probably not a good idea to stay there if you are travelling with children.

Having said that, there are a couple of landmarks. The **El Alamein Fountain**, on the corner of Darlinghurst Road and Macleay Street, was built to commemorate the men of the Australian 9th Division who fought in North Africa during World War II. It is an unusually shaped ball of a fountain, and there are always hundreds of people in the park surrounding it.

A short walk away, although in a different suburb, is **Elizabeth Bay House**, at 7 Onslow Avenue, Elizabeth Bay, ☎9356 3022. It was built for the Colonial Secretary, Alexander Macleay and his wife Eliza, and is presently furnished to the period, 1839-1845. In its day it was considered to be the finest house in the colony, and its views over the harbour would have been even more impressive then than they are now. It is a two-storey house with a grand winding staircase, and is maintained by the Historic Houses Trust. It is ⊙open Tues-Sun (Monday when a public holiday) 10am-4.30pm (except Christmas Day and Good Friday) and admission is ❸$7 adult, $4 child, $17 family.

Paddington is another suburb that seems to be part of the city, but it is a charming part. It has many crooked streets lined with pretty terrace houses that are decorated with Paddington Lace, a distinctive wrought-iron trimming. The original village was established in the 1840s and housed the workers building the Victoria Barracks. Parts of the original little town can be seen in the area bounded by Shadforth, Prospect and Spring Streets.

Darlinghurst Road links Kings Cross with Paddington, or you can follow Oxford Street from the city.

Attractions in the area include numerous antique shops along Queen Street, and art galleries sprinkled along Oxford Street and the side streets. The Paddington

Village Bazaar is held in the Uniting Church grounds every Saturday (see *Shopping*).

Victoria Barracks in Oxford Street, next to the Town Hall, ©9339 3170, is a Georgian-style building (1841-1848) and a living history of Australia's military. The Army Museum is ⊙open on Sunday 10am-3pm.

The **Sydney Cricket Ground** is a little further south, in Driver Avenue, Moore Park, ©9360 6601. This famous and historic site continues to play host to many notable sporting events. A *Sportspace Tour* is available, guiding visitors through the complex and its memorabilia for ❂$20 adults, $13 children and $52 for families, ©9380 0383 (bookings essential).

Centennial Park in Oxford Street, was founded in 1888 to celebrate the centenary of the colony. The park is open daily sunrise-sunset, and there are facilities for hiring horses and bikes (see *Sport*).

Double Bay, one of the most up-market suburbs in Sydney, is reached in a car by following New South Head Road from Kings Cross; or by bus from Elizabeth Street; or by train to Edgecliff and walking down New South Head Road.

Known by Sydneysiders who can't afford to shop here as 'Double Pay', it is the most exclusive shopping area in Sydney, and all the well-known, top-class designers have outlets. The surrounding areas of Darling Point, Point Piper, Vaucluse, etc, are populated by people who *can* afford to shop here, and it is worth a visit.

New South Head Road continues through **Rose Bay** and on to **Vaucluse** where it is worth visiting **Vaucluse House**, which dates from 1803. It was the home of William Charles Wentworth, one of the intrepid trio who first crossed the Blue Mountains, and the father of the Australian Constitution. He, and his wife Sarah and their children, lived here from 1829 to 1853, and it's furnishings still recall that period. The house is set in 11ha with gardens, bushland and a harbour beach frontage, and has outbuildings and stables. The house is ⊙open Tues-Sun 10am- 4.30pm and Monday if it is a public holiday. Admission is ❂$6.50 adults, $2.50 children, $15.50 family. There are tearooms in the grounds, and they serve a-la-carte lunches, and Devonshire teas that you would die for. If you are not driving, Bus 325 from Circular Quay stops at the front gate.

The end of New South Head road is **Watsons Bay**, which is on the Harbour, near South Head and the Harbour entrance. The area's most famous landmark is not, as some would say, the pub, nor is it Doyle's restaurant - it is **The Gap**, a cliff from which there are great views, and from where people have committed suicide by jumping into the ocean below. When things are not going too well for them, it is common for Sydneysiders to say that they are going to throw themselves off The Gap, although fortunately not many do.

Nearby is the anchor from the ill-fated *Dunbar*, a barque which was to carry passengers and goods on a regular basis between Sydney and England, but was wrecked on the rocks of The Gap on its second voyage in August 1857. It was Sydney's worst shipping disaster, with 121 lives lost and only one survivor.

From Watsons Bay you can follow Old South Head Road to **Bondi Junction**, or turn off Old South Head Road left onto Military Road and head for **Bondi Beach** and the other beaches to the south. Bondi Junction is about 2km from the beach, and is the main bus/train link for public transport throughout this area. It is also quite a good shopping centre, and its branches of David Jones and Grace Bros are linked by the Oxford Street pedestrian Mall, which has many specialty shops. Bus no 280 runs between Bondi Beach and Bondi Junction.

SOUTH

The southern suburbs are for the most part either industrial or residential, and if you arrived by air, you have already travelled through parts of them. However, there are a few places that are historically interesting on the shores of Botany Bay. The two main areas are **La Perouse**, on the north head of Botany Head, and **Kurnell** on the south head.

How To Get There
By Train
There is no direct train route to *La Perouse*.

To get to *Kurnell*, take the train to Cronulla, then local Bus 67 from the depot opposite the station, near Munroe Park.

By Bus
Bus no 398 runs from Circular Quay to *La Perouse*.

The best transportation route to *Kurnell* is detailed above.

By Car
To get to *La Perouse*, follow Anzac Parade all the way from Taylor Square in Oxford Street.

To get *Kurnell* from there, drive around the foreshores of the bay, crossing Endeavour Bridge and Captain Cook Bridge.

It is difficult to get to both places in one trip without a car.

Attractions
La Perouse
La Perouse is named after Jean-

Francois de Galaup, Comte de Laperouse, who was commissioned by Louis XVI in 1785, to set out on a voyage of discovery. The expedition consisted of two ships, *L'Astrolabe* and *La Boussole*. Two and a half years later, the two ships arrived in Botany Bay, a week after the arrival of the First Fleet. La Perouse and Captain Phillip apparently became good friends, and the Frenchman gave Phillip reports and letters to be sent back to his king. The French ships stayed in Botany Bay for a period of six weeks, then La Perouse set sail, never to be heard from again.

The whereabouts of the ships remained a mystery until the two wrecks were discovered on the reefs of Vanikoro, off the Solomon Islands, by Peter Dillon, an Irish trader and adventurer.

The **La Perouse Museum**, ✆9311 3379, is housed in the Cable Station, inside a circle formed by the end of Anzac Parade. It contains many artefacts from the wrecks, as well as relics from their time in the Bay.

The **Cable Station** was designed and built between 1880 and 1881 to provide accommodation, offices and telegraph facilities for the officers of the Eastern Extension Australasia and China Telegraph Company. The company's submarine cable between La Perouse and Wakapuaka in New Zealand terminated here.

On the bay foreshore, where La Perouse landed, there is an obelisk to commemorate his visit, and close by is the grave of Pere L.C. Receveur, a chaplain and naturalist with the expedition who has the honour of being the first Frenchman to be buried on the Australian continent.

The **Macquarie Watchtower**, also in the circle formed by the road, was built between 1820 and 1822, to prevent smugglers entering Botany Bay.

A causeway from the tip of the point leads to **Bare Island**, on which the fort was built in 1881, following Britain's decision to give self governing colonies the responsibility for their own defence. It only operated as a means of defence for 27 years, then it became a war veterans' home, then a museum with exhibits associated with its early history.

Kurnell

Kurnell has **Captain Cook's Landing Place**, an historic site of over 400ha. Cook landed at 3.00pm on April 28, 1770, and tradition maintains that the first person to step ashore was his wife's young cousin, Isaac Smith. The spot where he scrambled onto dry land is marked with a small obelisk, and there is a larger one dedicated to the discovery nearby.

The site is also a monument to the Gwiyagal People, the Aboriginal tribe who inhabited the area at the time of European discovery.

The **Discovery Centre**, in Captain Cook Drive, is ☺open Mon-Fri 11am-3pm and 10am-4pm on weekends and public holidays, ✆9668 9111. It is one of the major features of the site, with exhibits detailing Cook's life, exploits and achievements, including his notes and opinions on the country he had discovered.

There are also scenic walks, picnic and barbecue areas, and an historic walk, and the visitor centre has maps and leaflets on everything you can see and do.

WEST

The inner western suburbs were settled in the early days of the colony and therefore have many buildings and homes from a bygone era.

How To Get There

By Bus

Buses 438, 440, 470 travel south along George Street and pass the beginning of Glebe Point Road, Glebe, but the buses that actually drive down Glebe Point Road are 431, 433, and 434. Bus no 433 continues on to Balmain.

Bus 440 connects the city with Rozelle, passing through the suburbs of Camperdown, Annandale and Leichhardt.

By Road

To get to Glebe, drive south along George Street, which becomes Broadway, then turn right at the traffic lights on the corner of Glebe Point Road. Incidentally, at that point Broadway becomes Parramatta Road and the Great Western Highway.

Or, if you are crossing the Harbour Bridge, take the Western Distributor, stay in the left lane, follow the sign to the Western Suburbs, then take the first exit onto Bridge Road. The Fish Markets are off to the right and if you continue on you will find yourself in the heart of Glebe.

The best way to get to Balmain from the city is to drive south along George Street to Leichhardt, turn right at Norton Street, follow that street to its end, turn left, then right at the first traffic lights, and follow this street, which undergoes a few name changes before it becomes Darling Street and travels through the heart of Balmain.

If you are coming over the Harbour Bridge, take the Western Distributor, continue over the new Glebe Island Bridge, go with the major flow of traffic turning right into Victoria Road, then right into Darling Street, Balmain. This way by-passes Leichhardt.

By Ferry

Sydney Ferries travel between Circular Quay and three wharves in

Balmain - Darling Street, Thames Street and Elliott Street.

Attractions

The word 'glebe' means 'a gift to the church', and the suburb of **Glebe** was first settled in the late 1700s as a church-owned estate. The church in question was St John's Church, and it still stands on the corner of Glebe Point Road and St John's Road. Apparently by the 1820s the church had fallen on hard times, and the land was sold and subdivided. The high portions of Glebe, away from the insect-ridden Blackwattle Swamp (now known as Blackwattle Bay) were purchased by wealthy families. Grand houses with names such as Hereford House, Forest Lodge, Toxteth House and Lyndhurst were built. The land that was not so valuable became as area for worker's cottages, many of which have recently been restored.

By 1861, Glebe was Sydney's largest suburb and quite a stylish place to live, but by 1911 things had changed dramatically. The wealthier older families moved out, and the poor moved in, so by about 1930 there was nothing grand about giving your address as Glebe.

In a full turnaround, Glebe has become a trendy place to live again, and it has a small shopping centre with lots of art galleries and heritage shops. There are also many fine, cheap restaurants along Glebe Point Road, and a couple that are really up-market - *The Abbey*, ✆9660 4792, and *Darling Mills*, ✆9660 5666.

Unfortunately, many of the old historic homes are privately owned, so they are not open to the public, except on special tours arranged occasionally by the Glebe Society, ✆9660 7873.

If you are in Glebe on a Saturday or Sunday, you might like to visit the *Glebe Markets*, held in Glebe Public School, on the corner of Glebe Point Road and Derby Place. There are lots of stalls selling new clothes and jewellery, and others offering pre-loved treasures (see also under *Shopping*).

On Parramatta Road, opposite the start of Glebe Point Road, is Victoria Park, which has a wide expanse of lawns for picnics, and a public swimming pool, ✆9660 4181.

The University of Sydney, on Parramatta Road, adjoins Victoria Park, and is a sandstone blend of Tudor and Gothic architecture, with acres of green lawns. The Great Hall has a Royal Window which illustrates the monarchy from the Normans to Queen Victoria. The University's Fisher Library, ✆9351 2993, contains more than 400,000 volumes, and the Nicholson Museum has a quality collection of Egyptian, Etruscan, Greek and Roman art.

Leichhardt has a large Italian population, and consequently a large number of Italian restaurants are found in the main streets of Parramatta Road and Norton Street. Leichhardt Park, at the end of Mary Street, has several football ovals, acres of parkland, and an attractively sited public swimming complex, ⓒ9555 8344, with views over Iron Cove.

Trendy Norton Street's newest addition is the **Italian Forum**. Most residents used to think that the closest they would ever come to Italy on their own doorstep was to venture into Norton street and absorb the atmosphere of its Italian restaurant-lined sidewalk. Developers decided to go one step further. The Italian Forum is accessed through a narrow alley where buildings tower above and charming Tuscan flourishes grace the architecture. The end of the alley opens onto a stunning courtyard, surrounded by apartments, shops and restaurants, all mimicking something similar to the typical image of a quaint Italian village (except for the commercialism). This is no down-market immitation - the restaurants are top-class, the boutiques are expensive and the apartments exclusive. A statue of Dante, ornate waterscapes and a bright selection of flowers help to round off the European feel, and

transport you - at least temporarily - out of Sydney's lifestyle and into another. The Forum is located 100 metres from the intersection of Parramatta Road on the right-hand side.

The suburb of **Balmain** gets its name from Dr Balmain, who received the whole of the peninsula as a land grant. To give some idea of the size of his grant, his house was situated in Johnson Street in the suburb of Annandale. Balmain is a trendy area now, rivalling Paddington with its quaint terraces, art galleries and alternative lifestyle shops, but it wins hands down in the restaurant department. There are also many pubs that have outdoor beer gardens and live entertainment.

When driving to Balmain from Victoria Avenue, the *Dawn Fraser Swimming Pool*, named after Australia's swimming legend because this is where she began her swimming career, is in Elkington Park, ⓒ9555 1903. The park is opposite Young Street, which runs off Darling Street to the left. Further along Darling Street, there is a set of traffic lights, and a left turn will take you into Rowntree Street and lead to the less outrageous waterfront suburb of **Birchgrove**.

Balmain Saturday Market is held in the grounds of St Andrew's Congregational Church, on the corner of Darling Street and Curtis Road, ☻every Saturday 9am-4.30pm, ©0418 765 736.

Darling Street continues to Darling Street Wharf, where there is a nice little park at Peacock Point, and from where the ferries leave for Circular Quay.

Outlying Attractions

Parramatta

Parramatta Road terminates at Parramatta, the second oldest settlement in the country. The area was first visited by Governor Phillip and a party of explorers on April 24, 1788. It had become obvious that the soil in the area of Sydney Cove would not produce sufficient crops to feed the infant settlement, and in September 1788, Governor Phillip announced his intention to found another settlement. On November 2, 1788, he chose this area, and named the settlement Rose Hill, but on June 4, 1791, he renamed it Parramatta.

Parramatta became the site of Australia's first orchard, vineyard, tannery, legal brewery, woollen mills, observatory, steam mill, market place and fair. It also was the terminating point of the first road, ferry and rail links out of Sydney. And, most importantly, it saw the beginning of Australia's wool industry.

Although, strictly speaking, Parramatta is a suburb of Sydney, it is a city in its own right with a population of about 130,000. The *Parramatta Visitors Centre* has been incorporated into the Parramatta Heritage Centre, 346 Church Street, ©9630 3703, and is ☻open Mon-Fri 10am-5pm, Sat-Sun 10am-4pm. The Centre has a wealth of information on the city, and a detailed brochure covering walking tours, restaurants, transport details and more, with good maps on the area. The brochure is produced annually and is called *Discover Parramatta*. The self-guided tours include a walk through the heart of the central business district with an excursion into Parramatta Park and Old Government House; and another which passes the outskirts of the old town to the important historic houses of *Experiment Farm Cottage*, *Elizabeth Farm* and *Hambledon Cottage*. To take both tours requires a full day, and a certain amount of fitness, as there are many points of interest. At the end you will have a good idea of the historical importance of the city.

Parramatta Park is within easy walking distance of the central business area, and comprises about 85ha. In the Park are found Old Government House, the Governor's Bathhouse, The Tudor Gate House, Australia's first Observatory, and a

kiosk with boat and cycle hire. Nearby are *Parramatta Stadium* and the *Swimming Centre*.

Parramatta has an enormous shopping complex located near the train station, and a section of the main street, Church Street, is a shopping mall with shrubs, trees, paved pedestrian areas, a fountain and an amphitheatre.

The beautiful picnic area of Lake Parramatta Reserve is at the northern edge of the city, and a regular bus service and a sealed road provide access. The reserve covers about 65ha (160 acres), and the Lake covers 9ha (23 acres) in area. Along the drive on both sides of the Lake, and giving shade to the parking and picnic areas are splendid specimens of Blackbutts, Grey Gums, Red Mahoganies, Bloodwoods, Turpentines, Rough-Barked Angophoras and Sydney Red Gums. The Lake is very deep in parts, so boating is prohibited, but there is a fenced swimming pool and an artificial sandy beach. There are also fireplaces, tables, toilets and a kiosk.

Parramatta has many sporting facilities, including Rosehill Racecourse (see under *Entertainment*), very good restaurants, three cinema complexes, and a wide range of accommodation.

The city's main festival is the Wistaria Garden Festival, held in September each year.

North of Parramatta, in the suburb of **West Pennant Hills**, is *Koala Park Sanctuary*, ©9484 3141. Set in 4ha, the Park not only has plenty of koalas, there are also kangaroos, wallabies, wallaroos, wombats, dingoes, echidnas and emus. The Park is ©open daily 9am-5pm, and photo sessions with koalas are available at intervals throughout the day. Admission is ©$14 adults, $8 children and $32 for families. The Sanctuary is on Castle Hill Road, and to get there from Parramatta follow Pennant Hills Road to the Castle Hill Road turnoff. To get there from Sydney by road, travel along Epping Road which becomes Beecroft Road (or along the M2 to the Beecroft Road exit), to its end, then turn left onto Pennant Hills Road and a short distance along on the right is the Castle Hill Road turn-off. From Sydney by train, travel to the Pennant Hills Station, then take Bus 655 to the Park.

Ku-ring-gai Chase National Park

Located 24km (15 miles) north of the city, the Park has numerous bushwalks and some magnificent Aboriginal rock carvings in accessible spots. The higher parts of the park afford magnificent views across Pittwater.

On the edge of the park is *Waratah Park*, 13 Namba Road, Duffys Forest, home of 'Skippy the Bush Kangaroo' and many of her friends, including Tasmanian Devils, dingoes, wombats, wallabies, emus and koalas. Feeding times are on the hour between 11am and 4pm. There is a restaurant, a snack bar, and a souvenir shop, and the Park is ☉open every day 10am-5pm, ✆9450 2377. Admission is ✪$12.90 adults, $6.50 children and $34.90 for families. To get there by car, proceed north on the Pacific Highway to the suburb of Pymble, then turn right onto Mona Vale Road. Take the left turn to Duffy's Forest off Mona Vale Road at Terrey Hills, and follow the signs.

Wonderland Australia

Located near the M4, in outer western Sydney, Wonderland is 219ha (540 acres) of landscaped grounds in Wallgrove Road, Eastern Creek, and has Australia's longest wooden roller coaster, the Bush Beast. Other rides include The Demon, Space Probe and Snowy River Rampage. There are also many different kinds of theme shops, live shows and picnic spots. It is ☉open 10am-5pm every day, ✆9830 9100 or ✆9830 9106 (recorded information). Admission is adults ✪$39 and children $27.

The *Australian Wildlife Park*, ✆9830 9187, also at Wonderland, is ☉open daily 9am-5pm. Entry fees are ✪$18 adults, $12 children and $46 for families.

Shuttle buses run to the fun park from Mt Druitt, Fairfield, Blacktown and Rooty Hill train stations.

Also in Eastern Creek is the **Eastern Creek Raceway**, Brabham Drive, ✆9672 1000. This venue has accommodated the 500cc Motorbike Grand Prix, and hosts other races around the year.

Hawkesbury River

The River is 45km (28 miles) north of Sydney, and is dotted with historic towns such as Windsor, Richmond, Wilberforce, Pitt Town and Wisemans Ferry. It winds around Sydney's western outskirts through a natural forest area until finally meeting the sea at Brooklyn. One of the best ways to see it is to join the *Riverboat Postman* near the Hawkesbury River Railway Station in Brooklyn. This four hour cruise includes commentary and snacks. The cost is ✪$35 adults, $18 children and $72 for families, ✆9985 7566.

An alternative is to hire a house boat from the many on offer at Brooklyn, at the southern end of the Hawkesbury Bridge. Two such companies are Holidays Afloat Houseboats, ✆9985 7368, and House Boats Prestige, ✆9985 7744.

Royal National Park

History
Royal National Park was gazetted in 1879 as 'The National Park', and was the first public reserve in Australia to be so termed. In fact, the Park can lay claim to being the first in the world, because although Yellowstone Park in the USA was established in 1872, it was not officially gazetted as a national park until 1883. When Queen Elizabeth II first visited Australia in 1954, she bestowed the title 'Royal , but most Sydneysiders still refer to it as 'The National Park'.

The Park is situated south of Port Hacking, about 29km from the centre of Sydney, and covers 16,000ha of vegetation and landscape typical of the Sydney Basin sandstone.

The original inhabitants of the area were the Aboriginal people of the Dharawal tribe, who used the sandstone caves for shelter and lived off the land and waterways. Little detail is known of their life-style as rock engravings, axe-grinding grooves, charcoal drawings and hand stencils are the only physical remains of the culture.

The Royal National Park was established by the then NSW Premier, Sir John Robertson, who saw a need for a recreation space for Sydney, many parts of which had become infested with vermin and disease.

Audley was the site of the first European settlement in the Park. The native mangroves and mudflats were replaced by grassed parkland and exotic trees, and added to the local fauna were deer, rabbits and foxes.

Park Features
The Park has been shaped from a sloping sandstone plateau, which rises from sea level at Jibbon Point in the north, to over 300m at Bulgo in the south.

The Park scenery is magnificent and varied. The waves from the open sea have produced majestic cliffs, broken every now and then by small creeks and beaches. Deep river valleys have been formed by streams flowing north to Port Hacking and east to the Pacific Ocean. The upper slopes have woodlands that merge with the heath vegetation on the plateaux. Gorges and valleys have forest and rainforest, the tidal channels of the rivers have mangrove, and the swamps are covered in sedges.

There are numerous grassy areas along the *Hacking River valley*, and from July to November the wildflowers on the plateaux provide a riot of colour. There are waterfalls at *Wattamolla, Curracurrong, Uloola* and *National Falls*.

How to Get There
By Rail
Trains on the Illawarra-Cronulla line stop at Loftus, Engadine, Heathcote, Waterfall and Otford, and from these stations there are walking tracks into the Park.

By Car
From Sydney, follow the signs toward the Airport, and then follow the signs to Wollongong (Princes Highway) or President Avenue at Brighton-le-Sands, turn right and at the end of the street turn left onto Princes Highway keep going until you are past Sutherland. The Audley entrance to the Royal National Park is well signposted. You take a left turn of the Princes Highway just south of Sutherland.

From Liverpool City, take the Heathcote Road exit from the M5 motorway (before the toll booth). Turn right into Heathcote Road so you cross over the M5 Motorway and follow it all the way to the Princes Highway (between Engadine and Heathcote).

You can then do one of two things:
   Turn left and go back about 3km to enter the Park south of Sutherland (Audley entrance); or
   Turn right and head south to Waterfall and enter the Park there.

From Wollongong, drive north along the Princes Highway. After reaching Bulli continue along Lawrence Hargraves Drive (don't go up the escarpment). Another way is to follow the Mt Ousley Road to the Princes Highway and turn right at Stanwell Tops to go to Stanwell Park. At the top of the Bluff, turn left along Lady Wakehurst Drive, then continue to the Otford entrance of the Park.

By Ferry
Cronulla National Park Ferry Cruises, ©9523 2990, have a service from the wharf near Cronulla railway station to Bundeena, and the trip takes 25-30 minutes. The first ferry from Cronulla leaves at 5.30am Mon-Fri on the hour to 6.30pm, 8.30am Sat-Sun and public holidays on the hour to 6.30pm. The last ferry leaves Bundeena daily at 7pm (summer), 6pm (winter).

It should be noted that Bundeena is *not* within the Royal National Park.

Tourist Information
A Visitor Centre and Wildlife Shop is on Farnell Avenue, Audley. Call into the centre for advice on all aspects of your park visit. Permits for

camping are obtained here. It is ☺open daily 8.30am-4pm, ✆9542 0648. The shop sells books, film, maps, posters, gifts and souvenirs.

Park Entrance Fee

There is no charge for traffic travelling through and not stopping in the Park from Sutherland to places south of the Park.

For those that intend to stop within the park the following charges apply:

Bus - ✪$3.00 per adult, $1.00 for each school age child, under the age of 5 free, pensioners free. Must display pensioner card.

Cars - ✪$9.00 per vehicle.

Motor Bikes - ✪$3.00 per bike. There is no charge for people who hike into the park for the day.

Park Regulations

All fauna, flora, Aboriginal sites and rock formations are protected.

Wildfires can destroy lives and property, so be careful, especially during the bushfire danger period (normally October to March). Use only the fireplaces provided and observe Total Fire Bans. Portable fuel stoves are required for camping.

Pets and Firearms are not permitted in national parks.

Vehicles, including motorbikes must keep to formed public roads. Drive carefully.

Please use rubbish bins if provided; or take rubbish with you when you leave the park.

Camping

Caravans and car camping are permitted at the camping ground at **Bonnie Vale**, off Bundeena Road. It has toilet and shower blocks, but no powered sites. In fact, there are only 40 sites in all, and during school holidays and long weekends, ballots are held to allot them. There are so many applicants that this seems to be the fairest way. At other times there is not so much demand, and therefore there is a good chance of securing a site, but booking ahead is essential. For reservations, ✆9542 0648.

For site fees, you can expect to pay about ✪$10 per person for the first two people, and a couple of dollars per extra person. Children under 5 years of age are free.

There are lots of places for bush camping throughout the park, however booking and obtaining permits are essential. The permits must first be obtained from the Visitor Centre. They are free, but written on the back of them are the special conditions that apply to camping in a national park, and this is the best way of making sure that everyone is aware of them.

Activities

Weekends see many organised picnics arranged by sporting clubs, church groups and families with the addition of aunts, uncles, grandparents and third cousins, all taking advantage of the wide open expanse near the Audley causeway.

National Park Ranger guided activities are available. Bookings and more information can be obtained on ©9542 0649.

Picnicking

There are many picnic areas dotted throughout the park, but there are only barbecue facilities at Audley, Warumbul, Wattamolla, Bonnie Vale and Garie. Kiosks are found at Audley, Wattamolla and Garie Beach.

Swimming

Safe saltwater swimming is available at *Bonnie Vale*, *Jibbon*, *Wattamolla* and *Little Marley* beaches, and these are favourite spots for families.

Surfers head for *Garie*, *Era* and *Burning Palms* beaches, which are patrolled by surf lifesavers on weekends and public holidays during summer.

Freshwater swimming is possible at *Blue Pools*, *Karloo Pool*, *Deer Pool*, *Curracurrang* and *Crystal Pools*, but care should be taken when swimming in rock pools. The water always tends to be cold, so it is easy to get cramps. It is not always easy to judge how deep a rock pool is, so never jump or dive into these pools. Spinal injury units of hospitals are always warning people about the dangers of leaping headfirst into unknown waters.

Boating

The *Audley Boatshed*, ©9545 4967, has rowing boats, canoes, kayaks and aquabikes for hire, and only these may be used in Kangaroo Creek, and in the Hacking River above the causeway. Private boats can be used downstream from the Audley causeway.

The boat shed is ⊙open Mon-Sat 9am-5pm, Sun and public holidays 9am-5.30pm. A small refundable deposit is required for each craft.

Walking

The Park has over 150km of walking tracks that provide access to the wide range of scenery available, and the Visitor Centre has track pamphlets. Bungoona, Governor Game and Otford Lookouts offer chances to take spectacular photos, and National, Winifred and Curracurrong Falls are easily accessible.

Cycling

The best route for cyclists is Lady Carrington Drive, which is closed to motor vehicles, and is relatively flat. Ask at the Visitor Centre for directions. Bicycles and mountain bikes are only allowed on management trails. They are not permitted on walking tracks.

Sydney Tramway Museum

If you are visiting the Royal National Park on a Sunday or Wednesday, you might like to check out the Sydney Tramway Museum in Pitt

Street, Loftus, ☏9542 3646. It is ☺open Sunday and Public Holidays 10am-5pm, Wednesday 9.30am-3.30pm, but no one is admitted in the hour prior to closing.

Trams operated in Sydney for one hundred years to 1961, and a fleet of over 1500 vehicles provided the city with an efficient transport service. The Sydney Tramway Museum has an excellent collection of Sydney trams, and others from Brisbane, Ballarat, Melbourne and San Francisco, and also a selection of the buses which replaced them in Sydney. This fleet includes the last remaining double-decker trolley bus.

Every open day, a number of the museum's trams operate along a kilometre of track, each return trip taking about 15 minutes, but the San Francisco PCC Streetcar only operates on the first Sunday of the month. There is also a tramway waiting shed from Railway Square, the unique counterweight dummy from the Balmain line, and an extensive range of photographs and artefacts.

The museum has a shop with a range of books, post cards, video tapes and souvenirs, as well as snacks and drinks. There are also picnic facilities within the Museum grounds.

Admission is ✪$12 adult, $6 child, and includes unlimited tram rides and use of facilities.

Festivals

The **Festival of Sydney** is held during the entire month of January each year, and features include twilight and open-air concerts in the Domain, contemporary music at Hyde Park and Darling Harbour, outdoor movies at the Opera House, bike rallies, street theatre, and classical theatre performances at the Opera House, the Belvoir Theatre and the Seymour Centre.

Australia Day, January 26, sees the city come alive, especially around the harbour, with all kinds of displays, and a Ferrython in which all the Sydney ferries compete.

The Mardi Gras is organised by representatives of the gay and lesbian community, and is held on the first Friday in February each year. It is actually part of a month-long festival that centres around the Oxford Street section of the city.

The main attraction of the Mardi Gras for the thousands of spectators is the colourful parade of extremely imaginative floats and performers.

For visitors who are new to this scene, be aware that the parade's participants are often very expressive. Nudity and sexual insinuation are always prevalent here.

The Royal Easter Show was held at the Showground in Moore Park beside the SCG for decades, but that land is now occupied by Fox Studios. 1997 marked its last appearance at that site and Shows are now held at Homebush Bay, the venue of the 2000 Olympics.

The Show begins on the Friday before Good Friday and finishes on Easter Tuesday.

Advertised as *"when the country comes to town"*, there's something for everyone, with displays of horticulture, livestock, crafts and hi-tech machinery. For kids, there are rides and sample bags, and for all ages there is non-stop entertainment in the show ring with livestock judging, trotting races, equestrian events, the Grand Parade, bands, sky divers, clowns, rodeos, and fireworks displays.

The Show is well patronised by Sydneysiders with attendances on the public holidays reaching 100,000.

Anzac Day commemorates the actions of Australian and New Zealand troops involved in the conflict of the First World War, and the lives they sacrificed. The day falls on the 25 April, the same date that the soldiers landed on the shores of Gallipoli in 1914 and were overwhelmed by the Turkish resistance. Originally conceived as a lightning campaign, the conflict soon developed into an 8 month conflict during which time both sides sustained heavy casualties. Anzac Day services are held around the country and involve parades, marches, laying wreaths, minutes of silence, playing *The Last Post* and reciting the poem, *For the Fallen*. The opportunity is taken to reflect on all military losses since WWI. It remains a solemn and important day of remembrance in the Australian psyche.

The **National Folkloric Festival** is an annual multicultural event featuring dancers and musicians from many ethnic backgrounds. It is held in June, and begins with a Sunday parade that terminates at the Opera House, the scene for the many events of the following weekend.

St Patrick's Day seems to be gaining momentum every year. On the 17 March, thousands don a green item of clothing, grab a clover in one hand, and trot down to the nearest pub for a few pints or more of Guiness. The day is intended to mark the death of Ireland's patron saint and to commemorate his lifetime work of converting the country's entire population to Catholicism, but how this ties in with flagrant alcoholism remains something of a mystery. There is plenty of fun and good cheer, though halos are in scarce supply and the behaviour is often less than saintly!

The **Biennale of Sydney** is an international exhibition of contemporary art held every two years. Since its inception in 1973, the Biennale has brought the world's leading artists to Sydney, and more than 800 of them from over 45 countries have been exhibited.

The Biennale is not only confined to Sydney as visiting artists travel giving lectures, workshops and artist-in-residence programs, and special lectures and displays are organised.

The Sydney to Hobart Yacht Race can hardly be classed as a festival, but it does generate a lot of excitement. Every Boxing Day thousands of people line the vantage spots around the harbour to watch the mini and maxi yachts set off on their adventure, and there are so many boats of all sorts on the harbour, farewelling the entrants, that it is a wonder they ever get through the Heads. The race is closely monitored by news crews in light aircraft, and hourly reports are given on TV and radio as to who is in the lead, and by how much. Meanwhile, the people in Hobart get ready for the big welcoming party.

The City to Surf Fun Run is another annual event. Held every year in August, thousands of people of all ages assemble for the start of the run to Bondi Beach, and as the starting gun goes off, Park Street

becomes a sea of people. Of course, the race is always won by a professional marathon runner, but winning is not really what the spectacle is all about. Everyone who finishes receives a certificate, and their names are listed in the newspapers. Even those who don't finish are congratulated for entering, and there is a real spirit of comradeship as you watch people helping each other along the way.

In addition to the above, each municipal area of Sydney has its own festival, and there are other special annual events, such as the blessing of the fishing fleet.

Public Holidays

Christmas, Boxing Day, New Year and Easter are obviously celebrated at the same time as everywhere else in the world.

Other holidays that are enjoyed in Australia are:

Australia Day - January 26.

Anzac Day - April 25.

Queen's Birthday - the second Monday in June.

Labour Day - the first Monday in October.

Another day is *Bank Holiday*, which is held on the first Monday in August, but only banks, government offices, insurance companies and the like are closed.

Sport and Recreation

Boating

It should be noted that a licence is required to drive any mechanically driven vessel capable of 10 knots or more. There are several places around the harbour foreshores where bare boats can be hired. Here are a few names and addresses:

Abbotsford Point Boat Hire, 617 Great North Road, Abbotsford, ℂ9713 8621.

Australian Sailing School & Club, Parrawi Road, Mosman, ℂ9960 3077.

Balmoral Sailing and Kayaking School and Hire, 2 The Esplanade, Balmoral, ℂ9969 5344.

Eastsail, d'Albora Marinas, New Beach Road, Rushcutters Bay, ℂ9327 1166.

Rose Bay Marina, 594 New South Head Road, Rose Bay, ℂ9363 5930. If you are a marine enthusiast and wish to admire the yachts in the harbour, there are several wharfs along the shoreline. The ***Cruising Yacht Club*** at Rushcutters Bay is close to the city. Since the best way to enjoy the spectacular scenery of Sydney Harbour is by drifting luxuriously in its centre, a sailing craft is almost a necessity for those who can afford one, and on weekends the water's surface is laced with the tranquil patterns of whitewash. For the rest of the week, while corporate owners are in the city earning the money needed to pay for them, these yachts bob softly at the marina, their many masts forming an impressive sight against the skyscape.

Cycling

Australian Cycle Co., 28 Clovelly Road, Randwick, ℂ9399 3475, are ☉open seven days and are close to Centennial Park. They hire out bikes at reasonable prices.

Golf

Although Sydney has about 40 public golf courses, few are located close to the city centre. Here is a selection:

Moore Park Golf Club, is on the corner of Cleveland Street and Anzac Parade, ℂ9663 1064. This is the closest course to the city. It comprises 18-holes and is par 71 for 5790m. Eighteen holes will cost you ◎$24 on a weekday and $27 on weekends.

Cammeray Golf Course is located in Park Avenue, Cremorne, ℂ9953 2089. Another 9-hole course, at 2417m, par 33, Cammeray is built

on quality terrain that is always well-kept. A nine-hole round is ✪$11 and can be played between designated hours daily.

Bondi Golf Course, 5 Military Road, North Bondi, ✆9130 7170. This course is only a 2500m nine-hole course, but its hills and freak peninsula winds provide some challenges. Famous Bondi Beach sprawls below - a soothing sight after a terrible shot. It costs adults ✪$9 to play, and a further $9 to hire clubs. Children play for $5.

Balgowlah Golf Course, 506 Sydney Road, Balgowlah, ✆9949 2057, is another terrific nine-holer. This popular spot is not far from Manly Beach and is difficult enough to test good golfers whilst not crushing the dreams of intermediates. It is green and lush and can make for a pleasant couple of hours. The course is par 34, 2321m long, and costs ✪$12 for nine holes. Non-members have access to the course daily at designated hours.

Wakehurst Golf Club is on Upper Clontarf Street, Seaforth, ✆9949 3188. This is a full 18 hole, par 72 course built in the middle of cleared scrubland and dotted with water hazards. Its length is just over 6100m and its terrain can be tricky for any golfer to negotiate. A round on this scenic course will set you back ✪$22 on weekdays and $25 on weekends. Club hire is an additional ✪$15 and you can pick up a golf cart for $25.

The Australian in Rosebery and ***Royal Sydney*** in Rose Bay are nearby, while the ***New South Wales Golf Club*** is in La Perouse further south. However, the only way to make a divot on these exclusive fairways is to quickly make friends with a member, if you can find one.

For further information on Sydney's courses, find the listing in the Yellow Pages Telephone Directory or use the golf guide at 👁sydney.sidewalk.com.au

Horse Riding

Superior Horse, Pavillion A, Driver Avenue, Moore Park, ✆9360 5650, has horses for hire daily 9am-5pm. Centennial Park and adjoining Queens Park have a combined area 220ha (543 acres) - more than enough room to have a decent ride.

Lawn Bowls

There are bowling clubs in almost every suburb of Sydney, and one in the city. Bowling clubs are famous for their hospitality, and visitors are warmly welcomed. It is necessary, of course, to phone ahead to find out what days are reserved for social play, and to organise for a set of bowls. Bowling clubs are listed in the Yellow Pages Telephone Directory under *Clubs - Bowling*. If you are not sure which club is the closest to where you are staying, you could contact the Royal NSW

Bowling Association, ℂ9283 4555.

Scuba Diving

Gear can be hired and dives arranged from the following places:

Dive 2000, 2 Military Road, Neutral Bay, ℂ9953 7783.

Deep 6 Diving, 1057 Victoria Road, West Ryde, ℂ9858 4299.

Pro Dive, Head Office, 34/330 Wattle Street, Ultimo, ℂ9281 6166.

Swimming

The closest public swimming pools to the city centre are:

North Sydney Olympic Pool, Alfred South Street, Milsons Point, ℂ9955 2309;

Andrew (Boy) Charlton Pool, The Domain, Woolloomooloo, ℂ9358 6686;

Prince Alfred Park Swimming Pool, Chalmers Street, Surry Hills (near Central Railway Station), ℂ9319 7045.

The new *Cook and Phillip Park Recreation Centre*, is on the corner of Haig & Boomerang Streets, near St Marys, ℂ9326 0444. It has a 50m underground pool among its facilities.

The larger hotels have swimming pools, usually heated all year round.

Tennis

Tennis courts abound in Sydney's suburbs and most have lights for night play. Pages of available courts can be found in the L-Z Yellow Pages Telephone Directory, appropriately enough under *Tennis Courts For Hire*.

For spectators, the NSW Tennis Open is played at **White City** in Rushcutters Bay, ℂ9360 4113.

Ten Pin Bowling

The bowling centres close to the city are:

Balgowlah Bowling Centre, Condamine Street, Balgowlah, ℂ9948 7656. Other centres can be found in the A-K Yellow Pages Telephone Directory under *Ten Pin Bowling*.

Spectator Sports

Basketball (April-October)

Sydney's team in the National Basketball League (NBL) is *The Kings*, and they play their home games at the Superdome, Olympic Boulevard, Homebush. Phone ℂ9764 1300 for dates of the Kings' games.

Baseball (October-February)

The Sydney Blues is the local team in the National Baseball League and their home games are played at the Parramatta Stadium. The teams in the local competition play at various suburban venues, and for information on games, times, etc, contact the NSW Baseball League on ℂ9552 4635.

Cricket (October-March)

The Sydney Cricket Ground, near the Show-ground, is home to International matches, and is NSW's home ground in the competition played between the states. Grade matches are played on suburban grounds.

Football (March-October)

Rugby League is played on Saturdays and Sundays at various suburban grounds and at the Sydney Football Stadium, near the Showground.

Rugby Union is played on Saturdays at suburban grounds and at their headquarters at Concord Oval.

Soccer is played on Saturdays at various suburban grounds and Sydney Athletic Field, Anzac Parade, Kensington, ©9662 4390.

Australian Football is played on Saturdays at suburban grounds, and the *Sydney Swans* play their home games in the Victorian competition at the Sydney Cricket Ground.

Horse Racing

See Entertainment.

Sydney Olympic Park

Situated roughly in the geographic heart of metropolitan Sydney, the Olympic Park is 14km from the CBD, in the suburb of Homebush.

Facilities include Stadium Australia, Bicentennial Park, the Sydney International Aquatic Centre, the State Sports Centre, as well as Tennis, Hockey and Archery facilities. Other features include a major metropolitan park, called Millennium Park, a golf driving range and an Olympic Village which accommodated 15,000 athletes.

A concentration on modern architecture is the definitive element of the Olympic site. From a distance the domes, arcs and cylindrical shapes of the venue seem to make it spring like a spaceport from science fiction out of its green surrounds.

Stadium Australia

This enormous stadium was the venue for the Opening and Closing Ceremonies, and will host many other notable competition events into the future. It has a seating capacity of 100,000 people.

State Sports Centre

The Centre is a multi-purpose venue designed to present a full spectrum of events. The design enables the Centre to be used as: a competition venue for sporting events of State, National and International standard, and a training centre for these athletes; a sports education centre; and a venue for concerts, seminars and exhibitions.

The Arena, within the *Sports Hall*, is the focal point of the State Sports Centre, and is capable of staging a wide range of sports from gymnastics to showjumping, fencing to indoor cricket. It has seating for 5000, and a clear floor area of 57m x 38m.

Also in the Sports Hall is the *Hall of Champions* which honours Australia's champs in many sports.

The State Softball Centre has two floodlit fields, warm-up facilities and accommodation for 3000 spectators.

The State Hockey Centre has two synthetic pitches, flood lighting, and accommodation for 8000 spectators.

There are also outdoor netball courts, training centres and plans for many more sporting facilities.

For information about current programs at the Centre, phone the information line on, ©9763 0111.

Transport to Homebush

Transport to the Olympic Site is by car, bus, river cat or rail (O ympic Park station).

Guided tours of the Olympic Site are available, and perhaps the best way to explore this venue and all of the others in close proximity, is on the Olympic Explorer Bus (see under *Local Transport*).

Central Coast

The Central Coast is located north of Sydney. It begins at the Hawkesbury River and stretches northwards to the southern shores of Lake Macquarie, and westwards to historic St Albans.

The area is roughly divided into two - the City of Gosford with Brisbane Waters, and the Shire of Wyong with Tuggerah Lakes. Within these two districts there are many seaside and holiday centres.

Gosford City

Population 129,000
The City of Gosford is 88km (55 miles) north of Sydney. The natural beauty of the district and its close proximity to the major cities of Sydney and Newcastle has made it an attractive living and recreation area on the east coast of Australia. There are many popular surfing beaches and the Brisbane Waters are legendary for fishing, sailing and other recreational pursuits. Although for many years, it has been a popular holiday and retirement area, many young families are now settling in the district as an alternative to living in the outer suburbs of Sydney and Newcastle.

Climate

Average temperatures: summer max 25C (77F) - min 18C (64F); winter max 17C (63F) - min 10C (50F). Average annual rainfall is 1300mm (51 ins), average ocean temperature is 20C (68F).

How to Get There

By Bus
Interstate coachlines call at Gosford.

By Rail

There is a good electric train service from/to Sydney, and the State Rail Authority has mini-fares, family fares and combined rail/coach fares, ©131 500.

By Road

From Sydney via the Pacific Highway all the way to Gosford, or the F3 expressway from Hornsby to the Gosford turn-off, then the Pacific Highway.

Visitor Information

The Gosford Visitor Information Centre is in 200 Mann Street, Gosford, ©(02) 4385 4430 or ©1800 806 258, ©open Mon-Fri 9am-5pm, Sat-Sun 9am-2pm. Their email address is ✉theccast@cctourism.com.au and the web page is at ◉www.cctourism.com.au

If you are in Terrigal, the Visitor Information Centre is in Rotary Park, Terrigal Drive. It is ©open 9am-5pm Mon-Sat and 9am-3pm on Sunday during summer. They share contact details with the Gosford Centre.

The Centre has compiled some very good self-drive tours of the area, which encompass all the attractions. Visitors are well-advised to pick up these brochures.

Accommodation

Accommodation is not a problem in the area, although it is wise to book in advance during the summer holiday period. Here is a selection with prices for a double room per night, which should be used as a guide only. The telephone area code is 02.

Gosford

Metro Motor Inn Gosford, 512 Pacific Highway, ✆4328 4666. 50 units, licensed restaurant, swimming pool, spa, barbecue - ✪$105.

Bermuda Motor Inn, cnr Henry Parry Drive & Pacific Highway, North Gosford, ✆4324 4366. 17 units, swimming pool, barbecue - ✪$65-95.

Gosford Motor Inn, 23 Pacific Highway, ✆4323 1333. 36 units, heated swimming pool, barbecue - ✪$70-100.

Rambler Motor Inn, 73 Pacific Highway, West Gosford, ✆4324 6577. 55 units, playground, swimming pool, spa, barbecue - ✪$75-100.

Wyoming Caravan Park, 520 Pacific Highway, Wyoming, ✆4328 4358. (No pets allowed) - powered sites ✪$19 for two, cabins $55 for two.

Woy Woy

Glades Country Club Motor Inn, 15 Dunban Road, ✆4341 7374. 23 units, swimming pool, barbecue - ✪$80-120.

Ettalong

Motel Paradiso, cnr Schnapper & Ocean View Roads, ✆4341 1999.

1 room, licensed restaurant - ✪$75-140.

Ettalong Beach Village, Fassifern Street, ✆4344 2211. (No pets) - powered sites ✪$20-32 for two, cabins $60-110 for two.

Avoca

Bellbird Resort, 360 Avoca Drive, ✆4382 2322. 36 units, licensed restaurant, swimming pool, tennis court - ✪$80-100.

The Palms at Avoca, Carolina Park Road off the Round Drive, ✆4382 1227. (No pets allowed), barbecue, sauna, pool - cabins ✪$80-145 for two, villas $75-125 for two.

Terrigal

Country Comfort Terrigal, 154 Terrigal Drive, ✆4384 1166. 40 units, 7 suites, licensed restaurant, swimming pool, spa, sauna, tennis, barbecue - ✪$175-220.

Clan Lakeside Lodge, 1 Ocean View Drive, ✆4384 1566. 26 units, licensed restaurant (closed Sunday & Monday), barbecue - ✪$100-220.

Terrigal Beach House, 1 Painter Lane, ✆4384 1423. 9 units - ✪$45-90.

Bellbird Caravan Park, 61-69 Terrigal Drive, ✆4384 1883. (No dogs allowed) - unpowered sites ✪$20-25 for two, on-site vans $50-60for two, cabins $80-95.

Wamberal

Apollo Country Resort, 871 The Entrance Road, ✆4385 2099. 42

units (private facilities), licensed restaurant, swimming pool, spa, barbecue, tennis, gym - ✪$95-160.

Kincumber

Figtree Cottages, 247 Avoca Drive, ©4368 3056. 2 rooms, unlicensed restaurant, solar heated saltwater pool, fireplace, spa - ✪$120-130.

Eating Out

No matter which locality of the Central Coast you choose to stay in, you will find excellent restaurants. Here is a brief list, and the Information Centre can advise you further if you desire.

Gosford

Gosford Shoreline, Masons Parade, ©4325 0644. Fully licensed seafood restaurant with an a-la-carte selection. Open midday-2pm and 6pm-8.30pm Mon-Sat, and until 9.30pm Friday and Saturday nights, lunch only on Sundays, closed Public Holidays.

Gee Kwong Chinese Restaurant, 197 Mann Street, ©4325 2489. Open 11.30am-3pm and 4.30pm-9pm Mon-Sat, and until 10pm on Friday and Saturday nights, closed Sunday and Public Holidays.

Tohn Oor Sian Classic Thai, 26 Adelaide Street, Gosford East, ©4324 2887. Take-away available, dine-in BYO wine only. Open midday-2.30pm and 5.30pm-10.30pm 7 days.

Jaceys, 45 Imperial Centre, ©4324 2558.

Da Vincis, 1-2 Brisbane Waters Drive, Gosford West, ©4322 8000.

Saltwater, Shop 6 Brisbane Waters Drive, West Gosford, ©4323 7744.

Curry House, 104 Mann Street, ©4322 0223.

Peking Garden, in the Central Coast Leagues Club, Dane Drive, ©4324 3788.

Surrounding Areas

Paceys, 172 Avoca Drive, Avoca Beach, ©4382 3588. Seafood, a-la-carte. Open 6pm-9pm 7 days and midday-3pm weekends and Public Holidays.

Sirens, 1 Kurrawyba Avenue, Terrigal, ©4385 2602. Open 5pm-midnight every day.

Pizza One, 30 Ocean View Drive, Wamberal, ©4385 3311.

Ghandi Indian Restaurant, 189 Ocean View Road, Ettalong, ©4341 1994.

The Don's Italian Restaurant, 28 Kincumber Village, Avoca Drive, Kincumber, ©4363 1900.

Fishermans Wharf, The Boulevarde, Woy Woy, ©4341 1171.

For Pizza Hut deliveries, ©13 1166. Branches of McDonalds and KFC are found in all the major towns.

Points of Interest

The town site of Gosford was first referred to as the Township at Point

Above: Government House in the Botannical Gardens, Sydney   Below: Sydney Harbour

Sunset over Sydney Harbour

Frederick, then in February 1839, when the plan was sent to Governor Gipps for approval, as the Township of Brisbane Water. The plan was returned by the Governor in April marked as the Plan of Gosford, with no explanation to indicate the reason for its name. It was later discovered that the Governor had served with the Earl of Gosford in Canada, and had taken the opportunity to honour his friend.

Originally, timber cutting was the main economic product of the district, then from the 1880s, citrus orchards began to dominate the local farms in the Narara, Lisarow, Wyoming, Holgate and Ourimbah areas. These farms were close to the railway, but later as roads developed, farming spread on to Somersby plateau. By 1928-29, the district supplied 34% of the state's citrus crop.

The 1880s also saw the Gosford area become a tourist venue, with the completion of the railway in 1887, and visitors coming for the fishing, and for hunting trips.

In recent times Gosford's development has been influenced by other factors, such as the metropolitan expansion of Sydney, improvements to the roads, and changes in lifestyles.

The majority of people visit the area now for the surf, sun and sand, but there are quite a few attractions worth visiting.

Old Sydney Town, Pacific Highway, Somersby (west of Gosford) is the largest heritage park in New South Wales, and is a faithful recreation of Sydney as it was 200 years ago. There is live street theatre, and demonstrations of different crafts take visitors back to the 18th and 19th centuries. The park has many eateries, from fine restaurants to damper and billy tea places, or you can take your own food and make use of the barbecue facilities. Old Sydney Town is ☺open Wed-Sun and all state school and public holidays, 10am-5pm, ✆4340 1104. Admission fees are adults ✪$20, children $13. A family pass can be obtained for $55.

Henry Kendall Cottage & Historical Museum, 218 Gertrude Street, Gosford, ✆4325 2270, was built for the famous poet in 1836 by Peter Fagan. It is now an historical museum with displays of various items from the past. ☺Open Wed, Sat & Sun, and public and school holidays, 10am-4pm.

The Australian Reptile Park was the first major tourist attraction on the Central Coast, and is a popular science exhibit. Crocodile feeding in the impressive crocodile enclosure is by far the highlight of the day. Watch as the trainer holds a long pole over the water's edge while a croc emerges, leaps into the air, takes the dangling chicken from the end of the pole into its jaws, and thrashes back into the water again. The park supplies venoms to countries all over the world for antivenenes and other research. There are picnic and barbecue facilities, but note that the place is overrun by kangaroos, and the joy of their company can quickly turn into despair if one bounds up and pinches your lunch while you pat her! The park is hopen daily 9am-5pm, ©4340 1146, and is on the Pacific Highway, Somersby. Admission prices are ✪$16 adults, $8 children, $40 families.

The Starship Cruise & Ferry Service, 100 John Whiteway Drive, ©4340 1146, has two venues for cruises. The *Lady Kendall* departs from Gosford Wharf, Wed, Sat & Sun to cruise on the Brisbane Waters, and the *Trinity Queen* leaves from The Entrance Wharf for cruising Tuggerah Lakes and Wyong River, Wed-Sat 10.15am and 1pm. Both vessels operate daily during school holidays.

The Fragrant Garden, 25 Portsmouth Road, Erina, ©4367 7322, has a very large collection of fragrant plants, crafts, pot-pourri in an olde-worlde garden. There is a mud-brick gallery, waterfall and a herb roof, and souvenirs are for sale.

Central Park Family Fun Centre, The Entrance Road, Forresters Beach, ©4386 2466, has some-thing for everyone - ten-pin bowling, five giant waterslides, a mini golf centre, senior and junior Grand Prix cars, BMX track, maze, mini bikes, Sunday markets. ⊙Open daily 9am-5pm, Sat and holidays 9am-10pm.

Festivals

Gosford's Australian Springtime Flora Festival is held in September.

Facilities

Fishing, swimming, boating, diving, wind-surfing, water skiing, horse riding, ten-pin bowling, squash, lawn bowls, golf and tennis. The Tourist Information Centre will give you all the information for directions and bookings.

Outlying Attractions

Beaches

The coastal beaches in the Gosford area are Killcare, McMasters Copacabana, Avoca, Terrigal, Wamberal and Forresters. They each have their own attractions, and all are patrolled on weekends from October to April, with daily patrols during the school holiday periods. Apart from McMasters and Forresters, they have a choice of takeaway food outlets close to the beachfront.

The crystal clear waters right

along the Central Coast offer some of the best diving in Australia, and there are fascinating wrecks off Terrigal in reasonably shallow water. If you are interested in learning how to dive, the **Terrigal Diving Centre**, The Haven Terrigal, ©4384 1219, or **Pro Dive**, 96 The Entrance Road, The Entrance, ©4334 1559, are the places to visit. They teach diving, and after 5 days tuition, which costs around $450, you are awarded a C card. If you are already a qualified diver and have your certificate with you, a diving charter can be arranged instead. Fishing tours are also available for those who prefer to catch fish rather than rub noses with them (unless you are one of those fanatics who performs this ritual *after* catching a fish); one option is **Haven Fishing Charters**, 12 Lexington Parade, Green Point, ©4369 5673.

The **Blue Bead Arabian Stud**, ©4382 2346, is located at Razina Park in Picketts Valley Road, 5 minutes from Terrigal and Avoca Beaches. They have mountain trails

for the experienced, and instruct beginners and improvers. Bookings are essential, and the stud is open 7 days.

Tuggerah Lakes

The administrative centre of the Tuggerah Lakes district is Wyong, 22km (24 miles) north of Gosford on the banks of the Wyong River. The Lake system extends from Killarney Vale in the south to the township of Lake Munmorah in the north, and consists of three lakes - Tuggerah, Budgewoi and Munmorah. The biggest lake is Tuggerah Lake, and it has the only opening from the ocean, appropriately enough, at The Entrance. There are no sharks in the lakes.

Characteristics

One of the most popular holiday places in New South Wales, Tuggerah Lakes has grown like Topsy. Once it was strictly a fisherman's paradise with basic fishing shacks. Now there are first class motels, hotels, restaurants and sporting facilities.

How to Get There

By Rail
There is a regular electric rail service from Sydney to Wyong, and lo-

cal buses from the station to the other areas.

By Road

From Sydney, via the Pacific Highway, or the F3 from Hornsby to the various destination turnoffs.

Visitor Information

The Entrance Visitor Information Centre has its office in Marine Parade, and is ☺open daily 9am-5pm. It shares its contact details with the Gosford Visitor Information Centre.

Accommodation

As with any holiday centre, there is a great deal of accommodation to choose from in the Tuggerah Lakes district. Here is a selection with prices for a double room per night, not including GST, which should be used as a guide only. The telephone area code is 02.

Wyong

Central Coast Motel, cnr Pacific Highway & Cutler Drive, ✆4353 2911. 17 units, swimming pool - ✪$60-80.

The Entrance

El Lago Waters Resort, 41 The Entrance Road, ✆4332 3955. 40 units, licensed restaurant, swimming pool, spa, sauna, tennis - ✪$70-120.

Ocean Front Motel, 102 Ocean Parade, ✆4332 5911. 31 units, bar-

becue, undercover parking - ✪$80-150.

Sapphire Palms Motel, 180 The Entrance Road, ✆4332 5799. 20 units, swimming pool, spa, barbecue - ✪$55-95.

Tienda Motel, 309A The Entrance Road, ✆4332 3933. 30 units, swimming pool, spa - ✪$55-110.

Lake Front Motel, 16 Coogee Avenue, ✆4332 4518. 14 units, swimming pool, barbecue - ✪$55-110.

Blue Bay Camping and Caravanning Park, cnr Bay Road & Narrawa Avenue, ✆4332 1991. (No dogs allowed), 48 sites - powered sites ✪$23-30 for two, on-site vans $50-80 for two, cabins $60-100.

Dunleith Caravan Park, Hutton Road, North Entrance, ✆4332 2172. 180 sites - powered sites ✪$18-35 for two, cabins $65-180 for two.

Long Jetty

The Coachman Motor Inn, 33 Gordon Road, ✆4332 3692. 7 units, swimming pool, barbecue - ✪$50-110.

Palm Gardens Resort, 44 Kitchener Road, ✆4333 1000. 23 suites, swimming pool, spa, sauna, barbecue - ✪$70-170.

Buccaneer Motel, 398 The Entrance Road, ✆4334 3100. 14 units, swimming pool, barbecue - ✪$68-120.

Jetty Motel, 353 The Entrance Road, ✆4332 1022. 22 units,

swimming pool, spa, barbecue ✪$60-110.

Bateau Bay

Palm Court Motel, 61 Bateau Bay Road, ✆4332 3755. 10 units, unlicensed restaurant, swimming pool - ✪$60-110.

Bateau Bay Hotel/Motel, The Entrance Road, ✆4332 8022. 6 units, licensed restaurant - ✪$60-70.

Sun Valley Caravan Park, Bateau Bay Road, ✆4332 1107. (No pets allowed), 342 sites - powered sites ✪$21-30 for two, holiday flat $65-110 for two.

Budgewoi

Hibiscus Lakeside Motel, 2 Diamond Head Drive, ✆4390 9100. 13 units, barbecue - ✪$65-110.

Sunnylake Caravan Park, 2 Macleay Drive, ✆4390 9471. 130 sites - powered sites ✪$15-30 for two, cabins $90-170 for two.

Budgewoi Tourist Park, Weemala Street, ✆4390 9019. (Pets allowed on leash), 380 sites, barbecue - powered sites ✪$12-18.

Noraville

Sea'n'Sun Motel, 115 Budgewoi Road, ✆4396 4474. 12 units, mini golf, barbecue - ✪$55-100.

Toukley

Toukley Motor Inn, 236 Main Road, ✆4396 5666. 13 units, swimming pool - ✪$56-80.

Twin Lakes Motor Inn, 57 Main Road, ✆4396 4622. 11 units, swimming pool - ✪$50-85.

Eating Out

The district has several licensed RSL and bowling clubs, and these usually offer reasonably priced meals. There are also many takeaway and fast food outlets, both in the towns and on the beachfronts.

Rus Chinese Rendevous, 120 Railway Street, Wyong, ✆4353 2494.

Wyong Golf Club Restaurant, Pacific Highway, Wyong, ✆4352 1999.

Sounan Thai, 27 The Entrance Road, The Entrance, ✆4332 8806. Fully licensed restaurant with waterside views. Open 6pm-11pm 7 days and midday-3pm Wed-Sun, closed Public Holidays.

Jetty Indian Tandoori, 509 The Entrance Road, Long Jetty, ✆4334 2477.

Jans Chinese Malaysian Restaurant, Shops 5-6, 227-229 The Entrance Road, The Entrance, ✆4334 1333.

Mantas Seafood Restaurant, 347 The Entrance Road, Long Jetty, ✆4332 2548.

Beach Point, 19 Point Street, Bateau Bay, ✆4334 5070.

Carmelos Italian Restaurant, 61 Bateau Bay Road, Bateau Bay, ✆4334 5155.

Pizza Pit, 65 Scenic Drive Budgewoi, ✆4399 1035.

Silver Moon Chinese Restaurant, 105 Scenic Drive, Budgewoi, ✆4390 0489. Licensed, open 5pm-

9pm 7 days and for lunch midday-2pm every day except Monday.

Cactus Blues Mexican Restaurant, 245 Main Road, Toukley, ℰ4397 1557.

Starfish Seafood Restaurant, 200 Main Road, Toukley, ℰ4397 1300.

Points of Interest

The Forest of Tranquility, Ourimbah Creek Road, Ourimbah, is the home of Willy Wombat's rainforest walk, the best walk in a rainforest in the Sydney environs. There are gas barbecues, a children's playground, and picnic area, and rainforest plants are for sale. ☺Open Wed-Sun 10am-5pm and all public holidays, ℰ4362 1855.

Crackneck Lookout, in Hilltop Avenue, Bateau Bay, offers sweeping views of the coastline to Norah Head and Bungary Point, over the three lakes and the three power stations.

Bateau Bay Golf Practice Range, 468 The Entrance Road, ℰ4332 3277, is the largest golf range on the Central Coast, and venue of Australian Golf Schools. Practice facilities include grass tees, target greens, bunker and distance markers. ☺Open 7 days.

Long Jetty Catamaran Hire, cnr Tuggerah Parade and Pacific Street, Long Jetty, ℰ4332 9362, hires out catamarans, sailboards, canoes and pedal boats. They also have lessons in water skiing, and sell fishing tackle and bait.

The Entrance Aquaslide, ℰ4334 3151, adjacent to the Lakeside Plaza carpark, 19 Taylor Street, The Entrance, has The Space Spiral, Outer Orbit and Cosmic Crusher rides, and the good news is, the pool is heated.

Each afternoon at 3.30pm, near the children's playground in the **Memorial Park**, The Entrance, everybody gathers to feed the pelicans.

The pelican has been adopted as the symbol of the tourist industry on the Central Coast, and the daily feeding ensures that this symbol doesn't disappear. There is no doubt that they are fascinating creatures, with wing spans up to 2m, and those incredible beaks, but there are many locals who are not exactly enamoured of them. To start with, they eat fish and are not well mannered enough to limit themselves to the afternoon meals supplied by humans, but tend to fish for themselves in the lakes. And, they are much better at it than those people sitting in boats and on the shore with hooks and lines. Then they have lice, which they shed in the water to bite anyone who dares to swim in the area. It is not that the pelicans do this on purpose, but try selling that to a kiddy who is suffering from itchy

bites. Of course, the pelicans came before people starting feeding them, but not in such large numbers.

At **Dunleith Caravan Park**, Hutton Road, North Entrance, ©4332 2172, there is a Shell Museum, with an extensive display of shells and early photographs of the area, along with models of aquatic animals.

Norah Head Lighthouse, circa 1903, is open for visitors only by arrangement with the Visitor Centre. At Cabbage Tree Bay, the tiny settlement where the road to the light house commences, there are steps leading down to a lovely little rock pool, which is very popular with children. You can also drive down the steep road before the steps, but parking is usually a prob-

lem. There is a surfing beach alongside, but it is not patrolled, and there is a dangerous riptide.

Edward Hargraves Homestead, in Elizabeth Drive, Noraville, is not open for inspection, but can be viewed from the road. Edward Hargraves discovered gold near Bathurst in 1851, causing the first gold rush in Australia.

Toukley has a good-sized shopping centre, and the Toukley & District Senior Citizens Club in Hargraves Street, has loads of entertainment and things to do. Toukley RSL is also a very busy club, and visitors are always welcome, as they are at Toukley Bowling Club.

Warnervale Airfield, near the expressway (follow the road through Toukley, crossing the Pacific Highway) offers joy-flights every Sunday, and other days by appointment. Contact **Central Coast Helicopters**, Lot 1, Sparks Road, Warnervale, ©4352 2222, or **Warnervale Air**, Jack Grant Avenue, ©4392 5174.

Smokey Mountain Steam Railroad, in Mountain Road, Warnervale, offers a different day out for all the family with steam train rides through the surrounding picturesque valleys ⊙between 11am and 4pm. It operates on Sundays and public holidays from Boxing Day until the last Sunday in October, except Good Friday and days of total fire ban. For further information, contact them on, ©4392 7644.

Beaches

The coastal beaches in the Tuggerah Lakes area are: Bateau Bay; Shelly Beach; Toowoon Bay; The Entrance; North Entrance; Soldiers Point; Cabbage Tree Bay; Jenny Dixon; The Lakes Beach.

Jenny Dixon Beach and Cabbage Tree bay are not patrolled, and Jenny Dixon has some nude bathers, but the other beaches are patrolled every weekend, and all through the school holidays, and have handy food outlets. From the Lakes Beach, miles of sand and surf stretch northwards, but it should be remembered that the site of the beach club was chosen because it is the safest part of that stretch.

New South Wales – North

Newcastle

Population 138,200
Newcastle is situated on the Hunter River, 171km (106 miles) north of Sydney, and 827km (514 miles) south of Brisbane.

Climate

Average temperatures: January max 27C (81F) - min 18C (64F); July max 17C (63F) - min 6C (43F). Average annual rainfall: 1134mm (45 ins), and the rain falls evenly throughout the year.

Characteristics

Newcastle is the second largest city in New South Wales, and the sixth largest in Australia. The site was discovered when Lt Shortland was searching for convict escapees in the late 18th century, and discovered coal, which together with steel dominated Newcastle to the mid-1960s.

Newcastle is a city with international-style hotels, motels and shopping centres. It is an ideal base for visiting the holiday areas of Lake Macquarie, Port Stephens and the Hunter Valley.

The city was hit by a shocking earthquake on December 28, 1989, with the loss of lives and many buildings. A swift Novocastrian recovery has meant that few signs of the disaster remain.

How to Get There

By Air
The Newcastle Airport is at Williamtown, 23km from the city, and

there are plenty of taxis available for transport to the city centre.

Qantas, ©13 1313 have regular flights to Newcastle.

By Bus

Greyhound Pioneer, ©13 2030, and McCaffertys, ©13 1499, are among the coach companies that stop at Newcastle.

By Rail

Newcastle is on the Sydney/ Murwillumbah line with regular services, and connections from Murwillumbah to Brisbane and the Gold Coast, ©13 2232.

By Road

From Sydney, via the Pacific Highway and the F3 Expressway.

From Brisbane via the Pacific Highway through Tweed Heads and along the coast, or via the New England Highway through Glen Innes and Armidale.

Visitor Information

The Tourist Information Centre is located at 363 Hunter Street, ©(02) 4974 2999 or ©1800 654 558. ☺Opening hours are 9am-5pm Mon-Fri and 10am-3.30pm on weekends. The internet references are ✐ newtour@hunterlink.net.au or ✐ mail@ncc.nsw.gov.au for email, and ☞www.ncc.nsw.gov.au for the website.

Accommodation

As with any large city, moderately-priced accommodation places are in the suburbs, and the Tourist Office has a complete list of what is available. Here is a selection with prices for a double room per night, which should be used as a guide only. The telephone area code is 02.

City

Holiday Inn Esplanade Newcastle, Shortland Esplanade, ©4929 5576. 72 rooms, licensed restaurant - ✪$170-260.

Junction Motel, 121 Union Street, ©4929 6677. 30 units, licensed restaurant, pool - ✪$130.

Ridges City Central Hotel, cnr King & Steel Streets, ©4926 3777. 122 units, 6 suites, licensed restaurant, swimming pool, gym, spa - ✪$120-160.

Noah's On The Beach, cnr Shortland Esplanade & Zaara Street, ©4929 5181. 90 units, 1 suite, licensed restaurant - ✪$140.

Novocastrian Motor Inn, 21 Parnell Place, ©4926 3688. 47 units, licensed restaurant - ✪140-200.

Newcomen Lodge, 70 Newcomen Street, ©4929 7313. 1 room, unlicensed restaurant, pool - ✪$115.

Suburbs

Apollo International Hotel, 290 Pacific Highway, Charlestown, ©4943 6733. 42 units, 8 suites, tennis, swimming pool, barbecue - ✪$140-240.

Hospitality Motor Inn, 418 Maitland Road, Mayfield, ✆4967 1977. 28 units, licensed restaurant - ✪$120-130.

Sovereign Motor Inn, 309 Maitland Road, Mayfield, ✆4968 4405. 34 units, licensed restaurant, swimming pool - ✪$90-100.

Aloha Motor Inn, 231 Glebe Road, Merewether, ✆4963 1283. 29 units, barbecue - ✪$95-105.

Tudor Inn, cnr Tudor & Steel Streets, Hamilton, ✆4969 2533. 31 units, unlicensed restaurant - ✪$90-100.

Panorama Motor Inn, 256 Pacific Highway, Charlestown, ✆4943 3144. 33 units, licensed restaurant, barbecue, swimming pool - ✪$65-80.

Caravan Parks

Tomago Village Van Park, Pacific Highway & Tomago Road, Tomago, ✆4964 8066. (No pets allowed) - powered sites ✪$19 for two, cabins $45-70 for two.

Redhead Beach Holiday Park, 1A Kalaroo Road, ✆4944 8306. (No pets allowed) - powered sites ✪$19-25 for two, cabins $45-95 for two, on-site vans $45-55 for two.

Stockton Beach Tourist Park, Pitt Street, Stockton, ✆4928 1393. (No dogs allowed) - powered sites ✪$16-20 for two, cabins $35-60 for two.

There is a **Youth Hostel** in 30 Pacific Street (cnr King Street), ✆4925 3544. They have 22 rooms at ✪$24 per person twin share.

Eating Out

Finding somewhere to eat in Newcastle is not a problem. There are the licensed clubs (Newcastle Workers, Western Suburbs Leagues Club, Tubemakers Recreation Club, etc) which all offer restaurants, bistros and snack bars. There are also the hotels and motels, most of which have licensed or BYO restaurants, and coffee shops and takeaway food outlets. The Tourist Information Office has a complete list of restaurants, but here are some you might wish to try.

Hawaiian Sunsets, 171 Darby Street, ✆4926 1264. International menu, licensed. Open 6pm-midnight 7 days, closed Public Holidays.

Lans, 146 Darby Street, ✆4929 1565. Open 5pm-10pm every day except Mondays and Public Holidays (closed).

Delaney Hotel, 134 Darby Street, ✆4929 1627. Open 10am-midnight Mon-Sat and Sunday midday-10pm.

San Marco on the Park, 10 Pacific Street, ✆4926 3865. Fully licensed, open 12pm-3pm and 6pm-9pm Mon-Sat, closed Sunday.

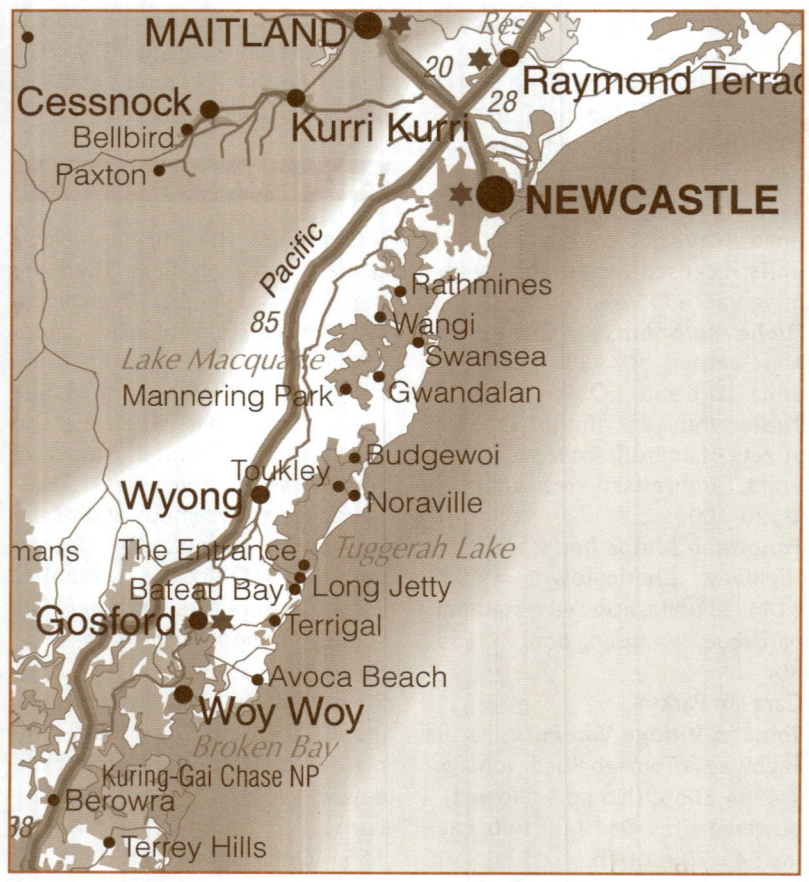

Harry's on Hunter, 672 Hunter Street, ℂ4926 2165.

Mercury Cafe, Mercury Hotel, 23 Watt Street, ℂ4929 2025.

Queens Wharf Brewery Restaurant, 150 Wharf Road, ℂ4929 6333.

Signatures, Radisson Hotel, cnr King & Steel Streets, ℂ4926 3777.

Thara Tong Thai, 541 Hunter Street, ℂ4929 6722.

Taco Bills Mexican Restaurant, 80 Darby Street, ℂ4929 2971.

Maharaja Indian Restaurant, 653 Hunter Street, ℂ4926 1665.

Elizas, Shortland Esplanade, ℂ4929 5576.

Newcastle Happy Gardens Chi-

nese Restaurant, 133 Scott Street, ©4926 2707.

McDonalds are on the corner of King & Steel Streets. KFC is at 227 Hunter Street and Pizza Hut is located at 500 Hunter Street, ©13 1166 for delivery.

Points of Interest

City Hall, in King Street, is the office of Newcastle's Lord Mayor, and is an impressive sandstone building with a tall clock tower. Opened in 1929, it was completely refurbished in 1970-80, and is now a Convention Centre.

Civic Park, opposite the City Hall, is a large park that is a favourite place for Newcastle's business people to relax during the lunchbreak. The special trees planted at the eastern and western ends are gifts from Newcastle's Sister City, Ube in Japan.

The Captain Cook Memorial Fountain forms a backdrop to Civic Park. It was built in 1966, and is illuminated at night.

The Newcastle Regional Art Gallery, in Laman Street, ©4974 5100, was opened in 1977 by Her Majesty, Queen Elizabeth II. It houses the city's Art Collection and features visiting exhibitions regularly. In front of the building is another gift from Ube, a stainless steel sculpture, 'Space Two'. The gallery

is ©open Tues-Sun 10am-5pm and entry is free.

Christ Church Anglican Cathedral overlooks the city from the top of **the hill**, and can be seen from harbour, sea and suburbs. The foundation for the first cathedral was laid in 1817 and was in use until 1884 when another (now the Cathedral Hall opposite) was erected. The present cathedral was dedicated in 1902, and was eventually completed, tower and all, in 1979. It is ©open from early morning until 6pm. Guides are available on Sat and Sun afternoons.

Hunter Mall became a pedestrian arcade in 1980, and is framed by fine Victorian and Edwardian buildings. As well as David Jones department store, it has many specialty stores.

Fort Scratchley, on Nobbys Road, is Australia's only fort that went to war. An historical fort, it was built in the mid-1880s near the site where Lt Shortland first landed on September 9, 1879. It is one of two remaining 19th century closed fort complexes in NSW. Believing that Newcastle was a place likely to be attacked from sea, the Government decided a major fort should be built on Signal Hill. It was largely completed in 1882. In June 1942, it was involved in an attack by a Japanese Submarine. The guns, now on display in the fort, returned the fire, causing the submarine to break off. This was the only time in Australian history that heavy guns were fired in hostility from coastal defences. The fort houses the **Newcastle Region Maritime Museum**, which has many interesting exhibits, and is ☉open week-ends and Public Holidays from midday-4pm.

The Ocean Baths, located at Newcastle Beach and at Merewether Beach, are the two largest saltwater baths in the Southern Hemisphere.

The Obelisk, up the hill just to the south of the city, is in the park bounded by Bindle Reserve Road, Ordnance Street & Wolfe Street. It marks the site of Newcastle's first windmill. The mill was erected in 1820 and became a navigational mark for ships approaching Newcastle. It was demolished in 1847, and the obelisk erected in 1850. In early 1987 it was struck by lightning, but has since been repaired.

The multi-million dollar **Queen's Wharf and Harbour** is a pleasant attraction. You can walk along the promenade, metres away from ships from all over the world, or hire a Daisy Trike or bike and pedal your way around. The complex is only 50m from the Hunter Mall, and includes a marina, a seafood restaurant, a boutique brewery, the Tourist Information Centre and variety shops. From the top of the tower in the complex one has a view of the city, harbour and beaches north up to Port Stephens, and west to the Watagan Mountains. On weekends there are horse-drawn carriage rides available, bands playing, and a complete holiday atmosphere. Unique little 'shop barrows' are located along its foreshores.

At **Harbourside Markets**, cnr Wharf Road & Merewether Street, there's everything to buy, in the classic market style.

William the Fourth was the first Australian-built coastal steamship, and is now anchored at Queen's Wharf. It is available for historical cruises around Newcastle Harbour. See the Tourist Information Centre for all the details.

Newcastle Regional Museum, 787 Hunter Street, ✆4962 2001, is the leading Regional Museum in the country. It features exhibits about the industrial and technological heritage of the surrounding region, its social history, lifestyle and environment. The redevelopment of the former Castlemain & Wood Bros Brewery into the museum was a major Bicentennial project. The museum is ☉open Tues-Sun and public holidays 10am-5pm.

Supernova, Newcastle's Science and Technology Fun Centre is housed within the Regional Mu-

seum. It is hands-on science, a museum where kids are encouraged to touch the displays. Supernova is open the same hours as the Museum, and there is a moderate admission fee.

Nobbys Head was first described by Captain Cook as a "small clump of an island". It was reduced in 1826 by half its size to improve access by ships to the harbour. In 1846, it was connected to the mainland by the breakwater. On top of Nobbys is a lighthouse signal station, and Nobbys Beach is a popular surfing beach with the Novocastrians.

The Heritage Centre, ℂ4925 2265, next door to the Post Office in Hunter Street, is Newcastle's former Police Station (1859), and is operated by the Hunter Region National Trust. The centre features an environmental Gift Shop, ⊕open Mon-Fri 9am-5pm.

Beaches

Newcastle Beach offers safe swimming from the rocks at the northern end to the front of the club pavilion, and surfboard riding to the southern end. *Surfest*, one of the world's leading surfing events takes place here every November. The floodlit and patrolled Ocean Baths are here also.

Nobbys Beach is an excellent family beach. There is good surfing on the reef, at the northern end and at Cowrie hole to the south (patrolled).

Horseshoe Beach is Newcastle's only harbour beach, and is popular with trainers and their racehorses. It is also a good fishing spot.

Stockton Beach, is opposite the city, and offers safe swimming from the breakwater to Hereford Street, and good surfing from there to the north. The main beach is patrolled. Here you can check out the wreck of the *Sygna* (1974).

Bar Beach to the south of Newcastle Beach and the Bogey Hole, is also a good family beach with safe swimming from the northern end (Bar area) to the front of the pavilion, and surfboard riding from there to the southern end. There is plenty of parking. The beach is patrolled and floodlit.

Susan Gilmore Beach, is accessed from the extreme northern end of Bar Beach, via a path down the cliff face, or over the rocks at low tide. The beach was named after an American ship that was wrecked here. It is a nudist beach, and is not patrolled.

Merewether Beach is an excellent swimming beach with good beachbreak surfboard riding south

of the club house. The beach is patrolled and floodlit. There are Ocean Baths here too.

Dixon Park Beach offers safe swimming in front of the clubhouse, and is good for surfing, board and ski, in front of the cliff. The beach is patrolled.

Burwood and **Dudley Beaches** are excellent for swimming and board riding, but these nudists beaches are not patrolled.

Out-of-City Attractions

Shortland Wetlands Centre. The Centre is situated on 65ha (160 acres) of wetland along Sandgate Road, Shortland on the edge of Hexham Swamp. More than 170 species of birds have been recorded here, with at least 30 of these breeding. During the summer months, several thousand egrets nest in the paperbark trees in one of the shallow swamps. Facilities include a Visitors Centre with static and live animal displays and a souvenir shop that provides light refreshments; picnic tables; walking trails; and a bird observation tower. Canoes can be hired for exploring the 7km of waterways around Hexham Swamp. The Wetlands Centre is located less than 1km from the Shortland Shopping Centre along Sandgate Road, Shortland, and a 10 minute walk away from Sandgate Railway Station. The centre is ☻open daily 9am-5pm, with extended hours during holiday seasons. An small admission price applies. Phone ✆4951 6466 for more information. The Information Centre in Newcastle can arrange half day tours and twilight walks to Shortland Wetlands.

Blackbutt Reserve. A reserve of approximately 180ha, Blackbutt is situated in the middle of Newcastle's suburbia. It consists of open forest land intersected by four valleys running from west to east. One of the area's greatest attractions, apart from vegetation, animals and uncommon birds, is its seclusion from the City around it. The Reserve is a popular spot with the locals and a source of interest for overseas tourists keen to observe the exhibition of Australian indigenous wildlife, including wombats, koalas, kangaroos, emus, wallabies and native birds. Families can prepare a meal, relax or play in the grounds with the barbecue facilities, children's playground, several quaint ponds and marked bushwalking tracks available. It is ☻open all year, 10am-5pm for the wildlife exhibits, and there is no admission fee. The Maritime Model Club launch their ships on the biggest pond every Saturday. The Tourist Office has a leaflet setting out the various bushwalks and all the attractions, or you can call direct on ✆4952 1449.

Tours

The Tourist Office has details of tours in and around Newcastle, and of Hunter River and harbour cruises that are available. Here are two worth enquiring about:

Australian Scenic Tours, 50 Hunter Street, ✆4929 4333.

Free Spirit Charters, Level 4, 175 Scott Street, ✆4929 1908.

There are several helicopter flights over the city, the surrounding coastal areas, and further afield to the Vineyards and to Moffats Oyster Barn at Swan Bay. *Scenic Helicopter Flights*, cnr Hannel and Cowper Streets, Wickham, ✆4962 2240, is one company operating in the area.

Daily departures from Newcastle, Maitland and Cessnock to the Vineyards are available, visiting a range of wineries from small familyowned to large commercial, with numerous tastings. Two of these tours are *Hunter Vineyard Tours*, ✆4991 1659, and *The Wine and Cheese Tasting Tour*, ✆4938 5031.

Festivals

The Matarra Festival is held each September.

Facilities

Newcastle has all the facilities you

would expect of a city its size. Theatre and cinema programmes are in the daily newspapers, and the Yellow Pages Telephone Book has details of all sporting facilities. The Tourist Information Centre has all the details.

Outlying Attractions

Forster - Tuncurry

North of Newcastle, about 161km (100 miles), are the twin towns of Forster and Tuncurry, which are the major tourist areas of the Great Lakes, and are renowned for their beaches, fishing, seafoods and temperate climate all year around.

On land there is the **Booti Booti National Park** to explore, and the **Cape Hawke Bicentennial Walk** with its panoramic viewing platform. The popular beaches and lakes provide ample opportunites for swimming, fishing and sailing.

Forster has the Great Lakes Visitor Centre located in Little Street, ℂ(02) 6554 8799 or ℰ1800 802 692. It is hopen Mon-Fri 9am-5pm. They have a web page at ☜www.greatlakes.org.au and an email address at ✉tourglc@tpgi.com.au

Barrington Tops

The Barrington Tops National Park is about 110km (68 miles) northwest of Newcastle, travelling through Raymond Terrace and Dungog. The area is on the World Heritage List.

The fabulous Barrington Tops landscape is the drawcard. It is very mountainous country, with many 4WD and hiking tracks, but care should be taken as many people have become lost wandering off the beaten track. There are many excellent places to spend a few days in this marvellous setting, suiting a wide range of budgets and tastes.

A wonderful website covers this area in great depth: ☜www.barringtons.com.au

Dungog Visitors Information Centre is on the corner of Dowling and Brown Streets, Dungog, ℂ4992 2212, or email: ✉dungogvc@midac.com.au. It is ☉open Mon-Fri 9am-5pm and Sat-Sun 9am-3pm.

The Gloucester Visitor Information Centre is on the corner of Church & Denison Streets, Gloucester, ℂ6558 1408, or email: ✉glosinfo@tpg.com.au. It is ☉open 7 days 9.30am-4.30pm.

Port Stephens

Port Stephens is a 45 minute coastal drive north of Newcastle, and is regarded as one of the most attractive and unspoilt waterways anywhere in Australia. It proclaims itself as the 'Dolphin Capital of Australia', since more than 140 bottlenose dolphins reside in the port, which is more than twice the size of Sydney Harbour. Further upstream from where the Myall River flows into the Port are the Broadwater and the Myall Lakes systems with lovely waterways, tiny uninhabited islands, abundant bird life, a national park, and un-polluted beaches stretching north to the Smith's and Wallace Lakes systems.

What were once isolated fishing settlements around the Port's foreshores, have become connected with the influx of residents and tourist facilities. The main centres are Shoal Bay, Nelson Bay, Salaman-der Bay and Soldiers Point, and the smaller, and somewhat newer ar-eas are Lemon Tree, Mallabula, Tanilba Bay and Oyster Cove.

On the waterway's northern reaches are the holiday centres of Tea Gardens and Hawks Nest, both offering good accommodation, beaches and facilities.

Lying only a couple of hours away from Sydney by car, this is a boom-ing tourist area that bustles with visitors in the peak summer season. **Nelson Bay** is the Port Stephens service centre, with a variety of shops, a movie cinema, a supermar-ket, restaurants, banks, a pub, and plenty more. People flock to the scenic **Marina** for shopping, din-ing and entertainment.

There is no shortage of activities to occupy your time in Port Stephens, from all manner of watersports to a number of Hunter Valley wine tours.

The area also has theme parks ca-tering for children, including **Tobog-gan Hill Park** in Salamander Bay, ✆4984 1022; **Tomteland Australia** in Williamtown, ✆4965 1500; and **Oakvale Farm and Fauna World** in Salt Ash, ✆4982 6222.

The Port Stephens Visitor Infor-mation Centre is on Victoria Pa-rade, Nelson Bay, ✆(02) 4981 1579 or ✆1800 808 900. It is ☺open 9am-5pm Mon-Fri and 9am-4pm Sat, Sun and Public Holidays. You will find it at the drive-way en-trance to the Marina. Email them at ✉ tops@hunterlink.net.au or find the website at ✇www.port stephens.org.au

Hunter Valley

The beauty of the Hunter, with its rolling hills covered in rows of grape-vines and surrounded by tall mountains, surprises many visitors. There are over 1500ha (3705 acres) of vineyards under cultivation in the Lower Hunter-Pokolbin district near Cessnock, and more than 1600ha (3952 acres) planted in the Upper Hunter, centred around the towns of Muswellbrook and Denman.

Renowned for the production of top quality table wines, the Valley's

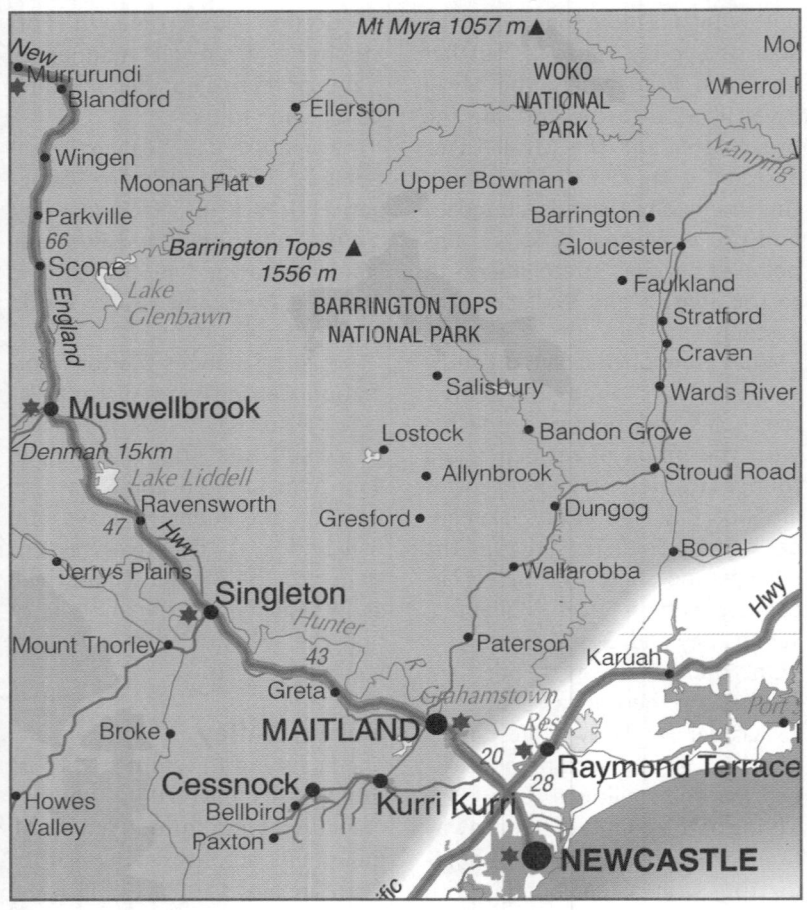

wineries range in size and production from small family affairs, where their entire vintage goes in their own tastings and cellar door sales, to large famous brand company bottlers whose award-winning labels have become household names.

In the last few decades, the rising popularity of the Hunter has produced a rapid development in ancillary visitor amenities with restaurants, craft shops, galleries and children's playgrounds becoming parts of many of the wineries.

Even if you are not in the grip of the grape, a day at Pokolbin Estate

Vineyard, or Hungerford Hill wine village, is good fun for all the family.

The main Tourist Information Centre for the area is in Cessnock, but there is another in Mait and, in King Edward Park, Banks Street East, ©(02) 4933 2611.

The Hunter Regional Tourism Organisation has a web page at ☞www.huntertourism.com/Online/home/main.html

Murrurundi

The town of Murrurundi on the Pages River occupies the northernmost point of the Hunter Valley, and has historic old buildings, many classified by the National Trust. Tales of bushrangers are intertwined with the region. Ben Hall was born here, and Thunderbolt roamed in the area in the latter part of the last century.

Sheep, cattle and horse breeding are the major interests, and the mountain scenery of the Liverpool Ranges, at the town's doorstep, gives an unparalleled view of the valley.

Scone

Scone was first settled during the 1830s by Scottish settlers who likened the countryside to their homeland, and named many spots after their birthplaces. The town is now a thriving commercial centre supporting important rural indus-

tries, and is well known for its thoroughbred horses, cattle and sheep from stud properties in the area. Scone is also the inland gateway to the Barrington Tops region, via the Scone-Gloucester Road.

Nearby **Glenbawn Dam** is well stocked with freshwater fish, and is ideal for boating, yachting, water skiing and swimming.

The **Burning Mountain**, off the New England Highway between Scone and Murrurundi, turn-off just north of Wingen, has been burning for thousands of years. According to Aboriginal legend, a tribesman was lighting his fire on the mountainside when he was carried off into the earth by the evil one. Unable to escape, he used his fire sticks to set the mountain alight so that the smoke might warn others to keep away. Today the mountain is easily reached via a two kilometre walking track.

Travelling south through **Aberdeen**, which once housed a thriving abbatoir, one comes to Muswellbrook.

Scone has a Visitor Information Centre on the corner of Susan & Kelly Streets, ☉open daily 9am-5pm. Email them at ✉stic@scone .nsw.gov.au or phone them on ©(02) 6545 1526.

Muswellbrook

The Muswellbrook area has

benefitted in recent years with the growth of the mining and power industries, and as well, the wine industry. The major rural activity, though, is dairy farming. Produce is supplied through the Hunter Valley Co-operative Dairy Company's processing plant at Muswellbrook.

The area boasts a number of **Art and Craft Galleries**, and the **Rainbow Zone Fun Centre** in Industrial Close, ©6541 4279.

For more information, the Muswellbrook Visitor Information Centre is in 87 Hill Street, ©(02) 6541 4050. ⊙Open 9am-5pm daily. A web page lets you explore the area at ☞www.muswellbrook.org.au

Denman

Situated in one of the most fertile areas of the Hunter Region, some 15km south-west of Muswellbrook off the New England Highway, Denman has many fine horse and cattle studs, and has become an acknowledged quality wine producing area.

Vineyards in the area are: **Arrowfield**, ©6576 4041, one of the largest in Australia; **Rosemount Estate**, ☎6549 6400; **McGuigan Wines**, ☎6547 2422; and **Horsehoe Vineyard**, ☎6547 3528.

The nearby **Widden Valley** is considered to be second only to America's famous Kentucky Blue Grass region for the breeding of racehorses.

Singleton

Back on the New England Highway we come to the geographical heart of the Hunter Valley, Singleton. It has the Hunter River flowing past its doorstep and irrigating the surrounding rich grazing land.

Nearby **Lake St Clair** offers boating and fishing, and maps of the waterways are available from the Information Centre.

The **Singleton Army Camp** includes the Royal Australian Infantry Corps Museum, which is ⊙open to visitors 9am-4pm Wed-Sun.

On the New England Highway, between Singleton and Muswellbrook, are the Liddell (©6542 1611) and Bayswater (©6542 1611) **Power Stations**, which are two of the biggest thermal power stations in the Southern Hemisphere. Visitor tours are available at certain times by arrangement.

The Singleton Information Centre at the southern entrance to the town, in the Shire Council, Civic Centre on Queen Street. They are ⊙open Mon-Fri 8.30am-4.30pm, ©(02) 6578 7267. The website is: ☞www.singleton.nsw.gov.au and the email address is ✉ssc@singletoncouncil.nsw.gov.au

Cessnock

The town of Cessnock is 52km (32 miles) from Newcastle and 185km (115 miles) from Sydney. It is the gateway to the wineries, with approximately 30 in the area. Cessnock is the major town in the area, but the satellite district of Pokolbin provides the real accommodation treats.

The historic village of **Wollombi**, 31km (19 miles) south-west of Cessnock, has a few interesting buildings worth visiting - the Court House, St John's Anglican Church and the two-storey Post Office.

The Visitor Information Centre is in Turner Park, Aberdare Road, and ☺opens 7 days, Mon-Thu 9am-5pm, Fri 9am-6pm, Sat 9.30am-5pm and Sunday and Public Holidays 9.30am-3.30pm. The Information Centre has a list of all the attractions in the town, and of the wineries which are open for tours and cellar door sales. They can be emailed at ✎info@winecountry.com.au or visited at the website ☞www.winecountry.com.au

Kurri Kurri

Kurri Kurri is the closest notable town in the Hunter Valley to Sydney (150km) and it lies fairly close to the end of the northern freeway, but really there are more picturesque places to stay in the region, so an extra drive is worth the time.

Near the town of Kurri Kurri is the **Richmond Vale Railway Museum** and the **Richmond Main Colliery**, but opening days are limited so phone ✆4937 5344 or ✆4936 1124 if you are fascinated by mid-nineteenth century mining and engineering accomplishments. The historic Kurri Kurri Hotel on the corner of Lang and Hampden Streets is also worth a visit.

New South Wales – North

Taree

Population 16,700
Taree is located on the banks of the Manning River, 330km (205 miles) north of Sydney.

Characteristics

Taree is the commercial centre of the Manning Valley, which offers a diversity of natural attractions from scenic lookouts and waterfalls that plunge deep into a box gorge, to some of the cleanest, whitest beaches on the east coast of Australia.

Climate

Average temperatures: January max 29C (84F) - min 17C (63F); July max 18C (64F) - min 6C (43F). Average annual rainfall: 1171mm (46 ins).

How to Get There

By Air
Qantas, ☎13 1313, has flights from/to Sydney.
By Bus
McCaffertys, ☎13 1499, and Greyhound Pioneer, ☎13 2030, stop at Taree on their Sydney/Brisbane runs.
By Rail
There is an XPT Countrylink service from Sydney to Taree and the trip takes 5 hours, ☎13 2232.
By Road
From Sydney (310km) and Brisbane (8 hours), via the Pacific Highway.

Visitor Information

The Manning Valley Visitor Information Centre is on the Old Pacific Highway, Taree North, 3km north of the Taree Shopping Centre, ©(02) 6552 1900 or ©1800 801 522. They are ☺open 7 days a week 9am-5pm, and the complex includes a restaurant, public toilets, and a 70-seat theatrette showing an audio-visual presentation. The email address is ✍ manningvic@gtcc.nsw.gov.au and the web address is ☜www.gtcc.nsw.gov.au/tourism

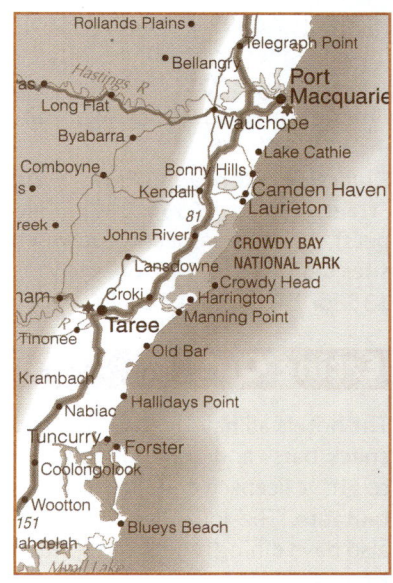

Accommodation

Taree has many motels, a few caravan parks, and houseboats for hire (available from Manning River Holidays Afloat, 36 Crescent Avenue, Taree, ©6552 3162).

Here is a selection of accommodation with prices for a double room per night, which should be used as a guide only. The telephone area code is 02.

Riverview Motor Inn, Old Pacific Highway, ©6552 2122. 21 units, 1 suite, licensed restaurant, swimming pool - ✪$100.

City Centre Motor Inn, 4 Crescent Avenue, ©6552 5244. 20 units, swimming pool, barbecue - ✪$80-90.

Best Western Caravilla Motor Inn, 33 Victoria Street, ©6552 1822. 27 units, licensed restaurant (closed Sunday), swimming pool - ✪$75-85.

In-Town Motor Inn, 77 Victoria Street, ©6552 3996. 20 units, spa bath, barbecue - ✪$70-80.

Marco Polo Motor Inn, Pacific Highway, ©6552 3866. 20 units, swimming pool, sauna, barbecue - ✪$100-110.

Agincourt Motel, 9 Commerce Street, ©6552 1614. 21 units - ✪$45-65.

Jolly Swagman Motel, 1 Commerce Street, ©6552 3511. 21 units, barbecue - ✪$55-90.

Chatham Motel, Pacific Highway, ©6552 1659. 10 units - ✪$40-45.

Arlite Motor Inn, cnr Bligh Street & Pacific Highway, ©6552 2433. 20 units, swimming pool - ✪$50.

Caravan Parks

Twilight Caravan Park, Pacific

Highway, ©0500 854 448. (Pets allowed under control), 65 sites - powered sites ✪$17-20 for two, on-site vans $30-40 for two, cabins $35-70.

Riverside Caravan Park, Reid Street, Croki, ©6556 3274. (No pets), 38 sites, barbecue - powered sites ✪$15-18 for two, on-site vans $35 for two, cabins $35 for two.

Eating Out

The hotels all have restaurants and snack bars, and some of the motels have licensed or unlicensed restaurants. The local licensed clubs also have dining rooms and bistros. Here are some restaurants you might like to try.

Thai Tarni, Albert Street, ©6552 2366. BYO dine-in or take-away. Open 5.30pm-9.30pm every day except Monday and for lunch 11.30am-2pm Tue-Fri.

Il Colosseo, 32 Oxley Street, ©6552 6289. BYO, Italian, also offers free pizza delivery within a 10km radius. Open 6pm-10pm every day except Monday, and until midnight Fri-Sun.

Shades, 23-25 Oxley Street, ©6552 1455. Fully licensed restaurant with an international menu. Open every day except Sunday 6pm-midnight.

Kowin Chinese Restaurant, 22 Chatham Avenue, ©6552 3482. Licensed, open 7 nights 5pm-9pm.

East Court Chinese Restaurant, 73 Victoria Street, ©6552 2465. Licensed, salad bar, banquets, open 7 nights 5pm-10pm.

Silhouettes, Shop 5, 103 Victoria Street, ©6552 1393.

Pelican, Old Pacific Highway, ©6552 2122.

Laurents, 33 Victoria Street, ©6552 5022.

Jin Hong Chinese Restaurant, 91 Victoria Street, ©6552 7199.

Seafood on Victoria, 166 Victoria Street, ©6552 8111.

McDonalds is on the corner of the Pacific Highway and Manning Street. You will find KFC at 38 Victoria Street. Pizza Hut is in Manning Mall, Manning Street. ©13 1166.

Points of Interest

Taree is, as we have mentioned, a holiday town, and there is not a great deal of sightseeing, just plenty of places to relax and take advantage of the river.

The riverside **Fotheringham and Queen Elizabeth Parks** offer the opportunity to feed the pelicans and seagulls, and to observe the river.

Manning River Cruises, ©6557 4767, have a cruise boat on the Manning, with informative commentary to accompany your charter. There are regular departures during school holidays.

The Big Oyster, Pacific Highway, North Taree, is like the other striking and largely ludicrous 'Bigs' in the country.

Festivals

The Taree Aquatic Festival is held each January, and the Taree City Festival is held every two years in June.

Facilities

An 18-hole golf course, several tennis courts, 4 bowling clubs, BMX track, Olympic swimming pool, basketball stadium, indoor cricket stadium, squash courts, ten pin bowling, greyhound racing and horse racing, and facilities for rugby league, rugby union, soccer, hockey, and netball.

The Manning Entertainment centre, ✆6551 0555, has a 505 seat auditorium, and local clubs have top local and interstate bands throughout the year. There is also a twin cinema.

Outlying Attractions

Harrington
The northern arm of the Manning River reaches the ocean at Harrington, and a long breakwall provides excellent fishing. The town is about 5km south of the east-side turn-off on the Pacific Highway.

Safe lagoon swimming is available, and there are barbecue and picnic areas.

From **Pilot Hill Lookout** there is a good view of the coastline. The graves near the lookout are those of pilots whose jobs were to guide the boats over the treacherous bar to enable the timber to be picked up at the ports of Wingham and Taree.

The Harrington Crowdy Tourist Information Centre is at 85 Beach Street, Harrington, ✆6556 1188.

Crowdy Head
4km (2 miles) north-east of Harrington is the quaint village of Crowdy Head, the home of the local fishing fleet.

There's good fishing from the headland, and a co-op if you don't have any luck yourself. The **lighthouse** is easily reached by a sealed road, and gives excellent views of the coastline, both north and south.

Crowdy Beach sweeps in a long arc through to Diamond Head in the National Park, and offers safe swimming.

The Harrington Crowdy Tourist Information Centre is at 85 Beach Street, Harrington, ✆6556 1188.

Manning Point
The township is a little over 35km (22 miles) from Taree, and is located

on an island near the mouth of the river. The sea and the north arm of the Manning River meet at Manning Point, with the ocean providing safe white sandy beaches for swimming, and the river providing excellent fishing.

Wingham

Situated 13km (8 miles) west of Taree, Wingham has a feeling of 'olde England', with its town common that is also the local cricket pitch. There are also about 13 buildings which have been classified by the National Trust for their historical significance, and most have been carefully reconstructed. They include the School of Arts, the Police Station and Court House, the Bank Building, Gibson & Skinner Butchery and the Australian Hotel.

Manning Valley Historical Society's Museum, corner Farquhar & Bent Streets, ☏6553 5823, ⏲open 10am-4pm, is also located within the town square area, and displays include Jimmy Governor's cell, together with various items relating to the history of the area.

Wingham Brush, located 500m from the shopping centre on Farquhar Street, is 7ha (17 acres) of coastal rainforest, with birds and native marsupials. The Brush is adjacent to the Manning River and has picnic tables, barbecues and boat launching facilities.

Use the resources of the Taree Information Centre to obtain further details of Wingham, ☏6552 1900.

Forestry Drives

Bulga Forest Drive is a scenic tour through timbered country north west of Wingham, passing the Ellenborough Falls near Elands. The round trip from Wingham takes visitors through three State Forests - The Bulga, Dingo and Knorrit.

Kiwarrak State Forest is 5km (3 miles) south of Taree, adjacent to the Pacific Highway. Highlights of this 16km (10 miles) sign-posted drive include the Pines picnic area and Breakneck Lookout.

Coopernook State Forest Drive includes Vincents Lookout, Newbys Creek Walk, Newbys Lookout, Starrs Creek, Big Nellie Mountain and Wautui Falls.

Middle Brother Forest surrounds Middle Brother Mountain (556m - 1824 ft). Several walking trails have been established within the Forest, and attractions include the largest Blackbutt trees in the State.

Old Bar

The town centre of Old Bar is only 16km (10 miles) from Taree's closest surfing beach. Old Bar's attractions, apart from the beach, are the mouth of the Manning River and the reserve/picnic area known as **Mud Bishops Reserve**, which offers shaded barbecue facilities.

Hallidays Point – Diamond Beach

Midway between Taree and the Great Lakes region is the coastal area of Hallidays Point - Diamond Beach. The Lands Department has established a **rainforest walk** encompassing the coastal landforms as well as rare tracts of coastal rainforest. The walk takes in two headlands, Black Head and Red Head, and is joined by Black Head Beach. The Visitor Information Centre in Taree has brochures on the Walk. **Nine Mile Beach** stretches southwards.

New South Wales – North

Port Macquarie

Population 33,700

Port Macquarie is situated at the mouth of the Hastings River on the North Coast of New South Wales, 423km (263 miles) north of Sydney.

Climate

Average temperatures: January max 25C (77F) - min 18C (64F); July max 18C (64F) - min 7C (45F). Average annual rainfall: 1563mm (62 ins). The CSIRO suggests that Port Macquarie has the most ideal climate in Australia. A warm off-shore current combines with the surrounding barrier of hills to form a pocket, and produce this small range of temperature.

Characteristics

A major coastal tourist resort and retirement area, Port Macquarie is the most historically significant town along the coast between Newcastle and the Queensland border.

In October, 1818, John Oxley reached the mouth of the Hastings River and described the area as "... a beautiful point of land, having plenty of good water and grass, and commanding a fine view of the interior of the port and the surrounding country". He named the inlet Port Macquarie in honour of the Governor of the Colony of New South Wales.

In 1821, the settlement of Port Macquarie was established by a pioneer party of soldiers and convicts.

How to Get There

By Air

Qantas, ©13 1313 provide flights from Sydney, Melbourne, Brisbane,

Newcastle, Taree, Coffs Harbour, Lismore, Ballina and Coolangatta.

By Bus

Greyhound Pioneer, ✆13 2030, and McCaffertys, ✆13 1499 stop at Port Macquarie.

By Rail

The XPT service from Sydney stops at Wauchope and a coach service connects with Port Macquarie, ✆13 2232.

By Road

From Sydney, via the Pacific Highway on a 400km trip. From Brisbane, either the Pacific Highway along the coast (510 km), or the Cunningham Highway to Warwick, the New England Highway and then the Oxley Highway back to the coast.

Visitor Information

The Port Macquarie Visitor Information Centre is on the corner of Clarence and Hay Streets, ✆(02) 6581 8000 or ✆1800 025 935. Their ☺opening hours are 8.30am-5pm Mon-Fri, 9am-4.30pm weekends. Their web page is at ☞www.portmacquarieinfo.com.au and they can be emailed at ✉vicpm@midcoast.com.au

Accommodation

There is a lot to choose from in Port Macquarie itself, and then there are the nearby resorts of Lake Cathie, North Haven and Laurieton. It is still advisable to book well in advance during the Christmas and school holiday periods.

The prices listed here are for a double room per night, which should be used as a guide only. The telephone area code is 02.

Sails Resort, Park Street, ✆6583 3999 or ✆1800 025 271. 83 guest rooms and suites, spa, sauna, mini golf, tennis, waterfront restaurant, cocktail bar - ✪$150-315.

Country Comfort Port Macquarie, cnr Buller & Hollingworth, ✆6583 2955 or 1800 065 064. 61 units, licensed restaurant, swim-ming pool, spa, barbecue - ✪$115-165.

El Paso Motor Inn, 29 Clarence Street, ✆6583 1944 or ✆1800 027 965. 55 units, licensed restaurant, swimming pool, spa, sauna, barbecue - ✪$100-115.

Best Western Macquarie Barracks Motor Inn, 103 Hastings River Drive, ✆6583 5333 or ✆1800 622 511. 14 units, swimming pool, barbecue - ✪$100-170.

Aquatic Motel, 253 Hastings Drive, ✆6583 7388. 21 units, swimming pools, barbe cue - ✪$80-150.

Rocky Beach Motel, 10 Pacific Drive, ✆6583 5881. 10 self-contained units, barbecue - ✪$65-90.

Arrowyn Motel, 170 Gordon Street, ✆6583 1633. 14 units, basic facilities, pool - ✪$55-95.

Port O'Call Motel, 105 Hastings River Drive, ✆6583 5222. 13 units, swimming pool, barbecue - ✪$70-115.

Narimba Lodge Motel, 4 Narimba Close, ✆6583 3839. 5 units with en suites and a range of facilities - ✪$55-80.

Holiday Units

Airlie Palms, 50 Pacific Drive, ✆1800 242 992. 6 units, air conditioning, comfortable facilities, barbecue, undercover parking - ✪$55-140.

Golden Sands Apartments, ✆6583 2067. 5 self-contained suites, barbecue, undercover parking, centrally located - ✪$50.

Blue Pacific Holiday Flats, 37 Pacific Drive, ✆6583 1686. Self-contained units, undercover parking - ✪$45-80.

Bed & Breakfast

Lighthouse Beach B&B Homestay, 91 Matthew Flinders Drive, ✆6582 5149. Self-contained, spa, swimming pool, barbecue, garage parking, guest library, adults only - ✪$110-150.

Belrina B&B, 22 Burrawong Drive, ✆6582 2967. Luxury accommodation with ensuite bedroom, barbecue, swimming pool - ✪$95-110.

Dolphin View B&B, 53 Matthew Flinders Drive, ✆6582 3561. Ensuite rooms, swimming pool, parking, adults only - ✪$110-145.

Joy's Doo Drop Inn B&B, 29

Laguna Place, ✆6583 3405. Situated on canal waters with private jetty available, solar heated swimming pool, barbecue - ✪$75-110.

Caravan Parks

Sundowner Breakwall Tourist Park, 1 Munster Street, ✆6583 2755. Swimming pool, games room, guest lounge, no pets allowed - powered sites ✪$19-32 for two, cabins $50-140 for two.

Hastings River Caravan Park, 268-270 Hastings River Drive, ✆6583 3387. En suite cabins, tent area, powered sites, barbecue, swimming pool - powered sites from ✪$18 for two, cabins from $45.

Lighthouse Beach Holiday Village, 50 Hart Street, ✆6582 0581. 24 self-contained cabins, 91 powered sites, no pets allowed - powered sites ✪$16-30 for two.

Melaleuca Caravan Park, 128 Hastings River Drive, ✆6583 4498. Budget to luxury accommodation, swimming pool and slide, barbecue, central location, no pets allowed - 81 powered sites ✪$18 for two, on-site vans $35-60 for two, cabins from $55-115.

There is a **Youth Hostel** at 40 Church Street, ✆6583 5512. It has 9 rooms at ✪$20 per person twin share.

Eating Out

There are many restaurants in the

Little Hills and Murrurundi as seen from the Pass on the crown of the Liverpool range

town, offering local seafood, French, Italian, Thai, Mexican, Chinese, Vegetarian and Aussie fare. Here are a few you might like to try.

Cray's Restaurant and Fish Cafe, 74 Clarence Street, ©6583 7885. Seafood specialists, licensed, lunch and dinner, quality takeaway available.

Scampi's on the Marina, Park Street, ©6583 7200. Seafood, dinner 7 days after 6pm, BYO, 'Seafood to Go' quality takeaway available for dinner 7 days.

Filou Restaurant, Mercure Sandcastle Motor Inn, 16-24 William Street, ©6583 4646. Licensed, French cuisine, breakfast, lunch and dinner daily.

Zephyrs on Clarence, 2 Clarence Street, ©6583 6822. Authentic Australian foods including crocodile, kangaroo and barramundi, licensed, open from 6pm.

Spinnakers Resort, Sails Resort, Park Street, ©6583 3999. A la carte dining, licensed, breakfast, lunch and dinner.

Al Dente, 74 Clarence Street, ©6584 1422. Licensed Italian restaurant on the waterfront, lunch and dinner.

Cafe 66, 66 Clarence Street, ©6583 2484. BYO, Italian fare, from snacks to meals, open late.

Toro's Mexican, 22 Murray Street, ©6583 4340. BYO, dine in or take away.

Pancake Place, cnr Clarence & Hay Street, ©6583 4544. BYO, open seven days from 10am, take-away and home delivery.

McDonalds is on the corner of Bay & Park Streets, opposite Settlement City and on the corner of the Pacific Highway and Oxley Street. KFC is on the corner of Horton and Hayward Streets. The phone number for Pizza Hut deliveries in the area is ©13 1166.

Shopping

Two major shopping centres in the town are:

Port Central Shopping Centre, Horton Street, ©6584 2988; and

Settlement City Shopping Centre, Bay Street, ©6581 7377.

Points of Interest

Peppermint Park, cnr Pacific Drive & Ocean Street (near Flynn's Beach), ©6583 6111, has landscaped parkland with water slides, pools, mini golf, aviaries, monkeys, 'Twista' Dodgems and roller skating. Barbecue facilities, a milk bar, and a fitness trail are other attractions. The Park is ©open Tue-Sun, and every day during school holidays. Adults ©$14, children $14, pensioners $9, family $50.

Sea Acres Rainforest Centre, Pacific Drive, ©6582 3355, has a

1.3km boardwalk within 6.2ha (15 acres) of coastal rainforest. There is also a theatre with continuous shows, a restaurant, gift shop and picnic area. The centre is ⊕open daily 9am-4.30pm. Adults ✪$10, children $6, pensioners $8, family $25.

The Church of St Thomas the Apostle, cnr Hay & William Streets, was built by convicts, completed in 1828, and has the original box pews made from local red cedar. In the church grounds is the old hospital dispensary, now a simple chapel. For a donation of a couple of dollars, two-hour tours are available on weekdays. The hospital was across the road, where St Agnes' Catholic Church now stands.

Fantasy Glades, Port Macquarie's Fantasy World, is in Parklands Close, off Pacific Drive, ✆6582 2506. Situated in 2.5ha (6 acres) of rainforest gardens, the Glades have ghosts, castles, dragons, witches, dwarfs, mini-cars and train rides. There are also barbecue and picnic areas and a coffee shop. A wonderful attraction for families. ⊕Open daily from 9am-5pm. Adults ✪$9, children $6.

Kingfisher Park, Kingfisher Road, off the Oxley Highway, has a large collection of Australian fauna and farm animals. There is also a coffee lounge and barbecue facilities. ⊕Open daily from 9am, ✆6581

0783. Adults ✪$9, children $6, family $25.

Billabong Koala & Aussie Wildlife Park, near the intersection of the Pacific and Oxley Highways, ✆6585 1060, is another place where you can cuddle a koala or pat a kangaroo. There are also indoor and outdoor displays and activities, a souvenir and gift shop, a barbecue courtyard, and Matilda's Restaurant. The Park is ⊕open every day 9am-5pm. Adults ✪$9, children $5.

The Hastings District Historical Museum, in Clarence Street near the corner of Hay Street, ✆6583 1108, won the Museum of the Year Award way back in 1981 and 1982. Its 14 rooms are ⊕open Mon-Sat 9.30am-4.30pm, Sun 1.30-4.30pm.

Port Macquarie Observatory, in Rotary Park, William Street, allows visitors to observe the Solar System with the aid of a Planetarium and telescope. ⊕Open Wed and Sun 7.30-9.30pm (8.15-10pm during Daylight Saving).

Both the Historic Cemetery Gardens and Kooloonbung Creek Nature Park are situated at the southern end of Horton Street. The cemetery has many old graves dating back over 150 years, and the nature reserve has landscaped gardens and walks along the creek.

Tacking Point Lighthouse, at

the end of Lighthouse Beach Road, is the third oldest in the country.

Macquarie Nature Reserve, Roto House off Lord Street, has an historic visitors' centre, and in the grounds you can picnic, spy on some healthy koalas, or visit some sick ones in the yard of the Koala Hospital a short distance away (the public is not permitted inside the complex itself). The koalas are fed daily at 8am and 3pm. The Koala Preservation Society of NSW is a voluntary organisation and your support will help save the koalas in Port Macquarie.

Old World Timber Art, 120 Hastings Drive, ✆6583 2502, is where you can watch craftsmen creating hand-crafted woodware and souvenirs from beautiful Hastings timbers. The complex is ⊕open Mon-Fri 8.30am-5pm, and the showroom is open Sat-Sun 10am-4pm.

Thrumster Village Pottery, is a pottery and craft centre situated 9km (6 miles) west of Port Macquarie on the Oxley Highway. Pottery, leatherwork, copper enamelling, hand made glassware and hand crafted works are on display. ⊕Open daily during school holidays, otherwise Thurs-Sun 9am-5pm, ✆6581 0885.

Cassegrain's Hastings Valley Winery, Pacific Highway, is ⊕open daily 9am-5pm, ✆6583 7777. They offer winery inspections, wine tasting and cellar door sales. There are also picnic and barbecue facilities, a children's play area, cooperage and souvenirs.

Surfing beaches are part of the city atmosphere. The best known is Lighthouse Beach, which has magnificent surf for boards and body surfing.

Tours

The Visitor Information Centre has details of many river cruises, boat hire outlets and deep sea fishing charter boats. They can also advise on bush and forest safaris. Here is a selection:

Port Explorer Bus, ✆1800 025 935 for details. Town Tour, ✪$15 adults, $12 children, $13 pensioner.

Eagle Iron Motorcycle Tours, ✆1800 025 935 for details. From ✪$34 for half an hour to $290 for a full day (7 hours).

At the southern end of Lighthouse Beach, **Camel Safaris**, ✆6583 7650, offer camel rides lasting from 20 minutes (✪$14 adult, $9 child) to overnight camping safaris ($195pp).

Everglades Waterbus, ✆6582 5009. 5 dolphin-spotting cruises on offer, from adult ✪$22 to $50.

Fantasea, ✆015 256 742. Adults ✪$19, children $8, pensioners $17, family $48.

Macquarie Mountain Tours, ✆1800 025 935 for details. Full day, adult ✪$85, child $50; River and Mountain Escape, adult ✪$80, child $40, Wine Tasting Tour, ✪$23.

Mansfield's Aussie Beach and Bush Tours, ✆1800 025 935 for details. Full day with two meals provided, ✪$80.

Port Macquarie Canoe Safaris, ✆1800 025 935. Short day tour, ✪$55 adult, $33 child. All day tour including lunch, ✪$85 adult, $45 child.

Port Macquarie River Cruises, ✆1800 025 935 for details. A number of choices including a 2hr scenic cruise, ✪$17 adults, $17 child, $9 pensioner.

Queens Lake Cruiser, ✆1800 025 935 for details. 2hr scenic cruise, adult ✪$16, child $8; 4hr lunch cruise, ✪$23 adult, $12 child.

Seaplane Joy Flights, ✆1800 025 935 for details. From ✪$45 adult, $22 child.

Wingaway Air Scenic Flights, ✆18000 025 935 for details.

Festivals

Port Macquarie has The Carnival of the Pines over the Easter period, and Wauchope (*see separate entry*) has Colonial Week in September.

Sports

Fishing

Mid Coast River Fishing Charters, ✆1800 025 935 for details 2 people full day, ✪$125.

Odyssey Charters, ✆6586 3132. Long Day Reef/Trolling ✪$155 (minimum 10 people), other packages available.

Port Macquarie Estuary Sportfishing Tours, ✆6582 2545.

SeaQuest Fishing Charters, ✆6583 3463. ✪$100 adult, $70 child.

Airborne

High Adventure Airpark, ✆1800 025 935 for details. Microlite flight (✪$145 for 1hr), tandem hanggliding (✪$160 for 20mins) and tandem paragliding (✪$145 for 30mins) are a few of the activities available.

Skydiving, ✆6584 3655. ✪$290 for a tandem jump.

Horse Riding

Cowarra Homestead Forest Trails, ✆1800 025 935 for details. 1hr ✪$28, 2hrs $45, several routes to choose from.

Watersports

Port Macquarie Kayak Adventures, ✆1800 025 935 for details. Half-day ✪$33.

Port Water Sports, ✆1800 025 935 for details. Parasailing ✪$50, coastal tour $39.

Golf

Supa Putt Golf, ✆1800 025 935

for details. Adult ✪$7, child $5 for 18 holes.

Outlying Attractions

South West Rocks

The largest seaside resort in the Kempsey Shire is South West Rocks, 32km (20 miles) north-east of Kempsey, near the mouth of the Macleay River. The town was so named because the pilot officer at Grassy Head, the old entrance to the river, advised masters of vessels to anchor in Trial Bay, south-west of the rocks to ensure their ships would be in deep water with room to manoeuvre under sail.

There are many beaches in the area, and two interesting places to explore: Trial Bay Gaol and Smoky Cape Lighthouse.

Trial Bay Gaol, overlooking Trial Bay, was opened as a prison in 1886, and later during World War I was an internment centre for 500 Germans. Guided tours are available through the gaol, or you can browse through the complex, with its museum pieces and restored cells. The gaol is ⊕open 9am- 5pm daily, ✆6566 6168.

Smoky Cape Lighthouse, on the border of Hat Head National Park, is the highest lighthouse on the NSW coast, standing 128m (420 ft) above sea level, and was opened in 1891. Visitors are welcome on ⊕Tuesdays and Thursdays, and you can chat to one of the light-keepers, and admire the outstanding views.

On the shores of the beaches around South West Rocks there are many **wrecks** of vessels dating back to 1816.

Kempsey

Situated 48km (30 miles) north of Port Macquarie, Kempsey straddles the Macleay River and is the heart of a fast growing valley renowned for its natural beauty and stress-free lifestyle.

Attractions include: The **Macleay River Historical Societies' Museum**, which can be found in the Information Centre complex on the Pacific Highway, South Kempsey, ⊕open daily 10am-4pm; The **Kempsey Shire Library and Les Graham Art Collection**, Elbow Street, West Kempsey, ⊕open Mon-Fri 10am-6pm, Sat 9am-noon; and **Kempsey Saleyards**, Kemp Street.

There are many bushwalks and drives in the **Macleay Valley**.

The area has facilities for every kind of **sport** imaginable on land and water.

The beaches in the Kempsey Shire offer safe, patrolled sections for families. The village of **Stuarts Point** is the focal point for the beaches that stretch north from the mouth of the Macleay River to the

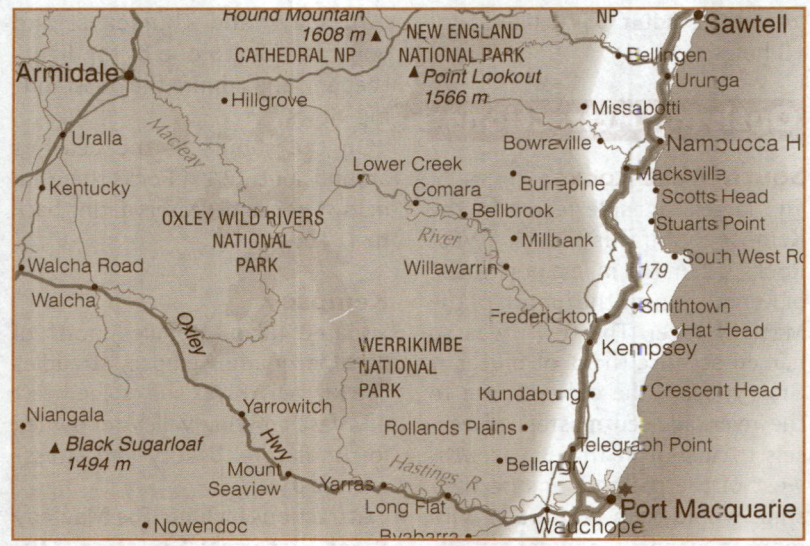

Shire's boundary above Middle Head.

The coastal village of **Hat Head** is regarded as one of the top fishing spots on the coast of NSW, because of its close proximity to the continental shelf. Hat Head is situated in the heart of the **Hat Head National Park**, and is the perfect base for a quiet family holiday, a fishing trip or a nature-lover's excursion.

The Kempsey Visitor Information Centre is on the Pacific Highway, South Kempsey, ☉open Mon-Fri 9am-5pm, weekends 10am-4pm. ✆(02) 6554 8799 or ✆1800 642 480 or email at ✉ktic@midcoast .com.au

Wauchope

Wauchope is 19km (12 miles) west of Port Macquarie on the Oxley Highway. At the centre of the region's timber industry, this historic town draws visitor mainly to its Timbertown theme park.

The main attraction is **Timbertown**, ✆6585 1866, an entire village recreated to demonstrate the struggles and achievements of the pioneers. It has a steam train, timber sawing, a bullock team, a woodturner and a general store selling the finished goods plus lollies from glass jars and liccrice by the yard, amongst other things from 'the good old days'. There is also a bakery offering freshly baked damper with home-made jams, and Devonshire teas. The houses and the church have been faithfully reproduced in the manner of the era (1880-1910), many with fine furniture and utensils brought out from the home country. You should allow 4 hours minimum for a visit, maybe more if it's a hot day and you spend some time in the *Maul and Wedge Hotel*. Timbertown is ☺open daily from 9am. It is 3km from Wauchope on the Oxley Highway.

Another attraction is the **Big Bull** in Redbank Farm, 50 Redbank Road, ☏6585 2044, just over the river. The Bull is 14m (46 ft) high, and in the complex there is a working dairy farm, an animal nursery, an educational display, hay rides, a restaurant, and a souvenir shop. It is ☺open daily 9am-5pm.

The Wauchope Information and Neighbourhood Centre is in Shop 3 Roland Plaza, 33 High Street, ☏6586 4055.

Laurieton

Laurieton is south of Port Macquarie on Ocean Drive, and is part of Camden Haven. It is another popular holiday spot, with a range of accommodation, restaurants and clubs.

This is a great area for fishing, and there are many good beaches to tempt you. The town is overlooked by **North Brother Mountain**, from which there are good views of the town and the coastline. **Kattang Nature Reserve**, a few kilometres east, and **Crowdy Bay National Park**, just south, are two pleasant natural features of the local environment.

Crowdy Bay National Park is located in the northern section of the Manning Valley, and covers some 6000ha (14,820 acres). Access to the park is via the Coralville Road at Moorland, some 35km (22 miles) north of Taree. Picnic and camping areas are available within the park and the main attractions are fishing and surfing. *Diamond Head* is the main camping area with barbecues and toilet facilities, however drinking water is not available within the Park.

Author Kylie Tennant often spent time at Diamond Head, where he built a hut from which he wrote *The Man on the Headland*. The hut was a gift to the National Park in 1976, and was restored in 1980.

Boorganna Nature Reserve is on the western edge of the Comboyne Plateau, 7km (4 miles) west of Taree. Access is along the Innes View Road from the Wingham/Comboyne Road. Brochures on both of these parks are available from the Tourist Information Centre in Taree.

The Camden Haven Neighbourhood Information Centre is in 1 Seymour Street, Laurieton, ☏6559 5676.

Coffs Harbour

Population 22,170

Coffs Harbour is situated on the coast of New South Wales, 578km (359 miles) north of Sydney and 427km (265 miles) south of Brisbane.

Climate

Average temperatures: January max 26C (79F) - min 19C (66F); June max 19C (66F) - min 9C (48F). Average annual rainfall: 1759mm (69 ins); wettest six months October to March.

Characteristics

Coffs Harbour is a popular year-round tourist destination. On one side there are the blue waters of the Pacific Ocean, while the western border area is the Great Dividing Range. The combination of golden sands, high mountains, dense luxuriant rainforests, steep banana plantations, clear rivers and streams make it a superb holiday area.

Coffs Harbour was originally called Korff's Harbour, named after Captain John Korff, who sheltered here in 1847. The harbour, being halfway between Brisbane and Sydney, was an extremely busy port facility for the many vessels plying the coastal trade. It was considered a dangerous port, however, and after a boycott by many ships' captains, the lighthouse was eventually built in 1878.

The surrounding lowlands and rolling hills were once a source of red cedar and other valuable timber when discovered some 150 years ago. The pastoralists followed in the tracks of the timber cutters and the area was given to cattle, dairying, vegetable growing and, of course, banana plantations.

How to Get There

By Air
The following airlines fly regional services into Coffs Harbour: Qantas, ☏13 1313 and Kendell, ☏9670 2677.

By Bus
Interstate coach lines operate daily in Coffs Harbour. Contact Greyhound Pioneer, ☏13 2030, or McCaffertys, ☏13 1499.

By Rail
XPT services operate daily from Sydney and overnight expresses operate from Sydney and Brisbane, ☏13 2232.

By Road
Travelling by the Pacific Highway, it is an 8 hour drive from Sydney, and about 6 hours from Brisbane.

Visitor Information

The Coffs Harbour-Tourism Holiday Coast Information Centre is located at the corner of Rose Avenue & Marcia Street, Coffs Harbour, ☏(02) 6652 1522 or 1300 369 070. It is ☺open 9am-5pm daily. Email them at ✎tourism@ coffscoast.com.au or check out the website at ☞www.coffs.net

Accommodation

Coffs Harbour has resorts, motels, holiday apartments, caravan parks, hotels, cabins/lodges and hostels. Here is a selection with prices for a double room per night, which should be used as a guide only. The telephone area code is 02.

Aanuka Beach Resort, Firman Drive, Diggers Beach, ☏6652 7555. 49 units, licensed restaurant, swimming pool, spa, sauna, gym, tennis, barbecue - ✪$205-400 including breakfast.

Coffs Harbour Motor Inn, 22 Elizabeth Street, ☏6652 6388. 35 units, licensed restaurant, swimming pool, spa, barbecue - ✪$90-130.

Big Windmill Motor Lodge, 168 Pacific Highway, ☏6652 2933. 39 units, licensed restaurant, swimming pool, spa, sauna, gym, barbecue - ✪$80-130.

Premier Motor Inn, Pacific Highway, ☏6652 2044. 32 units, licensed restaurant (closed Sun), swimming pool, barbecue - ✪$160-120.

Coachmens Inn, 93 Park Beach Road, ☏6652 2055. 41 units, swimming pool, spa - ✪$55-100.

Matador Motor Inn, cnr Grafton & Albany Streets, ☏6652 3166. 16 units, swimming pool - ✪$55-85.

Bananatown Motel, 15 Grafton Street, ☏6652 4411. 13 units, swimming pool, barbecue - ✪$50-90.

Caravan Parks

Coffs Village Caravan Park, 215 Pacific Highway, ©6652 4633. (No pets allowed), 52 sites - powered sites ✪$17 for two, on-site vans $25 for two.

Bananacoast Caravan Park, Pacific Highway, ©6652 2868. (Dogs allowed by arrangement), 105 sites - powered sites ✪$17-26 for two, cabins $35-105 for two.

Split Solitary Caravan Park, Split Solitary Road, ©6653 6212. (No pets during holiday period), 125 sites - powered sites ✪$15-20 for two, cabins $40-75 for two.

There is a **Youth Hostel** in 110 Albany Street, ©6652 6462. It has 15 rooms at ✪$20-22 per person twin share.

Eating Out

Coffs Harbour has many restaurants and fast food outlets, particularly down on the Marina. The restaurants range from many international cuisines to the family type catered for by the local clubs. Many of the motels and hotels have restaurants and bistros, and here is a taste of what else is available.

The Fishermans Katch, 394 High Street, ©6652 4372. Seafood platters and steak. Open 6am-8pm daily, closed Public Holidays.

Tequila Mexican Restaurant, 224 High Street, ©6652 1279. Fully licensed open 5.30pm-8pm every day.

Stetsons Steakhouse & Saloon, cnr Pacific Highway & Bray Streets,

©6651 9166. Open 5.30pm-10pm 7 days, closed Public Holidays.

Sawan Thai Restaurant, 376 High Street, Coffs Jetty, ©6652 9699. Vegetarian food is a speciality, Open 5.30pm-10.30pm Mon-Sat, closed Sunday and Public Holidays.

Star Anise, 93 Grafton Street, open 6pm-9pm Wed-Sun, 11.30am-2pm Thursday and Friday, closed Monday and Tuesday with selected hours on Public Holidays.

The Dragon, 108 Grafton Street, ©6652 4187. Cantonese cuisine with a seafood emphasis.

Ocean Oyster & Steak Grill, 394 High Street, ©6650 0444.

Sands, cnr Park Beach Road & Ocean Parade, ©6652 2666.

Taruah Thai Restaurant, 360 High Street, ©6652 5992.

The Village, 97 Park Beach Road, ©6652 2055.

McDonalds have a branch on the corner of the Pacific Highway and North Boambee Road and one in the High Street Mall. There is a Pizza Hut on the corner of High and Gordon Streets, and you can call them for delivery on ©13 1166.

Points of Interest

The Big Banana, Pacific Highway, ©6652 4355 is the landmark of Coffs Harbour, and is 3km north of the town. There you will find an audio-visual theatrette, Aboriginal Dreamtime Cave, historical exhibits, hydroponics glasshouse, banana packing shed, Triffid Forest, Time Tunnel, Future Culture Space Station, Greenhouse Food Fair/Souvenir complex, display gardens, machinery museum/ocean lookout, and a farmers' market.

Pet Porpoise Pool, ©6652 6133, in Orlando Street, has performing dolphins and sea lions, native fauna, marine animals, live sharks and reef tank, a kiosk and souvenir outlet. It is ☉open daily 9am-5pm. Shows are at 10.30am and 2.15pm.

North Coast Regional Botanic Garden, ©6648 4188, in Hardacre Street in the centre of town, has 19ha (47 acres) featuring native and exotic plants, ☉open daily.

Within an hour's drive of Coffs Harbour, and covered with magnificent rainforest, is **Dorrigo National Park**, which has many walking trails.

From Coffs Harbour there are a half-a-dozen **drives** that are recommended by the Tourist Office:

1 North along Pacific Highway, including the Big Banana, then continue north to Bruxner Park (Sealy Lookout) and Rainforest, back south, left at the Big Banana through residential areas returning via Macauleys Headland.

2 Starting at the Post Office, go east to Beacon Hill Lookout then down to the harbour area, Muttonbird

Island nature walk, out to Pet Porpoise Pool, Park Beach Surf Club development.

3 West along Coramba Road to Red Hill, Karangi, Coramba, Glenreagh, returning via Nana Glen, Lower Bucca and Moonee to Coffs Harbour.

4 South along Pacific Highway, turn left into Sawtell Scenic Drive, including Boambee Creek, Sawtell Beach and Bonville Lookout. Then on to Storyland Gardens, Pine Creek State Forest, Mylestom and Urunga then return.

5 South along Pacific Highway including Bellingen, Dorrigo National Park, Dangar Falls, and return via Thora to Coffs Harbour.

6 North along Pacific Highway including Big Banana, continue north to Kumbaingeri Wildlife Sanctuary, further north to Woolgoolga, see the Sikh Temple, Woolgoolga Art Gallery, return to Coffs via Lake Russell Gallery.

There are seven State Forests in the area. Sealy Lookout is a must when visiting Bruxner Park Flora Reserve, as it offers panoramic views of the city, Pacific coastline and banana-clad hillsides. The **Dorigo National Park and Rainforest Centre** is on the corner of Dome Road and Lyrebird Lane, ℂ6657 2309.

Several art and opal galleries are in and around the town. The Tour-

ist Information Centre in Hickory Street, Dorrigo, ℂ6657 2486, can provide you with details if you are interested in browsing through these places.

Joy flights over Nambucca Heads, Bellingen, Orara Valley, Woolgoolga and the Solitary Islands, are available (**Skylink Helicopters**, Aviation Drive, ℂ6658 0899; **Wingaway Air**, Airport Drive, ℂ6650 0655), as are deep sea fishing trips (**Adriatic Fishing Trips**, Shop 5 International Marina, ℂ6651 1277; **Cougar Cat 12 Fishing Trips**, ℂ6651 6715.

Storyland Gardens, ℂ6653 1400, 10km south of Coffs Harbour on Lyons Road, Sawtell, has a giant Old Woman's Shoe, surrounded by popular fairytale settings such as Snow White and Little Red Riding Hood. It is open 10am-4pm Thu-Sun and every day during school holidays.

And of course, there are the **beaches**. Coffs Harbour has many, and they range from those with full-blooded rolling surf that boardriders and body surfers love, to the sheltered, lagoon-type that are perfect for toddlers, to some secluded beaches used for nude bathing.

Festivals

The Agricultural Show is held in May.

Facilities

Two golf courses, five lawn bowling clubs, three surf clubs, a yacht club, a deep sea fishing club and racecourse. Tennis, squash, ten-pin bowling, croquet and indoor cricket facilities are available. An indoor stadium caters for basketball, badminton, indoor hockey and many other indoor sports.

Outlying Attractions

Woolgoolga

Situated 25km north of Coffs Harbour, Woolgoolga has a large Sikh community and they have built a lavish temple, called Guru Nanak.

The **Raj Mahal Emporium**, ©6644 1149, an Indian Theme Park on corner of Pullen Street and the Pacific Highway, has Indian artefacts and food.

The **Woolgoolga Art Gallery**, Turon Parade, ©6654 1064, has a treasure trove of fine art, pottery, batikwork and woodcraft, and is open daily 10am-4pm.

Whitewater rafting on the **Nymboida River** is available for the adventurous.

George's Gold Mine, ©6654 5355, 782 Moleton Road, Moleton, is open Wed-Sun 10am-5pm, and has inspections of the Bayfield gold mine and original equipment. There are picnic and barbecue areas, and food is available.

Valery Trails, 758 Valery Road, Valery, ©6653 4401, offer escorted trail rides through the Pine Creek State Forest, catering for both experienced and inexperienced riders.

Nambucca Heads

Situated 114km (71 miles) south of Coffs Harbour, Nambucca Heads is another popular holiday resort, and has a wide range of accommodation from premier hotels to flats and caravan parks.

It is a farming and timber district, and there are facilities for boating, lawn bowls, fishing (river, rock, beach and deep sea), golf, surfing and tennis. Attractions include the Nambucca Historical Museum; Mary Boulton's Pioneer Cottage; The Pub with No Beer; Taylor Arm - venue for the Easter Country Music Festival and Fair; the historical Star Hotel; Kew House Toy and Doll Museum; and the Worm Farm, Valla Road, Valla, which has worm picking, packing and racing.

The Nambucca Valley Visitor Information Centre can be found at 4 Pacific Highway. They are ☺open 9am-5pm daily, and have all the information you will need, ✆(02) 6568 6954 or ✆1800 646 587.

Grafton

Population 16,500
Grafton is situated on a bend of the Clarence River, 660km (410 miles) north of Sydney, 320km (199 miles) south of Brisbane, and 160km (99 miles) east of Glen Innes.

Climate

Average temperatures: January max 32C (90F) - min 19C (66F); July max 17C (63F) - min 7C (45F).

Characteristics

Grafton, the Jacaranda City, has tree lined streets and graceful o d buildings. The district was origir ally discovered by the escaped convict Richard Craig in 1831. For a pardon and one hundred pounds, he brought a party of cedar getters to log the huge cedar stands. The stories of the 'red gold' spread, and John Small arrived in 1838 and first occupied land on Woodford Island.

The settlement was established shortly after, and the first sale of town blocks took place in 1851. Governor Fitzroy officially named the town after his grandfather, the Duke of Grafton, and it was proclaimed a city in 1885.

How to Get There

By Bus
Greyhound Pioneer and McCaffertys stop at Grafton on the Sydney/Brisbane routes.

By Rail
There are daily Countrylink services from Sydney to Grafton.

By Road

From Sydney and Brisbane, via the Pacific Highway.

Tourist Information

The Clarence River Tourist Association is on the corner of Spring Street and the Pacific Highway, ©6642 4277. They can give tips on the best parts and offer you directions on how to access them, and whether road conditions require 4WD at your time of visit.

Accommodation

For a holiday with a difference, visitors can hire a houseboat accommodating up to eight adults in comfort, and cruise up and down the Clarence River, stopping at many of the 100 islands. No licence is required to operate local houseboats. For more information contact Clarence River Boats, Clarence Street, Brushgrove, ©6647 6232.

As regards more conventional accommodation, Grafton has motels and hotels, and South Grafton has motels, hotels and caravan parks. Here is a selection, with prices for a double room per night, which should be used as a guide only. The telephone area code is 02.

Reilley's Hideaway Grafton Farmstay, 218 Reilley's Lane off Pacific Highway, ©6642 6008. 3 rooms,

cooking facilities, fireplace playground, table tennis, pool, spa - ✪$110.

Bent Street Motor Inn, 62 Bent Street, ©6643 4500. 20 units, barbecue, licensed restaurant, car parking, spa, pool - ✪$70-90.

Abbey Motor Inn, 59 Fitzroy Street, ©6642 6122. 24 units, breakfast room service - ✪$65-70.

Fitzroy Motel, 27 Fitzroy Street, ©6642 4477. 21 units, spa, pool - ✪$70-105.

Hi-Way Motel, Pacific Highway, ©6642 1588. 31 units, playground, pool - ✪$55-75.

Roches Family Hotel, 85 Victoria Street, ©6642 2866. 14 rooms, licensed restaurant, barbecue - ✪$40.

Caravan Parks

The Gateway Village, 598 Summerland Way, ©6642 4225. 90 sites, pool, practice golf, barbecue - powered sites ✪$20 for two, cabins $60-85, on-site vans $40-45 for two.

Grafton Sunset Caravan Park, 302 Gwydir Highway, ©6642 3824. (Pets allowed by arrangement) 70 sites, barbecue, kiosk, pool - powered sites ✪$15 for two, on-site vans $30-35 for two, cabins $40-45 for two.

Eating Out

Most of the hotels are open for

counter lunches and counter teas from Monday to Saturday, and the Bowling Club, in Kemp Street, is open for lunch and dinner Mon-Fri, while the District Services Club in Mary Street, is open for lunch and dinner daily. In South Grafton, the Golf Club is open for dinner Wed-Sat.

Here is a selection of restaurants you might like to try.

New Oriental Chinese Restaurant, 127 Prince St, ☏6642 7888.

Kuppazz Family Restaurant, Shopping World Shop 40, ☏6643 1003.

Lea-Mar's Bistro, 93 Prince St, ☏6643 2290.

Clancys Restaurant & Bistro, Grafton Hotel, 97 Fitzroy St, ☏6643 3411.

Jarmers Restaurant, 85 Victoria St, ☏6642 2866.

KFC, Fiztroy Street, ☏6642 1621.

Points of Interest

Grafton has a bus service operating hourly tours that pass many of the historic buildings and points of interest (no service Sun or after noon Sat), ☏6642 3111. Buses leave Market Square at 20 minutes past the hour. There are also regular bus services to Yamba, Maclean, Ulmarra, Lismore and Glen Innes.

Clarence River Ferries, ☏6646 6423, have a fleet of three passenger ferries with individual capacities up to 160 people, servicing the needs of residents and visitors from Grafton to the river mouth, during special events like the Jacaranda Festival. Every day a minimum of four return trips connect Iluka and Yamba. The 30 minute river crossing is a popular scenic alternative to the lengthy road journey. The services from Yamba are met at

Iluka by a courtesy bus provided by Iluka's Sedger's Reef Hotel, where passengers can enjoy a top seafood luncheon.

Regular **river cruises** also operate from Yamba and Iluka including a weekly visit to Maclean (Monday) and Harwood Island (Wednesday and Friday). There are plans to have regular river cruises and ferry services to Susan Island from the wharf at the river-end of Prince Street, beginning in 1991.

Susan Island is situated in the Clarence River, with its tip almost opposite Prince Street. The northern end of the island has a rainforest with walking tracks, and the largest fruit bat colony in the southern hemisphere. It is a spectacular sight when the colony departs at dusk each summer evening. The southern section of the island has barbecues, picnic and toilet facilities.

Grafton Regional Art Gallery, 158 Fitzroy Street, occupies the restored Prentice House (1880), and has a variety of exhibitions from many notable artists and crafts people. It is ☉open 10am-4pm Wed-Sun.

Schaeffer House Museum, 192 Fitzroy Street, is in another fine old homestead, and has exhibits tracing the history of Grafton and the Clarence Valley. ☺Open 2-4pm, Tues, Thurs & Sun.

Christ Church Cathedral (1884), is designed along Gothic lines with towering arches and a spacious interior. The Cathedral is ☉open 7am-5.30pm daily.

Saraton Theatre in Prince Street, is a restored traditional picture theatre which also hosts live shows, conventions and community functions.

The **National Parks** of the Clarence Valley are Yuraygir, Bundjalung, Gibraltar Range and Washpool. Yuraygir and Bundjalung are coastal parks and Gibraltar Range and Washpool to the west offer a variety of scenic drives, camping areas and walking tracks.

Grafton is very proud of its trees, and 7000 of them line the avenues and shade the 24 well-maintained parks. The Visitor Centre has a brochure on trees and parks, but the most popular parks are: Market Square, adjacent to the clock tower in Prince Street; Memorial Park and Boulevarde, river end of Prince Street; South Grafton Boulevarde, Through Street; See Park Arboretum, Pound Street.

Festivals

The Jacaranda Festival was first held in 1935, and is Australia's longest running festival. The Jacaranda Queen is crowned on the last Saturday in October each year, heraldinging the start of the major festival week. On the first Saturday in November there is a spectacular street parade for the close of the Festival, but not the end of festivities, as people flock for weeks before and after to view the trees and the many exhibitions and events.

Facilities

Horseback trail rides can be taken through the coastal forests; the Grafton racetrack has over 40 meetings a year, with the July Racing Carnival rating as the richest country carnival in the nation; the July Carnival at the nearby greyhound track is also a major event; lawn bowls are catered for at four licensed clubs; the Big River Squash and Fitness Centre, Hoof Street, ✆6642 6633, has a gym, swimming pool, sauna, aerobic classes, masseurs and Tae-kwan-do training; Grafton Squash Centre, 39 Queen Street, ✆6642 2989, welcomes visitors; tennis courts are in Prince Street, ✆6642 5666; the Grafton Olympic Pool in Oliver Street has a waterslide, and there is a heated pool in Armidale Street; Big River Ski Lodge at Seelands caters for skiers and hires out boats, ✆6644 9324; and the Visitor Centre can advise on local sailing clubs.

Outlying Attractions

Ulmarra

Situated 13km (8 miles) north of Grafton, Ulmarra is a fine example of a 19th century river port, and the township is classified by the National Trust. It was chosen in 1986 as the location for the filming of the TV mini series Fields of Fire, a story based on life in a 1929 Queensland cane town.

In the early 1900s, Ulmarra was a bustling town with 4 blacksmiths, a killing factory and bacon works, general stores, hospital, two hotels, two schools and three permanent policemen to maintain law and order. Ulmarra wharf was a major pick-up point for steam and sailing vessels serving Sydney markets. The town thrived, but improved road systems and advancing technology eventually finished Ulmarra as a major river port.

The Commercial Hotel is a magnificent old style country pub on the river bank. Ulmarra boasts numerous antique, arts and crafts, and bric-a-brac shops, and cosy little tearooms.

Maclean

"The Scottish Town in Australia," Maclean, 34km (21 miles) north of Grafton, was first settled by Scottish immigrants, and the town's annual Highland Gathering over the

Easter period, and Free Presbyterian Church (the oldest in Australia) are legacies of this past.

During September, the Cane Harvest Festival is celebrated with a Queen Crowning, a street parade, and plenty of fun. A local cane farm can be inspected every Friday, throughout the year.

The Clarence River is one of only two NSW rivers trawled for prawns, and the river fleet works from the Ulmarra ferry to the river mouth using Maclean as its base.

For tourist information look out for places displaying the blue "I" sign, or call in at Scottish Corner souvenir shop in River Street. Attractions include Maclean Lookout, The Pinnacle Rocks, and the Bicentennial Museum, all in Wharf Street, and a number of historic buildings.

Water skiing, sailing and fishing are popular pastimes.
The Lower Clarence Visitors Centre is in Ferry Park, Pacific Highway, ©6645 4121, email ✉ crta1@nor.com.au. It is ⏰open 9am - 5pm daily.

Yamba

Yamba is the largest coastal resort in the Clarence Valley, and is 14km (9 miles) off the Pacific Highway, and 62km (39 miles) north-east of Grafton. It is primarily a holiday town with motels, caravan parks and hundreds of holiday flats and cottages. In the July school holidays the Family Fishing Festival is held, and tonnes of fish are caught.

Yamba's main beach is patrolled during the summer season and has an adjoining rock pool which is popular throughout the year. Neighbouring beaches are also popular for boardriding, sunbaking and fishing.

South of Yamba is the village of Angourie, famous for its surfing, and natural freshwater swimming at the Blue Pool. Angourie marks the northern limit of the Yuraygir National Park.

A daily passenger ferry service operates between Yamba and Iluka, with a minimum of four return services a day. There are also river cruises on Wednesday and Friday.

Iluka

The town of Iluka is situated on the opposite headland to Yamba, and is connected by the ferry service. Nearby is a rainforest that is World Heritage listed. It has excellent walking tracks, with interpretive signs for the most notable features.

West of Iluka is the world's southernmost coffee plantation, and they have tours of the plantation on weekends and during school holidays. At the plantation there is an intimate coffee house, and an arts and crafts shop.

Wooli

The third largest beach resort in the Clarence Valley is located 45km (28 miles east of Grafton with access from Ulmarra, or from the Pacific Highway 12km (7 miles) south of Grafton at the Airport turnoff. On the way to the village you pass by Lake Hiawatha. Wooli is bounded by the Wooli River to the west and the Pacific Ocean to the east. The river and beach offer many ideal swimming and fishing spots.

Wooli River is probably the most unpolluted river in Australia, as it flows completely through National Park. Party pontoon boats can be hired from Bushland Caravan Park.

New South Wales – North

Lismore

Population 27,200

Situated between rainforest and sea, Lismore is in northern New South Wales, inland from Ballina on the Bruxner Highway.

Climate

Average temperatures: January max 30C (86F) - min 19C (66F); July max 20C (68F) - min 6C (43F). Average annual rainfall, 1349mm (53 ins); wettest months December-May.

Characteristics

The commercial, cultural and sporting capital of the North Coast region. Lismore is the administrative centre for Federal and State Government departments, as well as being the commercial and retail hub of the region. The surrounding countryside is extremely fertile and all types of agriculture are found in the region. Tropical fruits, such as bananas, avocados, pineapples and macadamia nuts, are widely grown. Dairying is also popular and the hills away from the coast are still timbered. There has been much controversy in past years over logging.

How to Get There

By Air

Hazelton Airlines, ℂ13 1713, fly to/from Sydney.

By Bus

Greyhound Pioneer, ℂ13 2030, stop at Lismore on their Sydney/Brisbane Pacific Highway route.

Kirklands Coaches, ℂ1300 367

077, provide daily services to/from Brisbane and nearby regional centres.

By Rail
There is a regular Countrylink service from Sydney to Lismore, ✆13 2232.

By Road
Via the Pacific Highway and the New England Highway from Sydney (787km - 489 miles) and Brisbane (222km - 138 miles).

Visitor Information

The Lismore Visitor Information Centre, cnr Ballina & Molesworth Streets (the main street), ✆(02) 6622 0122 or ✆1300 369 795, has literature, maps, souvenirs and accommodation booking services, and is ⏰open 9.30am-4pm Mon-Fri, 10am-3pm weekends and 9.30am-4pm on Public Holidays.

The online references for more info are: email ✉tourism@liscity.nsw.gov.au and website ☞www.liscity.nsw.gov.au

Accommodation

Here is a selection of accommodation available in Lismore, with prices for a double room per night, which should be used as a guide only. The telephone area code is 02.

Sisleys Inntown Motel, 111 Dawson Street, ✆6621 9888. 8 units, comfortable facilities - ❂$70-100.

Dawson Motor Inn, cnr Dawson & Orion Streets, ✆6621 8100. 19 units, swimming pool - ❂$65-85.

Karinga Motel, 258 Molesworth Street, ✆6621 2787. 31 units, licensed restaurant (Mon-Thurs) - ❂$65-80.

Arcadia Motel, cnr James Road &

Ballina Road, Goonellabah (to the east of the city), ✆6624 1999. 10 units, swimming pool - ❂$65.

McDermotts's B&B, cnr Dawson & Magellan Streets, ✆6624 1158. 2 rooms, comfortable facilities - ❂$65-75.

Caravan Parks

Lismore Tourist Caravan Park, Dawson Street, ✆6621 6581. (Pets allowed by discretion), 92 sites, barbecue - powered sites ❂$17 for two, on-site vans $30-35 for two, cabins $40 for two.

Lismore Lake Caravan Park, Bruxner Highway, ✆6621 2585. (Pets on application), 138 sites, pool, barbecue - powered sites ❂$13 for two, cabins $35-45 for two.

Road Runner Caravan Park, Caniaba Road, ✆6621 6705. (No pets allowed), 133 sites, tennis, pool - powered sites ❂$14 for two, cabins $40 for two.

Eating Out

The Gollan Hotel, cnr Woodlark and Keen Streets, serves meals, as do most of the hotels. For tasty and reasonably priced meals, try the Golf Club and the local RSL Club. A few additional suggestions are:

Mandarin Palace Chinese Restaurant, 153 Keen Street, 11.30am-2pm and 5pm-8pm 7 days, closed Public Holidays.

Ho Ho International, 67 Wyrallah Road, ✆6621 5518. Chinese and international cuisine, open 11am-2pm and 5pm-9pm every day except Tuesdays

Paupiettes, 56 Ballina Street, ✆6621 6135. Open 6.30pm-9.30pm Tue-Sat only.

Mexican Magic, 6 Carrington Street, ✆6621 8206.

Giorgios Vegetarian Italia, 73 Magellan Street, ✆6622 3177.

The Tempted Palate, 34 Molesworth Street, ✆6621 6566.

Lismore Seafood Inn, 25 Eggins Lane, ✆6621 3736.

The Loft, 6 Nesbitt Lane, ✆6622 0252.

Bangkok Lismore, 44 Ballina Street, ✆6621 3375.

Thai Lotus Classic, 207 Ballina Street, ✆6622 0062.

If the budget is wearing thin, look for McDonalds on the corner of Laurel Avenue and Brewster Street or call Pizza Hut on ✆13 1166. Otherwise try another of the several take-away establishments in the city, most of which are on Keen, Ballina and Union Streets.

Points of Interest

Lismore was the queen of the river towns last century, as it was as far up river as the trading schooners could reach. The red cedar and other rainforest timber logs from

'The Big Scrub' were floated downstream to Lismore.

Cedar Log Memorial - a giant cedar log is displayed in the small park behind the City Hall as a permanent memorial to the first cedar loggers of the Richmond Valley.

Claude Riley Memorial Lookout, 3km north-east along the New Ballina Cutting, offers a fine view of the city.

Robinson's Lookout, also called Girard's Hill Lookout, is 2km south of the city centre. It offers views of the city, the river and the surrounding countryside.

There is a walking track that joins onto **Wilson's walk**, which starts at Albert Park and is 6.5km (4 miles) long. It takes you through Wilson's Park, a rainforest remnant with many trees identified by plaques where you can spot local bird life.

The Lismore Visitor and Heritage Centre, ©6622 0122, established during the Bicentennial Year, features an unusual walk-through, indoors 'rainforest experience'. Also incorporated in the centre are 'hands on' displays, models and photographic features of Lismore's history.

Lismore Lake is 2.5km from Lismore on the Casino road. There are gas barbecues and a swimming pool, children's playground and a BMX track. It is popular with water skiers.

Heritage Park, near the Visitors Centre, has toilets and gas barbecues.

The Richmond River Historical Society Museum, 165 Molesworth Street, ©6621 9993, contains a fascinating collection of Aboriginal artifacts and pioneer relics, as well as geological specimens.

The Regional Art Gallery, 131 Molesworth Street, ©6622 2209, houses fine collections of paintings, pottery and ceramics.

An **Aboriginal Bora Ring** adjoins Tucki Tucki Cemetery. The Ring overlooks the Steve King's Plain and the mid-Richmond valley. It is one of several tribal ceremonial grounds in the district, and has been fenced and marked with a description board.

Historic River Cruises aboard MV *Bennelong*, a fully licensed cruise boat, sail regularly from Lismore. For bookings, call into their office in Boat Harbour Road, Ballina, or ©0414 664 552 (mobile).

At Alphadale, on the eastern edge of the city, Cowlong Road, is **Macadamia Magic**. This is a macadamia nut processing complex where factory inspections are welcome. The tourist annex specialises in macadamia products and provides refreshments and souvenirs daily, ©6624 2900. It is ☉open 9am-5pm weekdays and 10am-4pm open weekends.

Festivals

September is the month when it's all happening: The Spring Orchid Show; The Lismore Cup, which is the highlight of the racing calendar in Lismore; The Cedar Guitar Awards; The Spring Greyhound Racing Carnival and the Annual Spring Garden Competition.

The North Coast National Show is held in the third week of October each year.

Facilities

Rolling skating at Summerland Skate Centre, North Lismore; Lismore Grand Prix, South Lismore, is a racing circuit where you are the driver, or where you can enjoy mini-golf.

You can learn to water ski at the Lismore Lake Ski School; The Lismore Bowl is ⊕open daily 9am-midnight for ten-pin bowling.

Lawn bowls, tennis, swimming, squash and golf are all catered for, as well as the traditional spectator sports and seasonal activities, such as the Speedway and Karting programmes.

Outlying Attractions

Murwillimbah Region

If you wish to visit the Murwillumbah region, drop into the World Heritage Rainforest Visitor Information Centre Murwillumbah, cnr Pacific Highway & Alma Streets, ⊕open Mon-Sat 9am-4.30pm, Sun 9.30am-4pm. They share a web page with Tweed Heads Information at ☞www.tactic.nsw.gov.au, and you can email them here at ✉info@tactic.nsw.gov.au

Mt Warning, 1157m (3796 ft), which towers above the Tweed Valley behind Murwillumbah, dominates the scenery for miles around. It was named by Captain Cook in 1770. The area is a National Park, and a walking track winds its way to the top for panoramic views of the Tweed Valley and the coast. The lower slopes are rainforest with heathlands higher up. Ask at the Information Centre about where to start and the current conditions of the climb.

Nimbin

Situated inland, in the centre of an area where the 'hippy' approach to life is very popular, one could say Nimbin was the birthplace of alternative lifestyle in Australia in the late 1960s. It is 30km from Lismore.

The town has a unique style and character of its own, and unusual local crafts may be purchased at the **Nimbin School of Arts Gallery**, 47 Cullen Street.

Nimbin Rocks, or Needles, are unusual rock formations 3km on the Lismore side of Nimbin. They are a sacred site of the Bundjalung Aboriginal Tribe.

The **Tuntable Falls**, 13km (8 miles) from Nimbin, can only be reached by a three hour return hike along the creek bed, and it is a walk only for the fit and healthy.

The website at ☜www.nimbin. net will give you an idea of the limited facilities the town offers and a taste of the prevailing attitudes of this small rural community. The email address is: ✎thecrew@ nimbin.net.au

Kyogle

Kyogle is a small town 50km (31 miles) inland north-west of Lismore that is known as the Gateway to the Rainforest. From the township it is an easy drive to the spectacular **Border Ranges National Park**. The town has an Information Centre at the Shire Council in Strathedon Street, ✆(02) 6632 1611.

The Channon

This is a charming village on Terania Creek, 20km (12 miles) north of Lismore.

On the second Sunday of every month, the famous The **Channon Craft Market**, the original country market in the area, is held. Only hand-made articles and produce are sold. There is always a colourful crowd with buskers and street theatre, pony rides and games for the kids.

Terania Creek, about which there was so much controversy in the 1970s, is now part of the **Nightcap National Park**, in which there are many walking tracks through tropical rainforest and to Protesters' Falls.

The **Wyymara Protea Plantation**, 8 Cooks Lane, Dalwood, ✆6629 5270, has 2000 protea shrubs in production, with many different varieties of fresh and dried protea flowers.

Brunswick Heads

Going back to the coast, Brunswick Heads is a fairly quiet tourist resort. It is 21km (13 miles) from Byron Bay, and is popular with keen fishermen and families. Apart from the attraction of the beaches, you will find a sub-tropical **Nature Reserve** located near the Brunswick River. Just north of the town is an alternative route along the coast, passing many popular surfing and fishing beaches, to Kingscliff. When in town, drop into Brunswick Valley Coach and Travel, Park Street, ✆6685 1385, for local information. There is a good website at ☜www.tropicalnsw/ brunswickheads

Byron Bay

42km (26 miles) from Lismore is idyllic Byron Bay - New South Wales' worst-kept secret. More

than 500,000 tourists flock here each year, making it the most visited destination outside Sydney. The city is renowned for its relaxed, peaceful atmosphere.

The focus here is on recreation and relaxation, so most of the town's services fall into one of these categories. Visit or contact the Information Centre to find the interests that most appeal to you.

Cape Byron is the most easterly point of Australia, topped by an extremely powerful lighthouse built in 1901. The Lighthouse is ☉open daily 8am-6.30pm.

For further details, the Byron Bay Visitor Information Centre is located at the Old Railway Cottage, Johnson Street, ✆(02) 6685 8050.

It is ☉open 9am-5pm daily. You will find a useful internet reference at 👁www.byronbayvbo.com

Alstonville

An attractive village that boasts a nice little bookshop, Alstonville is 19km (12 miles) from Lismore on the way to the coast.

Near the village is the **Victoria Park Nature Reserve**, a remnant of the 'big scrub' which once covered most of the district.

The **Summerland House With No Steps**, Wardell Road, ✆6628 0610, is a unique project providing job skills and training for the handicapped. It also has avocados, macadamia nuts, tropical stone fruit, custard apples, lychees and citrus fruits growing in plantations, and on sale, as well as a craft cottage, retail nursery and fruit packing house. Devonshire teas and light lunches are available ☼daily 9am-5pm.

At Bexhill, 10km north-east of Lismore, is an **open-air cathedral**. The pews are fashioned from logs, whilst behind the stone altar and cross are magnificent views of the Corndale Valley.

Ballina

A resort town, Ballina has all the usual tourist facilities. Take the coast road for a more pleasant drive to/from Byron Bay, rather than rejoining the Pacific Highway.

The **Big Prawn** can be seen several kilometres from town.

The **Maritime Museum**, Regatta Lane, ✆6681 1002, records the maritime history of the Richmond River and features the *Las Balsa Raft* which voyaged from South America to Ballina in 1973.

Shaws Bay Hotel, next to the caravan park, 2 Brighton Street, East Ballina, has a beautiful red cedar dining room and staircase which were carved in Spain, ☼open daily 10am-10pm, ✆6686 2034.

The **Broadwater Sugar Mill**, 19km (12 miles) south of Ballina, has tours during the crushing season (June to December).

The Ballina Visitor Information Centre is on the corner of La Balsa Plaza & River Street. They have a startling range of literature on tourist interests and should be your first point of contact. The centre is ☼open 9am-5pm Mon-Fri, 9am-4pm on weekends. Phone them on ✆(02) 6686 3484 or email them at ✉balinfo@balshire.org.au

Evans Head

A charming coastal town, Evans Head is 55km (34 miles) southwest of Lismore. North of the town is the Broadwater National Park, with unspoiled beaches and heathland that becomes a blaze of colour in spring. On the town's southern edge is the Bundjalung National Park, which is popular for surfing, boating, picnicking and bushwalking.

Blue Mountains

Population 70,800
The City of the Blue Mountains, comprising 26 towns and villages, stretches from Penrith, 53km (33 miles) from Sydney, to Mount Victoria, 122km (76 miles) from Sydney. The drive up to the region's major centre, Katoomba, only takes about an hour and a half, making this scenic area a comfortable distance from Sydney city for day trips or a weekend retreat.

Climate

The area has distinct seasons and is cooler than Sydney all year round. Occasionally snow falls in winter, usually July, but it does not last.

Characteristics

The Blue Mountains derive their name from the perpetual haze draped over them. Miniscule drops of eucalyptus evaporate from the leaves of the dense forest and are struck by the sunlight to produce this effect.

It was not until twenty-five years after the arrival of the First Fleet that the Blue Mountains were crossed in search of grazing land. The intrepid explorers who performed the feat in 1813 were Blaxland, Wentworth and Lawson, and three mountain towns bear their names.

In the 1920s and '30s, the Blue Mountains was the Holiday Capital of New South Wales, then it declined in popularity, as people travelled further afield. In recent years there has been a revival, and the Blue Mountains is once again a popular tourist centre.

How to Get There

By Rail
Electric trains depart from Central Station in Sydney every day with stops at Lapstone, Glenbrook, Blaxland, Warrimoo, Valley Heights, Springwood, Faulconbridge, Woodford, Hazelbrook, Lawson, Wentworth Falls, Leura, Katoomba, Medlow Bath, Blackheath and Mt Victoria.

CityRail have special off-peak fares to Katoomba - any train after 9am on weekdays, or any time at the weekend, with return before 4am the next morning, for ✪S11.80 adult. For further information ✆(02) 4782 1902.

By Bus
AAT Kings, ✆9666 3899, Newmans, ✆1300 300 036, and Australian Pacific Tours, ✆9247 7222, have daily tours departing from Sydney Day Tour Terminal, Circular Quay West at 9am.

Fantastic Aussie Tours, ✆9938 5714 (Sydney) or ✆4782 1366 (Katoomba) have three hour tours which connect with trains from Sydney at Katoomba Railway Station.

They also have full day tours of Jenolan Caves departing daily from Katoomba Station in the morning. The Blue Mountains Explorer Bus also operates daily and picks up and drops off in Katoomba and Leura at the main attractions and restaurants. It meets most trains from Sydney, and connects with trains returning to Sydney. On Wednesdays only, they offer trips to Australia's Wonderland, as well as Darling Harbour and the Olympic Site combined.

By Road
From Sydney, via Parramatta Road, the F4 Freeway and the Great Western Highway. From the west, the Great Western Highway.

Visitor Information

Echo Point Information Centre, ✆1300 653 408 and Glenbrook Visitor Information Centre, Great Western Highway, Glenbrook, ✆1300 653 408, are ◷open Mon-Fri 9am-5pm, Sat-Sun 8.30am-4.30pm.

Contact them by email on ✉info @bluemountainstourism.org.au

The official website of Blue Mountains Tourism, ✆1300 653 408, is ☞www.bluemountainstourism.org. au but another one to visit is ☞www.bluemts.com.au

Accommodation

Here is a selection of accommodation, with prices for a double room per night, which should be used as a guide only. GST is included. The

telephone area code is 02.

Katoomba

Alpine Motor Inn, cnr Great Western Highway & Orient Street, ✆4782 2011. 20 units, 4 suites, licensed restaurant, indoor heated swimming pool, sauna - ✪$200-255.

Mountain Heritage, cnr Lovel & Apex Streets, ✆4782 2155. 41 units, licensed restaurant, playground, swimming pool - ✪$180-420.

Katoomba Town Centre Motel, 218-220 Katoomba Street, ✆4782 1266. 18 units, spa - ✪$80-230.

The Cecil Traditional Blue Mountains Guest House, 108 Katoomba Street, ✆4782 1411. 23 rooms, unlicensed restaurant, barbecue, spa, playground tennis - B&B ✪$140-180.

Echo Point Motor Inn, Echo Point Road, ✆4782 2088. 37 units, licensed restaurant - ✪$70-130.

3 Sisters Motel, 348 Katoomba Street, ✆4782 2911. 20 units, unlicensed restaurant - ✪$65-120.

Leura

Peppers Fairmont Resort, 1 Sublime Point Road, ✆4782 5222. 210 rooms, 20 suites (private facilities), licensed restaurant, swimming pool, spa, sauna, gym, tennis, squash - ✪$240-340.

Mercure Resort Blue Mountains, Fitzroy Street, ✆4784 1331. 80 units, 9 suites, licensed restaurant, swimming pool, spa, sauna, gym, tennis, squash, putting green - ✪$130-170.

Above: An old abandoned homestead in rural Australi
Overleaf: Sheep enjoy the early morning winter sun in New South Wale

Medlow Bath

Hydro Majestic Hotel, Great Western Highway, ✆4788 1002. 63 rooms (private facilities), modern Art Deco and classic Edwardian style rooms available, very famous heritage hotel, licensed restaurant, swimming pool, tennis, spa (selected rooms) - ✪$220-1350.

Chalet Blue Mountains, 46 Portland Road, ✆4788 1122. 8 rooms, unlicensed restaurant, tennis, playground - ✪$130-150.

Mt Victoria

Mount Victoria Motor Inn, Station Street, ✆4787 1320. 12 units - ✪$95-160.

The Hotel Imperial, cnr Great Western Highway & Station Street, ✆4787 1233. 23 rooms, licensed restaurant - ✪$75-275 (a range of room standards offered).

Jenolan Caves

Caves House, ✆(02) 6359 3304. 50 rooms, licensed restaurant, playground, tennis, pool, barbecue - B&B ✪$80-200 a double; hotel section, 28 units - ✪$100-105 including breakfast.

Blackheath

Blackheath Motor Inn, 281 Great Western Highway, ✆4787 8788. 18 units, spa - ✪$90-135.

High Mountains Motor Inn, 193 Great Western Highway, ✆4787 8216. 21 units, unlicensed restaurant, swimming pool - ✪$70-120.

Caravan Parks

Katoomba Falls Caravan Park, Katoomba Falls Road, ✆4782 1835. (No pets), 68 sites, barbecue - powered sites ✪$25-30 for two, cabins $60-84 for two.

Leura Village Caravan Park, cnr Great Western Highway & The Mall, ✆4784 1552 (no pets) - powered sites ✪$13 for two, on-site vans $31-33 for two.

Blackheath Caravan Park, Prince Edward Street, ✆4787 8101. (No pets), 74 sites, - powered sites ✪$20-22 for two, cabins $38-55 for two.

Eating Out

If you would like a superb meal, try:

The Swiss Cottage Restaurant, 132 Lurline Street, Katoomba, ✆4782 2281. Undoubtedly one of the best restaurants in the Blue Mountains, *The Swiss Cottage* offers excellent meals in a warm atmosphere. The steaks and fish are superb, the soup is thick and rich, and, for dessert, the melted-Lindt-chocolate-soaked pudding is unbeatable (look for 'Death By Chocolate' on the menu). Your lively host Monique will make you

feel welcome and keep you chuckling as she serves up each course.

Grand View, 174 Great Western Highway, Wentworth Falls, ©4757 1001.

Fairmont Resort, 1 Sublime Point Road, Leura, ©4782 5222.

Hydro Majestic Hotel, Great Western Highway, Medlow Bath, ©4788 1002.

The Imperial, Station Street, Mt Victoria, © 4787 1788.

Guest Houses which serve good meals include:

Felton Woods Manor, cnr Lurline Street & Merriwa Streets, Katoomba, ©4782 2055.

Clarendon, 68 Lurline Street, Katoomba, ©4782 1322.

Mountain Heritage, cnr Apex & Lovel Streets, Katoomba, ©4782 2155.

Cecil, 108 Katoomba Street, Katoomba, ©4782 1411.

St Mounts, 194 Great Western Highway, Blackheath, ©4787 6111.

The Victoria & Albert, 19 Station Street, Mt Victoria, ©4787 1241.

For a touch of nostalgia make sure you visit the National Trust classified **Paragon Cafe** at 65 Katoomba Street, Katoomba, ©4782 2928, which is fully licensed and is the home of the famous Paragon Chocolates.

Local Transport

Bus

Pearce Omnibus, ©4751 1077, have services connecting Faulconbridge and Penrith; Springwood and Winmalee; Blaxland and Mt Riverview.

Katoomba Woodford Bus Company, ©4782 4213 operate services between Katoomba, Leura and Wentworth Falls; Bullaburra and Lawson; Hazelbrook and Woodford; Katoomba Falls, Scenic Railway and Skyway. (No service on public holidays)

Katoomba Leura Bus Service, ©4782 3333 links Leura, Katoomba, Echo Point, North Katoomba, Blackheath, Medlow Bath and Mt Victoria. (No service Saturday afternoon, Sunday or public holidays)

Car Hire

Thrifty, 80 Megalong Street, Leura, ©4784 2888

Taxi

Taxis Katoomba, ©4782 1311; Springwood Taxis, ©4751 1444; Blue Mountains Tax Cabs, ©4759 3000; Lawson Taxis, ©4759 3000.

Points of Interest

Penrith

Situated on the Nepean River, less than an hour's drive from Sydney,

Penrith is one of the most rapidly growing regions in Australia. The biggest tourist attraction is **Panthers**, set in 81ha (200 acres), where bona fide visitors are most welcome. The club has two cable water ski lakes, a miniature car racing track, swimming pool with water slides, tennis complex and a lake with canoes, windsurfers and paddle boats. It also has a motel, six restaurants, a huge variety of poker machines, cocktail bars and a Cabaret Room. It is located in Mulgoa Road, ✆4720 5555.

Other major attractions Penrith offers are the **Nepean Belle Paddlewheeler** (✆4733 1274), the **Museum of Fire** (✆4731 3000), **Warragamba Dam** and **Wonder-**land **Sydney** (✆9830 9100). For more information on these and other places contact the Tourist Information Centre in the carpark at Panthers, Mulgoa Road, ✆4732 7671. If you are in the mood for a show, there are two places you may wish to contact to find out what is on - the Q Theatre, ✆4721 5735 and the Joan Sutherland Performing Arts Centre, ✆4721 8832.

Lower Blue Mountains
Lapstone-Blaxland
Lapstone Zig-Zag Walking Track begins behind the RAAF base at Glenbrook, and follows the original railway cuttings with views of the arches of Knapsack Viaduct.
Blue Mountains National Park,

Glenbrook Area, has bushwalking, picnicking and camping. Information and advice plus publications are available from the Visitors Information Centre, Great Western Highway, Glenbrook, ©1300 653 408.

Lennox Bridge, Mitchell's Pass Road, Glenbrook, was built in 1833 and is the oldest bridge on Australia's mainland. The bridge is well sign-posted from the Great Western Highway.

Wascoe Siding, 15 Grahame Street, Blaxland, ©4739 9701, has a miniature railway and picnic area, and is open on the first Sunday of each month, except January.

Springwood

Two extremely good **bushwalks** originate in Springwood: the first, an easy 90 minute walk to Birdwood Gully, starts from Bednall Road; the second, to Sassafras Gully, is rated medium, and access is either from Holmdale Street, Sassafras Gully Road or Bee Farm Road.

The **Local History Centre** and a **Community Art Gallery** are in Braemar, an early Federation home which is classified by the National Trust, as are the Frazer Memorial Presbyterian Church and Springwood Railway Station.

In the cemetery is the grave of Sir Henry Parkes, the Father of Federation.

Faulconbridge

Norman Lindsay Gallery and Museum, Chapman Parade, ©4751 1067, is the home of this famous Australian artist and writer. There are displays of his paintings, etchings, ship models and family mementos, and a special Magic Pudding room. The house is set in delightful gardens with dozens of statues, some of which are also 'delightful'. There is a shop and a good coffee shop. ©Open Fri-Sun and public holidays 10am-4pm.

Central Blue Mountains

Bull's Camp, Great Western Highway, Linden, was used as a camp for convicts working on the road across the Blue Mountains. It is now a good picnic spot.

Selwood Science & Puzzles, 41 Railway Parade, Hazelbrook, ©4758 6235, is a mid-Victorian house which has been classified by the National Trust. It is ©open Thurs-Mon 9am-5pm, and has a fine collection of art and science features.

There are two interesting **bushwalks** emanating from Lawson: one begins at South Lawson Park, Honour Avenue, and goes to Adelina, Junction, Federal and Cataract Falls - 90 minutes, easy; the other starts in North Lawson Park, Bernards Drive, and walks along Dantes Glen and Lucy's Glen to Frederica Falls - 180 minutes, easy.

Wentworth Falls

Yester Grange, Yester Road, ©4757 1110, is a 19th century house with a collection of 19th century water colours, Victoriana and ceramics. The house is set in bush and parkland and Devonshire teas and light lunches are available. ⏰Open Wed-Fri 10am-4pm, Sat-Sun and public holidays 10am-5pm.

Wentworth Falls Lake, Sinclair Crescent, is a pleasant picnic spot with a playground and tame ducks. Row boats are available for hire.

There are several **walks** with good views in this area. From Falls Road to Fletcher's Lookout, Undercliff Walk, to Den Fenella - easy walk with views and wildflowers, 90 minutes. To Princes Rock with views of Wentworth Falls and Jamison Valley, 20 minutes. To the top of the Falls, 30 minutes. To Undercliff Walk, Den Ferella, Overcliff Walk to Valley of the Waters with panoramic views, 150 minutes.

Upper Blue Mountains
Leura

Sublime Point, at the end of Sublime Point Road, has great views of the Three Sisters and the Jamison Valley.

The Everglades Gardens, 37 Everglades Avenue, ✆4784 1938, is classified by the National Trust as one of the Great Gardens of Australia. There are unique sandstone terraces, magnificent mature trees and native flora, and a grotto pool, ⏰open daily 10am-5pm during spring and summer, and closing an hour earlier during the colder seasons. Admission is ✪$5 adults and $1 children.

Leuralla, 36 Olympian Parade, ✆4784 1169, is an historic art deco mansion with a collection of 19th century Australian art and a Memorial Museum to Dr H.V. Evatt, first President of the United Nations Organisation. There is also a toy and railway museum.

Gordons Falls Reserve is a pleasant picnic area with playground and toilets, and from it there is a walk to the Pool of Siloam and Lyrebird Dell.

Leura Cascades on Cliff Drive is another picnic area, and there are a number of bushwalks that start from this point, with the Round Walk taking about 40 minutes.

Katoomba

The best way to see the attractions of Katoomba is to follow **Cliff Drive**. From the Railway Station, take Lurline and Merriwa Streets to the Drive around the Jamison and Megalong Valleys. Along the drive there are many lookouts, all signposted, the most famous of which is undoubtedly **Echo Point**, from where there are the best views of **The Three Sisters**, Mennhi, Wimlah and Gunnedoo. These rock formations are very important in

Aboriginal legend, and are floodlit at night. From the point you can also see the Ruined Castle and Mount Solitary, and it is possible to pick out many animal shapes on the mountains on the other side of the valley.

From Echo Point the **Giant Stairway** of almost 1000 steps leads to the floor of the Jamison Valley and the Federal Pass, and the Prince Henry Cliff Walk leads left towards Leura or right towards the Scenic Railway Complex.

The Point has picnic facilities, a restaurant and a takeaway food outlet.

Katoomba Falls Reserve is another picnic spot because the cascades, and several walking tracks begin behind the kiosk.

The Scenic Railway and Skyway on Cliff Drive, ☏4782 2699, offer a ride down to the Jamison Valley, which is not for the faint-hearted, or a ride over the valley in the Skyway. The complex also has the cafeteria-style restaurant, a fun parlour and a souvenir shop, and

is ☉open daily 9am-5pm. Fares are ✪$5 for adults and $2 for children.

Also on Cliff Drive is **Cahill's Lookout**, another picnic spot, this time with views of escarpment and valley, and of Boar's Head Rock. The Drive ends at the Great Western Highway, at Katoomba Holiday Caravan Park.

Explorers' Tree, on the highway 2km west of Katoomba, commemorates the crossing of the Blue Mountains by Blaxland, Wentworth and Lawson. From behind the tree a Katoomba to Jenolan Caves walk begins, which takes 2-3 days. More information is available from the Tourist Information Centres.

Blackheath

Evans Lookout, Evans Lookout Road, offers superb views of the Grose Valley.

Govett's Leap, Govett's Leap Road, also has views of Grose Valley and of Bridal Veil Falls, the longest single drop fall in the Blue Mountains.

National Parks & Wildlife Service Heritage Centre, Govett's Leap Road, ☏4787 8877, has an exhibition on natural features of the Blue Mountains, and nearby Fairfax Heritage Track is suitable for disabled people.

Blue Mounts Rhododendron Garden, Bacchante Street, is set in native bushland. It is ☉open 9am-

5pm and admission is by a donation. There are easy walking tracks and picnic facilities.

From **Anvil Rock** and Wind-eroded Cave, Hat Hill Road, Blackheath, you can get good views of the Grose Valley.

Mount Victoria

A visit to the village of Mt Victoria is like taking a step back in time, with buildings of sandstone and iron lace, and others of colonial weatherboard housing antiques, crafts and tearooms. Attractions include the Post Office, Toll House and Railway Station, the Scenic Drive and Mount York where explorers Blaxland, Lawson and Wentworth realised they'd crossed 'The Impenetrable Barrier'. Victoria Falls, Mount Piddington and Pulpit Rock Reserve are also worth a visit.

The Mounts Area

Rich volcanic soils and high rainfall produce the lush vegetation for which the Mounts are renowned. A beautiful area with famous gardens, lookouts and walks.

Cathedral of Ferns, Mount Wilson, is a beautiful rainforest with nearby picnic area.

Mount Tomah Botanic Garden, Bells Line Road, ©4567 2154, was a Bicentennial project of the Royal Botanic Gardens, Sydney. It features cool-climate planting with sections representing specific geographic areas of the world. There are pano-ramic views and picnic areas, and the gardens are ☺open 10am-4pm March to September, and until 5pm during the other months.

Festivals

Lawson Festival - March;
Wentworth Falls Autumn Festival - April;
Yulefest - June/July;
Springtime in the Blue Mountains - September thru November;
Leura Gardens Festival - October;
Leura Village Fair - October;
Blackheath Rhododendron Festival - November;
Glenbrook Festival - November.

For dates and attractions for these festivals it is best to contact the Glenbrook Visitors Centre.

Facilities

Lawn bowls, bush walking, golf, horse riding, scenic drives, swimming pool, tennis, cinemas, squash, art galleries and craft shops.

Outlying Attractions

Hartley Historic Site, Hartley, ©6355 2117 includes the old Courthouse, churches and inns. The site consists of a relatively small cluster of mid-nineteenth century buildings preserved by the NSW National Parks and Wildlife

Service. Hartley is about 35km (22 miles) west of Katoomba.

Zig-Zag Railway

Situated about 7km east of Lithgow, the Railway is an engineering feat. It is a system of tunnels, cuttings and stone viaducts built 1866-69 to overcome the steep descent from the Blue Mountains to the Western Plains beyond. There are picnic areas, and rides are available on an old world steam train. Trains run ☉daily and the cost of a return journey is ✿$13 adults, $6.50 children.

Jenolan Caves

Probably the best-known limestone caves in NSW, the Jenolan Caves were discovered in the 1830s when the victim of a bushranger tracked his attacker to this hideout. The entrance to the caves is in a narrow gorge accessed through the Grand Arch, about 24m (79 ft) high. The view from Carlotta Arch, which overlooks the Blue Lake, is superb. Nine of the twenty-two caves are open for inspection, and guided tours are available. Phone the Jenolan Caves Reserve Trust on, ✆6359 3311 for more information.

Caves House, ✆6359 3322, right at the caves complex, is a charming hotel, with a restaurant, bar and accommodation. There are several bush walks in the area, and daily tours are run from Sydney and Katoomba.

New South Wales – West

Bathurst

Population 26,500
Bathurst is situated on the fertile western slopes of the Great Dividing Range, 208km (129 miles) west of Sydney.

Climate

Average temperatures: January max 27C (81F) - min 13C (55F); July 11C (52F) - min -1C (30.2F). Average annual rainfall: 629mm (25 ins); drizzle rain in winter and storms in summer.

Characteristics

Bathurst is Australia's oldest inland settlement and the centre of a large grain and pastoral district with many historic and distinctive buildings. When gold was discovered in the hills around Bathurst, many towns such as Hill End, Sofala and Hargraves sprung up. Most of them have either disappeared or are ghost towns.

How to Get There

By Bus
Greyhound Pioneer all have daily services to Bathurst from Sydney.

By Rail
There is a Countrylink service from Sydney to Bathurst and Orange.

By Road
From Sydney, either via the Great Western Highway, or via the Kurrajong Road through Bilpin and Bell to Lithgow.

From Melbourne, via the Hume

Highway to Seymour and then the Goulburn Valley Highway to Tocumwal, then the Newell Highway to West Wyalong.

From Adelaide, via the Sturt Highway through Renmark and Mildura to Hay, then via the Mid Western Highway to West Wyalong; or via the Barrier Highway through Broken Hill to Nyngan and then via the Mitchell Highway.From Brisbane, via the Cunningham Highway to Warwick and Goondiwindi, then via the Newell Highway through Moree to Dubbo; or via the New England Highway from Warwick to Tamworth then the Oxley Highway to Dubbo, then the Mitchell Highway.

Tourist Information

The Bathurst Visitor Information Centre is at 28 William Street, Bathurst. They have a website, ☜www.bathurst.nsw.gov.au, and an email address, ✎visitors@ bathurst.nsw.gov.au

Accommodation

Here is a selection of accommodation with prices for a double room per night, which should be used as a guide only. The telephone area code is 02.

James Cook International Motor Inn, cnr Mid Western & Great Western Highways, ©6332 1800.

50 units, licensed restaurant, swimming pool, bbq - ✪$110-135.
Sundowner Chain Motor Inn, 19 Charlotte Street, ©6331 2211. 37 units, licensed restaurant (closed Sunday), swimming pool - ✪$85-175.

Coachman's Inn Motel, cnr Great Western Highway & Oberon Road, ©6331 4855. 26 units, licensed restaurant (closed Sunday) - ✪$95.
Ben Chifley Motor Inn, 272 Stewart Street, ©6331 5055. 28 units, licensed restaurant pool - ✪$105.

Bathurst Motor Inn, 87 Durham Street, ©6631 3568. 53 units, licensed restaurant, swimming pool, spa, gym, room service - ✪$55-150.

Park Hotel, cnr George & Keppel Streets, ©6331 3399. 19 rooms (private facilities), licensed bistro - B&B ✪$70.

Caravan Park

Easts Bathurst Caravan Park, Sydney Road, ©6331 8286. (No pets) 145 sites, pool, tennis - powered sites ✪$18 for two, cabins $50-85 for two.

Eating Out

Many of the motels have restaurants, either licensed or BYO, and the licensed clubs have dining rooms or restaurants/bistros. There are also the usual number of takeaway food outlets, and the Tourist Office will have a complete list.

Points of Interest

The Visitor Centre has trained guides available to provide a commentary on historic buildings in Bathurst for tour groups, and makes brochures available to individuals.

The **Victorian Renaissance Court House**, with its double-storey portico and large octagonal central dome, faces Kings Square. It has two wings and the verandahed wing was built as a telegraph office. The Historical Museum is in the East Wing, and is ☉open Mon-Fri 9am-4.30pm, Sat-Sun 10am-4pm.

The **Bathurst Regional Art Gallery**, 70 Keppel Street, is ☉open Tues-Sat 10am-5pm, Sat-Sun 2-5pm.

Abercrombie House, built in the 1870s and classified by the National Trust, is ☉open for inspection on Sundays at 3pm, except in winter.

Ben Chifley's Cottage, the home of the former Prime Minister, is ☉open Tues-Sat 2-4pm, and Sunday 10am-noon.

Old Government Cottage, behind no. 1 George Street, is where Macquarie stayed during his farewell visit to Bathurst in 1821. It is ☉open Sundays 1.30-3.30pm.

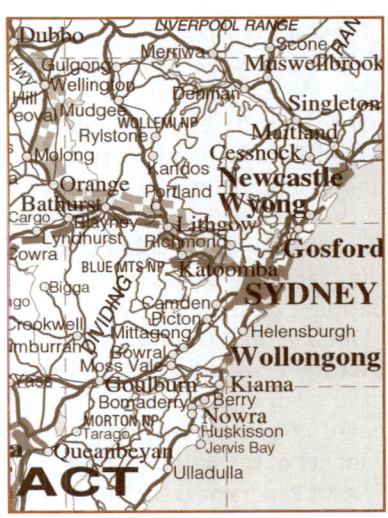

Miss Traill's House, 321 Russell Street, is also a National Trust property and is ☉open Tues-Sat 1pm-3pm and Sun 10am-3pm.

The **Holy Trinity Church** at Kelso was completed in 1835 and is the oldest consecrated Anglican Church in Australia.

St Michael and St John's Catholic Cathedral was completed in 1861. St Stanislaus' College has taken pupils since 1873, and is Australia's oldest Catholic Boarding School.

Ohkuma Japanese Garden is on the corner of Stanley and George Streets. Okhkuma is the sister-city of Bathurst, and this garden was laid out in 1998 as a symbol of the link.

Macquarie River Bicentennial Park is a popular spot for a picnic.

The 35 bells of the Carillon in **Kings Parade** plays every day at noon and 1pm. Also located within the park are three war monuments which commemorate the sacrifice of men from the Bathurst district.

Outside the Visitor Centre is the **Victors' Walk**, where brass plaques have been embedded in checkerboard concrete to commemorate winners of the Bathurst 1000.

At Mt Panorama is the Motor Racing Circuit which is used for the annual Bathurst 1000 motor race. Experience the excitement, disappointment and enjoyment that is motor racing in Bathurst at the **National Motor Racing Museum**, which is on Murray Corner and is ☉open daily 9am-4.30pm. It has a selection of memorabilia associated with the big race, collected over the years, from cars and trophies to souvenirs.

Located on Mt Panorama is the **Sir Joseph Banks Nature Park**, which has koalas, kangaroos and wallabies in a 41ha (101 acres) park, ☉open daily 10am-4pm.

The **Bathurst Sheep and Cattle Drome**, Rossmore Park, Limekilns Road, Kelso, is only an eight minute drive from the centre of town. There visitors can milk a cow or sit back in air-conditioned comfort and enjoy an 80 minute show of sheep shearing and wool classing. If the weather is fine, there will be a sheep dog in action. The newest addition to the Sheep and Cattle Drome is their Golf Practice Driving Range, open daily.

Bathurst Rotalactor is a modern rotary dairy that milks over 300 cows, situated in the picturesque Dunkeld Valley. There is a large, well-appointed, indoor viewing area, a cafe specialising in dairy products, and many educational displays on various aspects of the dairy industry. To get there, take the Blayney Road for 7km, then turn right for Dunkeld.

Festivals

The Bathurst 1000 Motor Race is held during the October long weekend (first Monday in October), with activities organised during the week leading up to the Race.

Facilities

There is an olympic swimming pool and water slide. Bathurst also has all the usual sporting facilities you would expect in a large town, including lawn bowls, golf course, tennis courts and squash courts.

Outlying Attractions

Orange

Situated 55km (34 miles) from Bathurst, Orange is a larger town than Bathurst, and the area produces 10% of Australia's apples, as well as cherries and other stone fruit, on the rich volcanic soil slopes of Mt Canobolas. The upper slopes of the extinct volcano are a flora and fauna reserve with picnic areas and walking trails. There is a lake in the crater, and canoeing, sailing and fishing are popular.

The Ophir gold find gave the early settlement a firm foundation, and it has grown into the largest town in the district. Bowen Terrace is a perfect and rare example of its period. The row of ironwork-decorated houses was built in 1876 by the owner of the first tannery. Endsleigh House, built in 1858, is thought to be the oldest house. The golf club is housed in the 1876 Duntryleague mansion.

A.J. (Banjo) Paterson, perhaps Australia's most popular poet and writer, was born along the Ophir Road in 1864 and an obelisk marks the spot. It is inscribed with a verse from Clancy of the Overflow.

Orange is the headquarters of the Ministry of Agriculture, and has a large agricultural college.

The Orange Visitor Information Centre is on corner of Byng and Peisley Streets, ✆6393 8226, email ✉ tourism@orange.nsw.gov.au. The website is ☞www.orange.nsw .gov.au

Ophir

Gold was first discovered in Australia in 1951 at Ophir, approximately 40km (25 miles) from Orange. Today the area is a reserve, and trails lead to old tunnels, sluices and other relics among the hills. The reserve is, naturally enough, popular with fossickers.

Abercrombie Caves

On the Goulburn Road, 72km (45 miles) from Bathurst, is one of the smaller but most spectacular limestone cave systems in Australia. The reserve has a camping/caravan park with picnic facilities, and cave inspection times and tours vary. For more information phone ✆6368 8603, visit ☞www.jenolancaves. org.au or email ✉abercrombie@ jenolancaves.org.au

Sofala

Set amongst the steep hills of the Turon Valley, Sofala is one of the old gold rush towns. It has a quaint store and some faded old-time buildings.

The Royal Hotel is the only hotel remaining of the forty which were operating during the gold rush era.

Hill End

The Parks and Wildlife Service have declared Hill End an historic site, and they publish an excellent information sheet 'Exploring Hill End Historic Site' which has a map on one side and an excellent walking tour on the other. Only a small community remains today. Miners dug up 701,000 ounces of gold here. Panning and fossicking are still popular, and gold pans may be hired in town. Hill End is 84km (52 miles) from Bathurst.

Mudgee

Situated 69km (43 miles) north of Hill End, Mudgee is the second oldest town west of the Blue Mountains, and was laid out in 1838. A score of handsome buildings, classified by the National Trust, dot the town, the oldest being the Catholic Presbytery, built in 1852. The church, St Mary's, was commenced five years later, and has an exceptional iron screen and stencilled decorations.

The Court House, St John the Baptist's Church, the Police Station and Post Office were all built in the early 1860s. The Colonial Inn Museum, Market Street, is ☉open Sat 2-5pm, Sun, school and public holidays 10am-5pm.

Mudgee is renowned for its honey, and visitors are able to watch honey processing at two factories.

There are also many wineries in the district, and all have cellar door sales. Mudgee is well known for its fine wines, and is gaining fame for its beautiful rose gardens. There is a Days of Wine and Roses Festival each year in September/October.

Mudgee Gulgong Tourism is at 84 Market Street, ✆6372 1020, email ✉tourist@mudgee.nsw. gov.au. It is ☉open 9am-5pm Mon-Fri, 9am-3.30pm Sat and 9.30am-2pm Sun.

Gulgong

Gulgong, 29km (18 miles) from Mudgee was, until the advent of plastic currency, the 'Town on the Ten Dollar Note'.

It has narrow streets which wind between quaint clapboard and iron buildings, complete with verandahs and iron lace. The Pioneers' Museum, in Medley Street, covers .4ha (1 acre) and includes an astonishing array of Australiana. The Henry Lawson Art Gallery is open during school holidays. The Phonograph Parlour, 69 Lee Street, has recorded sound equipment dating back to 1889. Gold is still found around Gulgong and panning is popular.

Dubbo

Population 33,700
Dubbo is situated in mid-western New South Wales on the Macquarie River, at the junction of the Newell and Mitchell Highways. The city is 416km (258 miles) from Sydney; 862km (536 miles) from Brisbane; 818km (508 miles) from Melbourne; and 1207km (750 miles) from Adelaide.

Climate

Average temperatures: January max 32C (90F) - min 18C (64F); July max 15C (59F) - min 3C (37F). Average annual rainfall - 584mm (23 ins); height above sea level - 262m (859 ft); average number of rainy days per year - 74.

Characteristics

Dubbo is known as the Hub of the West. It is a prosperous service centre for the fertile farmlands around it.

How to Get There

By Bus
Pioneer and Greyhound stop at Dubbo on their Melbourne/Brisbane/Gold Coast runs.

By Rail
There a Countrylink service from Sydney to Dubbo.

By Road
From Adelaide, via the Sturt Highway to Mildura, and then the Mid Western or the Barrier and Mitchell Highways.

From Brisbane, via the Cunningham Highway to Goondiwindi, and then the Newell Highway.

From Melbourne, via the Hume Highway to Seymour, the Goulburn Valley Highway to Tocumwal, and then the Newell Highway. From Sydney, via the Great Western Highway to Bathurst, and then the Mitchell Highway.

Tourist Information

The Dubbo Visitors Information Centre is on the corner of Macquarie and Erskine Streets, ✆6884 1422, email ✉ tourism@dubbo. nsw.gov.au. It is ⏱open daily 9am-5pm, but closed Christmas Day.

Accommodation

Here is a selection with prices for a double room per night, which should be used as a guide only. The telephone area code is 02.

Ashwood Country Club Motel, Whylandra Street, ✆6881 8700. 39 units, licensed restaurant, swimming pool, spa, tennis, barbecue - ✪$90-130.

Cascades Motor Inn, 147 Cobra Street, ✆6882 3888. 36 units, licensed restaurant, swimming pool, barbecue - ✪$85-95.

Australian Heristage Motor Inn, cnr Cobra and Brisbane Streets, ✆6884 1188. 22 units, licensed restaurant, bistro, swimming pool - ✪$105-145.

Blue Gum Motor Inn, 109 Cobra Street, ✆6882 0900. 24 units, swimming pool, barbecue - ✪$75-85.

Country Comfort Dubbo, Newell Highway, ✆6882 4777. 60 units, licensed restaurant, swimming pool, spa, tennis, bbq - ✪$90-150.

All Seasons Motor Lodge, 78 Whylandra Street, ✆6882 6377. 19 units, licensed restaurant, swimming pool, spa, sauna - ✪$70-75.

Forest Lodge Motor Inn, Myall Street, ✆6882 6500. 15 units, licensed restaurant (closed Sun & Mon), swimming pool, bbq - ✪$75-90.

Matilda Motor Inn, 231 Darling Street, ✆6882 3944. 38 units, licensed restaurant, swimming pool - ✪$60-80.

Castlereagh Hotel, cnr Brisbane & Talbragar Streets, ✆6882 4877. 13 rooms (some with private facilities), licensed restaurant (Mon-Thurs) - B&B ✪$55-70.

Caravan Parks

Dubbo City Caravan Park, Whylandra Street, West Dubbo, ✆6882 4820. (Pets allowed) 128 sites, good facilities, pool - powered sites ✪$18 for two, on-site vans $28 for two.

Poplars Caravan Park, Lower Bultje Street, ✆6882 4067. (Pets allowed) 69 sites - powered sites ✪$12 for two, on-site vans $26 for two.

Windmill Caravan Park, cnr Mitchell Highway & Sheraton Road, ©6882 4583. (Pets allowed on application) 78 sites, pool, barbecue, playground - powered sites ✪$14 for two, on-site vans $25 for two.

Midstate Motor Park, 21 Bourke Street, ©6882 1155. 53 sites, barbecue, golf, pool - ✪$16 for two, on-site vans $35 for two.

Eating Out

As mentioned in the Accommodation section, several of the motels and hotels have restaurants. Here are some others you might like try.

The Dubbo RSL Club, Wingewarra Street, ©6882 4411, welcomes visitors.

Jules Crepes Restaurant, 195 Macquarie Street, ©6882 9300, is fully licensed, and serves a wide variety of crepes in an old world atmosphere. It is open Mon-Sat noon-2.30pm, 6.30pm onwards.

Hing Wah, 143 Talbragar St, ©6882 4401.

Darbar Indian Restaurant, 215 Macquarie St, ©6884 4338.

Rose Garden Thai Restaurant, 208 Brisbane St, ©6882 8322.

Blue Lagoon, 81 Cobra St, ©6882 4444.

Golden Dragon Restaurant, 36 Victoria St, ©6882 6663.

Settlers Restaurant, Newell Hwy, West Dubbo, ©6882 4777.

Safari Lounge Restaurant, 78 Whylandra St, ©6882 1600.

McDonalds is at 22-24 Cobra Street.

Points of Interest

The city is best seen by following the signposted **Tourist Drive**, which starts at the Civic Centre, Darling Street.

Heritage Walk commences at the Museum and takes in many historic buildings around the city.

The **Old Dubbo Gaol**, ©6882 8122, in Macquarie Street between the State and Commonwealth Banks, is ⊙open daily 9am-5pm, and has many items of interest including animated robots, and the original gallows.

The **Museum**, 234 Macquarie Street, includes a village square with 14 shop exhibitions. It is ⊙open daily 9am-5pm.

Dubbo Regional Art Gallery in Darling Street, ©6881 4342, has changing exhibitions every four to six weeks, and you can book in advance for tours by trained guides. The Gallery is ⊙open Mon, Wed, Thurs, Fri 11am-4.30pm, Sat-Sun 10am-noon, 1-4pm.

Western Plains Zoo, Obley Road (6km south of the city), ©6882 5888, is Dubbo's main tourist attraction, and entry is ⊙daily 9am-4pm, but visitors are welcome to remain until 5pm. The Zoo, opened in 1977, is a sister zoo to Sydney's Taronga Park. It is administered by the Zoological Parks Board of New South Wales, and is Australia's only official open range zoo. Its 300ha (741 acres) of open bushland and landscaped exhibits are home to more than 2000 animals. Visitors can drive their own cars around the 6km sealed road in the Zoo, or hire a bike or mini moke, or fitness fanatics can walk. There are several picnic areas en route, as well as free gas barbecue facilities, or you can lunch at the licensed bistro, open noon-2pm, or grab a bite to eat from the fast food outlet.

The **Dubbo Military Museum**, Newell Highway, ℗6884 5550, has a whole range of WW2 military equipment in an open air setting. The museum is ℗open daily 10am-4.30pm.

Yarrabar Pottery and Gallery, Peakhill Road, ℗6884 2455, has a potter in action, and can make functional and decorative pottery to your requirements. The Gallery is ℗open daily 9am-5pm.

Facilities

Golf, lawn bowls, tennis, fishing, sauna, cinema, swimming pool, ice skating rink, ten pin bowling, slot car racing and horse racing. Paddle boats, canoeing and water skiing on the Macquarie River.

On the second Sunday of the month, Markets are held in the Showground, 10am-1pm, and hundreds of stall holders sell everything from plants and toys to furniture.

Festivals

The Orana Country Music Festival is usually held during the Easter period. The Dubbo Agricultural Show is held in May.

There are events held every month in Dubbo, and the Visitor Information Centre has all the details.

Outlying Attractions

Peak Hill

Located 71km (44 miles) southwest of Dubbo, on Roose Road, Peak Hill, is the site of an open cut gold mine, ℗6869 1733. It consists of two holes of enormous depth. When you view the mine from the lookouts, it is hard to realise that these holes were originally gouged out by hand. The walls of the holes reflect an array of colours due to the presence of iron, calcium, magnesium and other trace elements. To get to the lookouts, turn right at the Ex-Services Club and follow the signs.

Peak Hill Tourist Information is at 105 Caswell St, ℗6869 1981.

Parkes

Parkes is 121km (75 miles) south-west of Dubbo, and is the major centre of the Lachlan Valley, servicing the towns of Peak Hill, Alectown, Bogan Gate, Trundle and Tullamore.

Parkes has a town population of 10,100, and Parkes Visitor Information Centre is on the Newell Highway, ✆6862 4365 or email ✉ tourism@parkes.nsw.gov.au They are ◷open 9am-5pm Mon-Fri, 10am-4pm Sat-Sun.

The main attraction in the area is the Radio Telescope, and to get there travel north on the Newell Highway for 20km (12 miles), turn off the highway and follow Telescope Road for 6km (4 miles), then follow the signs. The Visitors Centre is ◷open daily 8.30am-4.15pm, ✆6861 1776, and you shouldn't miss the audio-visual show entitled "The Invisible Universe", which is screened daily from 8.30am, with the last show at 3.30pm. There is a moderate admission fee.

For those who love statistics: The radiotelescope is neither a tracking station for Earth-orbiting satellites, nor a communications station. It's for astronomy. It was built in a very quiet radio interference zone, near a large service town, close to Divisional headquarters in Sydney, and in a location with a low recorded average wind speed. The telescope was opened on October 31, 1961. The dish and drive mechanism weigh about 1,000 tonnes. The dish is 64m (210 ft) in diameter and 0.4ha (1 acre) in area. There are about 20 full-time staff, not all astronomers. Only 4 live on site, the rest live in and around Parkes. When the dish is pointing vertical to the zenith, the astronomers are not observing. The telescope is normally operational 24 hours a day, seven days a week.

Other attractions in Parkes include: Henry Parkes Historical Museum, 316 Clarinda Street, ✆622 815; Motor Museum - Craft Corner, cnr Bogan & Dalton Streets; BHP Gold Mine, 6km south-west of Parkes; Pioneer Park, a collection of agricultural machinery and road transport; Bushman's Hill Development, the restoration of the Bushman's gold mine adjacent to the Visitor Centre; and Mugincoble, a Wheat Terminal with inspections arranged by the Tourist Centre.

Forbes

35km (22 miles) south-west of Parkes on the Newell Highway, is Forbes, which has many well attended parks and gardens and historic buildings. Forbes Railway Arts and Tourist Centre, Union St, can be contacted on ✆6852 4155.

Forbes is Ben Hall country. The famous bushranger was part of the notorious Gardiner Gang who carried out a gold escort robbery at nearby Eugowra. He met his death in a hail of bullets at the age of 28 and is buried in the Forbes Cemetery. The Forbes Museum, in an old Music Hall which once formed part of the Osborn Hotel, houses an interesting collection of relics of the bushrangers, and outside of Forbes a plaque marks the spot where Ben Hall was killed.

Other interesting graves in the old cemetery are those of Kate Foster, sister of Ned Kelly, and Rebecca Shield, grand-niece of Captain Cook.

The Lachlan Vintage Village, ©6852 2655, is one kilometre from Forbes on the Newell Highway, and visitors can relive the past of an old gold town with exhibits dating from 1860 to 1900. Many of the early buildings and commercial businesses of the area have been reconstructed in a central part of the 81ha (200 acres) village to provide the visitor with a view of a country town from yesteryear. The complex also contains: the Lachlan Diggings, built on the site of the Forbes goldfield, where you can try your luck panning for gold in the creek; the Farming Museum, an 1860s farm complete with equipment, animals and the historic 'Nelungaloo' homestead with original furniture; Ben Hall's cottage; the home of the famous Australian poet, Henry Lawson; and the Trigalana Woolshed, the entry building which houses the Blackridge Restaurant and a souvenir shop.

Forbes also has three wineries, two of which have their own distilleries. For inspections and cellar door sales enquire at the Tourist Centre.

Wellington

Situated on the Mitchell Highway, 50km (31 miles) south-east of Dubbo, Wellington is famous for the Wellington Caves, 8km (5 miles) south of the town. There are tours of the caves every hour 9am-4pm, except 1pm, ©6845 1733, and accommodation is available in nearby *Caves Caravan Park*, ©6845 2970.

The Wellington Tourist Information Centre is at Cameron Park, ©6845 1733, and they have information on attractions in the town, which include a clock museum, a winery, and arts and crafts galleries. You can email them at ✓ wellvic@australis.aunz.com and they are ☺open 9am-5pm daily except Christmas Day.

The Burrendong Dam is 32km (20 miles) upstream from Wellington, and there you can waterski, sail, swim, fish, or relax in the sun. Burrendong's arboretum covers an area of nearly 160ha (395 acres),

set aside for the cultivation and preservation of plant life native to Australia. Mookerawa, another section of the Burrendong State Recreation Park, and Burrendong offer great facilities for visitors who love to camp.

Gilgandra

The town of Gilgandra is on the Newell Highway, 66km (41 miles) north of Dubbo, on the western side of the Warrumbungles. It was known originally as the town of windmills, and is home to one of the country's best privately owned observatories. The Gilgandra Visitor Information Centre is on the Newell Highway, ©6847 2045 email ✈ gilinfo@tpg.com.au It is

☺open 9am-5pm daily, closed Christmas Day. Drop in here for information on the attractions in the town, and available accommodation.

Coonabarabran

Situated 95km (59 miles) northeast of Gilgandra, Coonabarabran has a population of around 4000. The town name means 'Inquisitive Person' and the Visitors Centre is on the Newell Highway at the southern end of town, ©6842 144, email ✈ coonavic@lisp.com.au, ☺open daily 9am-5pm. They have enough information to satisfy any inquisitive person on accommodation and attractions, which include Miniland and Museum, and Crystal Kingdom.

New South Wales – West

Broken Hill

Population 24,466

Broken Hill lies in the Barrier Ranges in outback New South Wales, near the South Australian border. It is a long way from anywhere - 1170km (727 miles) from Sydney; 882km (548 miles) from Melbourne; 510km (317 miles) from Adelaide.

Climate

The city is 304m (997 ft) above sea level, and has an average rainfall of 235mm (9.25 ins) which is spread fairly evenly throughout the year with the greatest fall usually in June. As a rule the temperature only climbs above 38C (100F) eight or nine time a year. Maximum summer temperatures are generally in the low 30s (around 85F), but this causes little discomfort due to the low humidity. The nights are cold throughout the year. The winter months of May, June and July can be quite cold during the day as well.

Characteristics

Broken Hill is first and foremost a mining town, and in earlier days the dust problem appeared insurmountable, but due to a regeneration scheme started in 1930s, this problem has been largely overcome, at least as far as local storms are concerned. It has one of the richest silver and lead deposits in the world. Recently its popularity in the tourist market has grown.

Tourist Information

The Broken Hill Visitor Information Centre is on the corner of Blende and Bromide Streets, ✆(08) 8087 6077, email ✉ tourist@pcpro.net .au. It is ⏱open 8.30am - 5pm daily.

How to Get There

Pioneer have a Sydney/Adelaide service via Broken Hill.
Greyhound have a service from/to Melbourne.
Stateliner have a service from Adelaide.

By Rail
The Indian Pacific (Sydney/Perth) and The Alice (Sydney/Alice Springs) stop at Broken Hill.

By Car
From Sydney, via the Great Western Highway to Orange, the Mitchell Highway to Nyngan, then the Barrier Highway.
From Melbourne, via the Calder Highway to Mildura, then the Silver City Highway.
From Adelaide, via National Route 32.

Accommodation

Here is a selection of accommodation with prices for a double room per night, which should be used as a guide only. The telephone area code is 08.

Broken Hill Overlander Motor Inn, 142 Iodide Street, ©8087 7013. 12 units, heated swimming pool, spa, sauna, barbecue - ✪$85-105.

Daydream Motel, 77 Argent Street, ©8088 3033. 12 units, swimming pool, barbecue - ✪$65.

Charles Rasp Motor Inn, 158 Oxide Street, ©8088 1988. 20 units, swimming pool, spa, barbecue - ✪$95-110.

Miners Lamp Motor Inn, 357 Cobalt Street, ©8088 4122. 32 units, licensed restaurant, swimming pool, barbecue - ✪$90-100.

Silver Spade Hotel/Motel, 151 Argent Street, ©8087 7021. 14 units, licensed restaurant, swimming pool, barbecue - ✪$60-65.

Sturt Motel, 153 Rakow Street, ©8087 3558. 19 units, swimming pool - ✪$55-60.

Caravan Parks

Broken Hill City Caravan Park, Rakow Street, ©8087 3841. (Pets allowed in a restricted area) 173 sites, barbecue, heated pool - powered sites ✪$18 for two, on-site vans $32 for two.

Lake View Broken Hill Caravan Park, 1 Mann Street, ©8088 2250. (Pets allowed under strict control) 137 sites, pool - powered sites ✪$20 for two, on-site vans $30 for two.

Eating Out

Broken Hill has plenty of restaurants, cafes, clubs and hotels serving meals. Here are some you might like to try.

Pagoda Chinese Restaurant, 357 Cobalt Street, ©8087 3679.

Oceania Chinese Restaurant, 423 Argent Street, ©8087 3695.

Silver City Workingmen's Club, 402 Argent Street, ©8087 5337.

The Haven Restaurant, 577 Argent St, ©8088 2888.

Betina's, 271 Kaolin St, ©8088 2999.

Points of Interest

Broken Hill has two **Tourist Drives** - the Silver Arrow tour 1 and 2, and maps are available from the Tourist Centre.

Walking Tours depart from the Information Centre Mon-Fri and Sun at 10am, and are of approximately one and half hour's duration.

The **Sundown Nature Trail**, situated in the rocky Sundown Hills on the northern edge of the city Common, winds through the countryside for 2.8km (2 miles) and affords an opportunity to examine the sparse vegetation up close. It takes about one and a half hours, and is at its best just before sunset or just after sunrise.

Interesting and informative inspections of the surface workings of **North Mine** are conducted every afternoon Mon-Fri, and the Information Centre has details. NB solid footwear must be worn.

Underground tours are available Mon-Fri 10.30am and Sat 2pm, ©8088 1604, but children under 8 are not admitted. The Daydream Mine, ©8088 5682, near Silverton, 45 minutes away, also has underground tours with no age limit.

For tours of the **Royal Flying Doctor Base**, enquire on ©8080 1777. The School of the Air is open weekdays, and bookings for this are handled by the Information Centre.

At the **Whites Mineral Art and Mining Museum**, 1 Allendale

Street ©8087 2878, you can see life size replicas of current and old-time mining procedures.

The **Railway Mineral and Train Museum**, Blende Street, ©8088 4660, has a large display of old railway machinery.

Broken Hill has more than twenty-one Art Galleries open for public viewing. Here are a few names and addresses:

The Broken Hill City Art Gallery, cnr Chloride and Blende Streets, ©8088 5491, ⊕open Mon-Sat 9am-4pm, with guided tours Tues-Sat at 11.30am.

Pro Hart Gallery, ©8087 2441, 108 Wyman Street, ⊕open Mon-Sat 9.30am-5pm.

Hoppy Hopgood Gallery, 589 Fisher Street, ⊕open daily from 9am.

Facilities

Car Hire: Avis, ©8087 7532; Budget, ©8087 9151; and Hertz, ©8087 2719.
Taxi services: Yellow Radio Cabs, ©13 1008.
There are two laundromats, 3 Council run libraries, 3 swimming pools (one heated), golf, horse riding, lawn bowls, indoor cricket, squash and tennis.

The Royal Automobile Association of South Australia has an office at 261 Argent Street, ©8088 4999.

Outlying Attractions

Menindee

Situated 110km (68 miles) southeast of Broken Hill, there is a series of natural lakes stretching 50km (31 miles) north and 35km (22 miles) south of the town of Menindee, and areas have been developed for caravan parks, weekend cottages, speedboats, water skiing, sailing, safe swimming and good fishing.

The Kinchega National Park, on the western bank of the Darling River adjacent to Menindee, is a significant example of one of the major landscape categories of the arid and semi-arid regions of New South Wales.

The Menindee Regional Tourist Association is in the Railway Station, Maiden St, ©8091 4274.

Silverton

On a sealed road 25km (16 miles) north-west of Broken Hill, is Silverton, once a thriving community of over 3000, but now a ghost town where many films have been shot, eg A Town Like Alice, Mad Max II and Razorback, and several commercials and documentaries.

The Sturt National Park begins just north of Tibooburra, which is 337km (209 miles) north of Broken Hill, and reaches to the spot where the New South Wales, Queensland and

The main attraction, however, is the Anglo-Australian Observatory, in Siding Spring, whose visitor's gallery allows visitors to view some of the workings of this immense piece of equipment. On the site there is also a fascinating permanent exhibition, 'Exploring the Universe', which should not be missed. The Observatory is 28km (17 miles) west of the town, and is ☉open daily 9am-4pm, ©6842 6291.

35km (22 miles) from town is the Warrumbungle National Park, covering 21,004ha (51,880 acres) and containing magnificent scenery and prolific fauna and flora. The Park has spires and domes that are remnants of violent volcanic activity some 13 million years ago, and they are a spectacular sight. Food is not available in the park, and pets are prohibited. For further information ©1300 361 967 or visit ☞www.npws.nsw.gov.au

Between the Warrumbungle Mountains and the Namoi River is the Pilliga Forest and Nature Reserve, a vast flat area covering approximately 5400 sq km (2084 sq miles) of natural wild forest and scrublands known as the Pilliga Scrub.

The town of Baradine is the heart of the Pilliga, and there you can visit the Baradine Forest Centre, Lachlan Street, ©6843 1607, and find out details of the many forest drives, and the location of the numerous sandstone caves.

South Australian borders meet. At the three-state corner the dingo fence can be seen. It is part of the 'longest fence in the world'.

White Cliffs

The well-known opal field and township of White Cliffs is 295km (183 miles) north-east of Broken Hill. There you can try your luck at fossicking, see the superb opalised Plesiosaur skeleton, and the dug-outs where many of the residents live. Facilities include a hotel, motel, general store and cafe. Fossicker's Licences are available from the Tourist Information Centre in Karara Road, ©8091 6611.

New South Wales – North-West

Tamworth

Population 34,500
Tamworth is situated at the junction of the New England and Oxley Highways, on the banks of the Peel River. It is 411km (255 miles) from Sydney; 1152km (715 miles) from Melbourne; 1,446km (898 miles) from Adelaide; 589km (366 miles) from Brisbane.

Climate

Average temperatures: January max 30C (88F) - min 17C (63F); July max 16C (61F) - min 4C (39F). The town is 389 metres (1276 ft) above sea level and has an average rainfall of 650mm (25in). Occasional snow falls in winter on the hilltops around Nundle (60km [37miles]) to the south.

Characteristics

As well as being famous as the Australasian Country Music Capital, Tamworth was also the first city in the country to install electric street lighting. The city is in the heart of the biggest gemstone fossicking region of NSW, and is surrounded by picturesque countryside.

How to Get There

By Rail
An air conditioned Countrylink service operates daily to Tamworth. The Countrylink connects in Tamworth with a fleet of luxury coaches which travel over a large area of north-west NSW.

By Bus

Tamworth is on the main Brisbane/ Sydney, Brisbane/Melbourne and Brisbane/Adelaide routes which are covered daily by Greyhound Pioneer and McCafferty's.

By Road

Tamworth is approximately 5.5 hours drive from Sydney and 6.5 hours from Brisbane along National Highway 15 - the New England Highway. The city also has highway links to the Gold Coast, Melbourne, Port Macquarie and Adelaide.

Tourist Information

The Tamworth Visitor Information Centre is on the corner of Peel and Murray Streets, ✆02 6755 4300 or email ✎ tourism@tamworth.nsw. gov.au Their opening hours are ⏰8.30am-4.30pm Mon-Fri, 9am-5pm weekends.

Accommodation

Make sure you ask for a room away from the highway as trucks travelling at night can destroy your sleep. Here is a selection with prices for a double room per night, which should be used as a guide only. The telephone area code is 02.

Powerhouse Boutique Hotel, New England Highway, ✆6766 7000. 81 units, 2 licensed restaurants, swimming pool, sauna, spa, gym - ✪$115-125.

Tamwell Motel, 121 Johnston Street, ✆6766 2800. 16 units, unlicensed restaurant (closed weekends), secure parking - ✪$95-100.

Abraham Lincoln, 343 Armidale Road, ✆6766 1233. 15 units, swimming pool, barbecue - ✪$75-80.

Alandale Flag Inn, New England Highway, ✆6765 7922. 25 units, licensed restaurant, swimming pool, spa, half-court tennis - ✪$85-100.

Roydon's Motel, cnr New England Highway & Church Street, ✆6765 7355. 12 units, basic facilities - ✪$55-60.

Southgate Inn, cnr. Kathleen & Kent Streets, ✆6765 7999. 6 rooms (private facilities), unlicensed restaurant - ✪$60-65.

Tamworth Hotel, Marius Street, ✆6766 2923. 11 rooms, licensed restaurant - ✪$40.

Caravan Parks

City Lights Caravan Park, New England Highway, ✆6765 7664. (Pets allowed on application) 102 sites, pool, playground, barbecue - powered sites ✪$16-25 for two, on-site vans $30-45 for two.

Austin Caravan Park, 581 Armidale Road, ✆6766 2380. (Pets allowed on application) 104 sites, barbecue, pool, good facilities - powered sites ✪$19 for two, cabins $35-75 for two.

Eating Out

There are licensed clubs which provide lunch and dinner, and have activities and live entertainment for guests. Visitors are always welcome. There are a number of fully licensed restaurants mainly associated with the major hotels, and many fast food outlets such as McDonald's and the local cafes.

Valentino's Italian Restaurant, 2 Byrnes Ave, ✆6766 4246.

Empress Chinese Restaurant, 455a Peel St, ✆6766 1616.

Bangkok Thai Restaurant, Northgate Shopping Centre Shop, 18 Peel St, ✆6761 3098.

Deepka Indian Restaurant, 23 Brisbane St, ✆6766 1771.

83 Restaurant, 199 Marius St, ✆6766 2383.

Points of Interest

The Department of Lands has created a **Heritage Walk** and a **Nature Walk** in Tamworth. Maps of both walks are available from the Visitor Information Centre in Kable Avenue.

The **Powerstation Museum** in Peel Street celebrates Tamworth's centenary as Australia's first city with electric street lighting, and features working steam-powered electricity-generating equipment.

Calala Cottage in Denison Street was constructed in 1875 as the home of Tamworth's first Mayor, and today forms part of the local Historical Society complex.

Munro's Mill in Peel Street opened in 1863. Built from handmade bricks and hand-forged nails, it was the first commercial flour mill in New England. Today, it is an antique shop.

The **Country Collection**, ✆6765 2688, on the New England Highway offers an interesting combination of attractions including the Rock, Gem and Mineral Collection, a wax museum filled with legends of country music, and Britten's Boutique Brewery which produces a series of Tamworth ales.

Endeavour Drive, at the top of Brisbane Street, takes you to Oxley Park, a peaceful sanctuary for kangaroos and other native wildlife, with full amenities, picnic and barbecue facilities.

Bicentennial Park, in Kable Avenue, is a peaceful 'people's place' of parkland, pathways, fountains, pergolas, restaurant and a central pool. The pool is ringed by granite etched with depictions of the district's history and wildlife.

Tamworth City Gallery, ✆6755 4459, in Marius Street has a silver collection on permanent display. It also houses travelling exhibitions and is the site for the National Fibre Exhibition.

Festivals

The Australasian Country Music Festival is held over ten days each January. The festival normally has over 600 concerts and events.

The Tamworth Arts in Action Festival is held biennially in October. It includes concerts, displays of homecrafts, opera and live theatre.

Facilities

Excellent sporting facilities are available in Tamworth for just about every type of sport from ten-pin bowling to clay target shooting. At Lake Keepit you can water ski, canoe, fish, sail and bushwalk. There are also facilities for gliding (Keepit Soaring Club). The hilltop countryside around Tamworth is best appreciated on horseback. Four Wheel Drive enthusiasts will find the back roads around Manilla, Hall's Creek and Bendemeer challenging.

Outlying Attractions

Manilla

On the Namoi River, it is known for Dutton's Meadery in Barraba Street, where you can taste their honey-based alcoholic drink, which is reputedly mans' oldest liquor.

Kootingal

Pyramid Planetarium on the New England Highway features a working model of the solar system.

Moonbi

Braecroft Cottage Gallery, Braefarm Road is the home of the ceramic artist Fred Hillier and his range of ceramic figurines and Australian bush buildings.

Nundle

If you want to try your luck fossicking then try around this historic village especially in the 'Hills of Gold' area, after visiting Hanging Rock, and asking one of the locals for advice. The Nundle historical Museum is in Jenkins Street, ©6769 3292.

New South Wales – North-West

Armidale

Population 22,000

Armidale is situated in the New England Tablelands, part of the Great Dividing Range which stretches from around Newcastle to the Queensland Border. The city is surrounded by National Parks - Oxley Wild Rivers National Park, New England National Park, Cathedral Rock National Park and Beautiful Gorge Country. Distance from Sydney 563km (35 miles), Melbourne 1268km (788 miles), Brisbane 464km (288 miles), Adelaide 1636km (1017 miles).

Climate

Average temperatures: January max 26C (79F) - min 14C (57F); June max 14C (57F) - min 2C (36F). Average annual rainfall is 795mm (31 ins). Situated 1000m (3281 ft) above sea level. Armidale has definite seasons, and occasional snowfalls in winter.

Characteristics

The principal town of the area, it is an education centre with over 8 high schools and other institutions, and it is the site of New England University. The surrounding district produces fine merino wool, wheat and fruit.

How to Get There

By Bus

Border Coaches, Bus Australia, Trans City and McCaffertys have services to Armidale from Sydney and Brisbane.

By Rail

There is a daily Countrylink service from Sydney to Tamworth, with a connecting coach to Armidale.

By Road

From Sydney, via the New England Highway from Newcastle.

From Melbourne, via the Princes or Hume Highways to Sydney; or via the Newell Highway to Tamworth and then the New England Highway.

From Brisbane, via the Pacific Highway and then either Route 78 from Coffs Harbour; the Gwydir Highway from Grafton; the Oxley Highway from Port Macquarie; or the Bruxner Highway from Ballina via the New England Highway through Tenterfield.

Tourist Information

Armidale Visitor Information Centre is at 82 Marsh Street, ✆(02) 6772 4655 or email ✉ armvisit@ northnet.com.au ☺Opening hours are 9am-5pm Mon to Fri, 9am-4pm Sat, 10am-4pm Sun. It is closed on public holidays.

Accommodation

Here is a selection with prices for a double room per night, which should be used as a guide only. The telephone area code is (02).

Armidale Recency Hallmark Inn, 208 Dangar Street, ✆6772 9800. 40 units, licensed restaurant, swimming pool, spa, sauna - ✪$110-120.

Deer Park Motor Inn, 72-74 Glen Innes Road, ✆6772 9999. 24 units, licensed restaurant (closed Sun), swimming pool, spa, sauna- ✪$100-130.

Alluna Motel, 180 Dangar Street, ✆6772 6226. 20 units, licensed restaurant, swimming pool - ✪$65-75.

Acacia Motor Inn, 192 Miller Street, ✆6772 7733. 15 units, spa, barbecue, undercover parking - ✪$60-75.

Armidale Rose Villa Motel, New England Highway, ✆6772 3872. 10 units, undercover parking, barbecue - ✪$50-75.

Armidale Acres Motel, New England Highway, ✆6771 1281. 11 units (some with private facilities), pool, tennis, barbecue - ✪$55-60.

Caravan Parks

Pembroke Tourist and Leisure Park, 39 Waterfall Way, ✆6772 6470. (Pets allowed on leash) pool, barbecue, tennis, excellent facilities - powered sites ✪$20-25 for two, on-site vans $30-40 for two.

Highlander Van Village, 76 Glen Innes Road, ✆6772 4768. (Dogs allowed on leash) pool, barbecue, playground - powered sites ✪$16-

18 for two, on-site vans $35 for two.

Eating Out

As usual there are many places to eat in the main street, and the licensed clubs welcome visitors.

Armidale Cattleman's Motor Inn, 31 Marsh Street, ©6772 7788, has an a la carte menu, and you can select your wine from the public wine racks.

Moore Park Motor Inn, New England Highway, ©6772 2358, also has a licensed restaurant and cocktail bar which is open seven days.

Ming Court Restaurant, 11 Beardy St, ©6772 9363.

Squires Cottage Restaurant, 86 Barney St, ©6772 8511

Minio's Restaurant, 201a Brown St (Cnr Markham St), ©6771 4555.

Lizabeth's, 208 Dangar St, ©6772 9800.

Mandarin Restaurant, 213 Beardy St, ©6772 6535. .

Points of Interest

Central Park is attractive in all seasons, and contains a tourist directory, rotunda, a memorial fountain and picnic facilities.

There is a signposted **Tourist Drive** which takes in the main attractions.

University of New England, off Queen Elizabeth Drive, 5km north of town, west of centre, ©6773 3333, has 5 faculties and is ⊕open for inspection daily 9am-5pm. Booloominbah, an historic house, is the Administrative Centre. It also has a deer and kangaroo park.

The **Folk Museum**, cnr Rusden & Faulkner Streets, ©6770 3536, is classified by the National Trust and has displays of early transport, lighting, handicrafts, and more, ⊕open daily 1-4pm.

The **New England Regional Art Museum**, Kentucky Street, ©6772 5255, houses the famous Hinton, Armidale City and Coventry Collections, ⊕open Mon-Sat 10am-5pm, Sun 1-5pm. Other museums include the CB Newling Campus Educational Museum in Kentucky Street, the Museum of Printery, also in Kentucky Street, and the Museum of Antiquities in Queen Elizabeath & Madgwick Drive.

The **The Berry Best Cafe & Bakehouse** on the New England Highway towards the airport, is the largest hydroponic berry farm in Australia, ©6772 5974. They specialise in pies and strudels, and are ⊕open daily 8.30am-6pm.

From **Apex Lookout** you can obtain a view of the whole city.

St Mary's Roman Catholic Cathedral, Dangar Street near Central Park, is built in Gothic Revival style and has a fine spire, marble

sanctuary and Flemish bondwork, ☺open 7am-6pm daily. Nearby is **St Peter's Anglican Cathedral** (cnr Dangar & Rusden Streets), which has an Ecclesiastical Museum with exhibits relating not only to the church itself, but also to Armidale in general.

Festivals

Woolexpo is held annual in March, and the Arts Festival, lasting about a week, is held biennially in October.

Facilities

Lawn bowls, trout fishing, golf, squash, swimming pool and tennis.

Outlying Attractions

Dangar's Falls

The Falls and Lagoon, 22km (14 miles) south of Armidale, feature a large rock pool and many species of birds. Dumaresq Dam, 8km from town, has a boat ramp (only non-powered boats permitted) and swimming.

Ebor Falls

These are 74km (46 miles) to the east, and it is a delightful picnic spot. The falls are divided into two with a total drop of 115m (377 ft).

Hillgrove

An old ghost town about 27km (17 miles) east of Armidale, Hillgrove has been carefully restored to serve as an uncanny reminder of its vibrant and colourful past.

Wollomombi Falls

The highest falls in Australia, Wollomombi Falls have a drop of 460m (1509 ft).

For rockhounds and gem

fossickers: The area has numerous little pockets which contain sapphires, zircons, topaz, diamonds, gold, silver, tin, jelly beans, quartz, smokey quartz, grass stone, agate, rhodorite, tourmaline, petrified wood, and almost anything else you can think of. Inverell, to the north-west, is one of the more popular fossicking towns.

New South Wales – North-West

Lightning Ridge

Population 6,000 (est.)
Lightning Ridge is situated 770km (478 miles) north-west of Sydney and about 60km (37 miles) from the Queensland border.

Climate

The area has long hot summers and short cold winters, with summer temperatures dropping as much as 20C (68F) degrees at night.

Characteristics

An old fashioned, carefree, 'tomorrow will do if it can't be done today' atmosphere, which is treasured and preserved by local residents as a valuable way of life. The only place in the world where a wet pudding can be seen (the operation which is used to separate opal nobbies from the clay in which they are found). This area is world famous for its black and blue opals and that is why it has merited inclusion in this guide. It attracts many tourists.

How to Get There

By Rail & Coach
Trains and buses run from Sydney via Dubbo every day.

By Car
From Sydney travel along the Mitchell Highway to Gilgandra, and then north along the Castlereagh Highway. The road is bitumen sealed right into the town itself.

Tourist Information

The Lightning Ridge Tourist Information Centre is in Fred Reece Way ✆6829 0565. At 51 Morilla Street you will find the Opal Cave Tourist Centre, ✆6829 0333.

Accommodation

The standard of accommodation is comfortable. Prices included here are for a double room per night, which should be used as a guide only. The telephone area code is 02.
Black Opal Motel, Opal Street, ✆6829 0518. 11 units, basic facilities - ✪$70.
Lightning Ridge Motor Village, Onyx Street, ✆6829 0304. 41 units, licensed restaurant, barbecue - ✪$70.
Wallangulla Motel, cnr Morilla & Agate Streets, ✆6829 0542. 42 units, basic facilities - ✪$55-85.

Caravan Parks
Crocodile Caravan & Camping Park, Morilla St, ✆6829 0437. (Pets allowed on a leash) 30 sites, barbecue, pool - powered sites ✪$14 for two, cabins $45-55 for two.
Lightning Ridge Caravan Park, Harlequin Street, ✆6829 0532. (Pets allowed on leash) 84 sites, barbecue, basic facilities - powered sites ✪$14 for two, on-site vans $35 for two.
Lightning Ridge Motel Hotel, Onyx Street, ✆6829 0304. (Pets allowed on a leash) 47 sites, licensed res-

taurant, barbecue, pool - powered sites ✪$11 for two, cabins $40-50.

Eating Out

Take-aways or eat-in:
Miners Mate, Lot 4 Opal St, ✆6829 2725 - Chinese & Thai, open 7 days, licensed.
Nobby's Restaurant, Onyx St, ✆6829 0611.
Wong's Restaurant, 14 Opal St, ✆6829 2330.
Diggers Rest Bistro & Takeaway, Opal St, ✆6829 2410.

Points of Interest

Visitors can explore the mining fields and fossick for opal. At the **Big Opal Bazaar**, 3 Mile Road, you can see opals being cut, and at **Spectrum Mines**, Bald Hill Road, ✆6829 0581, there is a daily film show and an underground display.

At the **Bush Museum**, Hatters Flat, ✆6829 0016, there is memorabilia from the early mining days. At the **Drive-in Mine**, 13 Gem Street, old and new techniques used in mining for opals are displayed and the **Walk-in Mine**, 1 Bald Hill Field, has underground tours.

Other attractions include **Kangaroo Hill Wildlife Park**, ✆6829 0155, the **Bottle House Mining Museum**, ✆6829 0618, the **Bird** of **Paradise Art Gallery**, ✆6829 0538, and the **Lightning Ridge Bore Baths** in Pandora Street, ✆6829 0429.

Festivals

The Great Goat Race is held during Easter and the Opal Festival during the NSW September school holidays.

Facilities

The town has artesian baths, a children's park with a BMX track, a drive-in theatre, horse riding facilities, tennis courts, bowling club, golf course and a pistol club.

Outlying Attractions

Walgett

This town is near the junction of the Namoi and Barwon rivers and a little over 100km (62 miles) from Lightning Ridge. It is surrounded by pastoral properties stretching far in each direction. Irrigation has opened up large new areas to cotton, sorghum, maize and other crops. There is good fishing in the area.

Bourke

A town with its own folklore, Bourke is approximately 300km (186 miles) south-west of Lightning Ridge, 946km (588 miles) south-west of Brisbane, and 781km (485 miles) north-west of Sydney. It has been included in this section as it is even further from anywhere else. Its population varies but is generally in excess of 5,000 people with a large proportion being Aboriginal.

The town is 110m (361 ft) above sea level and has an annual rainfall of 325mm (13 ins). The area pro-

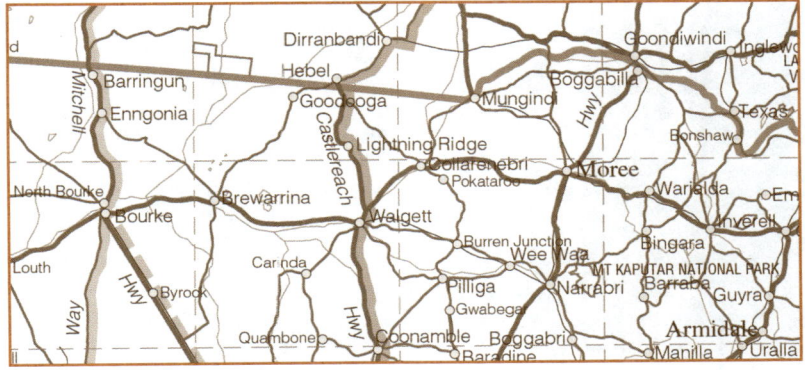

duces wool and beef, and in recent years cotton and other irrigated crops have been grown. A cotton gin operates in the area.

Bourke is situated on the upper banks of the Darling River, and its Post Office still flies the pennant indicating it is a port, from the days when boats would travel up and down the Darling transporting goods and produce. Now the wharves are broken up and hang in mid-air, a symbol of another era, whilst over the years the river has silted up making such transport impossible.

The town is considered to be the last before the vast empty centre. Just about everyone uses the expression "out the back of Bourke" when they want to describe the loneliness and emptiness of the centre of Australia.

The Bourke Visitor Information Centre is in Anson Street, ©6872 2280 or email ✎tourinfo@lisp. com.au ☉Opening hours are daily 9am-5pm.

New South Wales – South-West

Southern Highlands

Population 30,000
The Southern Highlands are south of Sydney, and the district includes, amongst others, the towns of Bowral, Mittagong, Moss Vale, Berrima, Bundanoon, Robertson and Kangaroo Valley.

Climate

Average temperatures: January max 25C (77F) - min 18C (64F); July max 10C (50F) - min -2C (28F). Average annual rainfall varies from 760mm (30 ins) in the north and west to 1140mm (45 ins) at Moss Vale and 1950mm (77 ins) at Robertson.

Characteristics

The rich, the famous and the powerful have long valued the Highlands as a rural retreat. The Governor of New South Wales used the Highlands as a 'holiday home' as early as 1868 when the Earl of Belmore rented Throsby Park. Later Hillview at Sutton Forest became a permanent vice-regal country residence, thus sealing the popularity of the area with the well-to-do citizens of Sydney. Many fine homes of the period remain. More recently, the Highlands have become a centre for artists and craft-workers, who find inspiration for their work in the quiet of the country and the beauty of their surroundings.

How to Get There

By Bus
All the major interstate bus companies stop in the Southern Highlands on their Sydney/Canberra/Melbourne routes.

There are regular bus services between Moss Vale and Canberra, and a daily service between Moss Vale and Nowra.

By Rail
There are daily services from Sydney and Canberra.

By Road
From Sydney, via the F5 Freeway from Liverpool, or the old Hume Highway - 1.5 hours. Or, via the Freeway to Wollongong, then the Illawarra Highway over Macquarie Pass, through Robertson, to Bowral - 2 hours.

From Canberra, via the Hume Highway through Goulburn - 2 hours.

From Nowra, via Kangaroo Valley and Fitzroy Falls - 1 hour.

Tourist Information

The Southern Highlands Visitor Information Centre is at 62 -70 Main Street, Mittagong, ✆(02) 4871 2888. You can email them at ✉wingtour@wsc.nsw.gov.au The ☺opening hours are 8am-5.30pm daily. There is a comprehensive website at ✇www.southern-highlands.com.au

Accommodation

Here is a selection of the available accommodation in each town, with prices for a double room per night, which should be used as a guide only. The telephone area codes are after the town names.

Mittagong
Mittagong Motel, 7 Old Hume Highway, ✆4871 1277. 28 units, unlicensed restaurant - ✪$55-90.
Poplars Motel, Hume Highway, ✆4889 4239. 15 units, licensed restaurant, barbecue - ✪$75-105.
Grand Country Lodge, Main Street, ✆4871 3277. 23 units, undercover parking, room service - ✪$85-135.
Melrose Motel, Old Hume Highway, ✆4871 1511. 16 units, barbecue - ✪$75-95.
Mittagong Caravan Park, Hume Highway, ✆4871 1574. 71 sites, basic facilities - powered sites ✪$18 for two, on-site vans $35 for two.

Bowral
The Briars Country Lodge, Moss Vale Road, ✆4868 3566. 30 units, licensed restaurant, swimming pool, tennis - ✪$165-220.
Boronia Lodge Apartment Hotel, Boronia Street, ✆4861 1860. 8 apartments, undercover parking, comfortable rooms- ✪$85-135.
Golf View Lodge, Boronia Street, ✆4861 2777. 28 units, swimming pool, barbecue, tennis - $90-135.
Port O'Call Motor Inn, cnr Bong Bong & Bundaroo Streets, ✆4861 1779. 20 units, licensed restaurant, good facilities - ✪$55-105.

Craigieburn Family Resort (guest house), Centennial Road, ✆4861 1977. 63 rooms (private facilities), fireplace, swimming pool, tennis, golf - ✪$195.

Links House Country Guesthouse, 17 Links Road, ✆4861 1408. 15 rooms, tennis, fireplace - B&B ✪$135-330.

Moss Vale

Bong Bong Motel, 238 Argyle Street, ✆4868 1033. 10 units, comfortable rooms - ✪$75-90.

Golf Ball Motel, cnr Arthur & Spring Streets, ✆4868 1511. 19 units, licensed restaurant (closed Sun-Mon), barbecue - ✪$60-85.

Lynton B&B, 618 Argyle Street, ✆4868 2552. 3 rooms - B&B ✪$110-180 .

Moss Vale Village Park, Willow Drive, ✆4868 1099. (Pets allowed under supervision) 114 sites, excellent facilities - powered sites ✪$15 for two, on-site vans $35 for two.

Berrima

Berrima Bakehouse Motel, cnr Wingecarribee Street & Hume Highway, ✆4877 1381. 19 units, swimming pool, barbecue - ✪$85-180.

Walden Wood, Old Mandemar Road, ✆4877 1164. 2 rooms, comfortable rooms - ✪$110-165.

Robertson

Robertson Country Motel, Illawarra Highway, ✆4885 1444. 6 units, basic facilities - ✪$60-85.

Ranelagh House (private hotel), Illawarra Highway, ✆4885 1111. 42 rooms (some with private facilities), unlicensed restaurant, swimming pool - DB&B ✪$4105-155 per person.

Bundanoon

Bundanoon Holiday Resort (motel), Anzac Parade, ✆4883 6068. 21 units, swimming pool, barbecue, tennis - ✪$75-100.

Morton National Park, Church Street, ✆4887 7270. (No pets allowed) - no power, advance site reservations only - ✪$10-18 for two.

Kangaroo Valley

Pioneer Motel Kangaroo Valley, 152 Moss Vale Road, ✆4465 1877. 23 units, licensed restaurant, fireplace, gym, heated swimming pool - ✪$95-185.

Big Bell Farm, 1666 Kangaroo Valley Road, ✆4465 1628. 2 cabins, comfortable facilities - ✪$70-90.

Kanagroo Valley Glenmack Caravan Park, Main Road, ✆4465 1372. (No pets allowed) 108 sites, barbecue, tennis, mini-golf - powered sites ✪$18-20 for two, cabins $50-75 for two.

Kangaroo Valley Tourist Park, Moss Vale Road, ✆4465 1310. (No dogs allowed) 60 sites, canoeing, playground, barbecue - powered sites ✪$17 for two, cabins $45-95 for two.

Eating Out

Following are some restaurants you might like to try in the various towns.

Mittagong

Lion Rampant, cnr Victoria Street & Hume Highway, ©4872 2980 - Bistro - ⊙open Wed-Sun 6-8.30pm, counter lunches noon-2pm.

Lesters Restaurant of Mittagong, 16 Bowral Road, ©4871 2696 - licensed, Italian - ⊙open Wed-Mon 5pm-10pm, plus Sun noon-2.30pm.

1890 Restaurant & Cafe, 84 Hume Highway, ©4871 1871 - licensed, French Continental a la carte - ⊙open Mon-Sat 6-9.30pm, Fri-Sun noon-2.30pm.

Mittagong Chinese Restaurant, 91 Hume Hwy, ©4871 1704.

B C's Italian Restaurante, 79 Hume Hwy, ©4872 1777.

The Blue Cockerel Bistro, 95 Hume Hwy, ©4872 1677.

Thonburi Thai Restaurant, Beaumont Gardens Shp 1/ Bowral Rd, ©4872 1511.

Bowral

House of Lowe, 236 Bong Bong Street, ©4861 2308 - licensed, Chinese and seafood - ⊙open daily for dinner from 5pm, and for lunch Wed-Sun noon-2pm.

Toshis Japanese Restaurant, Bong Bong Street, ©4861 4274.

Shanghai Restaurant, 265 Bong Bong Street, ©4861 1774.

Prego Trattoria Pizzeria, 412 Bong Bong Street, ©4862 5009.

Da Giacomo Cafe Restaurant, 275 Bong Bong Street, ©4862 2996.

Jack Style Thai Restaurant, Boolwey & Station Street , ©4862 1905.

Station Street Restaurant, 48 Station Street, ©4861 7171.

Moss Vale

Chow's Hong Kong Restaurant, 443 Argyle Street, ©4868 2208 - licensed, Chinese - open daily for lunch 11.30am-2.30pm, dinner Sun-Wed 5-9.30pm, Thurs 5-10.30pm, Fri-Sat 5-11pm.

Seafood Affair, 515 Argyle Street, ©4868 1726 - open Mon-Sat for dinner, Tues-Sat for lunch.

Cedar's Lebanese Restaurant, 490 -494 Argyle Street, ©4869 4600.

Peking Restaurant, Moss Vale Mall, ©4868 2366.

Argyle St Bistro, Argyle Street, ~4868 1599.

Sattahip Thai Restaurant, Shop 2/ 249 Argyle Street, ©4869 1891.

Berrima

Journeyman Bistro, Old Hume Highway, ©4877 1911 - licensed, specialise in flare-grill - open 7 days for lunch and dinner.

Victoria Inn, Jellore Street, ©4877 1475 - licensed, gourmet a la carte - open for dinner Wed-Sat, lunch Sun.

Old Breens Restaurant, Hume Hwy, ✆4877 1977.

Robertson

Robertson Country Motel, Illawarra Highway, ✆4885 1444 - BYO, country style cuisine - open 7 days 6.30-8.30pm, bookings essential.

Ranelagh House, Illawarra Highway, ✆4885 1111 - BYO, country style cooking - open 7 days for lunch and dinner (except when house closed for conferences).

Bundanoon

Highlander Restaurant, Anzac Parade, ✆4883 6242 - licensed, a la carte with German influence - open Wed-Sun from 6.30pm, Sun noon-2pm.

Tree Tops Guest House, 101 Railway Parade, ✆4883 6372 - BYO, International and Indian cuisine - open for dinner Fri-Sat.

Bundanoon Chinese Restaurant, 21 Railway Avenue, ✆4883 6368.

Kangaroo Valley

Restaurant Deville, Moss Vale Road, ✆4465 1314 - licensed, char grill, blackboard menu - open Wed-Sun 10am-3pm, Fri-Sat from 7pm.

Points of Interest

Mittagong

The area was one of the first settled by Europeans when the government allowed settlement south of the Cowpastures (now Camden). In 1821, William Chalker, principal overseer of government stock at the Cowpastures, was granted 200 acres of land on the Old South Road as a reward for service, and although he died before the grant was surveyed, his widow took up the grant, and his descendants still live in the area. In fact, in 1988 the family erected a cairn on the Old South Road to mark the site of the original grant, and from there you can get a good view of Mittagong and the surrounding countryside.

Many gracious sandstone buildings were constructed in the town in the 1860s, not only public buildings, but small cottages, and many of these can be found in the side streets between the Hume Highway and Lake Alexandra.

The town has many specialty craft outlets, that display and sell the works of both local and outside artists, including such items as tapestry, stained glass, woodwork, pottery and weaving.

In and around Mittagong there are several easily accessible **walking tracks**, including one to the old Box Vale Mine. There are also a number of trails around Mittagong's Lake Alexandra, which was built by damming drainage water from the town, and attracts a wide variety of domestic and wild birdlife. The Tourist Information Centre in Winifred West Park has full details of all the walks available.

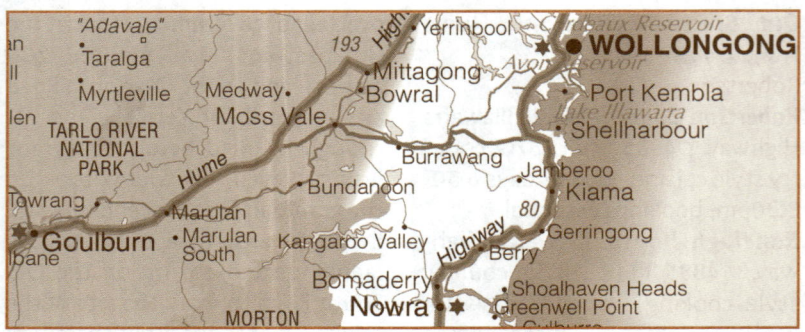

The Southern Highlands Visitor Information Centre is in Main Street.

Mount Gibraltar

The mount (863m - 2831 ft), known locally as The Gib, is the highest point between the Illawarra Coast and the Great Dividing Range beyond the Wollondilly River. It rises 240m (787 ft) above Mittagong to the north, and 180m (591 ft) above Bowral on its southern flank. From the summit, on clear days, there are views to the Sydney area (north), the Blue Mountains (north and north-west), the Cuckbundoon Range (south-west) and to Mt Keira above Wollongong.

The mountain and its lookouts can be reached by following Oxley Drive from Bowral or Mittagong, or there are fire trails and foot tracks for dedicated bushwalkers. The Tourist Information Offices have details of all the lookouts, and maps of the various tracks.

Bowral

Bowral was originally part of a property granted to the explorer John Oxley, and in 1859, 200 acres of his estate were subdivided by members of his family to coincide with the news of the coming of the railway. The village was first known as Wingecarribee (now the name of the Shire), then Burradoo, and finally in 1867, Bowral. The town was the site of the first store in the district, but development was slow until the opening of the railway. From 1870 onwards, the village grew rapidly, and by 1890 was considered a fashionable resort where Sydneysiders could retreat from the heat of summer.

Now, with a population of 8,500, the town is a blend of historic buildings, quaint old residential cottages and commercial premises. There is a uniformity to the architecture, and a large number of mature deciduous trees form a backdrop for magnificent public and private gardens.

Bendooley Street is subject to a Heritage Commission protection order, to prevent it from being altered. The Berrima District Historical Society has compiled an historical tour of Bowral, beginning at the Corbett Gardens, one block east of the main street, and visiting twelve attractions. The Information Centre has details.

The Bradman Museum, ✆4862 1247, is in St Jude Street, overlooking the Bradman Oval, and opposite his former home (52 Shepherd Street, which is a private residence), open daily 10am-4pm. It was on the Oval that Bradman played his first game of cricket when he was twelve, and where, in 1925, he scored a sparkling 234 for Bowral against the Wingello team that included bowler Bill O'Reilly.

The Museum has an incredible array of cricket-related material, ranging from an oak bat of the 1750s through to Allan Border's helmet used during the 1989 Ashes series. But, naturally, anything to do with the late Sir Donald (1908-2001) takes pride of place, and he has donated many objects, including the bat he used at Headingley in 1934 to score his second highest Test innings of 304. Admission is ✪$7.50 adults, $3.50 children and $20 for families. A website containing everything you want to know about The Don is: ✆www.bradman.org.au

For cricket fans, there is also The Bradman Walk, a self-guided tour through Bowral visiting some of the sites associated with the great cricketer. It begins at the Museum and Oval, and includes the school, St Simon & St Jude's Church, the Empire Cinema, his workplace in Bong Bong Street and two houses where he once lived.

Moss Vale

The town of Moss Vale stands on part of the original grant made to the district's first European settler, Charles Throsby, who played an important part in the exploration of New South Wales, opening up not only the Southern Highlands, but also the South Coast, Goulburn and Canberra regions. His nephew, also named Charles, came to live in the district and established Throsby Park as a well respected grazing property.

Throsby Park was inhabited by the family until 1990, and although originally a colonial Georgian home, it was added to in later periods, evident in the architecture, furnishings, decoration and garden. The site is open by arrangement and guided yours are available, contact The National Parks and Wildlife Service ✆4887 7270 for information and bookings. The is a small entry fee for park usage, with all proceeds going to the restoration and maintenance of Throsby Park.

Scenic attractions in the area include Belmore and Fitzroy Falls, and Morton National Park, with its 55km (34 miles) of river frontages and virgin bushland.

Fitzroy Falls

The falls are within 100m of the car park and visitor information centre in Morton National Park, one of the largest National Parks in New South Wales, covering an area of over 154,000ha (380,380 acres). The Falls cascade 82m (269 ft) to the valley below, and there are two scenic walking tracks, one on each side of the escarpment, that provide spectacular views from a series of lookouts along the way. Each track is approximately 3km in length, taking 1-2 hours walking. The visitor information centre has details of these, and of other attractions through the park.

Berrima

Situated 14km (9 miles) south of Mittagong on the Hume Highway, Berrima is considered the best remaining example of a small Australian town of the 1830s. The town was founded in 1829 by Sir Thomas Mitchell, the Surveyor-General of New South Wales, and in its heyday was an affluent community with a population of over 500. Many of the original buildings have been restored, and former hotels now trade as craft shops, galleries and restaurants.

The walking 2.5km tour of Berrima begins at the Berrima District Historical Museum and Information Centre, and visits the following: Berrima House, built in 1835, and once host to bushranger Ben Hall; Berrima Bridge Nursery, formerly a private girls' school; Brian McMahon's Pub, 1840; The Coach and Horses Inn, 1835, now a private home; The Market Place Park; Victoria Inn, 1834; The Barn Gallery; The Large Oak Tree, planted by Sir Henry Parkes in 1890; Post Office, 1836; Surveyor General Inn, 1835, the oldest continuously licensed inn in Australia still trading within its original walls; Superintendent's House, built in the 1880s as the Governor's House for the Gaol; Berrima Gaol; Deputy Superintendent's House; Bulls Head Fountain; Lambie's Well, 1840; Court House, 1833; Sandstone Cottages in Argyle Street; Presbyterian Church; Bellview House; Ardleigh; Harper's Mansion, 1834; Old Well; Colonial Inn; The Berrima Gallery; the Old Bakery; Holy Trinity Church; Magistrate's House; The White Horse Inn; and St Francis Xavier Catholic Church, 1849.

There are also a few other walks that take visitors further afield, and the Information Centre has details.

Robertson

The town was named in honour of John Robertson who was responsible for the Land Act of 1861 under which land was thrown open for selection before survey. The Robertson Nature Reserve, located 300m south of the township, is easily accessible and is an important conservation area, containing about 5ha (12 acres) of the Yarrawa Brush vegetation which, prior to European settlement, covered about 2500ha (6175 acres) around what is now Robertson township. Up until the 1950s, farmers in the area were still clearing the native timber, and the casual visitor must wonder what made them persevere against such overwhelming odds.

Today the Robertson area is one of the most beautiful to be found anywhere, with its rolling red soil country and rugged bushland.

Bundanoon

The town of Bundanoon has been a holiday spot for decades, but still manages to retain a quiet village atmosphere. It is a bushwalker's paradise, with walks going to Glow Worm Glen, Fern Glen, Fairy Bower Falls, and the Amphitheatre, amongst other places. The Southern Highlands Visitor Information Centre has all the details on durations of walks, and fitness required.

In April, Bundanoon goes Scottish in more than name alone, with the popular annual "Brigadoon" festival. The entertainment is as you'd expect, the day filled with the unmistakable tune of bagpipes, traditional dancing and a host of highland games.

Kangaroo Valley

Kangaroo Valley is situated on a plateau between the Highlands and the coast, and is easily accessible. The Kangaroo River winds through the valley, and is crossed by the Hampden Suspension Bridge, built in 1898 of castellated stone by convict labour. The bridge is named after Viscount Hampden, Governor of New South Wales at that time. The river under the bridge is popular for swimming and canoeing. Barbecue and toilet facilities are provided.

Adjacent to the bridge is the Pioneer Settlement Museum, with a fully furnished old farm homestead, a dairy, and a machinery shed, set in picnic grounds with barbecue facilities. The museum is ☉open daily 9am-5pm.

Historic Barrengarry Store and Post Office is found 1km north of the Suspension Bridge. They were established in 1880 and retain the old-world charm of a pioneer general store that sells almost everything.

The Kangaroo Valley village has many coffee shops, craft shops and specialty stores, while the river offers many spots for picnicking, swimming, bushwalking and canoeing.

Bendeela Pondage and Pumping Station is 7km (4 miles) west of the Main Road, on Bendeela Road. Here water is pumped 127 (417 ft) vertically to a reservoir above Fitzroy Falls. A picnic area, barbecues and toilets are provided.

Kangaroo Valley can also be reached easily from Nowra.

Festivals

January - Bowral Horse Show.
February - Mittagong Dahlia Festival and Fun Run. Kangaroo Valley Show.
March - Robertson Show. Moss Vale Show.
Easter - Berrima Art Society Exhibition. Musica Viva (biennial).
April - Brigadoon Day, Bundanoon.
August - Bowral Horse Show.
September - Tulip Time Festival, Bowral. Bowral Fun Run.
October - Tulip Time Festival, Bowral. Berrima District Art Society Exhibition.
December - Moss Vale Summer Gymkhana.

Facilities

The towns have a wide range of facilities for all types of sporting activities, and the Tourist Information Centres have all the details.

Goulburn

Population 21,300
Goulburn, 638m (2093 ft) above sea level, is 197km (122 miles) south-west of Sydney and 94km (58 miles) north-east of Canberra.

Climate

Average temperatures: January max 26C (79F) - min 12C (54F); June max 12C (54F) - min 0.5C (32.5F). Average annual rainfall: 671mm (26 ins).

Characteristics

Goulburn is Australia's oldest inland city dating back to the earliest days of the colony. Many of the buildings in the town have beautiful cast iron lace work. Wheat was grown in the locality as early as the 1820s, and today primary industry is still important. Goulburn is also an administrative centre for several State Government Departments. It was the last town of the British Empire to become a city by virtue of the Royal Letters Patent in 1863. Goulburn is home to 'Rambo' the 14m (46 ft) high ram at the Big Merino complex.

How to Get There

By Bus
Most of the major coaches stop at Goulburn on the Sydney/Melbourne and Sydney/Canberra/Melbourne routes.

By Car
Travel via the Hume Highway from Sydney or Melbourne, or the Federal Highway from Canberra.

Tourist Information

The Goulburn Visitor Information Centre, 201 Sloane Street, ✆(02) 48 23 4492, is ☺open 9am-5pm every day except Christmas Day. The website is www.igoulburn.com and you can email ✉visitor@goulburn.nsw.gov.au

Accommodation

Places to stay in Goulburn are excellent and varied. Here is a selection, with prices for a double room per night, which should be used as a guide only. The telephone area code is 02.

Posthouse Motor Lodge, 1 Lagoon Street, ✆4821 5666. 38 units, licensed restaurant, swimming pool - ✪$85-105.

Lilac City Motor Inn, 126 Lagoon Street, ✆4821 5000. 28 units, licensed restaurant - ✪$75-90.

Clinton Lodge, 80 Clinton Street, ✆4821 4488. 22 units, comfortable facilities - B&B ✪$75-80.

Parkhaven Motel, 60 Lagoon Street, ✆4821 4455. 15 units - ✪$65.

Hillview Motel, 2 Cowper Street, ✆4821 3130. 20 units, basic facilities - ✪$45-50.

Alpine Heritage Motel, 248 Sloane Street, ✆4821 2930. 45 units, unlicensed restaurant - ✪$45-75.

Caravan Parks

Governors Hill Carapark, 77 Sydney Road, ✆1800 227 373. (No dogs) 60 sites, good facilties, barbecue - powered sites ✪$19-21 for two, on-site vans $35 for two.

Goulburn South Caravan Park, Hume Street, ✆4821 3233. (Pets allowed under supervision) 112 sites, basic facilties - powered sites ✪$17 for two, on-site vans $40-60 for two.

Eating Out

Goulburn has restaurants, coffee bars, family style cafes and licensed clubs, so whatever your budget you will find something to suit. Here are a few you might like to try:

Goulburn Italian Pizza Restaurant, 147 Auburn Street, ✆4821 5998.

Billabong Station Restaurant, cnr Hume Hwy & Lansdowne Street, ✆4822 8014.

Khun Lek Thai Restaurant, 150 Auburn Street, ✆4821 2025.

Riley's Restaurant, 148 Sloane Street, ✆4822 747.

Blue Plate Restaurant, Lagoon St, ✆4821 5666.

Hung Win Chinese Restaurant, 277 Auburn Street, ✆4821 8933.

McDonalds has two locations, one in North Goulburn on the corner of the Hume Highway and Common Street, the other in South

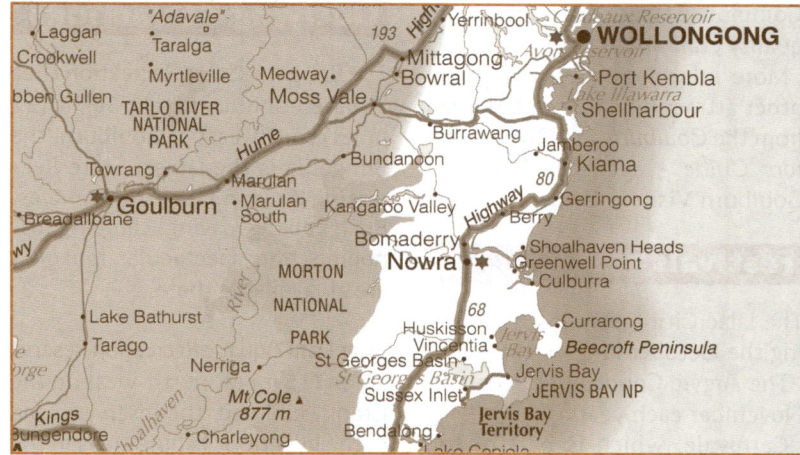

Goulburn on the Old Hume Highway.

Points of Interest

A **walking tour** of Historic Goulburn and a walking tour of the Wollondilly River are available to the traveller - brochures may be obtained from the Goulburn Visitors Centre.

Some of the historic buildings are open to the public, including the Court House, St Clair, St Saviours Cathedral and Riversdale.

Other attractions include the **Big Merino Complex**, on the corner of the Hume Highway and Lansdowne Street, ✆4822 8013, which has a craft centre, educational area, lookout and restaurant.

The Goulburn Yurtworks, ✆4821 5931, is the only producer of Yurts in Australia (yurts are roundhouses based on Mongolian tents).

The Rocky Hill War Memorial dominates the town and is Goulburn's landmark.

The Black Stag Deer Park, Gorman Road, ✆4821 4386, has fallow red deer as well as Australian wildlife.

The Goulburn Rail Heritage Centre, in Braidwood Road, features many pieces of industrial steam machinery, and is open the first weekend of every month.

The Goulburn Regional Art Gallery is in the Civic Centre, on the corner of Bourke and Church Streets, ✆4823 4443.

Gulsons Craft Village, located at the historic Gulsons brickworks,

Common Street, features many quality craft shops.

More information on these and other attractions may be obtained from the *Goulburn and District Visitors Guide* - available from the Goulburn Visitors Centre.

Festivals

The Lilac City Festival is held during the October long weekend.

The Argyle County Fair is held in November each year.

Carnivale, which is part of the NSW Government sponsored festival, is held in September each year.

Goulburn also stages an annual show and rodeo.

Facilities

There are many sporting facilities available in Goulburn, including squash courts, tennis courts, indoor cricket and sports centre, ten pin bowling centre, swimming pool and water slide. Lawn bowls, golf, darts, and fishing are also catered for. Contact the Visitor Information Centre for all the details.

Outlying Attractions

The Bungonia State Recreation Area
Situated approximately 35km (22 miles) south-east of Goulburn, the Bungonia is the largest State Recreation Area in New South Wales. Bushwalking, caving, climbing, canoeing, and spectacular lookouts are all available there.

Pejar Dam Aquatic Recreation Reserve
25km (15 miles) north-west on the Crookwell Road, the reserve is one of the best trout fishing areas in the south-east region. Only non-powered boats are permitted, and there is sailing, windsurfing and canoeing.

Wombeyan Caves
The caves are 77km (48 miles) north-east of Goulburn, and there are five cave tours. Many pleasant hours may also be spent strolling through the beautiful bushland reserve surrounding the caves. The road to the caves is very winding, so it is best to have the attitude that this excursion is a full day, and take your time. The Wombeyan Caves Visitors Centre and Caravan Park can be contacted on ©4843 5976.

New South Wales – South-West

Snowy Mountains

The Snowy Mountains are in the south-east corner of New South Wales, and the highest peak is Mt Kosciusko, 2230m (7316 ft). The mountains are home to the ski fields of New South Wales, and they conjure up visions of fashionable skiers hurtling down ski slopes before sipping their apres-ski drinks, but that is only one facet of the Mountains. One of Australia's engineering marvels is also to be found here, the Snowy Mountains Hydro Electric Scheme, which captures the water from the melting snow destined for the coast, and redirects it through mountain channels to the interior.

The mountains are a carpet of wildflowers in summer and there are numerous trails for bushwalkers. The many lakes and rivers are an aquatic paradise for those wishing to get away from it all. Lake Jindabyne (three times the size of Sydney Harbour) is ablaze with sailboard and catamaran sails, and the lakes and rivers abound with trout.

Cooma

Population 8,500
Cooma is where the Snowy Mountains begin, and is near the New South Wales-Victorian Border. Distance from Canberra 114km (71 miles); from Sydney 420km (261 miles); from Thredbo 97km (60 miles); from Charlotte Pass 105km (65 miles); from Perisher 98km (61 miles); from Adaminiby 52km (32 miles); from Mt Selwyn 99km (62 miles).

Climate

Cooma is 810m (2657 ft) above sea level. Average temperatures: January max 26C (79F) - min 11C (52F); July max 9C (48F) - min 1C (30F). Annual rainfall 450mm (17 ins).

Characteristics

If you are travelling to the snow by train or air, Cooma will be your port of call. It is a pleasant town and offers transport to Jindabyne and the snowfields.

Tourist Information

The Cooma Visitor Information Centre, 119 Sharpe Street, ℰ(02) 6450 1742, is ⏰open 9am-5pm daily. Email them at ✉cvc@snowy. net.au or visit the website, 👁www. snowymountains.com.au

How to Get There

By Road
Greyhound Pioneer have services from Sydney and Canberra. Snowliner Coaches, ℰ6452 1584, provide services from Bega and Canberra.

By Rail
There is a train service from Sydney via Canberra daily, with connections to Melbourne from Goulburn.

By Road
From Sydney via the Hume Highway, 420km (216 miles), or via Bega, 542km (336 miles).
From Melbourne via the coast 730km (454 miles), or via the Alpine Way 664km (400 miles).

Accommodation

Cooma has motels, hotels and caravan parks. Here is a selection with prices for a double room per night, which should be used as a guide only. The telephone area code is 02.
Kinross Inn - Cooma, 15 Sharp Street, ℰ6452 3577. 17 units, barbecue, undercover parking, indoor heated pool - ✪$70-110.
Alkira Motel, 213 Sharp Street, ℰ6452 3633. 13 units, undercover parking, barbecue- ✪$65-110.
Cooma Motor Lodge, 6 Sharp Street, ℰ6452 1888. 44 units, licensed restaurant, sauna, room service - ✪$60-150.
High Country Motel, 12 Chapman

Street, ✆6452 1277. 40 units, licensed restaurant, swimming pool, recreation room - ✪$60-80.
Hawaii Motel, 192 Sharp Street, ✆6452 1211. 23 units, unlicensed restaurant - ✪$50-60.
Alpine Country Guest House, 32 Massie Street, ✆6452 1414. 13 rooms (private facilities), unlicensed restaurant - ✪$30-60.

Caravan Parks

Snowtels Caravan & Camping Park, Snowy Mountains Highway, ✆6452 1828. (Pets allowed under supervision and by arrangement) 134 sites, good facilities, tennis, ski hire - powered sites ✪$20 for two, cabins $40-90 for two, on-site vans $35-55 for two.

Eating Out

Many of the motels and hotels have licensed and BYO restaurants, and the licensed clubs offer good family meals. There are several takeaway food outlets.
Grand Court Chinese Restaurant, Snowstop Village, Sharp Street, ✆6452 4525.
Cooma Truckstop Restaurant, 1 Polo Flat Road, ✆6452 5550.
Bahn Thai Noodle Restaurant, 178 Sharp Street, ✆6452 4277.
McDonald's is in Sharp Street.

Points of Interest

Tourist Drive markers signpost an easy drive through and around Cooma, taking in the town's many points of interest. The first marker is at Centennial Park near the Visitors' Centre, and from there it goes past Cooma Creek, Lions Lookout, the Murrumbidgee Water Filtration Plant, Snowy Mountains Authority Information Centre, the Snowy Memorial, Festival Pool, Nannygoat Hill, Cooma Cenotaph, Cooma Prison, Lambie Street, Raglan Gallery, Mt Gladstone, Alpenthaler Park, Southern Cloud Park, Christ Church, the Lookout, Polo Falt, and back to the Centre.

The **Snowy Mountains Hydro Electric Authority Information Centre**, Monaro Highway, ✆1800 623 776, ⊙open Mon-Fri 8am-4.30pm, Sat 8am-noon, has displays and models of the Snowy Mountains Scheme, and a film show, Mon-Fri at 11am and 3pm. Visit 👁www.snowyhydro.com.au for further details.

Snowy Mountain Scheme Tours to Adaminaby, Old Adaminaby, Providence Portal, Kiandra, Cabramurra, and Tumut underground Power Station, can be organised through the information centre.

For those who are energetic, there is the **Lambie Town Walk**, which passes through residential and

natural areas of scenic and historic interest in Cooma. One part of the walk is through the town area (5km) and the bushland section is also 5km, and takes approximately 2.5 hours.

Llama World, Snowy Mountains Highway, 19km (12 miles) from Cooma, has llamas and alpacas, a tractor ride through their paddocks, rides in llama-drawn sulkies, and the Inca Gallery, which sells souvenirs, South American and llama products including yarn, fleece and made-up garments. ☉Open Fri-Mon (weather permitting), ©6452 4593.

Festivals

Man from Snowy River Marathon in October each year.

Facilities

Bowling club, golf course, horse riding, swimming pool (heated), snooker, squash, tennis courts, gliding, ski hire shops, car hire depots and taxis.

Outlying Attractions

Adaminaby

The town of Adaminaby is 51km (32 miles) from Cooma, and is the home of The World's Largest Trout. The town was moved to its present site in 1956-57 to allow for the filling of Lake Eucumbene. Facilities include boating, fishing, sailing, snow skiing, tennis and water skiing.

Yarrangobilly Caves

The caves are just before the town of Yarrangobilly, and 6.5km (4 miles) off the Snowy Mountains Highway. They were carved out of the limestone by the Yarrangobilly River around 440 million years ago, and are a strange landscape of rugged bluffs and disappearing streams. Beyond the half light of the cave entrance is an underworld of unrivalled beauty.

The self-guiding Glory Hole Cave is ☺open daily, 10am-4pm. Guided inspections of either the North Glory, Jersey or Jillabenan Caves are conducted at 1pm each non-holiday week day. Additional tours are scheduled during weekends and school holidays. There are plenty of walking tracks in the area, and the Yarrangobilly Caves Visitor Information Centre, ✆(02) 6454 9597, has brochures and information, and is ☺open 7 days a week, 9am-4.30pm, 8.30am to 5.30pm in the peak season. Yarrangobilly is a day use area only, and camping is available at Yarrangobilly Village or Three Mile Dam.

Jindabyne

Population 1600
Situated 40km (25 miles) from Cooma, Jindabyne is the closest centre to the ski fields. Many people choose to stay in the town and drive to the fields each day. In summer time, Lake Jindabyne is the attraction for staying here.

Tourist Information

The Snowy Region Visitor Information Centre is in Kosciuszko Road, ✆(02) 6450 5600. Their ☺opening hours are 8am-6pm in the winter holidays and Easter, 8.30am-5pm the rest of the year. They can be contacted by email at ✉srvc@ npws.nsw.gov.au or you might like to visit the website at ☞www.kos .com.au for a preliminary look.

Accommodation

Here is a selection of the accommodation available, with winter prices for a double room per night, which should be used as a guide only. Never go to Jindabyne in the winter thinking you will be able to pick up accommodation without a booking, it is far too cold to sleep in the bus station. The telephone area code is 02.

Lake Jindabyne Motel Hotel, Kosciusko Road, ℘6456 2203. 39 units, licensed restaurant, bistro, indoor heated swimming pool, spa, sauna, barbecue- ✪$75-200.

Horizons Snowy Mountains, Kosciusko Road, ℘6456 2562. 109 apartments, licensed restaurant, bistro, indoro heated swimming pool, fireplace, undercover parking, spa, sauna - ✪$105-405.

Banjo Paterson Inn, Kosciusko Road, ℘6456 2372. 22 units (private facilities), licensed restaurant - ✪$65-750.

Alpine Resort Motel, 22 Nettin Circuit, ℘6456 2522. 29 units, good faciliites, unlicensed restaurant, barbecue, spa - ✪$100-300.

Lakeview Plaza Motel, 2 Snowy River Avenue, ℘6456 2134. 13 units, licensed restaurant, bar, spa - ✪$65-200.

Chesa St Moritz, Lot 10 Alpensee Weg, ℘6456 1856. 1 unit, basic facilities - ✪$65-190.

Yowi Lodge, 67 Gippsland Street, ℘562 547 - 14 units, unlicensed restaurant, swimming pool, spa, sauna - B&B ✪$60-170.

Caravan Park

Snowline Caravan Park, cnr Kosciusko Road & Alpine Way, ℘6456 2099. (No pets allowed) 178 sites, excellent faciltities, sauna, spa, cafe, barbecue, tennis - powered sites ✪$20-25 for two, cabins $40-205 for two.

Jindabyne Holiday Park, Kosciusko Road, ℘6456 2249. 200 sites, basic facilities - powered sites ✪$20-26 for two, cabins $55-130 for two, on-site vans $40-90 for two.

Eating Out

It is well known that cold weather makes everyone hungry, so there is no shortage of eating places in this neck of the woods. Here is a selection.

Pom's Balcony Bistro, upper level Petamin Plaza (Town Centre), ℘6456 2144 - fully licensed, steak and seafood, open daily 6pm-31m.

Chit Thai Restaurant, Snowline Caravn Park, cnr Kosciusko Rd and Alpine Way), ℘6456 2052.

Brumby Bar & Bistro, Kosciusko Road, ℘6456 2526.

Bacco Italian Restaurant, Nuggets Crossing, Shop 10, Kosciuszko Road, ℘6456 1420.

Gringo's Mexican Restaurant, Aspen Chalet, Kosciusko Road, ℘6457 2229.

Restaurant 14, Town Centre, Shop 14, Kosciuszko Road, ℘6457 2660.

Il Lago Restaurant, Nuggetts Crossing Shopping Centre, Shop 19a, Kosciusko Road, ℘6456 1171.

Ski and Equipment Hire

Ampol Jindabyne, Kosciusko Road, ✆6456 1177; BP Lakeside, Kosciusko Road, ✆6456 1959; Arlberg Ski Centre, Jindabyne Road, Berridale, ✆6456 3177; Jindabyne Sports Store, Shop 12, Town Centre, ✆6456 2216; Snowy Mountains Sports, Petamin Plaza, ✆6456 2530; Thredbo Sports, Nuggetts Crossing, ✆6459 4119; Wilderness Sports, Nuggets Crossing, ✆6456 2966.

Ski Fields
Mt Selwyn (1614m - 5295 ft)
The lowest field, Mt Selwyn is very popular with families and school groups. There is no accommodation at Mt Selwyn.

Ski lifts: 1 Double Chair, 4 T-Bars, 2 Pomas, 1 Platter and 4 Beginner Ropes and 1 Toboggan Lift.

Ski slopes: beginners 40%, intermediates 48%, advanced 12%.

Facilities/services: ticket office, ski school, ski hire, information centre, ski patrol, ski and souvenir shop, licensed cafeteria, resort booking centre.

Prices: half day ✪$35 adult, $20 child; full day $46 adult, $23 child; lift & lesson package $68 adult $45 child.

Information: ☞www.selwynsnow.com.au, ✉snowinfo@selwynsnow.com.au or ✆64549 488.

Perisher Blue
Includes Perisher/Smiggins (2034m

- 6673 ft), Mt Blue Cow (1980m - 6496 ft) and Guthega (1932m - 6339 ft) - an extensive 1250 hectares of skifields.

Accommodation: The Stables, ℂ6457 5755; Sundeck Hotel, ℂ6457 5054; Swagman Chalet, ℂ6457 5275.

Ski lifts: 4 Double Chairs, 6 Quad Chairs, 2 Triple Chairs, 22 T Bars, 4 J Bars, 11 others, 3 Ski carpet, Skitube

Ski slopes: beginners 22%, intermediates 60%, advanced 18%.

Facilities/services: ticket office, ski school, ski hire, information centre, resort booking centre, ski patrol, childminding, ski shops, Skitube train station, oversnow transport to lodges, bars, bistros, restaurants, coffee shops, takeaway food outlets (including on-slope), banks, post office, newsagents, chemist, supermarket, bottle shop, photographic services, medical services, souvenirs, lockers, ski-storage.

Transport: Skitube Trains depart frequently as required in peak times during winter. Below snowline on Alpine Way, so no chains required.

Bullock's Flat Terminal (Alpine Way) - free car parking for 3,000 cars and 250 buses. Ticket office for combined Perisher Blue and Skitube tickets. Ski hire, information centre, National Parks and Wildlife Service sales and information, souvenir and ski accessories shop, takeaway food outlet.

Perisher Valley Terminal: ticket office for Perisher/Smiggins and Mt Blue Cow plus train tickets. Ski minding and locker service, coffee shop, licensed bistro, ski equipment and accessories, children's clothing shop, gift shop, takeaway snack bar, full Medical Centre and Police Office, oversnow transport to Perisher Valley lodges.

Prices: check current prices at the time of your visit on the updated website.

Information and prices: ☞www. perisherblue.com.au, ☎1300 655 822.

Thredbo (2037m - 6683 ft)

Accommodation: Thredbo Alpine, ☎6459 4200; Snowgoose Lodge, ☎6457 6349; The River Inn, ☎6457 6505.

Ski lifts: 2 high-speed quad detachable chairlifts, 1 beginner quad chairlift, 3 double chairlifts, 7 T-bars, 2 rope tows.

Ski slopes: beginners 16%, intermediates 67%, advanced 17%.

Facilities/services: ticket office, ski school, ski hire, information huts, resort booking centre, ski patrol, ski shops, bars, bistros, restaurants (including on-slope), coffee shop, takeaway food outlets (including on-slope), bank, post office, newsagent, chemist, supermarket, bottle shop, photographic services, medical services, souvenirs, overnight ski storage.

Prices: full day ✪$75 adult, $41 child; lift & lesson $100 adult, $67 child; group lessons $40. Check current prices at the time of your visit.

Information: ☞www.thredbo.com .au, ☎6459 4100.

Charlotte Pass

Accommodation: Kosciusko Chalet, ☎1800 026 369; Arlberg Ski Lodge, ☎9453 2057; Snowbird Ski Resort, ☎1300 651 653. The ski lifts are virtually on the front doorstep.

Ski lifts: 1 triple chairlift, 1 T-bar, 2 poma lifts, 1 rope tow.

Transport: Charlotte Pass is the most isolated resort with access by oversnow transport (snowcats) from Perisher Valley. The journey takes about 35 minutes. If travelling by car, you have to park at the Skitube Terminal at Bullocks Flat and travel on the tube to Perisher. The snowcat part of the trip costs ✪$28 adults, $19 children each way.

Prices: full day ✪$75 adult, $48 child; half day $60 adult, $35 child. Check current prices at the time of your visit.

Information: ☞www.charlottepass .com.au, ☎1800 026 369.

Wagga Wagga

Population 42,900
The city of Wagga Wagga is situated on the banks of the Murrumbidgee River, 459km (285 miles) south-west of Sydney.

Climate

Average temperatures: January max 35C (95F) - min 18C (64F); July max 14C (57F) - min 5C (41F). Average annual rainfall: 669mm (26 ins).

Characteristics

The area was first settled by the largest Aboriginal tribe in New South Wales - the Wiradjuri. It is from their language that the city gets its name, Wagga (Wahga or Wahgam) means 'crow' and the repetition of the word expresses the plural.

In 1829, the land was explored by Captain Charles Sturt while he was on his famous expedition discovering the Murrumbidgee and Murray River systems. Settlement followed and Wagga Wagga was proclaimed a town in 1849. It became a city in 1948, and is the largest provincial city in New South Wales.

How to Get There

By Bus
Greyhound Pioneer have services daily from/to Sydney, Adelaide and Canberra.

By Rail
The Sydney-Melbourne and Melbourne-Sydney Countrylink stops at Wagga Wagga, daily.

Church in the Snowy Mountains New South Wales

Thredbo Creek, Snowy Mountain

By Road

From Sydney, via the Hume and Sturt Highways, 493km (306 miles).

From Canberra, via Barton, Hume and Sturt Highways, 248km (154 miles).

From Melbourne, via Hume to Albury, then via Olympic Way - Culcairn/Henty/The Rock, 443km (275 miles).

Tourist Information

The Visitors Information Centre is in Tarcutta Street ✆(02) 6926 9621. They have a website at ☞www.tourismwaggawagga.com.au and you can email them at ✉visitors@wagga.nsw.gov.au

The centre is ⏰open daily 9am-5pm.

Accommodation

Wagga Wagga has plenty of motels, hotels and caravan parks for a town its size. Here is a selection with prices for a double room per night, which should be used as a guide only. The telephone area code is 02.

Pavilion Motor Inn, 22 Kincaid Street, ✆6921 6411. 45 units, licensed restaurant, indoor heated swimming pool - ✪$130-190.

Heritage Motor Inn, 244 Edward Street, ✆6921 4099. 22 units, sauna, swimming pool, barbecue, spa - ✪$95-120.

Carriage House Motor Inn, Sturt Highway, ✆6922 7374. 37 units, licensed restaurant, swimming pool, spa, sauna, tennis, bbq - ✪$120-170.

Townhouse International, Morgan Street, ✆6922 7374. 42 units, licensed restaurant, swimming pool - ✪$80-250.

Allonville Motel, Sturt Highway, Gumly Gumly, ✆6922 7269 - 29 units, licensed restaurant, swimming pool, bbq - ✪$51.

City Park Motel, 1 Tarcutta Street, ✆6921 4301. 26 units, barbecue - ✪$70-80.

Palm & Pawn Motor Inn, Hampden Avenue, ✆6921 6688. 25 units, licensed restaurant, tennis, barbecue- ✪$60.

Caravan Parks

Horseshoe Motor Village, 23 Horseshoe Road, ✆6921 6033. (Pets allowed by arrangement) 44 sites, good facilities, pool - powered sites ✪$15 for two, cabins $45-50 for two.

Easts Van Park Riverview, 93 Hammond Avenue, ✆6921 4287. (No pets allowed)100 sites, good facilities - powered sites ✪$20 for two, on-site vans $45 for two.

Airport Caravan Park, Sturt Highway, Forest Hill, ✆6922 7271. (Pets allowed under control)14 sites, basic facilities, barbecue, playground - powered sites ✪$14 for two.

Eating Out

As with any city of its size, Wagga Wagga has a good selection of restaurants and takeaway food outlets. Here are some you might like to try.

Barter's Restaurant, 143 Fitzmaurice Street, ©6921 1922 licensed, traditional and nouvelle cuisine, seven nights a week.

Capers Restaurant, at the Country Comfort, cnr Morgan & Tarcutta Streets, ©6911 6444.

Reasonable, for the whole family
Montezumas Mexican Restaurant, 85 Bayliss Street, ©6921 4428 - licensed - open Wed-Fri noon-2pm, Tues-Sun from 6pm.

Golden Season Family Restaurant, 31 Forsyth Street, ©6921 1177.

Other restaurants worth considering:

Locksley Steak House, 137 Peter Street, ©6921 4886 - licensed, also serves seafood, chicken, etc - open Wed-Fri noon-2pm, Tues-Sat 6pm-midnight.

Indian Tavern Tandoori Restaurant, 176 Baylis Street, ©6921 3121.

Capers Restaurant, Morgan Street, ©6921 6444.

Olivers, 8 Day Street, ©6921 3646.
The Rivergum Restaurant, Sturt Highway, ©6922 7256.
La Porchetta Pizza Restaurant, 161 Baylis Street, ©6921 5122.

McDonalds and Pizza Hut are in Edward Street, and KFC is on the corner of Edward and Baylis Streets, and in Fitzmaurice Street.

Points of Interest

The Visitor Information Centre has maps of three **historic walks** through the city which were put together by the National Trust.

Amongst other places these walks highlight many of the historic buildings which date from 1865, including houses, churches, old gas works, police station, Lands Department, Court House, Post Office and the ANZ Bank.

The Centre also has copies of the 28km (17 miles) **Red Arrow Tour**, which takes about an hour by car, and the Wollundry Loop, a 10km (6 miles) loop following Wollundry Lagoon and the river bank.

In 1999 an impressive new **Civic Centre** was opened. It contains the regional art gallery, the Museum of the Riverina and the national art glass gallery. The city is proud of its civic centrepiece, and it is worth stopping in to have a look.

The **Wagga Wagga Regional Art Gallery**, on the corner of Bayliss

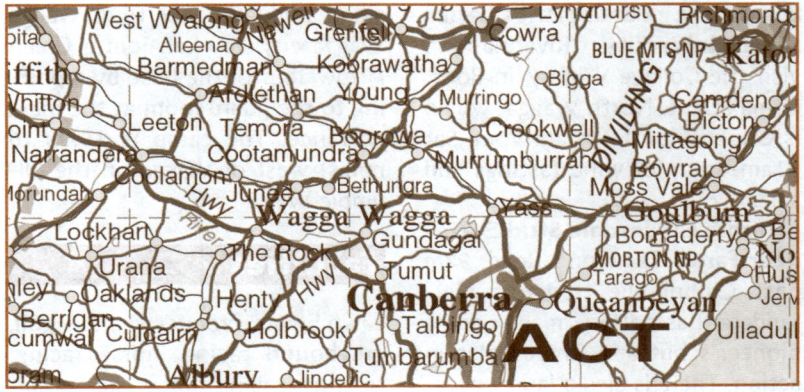

and Morrow Streets, has changing exhibitions of international, national and regional art. It is ☉open Mon, Wed-Sat 11am-5pm, Sun 2-5pm, ✆6926 9610.

The **Wagga Wagga and District Historical Museum** in Willan's Hill, ✆6925 2934, is open weekends, public holidays and school holidays, and ☉Tues-Wed from 2pm.

Wagga Wagga is the Garden City of the South, and the many parks and gardens range from the formal **Shakespearian Garden** to **Apex Park** located on the shores of Lake Albert.

The **Botanic Gardens**, ✆6923 5499, are set in 8.9ha (22 acres) on Willans Hill, and have many garden displays such as the Tree Chapel, with trees and shrubs of biblical significance, a rough-hewn cross and altar, complete with pews, which is a popular spot for weddings. Also in the Gardens are the Camellia, Cactus, Succulent and Shakespearian Gardens, and an Outdoor Entertainment Centre and Music Bowl which can accommodate a symphony orchestra and has seating for 3,000 people. A model railway runs through the gardens and features a station and booking office. The train operates on the 1st and 3rd Sundays of the month.

Wagga Wagga City Library is in Gurwood Street, and is the headquarters of a regional library. The service caters for 89,000 people in seven council areas - Coolamon, Cootamundra, Gundagai, Lockhart, Temora and Tumut. It is ☉open Mon-Fri 9am-8pm, Sat 9am-noon.

Sunday Markets are held from 8am-noon in Woolworth's Car Park.

Visitors are welcome to drive

through the grounds of the **Charles Sturt University** - Riverina, and visit the College Winery, in Boorooma Street, North Wagga, which is ☉open Mon-Fri 10am-4pm, Sat 11am-4pm, for wine tastings and sales.

Aurora Clydesdale Stud & Pioneer Farm, Cameron's Road, 9km past Collingullie, towards Narrandera, has antique machinery, a pioneer's hut and Clydesdales in action. There is also a large collection of birds and animals, ✆6928 2215 for information and times.

Murray Cod Hatcheries and Fauna Park on the Sturt Highway, ✆6922 7360, is home to Big Murray, a 52kg (115 lb) Murray Cod, who measures 1.37m (4.5 ft). The park also has Crab Eating Macaquehs (monkeys) from South East Asia, native snakes, camels, wombats, koalas, kangaroos, native fish and many native birds. There is a gift shop selling pottery, paintings and souvenirs, and a snack bar. Barbecues and playground equipment are set in the picnic area, and the complex is ☉open daily 8.30am-5.30pm.

Kapooka Military Camp invites visitors to view the parades held each Monday at 11am. The camp is the base for the Army's 1st Recruit Training Battalion. The Kapooka Band performs during the parades, and holds a series of Music at Midday concerts in Wagga Wagga city. You can join a Green Arrow Tour of the base by reporting to the guard room at the main entrance. The camp is 10km (6 miles) west of Wagga on the Olympic Way.

Facilities

Lawn bowls, croquet, fishing, golf, greyhound racing, horse racing, trotting, sailing, water skiing, sailing, swimming, boating and tennis. The city has 4 licensed Clubs with dining facilities and poker machines.

Festivals

The Gumi Festival is held on the last Saturday in February each year. Gumi is pidgin for 'rubber', and the Gumi Race consists of hundreds of craft made from inner tubes floating down the 11km course on the Murrumbidgee River.

The Wagga Wagga Agricultural Show is held over the long weekend in October (the first Monday in October sets the dates of the long weekend).

Outlying Attractions

Lockhart

Proceed south from Wagga Wagga along the Olympic Way to The

Rock, then turn left. Lockhart is 42km (26 miles) further on. The Rock (the town), originally named Kingston, is located 6km east of craggy outcrops which rise more than 360m (1181 ft) above the surrounding districts. The peak of the Rock Hill Nature Reserve is the only place in Australia where the Senecio wildflower is found. The Yerong Nature Trail within the Reserve takes about 3 hours to complete, and is worth the effort. The 3km track is gentle on the lower slopes, but fairly steep at the higher levels.

Lockhart has a well shaded caravan park, a motel and licensed Ex-Services, golf and bowling clubs. The centre of the town is an outstanding example of a turn-of-the-century streetscape, and has been classified by the National Trust. Also classified is the Old Urangeline Woolshed, which originally had 100 shearing stands. It is built from local timber with a shingle roof, and although on private property, is open for inspection by arrangement. Contact the Tourist Information Centre in Wagga Wagga, ©6926 9621, for details.

The Pioneer Memorial Gates, is an unusual structure set at the entrance of the Lockhart Showground. The 22 'wool bales' are branded with the stencils of original homesteads. The Lockhart Museum, in 45 Urana Street, ©6920 5674, contains many fine memories of the district's pioneering past.

Approximately 16km (10 miles) north of Lockhart is Galore Hill Recreation Reserve. The reserve comprises 510ha (1260 acres) of natural bushland, and Galore Hill rises to a height of 215m (705 ft) above the surrounding countryside.

Coolamon Shire

The shire includes the townships of Coolamon, Ardlethan, Ganmain, Beckom, Grong Grong, Matong and Marrar, and is the agricultural centre of the Riverina.

Ganmain, situated between Junee and Narrandera, is the centre of the chaff industry of Australia, and the residents, with the aid of the Shire Council, have constructed a building in Pioneer Park, Ford Street, to give the impression of a haystack. From the viewing area you can see a workable binder, a mural of a hay scene, photographs and history of hay in the district, and a video giving an insight into the hay industry.

Coolamon is 39km (24 miles) north-west of Wagga Wagga, and has many old world antique shops. The Coolamon Golf Club, ©6927 3178, welcomes visitors to play a round on the sand green course, and visit their Chinese restaurant.

Junee

The town of Junee is built to an

unusual plan with the railway running down the middle of the central business district. The railway has been important to the town as is shown by the impressive railway station, built in 1883.

Monte Cristo, a homestead in traditional Georgian design, is ☉open daily 10am-4pm, and is a museum of Victorian furniture and antiques.

Temora

Temora, a centre Harness Racing (Paleface Adios, the famous pacer, and winner of the Inter Dominion, was born here), was established after the 1880 gold rush when the famous Mother Shipton nugget weighing 258 ounces was found. The decline of gold saw the town become a major wheat growing district.

Most of the mining areas have disappeared, though several, including the Mother Shipton mine, are located off Moroney's Lane.

The Temora Rural Museum, ✆6977 1291, is ☉open daily 2-5pm, and is a .8ha (2 acres) complex with agricultural machinery, antique tractors and engines, a pioneer cottage with lifestyles of yesterday, and a rock and mineral display.

The Temora Visitor Information Centre is at 294 -296 Hoskins Street, ✆6977 1511.

Cootamundra

The town of Cootamundra, with a population of 6,600, is the home of the Cootamundra Wattle (Acacia Baileyana) and the birthplace of the late Sir Donald Bradman, Australia's famous cricketer. The cottage where he was born is privately owned but may be viewed from the street (89 Adams Street).

The focal point of the township is the Bicentennial Post Office Plaza, which incorporates the historical post office building and clock tower, and the old Peppercorn tree.

Pioneer Park, on the southern outskirts of Cootamundra, off the Olympic Way, commands extensive views of the town and district.

Bethungra Rail Spiral is 23km (14 miles) south-west of Cootamundra, and is a unique engineering feat. The rail line spirals around Bethungra Hill, crossing itself and the south line while traversing some of the deepest rail cuttings in Australia.

The Cootamundra Tourist Information Centre, Hovell Street, ✆(02) 6942 4212.

Gundagai

The famous Dog on the Tucker Box is, as every Australian knows, 5 miles (8km) from (north of) Gundagai, on the western side of the Hume Highway. Opposite the memorial to Mateship between man and dog, are copper representations of the Dog, and Dad, Dave, Mum and Mabel at Snake Gully, the characters of Steele Rudd.

The Gundagai Visitor Information Centre, 294 Sheridan Street, ✆(02) 69 44 1341, is ☉open daily Mon-Fri 8am-5pm, Sat-Sun 9am-5pm. You can contact them by email at ✉ztc1@gundagaishire.nsw.gov.au. The Centre houses the Rusconi Marble Masterpiece, a cathedral in miniature containing 20,948 pieces of NSW marble, built by Mr Frank Rusconi in his spare time over a period of 28 years. The Centre also has a gemstone collection, flood inundation maps and flood scenes of Gundagai.

The walking tour, devised by the Tourist Centre, takes in: the Dr Gabriel Gallery; the Court House built in 1859, where Moonlight the Bushranger was tried; the Gundagai Historic Museum; the Old Flour Mill constructed in 1849; and the two bridges, Railway Bridge, 1901, and Prince Alfred Bridge, 1866, the longest timber viaduct in Australia.

The Tourist Centre also has details of the Mount Parnassus Walking Tour, and can arrange coach tours and canoe tours of the Murrumbidgee and Tumut Rivers.

On the Hume Highway is the Tucker Box Tourist Centre, ✆(02) 6944 1450, which serves as an alternative information source.

Tumut

In 1824, Explorers Hume and Hovell crossed the Tumut River slightly south of the site of present day Tumut. The local natives called the area Doomat or Tumott, which meant "quiet resting place by the river".

In the early days, Tumut was squatter country, and was populated mainly by unfriendly Aboriginals. The town grew slowly, and by 1856 had one school, several slab and bark buildings, and three hotels. By 1870, the number of hotels had grown to 18. Dairy farming was the main industry then, but today, timber is big business, particularly softwood like Pinus Radiata, with 52,520ha (130,000 acres) being grown within 25km (16 miles) of Tumut.

Tumut is now a town of around 6,000 people, and the Festival of the Falling Leaf is held there every year in April-May. There are street parades, band recitals, Plaza Night and a Family Fun Day at the Sports Club.

Tumut is 128km (80 miles) west of Canberra, about midway between Sydney and Melbourne, and is the gateway to the giant Snowy Mountains Scheme. The town is surrounded very picturesque countryside, and the rivers and mountain streams within easy access are stocked with trout.

There are regular air and rail services to Tumut, the road access is very good, and the climate averages between 35C (95F) in summer to a low of 5C (41F). The Visitor Information Centre is at the Old Butter Factory, 5 Adelong Road, ✆(02) 6947 7025.

The Yarrangobilly Caves, which are covered in the Snowy Mountains section, are 77km (48 miles) south of Tumut.

Griffith

Located 196km north west of Wagga Wagga, Griffith is worth considering for a day trip or overnight stay. It is part of the Riverina district, its soil made rich and fertile by the irrigation scheme bringing water all the way from the Snowy Mountains. Wine, fruits, vegetables, rice, and poultry products are grown and cultivated here.

There are a number of interesting attrations, including the extensive Pioneer Park museum, the Regional Art Gallery, Catania Fruit Farm, and the natural wonders of Lake Wyangan and Cocoparra National Park.

Griffith Visitor Information Centre, cnr Banna & Jondaryan Avenues, ✆6962 4145 or ✆1800 681 141. You can email them at ✉ griffithvc@griffith.nsw.gov.au

New South Wales – South-West

Albury-Wodonga

Population 68,000
The twin cities of Albury-Wodonga sit astride the magnificent Murray River, touching the edges of the Upper Murray, North-East Victoria, the Riverina, the South-West Slopes of NSW and the Murray Valley. Distance from Sydney 592km (368 miles), from Canberra 195km (121 miles), and from Melbourne 300km (186 miles).

Climate

Average temperatures: January max 32C (90F) - min 15C (55F); June max 14C (57F) - min 2C (36F). Average annual rainfall: 796mm (31 ins) - wettest month August. Elevation - 195m (640 ft) above sea level.

Characteristics

Hume and Hovell carved their names in trees beside the Murray in 1824 and Hovell's still stands today. In 1836, Robert Brown arrived and constructed a punt to cross the river, built an inn, and the settlement was born. In 1974 Albury-Wodonga was designated the national growth centre.

How to Get There

By Bus
Greyhound Pioneer travel to/from Melbourne, Sydney, Canberra and Brisbane.

By Rail
Albury-Wodonga is three hours by

train from Melbourne on the Sydney/Melbourne route.

By Road

From Sydney and Melbourne via the Hume Highway; from Mildura along the Murray Valley Highway; from Brisbane via the Newell Highway and the Riverina Highway.

Tourist Information

Tourist Albury Wodonga Gateway Information Centre, is in Lincoln Causeway, ℂ6041 3875, freecall ℂ1800 800 743.

Accommodation

The twin towns have 50 quality hotels and motels and 7 caravan parks. Here is a selection with prices for a double room per night, which should be used as a guide only. The telephone area code is 02.

Country Comfort Albury, Dean Street, ℂ6021 5366. 140 rooms, licensed restaurant, heated swimming pool, spa, sauna - ✪$130.

Sundowner Chain Motor Inns, Hovell Tree, cnr Hume Highway and Hovell Streets, ℂ6041 2666. 40 units, licensed restaurant, swimming pool, spa, sauna, gym, undercover parking - ✪$115-205.

Elm Court Motel, 435 Townsend Street, ℂ6021 8077. 31 units, indoor heated swimming pool, spa, barbecue - ✪$80-85.

Matador Motor Inn, 617 Young Street, ℂ6021 1877. 60 units, licensed restaurant, indoor heated swimming pool, spa, gym, sauna, barbecue - ✪$85-100.

Commodore, 515 Kiewa Street, ℂ6021 3344. 40 units, licensed restaurant (closed Sunday) - ✪$80-85.

Sodens Australia Hotel/Motel, cnr David & Wilson Street, ℂ6021 2400. 50 units, licensed restaurant, barbecue - ✪$40-45.

Caravan Parks

Trek-31 Tourist Park, cnr Wagga Road & Catherine Crescent, ℂ6025 4051. (No pets allowed)119 sites, excellent facilities, pool, barbecue - powered sites ✪$19-22 for two, cabins $45-75 for two.

Albury Central Tourist Park, North Street, ℂ6021 8420. (Pets allowed under control) 127 sites, barbecue, tennis, playground, pool - powered sites ✪$16 for two, cabins $45-55 for two.

Eating Out

Albury-Wodonga offers a diverse range of cuisine styles from fine dining to fast service takeaway. Here are a few you might like to try.

Santino's Licensed Family Bistro, 14 City Walk, Dean Street, ℂ6041 1997 - caters for all seven days and nights.

Il Sogno Restaurant, 639 Dean Street, ©6023 4585 - proclaim themselves 'The Flavour of Italy'.

Puti Vegetarian Restaurant, 1083 Mate Street, ©6025 0086 - takeaway available.

One Six Eight, 1081 Mate Street, ©6025 9816 - Chinese cuisine.

Gourmet Inn Restaurant, 473b Dean Street, ©6021 4321.

Thai Grand Palace Restaurant, 592 Kiewa Street, ©6041 1238.

Indian Tandoori Restaurant, 449a Dean Street, ©6041 4705.

Beefeater's Bistro, 324 Wodonga Place, ©6041 1711.

Points of Interest

The most famous attraction is, of course, the Murray River, which starts as a tiny stream fed by melting snow high on the Australians Alps, near the NSW-Victorian border. Slowed by Lake Hume, the river's twists and turns divide the two cities of Albury and Wodonga. It then flows on to enter the Southern Ocean through Lake Alexandrina in South Australia, 2500km (1553 miles) from its source. The total Murray system, including the Darling and Murrumbidgee rivers and their tributaries, drains a seventh of the total area of Australia. The Murray supplies 49% of SA's domestic and industrial requirements, and almost all the water for irrigation.

The first industry of the area was established by Robert Brown in 1838, when he built a rough punt at the Crossing Place, followed by an accommodation house for travellers. This established a tradition for the district, and Albury-

Wodonga today has more 'accommodation houses' than any other Australian country centre.

Albury-Wodonga's river queen, the **PS Cumberoona**, was modelled on a former steamer of the same name that chugged up and down the Murray in the heyday of the paddelsteamer trade, and was the flagship of the Albury Steam Navigation Co. The new paddlesteamer operates daily from October through to May, depending on water flow and water level, which depends on the release of irrigation water from Lake Hume.

Other attractions are: **Kinross Woolshed**, which hosts bush dances and jazz nights; **Frog Hollow**, complete with a maze, minature golf and Mr F. Frog; **Hume Weir Trout Farm**, the largest trout farm in the area; and the restored **Cobb & Co** coaches that provide an alternative method of transport.

15km (9 miles) north of Albury is the original **Ettamogah Pub**. As their ad says, "the Ettamogah Mob needed a good excuse to work up a thirst...so we built a town around our Pub", and the end result is a complex which will keep every member of the family occupied for hours. For the kids, there is the Comedy Cop Shop (police station), dodgem cars, and a lock up if they misbehave. For the parents, there's a pottery and a bladesmith's, a souvenir shop selling only Aussie made, and the Winery with good quality wine at cellar door prices. For all, there is good Aussie tucker at the pub, and at the Ettamogah Cafe, or you might prefer Coopers Courtyard Restaurant next to the Winery. The Pub, ©6026 2366, is ☺open daily 9am-midnight, and the Winery is open Mon-Fri 9am-5pm, Sat 10am-5pm, Sun 9am-4pm.

At **Albury Pottery**, Lincoln Causeway, Wodonga, ©6041 6835, you can take a self-guiding tour and watch the potters at work - ☺open daily. If it's culture you seek, the **Albury Regional Art Centre**, 546 Dean Street, Albury, the **Museum**, 66 South Street, Wodonga, the **Pioneer Museum** in Urana Street, Jindera, and the **Albury Botanical Gardens** will get you off to a good start.

Albury's licensed **Clubs** provide meals, entertainment and, of course, poker machines. Thousands of people from Victoria travel to Albury to try and win the big one at the "pokies".

For **aquatic sport**, head for Lake Hume, only 12km (7 miles) upstream from town. It has 320km (199 miles) of shoreline, and is ideal for sailing, swimming, water skiing, canoeing, windsurfing, pedal boating and fishing. If you intend to fish, make sure you have both a NSW and Victorian Fishing Licence. The

Wyamah ferry links NSW with Victoria, and is operated by friendly folk. At Dora Dora there is a 130-year-old hotel which is more like an entertainment centre than a pub.

There is a lovely **Riverbank Walk** at Albury (Travel Centre has leaflets). The 7.5km (5 miles) marked trails from Nail Can Hill go along the river, over Monument Hill and past old gold diggings.

A visit to the **Flying Fruit Fly Circus** is a must - for booking and details, ✆6021 7044.

Facilities

The area has 14 licensed lawn bowls clubs. Canoes can be hired, and water skiing tuition is available on Lake Hume. Regular horse racing meetings are held in Albury/Wodonga. Other facilities include golf, tennis, fishing (cod, perch and trout) and swimming (pool and river).

Festivals

Winery Walkabout is held over the long weekend in June. and the Golden Horseshoe Festival is held at Easter.

Outlying Attractions

Howlong
A typical Murray River township,

Howlong is 26km (16 miles) west of Albury on the Riverina Highway. The town's river frontages are ideal for walking, horseriding and photography, and the river offers boating, fishing and swimming. The town gets its name, which means 'the beginning of the plain', from the Howlong run, a property of 20,000ha (49,400 acres) that fronts the river.

Corowa
Corowa is 56km (35 miles) west of Albury, and its wide main street extends to the Murray River's banks. The Tourist Information Centre is in Sanger Street, ✆6033 3221, and they have information on accommodation, and the many buildings of historical and architectural interest. They are ◷open 9am-5pm daily and can be emailed at ✎ corowa.tourinfo@albury.net.au. Additional information is available on the internet at 👁www.corowa. nsw.gov.au

Corowa is known as the birthplace of Australian federation. When Victoria broke away from NSW in 1835 to become a separate colony, it caused the constant irritation of dealing with customs officers stationed at every crossing place along the Murray River, the convenient natural border between the two colonies. The citizens of Corowa and Wahgunyah on the other side of the river, were particularly affected, and the first Border Federation League was established in Corowa in January, 1893. The historic conference of the various border leagues was held in July of that year, and together they continued to agitate until the referendum of 1898, when the decision in favour of federation was carried.

Anyone interested in Australian history should visit Corowa's Federation Museum in Queen Street, ☎6033 1568.

Mulwala

The town of Mulwala is 40km (25 miles) west of Corowa, and is renowned for its year-round mild climate. Nearby Lake Mulwala offers swimming, sailing and cruising.

Mulwala is often linked with Yarrawonga, on the other side of the river, and the Tourist Information is there on the corner of Irvine & Blemore Streets, ☎5744 1989 or ☎1800 062 260. There is a website at 👁www.yarrawongamulwalainfo.com and their email address is ✉ymt@cnl.com.au

Jindera

Only about 20km (12 miles) northwest of Albury, Jindera has a Pioneer Museum that is rated a world-class attraction. It is housed in an old store and home that belonged to the pioneering Wagner family, and the store is stocked with authentic goods of the 19th century. The Museum is ⏰open daily 10am-4.30pm, ☎6026 3622.

The Jindera district was settled in the 1860s by German migrants, the township was gazetted in 1869, and a century later a cairn was erected to honour these pioneering families.

Culcairn

Culcairn is 53km (33 miles) north of Albury-Wodonga, in the heart of 'Morgan' country. Other towns in the area are Henty, Walla, Jindera, Gerogery, Cookardinia, Morven and Walbundrie.

Bushranger Dan Morgan began his criminal career at Round Hill at Culcairn in June, 1864. Events surrounding the incident can be read at a site overlooking Round Hill, about 3km east on the Holbrook Road.

On August 28, 1864, Dan Morgan raided a police camp at Doodle Cooma, now Henty. Four policemen and a blacktracker who had spent all day searching for Morgan had retired to bed. When Sen-Sgt Smyth lit a candle after 11pm to read the Border Post newspaper, Trooper O'Connor pointed out the serious risk of having a light in the tent at such a late hour. Even before the candle could be extinguished, a bullet whistled through the tent. As the five men rushed outside a further six bullets tore through the canvas, and Smyth was hit. He died at Albury, and a magisterial inquiry found his death was wilful murder, recorded against Daniel Morgan.

A life-sized effigy of Dan Morgan is displayed in the Billabong Art and Crafts Centre's 'Mad Dog Morgan' art cellar. The effigy was made for the movie of the same name, filmed in the district in 1975, and the first Australian film to win an award at the Cannes Film Festival.

Holbrook

The Tourist Information Office is in the Woolpack Inn Museum, ✆(02) 60 36 2131, email ✉woolpack @dragnet.com.au, ☺open daily 9.30am-4.30pm. Behind the museum is an enclosed area with a vast array of horse-drawn vehicles and farming equipment. The museum also has a section devoted to the exploits of Cdr Norman Holbrook, after whom the town was named. In December, 1914, British submarine commander Lt Norman Holbrook guided a B11 submarine below a minefield to torpedo an enemy Turkish battleship, the Messudiya. The submarine was immediately attacked by destroyers and on-shore forts, and during the trip back through the minefields Holbrook and his crew were forced to stay submerged for nine hours, an incredible feat for a 1914 submarine.

At this time the town was called Germanton, but the wave of anti-German feelings caused by World War I had the citizens searching for a new name. The news of the extraordinary bravery exhibited by the British submarine crew ended their search, and the town became Holbrook.

Holbrook is midway between Sydney and Melbourne on the Hume Highway, and still provides a resting point for travellers, as it did in its early days as a staging post. Ten Mile Creek park divides the town, providing restful, attractive areas merging into a flora and fauna reserve.

It should be noted that the towns in the rest of this section are south of the New South Wales/Victorian border, and are therefore all in the state of Victoria.

Rutherglen

The heart of the North-East Winery centre, Rutherglen has thirteen wineries in the immediate area, that are well known for their fortified wines, and have wine tastings and cellar door sales. You can pick up a pamphlet in the town called 'Winemakers of Rutherglen', which shows where all the wineries are.

Special events in the town are:

The Tastes of Rutherglen, held over the Victorian Labour Day Weekend in March; Winery Walkabout, held over the Queen's Birthday Weekend in June; and Rutherglen Wine Show, in September. If you are visiting at these times, it is wise to book ahead.

Rutherglen is 42km (26 miles) from Wodonga, on the Valley Highway.

Lake Moodemere, 8km (5 miles) west of Rutherglen, is classified as a Wildlife Reserve, and is suitable for small boats and fishing. Picnic spots are nearby.

The Rutherglen Visitor Information Centre is at 13 -27 Drummond Street, ©(02) 6032 9166 or freecall ©1800 622 871.

Chiltern

Chiltern, in 1974, was the scene of the Walt Disney film *Ride Wild Pony* and the appearance of the town's centre was transformed to a 1920s setting. It was also the location for Crawford Productions mini-series *My Brother Tom*. Its other claim to fame was that the famous author Henry Handel (Florence Ethel) Richardson, who wrote among other titles, *The Getting of Wisdom* and *The Fortunes of Richard Mahony*, spent her childhood in Chiltern and described her experiences in *Ultima Thule*. Her home, Lake View, has been restored by the National Trust.

Yackandandah

First settled in the 1840s by miners, this old gold town, together with the surrounding hills, are classified by the National Trust. The appearance and pace of life in the town has changed little in the past hundred years. Today the centre of a renowned grazing district, the houses along the main street have a 19th century appearance and charm.

The surrounding countryside is very pretty with streams and valleys nestling between bush clad hills. There are plenty of places for fishermen to throw in a line.

Beechworth

Beechworth is 40km (25 miles) south-west of Albury, and 35km (22 miles) east of Wangaratta, and is Victoria's best preserved gold town, with 32 buildings classified by the National Trust. The Golden Horseshoe Festival held each Easter, recalls the early days. It gets its name from an incident in 1855 when, caught up in the excitement of their first parliamentary election, the Beechworth miners shod their new representative Daniel Cameron's horse with shoes made of pure gold. Cameron then rode through the town to the Star Hotel, and gave his policy speech from the balcony. A monument in Sydney Road marks the spot where the horse was shod.

The town also lays claim to being at the heart of Kelly Country. (Ned Kelly is Australia's best known Bushranger of the 19th century.) Ned made three appearances in the Court House, the last being on the charge of murder for which he was subsequently hanged.

The journey from Wodonga to Wangaratta, via Beechworth, along the 'Kelly Way', is only 5km (3 miles) longer than by the Hume Highway.

Local attractions include: Beechworth Cemetery with its Chinese Burning Towers and Prayer Altar, and a plaque dedicated to Dame Jean MacNamara, who introduced Myxamatosis to Australia in an effort to control the rabbit plague; But-But Tree, cnr Tanswell & Anderson Streets, one of Australia's largest trees; Fletcher's Dam; HM Training Prison that once hosted Ned Kelly; the Burke Museum, named after Captain Robert O'Hara Burke, of Burke and Wills fame who had been the superintendent of police in Beechworth; Gorge Road and One Tree Hill Scenic Drive, starts from the Golden Horseshoe's Monument, and a box near there has notes on the rest of the drive.

The Beechworth Tourist Information Centre is in 36 Camp Street, ✆(03) 5728 1374, email ✉ binfo@ dragnet.com.au. The website to visit is ☞www.beechworth.com

Wangaratta

Located at the junction of the Ovens and King Rivers, Wangaratta is a good base from which to explore the Wine and High Mountain Country.

The town was founded in 1838, and originally known as Ovens Crossing. The name was changed in 1863 to Wangaratta, which means 'Resting Place of the Cormorant'. Today it is a thriving town of around 17,000 people, with colonial style buildings side by side with recent designs.

The Wangaratta & Region Visitor Information Centre is on the corner of Tone Road (Hume Highway) and Handley Street, ✆(03) 5721 5711, and is ☉open seven days. There is a website at ☞www. wangarattaunlimited.vic.gov.au. The Centre has information on accommodation and restaurants, as well as sightseeing.

Attractions include: Bushranger Dan (Mad Dog) Morgan's grave, in the South Wangaratta Cemetery on the Hume Highway. Only his body is here, his head was sent to Melbourne for analysis after his execution!; the Pioneer Cemetery on the banks of the King River; Airworld, 7km (4 miles) south of town, the largest collection of flying antique civil aircraft in the world, with other collections of antique bicycles and Holden cars; Warby Range State Park; the Fire Station Museum in Ford Street; and Eldorado Dredge, the last remaining gold dredge in Victoria.

Glenrowan

The scene of Ned Kelly's last stand is 14km (9 miles) south of Wangaratta, and even if you haven't been caught up in the almost hero-worship of Ned, you can't help but be impressed by this town which is almost entirely devoted to his memorabilia.

There are seven wineries in the area as well, so why not pop in, taste some wine, and discuss the rights and wrongs of the 1880 execution.

The Glenrowan Tourist Centre is in the tourist attraction theme park on the Hume Hwy, ©(03) 5766 2367.

New South Wales – South

Wollongong

Population 219,800
Wollongong is situated on the coast of New South Wales, 80km (50 miles) from Sydney, and 238km (148 miles) from Canberra.

Climate

Average temperatures: January max 26C (79F) - min 18C (64F); July max 17C (63F) - min 9C (48F). Average annual rainfall: 1275mm (50 ins).

Characteristics

Wollongong is the seventh largest city in Australia, and the gateway to the Illawarra and Southern Highlands region. To its north, cosy mining villages dot the coastline against a dramatic backdrop of green escarpment. Here the Illawarra coastal plain is narrowest, at times reduced to nothing, as rocky sea cliffs reach right to the pounding waves.

In the seaside village of Thirroul, D.H. Lawrence wrote *Kangaroo*, and from Stanwell Park, aviator Lawrence Hargraves tested his kites.

How to Get There

By Rail
Electric trains run regularly between Sydney's Central Station and Wollongong, connecting with ongoing services to Port Kembla and south to Bomaderry on Nowra's northern outskirts, ✆13 2232.

By Bus
Greyhound Pioneer, ✆13 2030, and McCaffertys, ✆13 1499, stop at Wollongong daily on their Sydney/

Melbourne via the Princes Highway services.

By Road

From Sydney, via the Princes Highway to Waterfall and then the F6, or continue along the highway and turn off at the Stanwell Park signpost for a spectacular drive along the coast.

Another interesting route is via the National Park to Stanwell Park - turn off just past Sutherland.

Visitor Information

The Wollongong Visitor Information Centre, 93 Crown Street (corner of Kembla Street), ℂ(02) 4277 5545 or ✆1 800 240 737 (free call), is ☺open seven days a week 9am-5pm Mon-Fri, 9am-4pm Sat and 10am-4pm Sun. They can be emailed at ✉tourism@wollongong .nsw.gov.au and the website to explore is ☞www.wollongong.nsw. gov.au

Accommodation

The Illawarra coast boasts a comprehensive range of accommodation from caravan parks on many of the beaches and lakesides, to an international style resort hotel, leisure village, quality motels, hotels, holiday units and superb convention facilities. Here is a selection with prices for a double room per night, which should be used as a guide only. The telephone area code is 02.

Novotel Northbeach, 2 Cliff Road, ℂ4226 3555. 203 rooms, 17 suites, licensed restaurants, swimming pool, spa, sauna, gym, tennis, bicycling - ✪$230-360.

City Pacific Boutique Hotel, 112 Burelli Street, ℂ4229 7444. 61 rooms, licensed restaurant, swimming pool - ✪$75-250.

Boat Harbour Motel, 7 Campbell Street, ℂ4228 9166. 42 units, licensed restaurant (closed Sun and public holidays) - ✪$115-140.

Golden Pacific North Beach, 16 Pleasant Avenue, North Wollongong, ℂ4226 3000. 20 units, 2 suites - ✪$95-180.

Downtown Motel, 76 Crown Street, ℂ4229 8344. 31 units, licensed restaurant (closed Sun) - ✪$75-100.

Beach Park Motor Inn, 10 Pleasant Avenue, North Wollongong, ℂ4226 1577. 16 units, barbecue - ✪$60-170.

Caravan Parks

Corrimal Beach Tourist Park, Lake Parade, Corrimal, ℂ4285 5688. 397 sites, barbecue - unpowered sites ✪$15-25 for two, cabins $60-165 for two.

Windang Beach Tourist Park, Fern Street, ℂ4297 3166. (No pets) 259 sites, barbecue - unpowered sites ✪$15-25 for two, cabins $60-165 for two, bungalows $40-70 for two.

Bulli Beach Tourist Park, 1 Farrell Road, ℂ4285 5677. (No pets allowed), 269 sites - powered sites ✪$20-25 for two, cabins $60-165 for two.

Eating Out

Wollongong's cosmopolitan community offers you a wide choice of superb restaurants, snack bars and coffee lounges. Here are some you might like to try.

Fuji Yama Tepan Restaurant, 35 Flinders Street, ℂ4226 2609, specialise in Japanese barbecues.

Charcoal Tavern, 18 Regent Street, ℂ4229 7298. Modern Australian dining, seafood and steaks.

Nam, 4 Kenny Street, ℂ4228 3646. Vietnamese and Chinese food.

Beach House Seafood Restaurant, 16 Cliff Road, ℂ4228 5410.

Anchorage, cnr Campbell & Wilson Streets, ℂ4228 9166. A-la-carte menu and beach views.

Branches, Blackbutt Motel, Shellharbour Road, Shellharbour, ℂ4297 1323. Italian and seafood.

Zita's, 147-149 Corrimal Street, ℂ4227 1110. French, Italian and German cuisine with local seafood.

King's, 26 Flinders Street, North Wollongong, ℂ4228 6976. Chinese cuisine.

Amigos, 116 Keira Street, ℂ4229 8181. Mexican selection.

Bangkok Orchid Thai, Shop 1, 119 Corrimal Street, ℂ4229 6620.

Mammas Pizza Roma, 56 Crown Street, ℂ4229 9166.

Tandoori Village Indian Restaurant, Shop 2, 120 Corrimal Street, ℂ4225 7876.

During business hours a good place to eat is the Food Court, lower level of the Gateway on the Mall shopping complex, cnr Burelli & Keira Streets. They have tables in the centre and you can choose from Chinese, Italian, Austrian, Mexican, crepes, chicken, pies, kebabs, hamburgers, and so on.

McDonald's have outlets at 115 Corrimal Street and Wollongong Crown Central, Shop 97, 200 Crown Street. There are branches in all other Wollongong localities as well.

Pizza Hut have outlets in localities surrrounding Wollongong. You will find them on the corner of the Priness Highway and McGrath Street, Fairy Meadow, 32 Princes Highway, Dapto and on the corner of King Street and Kemblawarra Place in Warrawong.

KFC can be found at cnr Princes Highway & McGrath Street, Fairy Meadow; 74 Princes Highway, Unanderra; cnr Kemblawarra Road & King Street, Warrawong; 136 Princes Highway, Dapto; and Holm Place, Shellharbour Square.

Entertainment

For those who want to boogie the night away, there are many night clubs and discos, as well as the licensed clubs. The clubs in Wollongong itself are:

Collegians RLFC, 3A Charlotte Street,t, ℂ4229 7711.

Illawarra Master Builders, 61 Church Street, ℂ4229 6466.

Illawarra Leagues Club, 87 Church Street, ℂ4229 4611.

Wollongong Ex-Services, 82 Church Street, ℂ4228 8522.

For movie goers, Wollongong has two cinema complexes:

Regent Theatre, 197 Keira Street, ℂ4228 9238.

Town Cinemas, Burelli Street, ℂ4228 4888.

The *Illawarra Performing Arts Centre*, Burelli Street, ℂ4226 3366, has live theatre and musical presentations.

Points of Interest

Most historic buildings can be visited on a **walking tour** commencing at Flagstaff Hill (parking available). The sights visited are: Wollongong Head Lighthouse; Breakwater Lighthouse; Belmore Basin; Drill Hall; Throsby's stockman's hut monument; Market Square; Illawarra Historical Museum; Congregational Church;

Wollongong Courthouse; St Michael's Provisional Cathedral; Wollongong Uniting Church; The Town Hall; Wollongong East Post Office; Tour-ist Information office; St Francis Xavier's Provisional Cathedral; and Andrew Lysaght Park.

Mount Kembla Historic Village, 7km (4 miles) from Wollongong was the site of the 1902 mining disaster, but it is full of art and craft centres today.

Wollongong Botanic Garden, in Keiraville, is a pleasant spot for picnics and quiet walks, and offers many areas of interest - Sir Joseph Banks Plant Houses, where plants from the wet tropics, deserts and temperate regions are displayed; The Rose Garden; Woodland Garden; Flowering Trees and Shrub Garden; Succulent Plants from South Africa and Central America; Australian Plant Habitats; and The Herb Garden. The Garden is ☺open daily 7am-4.45pm Mon-Fri and 10am-4.45pm Sat-Sun. During winter the gardens close at 6.45pm.

The **Wollongong City Art Gallery**, 85 Burelli Street, ©4228 7500, has a fine collection of modern and traditional paintings, with changing exhibitions. It is ☺open Tue-Fri 10am-5pm, Sat-Sun noon-4pm.

Magnificent views of the coastline can be obtained from **Mount Kembla Lookout, Sublime Point** and **Bulli Lookout**, all of which are only about 15 to 20 minutes' drive from the centre of town.

Kelly's Falls, 2km off the Princes Highway at Stanwell Tops, has a picnic area and easy walking tracks to the falls. Flannel flowers are abundant in spring and early summer.

Nearby is **Symbio Wildlife Gardens**, 7 Lawrence Hargrave Drive, ©4294 1088, which has native and exotic animals, free barbecues, swimming and wading pools and lunchtime demonstrations of activities from milking a cow to handling reptiles. The gardens are hopen daily from 9.30am, and they advertise that feeding time is 'all the time'. To get to these attractions, take the old Princes Highway from Wollongong, not the F6.

While you are in the area, drive north for half an hour to **Bald Hill Lookout**, where there is a memorial to Lawrence Hargraves, and if the wind is favourable you will see many brightly coloured hang-gliders floating by.

Stanwell Park is in the valley below, and you can call in and browse through Articles Fine Arts Gallery, 111 Lawrence Hargrave Drive, ©4294 2491, and have a Devonshire tea on the outdoor terrace. The hang-gliders land in the part next to the sea.

South of Wollongong is **Lake Illawarra**, renowned for fishing and

prawning, and often ablaze with colourful sailing boats and sail boards. The lake is actually a lagoon covering an area of 35 sq km (14 sq miles), with its entrance at the foreshore suburb of Windang.

The **Illawarra Escarpment State Recreation Area** has many fine walking trails through the rainforest, ©9585 6444 for details.

Australia's largest steel mill is located around the foreshores of **Port Kembla Harbour**. The harbour sees millions of tons of coal exported each year from the surrounding mines, as well as steel from the steelworks.

Wollongong has two **bicycle tracks**. The one to the north starts at North Beach and goes to Corrimal, 14km (9 miles) away. The southern one starts near the Windang bridge and skirts the shores of Lake Illawarra.

Festivals

The Festival of Wollongong is held each year in November.

Facilities

Ten-pin bowling (8 Commerce Drive, Warilla), car rental depots (Auto Rentals, ©4229 7766; Avis, ©4228 4111; Budget, ©13 2727; Thrifty, ©4227 3000), catamaran and sailboard hire (Lake Illawarra & Belmore Basin), tennis, squash, horse riding (Otford Valley Farm,

©4294 2442), golf, joy flights (Albion Park Aerodrome), fishing, leisure centre with heated pools (Beaton Park, ©4229 6004), horse racing (Kembla Grange, ©4261 7211), greyhound racing (Bulli, ©4267 1467 and Dapto, ©4261 2449), harness racing (Bulli, ©4267 4224) and indoor cricket (Albion Park Rail, ©4256 6138 and Unanderra, ©4271 6685). Deep sea charter boats leave from Belmore Basin. Roller skating is available at Dapto, ©4261 6333.

New South Wales – South

Nowra

Population 11,600

Nowra is situated on the banks of the Shoalhaven River, on the south coast of New South Wales.

Climate

Average temperatures: January max 26C (79F) - min 18C (64F); July max 17C (63F) - min 9C (48F). Average annual rainfall: 1275mm (50 ins).

Characteristics

Nowra is the hub of the City of Shoalhaven, which has a population of around 83,000. The city area stretches from Berry to Durras North, and has 109 ocean, bay and lakeside beaches, lush rolling pastures, craggy mountain haunts and bush trails.

The town has produced two Melbourne Cup winners - Archer and Arwon.

How to Get There

By Rail

Bomaderry is the terminus of the South Coast Railway, and there are train services daily from and to Sydney, ✆13 2232.

Pioneer Motor Service operates a daily bus service which connects with the train, ✆13 3410.

By Bus

Greyhound Pioneer, ✆13 2030, have daily services from Sydney/Melbourne/Sydney which stops at Nowra.

By Road

From Sydney, via the Princes Highway - 162km (100 miles).

Visitor Information

The Shoalhaven Visitor Information Centre, cnr Princess Highway & Pleasant Way, ✆4421 0778 or ✆1800 024 261, is ◔open 9am-4.30pm daily. Their internet details are ✍www.shoalhaven.nsw.gov.au for tourist information and ✉beverlyc@shoalhaven.nsw.gov.au for email contact.

Accommodation

Here is a selection of available accommodation with prices for a double room per night, which should be used as a guide only. The telephone area code is 02.

Pleasant Way Motor Inn, Pleasant Way, ✆4421 5544. 22 units, swimming pool, spa, barbecue - ✪$95.

Parkhaven Motor Lodge, cnr Kinghorn & Douglas Streets, ✆4421 6444. 30 units, licensed restaurant, swimming pool - ✪$95-160.

Marriott Park, cnr Princes Highway & Douglas Street, ✆4421 6999. 16 units - ✪$70-85.

George Bass Motor Inn, 65 Bridge Road, ✆4421 6388. 10 units, comfortable rooms - ✪$80-100.

Cross Country Motel, 242 Kinghorn Street, ✆4421 7777. 18 units, swimming pool, barbecue - ✪$70-80.

Nowra Motor Inn, 202 Kinghorn Street, ✆4421 0555. 30 units, licensed restaurant, swimming pool - ✪$70-80.

Riverhaven Motel, Scenic Drive, ✆4421 2044. 22 units, licensed restaurant, indoor heated pool, barbecue - ✪$60-75.

Caravan Parks

Shoalhaven Caravan Village, Terara Road, ✆4423 0770. (Pets allowed under control) - powered sites ✪$17 for two, cabins $30-70 for two.

Rest Point Caravan Park, Browns Road, ✆4421 6856. (No pets allowed) 80 sites, playground, barbecue - powered sites ✪$20-24, cabins $55-100.

Eating Out

Nowra has a wide selection of restaurants, coffee shops, and four licensed clubs. Many of the motels also have restaurants. Some of the choices are:

Nowra Steak House, 16 Kinghorne Street, ✆4423 4193.

Captain's Table, 202 Kinghorne Street, ✆4421 0555.

Boatshed, Wharf Road, ✆4421 2419.

Trevi Fountain, 223 Kinghorne Road, ✆4423 0285. Italian cuisine.

Riverhaven, Riverhaven Motel, 1 Scenic Drive, ✆4421 2044.

Shoreline, Parkhaven Motel, cnr Kinghorn & Douglas Streets, ✆4421 5544.

Nowra Palace, 54 Berry Street, ©4421 4902. Malayasian and Chinese selection.

Theodore's Brasserie, 116 Kinghorne Street, ©4421 0300.

Leong's Chinese Restaurant, 83 North Street, ©4421 2131.

McDonald's is on the corner of Cambawarra Road, Bomaderry, and the Princes Highway & Browns Road, South Nowra, ©4421 1099. KFC is in Lot 22, Princes Highway, South Nowra. Pizza Hut is on the corner of McLean Street and the Princes Highway in Nowra, ©4421 4199.

Points of Interest

Cruises of the Shoalhaven River are available from Shoalhaven River Tours, 49 Greenwell Point Road, Greenwell Point, ©4447 1978.

The old **Shoalhaven River bridge** was erected in 1881. To cope with the heavy volume of traffic across the River, a second bridge was erected in 1980.

In **Moorhouse Park**, Bridge Road, there is an old flood rescue boat from Terara.

Nowra Olympic Pool and **Nowra Waterways** are in Scenic

Drive and are open from September to Easter, ☏4421 2093.

The Showground, in West Street, is the venue for the two-day agricultural show held in February each year. In the Showground there is the Council Youth Centre, and the Memorial gates, which were built to commemorate servicemen who died in action in the two World Wars.

At the western end of the Showground is **Hanging Rock**, a precariously positioned formation with views across the River and Nowra Golf Course.

Ben's Walk is a walking track which follows the river bank from the track head near Shoalhaven River Bridge to Nowra Creek, which is spanned by a suspension bridge.

On the corner of West and Worrigee Streets, is **Meroogal**, an historic house built by Robert Taylor-Thorburn in 1886. It is now owned by the Historic Houses Trust of New South Wales, and is ⊙open Sat 1pm-5pm and Sun 10am-5pm. For further information, ☏4421 8150.

Shoalhaven Historical Museum, cnr Kinghorn & Plunkett Streets, is ⊙open Sat-Sun 1-4pm, and on Mon, Wed and Fri during school holidays 1pm-4pm, ☏4421 2021.

Werninck Craft Cottage, 102 Plunkett Street, is ⊙open Mon-Fri 9.30am-3.30pm, Sat-Sun 10am-4pm, ☏4423 2419.

Situated on the corner of Kinghorn & Kalandar Streets is a **Sea Venom Jet**, which has been donated by HMAS Albatross. A short history of the aircraft and type of service is on a plaque at the site.

HMAS Albatross

Travel south from Nowra along the Princes Highway to the Kalandar Street intersection, turn right at the traffic lights and follow the signs.

The **Royal Australian Naval Air Station**, HMAS Albatross, 9km (6 miles) south-west of Nowra, is the home of the Fleet Air Arm. The fixed-wing section at the base was disbanded, due to the lack of an aircraft carrier, and the station now concentrates on helicopters. Educational tours can be arranged, ☏4421 1211 for more information. The **Naval Aviation Museum** at the Air Station has the finest collection of historic military aircraft in Australia, and a good collection of engines, aviation equipment, models, uniforms and memorabilia. Picnic, barbecue and toilet facilities are provided, and it is ⊙open daily 10am-4pm, ☏4421 1920.

Near the base is the **Nowra Hill Lookout**, with panoramic views of the Shoalhaven and Jervis Bay area. There is a pleasant stroll from there along Commodore's Walk to the Harry Sawkins Memorial Lookout.

Festivals

February - Nowra Agricultural Show.
November - The Shoalhaven Spring Festival.

Facilities

Lawn bowls, canoeing, fishing, golf, sailing, scenic drives, squash, swimming, tennis, water skiing, 4WD escapes and bushwalking tours. Check with the information centre.

Boats can be hired from the following outlets:
Aquatique, 125 Junction Street, ✆4421 8159 - canoes, scuba and diving gear, surf and wave skis.
Shoalhaven Caravan Village, Terrara Road, ✆4423 0770 - canoes.

Outlying Attractions

Shellharbour

The town of Shellharbour is around twenty minutes' drive south of Wollongong on the coastal road. There are caravan and camping areas, modern motels, one of the state's largest licensed clubs, an attractive corner pub, golf, bowls, great restaurants and beautiful beaches.

The name Shellharbour is derived from the many Aboriginal shell middens found here and at nearby Bass Point. The location is listed on the Heritage Commission Register, and is regarded as one of the two most important archaeological sites on the NSW coast.

Bass Point is a popular diving area, as part of its waters form a marine reserve. There is an airport at nearby Albion Park, and joy flights are offered. Nearby is the turnoff to Jamberoo Recreation Park, where you can play mini golf, go bobsledding, grass ski, or take the chairlift to the mountain top. There is also a maze, a licensed family restaurant, children's play area and a barbecue hut.

For more information contact the Shellharbour Visitor Information Centre, ✆4221 6169. They are located in Lamerton House, Lamerton Crescent, and are ◷open 8.30am-4.40pm Mon-Fri, closed weekends and public holidays.
They can be emailed at ✉tourism @shellharbour.nsw.gov.au and the web address is ☞www.shellharbour .nsw.gov.au

Kiama

Kiama is a seaside town 36km (22 miles) south of Wollongong.

The Blowhole is the main attraction, but nowadays it only seems to 'blow' in nasty weather. In any case, it is floodlit until 9.30pm.

The best way to explore Kiama is on foot, strolling around the foreshore area. First, visit the burial site of one of the members of the First Fleet, and then walk around the showground that overlooks Storm Bay's jagged rocks, to the town's popular Surf Beach. You can picnic in the adjoining park, or continue through the town centre taking in the historic grand old homes and commercial buildings on the way.

The Terraces, a row of historic timber cottages, are now gift and specialty stores, and a good place to pick up a bargain. Most of the stores are ⊙open daily 10am-5pm.

The **Family History Centre**, 7 Railway Parade, ✆4233 1122, has comprehensive in-house microform and data inventory to enable people to trace their family trees. The Centre is ⊙open daily 9.30am-4.30pm.

The **Quarry Leisure Centre**, Havilah Place, ✆4232 1877, has a 25m heated swimming pool, a wading pool, sauna, spa, aerobics, and facilities for indoor sports.

Minnamurra Falls. The Falls are 15km (9 miles) west of Kiama, in a dense subtropical rainforest, and plunge some 50m (164 ft) into a deep gorge. There is a delightful walk from the parking area through the rainforest to the Falls, and the round trip takes about an hour.

Barren Grounds Nature Reserve. The Reserve is 25km (16 miles) west of Kiama on the Jamberoo Mountain Road, and affords magnificent views from the lookout. There is a unique hanging swamp and bird observatory, and picnic and barbecue facilities.

The Kiama Visitors Centre is on Blowhole Point Road, ✆4232 3322 or ✆1300 654 262 (free call). ⊙Open 9am-5pm daily, they have information on accommodation available, and all the places of interest. You can check the area out on the web at 👁www.kiama.com.au and email them for more information at ✉kiamatourism@ozemail.com.au

Berry

Called the Town of Trees, Berry more than lives up to its name, and is 16km (10 miles) north of Nowra. The town has a population of around 1600, with shopping facilities, motel and hotel accommodation, restaurants, and many antique and craft shops.

The **Berry Historical Museum**, Queen Street, is ⊙open Sat 11am-2pm, Sun 11am-3pm and public holidays 11am-2pm, ✆4464 1551, and they can point out the other buildings in the town classified by the National Trust, such as the Court House and National Bank.

Berry Country Fair, featuring local crafts and second-hand goods, is held at Apex Park, cnr Princes Highway & Prince Alfred Street, on the first Sunday of the month.

Local information can be obtained from *Pottering Around*, on the corner of Queen and Alexandra Streets, ℭ4464 2177.

Shoalhaven Heads

The township of Shoalhaven Heads is at the southern end of Seven Mile Beach, about 13km (8 miles) east of Bomaderry. It is a popular holiday spot near Seven Mile Beach National Park. The town offers a bowling club, fishing facilities and a swimming pool. You can hire bicycles at Shoalhaven Heads Hardware Store, ℭ4448 7707.

Nearby is **Coolangatta Estate Historic Village Resort**, 1335 Bolong Road, ℭ4448 7131, the site of the first settlement in the Shoalhaven district. The complex comprises buildings erected by the district's founder, Alexander Berry, that have been restored as motel units. There is also a 9-hole golf course, a winery, and picnic areas and barbecues.

The **Coolangatta Craft Centre**, 1180 Bolong Road, is housed in the original school house, established in 1861. It is ☉open Wed-Mon 9am-5pm, and daily during school holidays, ℭ4448 7205.

Cambewarra Mountain Lookout. The lookout is on Tourist Road, Beamont, north of Bomaderry, and offers panoramic views of the Shoalhaven River Valley and the coastline. Picnic, barbecue and toilet facilities are provided. There is also a kiosk which is ☉open Fri-Wed 9am-5pm and daily during the Christmas school holidays, ℭ4465 1321.

Bomaderry/North Nowra

The town of Bomaderry is really a northern suburb of Nowra, separated from it by the river. It has a large shopping centre, Narang Road Supergrass Tennis Centre, Shoalhaven Sporting Complex, and a Basketball Stadium. Bomaderry Railway Station is the terminus of the South Coast Railway Line, ℭ4423 6416.

Bomaderry Creek Walk is a track that follows Bomaderry Creek from below the Ten Pin Bowling Centre in Narang Street. Walkers have a choice between a three hour walk and a one hour walk, and picnic and barbecue facilities are available at the track head.

Nowra Golf Club is situated under bush-covered escarpment, near the river in North Nowra, Greys Beach. The clubhouse has first class facilities, and the scenic 18-hole course offers a challenge. Visitors are welcome, ℭ4421 3900 (proshop ℭ4421 2249).

The **Grotto Walk**, west of the golf course, is an easy walk following the River, and beginning off Yurunga Drive.

Beach near Ulladulla, New South Wales south coast

Bateman's Bay, New South Wales

From **Rockhill Lookout**, off McMahons Road, you can get a spectacular view of the river.

Nowra Wildlife Park is set in 6ha (16 acres) off Rockhill Road, North Nowra, overlooking the river. You can walk amongst the animals, and have your photo taken with the resident koalas. The park has a well appointed picnic and barbecue area, a kiosk and a camping area, and is ☉open daily 8am-5pm, ✆4421 3949. Admission is ✪\$6 adults, \$3 children.

Huskisson

The town of Huskisson, on the shores of Jervis Bay, is 24km (15 miles) south-east of Nowra, and has a shopping centre, a modern RSL club and bowling clubs. It is a real holiday spot, and during the Christmas holiday period a movie theatre and carnival operate in the town. The sands of Jervis Bay are renowned as the whitest in the world, and each Easter Huskisson hosts the White Sands Carnival.

The **Lady Denman Heritage Complex** in Dent Street is worth a visit. The *Lady Denman* is an old Sydney ferry which was originally built at Huskisson, and saw many years of service on Sydney Harbour. After she retired she was sailed back to Huskisson, placed in the park at the Heritage Complex, and now contains the **Museum of Jervis Bay, Science and The Sea**. The park is ☉open daily 9am-5pm, and the museum is ☉open Tues-Fri 1-5pm, Sat-Sun and school holidays 10am-5pm. Nearby is **Lady Timbery's Aboriginal Arts and Crafts Centre**, ✆4441 5999.

Vincentia

Across the Moona-Moona Creek Bridge from Huskisson is the town of Vincentia, 30km (19 miles) south-east of Nowra. This is another holiday town, with shops, and a 9-hole golf course with superb views of Jervis Bay and the Pigeon House Mountain.

Plantation Point offers sweeping views of Jervis Bay to Bowen Island and Point Perpendicular, and there are barbecue and toilet facilities.

Jervis Bay Territory

This area is part of the Australian Capital Territory, and is 35km (22 miles) from Nowra. It contains the Royal Australian Naval College, HMAS Cresswell, the Jervis Bay Nature Reserve and Botanic Gardens Annex. The ruined lighthouse overlooking the ocean is quite interesting. It was built in the wrong place and proved to be a navigational hazard luring boats to their doom on the rocky coastline. The navy was requested to shell it!

At Jervis Bay Village you will find

a public telephone, police station, supermarket, general store and petrol station. The Administrative Office of Jervis Bay Territory is situated in the grounds of the village, ©4442 1217.

Booderee National Park is managed by Jervis Bay Administration, and there is a Visitors Centre on the left near the entrance, ©4443 0977. In keeping with the protection of the environment, spear guns, handspears, dogs and other domestic animals are not permitted in the reserve, and fires can only be lit in defined barbecue areas. For enquiries about camping in the park, call into the Visitor Centre, which is ©open 8.30am-5pm in the Christmas-Easter period, and 9am-4pm during the off-peak season. Entry into the park is ©$5 per car weekly.

Green Patch is a camping and picnic area within the National Park, and has a sheltered beach, toilets, hot showers, wood barbecues and picnic tables. There is prolific birdlife, many interesting bush walks, and a camping ground that allows a maximum of three weeks' stay.

Murrays Beach, Summer Cloud Bay and Cave Beach are other popular spots within the Reserve.

HMAS Cresswell was established as an officer training college in 1915, and visits to the grounds of the college are permitted on a limited basis (20 minutes on weekends and most public holidays), ©4429 7985 for details.

In the college is the **Royal Australian Naval College Historical Collection**, with a display of artefacts specifically related to the college and the Jervis Bay area, and Peter Webber's collection of model sailing ships. It is ©open on the last Sunday of each month, or by appointment, ©4429 7845.

The **Jervis Bay Annex** to the Australian National Botanic Gardens is 2km along the Cave Beach Road, and has a large variety of native plants collected from all parts of Australia. Facilities include nature walks, toilets and picnic area, but no barbecues are permitted. The annex is ©open Mon-Fri 8am-4pm, and the first Sunday of the month 10am-5pm. Hours may be extended during public and school holidays, ©4442 1122.

St Georges Basin

Sanctuary Point and St Georges Basin have a combined estimated population of 6000. There are some lovely spots in and around both places for picnics and all water sports. Catamarans, sailboards and small canoes can be hired from **Sanctuary Point Sail Centre**, 272 Grenville Avenue, ©4443 0205 (only available in Summer).

Lake Conjola

The town of Lake Conjola, is on the shores of the lake of the same name, about 55km (34 miles) south of Nowra.

Boats can be hired at the Post Office and General Store, Carrol Avenue, ©4456 1163, and at Conjola Boat Hire, ©4456 1563 (school holidays only). There are tennis courts, a bowling club, fishing and water skiing.

The Craft Corner in the General Store specialises in needlework and tapestry supplies and books, ©4456 1163.

Milton

Milton is 7km (4 miles) north of Ulladulla, and 61km (38 miles) south of Nowra. It was established in 1860, has many historic buildings, and in the Mick Ryan Park there is a giant fig tree that is estimated to be over 110 years old.

A flea market, featuring local crafts and second-hand goods, is held at the **Settlement Courtyard** on the first Saturday of the month.

Over the long weekend in October every year Milton celebrates the **Milton Settlers' Fair**, which consists of markets, art and craft exhibitions, music and dancing.

Mollymook

Mollymook is less than 5km (2 miles) south east of Milton, situated by the sea.

The surfing beach at Mollymook is patrolled daily, and surf skis are available for hire during the Christmas school holidays from the Surf Life Saving Club. Next to the Club is an 'Exersite' outdoor exercise area with equipment and instructions for strengthening and stretching exercises.

Mollymook Golf Club's picturesque 9-hole beachside course has superb sea views from the clubhouse and restaurant. Visitors are welcome, ©4455 1911. In addition, an 18-hole championship hilltop course is located in Maisie Williams Memorial Drive, with a pro-shop and snack bar facilities. Visitors are welcome here also, ©4455 2055.

The **Bogey Hole**, a circular natural rock pool, and Collers Beach are reached via Golf Avenue and Riversdale Avenue.

Ulladulla

Ulladulla is 68km (42 miles) south of Nowra, on the Princes Highway, and there is much to see around the harbour and wharf. Trawlers of the fishing fleet are anchored in the harbour behind the safety of the breakwater. Various small craft and the activity associated with fishing are fascinating. Each Easter Sunday, the traditional Blessing of the Fleet Ceremony is conducted on the harbour breakwater. This is a religious custom which has been practised by the Italian fishermen for many generations. Each year this ceremony has become quite a celebration which is worth seeing. Trawlers are decorated for the event and there is a carnival atmosphere.

The Royal Volunteer Coastal Patrol maintains full sea search and rescue facilities at Ulladulla, for the area from Jervis Bay to Batemans Bay. Radio cover is provided on 2182KHz, 2524KHz and VHF Channel 16 during weekends and holidays periods, and at any other time of day or night by arrangement. However, a continuous watch is maintained 7 days a week on 27880KHz. Pleasure craft owners are urged to lodge sailing plans with the Coastal Patrol Ulladulla either by telephone, ✆4455 3403, or by radio, to ensure they have an adequate radio cover while at sea, and then to advise the base of their safe arrival at their destination.

Pedal boats can be hired on the beach surrounding the harbour during holiday periods.

On **Wardens Head**, the southern point of Ulladulla Harbour, is the lighthouse, and from there you can get an uninterrupted view of the coast. A track leads from the lighthouse to the beach where there is good fishing and surfing.

South Pacific Heathland Reserve stretches from Dowling Street to Pitman Avenue, and features the Chris Humphries Nature Walk covering 12ha (30 acres).

Funland, 93 Princes Highway, ✆4455 3053, is one of the largest indoor fun parks in New South Wales. There are three floors of attractions, including dodgems, the 'sizzler' thrill ride, controlla boats, air hockey, slot cars, kiddy rides, and more. ⊙Open daily from 10am, closes 10pm Sat and school holidays, 5pm Sun-Fri.

The Ulladulla Visitors Centre, Civic Centre, Princes Highway, ✆4455 1269, is ⊙open Mon-Fri 10am-5pm, Sat-Sun 9am-5pm, and should be your first port of call. There is no shortage of accommodation or restaurants in the town, and the Visitor Centre has all the details.

New South Wales – South

Batemans Bay

Population 9600
Batemans Bay is situated on the Clyde River Estuary, at the foot of Clyde Mountain, 306 km (190 miles) south of Sydney.

Climate

Average temperatures: January max 23C (73F) - min 16C (61F); July max 16C (61F) - min 6C (43F). The average annual rainfall: 916mm (36 in). The hours of sunshine per day are 7 in summer and 6 in autumn, winter and spring.

Characteristics

Batemans Bay is a weekend and holiday retreat for people from Canberra. The beaches of the area are clear and clean with superb fishing. It has all the facilities of a beach resort but it is all very understated. It is the only place where the commercial fishing trawlers are permitted to sell their catch direct to the public. The general atmosphere is very friendly; strangers smile and say hello in the street.

How to Get There

By Air
Hazelton Airlines, ✆13 1713, fly to Moruya and Merimbula from Sydney, Melbourne, Brisbane and Adelaide, with at least two flights daily.

By Bus
Priors Scenic Express operates between Sydney and the Eurobodalla Coast, with a focus on the sightseeing opportunities of the trip, ✆1800 816 234.

Murrays offer daily services from Canberra, ℂ132 251.

V-Line have a combined road/rail service between Melbourne and Batemans Bay, ℂ132 232.

By Rail

The trains from Sydney, ℂ13 2232, terminate at Bombaderry, on the northern side of the Shoalhaven River, so you will have to organise an alternative form of transport to complete the trip south, be it a hire car or one of the coach services listed above.

By Car

From Sydney and Melbourne, via the Princes Highway - 279km (173 miles) from Sydney and 769km (478 miles) from Melbourne.

From Canberra it is 150km (93 miles) along the Kings Highway.

Visitor Information

The Eurobodalla Visitor Information Centre, cnr Princes Highway and Beach Road, Batemans Bay, ℂ(02) 4472 6900 or ℂ1800 802 528, is ⊙open daily 9am-5pm (closed Christmas Day). Email them at ✎ info@naturecoast-tourism. com.au or visit their website at 👁 www.naturecoast-tourism. com.au

Accommodation

Batemans Bay, as with most towns on the south coast of New South Wales, is well endowed with a variety of accommodation. Although motels and holiday units dominate, you can usually rent out cottages in the area at reasonable prices, outside of school holiday periods. Contact Estate Agents in the area or the local Visitor Centre.

Prices vary considerably depending on the standard of accommodation and the season. Here we have a selection, with prices for a double room per night, which should be used as a guide only. The telephone area code is 02.

Reef Motor Inn, 27 Clyde Street, ℂ4472 6000. 33 units, licensed restaurant, swimming pool, spa, barbecue - ✪$105-195.

Lincoln Downs Country Resort, Princes Highway, Surfside, ℂ4472 6388. 33 units, 7 suites, licensed restaurant, pool, tennis courts, barbecue - ✪$100-160.

Argyle Terrace Motor Inn, 32 Beach Road, ℂ4472 5022. 9 units, swimming pool, barbecue - ✪$155-160.

Hanging Rock Golf Club Family, Beach Road, ℂ4472 4466. 27 units, playground, barbecue, swimming pool - ✪$55-60.

Holiday Units

These listed are self contained units with all the 'mod-cons'.

Del Costa Holiday Villas, 54 Beach Road, ℂ4472 6260. 15 units - ✪$65-130.

The Beach House, 22 Myamba Parade, ©4472 4086. 1 cottage - ✪$95-130.
Caravan Parks
Easts Riverside Holiday Park, Wharf Road, ©4472 4048. (No dogs allowed) 47 sites - powered sites ✪$22-36, cabins $60-210.
Coachhouse Marina Resort, Beach Road, ©4472 4392. (No dogs allowed) - powered sites ✪$25-35 for two, on-site vans $40-100 for two.
Shady Willows Tourist Park, Old Princes Highway, ©4472 4972. (Dogs may be permitted on application) - powered sites ✪$15-25 for two, on-site vans $35-70 for two, cabins $40-100 for two.
There is a **Youth Hostel** on the corner of Old Princes Highway and South Street, ©4472 4972. It has 11 rooms at ✪$18 per person twin share.

Eating Out

The area boasts fine restaurants with particularly good fish dishes. Most of the larger motels have licensed restaurants which can be recommended. There are also a good number of Clubs - Bowling (©4472 4502), Golf (©4472 4967), Returned Servicemen (©4472 4847) - that also contain restaurants. Here are some additional venues.

Briars, Lincoln Downs, Princess Highway, ©4472 6388. Licensed, seafood and meat dishes, open daily.
Trappers Seafood Restaurant, 26 Princes Highway, ©4472 5888. Licensed, a la carte but seafood specialty, open daily.
Gallery, Catalina Country Club, part of the golf club, ©4472 4967. Licensed, a la carte, open daily. Also has the Garden Bistro, light snacks to grills with a kids' playground.
Innes' Boatshed, Clyde Street, ©4472 4052. BYO, family restaurant, seafood caught by the chef, open daily.
Rafters, 28 Beach Road, ©4472 4288. BYO, a la carte, open daily.
Mexican Munchies, Annetts Arcade, Orient Street, ©4472 8746. Authentic Mexican dishes.
Raymond's, 19 Clyde Street, ©4472 5700. Chinese cuisine, open daily.
Pinky's Pizza, 3 Clyde Street, ©4472 3073.
Vietnamese, Thai & Malaysian, Shop 7, Bay Plaza Centre, Orient Street, ©4472 7274.
McDonalds is on the corner of Hill and Vesper Streets and KFC is on the Princes Highway.

Points of Interest

The population increases to approximately 90,000 during the peak

holiday season (from about mid December to early February). Batemans Bay has **16 golden beaches**, with some sheltered calm waters. McKenzie's Beach is a small beach that has consistent small to medium waves, with the best area at Malua Bay, south of the Surf Club. To the north, there are several good beaches including South Durras near Wasp Head, and Depot, Pebbly and Merry beaches accessible through **Murramarang National Park**.

The **Clyde River**, which is quite a spectacular waterway, is navigable for 51 km (32 miles) from Batemans Bay up into the hills. Regular cruises are available up to **Nelligen**, which boasts a number of historically significant buildings.

The MV **Merinda** offers a great time out on the Clyde River (©4472 4052), or you can hire a boat in the town for your own 'explore and see', combined with a little fishing.

The area is well known for its **fishing**. Durras Lake, to the north of Batemans Bay, has flathead, whiting and bream, and various points and bays between there and North Head offer other good spots. Up from the town near the oyster beds and the mangrove flats on the Clyde River, many people catch whiting, mulloway and bream. There is also quite a deal of fishing from the bank around the town. To the south, Malua Bay and Pretty Point are perhaps the most popular spots.

There are many **National Parks** and **forests** in the region, and maps are available from the Visitors Centre. The nearest one to Batemans Bay is Murramarang, which lies between South Durras and North Head. Access is via the Princes Highway and Durras Road, and there are six well-defined walks beginning from the road.

Walks from the town include:
1. Beach walk from Clyde River to Cullendulla Creek - about 3 km (2 miles) long around the coast. Easy, okay for kids.
2. Guerilla Bay to the lighthouse - 1.5km (1 mile).
3. Along the Princes Highway to the Round Hill Fire Tower.

There are many other coastal walks recommended by the Visitors Centre.

The Birdland Animal Park at 55 Beach Road is ☺open 9.30am-4pm daily. It includes 'Wombat World', snake demonstrations, an animal nursery, a koala exhibit, and a scale model train. Admission is ✪$8 adults, $5 children and $7 for families, ✆4472 5364.

The **Historical Society Museum** is in the old court house, cnr Beach Road and Orient Street, and is ☺open Thu-Sat 1pm-4pm, ✆4472 8993.

The **Mogo Goldfields**, on the Tomakin Road near Mogo Village 15km (9 miles) from town, are ☺open weekend and school holidays, 10am-4pm. There is a guided tour of the old underground gold mine. You can camp here with all the amenities, ✆4471 7381. The Village is open most of the time and depicts a bygone era. It is well-known for its art and craft shops.

Festivals

The Neptune Festival is held each November.

Facilities

Boat, catamaran and sailboard hire, golf, tennis, lawn bowls and ten-pin bowling are all provided for in the area.

Outlying Attractions

Burrill Lake

Situated 5km (3 miles) south of Ulladulla, Burrill Lake is crossed by the Princes Highway at its eastern arm, but the main expanse reaches inland almost to the township of Milton. The inlet and beach are to the east of the Highway, and if you take the road to Dolphin Point and follow Seaside Parade you will come to the picnic area, rock platforms and popular fishing spots. Accommodation is available in caravan parks, motels and holiday units close to the lake and beach.

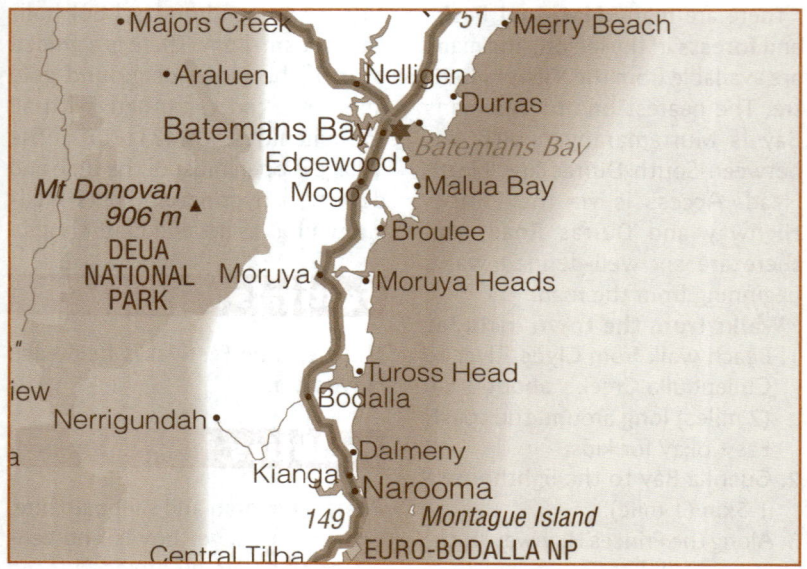

Burrill Lake offers boating, sailing, lake and beach fishing, surfing, swimming, windsurfing and prawning in season. Boats can be hired, and there are three launching ramps. A boat hire service, ©4454 0951 operates from the reserve on the foreshores in Moore Street.

At **Bungalow Park**, you can feed the lorikeets, which arrive at 8am and 3pm (during daylight saving 9am and 4pm), or play mini-golf on a course which is a replica of the Mollymook Hilltop Golf Course. There are also boats available for hire, ©4455 1621.

Moruya

The town of Moruya is 27km (17 miles) south of Batemans Bay on the Princes Highway. It has some fine old buildings, including the Wesleyan Church built in 1864 with local granite. The airport, which caters for the area, is on the north headland of the river entrance. South Moruya has a fine surf beach.

Accommodation is not plentiful in the area, since Batemans Bay to the north and Narooma in the south provide such facilities. If you are planning to stay here, however, there are a limited number of motels, lodges, guesthouses and B&Bs to choose from. Most are along the Princes Highway, so keep an eye out as you drive through.

The area has excellent **fishing** in the Deua River with its mangrove swamps, and along the various coastal headlands. **Surfing** is great from Moruya Heads to Congo, North Head, Broulee South, North Broulee, Pink Rocks (off the north face of Broulee Island - experienced riders only, 6m waves) and Mossy Point near the mouth of the Tomago River.

Behind Moruya, along the Araluen Road, is the 81,158 ha (200,460 acres) **Deua National Park** which extends up the coastal ranges to Batemans Bay. You can try hiking - good luck and be sure to let the ranger know your plans.

Moruya has an **Historical Museum** in 85 Campbell Street, ✆open Mon & Fri 11am-3pm and on Saturdays 11am-1pm (during peak Christmas and Easter seasons it open daily). Admission is ✆$2 adults and 50 cents for children.

Each Saturday from 9am the **Moruya Country Markets** are held in Shore Street, and the **Congo Crafts Gallery**, ✆4474 2931, is ✆open Wed-Mon 11am-5pm during school holidays, but it's best to phone beforehand.

Kiora House, along the Araluen Road, is a National Trust classified building that offers quaint old world charm. There is no public access to this building, but its recollections of colonial heritage can be admired from the street.

Moruya boasts a speedway, and a horse racing complex together with golf courses, tennis and bowling clubs.

Bodalla

24km (15 miles) south along the Princes Highway is the town of Bodalla, made famous by Bega cheese which uses it as a brand name. The **All Saints Church** is one of several photogenic buildings in this attractive little town. Just before Bodalla is the turnoff to **Tuross Head**, where you can hire boats for fishing and boating on the lake of the same name.

Narooma

This town is 44km (27 miles) south of Moruya, on the estuary of the Wagonga River. It is another popular fishing resort with excellent beaches for surfing (Mystery Bay, Handkerchief Beach, Narooma Main Beach, Bar Beach, Dalmeny Point, Potato Point, Blackfellows Point and Tuross Head). It has a narrow channel that leads to a small harbour. As with the other towns on the south coast, it offers excellent bushwalks and is very much a family holiday area.

Montague Island, 8km (5 miles) offshore, is a flora and fauna reserve, and the area around there is well known for its game fishing. The island is the halfway point in the Sydney to Hobart Yacht Race.

Contact the Narooma Visitors Centre, Princes Highway, ☺open every day except Christmas Day 9am-5pm, ✆(02) 4476 2881 or ✆1800 802 528, with any queries, or to assist in booking accommodation, restaurants or tours. Alternatively, you can email them at: ✎eurovcn@acr.net.au or visit the website at ☞www.naturecoast-tourism.com.au

Central Tilba

21km (13 miles) south is Central Tilba, which neighbors Tilba Tilba. Both of these tiny settlements are in the shadow of an ancient volcano, Mount Dromedary. Situated in rather pleasant hilly country at the base of **Mt Dromedary**, Central Tilba has become a tourist spot with art and craft shops, an old wooden general store, a cobblers cottage, a pub, and a quaint restaurant with displays of the traditional crafts. A pleasant day excursion from Narooma.

Cobargo

This village is 19km from Central Tilba. It has various cottage industries of pottery and leather, art and craft galleries, and a pub. You can turn off here for Bermagui, or it can be reached by turning off at Tilba Tilba and going along the coast road

and crossing Wallaga Lake.

Bermagui

Located on the coast 18km (11 miles) from Cobargo, Bermagui is the mecca for big game fishing in New South Wales, and was made famous in the 1930s by the novelist Zane Grey. Today a large fishing fleet operates out of Bermagui, and game fishermen from all over come for the sport between November and May.

Charter boats are available (for example, Blue Water Charters, Endeavour Drive, ✆6493 4540) for pleasure cruising or game fishing, and the harbour has a boat ramp and provision for trailer parking. Swimming and surfing are again the other main diversions - at Blue Pool, Horseshoe Bay and Wallaga Lake. Water skiing is the go on Wallaga Lake.

Bega

The town of Bega is 170km (106 miles) south of Batemans Bay, and 80km (50 miles) south of Narooma. It is the commercial centre of the district with a population above 4000. The district is famous for its dairy industry and cheeses.

The **Bega Cheese Heritage Centre** on the northern side of the Bega River, Lagoon Street, ✆6491 7777, is ☺open for inspection and tasting daily 9am-5pm.

The Bega Family Museum, cnr Auckland and Bega Streets, is ⊙open Mon-Fri 10.30am-4pm, Sat 10am-12pm, ✆6492 1453.

Brogo Valley's Rotolactor is 23km (14 miles) north of Bega on Baldwin Road, Brogo, and is ⊙open to the public Mon & Wed 2-5pm, with milking at 3pm, ✆6493 8330.

The **Grevillea Estate** winery and vineyards is on the Buckajo Road, ✆6492 3006.

Mumbulla Falls Picnic Area, 20km (12 miles) north of Bega off the Princes Highway along a gravel road, is a very pleasant spot for picnics and a swim. Because of the gravel road, only try it in dry weather.

The largest farm in the Bega Valley is **Kameruka Estate** which is classified by the National Trust. The homestead is set in extensive gardens, with its own church and clock-tower. It is ⊙open daily, ✆6492 0509.

Candelo Village, situated 20km (12 miles) south-west, still retains its old world charm with galleries and restaurants. It is a pleasant place for afternoon tea after a short drive.

Mimosa Rocks National Park, sprawls across its 17km coastal stretch north of Tathra and east of Mt Gearge Mountain. It is a perfect site for a picnic, and for enjoying the natural wonders of landscape and wildlife. Camping areas are also available, and it is best to discuss plans and ideas with the Tourist Information Centre, ✆6492 3313.

The Sapphire Coast Tourist Information Centre, Office 2, 163 Auckland Street, Bega, ✆(02) 6492 3313 or ✆1800 663 012, tends to be the arrival and departure point for coaches, and is the place to obtain assistance for accommodation and suggestions on where to dine. If you have internet access, or are planning your holiday from home, contact them at ✎info@ sapphirecoast.com.au, or visit the web page at ☜www.sapphirecoast. com.au

Tathra

Tathra is a quiet seaside village 18km (11 miles) east of Bega, with a beautiful beach and great fishing spots. Tathra offers the best of both worlds: beautiful beaches with ocean activities as well as the opportunity to explore the wildlife of nearby **Mimosa and Bournda National Parks**. There is a *campground* at Bournda National Park with very basic facilities for ❂$10-15 a night for two, ✆6495 4130. Tathra Tourist Centre on Tathra Wharf, Wharf Road, ✆6494 4062, is the best place to find out what you wish to know. The local people are very friendly and helpful.

Merimbula

This flourishing resort town on Lake Merimbula is 26km (16 miles) south of Bega. Merimbula is an activity-based centre, with surfing on Main Beach, Short Point and Tura Beach, sailboarding and water skiing on Lake Merimbula, golf at the 27-hole Pambula-Merimbula golf course, lawn bowls at the ubiquitous bowling clubs and a variety of other activities - tennis, canoeing, horseriding and cycling. It has an RSL club with 'pokies' and live entertainment.

The **Magic Mountain Family Recreation Park**, with its water slides, mini Grand Prix race track and mountain toboggan slide, is just north of the town on Coast Drive, ✆6495 2299. The park ◷opens at 10am and admission is ✪$22 adults, $14 children 5-7 years old and $18 children aged 8-11.

The area also boasts an **Aquarium** (Lake Street, ✆6495 4446), **Yellow Pinch Wildlife Park** (Princes Highway, ✆6494 9225), **Milingandi Leisure Farm** (✆6495 6125) and a **Museum** in Main Street.

The Tourist Information Centre is on Beach Street, ✆6495 1129, ◷open Mon-Fri 9am-5pm, Sat-Sun 9am-1pm. This is the place to get all the information on available accommodation, of which there is plenty.

Eden

Eden is situated some 61km (38 miles) south of Bega, on Twofold Bay. A former whaling station, it is now a deep water fishing port, and the fishing and timber industries are of utmost importance to the survival of the town.

The town's **Killer Whale Museum**, 94 Imlay Street, ✆6496 2094, gives an overview of Eden's history, and houses the skeleton of 'Old Tom' a legendary whale from the area. Also featured is the **Seaman's Memorial Wall**, commemorating those lost at sea. The museum has limited opening times daily.

The **Ben Boyd National Park** flanks Twofold Bay to the north, with its famous Red Cliffs, and borders historic Boyd's Tower to the south. You can camp in the park, and at East Boyd Bay the Forestry Commission runs the Edrom Lodge for students.

For more information on accommodation and things to do, contact the Eden Tourist Information Office, Princes Highway (at the round-about), ✆6496 1953. It is ◷open Mon-Fri 10am-4pm, Sat-Sun 10am-noon.

Wonboyn Lake

The locals are proud of Wonboyn Lake, some 30km (19 miles) south of Eden, and surrounded by Ben

Boyd National Park and Nadgee Nature Reserve. In addition to the stunning scenery of **Ben Boyd** and **Nadgee**, Wonboyn has a reputation for the finest lake fishing on the Sapphire Coast.

ACT

Canberra

Population 308,000
Canberra, in the **Australian Capital Territory**, is situated in the southern tablelands of New South Wales, 100km (62 miles) from the coast. It is 300km (186 miles) from Sydney, 654km (406 miles) from Melbourne, 1654km (1028 miles) from Brisbane, and 1201km (746 miles) from Adelaide.

Climate

Average temperatures: January max 28C (82F) - min 13C (55F); July max 11C (52F) - min -1C (30F). Average annual rainfall is 650mm (25 ins).

Characteristics

Canberra, Australia's national capital was founded in 1913. From its inception it has been developed as a garden city and is unique in that it was planned from the outset. In 1912, an American, Walter Burley Griffin, won first prize in a worldwide competition to design the new capital.

Since 1915, thousands of trees have been planted annually and the variation in the shades and colours of the leaves during spring and autumn leave a lasting impression. Over half of the city is parkland and open space dotted with picnic areas.

The Commonwealth Parliament did not sit in Canberra until 1927, when the provisional Parliament House was opened. The new Parliament House was completed in 1988, the Bicentennial Year.

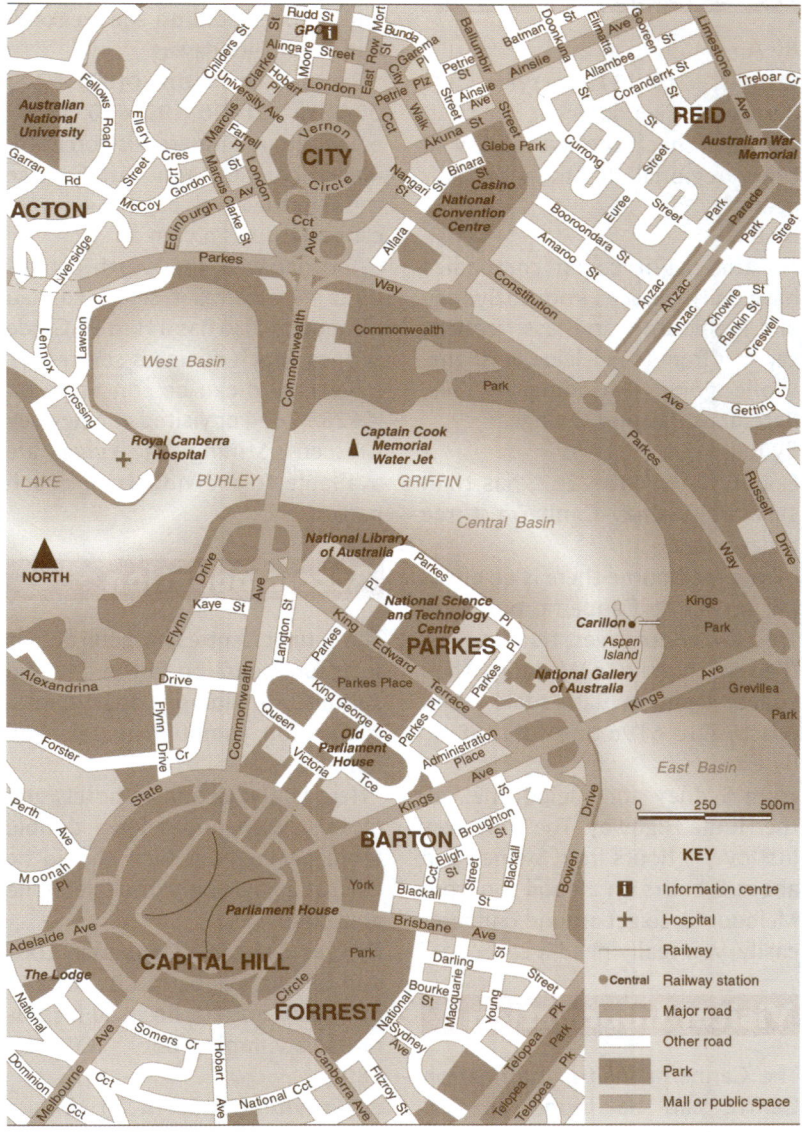

How to Get There

By Air

Qantas, ☎13 1313, service Canberra with their domestic lines, but you can check the availability of other regional flights with your agent.

By Bus

All the major coach companies have daily services from/to Sydney and Melbourne, and less frequent services from/to Adelaide, Brisbane, Wollongong, Cooma, Yass, Batemans Bay and Orange.

By Rail

Countrylink, ☎13 2232, has train services Sydney-Canberra three times a day.

From Melbourne there is no direct rail service to Canberra, but there are a few alternatives: train to Yass, then coach; train to Wodonga, then coach; train to Bairnsdale, then coach, ☎13 6196 or ☎13 1368.

By Car

From Sydney and Melbourne, via the Hume Highway. The trip takes just over 3 hours from Sydney and about 8 hours on a good run from Melbourne. To get around Canberra easily, you really need a car.

Visitor Information

The Canberra Visitor Information Centre can be found at 330 Northbourne Avenue in Dickson, and it is ◷open 9am-5pm Mon-Fri and 8.30am-5pm on the weekend and public holidays.

Contact them on ☎(02) 6205 0044 or ☎1800 100 660, or by email at ✉ canberravisitorcentre @msn.com.au. You can browse through their web page at ☞www.canberratourism.com.au

Another web site worth exploring is ☞canberra.citysearch.com.au

Canberra also has a Hire-A-Guide service which operates seven days a week, and can be contacted on ☎6288 7894 or visited at 4 Reveley Crescent, Stirling. The guides are available to individuals or coach parties.

Accommodation

The Tourist Centres have full details of accommodation in the city and suburbs, including apartments, cabins, on campus, hostels and farm stays.

Here is a selection of hotels and motels, with prices for a double room per night, which should be used as a guide only. The telephone area code is 02.

Rydges Lakeside Canberra, London Circuit, Canberra City, ☎6247 6244. 201 rooms, licensed restaurants, swimming pool - ✪$150-180.

Parkroyal Canberra, 1 Binara Street, Canberra City, ☎6247 8999.

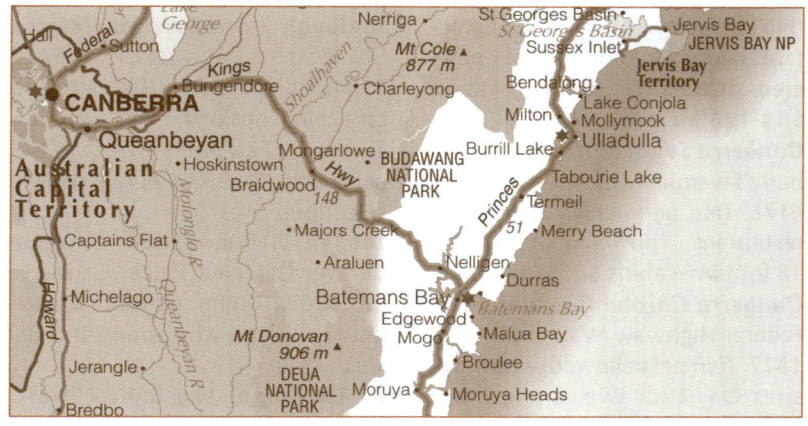

293 rooms (private facilities), licensed restaurant, bistro, swimming pool, spa, sauna, gym - ✪$160-290.

Capital Executive Apartment Hotel, 108 Northbourne Avenue, Braddon, ✆6243 8333. 83 units, licensed restaurant, sauna, gym - ✪$140-155.

University House Motel at Australian National University, Balmain Crescent, Acton, ✆6249 5211. 100 rooms (private facilities), licensed restaurant - ✪$120-130.

Quality Inn Garden City, Jerrabomberra Avenue, Cooma Road, Narrabundah, ✆6295 3322. 69 units, licensed restaurant, swimming pool, spa - ✪$120-150.

Tall Trees Motel, 21 Stephen Street, Ainslie, ✆6247 9200. 50 units - ✪$95-130.

Quality Inn Downtown, 82 Northbourne Avenue, Braddon, ✆6249 1388. 65 units, licensed restaurant, gym - ✪$110-150.

Embassy Motel, cnr Hopetoun Circuit & Adelaide Avenue, Deakin, ✆6281 1322. 86 units, licensed restaurant, air conditioning, sauna, pool - ✪$125.

Acacia Motor Lodge, 65 Ainslie Avenue, Braddon, ✆6249 6955 - 53 units, barbecue - ✪$85-95.

Australian Capital Motor Inn, 193 Mouat Street, Lyneham, ✆6248 5111. 54 units, licensed restaurant (closed Sunday), swimming pool - ✪$65-85.

Canberra Central Apartments, cnr Northbourne Avenue & Barry Drive, Turner, ✆6230 4781. 158 units - ✪$110.

Caravan Parks

Canberra Motor Village, Kunzea Street, O'Connor, ✆6247 5466.

(No pets allowed), licensed restaurant, barbecue, tennis, pool - powered sites ✪$20 for two, cabins $64-126 for two.

Canberra South Motor Park, Canberra Avenue, Symonston, ✆6280 6176. (No pets allowed), licensed restaurant - powered sites ✪$17-18 for two, cabins $45-75 for two.

Canberra Carotel Caravan Park, Federal Highway, Watson, ✆6241 1377. (No pets allowed) - powered sites ✪$12 for two, on-site vans $33 for two.

There is a **Youth Hostel** at 191 Dryandra Street, ✆6248 9155. It has 28 rooms at ✪$21-23 per person twin share.

Eating Out

Canberra's eateries cater for all tastes and pockets, and the Tourist Centres have complete lists. Here are some standard restaurants you may wish to try:

Charcoal, 61 London Circuit, Canberra City, ✆6248 8015. A quality steakhouse with seafood varieties available.

Great Wall, 113-119 Marcus Clarke Street, Canberra City, ✆6247 5423. Chinese food with yum cha lunches and a take-away option.

The Haig, cnr Northbourne Avenue & Girrahween Street, Canberra City, ✆6243 8121. Italian restaurant with al fresco dining.

Shalimar, Tasman House, Marcus Clarke Street, Canberra City, ✆6249 6784. Indian cuisine. A la carte and take-away options.

Tasuke, 122 Alinga Street, Canberra City, ✆6257 9711. Japanese selections.

Shogun, 70 Bunda Street, Gareema Centre, Gareema Place, Canberra City, ✆6248 8888. Traditional Japanese cooking with sashimi and sushi.

Tu Tu Tango, 124 Bunda Street, Canberra City, ✆6257 7288. Cafe & bar, woodfire pizzas a specialty. **Anatolia**, cnr Bunda & Mort Streets, Canberra City, ✆6257 1100. Turkish cuisine.

Canberra Vietnamese Restaurant, 21 East Row, Canberra City, ✆6247 4840.

Lemon Grass, 71 London Circuit, Canberra City, ✆6247 2279. Traditional Thai.

Taj Mahal, 39 Northbourne Avenue (upstairs), Canberra City, ✆6247 6528. Indian dining.

Zydeco, 173 City Walk, Canberra City, ✆6248 8709.

Rincon Latino, 5 Garema Place, Canberra City, ✆6247 0840.

Brindabella, 1 Binara Street, Canberra City, ✆6274 5506.

Ardeche, cnr City Walk & Ainslie Avenue, Canberra City, ✆6230 4800. If you can't make up your mind what you fancy to eat, take a trip to Glebe Park in Coranderrk Street,

Canberra City. There you will find eight food outlets - patisserie, hamburgers, refreshments bar, continental, Asian, Italian, carvery, seafood and bottle shop. The complex is open seven days, ✆0412 626 7252.

As in other cities, the Clubs offer good value for money, and welcome visitors. Some examples are:

The Canberra Club, 45 West Row, Canberra City, ✆6248 9000, has French cuisine in their restaurant.

Canberra Workers Club Bistro, cnr University Avenue & Childers Street, Canberra City, ✆248 0399, have a budget-priced bistro.

Ainslie Function Centre in the Ainslie Football Club, 52 Wakefield Avenue, Ainslie, ✆6248 8422, serves a Grand Seafood Buffet on Thursdays, but their extensive steak, seafood and salad menu should suffice on other days.

The **Canberra Labor Club**, Chandler Street, Belconnen, has an upmarket bistro at downmarket prices, ✆6251 5522.

KFC outlets are at Shop B07, Bunda Street, Canberra City; Bengendore Street, Queanbeyan; and 151 Canberra Avenue, Fyshwick.

McDonald's are found at the corner of Badham Street & Dickson Place, Dickson; 20-24 Wanniassa Street, Queanbeyan; cnr Namatjira Drive & MacNalley Street, Weston. Pizza Hut is in Woolley Street, Dickson and the Kippax Centre, Holt, ✆13 1166 for delivery.

Local Transport

Bus

Canberra has a public bus service, operated by Action Buses. The buses are large and orange and not easy to miss. The territory is divided into three zones, North, Central and South, and you will have to check your starting point against your destination to determine if you need a 'one zone' or 'all zone' ticket. The flat fares for adults are ✪$2 one zone and $4 all zone, but keep in mind that *Faresaver* tickets are available for extended use of this service.

Ticket agents can be found right across the area, and for more detailed information contact Action on ✆13 17 10 or for timetable information, either ✆6207 7611 or visit the website at ✆www.action. act.gov.au

Bicycle

Otherwise you can hire a bicycle at the Youth Hostel, Dryandra Street, O'Connor, ✆6248 9155; or Mr Spokes, near the Acton Ferry, Barrine Drive, ✆6257 1188.

Car Rental

Avis, 17 Lonsdale Street, Braddon, ✆6249 6088; Rumbles, 11 Gladstone Street, Fyshwick. Using a car is a good idea in Canberra.

Organised Tour

Round About Tours, ✆6262 8389; Canberra Region Tours, ✆6247 7281; Grand Touring Coach Charter, ✆6299 1600.

Points of Interest

Canberra has five sign-posted **Tourist Drives** which take in most of the sights. Each begins at the City Hill Lookout, and three concentrate on the central area of Canberra, while the others take in the popular stops on the city outskirts and beyond. The Visitor Centre will give you detailed information on these Drives.

Three popular tourist attractions in Canberra are Parliament House, the War Memorial and the National Library.

Parliament House, in keeping with Walter Burley Griffin's original plan, is the central landmark of Canberra. The building took eight years to complete, and was opened in 1988. While some might not be taken with the 81m (266 ft) stainless steel flagpole that dominates the city, all have to agree that the interior of the building is magnificent. There are imposing marble columns and stairs, extravagant halls, outstanding collections of paintings, sculptures, photographs and ceramics and well-worked timber masonry. Two halls are open to the public. In the Great Hall hangs one of the largest tapestries in the world, based on a painting by Australian artist, Arthur Boyd, that has to be seen to be believed.

Public galleries overlook the House of Representatives Chamber at the eastern side of the building, and the Senate Chamber to the west. The colours of the decor in both chambers reflect the natural green and red tones in native Australian flora. Visitors are welcome to view the Chambers between ⏱9am-5pm, and at all times when Parliament is sitting, even in the early hours of the morning. Guides are at key areas throughout the public areas of the building, and are happy to answer questions. There are also free guided tours available every 30 minutes. Facilities for visitors include a theatrette, an exhibition area, a post office, and on the first floor there is a cafeteria. The bookshop in the Foyer has many publications on Parliament and Parliament House, and a wide range of souvenirs. Pedestrian access is through the northern entrance, the side which overlooks the lake. Access to the underground carpark, which incidentally has room for 2000 vehicles, is via the ramps running off Commonwealth Avenue and Kings Avenue. Details on sitting hours of either of the Houses are available at the information desk in the foyer, or ℭ6277 7111.

The National Library, Parkes Place, is on the southern shores of Lake Burley Griffin. It has over 6 million books, periodicals and newspapers, thousands of paintings, maps, films, photographs, music scores, oral histories, and treasures. Exhibitions are held throughout the year, and tours of the Library are available on weekdays. The Library is ☼open every day except Good Friday and Christmas Day, and hours for the reading rooms, licensed bistro, shop and exhibition areas vary. For further information, ℭ6262 1111.

Australian War Memorial, Limestone Avenue, Campbell, commemorates the Australians who gave their lives for their country. The stylised Byzantine building houses a collection of relics, paintings, models, displays and records from all theatres of war. Exhibitions cover the history of Australians at war from Gallipoli to Vietnam. There is a free carpark and picnic areas, a licensed kiosk, and a shop selling a comprehensive range of military books, prints, posters and model kits and souvenirs. The memorial is ☼open daily 9am-4.45pm, ℭ6243 4211.

The National Gallery opened in 1982 and houses the national art collection. Eleven galleries provide more than 7000 square metres (8372 sq yds) of exhibition space spread over three levels. Sculpture is displayed in the garden. Regular lectures, film screenings and guided tours are available, and there are frequent special exhibitions, including some from overseas. Facilities include a shop, restaurant and snack bar. ☼Open daily 10am-5pm, ℭ6240 6502.

The High Court of Australia, Parkes Place, Parkes, is on the lake shore parallel to the Library. The building features extensive public areas, and is linked to the National Gallery by a pedestrian bridge. The three elegant courtrooms are open to the public. The court contains many interesting national murals and ceremonial plaques, and has a licensed cafeteria. ☼Open daily 10am-4pm. If you are in the mood for a meal, the *Sufficient Grounds* restaurant (ℭ6270 6820) can be found here - surely one of the most inventive theme names around!

Questacon, The National Science and Technology Centre, is located on the shores of Lake Burley Griffin, between the High Court and the Library. The Centre has over one hundred 'hands-on' exhibits, and visitors of all ages are entertained, intrigued and reassured about the science in our lives. Here you can experience an earthquake, operate a hovercraft, observe an active bee hive, and view a gallery of optical illusions, among other things. There is a cafe and science shop, and all are ☉open daily 10am-5pm, ✆6270 2800.

Seventy countries have diplomatic representation in Canberra, and most of their **Embassies** are in the suburbs of Yarralumla, Forrest and Red Hill. Two have special exhibitions open to visitors: Papua New Guinea, 39-41 Forster Crescent, ✆6273 3322 and Indonesia, 8 Darwin Avenue, ✆6252 8600. Some embassies are open for public inspection on occasions during the year, and the Visitor Information Centre has the details, as well as a brochure on all the embassies, and their addresses. Some of the embassies are built in their traditional style, including India, Thailand, Indonesia and China, and perhaps this explains the cattle that graze on the lawns of the New Zealand High Commission.

Government House, Dunrossil Drive, Yarra-lumla, the official residence of the Governor General, is not open for inspection, but there is a good view of the building from a lookout on Lady Denman Drive, south of Scrivener Dam.

The Prime Minister's Lodge is on the corner of Adelaide Avenue & National Circuit, Deakin, but it is not open to the public either.

Weston Park, Yarralumla, on the shores of the Lake, has picnic areas and gas barbecues. Features include a miniature railway, a mouse house and a maze. The maze takes about 15 minutes to negotiate and is suitable for all ages. ☉Open weekends and public and school holidays 11am-6pm. Miniature train rides are available 10.30am-5pm, ✆6282 2714.

Lake Burley Griffin is named after Canberra's designer, American architect Walter Burley Griffin. The lake was formed in 1963 by the construction of Scrivener Dam to hold back the waters of the Molonglo River. Over 400ha (988 acres) of parkland has been developed around the 35km (22 miles) foreshore, with numerous picnic areas and sailing boat launchings (power boats are prohibited). Swimming spots can be found at Black Mountain Peninsula, Yarralumla Bay and Springbank Island. Boat hire and cruises are available at Acton Terminal in West Basin, take Barrine Drive off Commonwealth Avenue.

The relatively inaccessible wetlands in East Basin, between Jerrabomberra Creek and the Molonglo River, provide a sanctuary for a variety of bird life.

Although they appear tranquil, Canberra's lakes can be dangerous for small craft as wind gusts can attain a velocity of 25 knots.

Weather bulletins issued by the media include wind forecasts, and boating enthusiasts should also heed orange spherical signals raised by water police, which indicate sailing conditions. The temperature of the water surface falls to 6.5C (44F) in winter, and obviously it is even colder below the surface, so this can also be a hazard.

The Captain Cook Memorial Water Jet, powered by two 560Kw motors, spurts a column of water 140m (459 ft) above central Lake Burley Griffin near Regatta Point. The jet and lakeshore Terrestrial Globe were built to mark the bicentenary of Captain Cook's discovery of eastern Australia in 1970. ⏱Operating times are 10am-noon and 2pm-4pm, subject to weather conditions.

The National Capital Exhibition is at Regatta Point in Commonwealth Park, ✆6257 1068. There are audio-visual presentations, photographs and displays explaining the history and development of the Nation's capital. Regatta Point provides an excellent vantage point of Lake Burley Griffin, and from the observation area and terrace restaurant there are views of the Captain Cook Water Jet, the Lake's Central Basin, and the Parliamentary Triangle. The Planning Exhibition is ⏱open daily 9am-5pm, and there is a gift and book shop.

St John's Church and **Schoolhouse**, Constitution Avenue, Reid, were built in the 1840s, and are Canberra's oldest surviving buildings. The schoolhouse features relics of Canberra's early history, ✆6248 8399. St John's is still an active parish.

Blundells Cottage is on Wendouree Drive, off Constitution Avenue, Parkes, and has a museum display of family life from the nineteenth century. The cottage was built about 1860 by Robert Campbell, and was part of his Duntroon Estate. The first long-term occupants were William and Mary Ginn, and their daughter, Gertrude, was the first child born in the cottage. Mr Ginn was the head ploughman on the Duntroon Estate. The farm house was occupied for 100 years until Mrs Oldfield, the final occupant, passed away on September 8, 1958. The cottage is ☉open Tue-Sun 10am-4pm, ☎6273 2667.

The Carillon, on Aspen Island, Lake Burley Griffin, Wendouree Drive, Parkes, is a three-column belltower, a gift from the British Government to mark Canberra's 50th jubilee. There are free 45 minute recitals in the afternoon daily, ☎6257 1068. The HMAS *Canberra* Memorial is nearby.

Royal Military College, Duntroon, is Australia's first military college and was founded in 1911. Tours of the grounds are available at limited times, ☎6265 9537 for details.

Civic Square is the civic heart of Canberra. Canberra Theatre Centre is at the head of the square and the famous old merry-go-round is in nearby Petrie Plaza. The statue of Ethos is in the foreground, flanked by government offices.

The **National Philatelic Exhibition**, Alinga Street, on the first floor of the GPO building, ☎6209 1680, has a gallery featuring Australia's largest and most valuable collection of stamps, including sheets of Australian stamps issued from Federation to the present.

The new, high-tech **National Museum of Australia** is on the Acton Peninsula, ☎6208 5000. It houses a vast and impressive collection in five permanent exhibitions and other temporary displays. Themes include *First Australian's*, *Tangled Destinies, Nation* and *Eternity*. An emphasis is placed on the unique people of Australia – historically and in the contemporary era. A visit to the museum is an interactive and immersive experience. There's plenty to see and do, with a range of engaging multimedia that means you'll probably come away learning something new. Plan to spend at least three hours exploring. A restaurant, cafe and shop are part of the complex. ☉Open 9am-5pm daily. Admission is free.

Scrivener Dam lookout is off Lady Denman Drive. Nearby is the **National Aquarium & Wildlife Park**, ☎6287 1211, with exhibitions of aquatic life, furry fauna and colourful birds. There is a walk-through oceanarium with sharks, rays, Barrier Reef fish, crocodiles, turtles and barracuda, though obviously not all in together. The complex also has a theatrette showing continuous films, a reasonably-priced Brasserie, seating 240 indoors and 300 outdoors, and a gift shop, all set in 5ha (12 acres) of landscaped grounds. It is ☉open daily 10am-5.30pm and admission is ✪$12 adults, $7 children and $35 for families.

The Royal Australian Mint, Denison Street, Deakin, is responsible for the production of Australia's circulating and collector coinage. The Mint also manufactures medals and medallions, and supplies coinage for several overseas nations. There is a display of past and present Australian coins and old minting equipment, and the Coin Shop offers a wide range of collector's coins and associated products. Ample parking is available, and the grounds are perfect for a picnic. The Mint is ☺open Mon-Fri 9am-4pm, Sat-Sun 10am-3pm, ©1300 652 020 or ©6202 6800.

St Christopher's Catholic Cathedral, 55 Manuka Street, near Manuka Park, ©6295 9555, has a Byzantine flavour to it.

The Free Serbian Orthodox Church, 32 National Circuit, Forrest, has vivid murals covering the walls and ceiling, the work of the late Karl Matzek, who painted them at the age of 87. The Church is not open to visitors on Sunday mornings, ©6295 1344.

The Telstra Tower is on the summit of Black Mountain, ©6248 1911, and from its lookout platforms, kiosk and restaurants, there are panoramic views of the whole region. Black Mountain Drive, the road to the Tower, runs off Clunies Ross Street, near the Botanic Gardens. Telstra Tower is ☺open daily 9am-10pm, adults ✪$4, concession $2. The kiosk and coffee shop provide refreshments and light meals, but for something special, the revolving restaurant in the

Parliament House

Tower offers international cuisine for lunch and dinner seven days a week, ✆6248 6162.

Australian National Botanic Gardens, also off Clunies Ross Street, Black Mountain, are devoted to growing Australian native plants and have over 6000 species. Special features include the Rainforest Gully, Eucalypt lawn and the Rockery. The Visitor Centre has displays and leaflets on walks around the gardens, and there is a kiosk and bookshop. ⏰Open daily, 9am-5pm, ✆6250 9540.

All Saints Anglican Church, 1 Bonney Street, Ainslie, was for 80 years the mortuary railway station at Rookwood Cemetery, Sydney. It was re-erected here stone by stone as the Parish Church of Ainslie, and is ⏰open daily, with tour guides on duty, ✆6248 7420.

The **Australian Institute of Sport**, Leverrier Crescent, Bruce, was the training ground of many athletes who took part in the 2000 Olympic Games in Sydney. It has become a popular tourist destination, particularly in recent years. Some tours are led by the athletes them-selves, and take the visitor through the modern facilities and sporting memorabilia, as well as provide an insight into gruelling training programs. Admission is ✪$10 adults, $5 children and $24 for families, ✆6214 1444.

Stromlo Exploratory, Cotter Road, Weston Creek, ✆6249 0232. This visitor centre is located in the Mt Stromlo Observatory and offers the latest in learning about outer space. Hands-on exhibits cover two floors, and there are giant-telescope tours and slides of spectacular solar system images. Admission into the Exhibition Hall is ✪$6 adults, $4 children and $14 for families. Public Observing Nights are only held once a month since they depend on the moon's phase, so phone the above number to check if this coincides with your trip and book your place.

Festivals

January - Multicultural Festival.
February - Royal Canberra Show. Canberra Travel Fair.
March - Canberra Festival. Autumn Flower Show. Black Opal Stakes. Canberra Antique Fair.
April - Canberra Marathon. ACT Heritage Week.
June - Trooping of the Colour - Duntroon. Embassy inspections.

Floriade Spring Festival - September
Canberra's parks and gardens come alive with spring colour during this very popular annual event. Talented gardeners and landscape architects create delightful patterns by plant-

ing a range of thousands and thousands of flowers. For information, ✆6205 0044, or visit 👁www.floriadeaustralia.com

October - Octoberfest.
November - Spring Show.

Facilities

Special, clearly marked cycleways have been provided in Canberra to separate cyclists from other traffic. A map of the metropolitan cycleways is available from the Canberra Visitors Centre. Cycles can be hired for an hour or a day around the lake (see under *Local Transport*).

Windsurfers, catamarans and other sailing craft can also be hired (Lake Burley Griffin Boat Hire, Acton, ✆6249 6861).

Golfers can choose from five courses (including Royal Canberra in Bentham Street, Yarralumla, ✆6282 7000), and another in nearby Queanbeyan.

Tennis courts can be hired in almost every suburb. There are also croquet lawns, squash courts, ten-pin bowling lanes and an ice rink.

The Visitor Information Centre has details of these and other sporting facilities, ✆1800 100 660.

Fishing
The streams in the ACT are divided into two categories - Open Fishing Water, which comprises the Murrumbidgee and Molonglo River below Coppins Crossing; and Trout Fishing Waters, which comprise all of the other waters in the ACT and Lakes Burley Griffin and Ginninderra.

No licences are required, and fishing is permitted in open fishing waters all year round. But trout and bass caught out of season must be returned to the water with the least possible injury. The bag limit is 10 fish per day.

The Open Season for fishing in trout fishing waters extends from the Saturday nearest October 1 to the Sunday nearest May 31 the following year.

Outlying Attractions

Gold Creek Road
The Gold Creek Road, a tranquil rustic setting embracing the historic Ginninderra Village, is only ten minutes' drive from Canberra City, following the Barton Highway. There are several interesting places to visit in the area.

Cockington Green, 11 Gold Creek Road, Nicholls, is Canberra's piece of Great Britain, and has accurate one-twelfth scale model buildings spread in acres of colourful fairy-tale-like gardens. A high speed train flashes by a station and across bridges as a nearby crowd watches a village cricket game. Not far away the people of Braemer Castle are enjoying the morning sun. Each model is a precise reconstruction, and each flower bed, lawn and hedge has been carefully manicured by Cockington Green's gardeners. There's a miniature steamtrain and a playground, both big enough for the kids, and a licensed restaurant that is adequate for discerning adults. Other facilities include an outdoor kiosk, gas barbecues and picnic areas. ⏰Open daily, 9.30am-5pm. Admission is adults ✪$12, children $6 and families $32.

Gems Gallery, is opposite Cockington Green, ✆6230 2740. The display in this museum is the largest presentation of Australian opals, and there is also a priceless collection of Aboriginal artefacts, some pieces being over 70 thousand years old. The cafeteria is open for meals daily, and there is an opal and souvenir shop. ⏰Open daily 9.30am-4.30pm.

Gold Creek Cultural Centre, O'Hanlon Place, has locally made crafts, Australian souvenirs, hand painted clothing, unique garden pots and other accessories from a variety of shops. ⏰Open daily 10am-5pm, ✆6241 8811.

Nearby is the **Ginninderra Gallery**, with paintings, pottery, woodturnings, glassware and leather works, all with an Australian theme. ⏰Open daily 10am-5pm, ✆6230 2922.

National Dinosaur Museum, on the corner of the Barton Highway, Gungahlin, ✆6230 2655. The museum houses more than 300 exhibits, including full-scale skeletal replicas and astonishing prehistoric facts. It is ⏰open daily 10am-5pm and admission is ✪$10 adults, $6 children and $25 for families.

George Harcourt Inn is an 'old English' pub, where you can dine outdoors, or in winter, inside before the open log fire. ⏰Open daily from 11am for lunch, and closes at midnight Thu-Sat, an hour earlier during the rest of the week. For further information, ✆6230 2484.

Canberra Walk-in Aviary, Federation Square, Gungahlin, ✆6230 2044. Hundreds of bird finches can be viewed in this unique environment, ⏰open daily 10am-4pm. Admission prices are ✪$6 adult, $3 children and $15 for families.

Bywong
Historic Bywong Mining Town is 33km (21 miles) north of Canberra, off the Federal Highway, Millyn Road, Gearys Gap. It is a gold mining village with areas classified by the Heritage Council. Guided tours of the village are available with an interesting commentary on geological and historical areas, including the open-cut mine shaft mines and

batteries. Panning tools can be hired. There is a kiosk, barbecue and picnic areas. ☉Open daily 10am-4pm, ✆6236 9183.

Ginninderra Gorge and Falls

The Falls are in Parkwood Road, the continuation of Southern Cross Drive, West Belconnen (NSW). There are spectacular views of Ginninderra Gorge and the Falls, scenic nature trails, canoeing, picnic facilities and camping. ☉Open daily 10am-5pm.

Cotter Dam

The source of Canberra's original water supply and first major construction work is located 22km (14 miles) west of the city, on Cotter Road. It is a very popular spot for picnics, camping and swimming in the river. There are playgrounds, a kiosk, shop, and licensed restaurant. ☉Open daily.

Tidbinbilla Space Centre

Situated 40km (25 miles) south of Canberra, off Paddys River Road, still in the ACT, the space tracking station is one of three such facilities located around the world to provide complete 24-hour tracking coverage. The other two are in the United States and Spain. ☉Open 9am-5pm, ✆6201 7838.

Tidbinbilla Nature Reserve

The Reserve is a wilderness area with marked trails and free-range wildlife enclosures, containing red and grey kangaroos, wallaroos, emus and water birds, and the occasional koala. The walking trails in the area are graded from easy to difficult, and you can walk 70m or 7km. The Reserve is off Paddys River Road and opens every day, except Christmas Day and days of total fire ban. At the Visitor Information Centre there are displays, audio visual presentations, literature and helpful staff who will answer your enquiries, ✆6205 1233. The Reserve is ☉open 9am-6pm daily, with extended hours in season, and are charged at ✪$9 per day for entry.

Corin Forest Recreation Area & Ski Facility

Corin Forest is off Tidbinbilla Road, Smokers Gap, a 30 to 40 minute drive from the city. It is home to Australia's longest bobsled/alpine slide (800m - 875 yds), which winds down through mountain forests, achieving a speed of up to 75km/h (47mph). During June through September, providing there is sufficient snow, there is skiing, ski hire and ski school, and snow tobogganing. ☉Open every weekend 10am-5pm, and all school and public holidays. There is also a licensed restaurant. For further information, ✆6247 2250.

Lanyon Historic Homestead

In Tharwa Drive, off Monaro Highway, Tharwa, the Homestead is classified by the National Trust, and is set in landscaped gardens and parklands on the banks of Murrumbidgee River. In the early days it assumed the proportions of a self-contained village. There is a coffee shop, gift shop, and the Sidney Nolan Art Gallery is close by. ⊙Open Tues-Sun 10am-4pm, with 1 hour tours available, ✆6237 5136. ✪$6 adults, $3 children and $14 families.

Cuppacumbalong Craft Centre

Another historic property in Naas Road, Tharwa, featuring three cottages, nine out-buildings and a private cemetery. There are craft galleries, studios, a restaurant, and picnic and barbecue areas near the river. ⊙Open Wed-Sun and public holidays 11am-5pm, ✆6236 5116.

Queanbeyan

Although Queanbeyan is in New South Wales, it is virtually a suburb of Canberra, with a population of around 25,700. The town has plenty of accommodation, and generally the prices are lower than in Canberra. Many people find it worthwhile to stay in Queanbeyan, and drive the 12km (7 miles) into the city to commence their sightseeing. The Queanbeyan Visitor Information Centre, 1 Farrer Place (cnr Lowe Street), ✆(02) 6298 0241 or ✆1800 026 192, is ⊙open Mon-Fri 8.30am-5pm, Sat 9am-1.00pm. The office has details of all accommodation, and also of tourist drives they have mapped for you to visit the interesting sights. You can email them at ✉tourist@qcc.nsw.gov.au, or go to the web page at ☞www.queanbeyan.nsw.gov.au

In Farrer Place there is a memorial commemorating the valuable work carried by the Father of the Wheat Industry, William James Farrer, and also the **Queanbeyan & District Historic Museum**. The museum is housed in the former police sergeant's residence, built in 1877, and has relics of early local families and items from pioneering days. There are also two rooms furnished in the style of the late 1890s. It is ⊙open Sat-Sun 2-4pm, ✆6297 1978.

The **Millhouse Gallery**, 6 Trinculo Place, was built in 1883 and restored and reopened in 1983. It is a unique building with rooms housing rare books, antique furniture and arts and crafts. The Gallery is ⊙open Wed-Sun 10am-2pm, ✆6297 8181.

Lookouts in the area include **Bungendore Hill**, 4km east of the city, and **Jerrabomberra**, 5km west.

Googong Dam was built south of the town to supply water to Queanbeyan, and to supplement

CANBERRA

MAP M

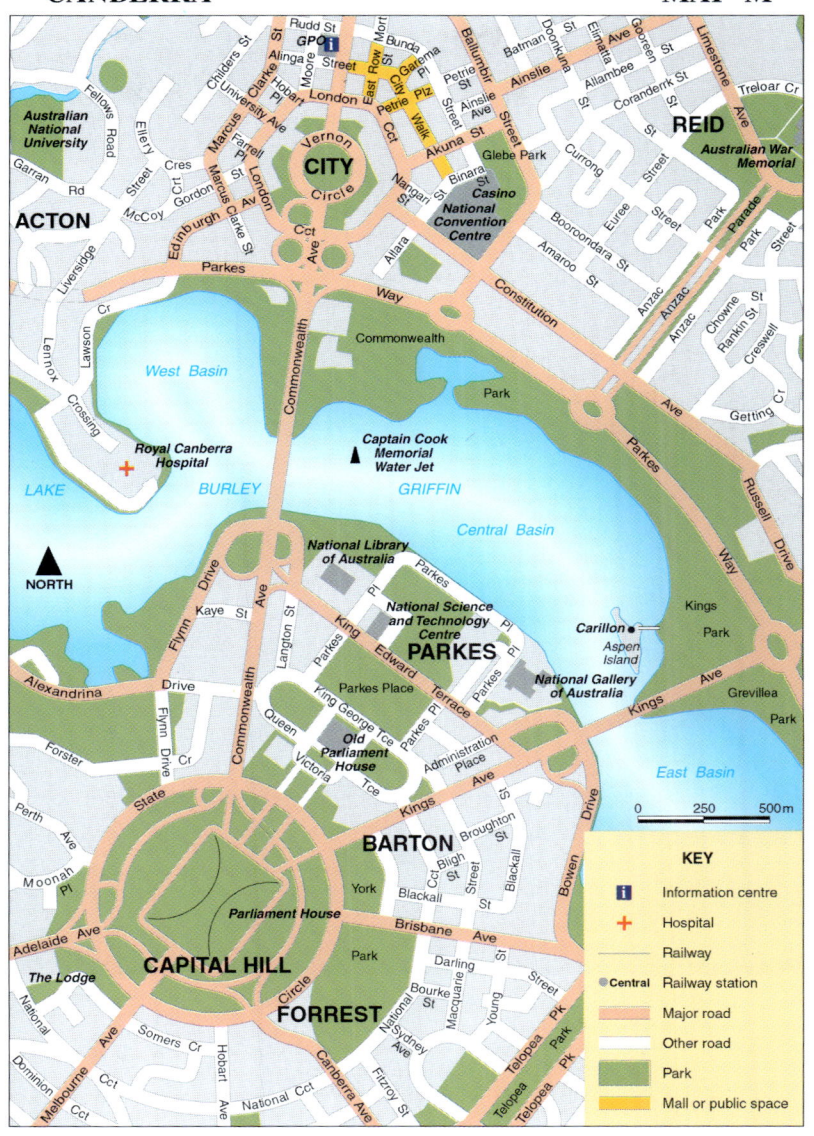

KEY

ℹ	Information centre
✚	Hospital
	Railway
●Central	Railway station
	Major road
	Other road
	Park
	Mall or public space

A Frosty Morning in the New South Wales countryside just north of the nation's capital, Canber

supplies to Canberra. The area is ☉open 8am-5pm and it is a good idea to drop into the Visitor Centre by the entrance for maps and recreational ideas, ✆6207 2779. Activities include canoeing, sailing, fishing and walking. Points of interest include London Bridge Homestead, a woolshed and shearer's quarters. The turnoff to the dam is about 10km along the Cooma Road.

Victoria

Melbourne

Population 2,942,000

Melbourne, the capital of Victoria, is situated on the shores of Port Phillip Bay. The Yarra River flows through the city.

Settlers in Van Diemen's Land (Tasmania) had known for years that there was good grazing land in the Port Phillip area, but had been refused permission to settle there. In 1835, John Batman ignored the ban, landed with a party, and 'bought' 600,000 acres of land from the local Aborigines for a few axes and other trade goods. He then returned to Launceston and formed the Port Phillip Association. (On the north side of Flinders Street, between Market and William Streets, there is a small plaque in the pavement marking the place where Batman stood when he declared that it was a good place for a village.)

In 1836, Governor Bourke vetoed Batman's purchase, and appointed Captain William Lonsdale as resident magistrate of the rapidly-growing settlement. Bourke visited the site in the following year, named the place Melbourne, had a street plan drawn up, and offered lots for sale.

The Australian Colonies Government Act was passed in August 1850, and constituted the Port Phillip district as a separate colony, with La Trobe as its first Lieutenant-Governor. Soon after, gold was discovered near Ballarat, and people came from all over the world seeking their fortune. The consequent Eureka Uprising gave the new government its first major challenge.

Climate

Melbourne's climate is midway between maritime and continental, and is very changeable. Average temperatures: January max 26C (79F) - min 14C (57F); July max 13C (55F) - min 6C (43F). Average annual rainfall: 656mm (26 ins). The driest months are June to August.

Characteristics

Victoria is called the Garden State, and its capital city certainly does its share to live up to that reputation. Melbourne has tree-lined boulevards, acres of parkland on the banks of the Yarra River, and parks and gardens galore in the suburbs.

How to Get There

By Air

Melbourne International Airport, at Tullamarine, is serviced by over 20 international carriers.

The domestic lines of Qantas, ✆13 1313, Ansett, ✆13 1300, and Impulse, ✆13 1381, have regular services from other cities in Australia. Aus-Air, ✆(03) 9580 6166, specialise in services to Tasmania and the southern islands of Flinders and King.

The airport is about 20km (12 miles) out of the city, and the Skybus operates between Tulla-

marine and the terminal at 58 Franklin Street, ✆9335 3066 or ✆9662 9275. The Frankston & Peninsula Airport Shuttle, ✆9783 1199, takes passengers to that area, and there are also shuttle buses for the eastern suburbs.

By Bus

Greyhound Pioneer, ✆13 2030, and McCaffertys, ✆13 1499, have regular services to/from Melbourne and Sydney, Adelaide, Canberra, Newcastle, Coolangatta, Brisbane, Alice Springs, Townsville, Perth, Cairns and Darwin.

By Rail

There are rail services from Sydney and Adelaide, with connections from other capital cities, ✆13 2232. The country and interstate terminal is Spencer Street Station.

V/Line

Rail and coach services operate from country Victoria to Melbourne daily. They also travel as far as Adelaide, Canberra and the Sapphire Coast of NSW. For further information, ✆136 196.

By Road

From Sydney, via the Hume Highway, 875km (544 miles); via the Princes Highway, 1058km (657 miles); via the Olympic Way, 961km (597 miles); via Canberra/Cooma/Cann River, 1038km (645 miles).

From Adelaide, via the Western and Dukes Highways, 726km (451 miles); via Princes Highway West, 910km (565 miles).

Visitor Information

The Victoria Visitor Information Centre is in the Melbourne Town Hall on the corner of Swanston Walk & Little Collins Street, ✆(03) 9658 9955. It is ☺open Mon-Fri 8.30am-5.30pm and weekends and public holidays 9am-5pm. They can be emailed at ✉visitor@melbourne .vic.gov.au

There are information booths in Bourke Street Mall, between Elizabeth and Swanston Streets, and Flinders Street Station, on the corner of Flinders and Swanston Streets.

The Victorian Tourism Operators Association is on Level 2, Rialto North Tower, 525 Collins Street, ✆(03) 9614 8877 or email ✉vtoa@vtoa.asn.au

Tourism Victoria is on Level 6, 55 Collins Street, ✆(03) 132 842.

City of Melbourne, is in Melbourne Town Hall, Swanston Street, ✆(03) 9658 9955.

The Travellers' Aid Society of Victoria is on the 2nd Floor at 169 Swanston Street, ✆(03) 9654 2600. They are ☺open Mon-Fri 8am-6pm and Sat-Sun 10am-4pm. They also have a Rail Room at Spencer Street Railway Station, ✆(03) 9670 2873.

Melbourne also has an Information Line available 7 days a week from 8am-6pm - ✆13 28 42.

The following websites will give you a detailed insight into the city of Melbourne, outlying regions and potential itineraries for travel around Victoria:

👁melbourne.citysearch.com.au
👁www.melbourne.org
👁www.tourism.vic.gov.au
👁www.theage.com.au
👁www.victrip.vic.gov.au

Accommodation

For a complete list of accommodation, contact one of the Tourist Offices above or explore the web pages.

As with any big city, accommodation is usually cheaper in the outer suburbs, and that is obviously where you find the caravan parks.

Here is a selection of city and inner suburban accommodation, with prices for a double room per night, which should be used as a guide only. The telephone area code is 03.

5-Star

Hotel Sofitel, 25 Collins Street, ✆9653 0000. 363 rooms, 52 suites, licensed restaurant, gym - ✪$310-1760.

Le Meridien at Rialto Melbourne, 495 Collins Street, ✆9620 9111.

242 rooms, 10 suites, licensed restaurant, swimming pool, spa, sauna, gym - ✪$425-1030.

Grand Hyatt Melbourne, cnr Exhibition & Lonsdale Streets, ✆9657 1234. 547 rooms, 26 suites, licensed restaurant, swimming pool, spa, sauna, gym, tennis - ✪$270-630.

Hilton on the Park Melbourne, 192 Wellington Parade, East Melbourne, ✆9419 2000. 398 rooms, 38 suites, licensed restaurant, swimming pool, spa, sauna, gym, barbecue - ✪$300-430.

4-Star

Rydges Melbourne, 186 Exhibition Street, ✆9662 0511. 363 rooms, 70 suites, licensed restaurant, undercover parking, pool, sauna, spa, gym - ✪$195.

Centra Melbourne, cnr Flinders & Spencer Streets, ✆9629 5111. 384 rooms, 13 suites, licensed restaurant, gym, heated swimming pool - ✪$195-275.

The Chifley on Flemington Melbourne, 5 Flemington Road, North Melbourne, ✆9329 9344. 227 rooms, 9 suites, licensed restaurant, bistro, swimming pool, gym, sauna - ✪$135-200.

3-Star

The Batmans Hill Hotel, 66 Spencer Street, ✆9614 6344. 85 rooms, licensed restaurant, undercover parking - ✪$140-160.

Hotel Ibis, 21 Therry Street, ✆9639 1988. 250 rooms, licensed restaurant - ✪$110-190.

Kingsway Motel, cnr Park Street & Eastern Road, South Melbourne, ©9699 2533. 40 units - ✪$115-135.

Treasury Motor Lodge, 179 Powlett Street, East Melbourne, ©9417 5281. 21 units - ✪$130-150.

Flagstaff City Motor Inn, 45 Dudley Street, West Melbourne, ©9329 5788. 39 units, spa - ✪$110-160.

Marco Polo Inn, cnr Harker Street & Flemington Road, North Melbourne, ©9329 1788. 70 units, licensed restaurant, swimming pool, sauna - ✪$110-200.

Hotel Enterprize, 44 Spencer Street, ©9629 6991. 150 rooms, licensed restaurant - ✪$100.

2-Star

City Square Motel, 67 Swanston Street, ©9654 7011. 24 units, basic facilities - ✪$105.

Melbourne Suburbs

Brunswick

Princes Park Motor Inn, 2 Sydney Road, ©9388 1000. 70 units - ✪$125-135.

Parkville Motel, 759 Park Street, ©9388 1500. 20 units - ✪$90.

Coburg

Coburg Motor Inn, 726 Sydney Road, Coburg North, ©9350 1855. 26 units, swimming pool, undercover parking - ✪$85-95.

Coburg Coach Motel, 846 Sydney Road, Coburg North, ©350 2844.

27 units, licensed restaurant (closed Sunday), swimming pool - ✪$75.

Footscray

Footscray Motor Inn, 90 Droop Street, ©9687 6877. 30 units, licensed restaurant (closed Sunday) - ✪$120-155.

Mid Gate Motor Lodge, 76 Droop Street, ©9689 2300. 25 units - ✪$85.

St Kilda

Cabana Court Motel, 46 Park Street, ©9534 0771. 16 units, 16 suites - ✪$100-120.

Crest on Barkly Hotel Melbourne, 47 Barkly Street, ©9537 1788. 60 units, sauna - ✪$110-160.

Serviced Apartments

South Yarra Place Apartments, 41 Margaret Street, South Yarra, ©9867 6595. 18 studio apartments - ✪$70-165.

Caravan Parks

Melbourne Holiday Park, 265 Elizabeth Street, Coburg, ©9354 3533. (No pets allowed), 120 sites, heated pool - powered sites ✪$23 for two, cabins $90-95 for two.

Ashley Gardens Holiday Village, 129 Ashley Street, Braybrook, ©9318 6866. (No pets allowed) 106 sites, tennis, heated pool - powered sites ✪$23, cabins $70-100 for two.

Sylvan Caravan Park, 1780 Hume Highway, Campbellfield, ©9357 0009. (No dogs or cats) 101 sites -

powered sites ✪$20 for two.

There is a **Youth Hostel** in 78 Howard Street, North Melbourne, ☎9329 8599. It has 34 rooms at ✪$25-35 per person twin share. Another is at 76 Chapman Street, North Melbourne, ☎9328 3595. It has 59 rooms at ✪$18 per person twin share.

Local Transport

The Met, Melbourne's public transport system, covers trains, trams and buses, and is operated by the Public Transport Corporation. Melbourne is divided into three zones and your ticket type depends on which zone you are going to travel in, and for how long. Two-hour, daily, weekly, monthly or yearly tickets are available.

The routes of the various forms of transport are indicated on the Met map, available from railway stations, newsagencies and some book shops. Further information is available from the Met Transport Information Centre, 589 Collins Street, ☎13 1638 (☉open 7am-9pm), or from The Met Shop at 103 Elizabeth Street.

Melbourne's metropolitan public transport website for Bayside Trains is 👁www.met.vic.gov.au

Victoria's official public transport site, containing timetables and fares for trams, buses and trains, is 👁www.victrip.com.au

Trams

Trams are just about the 'symbol' of Melbourne, and are a big drawcard for visitors. These vehicles, some old-fashioned and some sleek and new, continue to provide transport for thousands of commuters.

They are an interesting, reliable and efficient way to see the city. The Visitor Centres can provide you with a brochure outlining the routes, stops, zones and fares, with explanations to assist your reading of tickets (Metcards) and timetables.

Here are a few hints: remember to take coins with you, as this is the only form of currency which ticket vending machines accept. You can purchase a daily ticket for ✪$4.40, allowing you unlimited travel in Zone 1, which covers the city and immediate surrounds. Keep an eye out for retailers displaying the Metcard Sales Flag, because daily tickets must be pre-purchased. In the city centre, there is a free tram service, the Free City Circle, which skirts the rectangular perimeter of the CBD and may be useful for reducing your legwork while shopping or sightseeing.

Taxis

These can be hired off the street, at taxi ranks, major hotels, or by phoning one of the taxi companies.

Initial flagfall is ✪$2.60 and the

meter clicks over at ✪$1 per kilometre, or at 41.6 cents per minute if the speed of the vehicle drops below 25km/h. There is a booking fee of $1 and also a late night surcharge of $1. Be aware that CityLink tolls will be added to the fare if you choose to travel on certain roads - both the Western and Southern Links are ✪$2 for taxis.

Following are some of the companies operating in Melbourne: Arrow Taxi Service, ✆13 2211; Astoria Taxis, ✆9347 5511; Black Cabs Combined, ✆13 2227; Embassy Taxis, ✆13 1755; Frankston Radio Cabs, ✆9786 3322; North Suburban Taxis, ✆13 1119; Regal Corporate Cars, ✆9326 6600; Silver Top Taxi Service, ✆13 1008; West Suburban Taxi, ✆9689 1144; Yellow Cabs, ✆13 19 24.

Water taxis include: River Yarra Water Taxis, ✆0416 06 8655; and Melbourne Circle Water Taxis, ✆9686 0914.

Car Hire

There are plenty of car rental agencies, and they accept current international licences.

Airport Rent A Car, ✆9335 3355; All Cheap Car Rentals, ✆9429 6999; Atlas, ✆9633 6233; Avis, ✆9330 4011; Budget, ✆1300 362 848; Crown, ✆9682 2266; Delta, ✆9330 6122; Hertz, ✆13 3039; Murphy, ✆9602 2265; National, ✆9696 9000; Pacific, ✆9347 9600;

Thrifty, ✆1300 367 2277.

When driving in Melbourne, there are a few rules about the trams. Drivers must not obstruct trams, and there are yellow lines on roadways indicating streets in which drivers must keep clear of the tracks when trams are approaching. Drivers must also stop when a tram is picking up or setting down passengers, if there is not a central traffic island. Making a right hand turn can sometimes be dicey in the city centre. If the intersection has a 'hook turn' sign, the turn has to be made from the left-hand lane when the lights change, to leave the centre of the intersection clear for trams.

Tollways

Citylink is a system of roads that connects some of Melbourne's motorways together. At the time of writing, Citylink tolls are applicable on the Monash Freeway, Tullamarine Freeway and the Bolte Bridge. No other motorways in Melbourne have tolls on them.

Leave your change in your pocket, though, because tolls are collected electronically. Most people visiting Melbourne will only want to use Citylink a couple of times at most. It is possible to buy up to twelve day passes per year on Citylink. Day passes cost ✪$3.85 and can be paid for with a Visa, Mastercard or Bankcard over the phone or bought at selected Shell service stations. Day passes can be bought up until 12pm the day after travel, but an extra fee for late day passes applies. The Citylink customer service number to pay for the pass is ✆13 26 29.

Bicycle Hire

Melbourne has quite a few bike tracks, and to hire a bike it is best to get in touch with Bicycle Victoria, 19 O'Connell Street, North Melbourne, ✆9328 3000.

Eating Out

Melbourne has over 3200 restaurants representing 70 national cuisines. The most plentiful choice of Asian restaurants is found in Chinatown's Little Bourke Street; for Italian food, try Lygon Street, Carlton; for Greek, Lonsdale Street; and for Vietnamese, Victoria Street, Richmond. South Yarra is another restaurant centre.

Here is a selection of highly recommended restaurants.

Asian

Flower Drum, 17 Market Lane, ✆9662 3655. This is the number one Chinese restaurant, with a legendary status in Melbourne culinary circles. The question, however, is whether the justifiable fame, outstanding cuisine and impeccable service are worth the average $150 bill for two. The Drum is open for dinner 7 days and lunch Mon-Sat, licensed.

Mask of China, 117 Little Bourke Street, ✆9662 2116. Licensed, excellent seafood and wine list, dinner served daily from 6pm, lunch on Sunday from midday.

Empress of China, 120 Little Bourke Street, ✆9663 1833. Open for dinner 6 days and lunch on Sundays.

Bamboo House, 47 Little Bourke Street, ✆9662 1565. Licensed. Peking duck and spicy seafoods are specialties. Open daily from 5.30pm and for lunch Mon-Fri.

King of Kings, 209 Russel Street, ✆9663 2895. Inexpensive meals of a good quality, open daily 11am-2.30am.

Isthmus of Kra, 50 Park Street, South Melbourne, ✆9690 3688. Gernerally considered one of the finest Thai restaurants in Melbourne. Licensed, wonderful wine list, varied menu, open for dinner 7 days and lunch Mon-Fri.

European

Austria Haus Edelweiss, 419 Spencer Street, ✆9329 5877. Licensed, open 7 days for lunch and dinner, with Viennese Sunday luncheon.

Casa Di Iorio, 141 Lygon Street, Carlton, ✆9347 2670. Italian cuisine restaurant and pizza house, plus takeaway.

Da Salvatore, 29 Gratton Street,

Carlton, ©9663 4778. Pizza, pasta and steaks, quick service, open 7 days for lunch and dinner.

Bonum, 2 Collins Street, City, ©9650 9387. Licensed, up-market restaurant with inventive and exotic dishes at prices around $25 for a main course. Open for dinner Mon-Sat and for lunch Mon-Fri.

2bc, 177 Greville Street, Prahran, ©9529 4922. Busy and trendy establishment that serves Mediterranean-style meals at reasonable prices. It is licensed and open for lunch 7 days and dinner Mon-Sat.

Akvavit, Ground Level 3a, 2 Southgate, Southbank, ©9699 9947. Swedish restaurant with views of the river and city. Licensed or BYO, open daily for lunch and dinner. Two people can escape here paying around $40 for meals plus drinks.

International

O'Connels, 407 Coventry Street, South Melbourne, ©9699 9600. A changing menu that ranges from North American to Middle Eastern cuisine. Licensed, open for lunch and dinner 7 days.

Blakes, Ground Level, 2 Southgate, Southbank, ©9699 4100. Extensive menu offering a variety of unique flavours. Wonderful views of the Yarra and city. Open daily for lunch and dinner.

Harvey's, 10 Murphy Street, South Yarra, ©9867 3605. Predominantly Asian and Italian flavours. Open

daily for lunch and dinner, from 7am Mon-Fri.

Becco, 11-25 Crossley Street, ©9663 3000. Efficient service, strong wine list and an extensive menu. Open daily 9am-11pm.

Chinois, 176 Toorak Road, South Yarra, ©9826 3388. Expensive but elegant modern restaurant. Licensed, open for lunch and dinner Mon-Fri.

Abla's, 109 Elgin Street, Carlton, ©9347 0006. Considered to be the best Middle Eastern restaurant in Melbourne. Set menu with a variety of complementary flavours. Open Thu-Fri for lunch and Mon-Sat for dinner.

est est est, 440 Clarendon Street, South Melbourne, ©9682 5688. Short but innovative menu with good wines to match. An expensive venture. Licensed and open Mon-Sat from 6pm.

Theatre Restaurants

Hofbrauhaus, 18-24 Market Lane, Melbourne, ©9663 3361. Bavarian beerfest. Affordable lunch menu. Licensed, open daily midday to midnight.

Dirty Dick's Medieval Madness Restaurant, 45 Dudley Street, West Melbourne, ©9325 3999. Licensed, medieval banquet.

The Comedy Club, 380 Lygon Street, Carlton, ©9348 1622. Open 9am-5pm Mon-Fri. Fully, licensed, cabaret environment, dinner and show packages available.

Witches in Britches, 84 Dudley Street, West Melbourne, ✆9329 9850. Bar, three course meal and a two-hour show to follow. Open 7pm-1am 7 days.

Dracula's Theatre Restaurant, 169 Exhibition Street, Melbourne, ✆9663 1754. Comic Transylvanian theme. Centrally located in the city. At the other end of the scale, KFC is at 201 Bourke Street and 37 Swanston Street. Pizza Hut is on the corner of Elizabeth and Bourke Streets (✆13 1166 for delivery). There are no less than 11 McDonalds branches, with 4 on Bourke Street, 2 on Collins Street, 2 on Elizabeth Street, and one each on Lonsdale, Swanston and St Kilda. Of course, the suburbs are represented by additional branches of each of the above.

You will find many other types of fast food outlets in the city centre. Going hungry in Melbourne is almost impossible, except in cases when you remain indecisive for hours, overwhelmed by the wide choice of venues. But this seldom occurs.

Entertainment

Melbourne's nightlife conjures up images of excitement, colour, action and entertainment. There is a comprehensive range of nocturnal activities to select from including discos, wine bars, concerts, theatre, cinema, live bands, nightclubs and much more.

Here is a selection of entertainment venues in the city.

Cinemas

Hoyts Cinema Complex, 140 Bourke Street, ✆9663 3303.

Village Centre, 206 Bourke Street, ✆9667 6565.

Chinatown Cinema, 200 Bourke Street, ✆9662 3465.

Crazy Horse Cinema, 34 Elizabeth Street, ✆9654 8796.

Greater Union, 131 Russell Street, ✆9654 8235.

Kino Cinemas, 45 Collins Street, ✆9650 2100.

Lumiere Cinemas, 108 Lonsdale Street, ✆9639 1055.

Moonlight Cinemas, Level 10, 140 Bourke Street, ✆9663 9555.

Theatres

The **Half-Tix** kiosk is in the Bourke Street Mall, ✆9650 9420.

Princess Theatre, 163 Spring Street, ✆9662 2911.

Victorian Arts Centre, 100 St Kilda Road, ✆9281 8000.

Athenaeum Theatre, 188 Collins Street, ✆9650 1500.

Comedy Theatre, 240 Exhibition Street, ✆9209 9000.

Playbox Theatre Company, 113 Sturt Street, South Melbourne, ✆9685 5111.

Melbourne Theatre Company, 129 Ferrars Street, Southbank, ✆13 6166.

Her Majesty's Theatre, 219 Exhibition Street, ✆9663 3211.

Forum Theatre, 154 Flinders Street, ✆9299 9700.

Princes Theatre, 163 Spring Street, ✆9299 9800.

Regent Theatre, 191 Collins Street, ✆9299 9860.

Sidney Myer Music Bowl, Kings Domain, ✆9281 8360.

Nightclubs

Chevron, 519 St Kilda Road, ✆9510 1281. ⏰Open Thu 9pm-5am, Friday midnight-10am. Cover charge ✪$12.

Melbourne Metro, 20-30 Bourke Street, ✆9663 4288. ⏰Open Thu-Sat. Cover charge ✪$6 Thursday, $10 Friday & Saturday.

Revolver Upstairs, 229 Chapel Street, Prahran, ✆9521 5985. ⏰Open Mon-Thu midnight-3am, Fri-Sun 24hrs.

The Dome, 19 Commercial Road, Prahran, ✆9529 8966. ⏰Opens daily from 10pm with a cover charge of ✪$10.

Grainstore Tavern, 46 King Street, ✆9614 3570. Live acts upstairs, video dance club downstairs.

The Ivy, 145 Flinders Lane, ✆9650 1855. Open Thurs-Sat, four floors, dance, bar, band and VIP Bar upstairs.

Club V, 371 Chapel Street, South Yarra, ✆9827 1771. ✪$10 cover charge.

Salt, 14a Claremont Street, South Yarra, ✆9827 8333. Melbourne's newest and most sophisticated nightclub.

Billboard, 170 Russell Street, ✆9639 4000. ⏰Open Mon, Thurs-Sat 9pm-7am.

Club UK, 169 Exhibition Street, ✆9663 2075. Geared towards the backpacker sector - perhaps those who are feeling a little homesick. ⏰Open Wed-Sun 5pm-3am and there is no cover charge.

Monsoon's, in the Grand Hyatt Melbourne, 123 Collins Street, ✆9653 4516.

P O D, 241 King Street, ✆9642 8100. As the name indicates, this venue is quite simply a 'Place Of Dance'.

Chaise Lounge, 105 Queen Street, Melbourne, ✆9670 6120. Good music, plenty of seating, vibrant atmosphere and post-modern decor. ⏰Open from 4pm Tue, Wed & Fri and from 9am on Saturday, closing at 3am.

Bars & Pubs

Up Top Bar, First Floor, 163 Russell Street, ✆9663 8990. ⏰Open from 4pm until late the following morning Wed-Sun. Nostalgic '50s decor revised in trendy style. Impressive list of alcoholic beverages. Entry is free.

Gin Palace, 191 Little Collins Street, ✆9654 0533. Characterised by an eclectic mix of furniture fashions and cocktail concoctions (try an 'Industrial Revolution', for example!). ☺Open daily 4pm-3am.

Hairy Canary, 212 Little Collins Street, ✆9654 2471. An inviting complement of food is on offer for those who feel that they need something to wash down with their drink. ☺Open 7.30am-3am 7 days.

The Bullring, 95 Johnston Street, Fitzroy, ✆9416 0022. Lively atmosphere with music and dance of Latin American derivation. ☺Open from 6pm-late, entertainment begins at 10.30pm. ✪$5 cover charge.

Walters Wine Bar, Upper Level, Southgate, Southbank, ✆9690 1211. Popular after-dark venue with stunning city views across the Yarra River. Good meals also available. ☺Open midday every day and closes Sun-Thu at 1am and Fri-Sat at 3am.

Bell's Hotel, 157 Moray Street, South Melbourne, ✆9690 4511. Meals from 6pm.

Redback Brewery, 75 Flemington Road, North Melbourne, ✆9329 9400. ☺Open Mon-Thurs 11am-midnight, Fri-Sat 11am-1am, Sun 11am-11.30pm. Meals Mon-Sun noon-3pm and 6-10pm.

Edward's Tavern, 221 High Street, Prahran, ✆9510 9897. 3 main bars and live entertainment. ☺Open from 7pm Fri-Sun & Tues, 9pm Mon & Thurs, closed Wednesdays.

Music Venues
Rock
Wayside Inn, 466 City Road, South Melbourne, ✆9699 8469.

Central Club Hotel, 246 Victoria Street, North Melbourne, ✆9329 7482.

Jazz
Dizzy's Jazz Bar, 90 Swan Street, Richmond, ✆9428 1233. A deservedly famous centre for jazz lovers. ☺Open Thu-Sat 8pm-1am. Cover charges are ✪$8 on Thursday and $10 on Friday & Saturday.

Moylans, 384 Flinders Lane, Melbourne, ✆9629 1030. Smoke-free environment, and a magnet for talented jazz musicians.

Ozcat, at the Parkview, cnr Scotchmer Street & Georges Road, Fitzroy North, ✆9489 8811. This venue will be used only for special concerts, while the main features of the Australian Catalog of Independent Artists will be played at Moylans (*see above*).

Rhythm & Blues
The Next Blue, at the Crown Casino, 8 Whiteman Street, Southbank, ✆9292 7007.

Shopping

Melbourne is Australia's fashion capital, and has an enormous selection of clothes and accessories boutiques.

Collins Street has many designer

label boutiques, and is linked to Bourke Street by a network of arcades and alleys with boutiques and specialty shops. Explore the sidewalks along Collins Street between Swanston and Spring Streets for some exclusive up-market clothing stores.

234 Collins, located at that address, is a complex dedicated to fashion.

Australia on Collins is another fashion mecca. It joins Collins and Little Collins Streets and boasts an elaborate food court.

The 19th century **Block Arcade**, with its high domed ceiling and mosaic tiled floor, runs from 282 Collins Street to Little Collins Street, or you can enter from Elizabeth Street.

The **Royal Arcade**, the oldest arcade in Melbourne, links Little Collins Street and Bourke Street Mall, and also has an entrance in Elizabeth Street.

The **Galleria Plaza** is a centre for fashion and also a good place to find gifts. It is on the corner of Elizabeth and Little Collins Streets.

The **Bourke Street Mall** in the heart of the city, between Swanston and Elizabeth Streets, offers very good shopping, and is dominated by David Jones and Myer Department Stores. Other arcades running off the Mall are the **Centrepoint Mall** and **The Walk**. Although the Mall

is classed as a pedestrian area, trams do run through its centre.

Midtown Plaza is on the corner of Bourke & Swanston Streets.

If you are searching for **duty free** shopping, head to the stretch of Elizabeth Street between Bourke and Lonsdale Streets.

The bazaar-like character of: the **Queen Victoria Market**, cnr Victoria and Elizabeth Streets; the **Prahran Markets**, Commercial Road, just off Chapel Street; **South Melbourne Markets**, York Street, off Ferrars Street; and the **Victorian Arts Centre Sunday Markets**, 100 St Kilda Road, South Melbourne, each offer an alternative and entertaining shopping experience.

Toorak Village, in Toorak Road from Punt Road to Williams Road has restaurants, boutiques and expensive furniture stores.

A little further out in Campbellfield at 400 Mahoneys Road, just off the Hume Highway, is the **Pipeworks Fun Market**, ✆9357 1155, with 600 shopping stalls, fun rides, live entertainment, mini-golf and bungee jumping.

Many **shopping tours** are available to factory outlets. Here are a few of the options:

Shopping Spree Tours, 2/77 Asling Street, Gardenvale, ✆9596 6600. 8.30am-5pm daily, ✪$50 a head.

Special Buying Tours, 198 Cotham Road, Kew, ✆9817 5985. 9am-5pm

Mon-Sat, ✪$15-40 a head.
Melbourne Shopping Tours, 7 Almeida Crescent, South Yarra, ✆9826 3722.

Points of Interest

City Explorer Bus. Taking a tour on the City Explorer Bus is a good way to get your bearings. This red and white double-decker leaves from Swanston Street, just outside the Visitor Information Centre, on the hour between ⏰10am-4pm and visits most of the main city attractions with its 16 stops. There are discounts on entry into nominated venues and other perks that might appeal. The costs are ✪$22 adults, $10 children and $50 for families. For additional infor-mation, ✆9650 7000. Enquire also about the evening City Lights Tour or the Half-Day Tours which include Australian Wildlife, Shrine of Remembrance & Botanical Gardens and All Around Melbourne.

Melbourne Museum. The Melbourne Museum replaced the Museum of Victoria, formerly in Swanston Street, which is now closed as a result. This $263 million project places Victoria's newest museum to the north of the Royal Exhibition Building in Carlton Gardens, off Nicholson Street. Its exhibits focus on the natural environment and new technologies.

Among the many facilities are an Aboriginal Centre, a Forest Gallery, a Mind and Body Gallery, Technology Exhibitions and a Science Gallery, ✆8341 7777. Adults ✪$12, children $5, families $30. Apart from the attractive garden surrounds, an **IMAX Theatre**, off Rathdowne Street, opened on the site in 1998, ✆9663 5454. The nearby **Royal Exhibition Building**, built in 1880, is itself worth a visit for its history and architecture, ✆9270 5000 for enquiries.

Immigration Museum. The museum is located in Old Customs House, on the corner of 400 Flinders Street and William Street, ✆9927 2700. This musuem takes visitors through a cultural tour using interactive computer displays and permanent physical exhibits. Personal stories are recounted by immigrants themselves, providing insights into the emotions and memories of immigration experiences. The museum is ⏰open between 10am and 5pm and admission is ✪$7 adults, $5.50 concession, $3.50 children and $20 for families. The best method of transport is the Free City Circle tram, which passes nearby on Flinders Street between 10am and 6pm.

Hellenic Antiquities Museum. Located on the second floor of Old Customs House, this museum is designed to host periodical exhibits of ancient Grecian and Byzantine treasures, and is a joint venture of the Victorian and Greek governments. It shares opening times and entry fees with the Immigration Museum on the ground floor, ℡9927 2700 for current and upcoming showcases.

Scienceworks Museum. Science-works is a short 10 minute drive from the city centre, and occupies the futuristic cylindrical building in 2 Booker Street, Spotswood, which cannot be missed. Exhibitions include a detailed exploration of the human body and its mechanics (*Stayin' Alive*), and a 'behind-the-scenes' look at producing special effects for movies and television (*The Sequel*). Also included in the complex is the fascinating Melbourne Planetarium. Admission is ✪$8 adults, $6 concession and $4 children, and the museum is ◷open 10am-4.30pm, ℡9392 4800 for more details.

State Library. The oldest public library in Australia, established in 1856, is on the corner of Swanston and La Trobe Streets. It contains over one million books and periodicals, as well as overseas manuscripts, maps, microfilms, a multimedia catalogue, paintings and photographs. The La Trobe Library is located in a special wing opened in 1965. It is ◷open Mon-Thurs 10am-9pm, Fri-Sun 10am-6pm, ℡9669 9888.

Rialto Towers. An excursion to the top of Rialto Towers, 525 Collins Street, ℡9629 8222, is absolutely imperative for any visitor. The magnificent panoramic vista, completely unobstructed from mountain to ocean and everything in between, is undoubtedly the best way to see Melbourne and its surrounds. At 253m in height, it is the tallest office building in the Southern hemisphere. The Observation Deck is accessible ◷Sun-Thu 10am-10pm and Fri-Sat 10am-11pm, adults ✪$7, children $5.

Old Melbourne Gaol. The National Trust has preserved one remaining cell block as a penal museum, which has a unique collection tracing the story of transportation, convicts, and the development of Victoria's penal system. It is believed that 104 hangings were carried out at the gaol, including that of Ned Kelly on November 11, 1880. The gaol is located in Russell Street, near Victoria Street, and ◷opens daily 9.30am-4.30pm, with admission ✪$9 adults, $6 children and $25 for families, ℡9663 7228. For ✪$15 adults, $8 children and $39 families, shows are conducted on Wednesday and Sunday nights - but some may consider them to be suggestively violent in nature, so be warned if you plan to take young children.

Chinatown. Chinatown is in Little Bourke Street, and extends from Exhibition Street to Swanston Street. It contains many restaurants from the most economical to the extremely expensive. The **Chinese Museum** is in 22 Cohen Place, and is one of the best small museums in Melbourne. It is ☼open Sat midday-4.30pm, Sun-Fri 10am-4.30pm, and entry fees are ✪$5 adult and $3 concession, ✆9662 2888.

Fire Services Museum Victoria. The museum, on the corner of 39 Gisborne Street and Victoria Parade, East Melbourne, was once the Eastern Hill Fire Station. Now it has displays of restored fire fighting equipment used by fire brigades throughout the city. The museum is ☼open Fri 9am-3pm, Sun 10am-4pm, with admission ✪$5 adults, $2 children and $10 for families, ✆9662 2907.

Parliament House. The State Houses of Parliament in Spring Street, at the top of Bourke Street, were built in stages between 1856 and 1930, and have never actually been finished as the dome and facades to the side and rear were never added. Guided tours of this Victorian construction are available at 10am, 2pm and 3pm Mon-Fri when Parliament is in recess, ✆9651 8911.

The Old Treasury. This fine public building was restored, converted to a museum and re-opened in 1994. It is situated in Spring Street, at the top of Collins Street, ✆9651 2233. There are three permanent exhibitions which encompass the past history and contemporary life of the city, its art, culture and architecture. The layout of the museum is designed for self-guiding, but guided tours are offered at 1pm and 3pm. The Treasury is ☼open 9am-5pm Mon-Fri and 10am-4pm on weekends and public holidays. Admission is ✪$5 adults, $3 children and $13 for families.

St Patrick's Cathedral. This Gothic Revival cathedral is in 1 Cathedral Place, which runs off Lansdowne Street, East Melbourne, and is constructed of Footscray bluestone. It was completed in 1897, except for the spires, which were added in 1936. There is a statue in the churchyard of the great Irish liberator, Daniel O'Connell, which is a replica of that which stands in O'Connell Street, Dublin. The Cathedral contains many beautiful works of art and is ☼open 9am-5pm Mon-Fri, ✆9662 2233.

Fitzroy Gardens. Bounded by Albert, Clarendon, Lansdowne Streets and Wellington Parade in East Melbourne, Fitzroy Gardens are delightful nineteenth century gardens. The gardens contain **Cooks' Cottage**, ✆9419 4677, which was transported to Australia in 1934 and rebuilt block by block.

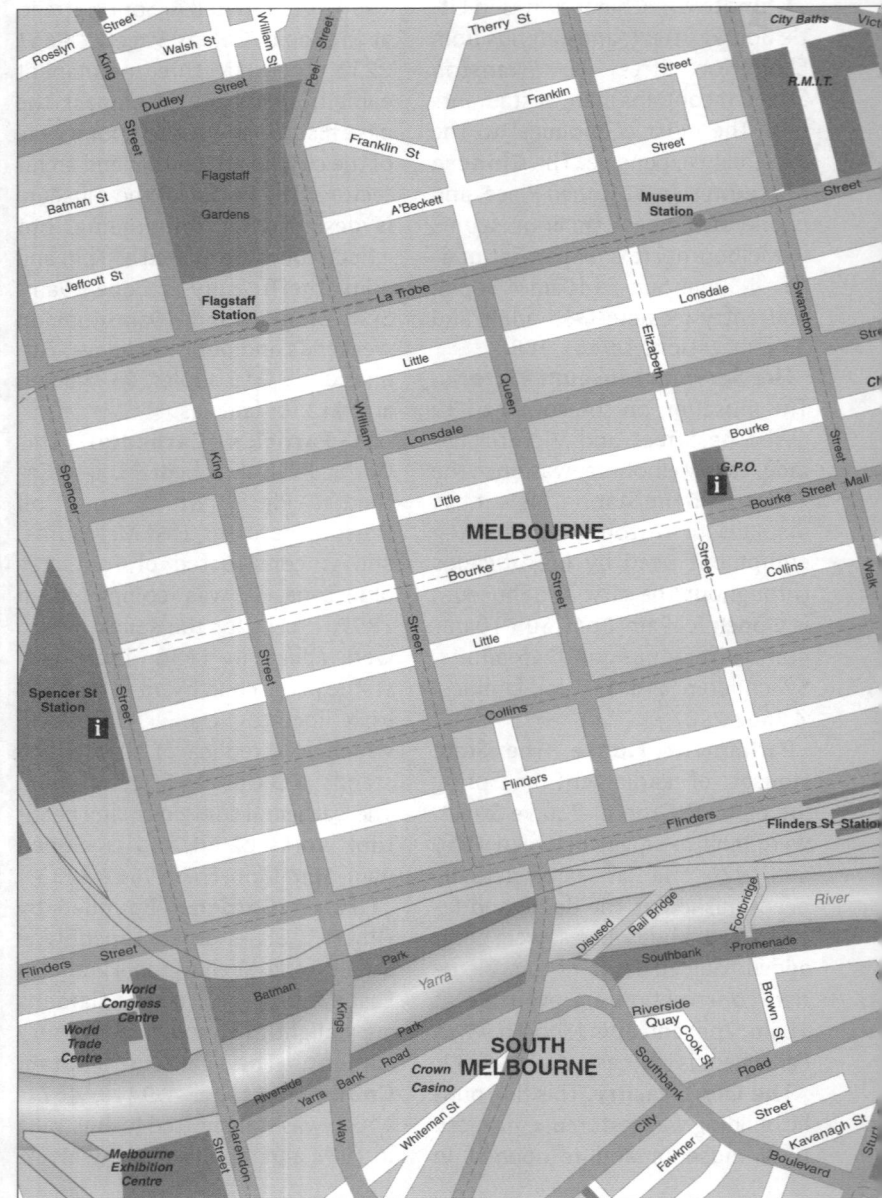

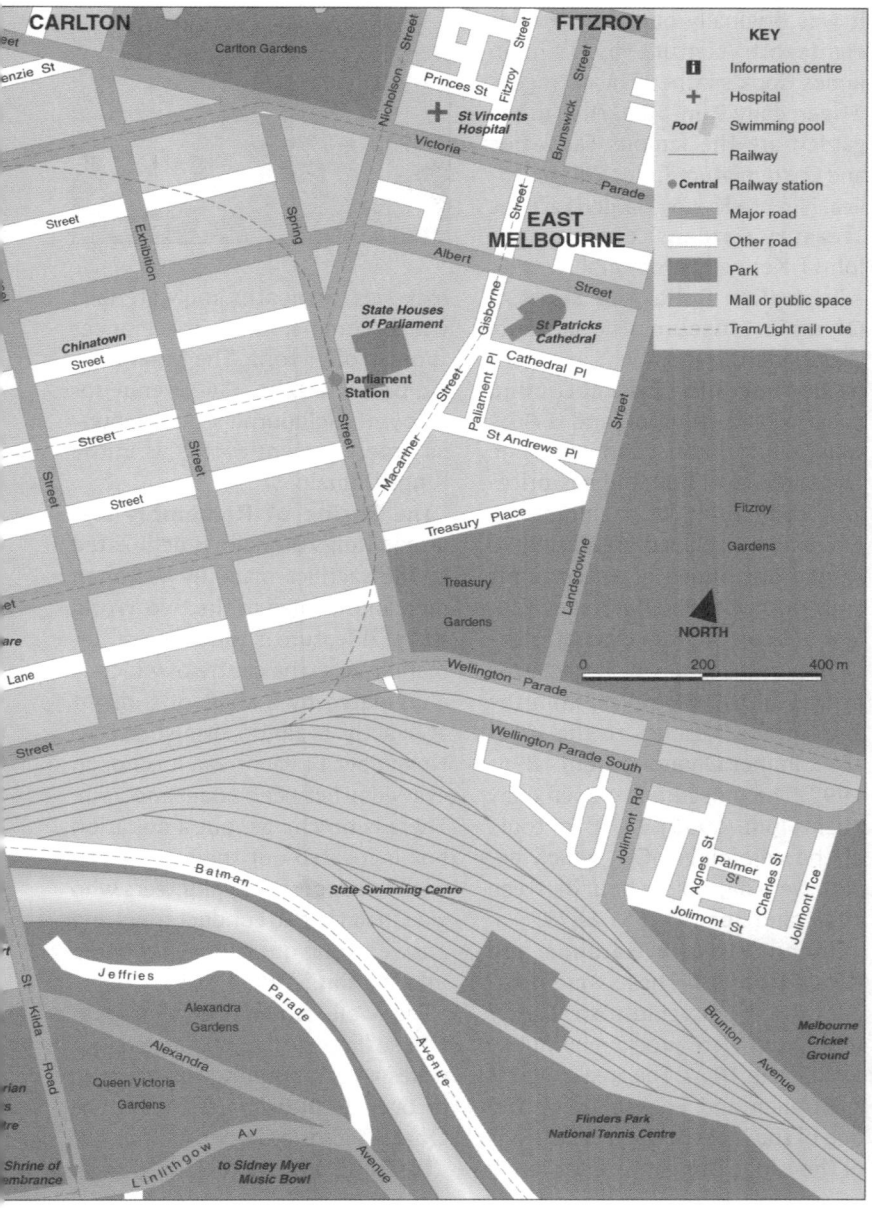

KEY

ℹ	Information centre
✚	Hospital
Pool	Swimming pool
——	Railway
● Central	Railway station
	Major road
	Other road
	Park
	Mall or public space
– – –	Tram/Light rail route

NORTH

0   200   400 m

It was originally built in the mid-eighteenth century by Captain James Cook's father. The cottage is ☉open daily 9am-5pm. Also in the garden are the famous Fairy Tree and the miniature Tudor Village replica. Next to Fitzroy Gardens are the **Treasury Gardens** containing the John F Kennedy Memorial.

Australian Gallery of Sport & Olympic Museum. The museum is outside the member's entrance to the **Melbourne Cricket Ground** in Yarra Park, Jolimont, and is Australia's first multi-sport museum. The three level building has priceless collections of memorabilia, which are displayed graphically in exhibitions aimed at entertaining and educating. The Australian Gallery of Sport now incorporates the Olympic Museum, which traces the history of the Olympics, from the ancient Greek games to the Modern Summer Olympics from 1896-1992. The museum is ☉open daily 10am-4pm, ☏9657 8879. For tours of the adjoining MCG, which depart every day on the hour between 10am and 3pm, ☏9657 8879.

Queen Victoria Gardens and Kings Domain. These were originally the site of a gold-rush shantytown, and were proclaimed public parkland in 1854. The area contains Australian and English trees, and one of the most attractive sections of the Kings Domain is a garden of

rockeries, tiny paths and waterfalls which commemorate the Pioneer Women of Victoria. The **Myer Music Bowl**, ☏9281 8360, venue for many of Melbourne's most popular entertainment events, is in the Kings Domain.

The **Shrine of Remembrance**, also in Kings Domain, is dedicated to the sacrifice made by Victorian men and women in the two World Wars. A feature is the Stone of Remembrance, the centre of which is illuminated by a shaft of sunlight at exactly 11am on Armistice Day, November 11 each year. It is ☉open every day between 10am and 5pm. There is no charge, but a donation box is located out the front if you wish to support the volunteers who give their time to conduct tours and answer your questions. For more information, ☏9654 8415.

The well-known **Floral Clock**, whose floral design is changed four times a year requiring the planting of over 30,000 flowers, is in the Queen Victoria Gardens.

La Trobe's Cottage. The Cottage,

on the corner of Birdwood Road and Dallas Brooks Drive, in the Domain, South Yarra, was the colony's first Government House. La Trobe brought the house with him in the ship *Fergusson*, along with his family and possessions. The National Trust supervised the re-creation of the buildings, and they contain many of the original furnishings. The Cottage is ☺open 11am-4pm Mon, Wed, Sat & Sun, ✆9654 4711.

Victorian Arts Centre Complex. On the banks of the Yarra River, at 100 St Kilda Road, the Centre comprises the theatres, the Melbourne Concert Hall, the Performing Arts Museum and the National Gallery of Victoria. As well as the performance and exhibition spaces, the Victorian Arts Centre has several restaurants. The **George Adams Gallery** has an extensive collection and is ☺open Mon-Sat 9am-11pm, and Sun 10am-5pm, ✆9281 8194. The **Performing Arts Museum** has regularly changing exhibitions, free entry and is ☺open Mon-Sat 9am-11pm, Sun 10am-5pm, ✆9281 8000. Guided tours of the Centre are available at limited times, ✆9281 8198.

Princes Bridge. The bridge is Melbourne's oldest and grandest, and is located at the point where Swanston Street becomes St Kilda Road. It was built around 1886, replacing a wooden bridge that had

been opened by La Trobe in 1850.

Young & Jackson's Hotel. Also known as Princes Bridge Hotel, the pub is at 1 Swanston Street, ✆9650 3884. Its claim to fame is that the upstairs lounge is home to the infamous painting 'Chloe' which caused a scandalized public outcry when it was first hung in the Melbourne Art Gallery in the 1880s. She may have caused a stir then, but now she hardly manages to raise an eyebrow.

St Paul's Cathedral. This Gothic Revival Anglican cathedral is on the corner of Swanston and Flinders Streets, on the site of the first official church service in Melbourne. The Cathedral was completed in 1891, and the spires added between 1926 and 1931. The doors are ☺open Mon-Fri 9am-5pm, ✆9650 3791.

Capitol Theatre. The astonishing ceiling of the theatre, at 113 Swanston Street, was designed by Walter Burley Griffin, the architect of the city of Canberra. Entry is ✪$8 adults, $4 children, ✆9654 4422.

Melbourne Town Hall. The Town Hall, in Swanston Street Walk, ✆9658 9779, was built between 1867 and 1870, and the portico added in 1887. It is worth going inside the main hall to see the chandeliers, murals and organ and the rest of its recenty restored interior. The Town Hall was one of the main venues for concerts before the advent of the Concert Hall in St Kilda Road.

Polly Woodside Maritime Museum. The barque *Polly Woodside*, in Lorimer Street East, Southbank, is a deepwater, square-rigged, commercial sailing ship built of riveted iron in 1885. Seventy years ago, she was one of the fast fleet of windjammers, today she is fully restored and is the centrepiece of a display of Australia's maritime history. ☺Open 7 days 10am-4pm, admission ✪$7 adults, $4 concession and $15 for families, ✆9699 9760.

Melbourne Exhibition and Events Centre. At 28 Clarendon Street, South Melbourne, ✆9205 6400, this complex is the largest and most modern of its kind that Australia has to offer, and plays host to a wide range of exhibitions throughout the year. Its unique exterior design is worth a glance.

Crown Entertainment Complex. The complex is often described as 'the city under one roof', and indeed its restaurants, theatres, cinemas, Crown Towers Hotel, bars, nightclubs, showrooms, cocktail lounges, cafes, ballrooms, shopping boutiques and unabated gambling opportunities at the **Crown Casino**, do give the impression of a mini metropolis. The complex is in Southbank, and the Casino is at 8 Whiteman Street, ✆9292 8888.

Melbourne Aquarium. This Aquarium, situated on the corner of King Street and Queenswharf Road, City, ✆9620 0999, is a very sophisticated and impressive way to view ocean creatures. It has the enormous Oceanarium viewing tank, modern computer interactions, aquatic feeding facilities and a simulator. The complex is ☺open daily 9am-6pm (until 9pm during summer), and costs adults ✪$17.50, concession $12.50 and children $8.50.

Suburban Attractions

Royal Botanic Gardens. The Royal Botanic Gardens are in Birdwood Avenue, South Yarra, and have 41ha (101 acres) of lawns, gardens and ornamental lakes. The Gardens are regarded as one of the finest examples of landscape gardening in the world. Their development commenced in 1846 under the direction of the then Superintendent of the Colony, Charles Joseph La Trobe, and now features 12,000 plant species. Brochures are available on special seasonal walks through the Gardens. **Como House**, Como Park, is an elegant colonial mansion, built in 1847, which has been classified by the National Trust and is ☺open for inspection daily 10am-5pm, ✆9827 2500.

St Kilda

St Kilda is Melbourne's equivalent

of Sydney's Kings Cross, only more so. Developers would like to move in and restore the area to the fashionable and wealthy resort it once was, but they are meeting resistance from long-established residents. From Swanston Street, there are many trams that run to St Kilda, including Tram 16 from Swanston Street, and from Bourke Street, Tram 96 goes through South Melbourne to St Kilda. From Richmond, take Tram 79, which travels along Church Street, and Chapel Street in Prahran, then continues on to St Kilda Esplanade. By road, St Kilda is reached by the West Gate Freeway from the west, Punt Road from the north. **The Esplanade** runs along the beach, which is not very inviting, and leads to the St Kilda Pier, which has a kiosk built in 1904 at the corner. The St Kilda hot sea baths are nearby, and are very popular. **Luna Park** is in 18 Lower Esplanade, next door to the Palais Theatre, and has been run as a fun palace since the 1920s. There is a restaurant behind the Palais that was originally a bathing shed. Rides such as the Mad Mouse, the Ghost Train and the Scenic Railway have been entertaining young ones for years. Entry is free into the Park but rides are priced at around ✪$2 or $3. It ◷opens 11am daily and closes at 5pm Mon-Thu & Sun and 11pm Fri-Sat. **Rippon Lea**, 192

Hotham Street, Elsternwick, is a brick mansion built between 1868 and 1887, and has 33 rooms, iron carriage gates and a conservatory. It is set in a beautiful garden with a lake, and is one of the National Trust's pride and joys. It is ◷open Tues-Sun 10am-5pm, ✆9523 6095. **Ripponlea Railway Station** is a fine example of early twentieth century architectural style.

Parkville

Parkville is a student area with colleges, halls of residence and student flats set amidst fashionable homes, office buildings and Victorian terraces. Its main attractions are the Melbourne Zoo and the nearby University of Melbourne.

The **Melbourne Zoo** is in Elliot Park, ✆9285 9300. It has a lion park, walk-through aviary and native fauna park, and a butterfly enclosure. More than 350 species are represented here in Australia's longest-standing zoo (since 1862). The *Lakeside Restaurant* serves 'meals with a view', looking out to Gibbon Island. Standard opening times are ◷daily 9am-5pm, but some exhibits and special events have alternative times. It is recommended that you allow at least four hours to fully appreciate this attraction, and you can phone the above number for feeding times and other points of interest to better plan your visit. Admission is adults

✪$14.50, children $7.20 and $39.30 for families.

The **University of Melbourne**, Gratton Street, ✆9344 4000, dates back to the 1850s, and contains, among other interesting buildings, **The Grainger Museum**, Gate 13, Royal Parade, ✆9344 4270, which is ☉open Mon 10am-1pm, Tue 10am-4pm and Wed-Fri 10am-4pm.

Flemington

Flemington Racecourse is one of the most beautiful courses in the world, and is worth a visit even if you are not into betting. Unfortunately, it is only open to the public on race days, but the crowds add to the atmosphere anyway. The daily papers have details of race meetings in the sports pages. The famous Melbourne Cup is run here on the first Tuesday of November.

Tours

The Visitor Information Centre has details of all tours that are available in and around Melbourne. Here are some examples.

Melbourne Discovery Pass
Duration: ☉12pm-5pm daily.
Attractions: Lunch at Rialto Towers, cruise on the *Melba Star* past Southbank and the Royal Botanic Gardens, Como Historic House, afternoon tea and return.
Cost: ✪$45

Operator: Rialto Towers Observation Deck, ✆9629 8222.
City Tour
Duration: ☉9am-12pm daily.
Attractions: City, Chinatown, Parliament House, Fitzroy Gardens, Captain Cook's Cottage, Melbourne Cricket Ground, National Tennis Centre, Albert Park, Westgate Bridge, Botanic Gardens, Shrine of Remembrance and return.
Cost: ✪$45.
Operator: Gray Line, ✆9663 4455.
Melbourne Highlights
Duration: ☉1.30pm-5.30pm daily
Attractions: City, Chinatown, Shrine of Remembrance, South Yarra, Toorak, Dandenong Ranges, Sher-brooke Forest, Mt Dandenong and return.
Cost: ✪$46.
Operator: Gray Line, ✆9663 4455.
Best of Melbourne
Duration: ☉12.15pm-7.15pm daily
Attractions: Same as Melbourne Highlights but with the addition of dinner on the Colonial Tramcar Restaurant, which tours Melbourne streets at night while you eat.
Cost: ✪$122.
Operator: Gray Line, ✆9663 4455.
Penguin Parade and Seal Rocks
Duration: ☉Fluctuates with season, daily.
Attractions: Phillip Island by coach, Koala Conservation Centre, dinner at Cowes (price not included), viewing of Penguin Parade, Seal Rocks Seal Life Centre and return.

Cost: ✪$106.
Operator: Gray Line, ✆9663 4455.
Penguin Express
Duration: ⏱5.30-11.30 daily between March and November.
Attractions: Express coach to penguin viewing on Phillip Island then return.
Cost: ✪$72.
Operator: Gray Line, 9663 4455.
Melbourne's Best Tours
Duration: ⏱Seasonal (late afternoon until late)
Attractions: Hotel pick-up in Melbourne, South Gippsland, Western Port Bay, Australian Wildlife, San Remo, tour of Phillip Island, Seal Rocks, Mutton Bird, Penguin Parade and return.
Cost: ✪$75.

Operator: Melbourne's Best Tours, ✆1300 130 550.
Blue Dandenongs
Duration: ⏱8.40am-5.30pm daily.
Attractions: Dandenong Ranges, Puffing Billy train ride, lunch at Fergusson's Winery, Healsville Sanctuary and return.
Cost: ✪$112
Operator: Gray Line, ✆9663 4455.
Sovereign Hill
Duration: ⏱9am-5.30pm daily.
Attractions: Coach to Ballarat, Sovereign Hill Historical Park, gold panning, provincial town tour and return.
Cost: ✪$90
Operator: Gray Line, ✆9663 4455.
Winery Tour - Yarra Valley
Duration: ⏱8.30am-5pm daily.

Attractions: 3-6 wineries, lunch, Badger Weir Park and return.

Cost: ✪$118

Operator: Victorian Winery Tours, ©9653 9749.

Additional tours of the Great Ocean Road, Grampians, Murray River and extended trips to Phillip Island are also available, and the Visitor Information Centre will supply you with details of all of them.

The **National Trust (Victoria)** produces a brochure which you can pick up at the Visitor Information Centre. It outlines buildings of particular historical significance and includes all the relevant details for visiting them.

Apart from their regular city service, the **City Explorer Bus** offers a number of different tours in the Melbourne area and to outlying regions, ©9650 7000 to enquire further.

Cruises on the Yarra are also available. Here are a few companies which operate such services:

Melbourne River Cruises, Vault 18, Banana Alley Jetty, ©9614 1215.

City River Cruises, 3 Princes Walk, Melbourne, ©9650 2214.

Southgate River Tours, Southgate, Southbank, ©9682 5711.

Festivals

The Moomba Festival is held in March each year.

A parade is held before the Grand Final of the AFL competition in September.

The Melbourne Cup is held on the first Tuesday in November each year.

Sporting Facilities

Melbourne has four venues for horseracing - Flemington, ©9258 4666; Caulfield in Station Street, ©9257 7200; Moonee Valley in McPherson Street, Moonee Ponds, ©9373 2222; and Sandown in Racecourse Drive, Springvale, ©9546 9511.

In summer, many International Tests, one day International and Sheffield Shield Cricket matches are played at the Melbourne Cricket Ground (MCG), Yarra Park, Jolimont.

There are two major venues for greyhound racing - Melbourne Park on Monday nights and Sandown Park on Thursday nights.

Harness Racing's main venue is Moonee Valley in Moonee Ponds, and races are held every Saturday and some Mondays.

Australian Rules Football (AFL) is played every Saturday during the season (March to September) at various grounds around the city, including the MCG.

Soccer's main venue is Melbourne Park, Swan Street, Melbourne, ©9286 1600.

The Australian Tennis Open is held each year at the National Tennis Centre in Batman Avenue, East Melbourne, ✆9286 1600.

Calder Park Thunderdome, Calder Highway, Keilor, is Australia's only super speedway. For information on race meetings, ✆9217 8800.

The Australian Motorcycle Grand Prix is held at the Phillip Island Motor Racing Circuit, Back Beach Road, ✆5952 9400.

The Formula One Grand Prix is held at Albert Park in March, ✆9258 7100 for more information.

Melbourne has facilities for every type of sport, and venues and clubs are listed in the Yellow Pages telephone directory.

Outlying Attractions

Phillip Island

Phillip Island is 129km (80 miles) from Melbourne, and is the home of the fairy penguins. At dusk, the famous penguins emerge from the surf, completely ignoring the thousands of curious onlookers. The Island has a Phillip Island Nature Park, which is divided into a number of outlets for wildlife viewing and information, including koalas, fur seals, pelicans, mutton birds, and the famous fairy penguins.

There are more than fifty places to stay in Cowes alone, the main tourist centre of Phillip Island. The districts of Newhaven, Rhyll and San Remo offer several alternatives. All types of accommodation are available.

The **Penguin Parade Visitors Centre**, off Ventnor Road, ✆5956 8300, is open daily from 10am and you can view the seasonal nightly pilgrimage of the cute creatures as they waddle their way onto the beach and up the sand dunes. It costs adults ✪$11.50, children $6 and families $29.

The Koala Conservation Centre is located at Fiveways on Phillip Island Road, ✆5952 1307. It ⏰opens at 10am 7 days a week and costs ✪$5 adults, $2 children and $12 families.

Churchill Island, accessed via Newhaven, off Phillip Island Road, is popular for its tranquil gardens and stunning array of bird life. Costs are ✪$5 adults, $2 children and $12 for families.

The Seal Rocks Life Centre, Penguin Reserve, The Nobbies, ✆9793 6767, has amazing educational displays and panoramic views. Entry is ✪$10 adults, $5 children and $28 for families.

A Four Park Pass gives access to all four attractions listed above for the one price: ✪$25 adults, $12 children and $65 for families.

At the **Australian Dairy Centre**, Phillip Island Road, Newhaven, there is a museum explaining the history of the dairying industry, and a cheese factory with sales section and tastings. The cafeteria sells dairy-based light meals and snacks, ✆5956 7583.

Other attractions include great surfing beaches and restaurants.

French Island National Park, which can be reached by ferry either from Cowes at Phillip Island or from Stoney Point on the Mornington Peninsula, is larger than Phillip Island although less developed.

In Korumburra, on the South Gippsland Highway east of Phillip Island, is **Coal Creek Heritage Village**, a re-creation of an 1890s coal mining/railway town, with 40 buildings, including a mine, blacksmith, printer, stores, and a saw mill, ✆5655 1811.

For more information on Phillip Island attractions, contact the Phillip Island Information Centre, ✆5956 7447, or drop into their outlet at Newhaven on Phillip Island Tourist Road. It is ⊕open 7 days a week, 9am-5pm.

You can take advantage of the comprehensive web page at ☞www.phillipisland.net.au, or the Centre's accommodation booking service on ✆1300 366 422. Contact them via email at ✉info@phillipisland.net.au

Another good website for plan-

ning and attractions details is ☞www.penguins.org.au which includes an email form at ☞www.penguins.org.au/trip/index.html

Tynong

Tynong is a town on the Princes Highway, and can be visited on the way to Melbourne from Sale.

Here you will find **Victoria's Farm Shed**, Australia's leading farm animal theatre featuring parades, milking, shearing and sheep dog displays. Show times are 10.30am and 2pm daily. For more information, ✆5629 2840.

Also at Tynong is **Gumbuya Recreation and Leisure Park**, a 174ha (430 acres) recreation park with toboggan slide, minicars, pony coach and trail rides, mini golf, adventure playground, water slide, half court tennis, barbecue and picnic areas, and a restaurant, ✆5629 2613. The park is ⊕open every day 10am-6pm (rides in operation 11am-4pm) and admission is ✪$6 adults, $3.50 children and $19 for families.

Bass

Bass is located on the Bass Highway and can be visited on the way to Phillip Island from Melbourne.

The Giant Worm Museum, on the Bass Highway, is a unique attraction and education facility. They do actually have giant worms (including one you can walk through!), and many other historical and hands-on displays, ✆5678 2222.

Mornington Peninsula

The Nepean Highway follows the eastern shore of Port Phillip Bay for 97km (60 miles) to the seaside resort of Portsea. On the way it passes picturesque peninsula beaches such as Dromana, Rosebud and Sorrento.

At Dromana, the **Arthur's Seat Scenic Chairlift** ride offers great views of Melbourne, Port Phillip Bay and the Mornington Peninsula. It ⏰opens at 11am daily September-April, and only on weekends and holidays during winter, ✆5987 2565.

The MV *Peninsula Princess*, a car assenger ferry, operates every day linking the Mornington and Bellarine Peninsulas, from Queenscliff to Sorrento.

Ashcombe Maze, Red Hill Road, Shoreham, ✆5989 8387, is a large hedge maze believed to be the only significant one of its type in Australia. There are tea rooms surrounded by extensive gardens. It is ⏰open from 10 am every day and costs ✪$6 adults, $4 children.

The Visitor Information Centre for Peninsula Tourism is at 359B Point Nepean Road, Dromana, ✆5978 3078. For web information ✏www.melbourne.citysearch.com.au in-

cludes the Mornington Peninsula region.

Dandenong Ranges

The Dandenongs are only 35km (22 miles) east of Melbourne, and the area is ideal for picnics, bushwalks and wildlife observation. It is an extremely popular destination with Melbournians and tourists for both daytrips and weekend escapes. Mt Dandenong (630m - 2067 ft) offers a panoramic view of Melbourne from its strategic lookout points.

One of the most popular attractions is Puffing Billy, Old Monbulk Road, Belgrave, ✆9754 6800, an historic narrow gauge train that runs through 13km (8 miles) of mountain scenery between Belgrave and Lakeside (Emerald Lake) in the Dandenong Ranges every day of the year, except Christmas Day. Return fares are adults ✪$17.50, children $9 and $49 for families. The line opened in 1900, and it is the ideal way to view the Dandenongs at close range. The suburban trains from all stations connect with Puffing Billy at Belgrave, one hour's easy drive from Melbourne.

The famous **William Ricketts Sanctuary**, Mt Dandenong Tourist Road, ✆13 1963, is set in the lush surrounds of the Dandenong Ranges and comprises the inspired sculptures of one artist. Encapsulating the spirituality of Aboriginal culture and expressing an affinity with nature, these startling images bear a powerful mystique. The Sanctuary is ☉open daily 10am-4pm and entry is ✪$5 adults, $2 children and $12 for families.

The Dandenongs are covered in 👁www.melbourne.citysearch.com.au

Victoria – East

Lakes Entrance

Population 4,600

Lakes Entrance is at the gateway to the Gippsland Lakes, Australia's largest inland water system. It is 360km (224 miles) east of Melbourne, 840km (522 miles) south of Sydney and 429km (267 miles) south-west of Canberra.

Climate

Lakes Entrance has a temperate climate. The average maximum temperature in summer is 33C (91F), in winter 21C (70F). There is some rain in July and August, and occasional overnight showers in summer.

Characteristics

The largest town on Ninety Mile Beach, Lakes Entrance is a popular holiday destination. It has a spectacular hinterland with mountains (snow in winter), rivers and forests. Wildlife in the area includes dolphins and water birds, kangaroos, wombats, koalas and bush birds.

How to Get There

By Bus
Greyhound Pioneer, ©13 2030, provides interstate connections.
By Rail
V/Line, ©13 6196, offer a road and rail combination to Lakes Entrance.
By Road
Access is via Princes Highway from Melbourne and Sydney, and the Cann Valley Highway from Canberra.
By Air
Flying is not the preferred method of access to this area, but regional connections can be made throughout the district and the Visitor In-

formation Centre will be able to advise on the timetables and routes that suit your itinerary.

Visitor Information

The Lakes Entrance Visitor Information Centre is on the corner of Marine Parade and The Esplanade, ✆(03) 5155 1966. They are ☺open 9am-5pm daily. Contact them over the internet at ✉ lakes@lakes andwilderness.com.au or simply explore the web page at ☞www. lakesandwilderness.com.au

Accommodation

As mentioned, Lakes Entrance is a popular holiday spot, so there is plenty of accommodation from which to choose, in fact over 60 places in the town. The Information Centre has a complete list, but here are a few examples with prices for a double room per night, which should be used as a guide only. The telephone area code is 03.

Banjo Paterson Motor Inn, 131 Esplanade, ✆5155 2933. 22 units, licensed restaurant, heated swimming pool, barbecue - ✪$115-190.
Abel Tasman Motor Lodge, 643 Esplanade, ✆5155 1655. 11 units, heated swimming pool, barbecue - ✪$70-165.
Golden Beach Motor Inn, 607 Esplanade, ✆5155 1666. 29 units,

swimming pool, unlicensed restaurant - ✪$55-100.
Lakes Central Hotel, 321-333 Esplanade, ✆5155 1977. 16 units, licensed bistro, swimming pool, spa, barbecue - ✪$55-95.
Albatross Motel, 661 Esplanade, ✆5155 1779. 8 units, heated swimming pool, barbecue - ✪$50-135.
Lakeside Motel, 164 Marine Parade, ✆5155 1811. 27 units - ✪$45-90.
The Esplanade Motel, 251 Esplanade, ✆5155 1933. 40 units, car wash, heated swimming pool, spa, barbecue - ✪$40-125.
Lakes Seaview Motel, 12 New Street, ✆5155 1318. 11 units, barbecue - ✪$40-80.
Caravan Parks
Silver Sands Tourist Park, 33 Myer Street, ✆5155 2343. (No pets allowed) 37 sites, spa, pool, barbecue - powered sites ✪$18-30 for two, on-site vans $30-80 for two.
Riviera Country Caravan Park, 29 Palmers Road, ✆5155 1236. (No pets allowed) 62 sites, barbecue - powered sites ✪$17-26 for two, on-site vans $35-70 for two, cabins $40-90 for two.
Echo Beach Caravan Park, 33 Roadknight Street, ✆5155 2238. (Pets allowed under control) 25 sites - powered sites ✪$18-32 for two, cabins $45-110 for two.
Lakes Haven Caravan Park & Flats, 3 Jemmeson Street, ✆5155

St Kilda Pier, Melbourne

MELBOURNE

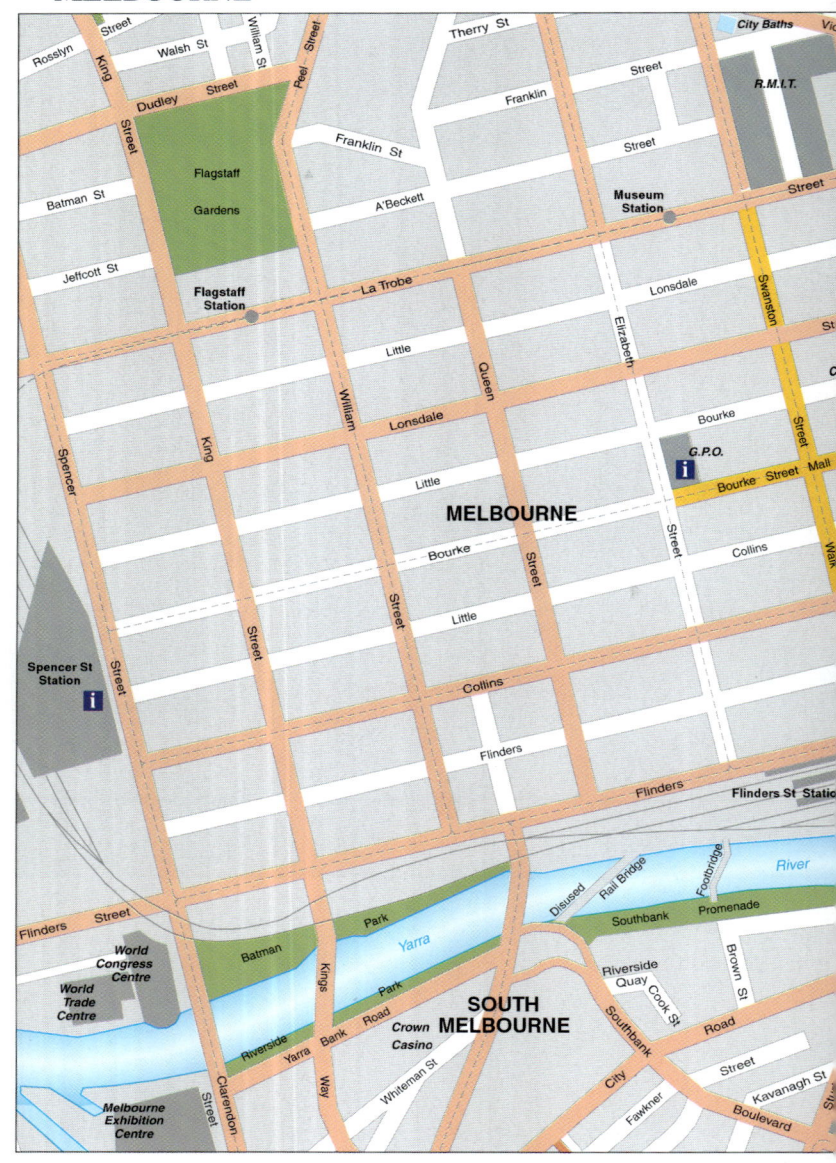

CARLTON

Carlton Gardens

ie St

Nicholson Street

Princes St

Fitzroy Street

Brunswick Street

FITZROY

St Vincents
Hospital

Victoria

Parade

Street

EAST
MELBOURNE

Street

Spring

Street

Exhibition

Albert

Street

Gisborne

St Patricks
Cathedral

Chinatown

Street

State Houses
of Parliament

Paliament Pl

Cathedral Pl

Street

Street

Parliament
Station

Paliament

St Andrews Pl

Street

Macarthur

Street

Street

Street

Street

Treasury   Place

Fitzroy

Gardens

Treasury

Gardens

Landsdowne

NORTH

0   200   400 m

ne

Wellington   Parade

street

Wellington Parade South

Jolimont Rd

Agnes St

Palmer
St

Charles St

Jolimont Tce

State Swimming Centre

Jeffries

Parade

Batman

Jolimont St

Alexandra
Gardens

Alexandra

Brunton

Avenue

Melbourne
Cricket
Ground

St · Kilda

Road

Queen Victoria

Gardens

Avenue

Flinders Park
National Tennis Centre

ine of
brance

A v

Linlithgow

to Sidney Myer
Music Bowl

Avenue

KEY

i   Information centre

+   Hospital

Pool   Swimming pool

———   Railway

● **Central**   Railway station

Major road

Other road

Park

Mall or public space

- - - - -   Tram/Light rail route

2254. (No pets allowed) 17 sites, barbecue - powered sites ✪$17-28 for two, cabins $40-85 for two, holiday flats $45-105 for two, on-site vans $30-65 for two.

Lakes Entrance Tourist Park, 127 Princes Highway, ✆5155 1159. (Pets by arrangement) 100 sites, barbecue, heated pool - powered sites ✪$18-30 for two, cabins $35-95 for two.

There is a **Youth Hostel**, **Riviera Backpackers**, in 5 Clarkes Road, Lakes Entrance, ✆5155 2444. It has 19 rooms at ✪$15 per person twin share.

Eating Out

There is the usual range of takeaway outlets, and most hotels serve counter meals. Local seafood is often the specialty on the menu. Some of the motels have restaurants, but here are the addresses and phone numbers of other restaurants you might like to patronise.

For a special dining experience try **Nautilus Floating Dockside**, Western Boat Harbour, The Esplanade, ✆5155 1400. It is licensed, has a seafood specialty, and boasts an outstanding waterside location with views. This award-winning restaurant is open Mon-Sat from 6pm for dinner.

Egidio's Wood Oven, 573 The Esplanade, ✆5155 1411. Licensed, Italian menu.

Ocean Dragon, 601 The Esplanade, ✆5155 1349. Chinese cuisine.

Tres Amigos, 521 The Esplanade, ✆5155 2215. Authentic Mexican flavours.

Shang Hai Garden, 215 The Esplanade, ✆5155 2602.

Skippers, 481 The Esplanade, ✆5155 3551.

The Scallop Pot, 221 The Esplanade, ✆5155 1555.
Miriams, Shop 2, Level 1, 3 Bulmer Street, ✆5155 3999.
Cafe Pelicano, 171 The Esplanade, ✆5155 2166.
Pinocchio Inn, 569 The Esplanade, ✆5155 2565.
McDonalds is at 359 The Esplanade. Although there are no KFC or Pizza Hut branches here, you will find an abundance of alternative fast food outlets along The Esplanade.

Points of Interest

The artificial entrance of the lakes to the ocean was completed in 1889, and there are still visible signs of the equipment used to bring logs and rocks from inland for the construction.

A short walk across the footbridge brings you to the Entrance and Bass Strait, with **Ninety Mile Beach** stretching away into the distance. A section of the beach is patrolled by the Surf Lifesaving Club during the holidays.

Nyerimilang Park on Lake King, Kalimna West Road, Nungurner, overlooks Rigby, Fraser and Flannagan Islands. It has bullock driving demonstrations and field days, and there are bushwalks, as well as barbecue and picnic facilities, ✆5156 3253. Nyerimilang is Aboriginal for Chain of Lakes.

Kinkuna Country Fun Park & Zoo, Princes Highway, ✆5155 3000 has waterslides, a toboggan ride with electronic timing, kiosk, sou-venirs, crafts and games room. It is ⏰open daily from 10am (weather permitting) and the entry fee includes barbecues, toddlers' pool, the jumping castle and wildlife area. The lions are hand-fed (not fed hands) at about 1pm on most days. Entry is ❂$4.50 adults, $4 children and toddlers under three are free.

Griffiths' Sea Shell Museum and Marine Display, 125 Esplanade, ✆5155 1538, also has a gift shop and a model railway display. Over 90,000 shells from around the world are featured, and there is also a model railway room for locomotive enthusists. The complex is ⏰open daily.

The Lakes Entrance Aboriginal Art & Crafts, 239 The Esplanade, ✆5155 3302, has genuine Aboriginal artifacts on display and for sale. ⏰Open 9am-5pm daily.

Festivals

Here are a few of the major events in the East Gippsland area:
January - the Metung Regatta, and the New Year's Eve fireworks at Lakes Entrance.
February - the Canni Creek Races near Buchan, the Cattlemen's Cup

(every year in the high country, once every four years at Omeo).

March - the Marlay Point Overnight Yacht Race and the Bairnsdale Festival.

Easter - Rodeos at Omeo and Buchan, the Kinkuna Festival and Blessing of the Fleet at Lakes Entrance.

June - the Wildtrek at Dinner Plain.

November - the Flat Water Classic (windsurfing) at Paynesville.

Facilities

Boat cruises from Lakes Entrance, Metung, Lake Tyers, Paynesville. Sail and motor boat hire, daily or longer term, from Lakes Entrance, Metung, Paynesville, Lake Tyers, Johnstonville. Fishing from jetties, shoreline, from hired boats, or on organised fishing trips. Swimming in lakes and sea. Viewing the hot pools at Metung. Rafting and canoeing on rivers. Horse-riding - full day and extended trail rides. 4WD tours, bushwalking, tennis, lawn bowls, golf.

The Visitor Information Centre has all the information on times and locations, ℂ(03) 5155 1966.

Outlying Attractions

Mallacoota

Reached via Genoa on the NSW/Vic border, Mallacoota is surrounded by the Croajinolong National Park. Mallacoota is situated in one of Victoria's most remote and peaceful lakeland settings. There are many walking tracks through the **Croajinolong National Park**, which has prolific birdlife.

If you wish to explore the natural wonders here, contact the Park Office, Genoa Road, Mallacoota, ℂ(03) 5158 0263 or the Information Centre in nearby Cann River, ℂ(03) 5158 6351.

Orbost

Orbost is the railhead for East Gippsland, and is situated on the Snowy River 16km from the coast. It is the gateway to Marlo where the Snowy meets the Brodribb River and where a sandbar allows the rivers to reach the sea. Scenic drives and walks are the main attraction of this stunning region. Cape Conran, reached via Marlo, has camping, picnic and walking facilities.

For ideas on the best places and routes to explore, the Snowy River Visitor Centre in Lochiel Street can be contacted on ℂ(03) 5154 2424 or emailed at ✍ orbost@lakesandwilderness.com.au

Omeo

Omeo is on the way to the snowfields at Mt Hotham, about

one-and-a-half hours drive from Bairnsdale. The town's history lies in timber, gold and cattle, and the town is like the backdrop for a movie set in the 1880s. Omeo is an ideal place to stop for a meal and to hire skis and chains during winter, and even close enough to stay in the town and visit the snow of Alpine National Park daily. Many people visit Omeo for trout fishing, bushwalking and canoeing.

Buchan

In the foothills of Snowy River Country, 56km (35 miles) from Lakes Entrance, lies the town of Buchan which is probably best known for its limestone caves.

The **limestone caves** were discovered in 1907, and the reserve surrounding them has picnic facilities, barbecues, and lots of kangaroos. There is also a swimming pool fed by an extremely cool underground stream. The rangers conduct tours through the caves during the day.

The Visitor Centre in Lakes Entrance produces a very good pamphlet detailing activities and attractions in the area, including a comprehensive driving map, ☎5155 1966.

Nowa Nowa

Situated approximately 24km (15 miles) from Lakes Entrance, Nowa Nowa is predominately a timber milling town. Numerous forest drives off the Princes Highway lead to delightful barbecue spots. Close by are the trestle bridge and the Mundic Creek waterfall at **Cosstick Weir**. The arm from **Lake Tyers** extends to the town, offering good fishing.

Bairnsdale

Bairnsdale, just over 30km west of Lakes Entrance, was the port for its pastoral hinterland in the days before road transport. Now it supports a number of secondary industries.

St Mary's Roman Catholic Church, ☎5152 2942, built in 1913 and extended in 1937, has unique murals by Frank Floreani, an incredible painted ceiling and other works of art.

The **Court House**, built in 1893 and classified by the National Trust, has delightful architecture, but it can only be viewed from the street.

The Historical Museum, Macarthur Street, has some interesting memorabilia on display, ☎5152 6363. It is ⏰open Wednesday, Thursday and Sunday 1-5pm.

The Tourist Information Centre is at 240 Main Street, ☎(03) 5152 3444, and they have brochures and details of all attractions. You can email them at ✉bairnsdale@lakesandwilderness.com.au

Eagle Point

Eagle Point is only 15 kilometres, following the coastline south then east, from Bairnsdale. The well known Mitchell River silt jetties are found at Eagle Point. Eagle Point is also known for its fishing, both in Lake King and the Mitchell River.

Paynesville

Known as the boating capital of the Gippsland Lakes, Paynesville is 18km (11 miles) south-east of Bairnsdale, with a well-marked turn off the Princes Highway. McMillan Strait, Newlands Arm and canals provide sheltered moorings for many pleasure and commercial fishing boats.

From Paynesville there are many places to go by boat - the **Lakes National Park**, with its picnic grounds and kangaroos, the beautiful **Duck Arm**, and three of Victoria's best **bream rivers**: Mitchell, Nicholson and Tambo. There is also a ferry that runs from Paynesville to **Raymond Island**, which is inhabited by kangaroos, koalas and water and bush birds.

Stratford

Stratford is a town located on the Avon River 17km north of Sale. A **Shakespearean Festival** is held here in April every year. For more details, ©(03) 5145 6133, email ✎ dmccubb@netspace.net.au or visit the website at ☜home. bicnet.au\~shakes

Gippsland

In general terms, the Gippsland area stretches from the east of Bairnsdale to Phillip Island, and north of Morwell and Traralgon down to Wilsons Promontory and Ninety Mile Beach on the southern coast, taking in just about everything in between. It covers the beautiful landscapes of fertile countryside and is full of various natural wonders from mountains and forests to rivers and beaches.

The best way to explore the Gippsland is by driving through it at a leisurely pace and absorbing its scenic qualities.

The Visitor Centres can provide you with a range of material comprising the eight uniquely-themed drives listed below.

1. **Gippsland Heritage Track** - museums, historic buildings, shipwrecks, gold mines, antique shops and more.

2. **Walhalla and Mountain Rivers Trail** - Long Tunnel Extended Mine, Walhalla Cemetery, Stringers Creek Gorge, Walhalla Goldfields Railway.

3. **Wildlife Coast Nature Track** - Victoria's south coast including Phillip Island, National Parks, Ninety Mile Beach, walking trails, Wilsons Promontory.

4. **The Grand Ridge Road** - Strzelecki Ranges, rainforest and bushwakling areas.

5. **The High Country Adventure** - a journey through mountainous peaks providing breathaking views of rugged valleys below.

6. **The Country Road** - Great Dividing Range Hinterland, rural country, charming pubs, Alpine National Park.

7. **Gourmet Traveller Track** - sampling seafood, meat products, dairy selections, fresh vegetables and fine wines cultivated in the prosperous Gippsland soil.

8. **Power Track** - traces the history of coal mining in the region and takes you past the massive power generation facilities of the LaTrobe Valley.

Plenty of touring material is produced covering the Gippsland region. There are detailed maps, driving routes, accommodation listings and current news and events. Two information outlets are:

Gippsland Country Tourism Information Centre, Shop 1, Southside Central, Princes Highway, Traralgon, ☎5174 3199 or ☎1800 621 409 (toll free).

South Gippsland Visitor Information Centre, cnr South Gippsland Highway & Silkstone Road, Korumburra, ☎5655 2233 or ☎1800 630 704 (toll free).

For online information visit 👁www.gippslandtourism.com.au or email ✐information@gippsland tourism.com.au

Sale

Situated on the Melbourne side of Lakes Entrance, Sale is the operations centre for the nearby Bass Strait oil fields of Esso-BHP. There is also a large RAAF training base located here.

Cullinen Park, off Foster Street, is the site of the historic Port of Sale where, in days of yore, steamers tied up after their long trip from Melbourne. From Sale there are roads leading to the southern end of Ninety Mile Beach.

Apart from the historical interest of the town centre, including the **Gippsland Art Gallery** (68 Foster Street, ☎5142 3372) and the **Historical Museum** (Foster Street, ☎5144 5994), Sale is surrounded by attractive natural areas which include a **Wildlife Refuge** and the **David Morass State Game Reserve**.

The Central Gippsland Visitor Information Centre can be found in 8 Foster Street, ☎(03) 5144 1108. Email them at toursale@i-o.net.au

Healesville & the Yarra Valley

Population 8,150
Healesville is 62km (38 miles) east of Melbourne, in the foothills of the Great Dividing Range.

Climate

The climate can be brisk in winter, with snow on the higher peaks.

Characteristics

Healesville is the gateway to towering ash forests, waterfalls and fern bowers. The township is surrounded by high mountains, and one of Victoria's most picturesque mountain highways climbs from Healesville to Marysville over the Black Spur through forests of mountain ash, beech and wattle.

How to Get There

By Rail
From Melbourne's Flinders Street Station, take a train to Lilydale, which connects with a V/Line coach to Healesville.

By Road
From Melbourne, via the Maroondah Highway.

Tourist Information

The Yarra Valley Visitor Information Centre is in The Old Courthouse, Harker Street, ✆(03) 5962 2600, email ✎info@yarravalleytourism. asn.au, online at ☞www.yarra valleytourism.asn.au

Accommodation

Healesville does not offer a wide choice of accommodation, but here is a selection, with prices for a double room per night which should be used as a guide only. ℭThe telephone area code is 03.

Healesville Motor Inn, 45 Maroondah Highway, ℭ5962 5188. 14 units, bbq - ✪$75-140.

Healesville Maroondah View Motel, 1 McKenzie Ave, ℭ5962 4154. 10 units, unlicensed restaurant, swimming pool - ✪$70-75.

Sanctuary House Healesville (Motel), 326 Badger Creek Road, ℭ5962 5188. 12 units, unlicensed restaurant, swimming pool, spa, sauna - ✪$65-80.

Yarra Gables Motel, 55 Maroondah Hwy, ℭ5962 1323. 5 units (private facilities) - ✪$99-140.

Caravan Parks

Badger Creek Caravan & Holiday Park, 419 Don Road, ℭ5962 4328. (No pets allowed) - powered sites ✪$20-24 for two, no on-site vans.

Ashgrove Tourist Park & Holiday Units, 322 Don Road, ℭ5962 4398. (Pets allowed by prior arrangement) - powered sites ✪$20-22 for two, no on-site vans.

Eating Out

Some of the motels have BYO restaurants, and the hotels have licensed restaurants or bistros. Here are a few others you might like to try.

Mount Rael Restaurant, Healesville/Yarra Glen Road, ℭ5962 4107- BYO, Australian cuisine.

Strathvea Country House, Myers Creek Road, ℭ5962 4109 - BYO, Australian cuisine.

Ming Gardens Restaurant, 271 Maroondah Highway, ℭ5962 5067

Montiverdi Pizza Restaurant, 335 Maroondah Highway, ℭ5962 4455 - BYO and licensed, eat in or takeaway.

Healesville Piquant Palate, 278 Maroondah Highway, ℭ5962 3625, is a deli and restaurant. They specialise in Teddy Bears Picnic Baskets, specially prepared for a relaxing day in the country. They ask if orders for the baskets could be placed the day before they are needed.

Points of Interest

One of the most popular attractions is the **Healesville Sanctuary** in Badger Creek Road, ℭ5957 2800. The sanctuary is the only place where the platypus has been bred in captivity, and they are on display here ⊕between 11.30am-3.30pm. There are also koalas, wombats, kangaroos and emus, and a Nocturnal House with some of Australia's least-seen animals such as the Leadbeater possum, kowari, sugar gliders and potaroos. The Reptile House has a selection of Australia's venomous snakes, and in another area there are lyrebirds, that have also been successfully bred here. The Sanctuary has a catering centre for picnic lunches, a licensed bistro, and a gift shop. ☺Open daily 9am-5pm.

Hedgend Maze, at 163 Albert Road, is a giant hedge carved into a maze, with cryptic messages to solve on the way to help you get through. The grounds make for a pleasant picnic setting. It is ☺open daily from 10am, ✆5962 3636.

Maroondah Reservoir is a popular place, and is set in a landscaped park of exotic and native trees, shrubs and flowers.

Badger Weir and **Donnelly's Weir** also provide beautiful bushland walks and superb picnic-barbecue areas. For the more energetic, walking tracks explore local National Parks and Forests.

Queen's Park, in the centre of the township, is ideal for picnics, and has a sports oval, tennis courts, children's playground and swimming pool.

11km (7 miles) west of Healesville is the township of **Yarra Glen**, and the Yarra Valley Tourist Railway winds between the two towns. A group of volunteers are in the proc-

ess of making the railway a premier tourist attraction. Trolley rides can be taken from Healesville Station through a 100m old, brick-lined tunnel. Just out of Yarra Glen is the historic Gulf Station, which is worth a visit.

Toolangi, about 30km (19 miles) north of Healesville, was the home of C.J. Dennis, author of *The Sentimental Bloke*. Arden, the 'Singing Garden' he and his wife Biddy created, is ☺open daily 10am-5pm. The 1.5ha rhododendron gardens are a delight, and there are Tea Rooms where you can spend some time admiring them, and enjoying a light lunch. Across the road is Toolangi Pottery, where master potter David Williams produces and displays his stoneware and crystalline pottery. His work has been exhibited in the National Gallery of Victoria.

Wineries

The Yarra Valley has many wineries, and here they are listed, with the cellar door hours.

Yarra Burn Vineyard, Settlement Road, Yarra Junction, ✆5967 1428 -☺open daily 10am-6pm.

McWilliams Lillydale Vineyards, Davross Court, Seville, ✆5964 2016 - ☺open daily 11am-5pm.

Five Oaks Vineyard, Aitken Road, Seville, ✆5964 3704 - ☺open daily 10am-5pm.

Kelly Brook Winery, Fulford Road, Wonga Park, ☎9722 1304 - ⏰open Wed-Sat 9am-6pm, Sun 11am-6pm, Mon 9am-6pm.

Bianchet Winery, Victoria Road, Lilydale, ☎9739 1779 -⏰open Mon-Fri please phone prior to visit, Sat-Sun 10am-6pm.

Warramate Vineyard, Maddens Lane, Gruyere, ☎5964 9219 - ⏰open daily10am-6pm.

St Huberts Vineyard, St Huberts Road, Coldstream, ☎9739 1118 -⏰Mon-Fri 9.30am-5pm, Sat 10.30am-5.30pm, Sun 11.30am-5.30pm.

Eyton On Yarra Winery & Restaurant, cnr Maroondah Highway & Hill Road, Coldstream, ☎5962 2119 - ⏰daily 10am-5pm.

Fergusson's Winery & Restaurant, Wills Road, Yarra Glen, ☎5965 2237 - ⏰ Mon-Fri 9am-5pm, Sat-Sun 11am-5pm.

De Bortoli Winery & Restaurant,

Pinnacle Lane, Dixons Creek, ☎5965 2271 - ⏰daily10am-5pm.

Shantell Vineyard, Melba Highway (60km post), Dixons Creek, ☎5965 2155 - ⏰Thu-Mon 10.30am-5pm.

Broussard's Chum Creek Winery, Cunninghams Road, Healesville, ☎5962 5551 - ⏰Sat-Sun 10am-6pm.

Long Gully Estate, Long Gully Road, Healesville, ☎9510 798 - ⏰Mon-Fri please phone prior to visit, Sat-Sun noon-5pm.

Festivals

The Yarra Valley Expo, celebrating the regions wine, food and farmlife, is held in March.

Facilities

Lawn bowls, swimming, tennis, golf, fishing, greyhound racing, horseracing, harness racing and squash. There is a cinema on the highway.

Outlying Attractions

Marysville

Situated 36km (22 miles) northeast of Healesville, Marysville is high in the Great Dividing Range, 500m (1640 ft) above sea level. It has great forests and tree-fern gullies, and is a cool and welcome retreat. In winter, nearby Lake Mountain offers one of the best cross-country ski areas outside Scandinavia.

There is an 18-hole golf course, and horse riding on mountain trails is available. Bushwalking is also a popular pastime.

Steavenson Falls, the tallest in Victoria, cascade 82m (269 ft) in three leaps and are floodlit at night.

Accommodation is available in guesthouses, holiday lodges, cabins and motels, as well as a camping and caravan park beside the Steavenson River. For more information on Marysville, contact the Visitor Information Centre, 11 Murchison Street, ✆(03) 5963 4567.

Eildon and Alexandra

These towns are the gateways to Lake Eildon and Fraser National Park. Both have facilities for fishing, bushwalking, camping, water skiing, swimming, sailing, cross country skiing, golf, tennis, squash and bowls, and accommodation is plentiful.

Alexandra is 69km (43 miles) north of Healesville, and Eildon is 26km (16 miles) east of Alexandra.

There are quite a few attractions - art and craft shops and galleries; fauna parks with native animals, deer and camels; The Timber Tramway & Museum at the old railway station, Alexandra, ✆5772 2392; and the Visitor Centre at 45a Grant Street, Alexandra, ✆(03) 5772 1100 will assist with further enquiries.

Bright & the Victorian Alps

Population - 1,800
Bright is situated on the Ovens River, in the foothills of the Victorian Alps. It is 310km (193 miles) from Melbourne, 700km (435 miles) from Sydney, 940km (584 miles from Adelaide, 74km (46 miles) from Wangaratta, and 116km (72 miles) from Albury.

Characteristics

Bright is truly a town for all seasons. In Summer, there is the river for safe swimming and fishing, and horseriding and bush walking are very popular. In Autumn, the European and Asian trees left by the pioneers become a blaze of gold, orange, red and yellow, and the town celebrates with the Autumn Festival. Winter brings snow to the mountains surrounding Bright, and the skiers arrive in their thousands for the slopes in the three close alpine resorts. And in Spring, the elms, poplars, wattles, fruit trees, etc, create the brightest Bright of all.

How to Get There

By Bus
Greyhound Pioneer travel to Albury-Wodonga from Sydney and Melbourne, and connect with a local bus service to Bright.

By Rail
Regular train services run from Melbourne and Sydney to Wangaratta, and then V-line buses to Bright.

By Road
From Melbourne, either via the Hume Highway to Wangaratta and

then the Ovens Highway, or via the Princes Highway to Bairnsdale and then the Omeo Highway.

From Sydney, via the Hume Highway to Albury, then the Kiewa Valley Highway.

Tourist Information

The Bright Tourist Information Centre is at 119 Gavan Street, ✆(03) 5755 2275 or ✆1800 500 117, ✉ email bright@dragnet.com.au

Two websites to visit are 👁www.brightdistrict.com.au (for limited local information) and 👁www.alpinelink.com.au

Accommodation

Bright's main industry is tourism, so there is no shortage of accommodation. Here we have a selection, with prices for a double room per night, which should be used as a guide only. ✆The telephone area code is 03.

Barrass's John Bright Motor Inn, 10 Wood Street, ✆5755 1400. 20 units, swimming pool, spa, bbq - ✪$85-145.

High Country Inn, 13 Gavan Street, ✆5755 1244. 32 units, licensed restaurant, swimming pool, spa, sauna, bbq - ✪$89-112.

Acacia Motor Lodge, 85 Gavan Street, ✆5755 1441. 12 units, swimming pool, bbq - ✪$77-125.

Bright Avenue Motor Inn, 87 Delany Avenue, ✆5755 1911. 13 units, bbq - ✪$77-130.

Ovens Valley Motor Inn, cnr Great Alpine Rd & Ashwood Avenue, ✆5755 2022. 24 units, licensed

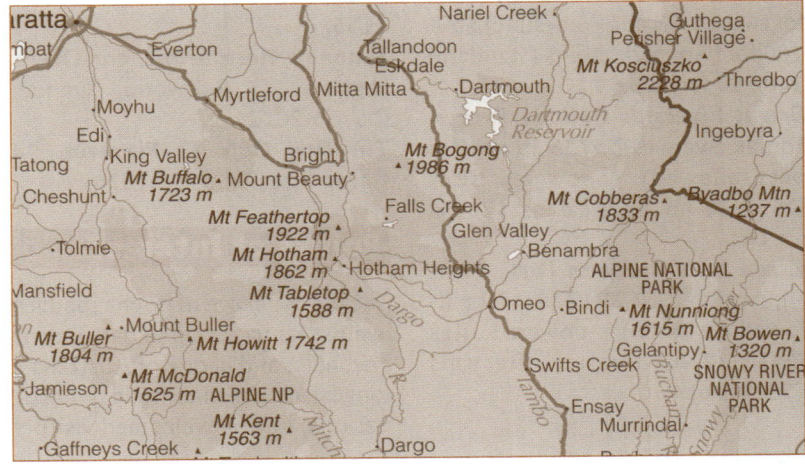

restaurant, swimming pool, spa, sauna, bbq - ✪$75-95.

Bright Motor Inn, 1 Delany Avenue, ✆5750 1433. 26 units, licensed restaurant, bbq - ✪$60-75.

Riverbank Park Motel, 69 Gavan Street, ✆5755 1255. 24 units, unlicensed restaurant, swimming pool - ✪$88-100.

Bright Colonial Inn Motel, 54 Gavan Street, ✆5755 1197. 18 rooms (private facilities), unlicensed restaurant, bbq - ✪$77-88.

Caravan Parks

Alpine Cabins & Caravan Park, 1 Mountbatten Avenue, ✆5755 1064. (No pets allowed) - powered sites ✪$20-25 for two, cabins $57-115 for two.

Bright Caravan Park, Cherry Avenue, ✆5755 1141. (No dogs allowed Christmas, January and Easter) - powered sites ✪$17-25 for two, park cabins (en-suite) $50-100 for two, park cabins (standard) $40 -56 for two.

Bright Riverside Holiday Park, 4 Toorak Avenue, ✆5755 1118. (No pets allowed) - powered sites ✪$17-26 for two, cabins $25-33 for two.

Green Hills Caravan Park, Great Alpine Rd, ✆5750 1218. (Pets allowed on leash) - powered sites ✪$16-22 for two, on-site vans $29-41 for two.

Eating Out

Many of the hotels and motels have dining rooms, and there are the usual amount of takeaway outlets for a holiday town. Here are some you might like to try:

Lawler's Hut, 100 Gavan St, Bright, ✆1800 813 992 - licensed, high quality local produce - a la carte - ☺open for breakfast and dinner.

Poplars, 8 Star Road, Bright, ✆5755 1655 - BYO and licensed, a la carte and seafood - ☺open daily from 6.30pm.

The Cosy Kangaroo, Gavan Street, ✆5750 1838 - good value family restaurant.

Ned's Rstaurant & Bar, 13-17 Gavan Street, ✆5755 1244 - licensed, country-style dining - ☺open Tue-Sat for dinner.

Golden Bright Chinese Restaurant, 108 Gavan Street, ✆5750 1155.

Simone's Restaurant, cnr Ovens Highway & Ashwood Avenue, ✆5755 2022.

Tin Dog Cafe & Pizzeria, 94 Gavan Street, ✆5755 1526.

Points of Interest

The pretty village of Bright sparkles against its backdrop of dark green-clad hills, and is one of Australia's longest established holiday destinations, having welcomed visitors for more than a century. Bright's first guide book was published in 1887, and included maps of walking tracks and bridle paths, specially marked and graded according to degree of difficulty. These are still popular today, and current maps are available at the Tourist Information centre. Some of the most popular walks are to the Clearspot, Huggins and Mt Porepunkah lookouts, which offer a panoramic view of the village.

The **Historical Museum of Bright** has been established in the town's disused railway station. It is ☉open 2-4pm Tue, Thu & Sun during school holidays and festivals, and 2-4pm Sun from September to May.

The **Bright Art Gallery & Cultural Centre**, 28 Mountbatten Avenue, ☎5750 1660, has a comprehensive art collection and a gem and rare mineral collection, as well as the largest cuckoo clock in Australia. It is ☉open Mon-Sat 1-5pm, Sun 9am-5.30pm, and daily during school holidays.

Gallery 90, 90 Gavan Street, ☎5755 1385, has original paintings, pottery, leather, handpainted clothing, jewellery, handpainted porcelain, traditional cottage crafts, and much more. The gallery is housed in a restored local granite and bluestone cottage that dates back to 1881, and is ☉open Mon-Sat 9.30am-5.30pm, Sun 11am-5.30pm. During the Autumn Festival the hours are extended to 9am-5.30pm daily.

Walks around Bright are marked by sign posts and yellow track markers fixed to trees and posts. Maps and guides are available from the newsagent and the Tourist Information Centre for walks further afield, and if venturing up in the hills you should remember to take some warm clothing, as it will be colder there than down in the valley. The climb to **Mt Buffalo** commences at the Park entrance and climbs through 11km (7 miles) of varied scenery, to arrive at the oval below the *Mt Buffalo Chalet*.

For the less energetic, there is a wide variety of **tours**, both half and full day, to various attractions around Bright and the high country. For further information and bookings, contact the Tourist Information Centre. If you are in Bright in the winter, enquire about ski packages and snow trips.

Festivals

The Bright Autumn Festival is held during the last week of April and the first week of May each year, and one of the main features is Gala Day with street processions and stalls. The entrants for Miss Autumn Festival are received at the Presentation Ball and the judging and crowning takes place.

Among the many events that are part of the Festival are: the opening of the Autumn Art Exhibition; conducted tours of tobacco farms; gold panning exhibitions; historic tours of Wandiligong and surrounding districts; tours of the forests by the Forest Commission; a Family Picnic; an Old Time Music Hall; and wine and cheese tastings.

The Springtime in Bright Festival is held during October and November, and co-ordinates a whole range of events and activities.

Outlying Attractions

Porepunkah

The small town of Porepunkah is 6km (4 miles) from Bright, at the junction of the Buckland and Ovens Rivers, and the turnoff to Mount Buffalo National Park. Originally named Port Punka, the area was part of a cattle station which reached from Eurobin to Bright. During the gold mining era, the township site was known as The Ovens Crossing. It is a quiet, peaceful spot, and has a hotel, post office, petrol station, general store, several riverside caravan parks, and a growing number of flats and motels. The two rivers provide excellent fishing for trout.

The Snow Country

The major ski centres are Falls Creek, Mt Buffalo and Mt Hotham. The website 👁www.ski.com.au gives the latest information about the weather and skiing conditions at all the Victorian ski resorts. Ski packages and snow trips to the three resorts can be arranged thorough various outlets, and the Tourist Centre can provide you with a list of operators and prices.

Mount Buffalo

The mountain is 32km (20 miles) from Bright, and 320km (199 miles) from Melbourne. Accommodation on the slopes is available at Mount Buffalo Chalet and Lodge, and inclusive packages are offered.

Operating only 3 poma lifts and 2 chairlifts, Mt Buffalo is a small, sheltered ski field that focuses on laid-back family enjoyment. It is comprised mainly of gentle downhill slopes. Serious skiiers looking for a challenge should head elsewhere, although cross-country ski trails are available here in Mt Buffalo National Park.

Lift ticket prices are $39 adult, $25 child for one day; $180 adult, $120 child for 5 days; and $199 for a season pass.

Mount Buffalo Chalet, ✆(03) 5755 1500, 👁www.mtbuffalo chalet.com.au. You can choose from the guesthouses, which have shared facilties, or the View and Tower rooms, which are private. Prices include dinner, breakfast, activities, guided walks, shuttle transfers daily, entry into the National Park, and use of all Chalet facilities. They should be used as a guide only.

Guesthouse - 2 nights $260 adult, $140 child; 5 nights (including lunch) $670 adult, $350 child.

View Room - 2 nights $370 adult, $160 child; 5 nights $865 (including lunch) adult, $395 child.

Tower Room - 2 nights $395 adult, $160 child; 5 nights (including lunch) $920 adult, $395 child.

The nearby Mount Buffalo Lodge offers motel and lodge-style accommodation with breakfast, use of facilities and National Park entry included, and backpacker rooms with meals not included.

Motel - 2 nights $130 adult, $55 child; 3 nights $180 adult, $85 child.

Lodge - 2 nights $105 adult, $55 child; 3 nights $150 adult, $85 child.

Backpackers - 2 nights $40 adult, $35 child; 3 nights $65 adult, $50 child.

Ski hire is available and ski lessons can be booked.

Dingo Dell

Ski runs are 6km (4 miles) south of the Chalet, and are ideal for beginners and family groups. There are two poma lifts and a portable beginners' lift.

Amenities and services include the large car park within easy walking distance of the slopes; ski instruction; Keown Lodge, a visitor centre which is used as a day lodge and provides takeaway and eat-in meals, changing rooms, toilets and first aid facilities.

Cresta Valley

Ski runs are 4km (2 miles) south of Dingo Dell, and are around the Mt Buffalo Lodge & Alpine Resort, ©5755 1988, at about 1525m (5003 ft) above sea level. There are eight runs served by 5 lifts catering for beginner, intermediate and advanced skiers. The degree of difficulty of a slope can be identified by the coloured markers at the runs. Easiest runs are marked by green circles and are served by the Gully Poma and Novice Poma. More difficult runs are marked with blue squares and suit intermediate skiers. The Valley and Cresta Chairlift runs are in this category. The most difficult runs are marked by black diamonds and are reached by riding the Cresta Poma.

The Cresta Day Visitor Centre houses the resort management office, ski school, ticket office, National Park information area, medical centre and a cafe offering takeaway.

Cross Country Trails are graded Beginner and Intermediate, with access to Cresta Valley graded Intermediate to Advanced. Lift Tickets: Ticket boxes have single ride, half-day and full day; Cresta Office has a season pass (photo required); and The Chalet and Tatra Inn have 1-day, 2-day, 3-day, 5-day and 7-day packages.

Falls Creek
👁www.fallscreek.com.au

Falls Creek is 62km (39 miles) from Bright, 32km (20 miles) from the township of Mount Beauty, and 356km (221 miles) from Melbourne. There are many guest houses to choose from, and several offer ski packages.

Falls Creek has snowmaking machines, and the system covers 10ha (25 acres). It is installed on Towers Duplex, Panorama, Playground, Tom Thomb and at the top of Eagle, Halley's Comet and Scott Chairlifts.

Following is a brief description of the ski runs -

Novice
Nursery Pomas/Dogpatch Pomas - in the bowl area, near the Ski School. Ideal for beginners.

Saddle Linklift - an easy T-Bar for skiers of all standards. Also gives access to the Ruined Castle area.

Headwater Poma, Playground Pomas, Tom Thumb - gentle and have easy access via the Eagle Chair and Halley's Comet Quad Chair, returning via the Broadway Hometrail and the Wombat's Ramble Hometrail.

Halley's Comet Quad Chairlift - a fast access lift from the carpark to the slopes of Sun Valley. Novice skiers return via the Wombat's Ramble Hometrail and intermediates return via the Last Hoot Hometrail. At the top of Halley's Comet is the Cloud Nine Restaurant with bar, dining and restroom facilities.

Intermediate
Gully Triple Chairlift - an access lift from the carpark to the bowl. Gully slopes are not suitable for novices.

Village T-Bar - forming part of the sheltered bowl, these runs are ideal for easy intermediate skiing.

Panorama Poma, Towers Duplex T-Bar, Lakeside Poma, Scott Quad Chairlift, Ruined Castle Poma - these five lifts offer a variety of intermediate skiing. The valley holds a good cover of dry snow on interesting gullies and lightly wooded trails.

Eagle Triple Chairlift - a fast access lift from the bowl to the slopes of Sun Valley. Return via the Broadway Hometrail.

Advanced
Big Dipper Duplex T-Bar - a good length run for intermediate skiers.

However, on the right-hand side is a large cornice with deep soft snow.

Summit T-Bar - known traditionally as the advanced skier's paradise, the finest bumps run in Australia.

International Poma - a fast lift providing challenging skiing for advanced skiers. Also provides access to the Bowl, the Summit, and the slopes of Sun Valley.

Lift Tickets
A full range of lift tickets is available early in the morning at Bogong Ski Centre, Kiewa Valley Highway, Mt Beauty, and at JD's Mountain Sports, cnr Burke & Anderson Streets, Bright. They can also be purchased in the Sun Valley area. Passport type photographs are required for Season and 4, 5, 6 and 7 day lift, and lift and lesson packages. Instant photos can be taken at Cumings, The Hub, Gebi's, Snowland and The Creek Photo Service. 4, 5, 6 and 7 days lift, and lift and lesson tickets can be purchased after 4pm on day prior to the first day of use.

Approximate prices are: Half day - $56 adult, $29 child; 1 day - $75 adult, $39 child; 2 day - $144 adult, $74 child; 3 day - $212 adult, $108 child; 4 day - $273 adult, $140 child; 5 day - $328 adult, $171 child; 6 day - $383 adult, $199 child; 7 day - $420 adult, $218 child.

Season tickets cost between $400 and $900, depending on the time of purchase - the earlier the better.

A one day lift & lesson package costs $105 adult, $70 child. Ski hire is available.

Accommodation
Below is a selection of what is available in the heart of Falls Creek. All have outstanding views of the surrounding mountains.

Alpha Lodge, ✆5758 3488, from $23 for shared rooms and $41 for a single room, per person.

Falls Creek Country Club, ✆5758 3391, from $135 for a double room.

Alpine View & Cumings Apartments, ✆5758 3461, from $420 for a 4-room apartment.

Attunga Alpine Lodge & Apartments, ✆5758 3255, from $100 for a double room, including breakfast.

Alpine Woodsmoke, ✆5754 1138, www.woodsmoke.com.au, apartments from $200 per night.

Mount Hotham
👁www.mthotham.com.au
Mount Hotham is 55km (34 miles) from Bright, and 354km (220 miles) from Melbourne. It is Australia's highest alpine village at 1750m (5741 ft), and all accommodation is only minutes from the ski runs. The runs are classified as 27% beginner, 36% intermediate and 37% advanced.

More information can be obtained

from the Mount Hotham Alpine Resort Management Board, Great Alpine Road, Mount Hotham, ©(03) 5759 3550, email ✐mhar@mthotham.com.au

There are over 40 marked and groomed runs on the slopes, and the ski school, ticket sales, ski shops and ski hire are all in easy walking distance from the car parks, and one short step from the slopes.

Above the Village
Summit - a high altitude slope of south-easterly aspect, and a reliable beginners' area. Served by the Summit quad chairlift, and on the summit is the Doppelmayr T-Bar.

Big D - at the southern end of Mt Hotham village, with reliable snow and gentle beginners' slopes.

Below the Village
Sun Run - opposite the Summit, the Sun Run is for skiers progressing to intermediate. Served by a T-Bar lift.

Basin - a sheltered bowl opposite the main day car-park offering skiing for beginners and intermediates. Served by a Doppelmayr platter lift.

Playground - several trails for intermediate and advanced skiers down to Swindlers Creek.

Heavenly Valley
The Heavenly Valley quad chairlift provides access to vast areas of skiing terrain for confident intermediates and advanced skiers.

Blue Ribbon - served by a Doppelmayr triple chairlift, offers sustained and sheltered fall line skiing for intermediate and advanced skiers.

Mt Hotham Village offers a range of shops and services including ski hire, ski shop, licensed restaurants (Italian, international and modern Australian), pizzeria, a supermarket, bistro, post office, nightclub and information desk.

Lift Tickets

Lift passes are available from the Mount Hotham Skiing Company, ©5759 4444, which has an office on the mountain.

The following are prices for lifts only. Half day - $56 adult, $29 child; 1 day - $75 adult, $39 child; 2 day - $144 adult, $74 child; 3 day - $212 adult, $108 child; 5 day - $328 adult, $171 child; 7 day - $420 adult, $218 child; Season - from $870 adult, $440 child.

Myrtleford

Situated 29km (18 miles) north-west of Bright on the Ovens Highway, Myrtleford is at the foot of Mount Buffalo. The district's main industries are timber, hops, tobacco and cattle.

The town has 3 hotels, 2 motels, a caravan park, 2 camping reserves, bunkhouse and lodge accommodation. There are facilities for swimming, tennis, golf, bowls, bocce, croquet, fishing (trout and redfin), horse riding, hang gliding, bushwalking, and of course, skiing.

Victoria – North

Shepparton

Population 32,000
Shepparton is located in the Lower Goulburn Valley in the northern 'centre' of Victoria, 178km (111 miles) north of Melbourne.

Climate

Average temperatures: January max 30C (86F) - min 14C (57F); July max 13C (55F) - min 4C(39F). Average annual rainfall: 502mm (20 ins). Shepparton averages more than 7 hours of sunlight per day.

Characteristics

Shepparton was declared The Solar City by the Solar Council in 1986, due to the large amount of sunshine it averages, and the city has a solar heated swimming pool (in summer), some solar powered street lighting in areas, a solar powered telephone outside the Tourist Information Centre, and some solar powered parking meters. It is the major city of the Goulburn Valley, one of the food bowls of the nation. The area produces enormous quantities of fruit, vegetables and dairy products, as well as cereal crops, grapes, wine, beef, wool and lamb.

How to Get There

By Rail
V/Line Trains have services Mon-Fri from Spencer Street Station in Melbourne, ⊕leaving at 9.10am and 6.15pm. On Saturday the trains leave at 9.10am and 6.10pm, and on Sunday at 9.50am and 6.05pm.

By Bus

Greyhound Pioneer stop at Shepparton on their Melbourne/ Brisbane service. V/Line coaches have services from Melbourne daily except Saturday.

By Road

From Melbourne, via the Hume Highway to north of Shepparton, then the Goulburn Valley Highway.

From Sydney, via the Hume Highway to Benalla, then the Midland Highway.

Visitor Information

The Tourist Information Centre, Victoria Park Lake, 534 Wyndham Street, ©(03) 5831 4400 or ©1800 808 839, is ©open 10am-3pm daily. Further information is available online at ☞www.shepparton.vic. gov.au and you can email ✎visitor@ shepparton.vic.gov.au

Accommodation

There is a wide range to choose from, and here is a selection with prices for a double room per night, which should be used as a guide only. ©The telephone area code is 03.

Parklake Motor Inn, 481 Wyndham Street, ©5821 5822. 70 units, licensed restaurant, swimming pool, spa, sauna - ✪$116-176.

Pines Country Club Motor Inn, 103 Numurkah Road, ©5831 2044. 20 units, licensed restaurant (closed Sunday), swimming pool - ✪$110-130.

Paradise Lakes Motel Resort, 7685 Goulburn Valley Highway, Shepparton South, ©5823 1888. 26 units(private facilities), swimming pool, spa, bbq - ✪$80-115.

Tirana Motor Inn, 33 Wyndham Street(Goulburn Valley Hwy), ©5831 1766. 24 units, swimming pool, bbq - ✪$80-90.

The Bel-Air Motor Inn, 630 Wyndham Street (Goulburn Valley Hwy), ©5821 4833. 30 units, licensed restaurant (closed Monday), swimming pool, spa, sauna - ✪$65-80.

Country Home Motor Inn, 11 *Wyndham Street*, ©5821 7711. 15 units, swimming pool, bbq - ✪$65-80.

Overlander Hotel/Motel, 97 Benalla Road (Midland Hwy), ©5821 5622. 30 units, licensed restaurant, swimming pool - ✪$65-70.

Apex Motel, Goulburn Valley Highway, ©5821 4472. 16 units, swimming pool, bbq - ✪$45-50.

Victoria Hotel Shepparton, cnr Wyndham & Fryers Streets, ©5821 9955. 37 rooms, licensed restaurant - ✪$40-65.

Caravan Parks

Pine Lodge Caravan Park, cnr

Midland Highway & Orrvale Road, ©5829 2396. (No pets allowed) - powered sites ✪$19-22 for two, no on-site vans.

Shepparton Riverview Caravan Park, Melbourne Road (Goulburn Valley Hwy), ©5823 1561. (Dogs allowed at manager's discretion) - powered sites ✪$16 for two, no on-site vans.

Strayleaves Caravan Park, cnr Mitchell Street & Old Dookie Road, ©5821 1232. (No dogs allowed) - powered sites ✪$16 for two, on-site vans $29 for two.

Eating Out

Cellar 47 Restaurant, 166 -170 High Street, ©5831 1882, is ◷open for lunch Tues-Fri noon-2pm, dinner Tues-Sat from 6pm.

Shepparton Family Restaurant, City Walk, ©5821 3737, specialise in Chinese and Australian smorgasbord - ◷open for lunch Mon-Sat 11.30am-2.30pm, dinner every day 5.30-9.30pm.

Parklake Motor Inn Cafe Bar Restaurant, at the Parklake Motor Inn, 481 Wyndham Street, ©5821 5822, is ◷open for dinner nightly from 6pm, and has a dinner dance on Saturdays.

La Porchetta, 264 Maude Street, ©5821 0800 - Italian and pizza.

Casablanca Pizza Restaurant, 125 High Street, ©5821 1115 - takeaway available.

New China Restaurant, 55 Fryers Street, ©5831 1166.

Calzoneys Restaurant, 30 North Street, ©5831 3578.

Aloi Thai Restaurant, 630a Wyndham Street, ©5831 6613.

Riviera Pizza Restaurant, 117a Wyndham Street , ©5821 4402.

Pizza Hut is at 525 Wyndham Street, ©5822 2111, and **KFC** has two outlets in Wyndham Street at nos 620 and 465.

Points of Interest

Victoria Park Lake, near where the Tourist Information Centre is found, has picnic, barbecue, water skiing, windsurfing and cycling facilities. It is the leisure centre of the city.

The **Eastbank Centre** in Welsford Street, which houses the town hall, art gallery, theatre and municipal offices, is one of the most outstanding in any rural city in Australia. It was designed by architecture students from the University of Melbourne.

The **Shepparton Art Gallery**, in the Eastbank, has an extensive collection of ceramic works by well known artists, and around 150 paintings including pieces by McCubbin. It is ◷open 10am-4pm seven days, and admission is free, ©5832 9861.

The **Historical Museum**, cnr

Welsford & High Streets, is ⏰open on irregular Sundays 1-4pm (☎5831 4400), and has exhibits of local memorabilia from Aboriginal and European heritage to current events.

The **Telecommunications Tower** in Fraser Street, West Walk of the Maude Street Mall, has an observation platform which allows 360 degree views of the district. At the base of the tower is a Human Sundial, which accurately tells the time when you stand on the point corresponding to the day's date.

Maude Street Mall is in the heart of the city and is a shopping centre with many features including entertainment areas, loads of trees and flower beds, and plenty of parking.

Shepparton Preserving Company (SPC), Andrew Fairley Avenue, has a sales outlet ⏰open Mon-Fri, and factory tours during the canning season, January-April.

Driver Education Centre of Australia (DECA), Wanganui Road, ☎5821 1099, has courses for people of all ages, and tours of the complex are ⏰available Mon-Fri 8am-5pm.

In the **Shepparton Sports Stadium**, near McEwan Reserve, is a Maze which will keep all the family involved for a while.

Radio Australia in Verney Road, Lemnos, is home of the international broadcasting station. Tours are by appointment only, ☎5829 9202.

The **Dookie College of Agriculture and Horticulture**, is midway between Shepparton and Benalla. The buildings are situated at the foot of Mt Major, on the fringe of the Goulburn Valley, and have excellent accommodation, conference and seminar facilities, ☎5833 9200.

Festivals

The Sun City Festival is held over seven days in March/April, and the Shepparton Show is in October.

Kialla West Strawberry Festival is held in November.

Facilities

Sporting facilities include horse-racing, trotting, greyhound racing, tennis, squash, lawn bowls, golf, and water sports. There is a cinema, cnr Maude & Stuart Streets, and a drive-in theatre in Melbourne Road, South Shepparton.

Outlying Attractions

Numurkah

Situated 35km (22 miles) north of Shepparton on the Goulburn Valley Highway, Numurkah has a population of around 3000, and is on Broken Creek. The town is surrounded by mostly irrigated farmland, with a wide range of crops. There is also wool and beef production, and a large dairying industry.

The town is about the same distance from the Murray River, and its attractions include the Barmah Forest, Monichino Wines (✆5864 6452), Brookfield Historic Farm (✆5862 2353), and of course, the Murray River beaches.

The Numurkah Visitor Information Centre is at 25 Quinn Street, ✆(03) 5862 3458.

Tocumwal

This is the first New South Wales town on the Newell Highway, and is situated on the banks of the Murray River. It offers a blend of old with new, from Federation era buildings with stained glassed windows to modern licensed clubs, business and accommodation developments.

The town has a population of around 1400, but this is regularly swelled with visitors stopping off on their north or south journeys. There is a golf club and a bowling club with first class facilities, restaurants, and being in New South Wales - poker machines. The main street of the town and the river are divided by parklands with camping sites, water skiing, swimming, boating, sailing and fishing facilities, and houseboat cruises departure points. About 2km from town there is a wartime aerodrome where Sportavia Soaring (Gliding) Centre offers year-round gliding, ✆5874 2063.

The Visitor Information Centre is in Foreshore Park, ✆(03) 5874 2131.

Benalla

Benalla is 61km (38 miles) south-east of Shepparton, at the junction of the Hume and Midland Highways. The Visitor Information Centre is at 14 Mair Street, ✆(03) 5762 1749.

Benalla was the base of operations in the 1870s for the Kelly Gang, and many mementoes of the Gang can be found in the Kelly Museum in Bridge Street. Enquire at the Visitor Centre about opening times.

Benalla is also famous for its roses, and from late October until early April the Benalla Gardens provide the finest display of that bloom in the State. The Rose Festival is held each November.

The Benalla Art Gallery, in the Benalla Gardens, ☎5762 3833, has an impressive collection of Australian art, including several paintings from the Heidelberg School by Roberts, Streeton and McCubbin.

Mansfield

Situated 63km (39 miles) south of Benalla, at the terminus of both the Maroondah and Midland Highways, Mansfield is the gateway to the Mount Buller alpine resort.

The town is also close to the north arm of Lake Eildon, and to Lake Nillahcootie, so in summer is a popular spot for fishing, sailing, water skiing and white water canoeing. In winter the skiers move into town. This area was the setting for the classic *The Man From Snowy River* movies, and that beautiful scenery was not trick photography, as visitors soon discover.

Call in at the Mansfield Visitor Information Centre at the Railway Station on the Maroondah Highway, ☎(03) 5775 1464.

Mount Buller

👁www.mtbuller.com.au
The ski village is 47km (29 miles) from Mansfield, and is situated at 1600m (5249 ft), with the highest lifted point at 1788m (5866 ft). There are 5 Poma, 8 T-bar, 4 Triple chair and 7 Quad chair lifts, with a capacity of 38,500 people an hour.

The downhill skiable area is 162ha (400 acres), and is graded 24% Beginner, 34% Intermediate and 42% Advanced, with the longest run 2500m (2734 yds).

The Cross-Country areas are Village Loop (Beginner) and Corn Hill (Beginner), with total trails of 10.9km (7 miles).

Lift Tickets: Day - adult $70, child (under 16) $40; Half day - adult $60, child $30; Five day - adult $300, child $200; Seven day - adult $420, child $280; Season - adult $1000, child $560.

Accommodation is available in the village area at **Pension Grimus**, ☎5777 6396 - $390-440 for a double room; and **Arlberg Hotel**, ☎1800 032 380 - DBB one person $140 per night twin share. Contact Mt Buller Resort Management for other accommodation options, ☎(03) 5777 6077 or email ✎info@mtbuller.com.au

Violet Town

Situated 13km (8 miles) west of Benalla, Violet Town is on Honeysuckle Creek and at the foothills of the Strathbogie Ranges. It is the oldest surveyed inland town in Victoria, having been surveyed in 1838, but there was no permanent settlement until 1846. There is a caravan park, hotels, a swimming pool, and many sporting facilities. Head out to the Stonecrop Fine Art Gallery on Harry's Creek Road, ©5798 1444, ⊕between 11am and 5pm any day, and enjoy their dispays and garden surrounds.

Euroa

Euroa is 45km (28 miles) west of Benalla. The Euroa district is steeped in history from the time of early settlement in the 1800s, prospering from people heading for the goldfields. The first flock of Saxon Merino sheep in the State was driven overland from New South Wales to Euroa, and since that time wool has played the major part in the development of Euroa.

Seven Creeks winds through the town with parkland on both banks, and the "Seven Creeks Run" has been established, a project depicting the history of the wool industry. International shearing competitions are conducted in Euroa, and Wool Week has become an event known throughout Australia.

The surrounding district, which includes Forlonge Memorial and Strathbogie Ranges, appeals to the trout fisherman and the bushwalker.

Seymour

Situated at the northern foothills of the Great Dividing Range on the Goulburn River, Seymour is 84km (52 miles) south of Shepparton, and only one hour's drive from Melbourne. The Panyule Fauna Park & Tourist Information Centre, on the corner of Seymour-Tooboorac and Pyalong Roads, can be contacted on ©(03) 5799 0043.

A short distance to the north of the town is Mangalore Airport, originally built as an alternate airport for Melbourne. It is now the headquarters of the Australian Sport Aviation Council, and the Mangalore Air Spectacular Show is held annually over the Easter weekend.

Attractions in the area include:

Trawool Valley has been classified by the National Trust for its scenic beauty. There is an international standard resort, and tea rooms and a gallery. The century-old former Trawool Chool is an art gallery, ©5792 3118. Riddy's Trawool Valley Tours, ©5792 1654, is one way to see the area in full.

Avenel is a small township on Hughes Creek, some 20km (12 miles) from Seymour. It has a number of historical buildings, four of which have been classified by the National Trust, and the grave of Ned Kelly's father. Look out for the old Harvest 'Home Hotel, built in the 1860s and now a restaurant, ©5796 2339.

Puckapunyal Army Camp is 13km (8 miles) west of Seymour, off the Hume Freeway. The camp has the Royal Australian Armoured Corps Tank Museum, which may be viewed 10am-4pm daily, ©5793 7285.

Nagambie

The gateway to the Goulburn Valley, Nagambie is 28km (17 miles) north of Seymour. The township was founded in the mid-19th century and has a number of important historical buildings, seven of which are classified by the National Trust. The eastern shore of Lake Nagambie abuts the main street, with grassy picnic areas on its banks. Buckley Park, at the southern entrance of the town has a shady picnic area, boat launching ramp, and swimming area.

Lake Nagambie was created by the construction of the Goulburn Weir, which was built with manual labour in 1890. The River and Lake combine to offer over 40km (25 miles) of waterways for boating, and there are many picnic areas. The Nagambie Lakes Visitor Information Centre is at 145 High Street, ©(03) 5794 2647 or ©1800 444 647, and they have information on the many wineries in the area.

Bendigo

Population 40,340
Bendigo is almost in the centre of Victoria, at the junction of the Calder, McIvor, Northern and Loddon Valley Highways. It is 151km (94 miles) from Melbourne, 661km (411 miles) from Adelaide, 892km (554 miles) from Sydney and 653km (406 miles) from Canberra.

Climate

Average temperatures: January max 29C (84F) - min 14C (57F); July max 12C (54F) - min 3C (37F). Average annual rainfall: 550mm (22 in).

Characteristics

Bendigo was once one of the richest gold mining towns in Australia. It is proud of its mining history and has preserved relics of the period for present and future generations. The most tangible of these is a complete mine in working condition, in the town - the Central Deborah Mine.

How to Get There

By Bus
Greyhound Pioneer stop at Bendigo on their Melbourne/Mildura routes. A mini-bus service operates between Ballarat and Bendigo.

By Rail
A regular daily service operates between Melbourne and Bendigo, and the journey takes two hours. Bendigo is also linked by rail to Echuca, Cohuna, Swan Hill and Charlton.

By Road

From Melbourne by the Calder Highway is a two hour trip. From Albury/Wodonga, take the Hume Highway, then the Midland Highway for the 279km (173 miles) trip to Bendigo.

Tourist Information

The Bendigo Visitor Information & Interpretive Centre is located in the Historic Post Office, 51-67 Pall Mall, ✆(03) 5444 4445 or ✆1800 813 153. It is ◷open seven days a week 9am-5pm. Email them at ✉tourism@bendigo.vic.gov.au or visit the website ⊕www.bendigo tourism.com Another website, for the wider region, is ⊕www. goldfields.org.au, but it is less detailed.

Accommodation

There are 24 motels, 7 hotels, 10 caravan parks and a youth hostel. Here is a selection, with prices for a double room per night, which should be used as a guide only. ✆The telephone area code is 03.

All Seasons International Motor Inn, 171 McIvor Highway, ✆5443 8166. 49 units, licensed restaurant (closed Sunday), swimming pool, spa - ✪$125-180.

Bendigo Colonial Motor Inn, 483 High Street, ✆5447 0122. 30 units, licensed restaurant (closed Sunday), indoor swimming pool, spa, sauna - ✪$120-180.

Central Deborah Motor Inn, 177 High St (Calder Hwy), ✆5443 7488. 26 units, licensed restaurant (closed Sunday), spa - ✪$95-115.

Lakeview Motor Inn, 286 Napier Street, ✆5442 3099. 33 units, licensed restaurant (closed Sunday), swimming pool, spa, bbq - ✪$95-110.

Bendigo Motor Inn, 232 High Street, Kangaroo Flat, ✆5447 8555. 32 units, licensed restaurant (closed Sunday), swimming pool, spa, sauna, playground, bbq - ✪$75-90.

Shamrock Hotel Bendigo, cnr Pall Mall & Williamson Street, ✆5443 0333. 30 rooms, licensed restaurant - ✪$70-145.

The Elm Motel, 454 High St, ✆5447 7522. 15 rooms (private facilities) - ✪$55-70.

Calder Motel, 296 High Street (Calder Hwy), Kangaroo Flat, ✆5447 7411. 12 units, swimming pool, bbq - ✪$50-65.

Caravan Parks

Ascot Lodge, 15 Heinz Street, White Hills, ✆5448 4421. (No pets) - powered sites ✪$20-22 for two, cabins (en-suite) $60-90 for two, cabins (standard) $45-55 for two.

Robinley Caravan Park, Calder

Hwy, Maiden Gully, ✆5449 6265. (No pets) - powered sites ✪$15-20 for two, on-site vans $35-40 for two.

Central City Caravan Park, 362 High Street (Calder Hwy), Golden Square, ✆5443 6937. (Dogs allowed on leash) - powered sites ✪$17 for two, on-site vans $35 for two.

Eating Out

There's a good range of restaurants and cafes in Bendigo, offering various types of cuisine. Pub lunches are widely available and usually represent good value. They range from the humble ploughman's lunch to hearty steak and vegies. Good restaurants include:

Bazzani, Howard Place, ✆5441 3777 - licensed - ☼open 7 days.

Whirrakee Restaurant, 17 View Point, ✆5441 5557 - overlooks Alexandra Fountain - licensed - modern Australian cuisine.

Jo Joes, 4 High Street, ✆5441 4471 - international cuisine - changing menu - ☼open 7 days for lunch and dinner.

The Boardwalk Restaurant & Cafe, Nolan Street, ✆5443 9833 - lakeside dining, ☼open for breakfast lunch and dinner 7am-7pm daily - licensed.

Cafe Tram, 76 Violet Street, ✆5443 8255 - licensed - bookings essential - ☼open for dinner Fri & Sat, lunch on Sun.

Malayan Orchid Restaurant, 157 View Street, ✆5442 4411 - Thai, Cantonese and Malaysian curries - ☼open Mon-Fri 12-2pm, dinner seven days.

Fortunes Restaurant, 171 McIvor Road, ✆5443 8166 - open 7 days - a la carte - lunch and dinner - licensed.

There is also a *Pizza Hut* on the corner of High & Violet Streets, ✆5443 2122, and *McDonald's* is at 63 High Street.

Points of Interest

The heart of Bendigo is well worth exploring on foot, with much to see and admire in the busy shopping area and nearby parks. The Vintage Talking Trams will take you to many other places of interest. A Bendigo Heritage Walk leaflet is available from the Information Centre.

Bendigo has been described as, architecturally, the most interesting and integrated provincial city in Australia. Solidly built with the wealth that gold gave it, the city has some of the best preserved Victorian-era buildings and streetscapes to be found anywhere.

Pall Mall is Bendigo's main boulevard, and has some of the city's grandest Victorian buildings. Take note of: the Italianate post office

Land in south east Australia used mainly for grazing cattle and running sheep

A wave caught in the afternoon light on the East Coas

(1887) and law courts (1896); the Shamrock Hotel (1897); Alexandra Fountain (1881); the Beehive Store (1872); National Bank (1887) and Grand United HBS building (1886). Other buildings nearby include: the Bendigo Town Hall (1885); Bendigo Gaol (1864); Old Police Barracks (1859); St Paul's Cathedral (1868); Goldmines Hotel (1857); Specimen Cottage (1856).

View Street begins at the Alexandra Fountain, and also has some impressive 19th century buildings: Atkinson Building (1877); Bendigo Trades Hall (1885); Bendigo Art Gallery (1890); Capital Theatre (1874); Dudley House (1858); National Australia Bank (1863); Old Fire Station (1899); Rifle Brigade Hotel (1887); Sandhurst Trustees (1891).

Alexandra Fountain is situated at the head of Bendigo's Pall Mall, Charing Cross. The fountain was a gift from George Lansell 'the quartz king'. Designed by W.C. Vahland and erected in 1881, it is made from 20 tonnes of Harcourt granite and features seahorses and nymphs.

Chinse Joss House, Finn Street, Emu Point, ©5442 1685. The original Chinese temple was built in the 1860s of handmade bricks and timber, and painted red, the traditional Chinese colour for strength. To get there, follow the tram tracks towards Echuca, then turn at Lake Weeroona. The Joss House is operated by the National Trust, and is open daily 10am-5pm. Admission is adults ✪$3, children $1.

Golden Dragon Museum and Chinese Gardens, 5 - 13 Bridge Street, ✆5441 5044. Trace the history of Chinese influence in Bendigo, going right back to the gold rush days, in this impressive setting. Entry is ✪$7 adult, $4 child, and the complex is ☉open daily 9.30am-5pm.

Central Deborah Gold Mine, 76 Violet Street, ✆5443 8322. The last deep-reef goldmine in Bendigo - sunk in 1909, closed in 1954 - has been restored and is open for inspection. It is 411m (135 ft) deep with 17 levels. The tourist level at 61m (200 ft) includes a 350m (383 yds) circuit which illustrates the various geological features of the Bendigo region, and the machinery used in the gold retrieval process. Above ground there are many exhibits to be inspected. The mine is ☉open daily 9.30am-5pm, the tour takes about 1.5-2 hours, and there is an admission charge.

Vintage Talking Trams, 1 Tramways Avenue, ✆5442 2821. The Bendigo Trust has a collection of 34 vintage trams, and they are one of Bendigo's most popular tourist attractions. They run through the city centre, via Pall Mall, and along the 8km route between Central Deborah Mine and North Bendigo. A recorded commentary highlights more than 50 features along the way, and a stop at the Tram Museum in Tramways Avenue, ✆5442 2821, is included in the tour. The trams ☉depart from Central Deborah Mine Mon-Fri 9.30am, 1 and 2pm, hourly on weekends and school and public holidays from 9.30am-4.30pm. The tour takes approximately one hour.

Hargreaves Mall is a retail shopping area in the city centre, and has a wide selection of specialty shops and boutiques.

Lake Weeroona, cnr Midland Highway & Nolan Street, is a delightful ornamental lake close to the city centre. Surrounded by trees and gardens, there are boat hire, picnic and barbecue facilities.

Discovery & Science Technology Centre, 7 Railway Place, ✆5444 4400, has hands-on exhibits and a vertical slide. Admission is ✪$7.50 adult, $4.50 child and it is ☉open daily 10am-5pm.

Within a few minutes drive from the city centre there are many interesting places to visit -

Bendigo Pottery, Midland Highway, Epsom, ✆5448 4404, ☉open daily 9am-5pm, with guided tours at 10.30am and 2.30pm. Admission is free.

Bendigo Market Place, 116 - 120 Mitchell Street, Bendigo, ✆5441 6906, ☉open daily.

Kennington Reservoir, Reservoir

Road, Bendigo - swimming, boating, windsurfing and canoeing. Barbecue and picnic grounds.

Espsom Market, off Midland Highway at Epsom past the Bendigo Pottery, ℃5448 8411, ⏰open every Sunday 8.30am-3pm. Country Victoria's largest undercover market.

Eaglehawk, an historic town 8km north-west of Bendigo, and the site of a gold rush in 1852.

One Tree Hill Lookout, 8km south of Bendigo - from the Fountain follow Mitchell Street, then Carpenter Street, into Spring Gully Road. Continue south and the turn-off is just before Tannery Lane.

Wineries in Bendigo include: *Balgownie Vineyards*, Hermitage Road, Maiden Gully, (8km west), ℃5449 6222, closed Sunday; *Chateau Leamon*, Calder Highway, Big Hill, 10km south of Bendigo, ℃5447 7995, closed Tuesday; *Chateau Dore Vineyard*, 8km south-east of Bendigo at Mandurang Valley, ℃5439 5278, closed Monday.

For information on other wineries in the surrounding districts, contact the Visitor Information Centre.

Festivals

The Easter Fair has been staged for more than a century. The ten day festival commences with a street carnival on Easter Saturday, a 'waking of the dragon' ceremony takes place on Easter Sunday when a small lion wakes 'Sun Loong' with fireworks. Sun Loong is 100m long and is the largest known ceremonial Chinese dragon in the world. It is a colourful feature of the major procession on Easter Monday.

Facilites

Lawn bowls, ten-pin bowling, ice skating, roller skating, golf, tennis, swimming, croquet, indoor cricket, squash, horse racing and trotting and greyhound racing.

Outlying Attractions

Castlemaine
Nestling in a dip of the Great Dividing Range 38km (24 miles) south of Bendigo, Castlemaine is another gold mining town.

Attractions in and around town include nineteenth-century Buda Historic Home & Garden in Hunter Street; Skydancers Butterfly Sanctuary on the Midland Highway, Harcourt; Kyirong Emu Farm on Strathlea Road, Strathlea; and Maldon Porcupine Township, a recreation of life in early Victoria, cnr Bendigo and Allan Roads, Maldon, ℃5475 1000.

The Castlemaine Visitor Information & Interpretive Centre is in Market Building, Mostyn Street, ℃5470 5566 or ℃1800 171 888.

Echuca-Moama

Population 9,000 and 2,500 respectively

Echuca-Moama is located near the junction of the Murray, Campaspe and Goulburn Rivers, 205km (127 miles) from Melbourne.

Climate

Average daily temperatures: January max 32C (90F) - min 17C (63F); July max 15C (59F) - min 4C (39F). Average annual rainfall: 451mm (18 ins).

Characteristics

More than 130 years ago two ex-convicts, Henry Hopwood and James Maiden established the twin towns of Echuca-Moama on opposite sides of the Murray River. For about 40 years, from 1860 to 1900, Echuca was a busy port with hundreds of paddlesteamers and barges carrying supplies to stations along the Murray, Darling and Murrumbidgee Rivers. Much of the romance of this era was captured in the television mini-series All The Rivers Run.

The name Echuca is Aboriginal for 'meeting of the water'.

How to Get There

By Bus

V/Line have a service from Melbourne on Tues, Wed, Thurs and Sat.

Greyhound Pioneer stop at Echuca on their Sydney/Adelaide run.

By Road

Echuca is near the junctions of the

Murray Valley, Northern and Cobb Highways.

Tourist Information

Echuca-Moama District Tourism is at 2 Heygarth Street, Echuca, ✆(03) 5480 7555 or 1800 804 446. They can be emailed at ✎ emt@origin .net.au and the website is ☞www. echucamoama.com

Accommodation

Echuca-Moama has motels, hotel/ motels, a guest house, caravan parks, and self-contained unit accommodation. Here is a selection with prices for a double room per night, which should be used as a guide only. ✆The telephone area code is 03.

Philadelphia Motel Inn, 340 Ogilvie Avenue (Murray Valley Hwy), ✆5482 5700. 24 units, licensed restaurant (closed Sunday), swimming pool, bbq - ✪$88-120.

Riverboat Lodge Motor Inn, 476 High Street, ✆5482 5777. 19 units, swimming pool, spa - $90-115.

All Rivers Motor Inn, 115 Northern Highway, ✆5482 5677. 31 units, licensed restaurant (closed Sunday), swimming pool, bbq - ✪$90-140.

Pevensey Motor Lodge, 365 High Street, ✆5482 5166. 20 units, swimming pool, bbq - ✪$85-120.

Old Coach Motor Inn, 288 Ogilvie Avenue, ✆5482 3155. 19 units, swimming pool, spa, bbq - ✪$65-115.

Big River Motel, 317 High Street, ✆5482 2522. 15 units, bbq - ✪$60-85.

Fountain Motel, 77 Northern Highway, ✆5482 3200. 13 units, swimming pool, bbq - ✪$55-105.

Highstreet Motel, 439 High Street, ✆5482 1013. 11 units - ✪$60-70.

Pastoral Inn Hotel Motel, 100 Sturt Street, ✆5482 1812. 15 units, licensed restaurant - ✪$55-65.

Caravan Parks

Echuca Caravan Park, Crofton Street (Victoria Park), ✆5482 2157. (No pets allowed) - powered sites ✪$15-20 for two, on-site vans $35-45 for two.

Rich River Caravan Park, Crescent Street, ✆5482 3658. (No pets allowed) - powered sites ✪$15-25 for two, cabins $52-80 for two.

Yarraby Caravan Park, River Avenue, ✆5482 1533. (No dogs allowed) - powered sites ✪$15-20 for two, cabins (en-suite) $53-125 for two, cabins (standard) $40-53.

Riverlander Caravan Park, 48 Pianta Road, ✆5482 2558. (No pets allowed) - powered sites ✪$17 for two, cabins $47-90 for two.

For something different you could hire a houseboat from Magic Murray Houseboats, ✆5480 6099, or Rich River Houseboats, ©5480 2444.

Eating Out

You can enjoy surprisingly fine dining in Echuca-Moama. The Tourism Centre has information on all the dining establishments in Echuca-Moama, and here we have a few names and addresses:

Oscar W's Wharfside, Red Gum Grill & Deck Bar, 101 Murray Esplanade, Echuca, ©5482 5133 - popular and highly recommended restaurant, described by critics as Echuca's best.

Wistaria Tea Rooms, 51 Murray Esplanade, Echuca ©5482 4210 - licensed - lunch, morning and afternoon teas, children welcome.

Top of the Town, High Street, Echuca, ©5482 4600 - excellent quality fish and chips available from this take-away shop - ☺open seven days.

Fiori, 554 High Street, Echuca, ©5482 6688 - licensed - Italian.

Cock 'n'Bull Restaurant, 17 Warren Street, Echuca, ©5480 6988 - modern Australian - licensed - ☺open 5.30pm Tue-Sat.

Riverview Estate Restuarant, 2 Merool Lane, Moama, ©5480 0126 - riverside dining.

Radcliffe's, Radcliffe Street, Echuca, ©5480 6720 - Mediterranean cuisine, licensed.

Giorgio's on the Port, 527 High Street Echuca, ©5482 6117 - open every night for dinner - award-winning - authentic Italian food.

MV Mary Ann, ©5480 2200 - licensed luxury cruising restaurant - lunch and dinner cruises.

Points of Interest

The **Port of Echuca**, ©5482 4248, was once Australia's largest inland port, and the wharf, river boats, barges and century-old buildings have been restored. The Port is open daily and tickets for the Port Tours cost $10 adult and $6 child. A full ticket ($20 adult, $11 child), allows you to board the *Pevensey* (better known as the *Philadelphia* from *All The Rivers Run*) or the *Alexander Arbuthnot* which carries passengers during holiday periods and the last Sunday each month. *The Adelaide*, an historic logging boat, gives demonstration runs monthly, towing the D26 barge. Other features include a 10 minute film telling the Port story, an escape tunnel from the former cellar bar in the Star Hotel, the Paddlesteamer Gallery and the upstairs gallery in the Bridge Hotel.

The Historical Society Museum, opposite the Hopwood Gardens, has old River Charts, photographs, etc, and is ☺open weekends, Mon, Wed, public and school holidays 1-4pm, or by appointment, ℂ5480 1325.

Echuca also has the **World in Wax Museum**, Australia's largest collection of wax figures by international artists, situated in the High School. ☺Open daily 9am-5pm, ℂ5482 3630.

There are one hour **cruises** on the *PS Canberra*, ℂ5482 2711, and *PS Pride of the Murray*, ℂ5482 5244. *MV Mary Ann* is a cruising restaurant that offers two hour luncheon and 3-4 hour dinner cruises. Also available is a river cruise for 2 day/nights aboard the *PS Emmylou*, ℂ5482 4248.

Sharps Magic Movie House and Penny Arcade, opposite the Wharf, Bond Store, Port of Echuca, ℂ5482 2361, have 30 penny arcade machines to play, the largest collection in Australia. You can also watch the old time movie shows dating from 1890. ☺Open daily 9am-5pm.

The **Murray River Aquarium**, 640 High Street, ℂ5480 7388, has fish and reptile displays.

Njernda, the Aboriginal Cultural Centre, is in the Old Court House in Law Place, ℂ5482 3904, and has displays of local and traditional artifacts and videotapes/language tapes of the local area. For sale are traditional crafts by people descended from the Yorta Yorta and Wemba Wemba tribes. The Centre is ☺open daily, 10am-4.30pm.

Tisdall Winery is ☺open daily for tastings and cellar sales, Mon-Sat 10am-5pm, Sun 11am-5pm, ℂ5480 1349. It is in Murray Esplanade, one block down from the Port of Echuca.

Visitors can enjoy a 'flutter on the pokies' (play the slot machines) at one of the 4 licensed clubs in Moama, which also have dining facilities.

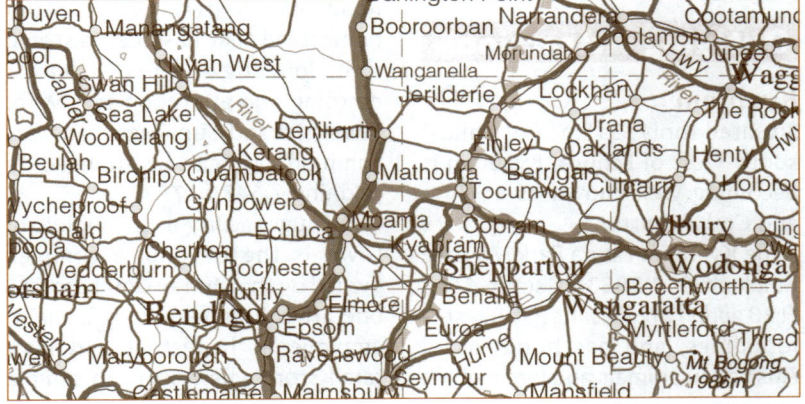

Festivals

The Rotary Steam, Horse and Vintage Rally is held over the Saturday and Sunday of the Queen's Birthday weekend in June. It features working exhibits of Clydesdale horses, vintage and veteran vehicles and steam traction engines, allowing everyone to experience the sights and sounds of a by-gone era.

The Port of Echuca Heritage Steam Festival is staged over a weekend in late October. It is involves a cavalcade of riverboats and a fireworks display.

Facilities

Boating, bowls, bush walking, croquet, fishing, golf, horse racing, horse riding, sailing, swimming, trotting, water skiing, bingo, and bicycle and canoe hire are available.

Outlying Attractions

Kyabram

Situated only 31km (19 miles) south-west of Echuca, Kyabram is becoming well known as an Arts and Crafts centre.

The Kyabram Fauna Park, 75 Lake Road, ✆5852 2883, is set in 55ha (128 acres) of pleasant natural surroundings, and has hundreds of Australian animals and birds which roam freely around the park. It also has a miniature railway, playground and kiosk, and is ⏰open daily 9.30am-5.30pm.

The Barmah Forest

The Forest is a 20 minute drive from Moama, and the Visitor Information Centre in Echuca has leaflets giving directions.

The Dharyna Centre, Sandridge Road, Barmah, ✆5869 3302, is a visitor centre which also provides live-in educational opportunities for groups in the Barmah Forest, the largest Redgum Forest in the Southern Hemisphere.

Rochester

The town of Rochester is 24km (15 miles) south of Echuca on the Northern Highway. It is the Hub of the North, and has palms, peppercorns, quaint shops and sleepy streets. Random House, situated in on the Campaspe River in Bridge Road, is a stately 19th century homestead that has been restored to its former glory. It is ⏰open for morning and afternoon tea, Wed, Thurs, Fri and Sun. Meals and accommodation can be arranged by phoning ✆5484 1792.

The huge facility in the middle of town is the Devondale complex owned by the Murray Goulburn Co-operative Company. It is a major employer in the district, and has a retail store where you can sample and buy some of their products.

Ballarat

Population 80,000

Ballarat is the main centre of the Victorian Central Highlands, which have a decidedly Scottish flavour to them. Ballarat was made famous through the Eureka Stockade, the bloody miners' rebellion in 1854.

The city is 113km (70 miles) from Melbourne, 985km (612 miles) from Sydney, 637km (396 miles) from Adelaide, and 747km (464 miles) from Canberra.

Characteristics

Over the years Ballarat has been known as 'The Goldfields', the 'Garden City', the 'City of Statues' and the 'Historical City', and it is all these and more.

The city is one of the best preserved in Australia, and also one of the most fascinating. Steeped in history, it is a monument to the pioneering adventurers who left their distant homelands in search of prosperity in the gold rush of the 1850s.

Incidentally, is it Ballarat or Ballaarat? The original spelling came from the aboriginal 'Balla-arat', meaning 'elbow place'. Over the years the second 'a' was dropped for convenience. In early 1990 the Ballaarat Council officially re-adopted the original spelling and it is now officially the City of Ballaarat, although for commercial or other purposes either spelling is acceptable.

How to Get There

By Bus
Greyhound Pioneer stop at Ballarat on their Melbourne/Adelaide/Perth and Melbourne/Adelaide/Alice Springs routes.

V/Line buses run from Melbourne

to Ballarat, and the trip takes about two hours.

By Rail
There is a regular service Melbourne-Ballarat.

By Road
From Melbourne, via the four lane Western Freeway.

Tourist Information

Ballarat Tourist Information Centre is at 39 Sturt Street (cnr Albert Street), ✆(03) 5320 5741 or ✆1800 446 633. For further information email them at ✎tourism@ballarat.vic.gov.au or see the website ☞www.ballarat.com

Accommodation

Victoria's largest inland provincial city has a wide range of accommodation, and here we have a selection, with prices for a double room per night, which should be used as a guide only. ✆The telephone area code is 03.

Mercure Inn Ballarat, 1845 Sturt St, ✆5334 1600. 76 units, licensed restaurant, swimming pool - ✪$85-130.

Sundowner Chain Motor Inns, 312 Main Road, ✆5331 7533. 25 units, licensed restaurant (closed Sun), swimming pool, spa - ✪$95-150.

Park View Motor Inn, 1611 Sturt Street, ✆5334 1001. 46 units, licensed restaurant, swimming pool - ✪$75-100.

Ballarat Mid City Motor Inn, 19 Doveton Street North, ✆5331 1222. 73 units, licensed restaurant (closed Sun), swimming pool, sauna - ✪$100-125.

Begonia City Motor Inn, 244 Albert Street, Sebastopol, ✆5335 5577. 15 units, swimming pool, bbq - ✪$85-110.

Ambassador Motel, 1759 Sturt Street, Alfredton, ✆5334 1505. 22 units, licensed restaurant (closed Sun), swimming pool, spa, sauna, bbq - ✪$75-115.

City Oval Hotel/Motel, cnr Pleasant & Mair Streets, ✆5332 1155. 8 units, licensed restaurant - ✪$64.

Caravan Parks

Ballarat and A Welcome Stranger Caravan Park, Cnr Water St & Scott Parade, ✆5332 6818. (No pets allowed) - powered sites ✪$20 for two, cabins (en-suite) $62-94 for two, cabins (standard) $50-60 for two.

A Ballarat Windmill Caravan Park, Avenue of Honour, Western Highway, Alfredton, ✆5334 1686. (No dogs allowed) - powered sites ✪$25-30 for two, on-site vans $44 for two, cabins $60-120 for two.

Shady Acres Caravan Park, Melbourne Road (Western Hwy),

✆5334 7233. (No dogs allowed) - powered sites ✪$18 for two, park cabins (en-suite) $60-72 for two, park cabins (standard) $25-35 for two.

Ballarat Goldfields Holiday Park, 108 Clayton Street, ✆5332 7888. (No pets allowed) - powered sites ✪$21 for two, park cabins (en-suite) $65-70 for two.

Eating Out

As with any city of its size, Ballarat has a wide choice of restaurants, as well as those in the motels and hotels. Here are some names and addresses.

The Ansonia, 32 Lydiard Street, South Ballarat, ✆5332 4678 - international cuisine - licensed - breakfast, lunch & dinner available.
Golden Crown Chinese Restaurant, cnr Main Road & Barkly Street, ✆5332 2169 - ☉open for lunch & dinner seven days - licensed & BYO - takeaway available.
Europa Cafe, 411 Sturt Street, ✆5331 2486 - dishes in a variety of flavours - dinner Thu-Sat, breakfast & lunch daily - licensed.
Lillian's Restaurant, at the Sundowner Motor Inn, 312 Main Road, ✆5331 7533 - modern Australian - good value - licensed.
The Bonshaw, cnr Tait Street &

Ross Creek Road, ✆5335 8346 - licensed, seafood/steak in candlelit atmosphere - mains under $20 - ☼open Tues-Sat.

Peter Lalor Hotel, 331 Mair Street, ✆5331 1702 - licensed, full a la carte menu and smorgasbord - ☼open daily for lunch noon-2pm and dinner 6-8pm.

Boatshed Restaurant, 27 Wendouree Parade, ✆5333 5533 - open seven days - situated beside Lake Wendouree.

Robin Hood Family Bistro, 33 Peel Street, ✆5331 3348 - licensed, a la carte - ☼open seven days with piano bar on Thurs, Fri and Sat nights.

Mexican Terrace Restaurant, 71 Victoria Street, ✆5333 1435 - mexican, steak, vegetarian & children's menus - ☼open Tue-Sun from 6pm - licensed.

Pancake Kitchen, Grenville Street, ✆5331 6555 - BYO, family atmosphere.

There are also two branches of **McDonald's** in Ballarat.

Points of Interest

Gold was first discovered in the Ballarat area in 1851 by James Esmond, and the rush for gold was on. However, by the end of 1851, much of the surface gold had been depleted, and many diggers moved to the new fields at Bendigo and Castlemaine. Then, early in 1852,

new arrivals from England (mainly Cornwall and Wales) heard that the gold had run out but decided to see for themselves. They dug to the Ordovician bedrock, and uncovered a veritable treasure trove. The rush was on again in earnest, with people coming from all over the world.

The government of the day had imposed a licence fee for the right to dig, and were more than happy with the revenue they received. However they didn't administer the system well, and there was the usual claim-jumping and skirmishes.

Tempers became short amongst the original miners, and the fields became a virtual tinder box. The spark that set it all afire came when a digger, James Scobie, was murdered, and a hotel owner named Bentley was charged with the crime, but found not guilty, contrary to popular belief. On the spot where Scobie had been murdered, about 5,000 diggers met, formed a committee, and held a meeting, which began in an orderly fashion, but soon degenerated, and the hotel was burnt to the ground. Several people were arrested, and although they were only given short terms of imprisonment, the incensed diggers formed the Ballarat Reform League with Peter Lalor as their leader.

The Governor listened to the

grievances of the men, told them a franchise was being set up, and they returned to the diggings in a more reasonable state of mind - but not for long. An altercation between troopers and diggers caused many miners to burn their licenses in opposition to authority, thereby laying themselves open to conflict. Lalor and his men built a crude stockade of wagons, spikes, logs and slabs, and about 120 men were in this stockade, flying their own flag, on the night of December 2, 1854. The troopers attacked at dawn on the 3rd, and although the battle lasted barely twenty-five minutes, about 22 diggers and 6 soldiers were killed, and 114 prisoners were taken. The battle was lost, but the miners' rights improved as a consequence.

The **Eureka Stockade Centre**, cnr Rodier & Eureka Streets, ✆5333 1854, opened in March 1998 and cost $4 million to build. It involves a modern, interactive re-retelling of the story of the miner's brief but bloody uprising in 1854 Ballarat. The exhibition is well-done, and should be your first port of call to understand the city's past. It is ☉open daily 9am-5pm, and entry is ✪$8 adult, $4 child.

Opposite the exhibition is the **Eureka Memorial and Park**, near where the events actually occurred.

The **Ballarat Fine Art Gallery**, 40 Lydiard Street North, has the remains of the original Eureka Flag, depicting the Southern Cross, displayed in its own gallery alongside a changing display of related work. The flag was given to James Oddie, the gallery's founder and president, in 1895, by the widow of John King, a trooper who had taken part in the attack on the Stockade. The gallery was the first provincial art gallery to be established in Australia. The foundation stone for the present building was laid in 1887. It is ☉open daily 10.30am-5pm. Admission is ✪$4 adult, children free.

Historic Montrose Cottage, 111 Eureka Street, was built in 1856 and is the oldest remaining bluestone miner's cottage in Ballarat. Classified by the National Trust of Australia (Vic), the Cottage is also on the Australian Heritage List. It is ☉open daily 9am-5pm, as is the adjacent **Eureka Museum**, which gives an insight into life on the goldfields, with an array of personal and household items dating from the 1850s. Outside is a cottage garden featuring old roses, herbs and other aromatic plants, and next door is Priscilla's Cottage, offering morning and afternoon teas and snacks. This is Ballarat's oldest attraction and a multi-award winner.

Ballarat Wildlife Park, cnr Fussel and York Streets, ✆5333 5933, is set in 15ha (37 acres) of parkland,

and attractions include a large collection of Australian animals, barbecue and picnic areas, children's adventure playground, tropical reptile house, large salt water crocodiles, kiosk and wildlife souvenir shop, a cafe and takeaway food shop. The Park is ⊙open every day from 9am-5.30pm. Admission is ❸$13.50 adult, $7.50 child, $38 family.

Sovereign Hill, in Bradshaw Street, ©5331 1944, offers a trip back in time to the period of Ballarat's gold rush days. It is a re-created gold mining town complete with Main Street, busy with people in olden day dress and horse-drawn vehicles; a blacksmith; coach-builder; tinsmith; potter; furniture maker; Clarke Brothers' Grocery; the Apothecaries Hall; Spencer's Sweetshop; and the Hope Bakery. You can pan for gold, or take a guided tour of the underground mine, play bowls at the Empire Bowling Saloon, or be photographed in period costume. There is something for everyone at Sovereign Hill, and plenty of places to eat or be entertained. The complex is ⊙open daily 10am-5pm. Entry is ❸$25 adult, $12 child and $65 for families.

Blood on the Southern Cross is described as a "Night-time Sound and Light Spectacular". It is an unique and engaging re-creation of the Eureka Stockade, a turning point in Australia's history, which takes place on Soveriegn Hill - ©5333 5777 for booking and information.

The **Gold Museum** is opposite Sovereign Hill in Bradshaw Street, and is run by the Ballarat Historical Society. The museum has a collection of rare gold coins, including a ducat, a denarius and a doubloon, and an exhibition of Chinese bronze and porcelain, watercolours, jewellery and clothing. There is also an historical pavilion with Aboriginal artefacts, relics of the wool industry, old signs and store fronts, bric-a-brac, and memorabilia of both Ballarat and Victoria. The Museum is ⊙open 9.30am-5.20pm daily.

The **Central Business District** of Ballarat is a treasury of architectural elegance - Lydiard Street has the 1872 Alexandria Tearooms, Old Colonists Hall (1887-89), former Mining Exchange (1888), Reid's Coffee Palace (1886 - now a private hotel), and the George Hotel, originally built in 1853 but the present building dates from 1903.

Sturt Street has the Post Office (1863-1885), the Town Hall (1870), and a pagoda-like pavilion that was erected as a memorial to the bandsmen who played as the Titanic went down.

The Tourist Information Centre has information on other buildings of architectural merit.

At the western end of Sturt Street (Western Highway) is an unusual war memorial - the **Arch of Victory** and the **Avenue of Honour**. The Arch is across the highway, near the golf club, and is floodlit by night. Immediately west an avenue of around 4000 trees reaches to Lakes Burrembeet and Learmonth, each one bearing a name honouring one of the fallen.

The **Botanical Gardens** in Gillies Street are noted for the many specimens of mature trees ranging in age to over 120 years. About 46 of them have been registered on the National Trust register of Significant Trees. There is an informative free brochure on the gardens, that is available at most tourism outlets and accommodation, which lists the various attractions such as: Adventure Playground, the Avenue of Prime Ministers; the Begonia display (best in March); Lake Wendouree; and the Tram Museum.

Lake Wendouree was originally called Yuille's Swamp, named after Archibald Yuille, who in turn had named his run Ballaarat after the local Aborigines. The Lake is the focus of recreation in Ballarat, with its beautiful gardens, boat sheds, shady trees and picnic spots. It was used in 1956 for the rowing events of the Olympic Games. There are ducks, swans and other water birds, and, as is the way these days,

plenty of joggers. The swans are exceptionally friendly at most times, but can become quite feisty when they have cygnets with them, so take care.

The **Ballarat Tramway Museum** is operated by a volunteer group over an original section of track. The 1.3km of track began in 1887 as a horse-tramway, then the route was electrified in 1905 and officially closed in 1970-71. Rolling stock at the depot/museum includes 10 tramcars and horse tram No 1, and there is a photographic display. The trams run ⊙every weekend, public holidays and school holidays from noon-5pm, ✆5334 1580.

The **Dinosaur World Fun Park & Fossil Museum**, Midland Highway, Creswick, ✆5345 2676, is set in 12ha (30 acres) of bushland. 18 life-size dinosaurs and Model Land are features inside the complex. Ouside there are 36 picnic tables (many under cover), 16 barbecues, a takeaway kiosk, and plenty to see and do ⊙every day 9.30am-5pm.

The **Tuki Fishing Complex**, "Stoney Rises", Smeaton, ✆5345 6233, is about 25 minutes from Ballarat, and you can hire all the necessary equipment and catch your trout for lunch. There are eight ponds and two lakes, all brimful with fish, and from the complex there are panoramic views over the Loddon Valley. ⊙Opening hours are daily 11am-6pm.

Kryal Castle is 8km (5 miles) east of Ballarat, off the Western Highway, and is ☺open daily 9.30am-5.30pm, ✆5334 7388. The castle occupies 2.4ha (6 acres) within a walled area, with 73 buildings, displays, museums, facilities and services. The castle opened in 1974, and is well worth visiting. There are gothic towers, turrets, parapets, battlements complete with moat, drawbridge, porticos, keep, tavern, craft shops, stables and dungeons. Live exhibitions include the 'Hanging of the Villain', 'Whipping of the Wench', and various changing shows. Whatever you do, don't miss the graveyard, and make sure you read the headstones. The Castle also has the *Golden Eagle Tavern*, where you can wine and dine like the knights of old. Entry is ✪$12.50 adult, $7.50 child.

Festivals

The Begonia Festival is held over 10 days in March, and is one of the best known in Victoria.

The Ballarat Agricultural Show is held on the Friday, Saturday and Sunday of the second weekend in November.

Facilities

Lawn bowls, croquet, fishing, gold panning, golf, greyhound racing, horse racing, rowing, sailing, squash, swimming, tennis and trotting.

Outlying Attractions

Clunes

Situated 40km (25 miles) north of Ballarat, Clunes was the first place where gold was discovered in Victoria. A small rush followed but no permanent development occurred until 1856. Commercial development began in 'Lower' Fraser Street in the 1860s, and by the 1870s, many of the fine civic buildings you see today were constructed. Mining ceased in the 1890s and a tree planting programme began, creating one of the prettiest small towns in Victoria.

The town has a museum, a motel, hotels, historic buildings, a supermarket, and a golf course. For more local information, contact the Clunes Museum on ✆(03) 5345 3592.

Daylesford

John Egan first discovered gold at a site known as Wombat Flat Diggings, in August 1851. The township of Daylesford was surveyed and laid-out in 1854. A settlement, including Chinese market gardens, remained at the diggings site until 1929, when the area was flooded to create Lake Daylesford.

You will find the Daylesford Regional Visitor Information Centre in Vincent Street, ✆(03) 5348 1339.

Hepburn Springs

John Hepburn was credited with discovering the area in 1837, and he said it was the loveliest spot he had seen in his travels. He established an extensive sheep squat on Smeaton Hill (now Kooroocheang). The springs were known to the Aborigines of the area, and discovered by early settlers, but the true worth of their presence was overshadowed by the mining boom. However, when the gold ran out, the quality of the waters was found to equal that of Europe's famous health resorts, and soon attracted growing numbers to drink and bathe in the springs.

The Hepburn Spa Resort, Mineral Springs Reserve, has hot mineral water, herbal, mud, bubble and sinusoidal electric baths, and these are becoming the tourist mecca they were at the turn of the century, ✆5348 2034.

Maryborough

Situated 88km (55 miles) from Daylesford, Maryborough has a population of 8,500. It was occupied by graziers until 1854 when there was a gold rush to nearby White Hills, 5km to the north. By 1856, Maryborough's main street was a thriving thoroughfare serving some 50,000 diggers. By 1918, the gold had petered out, and secondary industry took over, making it one of the most highly industrialised towns in Australia. A town tour will give an insight into the town, and its historical attractions. For more information, get in touch with the Central Goldfields Shire Office, 2 Neill Street, Maryborough, ✆(03) 5461 0610, ✉email mail@ cgoldshire.vic.gov.au or visit 👁www .centralgoldfields.com.au

Avoca

This is another former mining town in the foothills of the Pyrenees Range at the junction of the Sunraysia and Pyrenees Highways, on the banks of the Avoca River. Its quiet hills teem with black wallabies and grey kangaroos, and there is a growing colony of koalas. The Pyrenees Tourist Association is at 122 High Street, ✆(03) 5465 3767.

Wineries around Ballarat

Yellowglen Winery, Whites Road, Smythesdale, ✆5342 8617 - ⏰open Mon-Sat 10am-5pm, Sun noon-5pm.

Mount Avoca Vineyard, 45 minutes along the Sunraysia Highway from Ballarat, ✆5465 3282 - ⏰open Mon-Sat 10am-5pm, Sun from noon.

Redbank Winery, at the 200km post on Sunraysia Highway, ✆5467 7255 - ◷open daily 9am-5pm. The following wineries are open weekends and public holidays. For other times phone ✆5368 7209..

Chepstowe Vineyard, Fitzpatricks Lane, Carngham, ✆5344 9412.
Leura Glen Estate, 260 Green Gully Road, Glenlyon, ✆5348 7785
Whitehorse Wines, 4 Reid Park Road, Mt Clear, ✆5330 1719.

Ararat &
The Grampians

Population 10,100
Ararat is situated near the Hopkins River, 203km (126 miles) north-west of Melbourne, in the central highlands of Victoria. It is the gateway to the Grampians.

Characteristics

The Ararat district was founded and settled around 1839-40 and gold was discovered in the area in 1854. Evidence of the extensive mining in the surrounding district still exists for the interested to see. The Municipality was declared a Borough in 1858, became a Town in 1934 and was declared a City in 1950.

Ararat is an important service centre for a rich farming and wine growing area. It boasts some of the finest agricultural and wine growing land in Victoria, and produces the State's top fine Merino wool, and has the largest sheep production in Australia.

Many visitors to the region use Ararat as a base to explore the magnificent natural resources in the Mount Cole Forest Ranges and the popular Grampians National Park.

How to Get There

By Bus
Greyhound Pioneer call into Ararat on their Melbourne/Adelaide runs.

By Train
Ararat is connected by rail with Geelong, Portland, western, north western and central Victoria.

By Road
Ararat is on the Western Highway, 545km (339 miles) from Adelaide

and 203km (126 miles) from Melbourne.

Tourist Information

Ararat and Grampians Visitor Information Centre, 91 High Street, ✆(03) 5355 0281 or ✆1800 657 158. Email ✉ tourinfo@ararat.vic.gov.au or visit 👁www.ararat.asn.au
There is also the Ararat Tourist Information Centre in Barkly Street, ✆(03) 5352 2096.

Accommodation

Ararat has motels, hotels and caravan parks. Following is a selection, with prices for a double room per night, which should be used as a guide only. ✆The telephone area code is 03.

Ararat Colonial Lodge & Pyrenees Restaurant, 6 Ingor Street, ✆5352 4644. 19 units, unlicensed restaurant, swimming pool, bbq - ✪$90-105.

Statesman Motor Inn, Western Highway, ✆5352 4111. 19 units, licensed restaurant - ✪$85-100.

Ararat Central Motel, 249 Barkly Street, ✆5352 2255. 22 units, unlicensed restaurant, swimming pool - ✪$65.

Mount Ararat Motor Inn, 367 Barkly Street, ✆5352 2521. 9 units, bbq, playground - ✪$60.

Chalambar Motel, 132 Lambert Street, ✆5352 2430. 10 units, bbq, playground - ✪$45.

Caravan Parks

Acacia Caravan Park, 6 Acacia Avenue, ✆5352 2994. (Pets allowed by arrangement) - heated pool, powered sites ✪$16 for two, on-site vans $33-42 for two, cabins (en-suite) $55-90 for two, cabins (standard) $35-50 for two.

Pyrenees Caravan Park, 67 Pyrenees Highway, ✆5352 1309. (Pets allowed at manager's discretion) - powered sites ✪$16 for two, on-site vans $30-50 for two, cabins $55-80.

Eating Out

There is not a wide range of choices in Ararat, but the following provide good meals at reasonable prices, and will give you an idea of what is on offer.

Man Hing Chinese Restaurant, 190 Barkly Street, ✆5352 3311 - BYO - lunch Mon-Sun 12-2pm, Dinner Sun-Thurs 5-10pm, Fri-Sat 5-11pm.

Noble Garden Restaurant, 204 Barkly Street, ✆5352 2019.

Sicilian's Bar & Restaurant, 102 Barkly Street, ✆5352 2627.

Vines Cafe & Bar, 74 Barkly Street, ✆5352 1744.

Statesman Motor Inn, Western Highway, ✆5352 4111.

Ararat RSL Club, 76 High Street, ✆5352 2794.

Points of Interest

The town was named by the first settler, Horatio Spencer Wills, who set off in a covered wagon with 5,000 sheep from the Murrumbidgee area in NSW, to a grazing site near the Grampian Mountains. After 11 months of travel, in March 1840, Wills rested on a large bald mountain, noted that he was only one day's travel from his destination, and called the mountain 'Mount Ararat' for as he said, "Like the Ark, we rested here".

Ararat has many historical buildings classified by the National Trust, and the Tourist Information Centre has a brochure setting out a City Area Walk which takes in the splendid architecture of yesteryear. It commences at the **Art Gallery**, on the corner of High & Vincent Streets, ⏰open Mon-Fri 11am-4pm, Sat closed (except school holidays 12-4pm), Sun 12-4pm. You then visit the **Town Hall**, which incorporates the Arts Centre; the Shire Hall; the **Langi Morgala Museum** (⏰open Sat-Sun 2-4pm); the **YMCA**; the **Mural** by Artist Hugh Anderson in High Street; **Pyrenees House**; the **Old Gaol**; **Alexandra Gardens**; the **Old Post Office and Sub Treasury**; the **Court House**; the **Edith Cavell Memorial**; and a **Grape-vine** that has survived since 1856 when it was planted by G.W.H. Grano. The walk can take from 1/2 hour to 2 hours, depending on how much time you spend at each stop.

The Information Centre also has three **Driving Tours from Ararat**, which travel a bit further afield, and apart from the places visited on the walk, visit the following: One Tree Hill scenic lookout; McDonald Park approximately 4km from city centre; Copes Hill scenic view; Cathcart Ridge Winery ℰ5352 1997; Carrol's Cutting with views to the Grampians; Pinky Point where gold was first found; Norval Dam for fishing, swimming and yabbying; Montara Winery ℰ5352 3868; and Green Hill Lake.

Green Hill Lake, 4km from the city centre, is stocked with perch, trout and yellowbelly. There are gas barbecues, shade shelters, adult playground equipment and a boat ramp. The lake also has canoe channels and islands.

Alexandra Gardens have a Fernery and Glass House, which is used for growing orchids, and in fact, Ararat is known as the orchid centre of the west and has an annual orchid display in the town hall during October.

Ararat has eight district **wineries**, with most open for cellar sales and tastings. The Seppelts guided tour is a highlight of a visit to the area. Tours are Mon-Sat 10.30am, 1.30pm and 3pm and the cellar door is ⊙open 10am-5pm Mon-Sun, ℰ5361 2239.

Festivals

The Great Western Vintage Races are held on the Australia Day weekend in January.

Ararat Highland Sports, featuring the Ararat Gift (foot race) are held on the Labour Day Weekend in March.

Golden Gateway Festival is over ten days in October.

Facilities

Lawn bowls, croquet, horse racing, trotting, swimming, tennis and squash.

Outlying Attractions

Mount Cole Forest

The Forest straddles the Great Dividing Range about 20km (12 miles) east of Ararat. Mount Cole and Mount Lonarch Forests are excellent examples of forests resulting from multi-use management, and in area total about 12,150ha (30,010 acres). They produce a steady supply of high quality milling timbers to local sawmills, while providing wildlife habitat and recreational opportunities. The area also has another important value as its timbered slopes act as catchments for the streams that supply water to neighbouring towns. Road surfaces throughout the forest are good, but narrow, and allowances for slower speeds should be made.

Mount Cole Forest has become one of the most popular spots in Australia for Hang Gliding enthusiasts to practise. There are three sites used for take-off – Ben Nevis, Mt Buangor and Mt Langi Ghiran. While you might not be interested in jumping off a mountain yourself, it is exciting to watch others risking life and limb.

For those interested in nature, the things to look out for are: wildflowers, including Rare Gre-villea; kangaroos and wallabies; platypus (experts guarantee they are around in the streams, but don't get your hopes too high); echidnas, koalas, deer, tree ferns and waterfalls.

Grampians National Park

The Grampians became Victoria's largest National Park on July 1, 1984.

The start of the Park is about 25km (15 miles) from Ararat, west of the township of Moyston. There are several ways to enter the Park from Moyston, through Pomonal to Hall's Gap, or west from Moyston to Mafeking and Mt William. The Park consists of 167,000ha (412,490 acres) and has a rich variety of native flora, wildlife, and Aboriginal rock art sites. The eastern slopes of the Grampians present some of the most beautiful scenery in the area with an abundance of heath, wildflowers and the tall eucalypt forest with the red gum woodland in Victoria Valley a special feature.

The Park supports over 860 native plant species. Kangaroos, koalas, echidna, possums and gliders are common, and over 200 bird species have been recorded.

More information on the Grampians is available from Parks Australia, ☎131 963 or by dropping into the information centre on Dunkeld Road near Halls Gap, ☎5356 4381.

West of Moyston, about 20km (12 miles) is the Mafeking Reserve where the 'discovery of gold' Cairn is located depicting the site of the 1900 gold rush to the area. It is reported that over 7000 miners were in the area then, and today you can still see the sluiced gullies and disused shafts. Special care should be taken in the area, as the shafts can be dangerous.

The Mount William picnic area on the eastern slopes of the Grampians is a delightful spot, with the Kalymna Falls a short walking distance away.

The main wildflower season is in Spring (September-November), but Autumn is also a popular time to visit.

Great Western

Midway between Ararat and

Stawell is the little township of Great Western, which gives its name to fine wines, including the champagne-style Great Western Special Reserve, which matures in the cellars beneath the sloping hills of Seppelts vineyards. There are many wineries in the town, all offering cellar door sales and tastings, and information can be obtained from the Tourist Information Centre in Stawell.

Stawell

A former gold mining town 30km (19 miles) west of Ararat, Stawell is probably better known now for the Stawell Gift, the world's richest professional foot running race. It is held for 3 days over the Easter break, and is a handicap race over 120m (131 yds). Since 1986, the carnival has been open to professional and amateurs, and attracts top Australian and international competitors. In Lower Main Street is the Stawell Gift Hall Of Fame, with videos, photographs and equipment covering over a century of history, ◷open Wed-Sun 10am-4pm, or by appointment, ✆5358 1326.

The Stawell & Grampians Tourism Information Centre is at 54 Western Highway, ✆(03) 5358 2314, and is ◷open Mon-Fri 9am-5.30pm, Sat-Sun 9.30am-5pm. From the office you can get a brochue which shows visitors the attractions of Stawell.

The Walk starts in Stawell's 'World in Miniature' in London Road, ✆5358 1877. This Tourist Park features a unique presentation of world cultures, and Australian and local history displayed in dioramas and working models, both indoor and outdoors in landscaped gardens. You might also like to stroll through the Historic Precinct, and the Visitor Centre will guide you.

Halls Gap

Halls Gaps is the heart of the Grampians National Park in the picturesque Fyans Valley. The township offers a variety of accommodation, a comprehensive shopping centre and facilities including tennis courts, swimming pool, restaurants, horse riding, walks, scenic 4WD tours, golf course, fun park, nurseries, nearby wildlife park, winery and National Park visitor centre, ✆5356 4381.

The sandstone ranges of the Grampians National Park surround Halls Gap, providing views of rugged escarpments and a tranquil atmosphere. The ridges and valleys are filled with Australian fauna, wildflowers, treefern gullies, strange rock formations, Aboriginal rock art, crystal clear rock pools, and many waterfalls, such as the McKenzie Falls.

Mildura

Population 19,360
Mildura is situated on the Murray River at the junction of the Sturt, Silver City and Calder Highways. It lies 560km (348 miles) from Melbourne, 398km (247 miles) from Adelaide, 1068km (664 miles) from Sydney, and 780km (485 miles) from Canberra.

Climate

Mildura has a dry, mild winter climate and 400 hours more sunshine each year than Surfers Paradise in Queensland. The average summer temperature is 32C (90F) with most days around 29C (84F).

Characteristics

The north-west of Victoria is known as Sunraysia, and Mildura is the main town. It is a great place to relax as well as being the threshold of the great outback, which begins just beyond the far banks of the Murray. Mildura is called 'The Oasis in the Desert', with mile upon mile of lush, productive vineyards and orchards, in the midst of dry, harsh Mallee country.

How to Get There

By Air
Mildura has a budy regional airport, ©5022 2777 for information on flight services and schedules.
By Bus
V/Line and Greyhound Pioneer have daily services from capital cities.
By Rail
The Vinelander from Melbourne daily except Saturday (overnight 10 hours). V/Line services the region daily.
By Road
From Adelaide by the Stuart Highway.

From Sydney by the Mid-Western Highway.

From Melbourne by the Calder/Sunraysia Highway.

Tourist Information

The Mildura Visitor Information & Booking Centre is located at 180 - 190 Deakin Avenue, ✆(03) 5021 4424 or ✆1800 039 043 (bookings). Additionally, you can email them at ✉tourism@mildura.vic.gov.au or explore the website at ⌨www.milduratourism.com

Accommodation

Mildura has plenty of motels, hotels guest houses, serviced apartment buildings and caravan parks/camping grounds. Here is a selection, with prices for a double room per night, which should be used as a guide only. ✆The telephone area code is 03.

Chaffey International Motor Inn, 244 Deakin Avenue, ✆5023 5833. 32 units, licensed restaurant (closed Sunday), swimming pool, spa - ✪$100-175.

City Colonial Motor Inn, 24 Madden Avenue, ✆5021 1800. 14 units, bbq, swimming pool - ✪$75-105.

Sandors Motor Inn - Mildural, 179 Deakin Avenue, ✆5023 0047. 30 units, licensed restaurant, swimming pool - ✪$100-105.

City Gate Motel, 89 Seventh Street, ✆5022 1077. 22 units, bbq, swimming pool, spa - ✪$70-90.

Mildura Grand Hotel, Seventh Street opposite the railway station, ✆5023 0511. 108 rooms, licensed restaurant, bistro, swimming pool, spa, sauna - ✪$110-143.

Mildura Park Motel, 250 Eighth Street, ✆5023 0479. 28 units, bbq, swimming pool - ✪$50-100.

Orana Motor Inn, 2101 Calder Highway, Irymple, ✆5024 5903. 12 units, swimming pool - ✪$50-70.

Caravan Parks

Golden River Caravan Gardens, Flora Avenue, ✆5021 2299. (No dogs allowed) - powered sites ✪$20 for two, cabins (en-suite) $50-130 for two, cabins $50 for two.

Cross Roads Holiday Park, cnr Deakin Avenue & Fifteenth Street, ✆5023 3239. (No pets allowed) - powered sites ✪$19-20 for two, cabins (en-suite) $50-100 for two.

Sunraysia Holiday Park, cnr Walnut Avenue & Sturt Highway, ✆5023 1914. (No pets) - powered sites ✪$15 for two, cabins $ 40-60 for two.

Desert City Tourist and Holiday Park, Calder Highway, ✆5021 1533. (No pets allowed) - powered sites ✪$15-22 for two, cabins (en-suite) $40-86 for two, cabins (standard) $40-90.

House Boats

For a holiday with a difference, get a few friends together and hire a houseboat, to cruise down the mighty Murray. The boats range from 6 berth to 12 berth units, from budget price to luxuriously equipped top of the range. For further information on this alternative accommodation, contact the Mildura Visitor Information & Booking Centre, ✆(03) 5021 4424, or one of the following:

Adventure Houseboats, Sturt Highway, Buronga, ✆5023 4787.

Mildura Holiday Houseboats, 842 Fifteenth Street, Mildura, 3502, ✆5021 4414.

Sunraysia Houseboats, 48 Wentworth Street, ✆5027 3621.

Sunseeker Houseboats, 189 Game Street, Merbein, 3502, ✆1800 035 529 (free call).

Eating Out

Whether you prefer French, Italian, Mexican, Chinese or Vegetarian, a la carte, bistro, or casual, Mildura has the restaurant to suit your taste, and your pocket. Here is a selection:

Doms Tavern Restaurant, 28 Langtree Avenue, ✆5021 3822 - open Mon-Sat, 6-30pm till late. Upstairs is the Carlyle Night Club, open Thurs, Fri and Sat, 9pm-3am.

Rendezvous Restaurant, 34 Langtree Avenue, ✆5023 1571 - French cuisine, with bistro and wine bar - ☺open for lunch Mon-Fri, dinner Mon-Sat.

Mildura Settlers, 110-114 Eighth Street, 5023 0474 - open Mon-Wed 8.30am-midnight, Thu-Sat 8.30am-2am - modern Australian - licensed.

Fasta Pasta, 30 Langtr ee Avenue, ✆5022 0622.

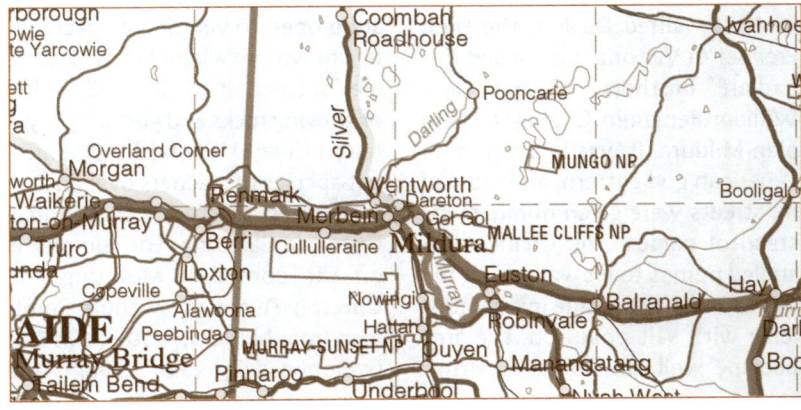

Reef & Beef Restaurant, Deakin Avenue, ℂ5023 5023.

Marias Pizza & Pasta Palace, 210a Deakin Avenue, ℂ5023 7713.

Belvue Restaurant, at the Commodore Motor Inn, cnr Deakin Avenue & 7th Street, ℂ5023 0241.

Regal Chinese Restaurant, 224 Deakin Avenue, ℂ5021 3688.

Barneys Seafood Restaurant, 360 Deakin Avenue, ℂ5021 2166.

Dragon Tower Chinese Restaurant, 29 Langtree Avenue, ℂ5023 1925.

Wirraway Bistro, 130 Madden Avenue, ℂ5023 1187.

Dom's Tavern Restaurant, 28 Langtree Avenue, ℂ5021 3822.

Bel-Jardin Restaurant, 376 Deakin Avenue, ℂ5023 7377.

And, of course, we can't forget *McDonald's*. The local branch is at 395 Deakin Avenue, ph 222 544.

Points of Interest

In 1885, Alfred Deakin, the then Premier of Victoria, persuaded Canadian brothers, George and William Benjamin Chaffey to help plan Mildura. It was laid out in an American grid pattern, and most of its streets were given numbers instead of names. The Chaffeys installed pumps to lift water from the Murray, and after some initial problems with salt pollution, the area became well known for its fruit.

Much of Mildura's history is preserved in the **Museum of Local History**, which is housed in Rio Vista, the stately home of W.B. Chaffey in Cureton Avenue - open 6 days. Also there is the **Mildura Arts Centre**, one of the best provincial galleries in Australia, ℂ5018 8330.

Dolls on the Avenue is a collection of hundreds of dolls from every decade, and is ☺open daily 10am-4pm. It is in Benetook Avenue, ℂ5025 7113.

Golden River Zoo, 4km from Mildura on the banks of the Murray River is a fine privately owned zoo. Open daily 9am-5pm on Flora Avenue, off 11th Street. For information on animal show times ℂ5023 5540. Entry is $12 adults, $6 children.

Woodsie's Gem Shop is Australia's largest jewellery manufacturing complex, and one of Mildura's top attractions. It comprises: a workshop open to visitors; a spectacular showroom where finished items are for sale; an Aladdin's Cave full of glowing rocks and glittering crystals; a Crazy Maze with 100 different species of creepers over an acre of land to test your skill; and a Cave-Inn Cafeteria. The complex is on the corner of Morpung and Cureton Avenues, Nichols Point, 6km from Mildura, ℂ5024 5797. It is ☺open daily 9am-5.30pm, and there is a modest admission fee to the Cave and Maze Section. The rest of the complex is free.

Orange World, 7km from Mildura on the Silver City Highway, is a fully operational citrus property with: ☉Tours on Tractor Train, 10.30am and 2.30pm; Citrus Tour; Red Emperor Tour, including a tour of Stanley Winery, 11.30am. Tours run daily, with extra tours during school holidays. For further information ☏5023 5197.

River Cruises

You can experience the old river boat era when you sail down the Murray on a paddleboat, and there are plenty of day and half-day cruises available. Details of current sailings are provided on noticeboards on Mildura Wharf, but here are a few examples.

PS Melbourne, ☏5023 2200, the only original steam driven Paddlesteamer (built 1912) ☉departs Mildura Wharf 10.50am and 1.50pm for a 2 hour cruise, which goes through Lock 11.

PV Loyalty, 5027 3224, has daily cruises (except Saturdays) on the Darling River, ☉departing from behind Wentworth Services Club at 1.45pm (returns 3.45pm).

PV Rothbury specialises in day cruises, including lunch. Cruise to the Golden River Zoo ☉leaves 9.50am on Wednesdays, and returns 3pm. Cruise to Trentham Estate Winery, leaves 10.30am Thursdays and returns 3.30pm. There are additional cruises during school holidays. The boat is also available for charter day or night cruises, ☏5023 2200.

Facilities

Olympic swimming pool, 12th Street; putt putt golf course, cnr 7th Street and Orange Avenue; ten pin bowling, King Avenue; old time dance at Nichols Point Hall, ph 232 208, Saturday 8pm-midnight; tennis, golf, lawn bowls, squash, skating, boating, water skiing, fishing, croquet, and badminton.

Outlying Attractions

Red Cliffs

15km (9 miles) south of Mildura along the Calder Highway on the way to Melbourne, lies the town of Red Cliffs which is currently enjoying a surge in development. The town gets its name from the nearby striking red cliffs which dominate the Murray River. In the early 1890s, George Chaffey bought 6060ha (15,000 acres) of rich mallee land above the cliffs to grow vines, but the cliffs proved too steep for pumping irrigation water, and it was not for another 30 years that prosperity reached the town.

That was when more than 700 soldiers were re-settled in the area after World War I, and today the area is an important part of the citrus and dried fruits industries.

Using Red Cliffs as a base, the visitor has a great variety of attractions to see, ranging from the huge Southcorp Karadoc Winery, to various handcraft, art and gemstone displays. In the heart of the town, in Barclay Square, is Big Lizzie, the largest traction engine ever built in Australia, which took two years to make the journey from Melbourne.

Hattah-Hulkyne National Park
Murray-Kulkyne National Park

This vast Mallee park is about 70km (43 miles) south of Mildura and provides striking contrasts teeming with birdlife, kangaroos, emus and colourful wildflowers. The park information centre can be reached from the Calder Highway turn-off at Hattah (look for the store) - also enter through Nangiloc/Colignan, ✆13 1963.

Mungo National Park

The Park contains the unique Walls of China, a range of dunes up to 46m (150 ft) high shaped by erosion into a barrier 27km (17 miles) long, leaving a foreground likened to a lunar landscape, or part of the Sahara Desert. Many geological and archaeological discoveries have been made in the area, and Aboriginal ovens can be seen. There is also an old shearing shed, built by Chinese labourers more than a century ago. The site is about 110km (68 miles) north-west of Mildura, on a dry weather road. Phone ✆5029 7292 for more information.

Wentworth

The historic town of Wentworth NSW, is situated where the Darling River joins the Murray, and is a 20 minute drive from Mildura. The Wentworth Tourist Information Centre, 66 Darling Street, ✆5027 3624, is ☺open seven days a week (9.30-4p, Mon-Fri and 10am-2pm on weekends), and will provide details of scenic attractions. You can email them at ✉tourism@wentworth.nsw.gov.au or visit the website ☞www.wentworth.nsw.gov.au

One site that you must not miss is the Old Wentworth Gaol, 1879-1927, in Beverley Street. It was designed to serve a vast outback region, and now stands as a vivid reminder of those harsh and uncompromising days when Wentworth stood on the edge of the lonely Australian inland. Classified as essential to the preservation of Australia's heritage, the gaol is a tribute to the craftsmanship of the pioneer builders and to the unfortunate inmates. The gaol also houses the Nanya Exhibit, dedicated to the courage and ingenuity of a remarkable man, and the beautiful Morrison collection. ⊕Open daily 10am-5pm, ✆5027 3337.

A walk through town will take you padst quaint and notable buildings, some of whch are heritage listed. After visiting the Old Wentworth Gaol, stop in at the Museum, also in Beverly Street, for its fascinating fossil collection.

Wineries

Capogreco Wines, Riverside Avenue between 17th and 18th Streets, South Mildura. ⊕Tastings, sales and inspections Mon-Sat 10am-6pm, ✆5022 1431.

Southcorp Winery, Karadoc. Guided tours Mon-Fri 11am, 2pm and 3.3-pm. ⊕Tastings and sales Mon-Fri 9am-5pm, Sat 10am-4.30pm, ✆5051 3333.

Mildara Blass Winery, Wentworth Road, Merbein. ⊕Guided tours Mon-Fri aa1m, 2pm, 3.30pm. Tastings and sales Mon-Fri 9am-5pm, Sat 11am-4pm, Sunday noon-4pm, ✆5025 2303.

Buronga Hill Winery, Silver City Highway, Buronga. ⊕Tastings and sales Mon-Fri 9am-5pm, Sat 10.30am-4pm, Sun noon-4pm. Winery tours by appointment, ✆5022 5100.

Trentham Estate Winery, Sturt Highway, Trentham Cliffs. ⊕Tastings and sales Mon-Fri 9am-5pm, Sat-Sun 10am-5pm, ✆5024 8888.

Victoria – South-West

Warrnambool

Population 28,000
Warrnambool is situated on the coast, 263km (163 miles) south-west of Melbourne, where the Princes Highway meets the Great Ocean Road.

Climate

Average temperatures: January max 23C (73F) - min 13C (55F); July max 14C (57F) - min 6C (43F). Average hours of sunshine: summer 8, autumn 4, winter 3, spring 5. Wettest six months May-October.

Characteristics

Warrnambool was popular with the old whalers and sealers, as they could repair their boats and process their catches on its wide beaches. Due to reduced hunting, Warrnambool is now visited each year by a herd of the rare Southern Right whales, and a viewing platform has been erected at Logan's Beach to enable visitors to obtain a better view of the whales, which usually remain in the area for several weeks.

How to Get There

By Bus
Greyhound Pioneer, ☏13 2030, stop at Warrnambool on the Melbourne/Adelaide coastal route.

By Rail
There is a regular V/Line service between Melbourne and Warrnambool, ☏13 6196.

By Road
From Melbourne, travel to Geelong

The Twelve Apostles, Victoria

The Victorian coast , viewed from the Great Ocean Roa

and then take the Princes Highway if you are in a hurry, but if you have more time, then take one of Australia's really beautiful roads, the Great Ocean Road which follows the coast and passes through Lorne.

Warrnambool is 263km (163 miles) from Melbourne via the Princes Highway, 211km (131 miles) from Mt Gambier, and 654km (406 miles) from Adelaide.

Visitor Information

The Tourist Information Office is at 600 Raglan Parade, ✆(03) 5564 7837, and it is ⏰open daily 9am-5pm, or you can email the manager at ✉nan_adams@wcc.mav.asn.au

The website to visit is 🖥www.warrnambool.org

In addition, Shipwreck Coast Tourism can be found at 174a Timor Street, ✆5561 7894.

Accommodation

Here is a selection of accommodation, with prices for a double room per night, which should be used as a guide only. The telephone area code is 03.

Guthrie Heights Apartment, 8/148 Merri Street, ✆5562 1600. 1 unit, 3 queen ensuites, sea views, barbecue - ✪$160.

Warrnambool Heritage Cottage, 26 MacDonald Street, ✆5562 6531. Private courtyard, barbecue - ✪$120-160.

Sundowner Chain Motor Inn, 525 Raglan Parade, ✆5562 3866. 60 units, licensed restaurant, swimming pool, spa - ✪$110-200.

Tudor Motel Warrnambool, 519 Raglan Parade, ✆5562 8877. 22 units, licensed restaurant (closed Sunday off-season), spa - ✪$100-150.

Olde Maritime Motor Inn, cnr Merri & Banyan Streets, ✆5561 1415. 37 units, licensed restaurant, spa - ✪$90-170.

Western Coast Motel, 349 Raglan Parade, ✆5562 2755. 21 units, restaurant - ✪$80-120.

Warrnambool Gateway Motor Inn, 69 Raglan Parade, ✆5562 8622. 26 units, *Quigley's* licensed restaurant (closed Sunday), barbecue, heated swimming pool - ✪$90-125.

Warrnambool Hotel, cnr Koroit & Keppler Streets, ✆5562 2377. 16 rooms, a la carte restaurant - ✪$70 including breakfast.

Motel Downtown Warrnambool, 620 Raglan Parade, ✆5562 1277. 58 units, heated swimming pool, spa - ✪$70-200.

Western Hotel, cnr Timor & Kepler Streets, ✆5562 2011. 20 units, standard facilities - ✪$60.

Bed and Breakfast

Merton Manor B&B, 62 Ardlie Street, ✆5562 0720. 6 rooms, barbecue - ✪$150-170.

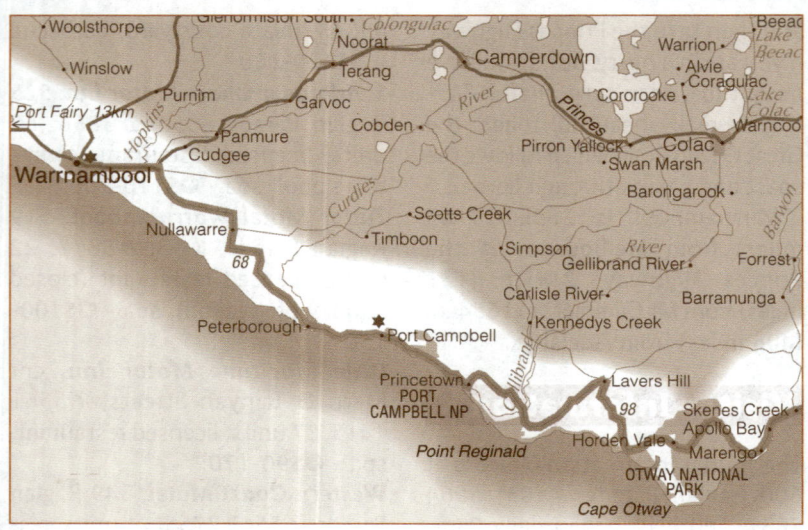

Casa D'Oro B&B, 42 Shady's Lane, ✆5565 4243. 3 rooms, barbecue, comfortable rooms - ✪$90.

Whalesway, 6 Florence Street, ✆5661 2660. 2 rooms, barbecue - ✪$75-80.

Caravan Parks

Ocean Beach Holiday Village, Pertobe Road, ✆5561 4222. 58 sites, 26 cabins, no pets, barbecue, heated pool - powered sites ✪$22-30 for two, cabins $60-110 for two.

Warrnambool Holiday Park, cnr Raglan Parade & Simpson Street, ✆5562 5031. 17 sites, 17 cabins, no dogs, barbecue, heated pool - powered sites ✪$20-26, cabins $60-85.

Fig Tree Holiday Village, 33 Lava Street, ✆5561 1233. 72 sites, 23 cabins, no pets, barbecue - powered sites ✪$17-30 for two, cabins $55-90.

Caravarna Lodge, 81 Henna Street, ✆5562 3376. 42 sites, 4 cabins, barbecue, heated pool - powered sites ✪$14-17 for two, on-site vans $25-40 for two, cabins $30-50.

Hostels

Warrnambool Beach Backpackers, 17 Stanley Street, ✆5562 4874. 6 rooms, cooking facilities, guest dining - ✪$15.

Backpackers Barn, 90 Lava Street, ✆5562 2073. 15 rooms, cooking and dining - ✪$14.

Eating Out

There are over 50 places to have a meal in Warrnambool, from cafes to quality restaurants, and the Tourist Information Office will have details. Here is a selection.

Balenas Cafe, 158 Timor Street, ✆5562 0900. Contemporary Australian cuisine as well as seafood and steaks with Italian, Mediterranean and International influences. Open 7 days.

Jukes Cafe Restaurant, 525 Raglan Parade, ✆5562 3866. A-la-carte menu with entertainment on Saturday evening. Licensed, open seven days for breakfast and dinner.

Oriental Restaurant, 80-82 Leibig Street, ✆5562 7079. BYO, Chinese and Australian fare, lunch and dinner, open 7 days.

Mahogany Ship, 91 Merri Street, ✆5561 3866. Australian seafood steak and pasta is served in this Scottish themed restaurant. A-la-carte dining with sea views.

Bojangles, 61 Liebig Street, ✆5562 8751. Award-winning Italian restaurant offering wood-fire pizzas and pastas as a specialty. Licensed, open for dinner only.

Beach Babylon, 72 Leibig Street, ✆5562 3714. Seafood with Mediterranean and Australian flavours. Open every day.

Restaurant Malaysia, 69 Liebig Street, ✆5562 2051. Also has Thai, Indian and Chinese dishes, BYO, open 7 days, noon-2pm, 6pm to late. Yum Cha, Sun noon-2pm.

Freshwater, 78 Leibig Street, ✆5561 3188. Licensed restaurant serving modern Australian and International cuisine and offering local wines.

The Blues, 142 Timor Street, ✆5562 2033. Family oriented dining with live local music. Australian seafood and steaks.

Images, Liebig Street, ✆5562 4208. Licensed restaurant with a family atmosphere.

Breakers, 79 Banyan Street, ✆5561 3088. All types of seafood served in an Australian style.

Clovelly, cnr Banyan & Merri Streets, ✆5561 1415. A-la-carte menu with seafood, steak and pasta.

Dragon Inn, 219 Lava Street, ✆5562 1517. Chinese cuisine.

Points of Interest

Flagstaff Hill Maritime Museum, Merri Street, ✆5564 7841, recreates the atmosphere of an early Australian coa-stal port. The lighthouse and associated buildings, and the 1887 fortifications are the original features of the site, and around them the village has been created. The story of shipping and the sea unfolds for visitors as they tour the village. Each building portrays an important aspect of port life in the last century, whether it be the role of the Ship Chandler or the function of the Mission to Seamen Church. Among the relics on display there is the Loch Ard peacock: an 1851 Minton porcelain statue which was washed up (still in its packing case) in Loch Ard Gorge after a ship-wreck. The museum is ☉open daily 9.00am-5.00pm, adults ✿$9.50, child $4.50, pensioner $8, family $26.

Lake Pertobe Park has causeways, walking tracks, a maze, a flying fox, paddle boats and a well-equipped Adventure Playground behind the surf beach of Lady Bay.

Fletcher Jones Gardens, cnr Flaxman Street and Raglan Parade, are a colourful advocate for Victoria's claim as the Garden State of Australia. Thousands of visitors come each year to see these gardens.

The Performing Arts and Conference Centre, 185 Timor Street, is a modern-style building situated in landscaped grounds in the heart of the business and restaurant district. It has three main venues suitable for stage presentations, conventions, dinners, cabarets, exhibitions, lectures, classes and meetings. Check the daily newspapers for programmes, or ©5564 7904.

Warrnambool Art Gallery, 165 Timor Street, has a permanent collection of 19th and 20th century Australian and European paintings and graphics - ☉open daily noon-5pm, ©5564 7832.

The **Warrnambool Botanic Gardens** are on the corner of Botanic and Queen Streets.

Tower Hill State Game Reserve, 14km (9 miles) from Warrnambool, is the remains of a volcano whose crater walls collapsed inward during its dying stages 6000 years ago. They blocked the 3km wide crater, which later filled with water. There is a sealed road leading to the main island, from where bushwalks radiate. There is also a **Natural History Centre**, ☉open 9.00am to 4.30pm daily, which conducts tours, ©5565 9202.

Hopkins Falls, are 13km (8 miles) from Warrnambool, near Wangoom. Thousands of tiny eels (elvers) make their way up the falls to the quiet waters beyond, to grow to maturity before returning to the sea to breed.

There are several recommended **heritage walks** through the town and nearby regions, and the Tourist Centre can provide you with maps and other details.

Warrnambool also has **a mystery**! There have been several reported sightings of the wreck of a mahogany ship in the windswept sandhills west of the city. The last was in 1980, and several artefacts have been found in the area. It is said that the ship foundered 400 years ago with a complement of Dutch and Spanish sailors. If there is any substance to the story it means that Europeans set foot on Australian soil long before Captain Cook. In 1980 the City Council formed a Mahogany Ship Committee to compile all the known information, which is being fed into a computer in an endeavour to solve the mystery.

Festivals

Wunta Fiesta - February.
Racing Carnival - May
Melbourne-Warrnambool Cycling Classic - October.

Facilities

Aerobics, badminton, basketball, volleyball, bingo, boating, lawn bowls, indoor cricket, croquet, golf, greyhound racing, horse racing, swimming, mini golf, scuba diving, skin diving, squash, speedway, surfing, swimming, table tennis, tennis, ten pin bowling, waterskiing, windsurfing and yachting.
Here are a few specific activity venues:

Karting
Indoor Karting, Silverton Park, ℂ5562 2422. Open Wed-Fri noon-late, Sat-Sun 11am-late.

Golf
Mini Golf Lake Pertobe, 47 Pertobe Road, ℂ5562 0644. Open Dec-Jan - 10am-close, Feb-Nov - noon-5pm.

Horse-riding
Rundells Mahagany Trail Rides, Millers Lane, Dennington via Warrnambool, ℂ5529 2303. One and two hour trail rides, full day pub rides, twilight rides and riding lessons. Horse riding mainly along the beach.

Fishing
Warrnambool Trout Farm, 4km north of Warrnambool on Wollaston Road, ℂ019 94 3396. Catches guaranteed, equipment supplied free, fish feeding, barbecue. ☺Open every weekend 10.30am-5pm, 7 days during school holidays.

Tours

Regular tours on the new *Sprit of Warrnambool*, lasting from 1-1.5 hours return. ☺Open 10am-6pm with nighttime charters available. Adults ✪$10, children $5.
Southern Right Charters and Diving, ℂ5561 6222 or ℂ5562 5044, offer fishing charters, diving charters, whale watching tours and scenic tours.
Seeall Tours, 13 Barham Avenue, ℂ5562 5795, have six tours

through various locations, costing between ✪$10 and $50.

Warrnambool River Cruises, 2 Simpson Street, can be contacted on ©5562 7788.

Outlying Attractions

Great Ocean Road

The spectacular Great Ocean Road follows the coastline for much of its 250 kilometre (156 miles) length from Torquay to Peterborough. In some parts it is the only thing separating the mount-ains from the surf beaches.

The road was built by 3000 First World War veterans, and was dedicated to the memory of all those who fought in that war. Using picks and shovels, the men commenced work in 1919 and the road was opened in 1932.

Fully sealed, though narrow in

parts, it wends its scenic route through some of Victoria's most popular resorts. Pretty coastal towns like Lorne, Apollo Bay and Port Campbell swell to capacity in the high season. But it is in the winter, when massive breakers crash into the limestone cliffs, that the challenge which confronted the captains of the small coastal vessels can be understood. In the period to 1920, some 80 major shipping disasters were recorded between Port Fairy and Cape Otway. Of these the best known are the *Loch Ard* and the *Schomberg*, relics of which can be seen in the Flagstaff Hill Maritime Village at Warrnambool.

The road also passes through some of the richest forests in Australia. The Angahook Forest Park, the Otway National Park and the Lorne Forest Park are all extensive forest systems with prolific fauna.

We are starting our trip along the Great Ocean Road from Lorne, which is less than 2 hours' drive from Melbourne, and 218km (135 miles) from Warrnambool.

As an additional resource, the website that covers the general area is 👁www.greatoceanrd.org.au

Lorne

On the Erskine River, surrounded on three sides by forest ranges, and to the south by the Southern

Ocean, Lorne was the first place declared an area of Special Significance and Natural Beauty by the Victorian Government.

On a bay named after Capt Louttit, who sought shelter there around 1840 while retrieving cargo from a shipwreck, Lorne was first settled by William Lindsay, a timber-cutter. Subdivision began in 1869 and the town was named after the Marquis of Lorne. Much of its colourful history is preserved in the gracious homes which remain.

Lorne's attractions include **Lorne Angahook State Park**, **Erskine Falls**, **Pennyroyal Valley**, as well as numerous bushwalks leading through lush fauna to beautiful waterfalls.

The Lorne Visitor Information Centre is at 144 Mountjoy Parade, ©5289 1152. It is ☺open daily 9am-5pm. They can provide you with excellent information on absolutely everything you need to know to about this area, from where to stay and eat, to what to see and do. If you wish to contact them by email, the address is ✉lornevic@primus.com.au The web page to explore is ☜www.surfcoast.vic.gov.au

Apollo Bay

Apollo Bay was first visited in 1840 by the Henty Brothers, founders of Portland and Mount Gambier. They established a small whaling station on what is now the golf course. One of the three major centres along the Great Ocean Road, it has all facilities to offer the visitor - motels, hotels, holiday flats, lodges and caravan parks; several restaurants and take-away food places.

There are also many guest houses, B&Bs and cottages in Apollo Bay, so if you prefer these cosy kinds of accommodation, the Information Centre can give you an idea of what is on offer. The Visitor Information Centre is on the Great Ocean Road, ©(03) 5237 6529.

Apollo Bay is an ideal touring centre for the **Otway Ranges Forest Park**, **Otway National Park**, and **Melba Gully State Park**.

Princetown

Situated on the La Trobe Creek near Gellibrand River, the surrounding limestone cliffs contain interesting fossils and formations. Gemstones can sometimes be found along the coastline, and the area is rich in flora and fauna. Princetown was named after Prince Alfred and was proclaimed in 1885. Safe swimming, boating, fishing and water skiing are all features of this tiny settlement.

Given its location between the western boundary of the **Otway National Park** and the eastern boundary of the **Port Campbell**

National Park, Princetown is ideal as a base for touring both.

Port Campbell

At the heart of one of Australia's most famed and photographed natural attractions, Port Campbell is a very popular resort. Situated on Campbell's Creek, and named after Capt. Alexander Campbell, a Scotsman in charge of the Port Fairy whaling station, it began as a small fishing port with surrounding pastoral runs. In 1964, 700ha (1729 acres) around Port Campbell was set aside as a National Park, and in 1981 the park was extended from Princetown through to Peterborough. Port Campbell is roughly at the centre of the park.

The town is a crayfishing port near the mouth of the river and has a safe, sandy beach ideal for family swimming. Restaurants and take-away foods are available and fresh local crayfish is the specialty.

Of course the **Port Campbell National Park** itself is the attraction (see entry overleaf), but whilst in Port Campbell you can take a trip to the old cemetery on the northern edge of the town. It has many old graves of interest, including that of Captain Scott and some of his crew, shipwrecked off the coast in the barque *Newfield* in 1892.

A look-out on the western side of the river offers a scenic pano-

rama of the town and coastline.

The Port Campbell Visitor Information Centre, is in 26 Morris Street, ©5598 6089.

Port Campbell National Park

Recognised as one of Australia's most scenic sections of coastline, the 1750ha (4323 acres) Port Campbell National Park stretches 32km (20 miles) along the Great Ocean Road.

The best known features are the **Twelve Apostles**, **Loch Ard Gorge** and **London Bridge**. In early 1990 a span of London Bridge collapsed into the ocean, vividly demon-strating the ongoing erosion of wind and sea on the limestone cliffs of the park.

Gorges, arches, islands, blowholes and stark outcrops create a dramatic foreground to the stormy Southern Ocean which stretches to the Antarctic. Here and there a sandy beach glistens in sharp contrast to the sheer cliffs and deep inlets which offer some of the most interesting scenery and photography subjects you will find.

Further information on the park can be acquired by calling ©13 1963.

Peterborough

Situated at the mouth of the Curdie's River, Peterborough is a popular summer holiday town where you can get away from it all. River or beach swimming, and fishing for bream, mullet or crayfish are among the main pastimes, while the shipwrecks in the area provide good diving and aqualunging.

Port Fairy

The pretty town of Port Fairy is 29km (18 miles) from Warrnambool. The first stop for all visitors should be the Visitor Information Centre in 22 Bank Street, ©(03) 5568 2682, as this historic town has many attractions. Over 50 buildings have been classified by the National Trust, and there many art, craft and antique shops, picnic and barbecue areas, and facilities for golf, tennis, squash, lawn bowls and boat trips. There are heritage buildings outlined in brochures available from the Visitor Centre, and the Port Fairy History Centre in Gipps Street should satisfy anyone interested in nineteenth-century memorabilia.

High on the list of attractions, though, is not man-made. It is the **Mutton Bird Rookery** on Griffiths

Island. The bird gets its name from early settlers who utilised its fatty flesh for food, and as an oil source, but it is really the short-tailed shearwater (*puffinus tenuirostris*). They are not much to look at, but their lifestyle is fascinating. They arrive at Griffiths Island within three days of September 22 each year, returning to the nest burrow they had the previous year, with the same partner. They spend a few weeks renovating their homes, mate in early November, then fly out to sea for a couple of weeks. They return to Port Fairy about November 25, immediately lay their eggs (one per family), then both parents share in the incubation until the egg hatches in mid-January. After two or three days, the parents leave the chicks and forage at sea for food, firstly only for the day, regurgitating the food for the chicks at night, then gradually increasing the period and distance of food gathering until the chick has up to two weeks between meals. Nevertheless it gains weight rapidly and for a period becomes heavier than the adult birds. In mid-April the adult birds hear the call of the wild, commence their Pacific migration, and leave the young behind to fend for themselves. Hunger finally forces the chicks from the nest at night, and in early May they set off after the adults, somehow finding the migratory route with no help from mum or dad. Obviously, the mortality rate is high, and it is not helped by stray dogs and cats, and visitors who do not stick to the formed tracks, and tramp through the burrows instead. In fact, one year 80% of the young chicks were lost because some people were careless while exploring the area.

Victoria – South-West

Geelong

Population 145,300
Geelong is on the shores of Corio Bay, south-west of Melbourne.

Climate

Average temperatures: June max 25C (77F) - min 13C (55F); July max 14C (57F) - min 5C (41F).

Characteristics

Geelong is Victoria's premier regional city and, in fact, was a more important commercial centre than Melbourne in the 1840s. It is the natural gateway to the richest wool and wheat areas of the world. The city has many antique and arts and crafts shops.

How to Get There

By Air
Geelong has its own regional airport which can be contacted on ℃5264 1273.
By Rail
Trains run frequently between Melbourne and Geelong, ℃13 1368.
By Coach
V/Line services Geelong frequently, ℃13 6196.
By Car
From Melbourne, via the Princes Highway (74km-46miles).

Visitor Information

The Geelong and Great Ocean Road Tourist Information Centre is in Stead Park on the Princes Highway,

✆(03) 5275 5797. More information can be found at the Wool Museum on Moorabool Street, ✆5222 2900 or ✆1 800 620 888 (free call).

The website to visit is 👁www.greatoceanrd.org.au (there are no email contact facilities).

The Melbourne website 👁www.melbourne.citysearch.com.au also lists information on Geelong.

If you are wandering around the city, keep in mind that there is an information outlet in the Market Square Shopping Centre in Moorabool Street. Another can be found on the corner of Princes Highway and St Georges Road, Corio.

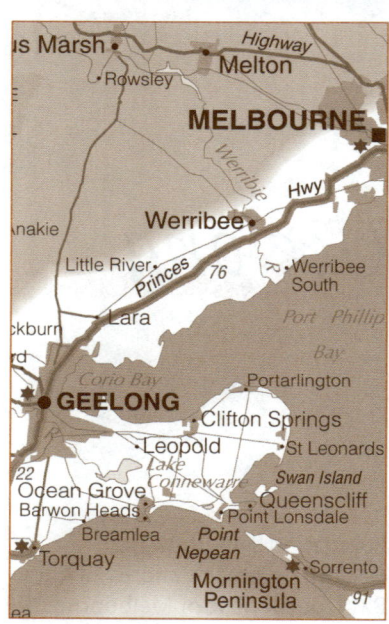

Accommodation

Following is a selection of hotels, with prices for a double room per night. Please use this as a guide only. The telephone area code is 03.

Mercure Hotel Geelong, cnr Gheringhap & Myers Streets, ✆5221 6844. 142 units, 3 suites, licensed restaurant, pool, spa, sauna - ✪$140.

Sundowner Chain Motor Inn, 13 The Esplanade, ✆5222 3499. 35 units, licensed restaurant, sauna, pool - ✪$105-175.

Flag Inn Eastern Sands, 1 Bellerine Street, ✆5221 5577. 25 units, licensed restaurant, carport parking - ✪$95-125.

Rose Garden Motor Inn, 14 Settlement Road (Princes Highway), ✆5241 9441. 15 units, spas, carport parking - ✪$85-115.

Aristocrat Waurnvale Motel, 90 Princes Highway, ✆5241 8211. 14 units, spa bath, pool, playground - ✪$70-85.

Huntsman Innkeepers Motor Inn, 9 Aberdeen Street, ✆5221 2177. 36 units, licensed restaurant (closed Sunday), pool, spa, sauna - ✪$75-90.

Colonial Lodge Motel, 57 Fyans Street, ✆5223 2266. 10 units - ✪$65-75.

The Ponds Hotel Motel, Princes

Highway, ℳ5243 1244. 15 units, licensed restaurant - ✪$65-70.

Kangaroo Motel, 16 The Esplanade, ℳ5221 4022. 10 units, licensed restaurant (closed Sunday) - ✪$70-75.

Caravan Parks

Barwon Caravan & Tourist Park, 153 Barrabool Road, ℳ5243 3842. (No pets allowed) 191 sites, barbecue, playground - powered sites ✪$20-25 for two, cabins $55-85 for two.

City Southside Caravan Park, 87 Barrabool Road, ℳ5243 3788. (No dogs allowed) 90 sites, barbecue, playground - powered sites ✪$18 for two, cabins $55-65 for two.

Billabong Caravan Park, 59 Barrabool Road, ℳ5243 6225. (No pets allowed) 97 sites, barbecue, playground, pool - powered sites ✪$18-20 for two, cabins $55-65 for two.

Sherwood Forest Caravan Park, 70 Bailey Street, ℳ5243 1068. (Pets allowed at owner's discretion) 120 sites, pool, playground - unpowered sites ✪$17 for two, cabins $40-45 for two.

Eating Out

Geelong has a good selection of restaurants, with all nationalities represented. Also remember that some of the motels have restaurants serving reasonably-priced meals.

Recommended restaurants are:

Bamboleo, 86 Little Malop Street, ℳ5229 2548. Licensed restaurant with Spanish cuisine.

Rheingold Cellar, 9 Malop Street, ℳ5222 2557. Traditional German and Continental dishes. The restaurant has an historic theme and light entertainment to liven the atmosphere.

Le Parisien, 15 Eastern Beach Road, ℳ5229 3110. Licensed restaurant that has an extensive wine list boasting more than 350 selections. Waterside frontage and seafood specialities.

Empire Grill, 66 McKillop Street, ℳ5223 2132. Licensed restaurant with regional wines and a-la-carte dining.

Mexican Graffiti, 43 Yarra Street, ℳ5222 2036. All types of Californian-style Mexican food available. Fully licensed. Open from 11am daily.

Mei Ling, 169 Malop Street, ℳ5229 7505. Chinese food with dine-in, take-away or home delivery options.

Fisherman's Pier, Bay end of Yarra Street, ℳ5222 4100. Fully licensed seafood restaurant overlooking Corio Bay. Outside dining, family oriented menu. Open daily for both lunch and dinner.

King Edward VII, above the Sailors Rest Tavern, 3 Moorabool Street, ℳ5224 2241. Modern inter-

national cuisine with alfresco dining and water views.

Pastels by the Bay, 13 The Esplanade, ☎5222 3499. Fully licensed, bay views, open daily for lunch and dinner.

Pearl of China Cafe, 154 Ryrie Street, ☎5229 8895. Take-away, home delivery or a-la-carte.

Sirinda, 93 Ryrie Street, ☎5221 5797. Thai restaurant.

Koaki, Bell Parade, ☎5272 1925. Traditional Japanese food.

Samraat, 137 Pakington Street, Geelong West, ☎5229 7995. Indian cuisine.

McDonalds have branches on the corner of Ryrie and Yarra Streets, Geelong; 400 Melbourne Road, Geelong North; and 230-236 Autumn Street, Geelong West.

Points of Interest

Geelong was first settled in the 1930s and has several historic buildings within walking distance of the city centre. The Information Centre has details of a Heritage Walk that starts from the Post Office on the corner of Ryrie and Gheringhap Streets.

The National Wool Museum, cnr Moorabool & Brougham Streets, ☎5227 0701, is housed in a bluestone wool store and traces the story of wool from the sheep's back to the finished garment. Wool auctions are still held here. ☺Open daily 9.30am-5pm, and admission is ✪$7 adults, $3.50 children and $18 for families.

Geelong Art Gallery, Little

Mallop Street, ℗5229 3645, has some fine examples of early Australian painters and a good contemporary collection. ℗Open Mon- Fri 10am-5pm, Sat-Sun 1-5pm. Admission is free.

Port of Geelong Maritime Museum, Eastern Beach Road, ℗5277 2260, has displays depicting 150 years of shipping in Corio and Port Phillip Bays. The museum is ℗closed on Tuesdays and Thursdays, and opens from 10am-4pm every other day of the week. Entry fees are ✪$2 adults, 50c children and $4 for families.

The Ford Discovery Centre, on the corner of Gheringap & Brougham Streets, ℗5227 8700, features the history of car design and engineering, and offers insights into the impact of global influences and environmental change on automobiles in the future. It is ℗closed on Tuesdays but opens 10am-5pm every other day.

Gabbinbar Animal Wildlife Park, 654 Torquay Road, ℗5264 1455. Many types of animals, both native and foreign, can be found in the park ℗open daily 10am-5pm.

Beaches. Apart from the still-water beaches in Corio Bay-Eastern Beach and St Helen's - there are the nearby still-water beaches of Port Phillip Bay - Portarlington, Indented Head, St Leonards, Queenscliffe and Barwon Heads. Then you come to the ocean beaches of Point Londsdale, Ocean Grove, Torquay, Jan Juc, Anglesea, Point Addis, Airey's Inlet, Fairhaven, Lorne, and the famous surfing mecca, Bell's Beach.

Festivals

The Springding Festival is held in November.

Facilities

There are facilities for over 150 sports, including football, basketball, horse racing, greyhound racing, golf, tennis, and all water sports.

Victoria – South-West

Portland

Population 12,000

Portland is situated on the coast of Victoria at Cape Sir William Grant, and is the only deepwater port between Geelong and Adelaide.

Climate

Average temperatures: January max 22C (72F) - min 13C (55F); July max 12C (54F) - min 8C (46F). Average rainfall: 840mm (33 in); wettest 6 months May - October. Average hours of sunshine: summer 8; autumn 4; winter 3; spring 5.

Characteristics

Portland was the first permanent settlement in Victoria, and is filled with historic buildings from the 1840s. The Henty Brothers settled here with their flocks of sheep in 1834 before Victoria was proclaimed a separate State.

Portland has become an important port serving a vast hinterland including the Mallee, Wimmera, Western District and the southeast of South Australia. It is also the site of the giant Portland Aluminium Smelter.

How to Get There

By Bus

There is a daily bus service to/from Mount Gambier which takes approximately 90 minutes.

By Rail

There is a rail service from Melbourne with a coach connection to Portland.

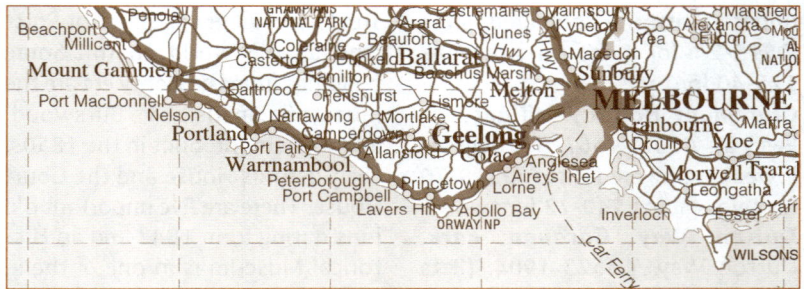

By Road

Either along the Princes Highway from Melbourne (362km - 225 miles), or via the Great Ocean Road from Melbourne.

Via the Princes Highway from Adelaide (568km - 353 miles), or the Calder and Henty Highways from Mildura (531km - 330 miles).

Tourist Information

The Portland Maritime Discovery and Visitor Information Centre can be found in Lee Breakwater Road, ✆(03) 5523 2671. They are ☼open daily 9am-5pm.

Accommodation

No shortage in this department in Portland. Here is a selection with prices for a double room per night, which should be used as a guide only. ✆The telephone area code is 03.

Mariner Motel, 196 Percy Street, ✆5523 2877. 12 units - ✪$55-70.

Admella Motel, 5 Otway Court, ✆5523 3347. 10 units, bbq - ✪$57.

Whaler's Rest Motor Inn, 155 Henty Hwy, ✆5523 4077. 13 units, swimming pool, bbq - ✪$80-105.

Melaleuca Motel, 25 Bentinck Street, ✆5523 3397. 16 units, unlicensed restaurant (closed Sunday) - ✪$55.

Grosvenor Motel, 206 Hurd Street, ✆5523 2888. 14 units, unlicensed restaurant (Mon-Thurs), bbq - ✪$65-85.

Caravan Parks

Centenary Caravan Park, 184 Bentinck Street, ✆5523 1487. (No dogs allowed) - powered sites ✪$18 for two, cabins $18 for two.

Portland Haven Caravan Park, 76 Garden Street, ✆5523 1768. (No dogs allowed) - powered sites ✪$14-16 for up to four, cabins $33-55 for up to four.

Henty Bay Caravan Park, Dutton Way, ✆5523 3716. (Dogs allowed under control) - powered sites ✪$15-25 for two, on-site vans $25-40 for two.

Claremont Holiday Village, 37 Percy St, ✆5521 7567. (No dogs allowed) - powered sites ✪$18-20 for two, cabins $40-72 for two.

Dutton Way Caravan Park, Dutton Way, ✆5523 1904. (Pets allowed at manager's discretion) - powered sites ✪$13-16 for two, on-site vans $30-33 for two.

Eating Out

Here are a few reasonably priced eateries you might like to try:

The Canton Palace BYO Chinese Restaurant, 7 Julia Street, ✆5523 3677.

Middle Kingdom Chinese Restaurant, 31 Henty Street, ✆5523 3666.

Poon's Restaurant & Cafe, 121b Percy Street, ✆5523 5071.

Sandilands Restaurant, 33 Percy Street, ✆5523 3319.

Counter meals are available at *Richmond Henty Hotel*, 101 Bentinck Street, ✆5523 1032; *Mac's Hotel*, 41 Bentinck Street, ✆5523 2188; and *Gordon Hotel*, 63 Bentinck Street, ✆5523 1121.

Points of Interest

There are around 100 historically-important buildings in the city, many classified by the National Trust, and all giving parts of Portland an old world charm. Some buildings from the Henty era are the bluestone mansions 'Burswood' and 'Claremont' built in the 1850s, the Customs House and the Court House. There are five important old inns dating from 1842 and an Historical Museum is in one of them, the Caledonian Inn. The Portland Club and the Visitors Centre are from the same period.

The Cottage in the Botanic Gardens, built in 1858, has been the home of six different curators over the years. It has now been restored and furnished in the period style of 120 years ago. The Cottage will be opened for inspection if you arrange an appointment, ✆5523 3820.

History House, the Old Town Hall, houses a collection of historical items, including the Henty plough. It contains, as well as large framed pictures of former mayors and prominent officials who were well known in the early days of the town, a fine collection of photographs and records of the early history of Portland. It ⏰open 10am-noon and 1-4pm every day, ✆5522 2226.

The 250km (155 miles) **Great South West Walk** provides an excellent introduction to the fascinating variety of scenery and wildlife in South-West Victoria. The walk begins and ends at the Visitor Centre and traverses forest, woodland, the Lower Glenelg National Park, the magnificent beaches at Discovery Bay, and the high limestone headlands at Cape Bridgewater and Cape Nelson. The walk is not solely for the hardy long distance walker, it can be undertaken in easy stages by young and old alike. A 2km section at Cape Grant has been sealed for the disabled.

Cape Bridgewater, is the home of the Petrified Forest, a tangle of weird tree forms fashioned by wind and water from the old root systems of the native scrub. The enormity of the rugged coastline can be experienced from cliff walks with the powerful ocean pounding the rocks below, and occasionally shooting up through blowholes.

Festivals

The Portland Summer Festival, Apex Fishing Carnival and Country and Music Festival are held in January. The Dahlia Festival is held in March.

Facilities

Boating, lawn bowls, bush walking, croquet, fishing, golf, horse riding, sailing, surfing, swimming (pool, river, beach) tennis, water skiing.

Outlying Attractions

Heywood

Situated 25km (16 miles) north of Portland, Heywood is a rural centre with hosts of apple orchards. The main attractions in the town are the Bower Bird Museum, ©5527 1660, the Cave Hill Gardens, and Lake Condah Aboriginal Mission.

Hamilton

Known as the Wool Capital of the World, Hamilton is 58km (36 miles) north of Heywood in the heart of fine wool grazing country. The Tourist Information Centre is in Lonsdale Street, ©5572 3746 or ©1800 807 056 (free call), and they have information on the town's attractions, which include the Hamilton Art Gallery ©5573 0460, Hamilton Historical Museum ©5572 4933, the Pastoral Museum ©5571 1595, Lake Hamilton and nearby Nigretta and Wannon Falls.

Macarthur

34km (21 miles) south of Hamilton, and 11km (7 miles) south of Byaduk Caves, Macarthur is also within easy reach of Mt Napier and its volcanic surrounds. Only a few kilometres south-west of the town is the Mt Eccles National Park, in which is found Lake Surprise. There are two first class walks around the crater of Mt Eccles, and camping and picnic facilities are available.

Nelson

Nelson is 70km (43 miles) west of Portland, and is a picturesque fishing hamlet at the mouth of the Glenelg River. It is a popular resort and has numerous bushwalks. A regular boat service takes visitors to the Margaret Rose Caves, which are ☉open daily for inspection, ☏8738 4191.

Tasmania

Hobart

Population 130,000
Hobart is situated on the Derwent River Estuary at Stormy Bay, at the foot of Mt Wellington, which is snowcapped in winter.

Climate

Average Temperatures: January max 22C (72F) - min 12C (54F); July max 11C (52F) - min 4C (39F). Average rainfall: 635mm (25 ins). Driest months January to March.

Characteristics

The suburbs of Hobart spread along both banks of the river and into the foothills of Mt Wellington, which is 1,354m (4,442 ft) high. The central part of the city is very attractive. Hobart is the second oldest capital city in Australia, founded very soon after Sydney. Its architecture reflects its age, with beautifully preserved sandstone buildings unsullied by pollution, and clean, clear streets. It is a great place for a holiday and is well served by many hotels, motels, caravan parks and camping places.

How to Get There

By Air

Hobart Airport is 16km (10 miles) from the city centre and Redline Coaches, ©6233 9466, operate a regular service to the city. Taxis are readily available.

By Bus

Redline Coaches have a service to/from Launceston/Devonport/Burnie/

Wynyard/Smithton and to Queenstown, ☏6233 9466.

Hobart Coaches have a Hobart/Swansea/Bicheno service, ☏6233 4232.

Peninsula Coach Service operate a Hobart/Port Arthur Service, ☏6250 3186.

By Road

It is virtually possible to travel to Hobart in less than a day from anywhere in Tasmania. The distance from Hobart in the south to Devonport on the north coast is less than 300km (186 miles), which gives you some idea of the size of the island.

Tourist Information

The Hobart Visitor Information Centre is in Davey Street, ☏(03) 6230 8233, email ✎tasinfo@discovertasmania.com, and the website is 👁www.discovertasmania.com.au

Accommodation

The prices for accommodation vary considerably depending on the standard offered and the season. Here we provide a selection with prices for a double room per night, which should be used as a guide only. The telephone area code is 03.

Wrest Point Hotel Casino, 410 Sandy Bay Road, Sandy Bay on the shore of the Derwent River, ☏6225 0112. 166 rooms, licensed restaurants, heated indoor pool, sauna, tennis courts, mini golf - ✪$242-264.

Hotel Grand Chancellor, 1 Davey Street, ☏6235 4535. 234 rooms, licensed restaurant, bistro, heated indoor pool, sauna, gym - ✪$260-290.

Lenna of Hobart, 20 Runnymede Street, Battery Point, ☏6223 2911. 50 units, licensed restaurant - ✪$170-195.

Salamanca Inn, 10 Gladstone Street, ☏6223 3300. 60 units, licensed restaurant, heated pool, spa - ✪$150.

Hobart Visa Hotel, 156 Bathurst Street, ☏6232 6255. 140 units, licensed restaurant - ✪$140.

Rydges Hobart, cnr. Argyle & Lewis Streets, North Hobart, ☏6231 1588. 63 units, licensed restaurant, pool, spa, sauna - ✪$135-180.

Hobart Mid City Hotel, 96 Bathurst Street, ☏6234 6333. 106 units, licensed restaurant - ✪$120-148.

Hobart Macquarie Motor Inn, 167 Macquarie Street, ☏6234 4442. 104 units, licensed restaurant, pool, spa, sauna - B&LB ✪$120.

Hadley's Hotel, 34 Murray Street, ☏6223 4355. 65 rooms, licensed restaurant, spa, sauna, gym - ✪$180-200.

TASMANIA

SOUTHERN OCEAN

TASMAN SEA

Large built-up area
○ Settlement
Road
Railway
National Park

0 25 50 75 100 km

Map drawn by MAPgraphics

Sandy Bay Motor Inn, 429 Sandy Bay Road, Sandy Bay, ✆6223 7355. 31 units, games room, bbq - ✪$99.
Theatre Royal Hotel Hobart, 31 Campbell St, ✆6234 6925. 8 units, licensed restaurant - ✪$65-100.
Argyle Motor Lodge, cnr Argyle &

Lewis St, ✆6234 2488. 36 units - ✪$88-102.

Budget
Globe, 178 Davey St, ✆6223 5800. 12 rooms - ✪$40.
Brunswick, 67 Liverpool St, ✆6234

4981. 20 rooms, licensed restaurant (closed Sunday) - ✪$50.

Adelphi Court YHA, 17 Stokes Street, New Town, ✆6228 4829. 16 rooms - ✪$20-63.

New Sydney Hotel & Backpacker Inn, 87 Bathurst Street, ✆6234 4516. Room only (dorm) $18 single.

Transit Centre, 1st Floor, Redline Coaches, 199 Collins St, ✆6231 2400. Room only ✪$17 single.

Narrara Backpackers, 88 Goulburn St, ✆6231 3191. Room only ✪$20 single.

Caravan Parks

Sandy Bay Caravan Park, 1 Peel Street, Sandy Bay, ✆6225 1264. 181 sites - powered sites ✪$19 for two, park cabins $66 for two, on-site vans $44 for two.

Treasure Island Caravan Park, 235 Bass Highway, Burnie, ✆6421 1925. 73 sites - powered sites ✪$9 for two, park cabins $63 for two, on-site vans $38 for two.

Eating Out

Hobart caters for all tastes, and like any major population centre, its food outlets vary from quick takeaway to the more sophisticated and sedate air of the restaurants listed below. Generally speaking, the fish dishes in the Hobart restaurants are something about which the city can boast.

Licensed Restaurants

Mure's Upper Deck, Victoria Dock, ✆6231 1999 - seafood - licensed - open daily.

Prossers on the Beach, Beach Road, Sandy Bay, ✆6225 2276 - a la carte & seafood - licensed - open Tues-Sat.

The Revolving Restaurant, Wrest Point Casino, 410 Sandy Bay Road, Sandy Bay, ✆6221 1719 - modern Australian - licensed - open Mon-Fri from noon.

Meehan's, Hotel Grand Chancellor, 1 Davey Street, ✆6235 4535 - delicious Tasmanian produce in a variety of flavours - excellent but not cheap - licensed.

Sisco's on the Pier, Level 1, Murray Street Pier, ✆6223 2059 - seafood - open Mon-Sat for dinner, Mon-Fri for lunch - licensed.

Le Provencal, 417 Macquarie Street, South Hobart, ✆6224 252

- French cuisine - licensed.

Gusto Italiano, 186 Collins Street, Hobart, ☏6223 3595 - Italian - open Mon-Sat for dinner, Mon-Fri for lunch - licensed & BYO.

Flavour of India, 196 Macquarie Street, Hobart, ☏6223 5733 - open for dinner seven days - take-away available - licensed & BYO.

The Astor Grill, 157 Macquarie Street, ☏6234 3809 - licensed.

Thai Hut, 80 Elizabeth Str eet, Hobart, ☏6234 4914 - licensed.

A Splash of Paris, Elizabeth Street Pier, ☏6224 2200 - modern menu with French influence - open daily - licensed.

Concetta's Pizza & Restaurant, 213 Elizabeth Street, Hobart, ☏6234 9901 - pizza & Italian - open daily.

Marti Zucco's, 364 Elizabeth Street, North Hobart, ☏6234 9611 - Italian - open seven days for dinner, Thu-Sat for lunch - licensed & BYO.

Blue Skies, Murray Street Pier, ☏6224 3747 - cafe, restaurant and bar - waterfront location and casual setting - a variety of international mains - licensed.

Anatolia, 321 Elizabeth Street, North Hobart, ☏6231 1770 - authentic Turkish flavours - BYO - dinner Tue-Sun.

Mit Zitrone, 333 Elizabeth Street, North Hobart, ☏6234 8113 - modern Australian dishes prepared with flair and moderately-priced - an award winner - open for dinner Wed-Sun, lunch seven days - BYO.

Local Transport

The Metropolitan Transport Trust buses depart from the central business district for the outer suburbs. Day Rover tickets are available for ☼$3.40 and may be used between 9am-4.30pm and after 6pm on weekdays, and all day on weekends.

Bicycle Hire

Derwent Bike Hire, Regatta Grounds, Queens Domain, ☏6268 6161.

Points of Interest

Hobart has more than 90 buildings which have been classified by the National Trust, 32 of them are in Macquarie Street and 31 in Davey Street, but apart from those there are numerous other well maintained buildings still in use today. They are some of the city's most attractive features.

The National Trust has regular walking tours of the city on Saturday mornings. They start at 9.30am and last 2-3 hours.

If you are not in Hobart on a Saturday some of the more interesting buildings are:

Parliament House, part of which was originally the Customs House

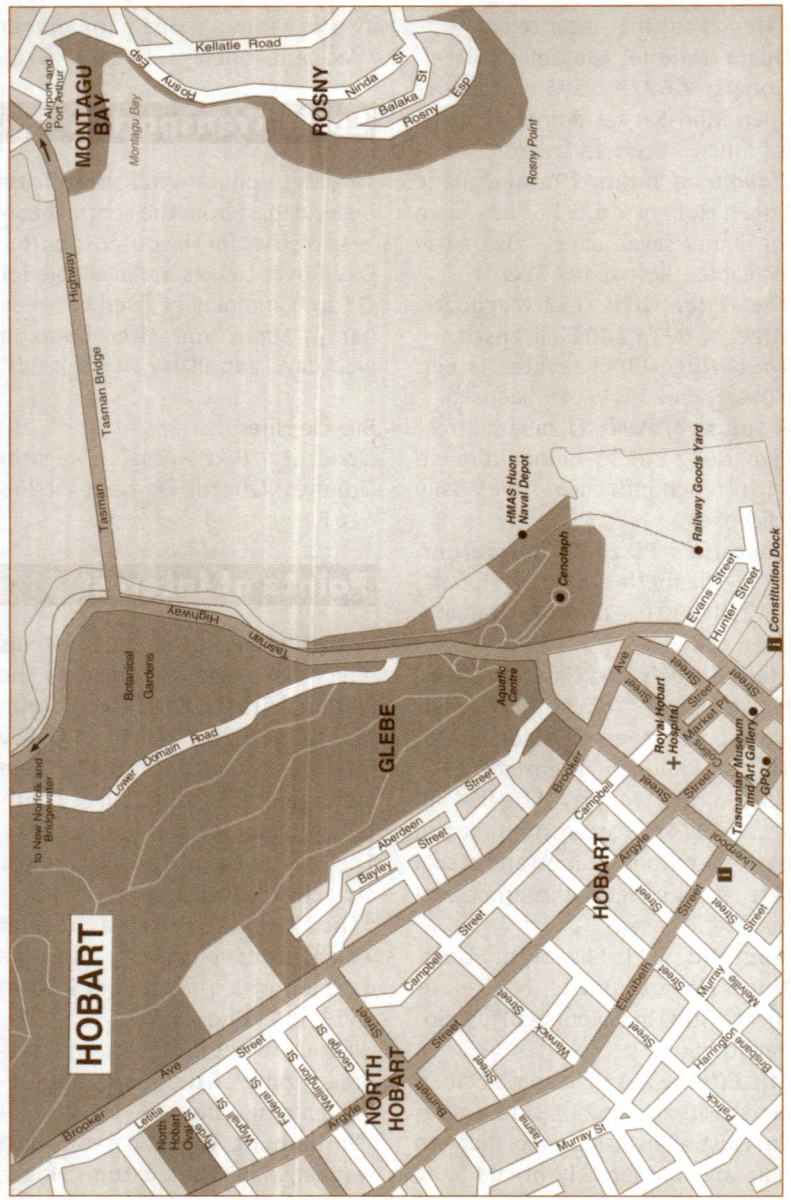

HOBART

MONTAGU BAY
To Airport and Port Arthur
Kellatie Road
ROSNY
Ninda St
Balaka St
Rosny
Rosny Point
Montagu Bay
Rosny Esp

Tasman Bridge
Tasman Highway

HMAS Huon Naval Depot
Railway Goods Yard
Cenotaph
Constitution Dock
Evans Street
Hunter Street

Tasman Highway
Botanical Gardens

to New Norfolk and Bridgewater
Lower Domain Road

GLEBE
Aquatic Centre
Davey Street
Brooker
Ava Street

Royal Hobart Hospital
Tasmanian Museum and Art Gallery
GPO
Market Pl
Bank Street

Aberdeen Street
Bayley Street
Street
Campbell Street
Liverpool Street

HOBART
Argyle Street
Molle Street
Murray Street
Elizabeth Street
Harrington
Patrick
Melville Street
Brisbane Street

Brooker Ave
Letitia Street
Wignall St
North Hobart Oval St
Federal St
Wellington St
George St
Argyle St
Burnett Street
Warrick Street
Tasma Street
Murray St
NORTH HOBART

Street
Campbell Street

built between 1835 and 1840. The stone for the building came from what is now a lake in the grounds of Government House. The cellars, once the bonded store, still display broad arrows on the brickwork. The Legislative Council chamber has housed that body since 1856. The House of Assembly chamber is housed in a wing built in 1939. Parliament House is situated at the lower end of Murray Street opposite the wharves and is fronted by spacious lawns and gardens.

Government House, ©6234 2611, is built in Tudor Gothic style. It has 70 rooms and 50 chimneys, and took from 1840 to 1858 to complete.

The **Theatre Royal** in Campbell Street - Australia's oldest theatre is built in the regency style and is a reminder of a more gracious era.

The **Customs House Hotel**, cnr Morrison and Murray Streets, ©6234 6645, was first licensed in 1846. This was the prototype for the hotels of the old Hobart waterfront of the 19th century.

Battery Point, save for the modern hotels, looks much the same as it did a century ago. Houses and cottages are packed into a jumble of narrow streets and lanes which gives the area a maritime atmosphere. The oldest building is the 1818 signal station which was used to relay messages from another sta-

tion on Mt. Nelson. There is a fine terrace of Georgian sandstone warehouses on one side of Salamanca Place which now house restaurants, galleries and some offices. Open-air markets are now held on the other side, where the "New Wharf" used to be, every Saturday in summer. In winter the markets move into one of the warehouses. St George's Church stationed nearby has Australia's oldest Classical Revival spire.

Other interesting churches include **St. Mary's Cathedral**, Harrington Street, **St. David's Anglican Cathedral**, cnr Macquarie & Murray Streets, the **Holy Trinity Church**, North Hobart and **The Scots Church and the Uniting Church** (formerly Congregational), New Town. All of these churches were built in the fine architectural tradition of the great cathedrals of Europe and Britain. The imposing St Mary's was built on the site of St. Virgilius, the first Catholic Church to be built in Tasmania. Much of St. Mary's sandstone work had to be rebuilt as the original foundations were faulty. St David's is an example of the Gothic Revival style. It's solid silver altar vessels were presented by King George III in 1803. Scots Church was first knows as St Andrews, and the 1830 building is notable for its heavy battlements. The New Town church was built in 1842 in Romanesque style.

The historic home **Runnymede** in Bay Road, New Town, was built in 1844. It was a family home from that time until the 1970s. It is now owned by the National Trust, and is ✆open for inspection daily 10am-4.30pm, except Good Friday, the month of July and Christmas Day. An admission fee of ✆$7.70 adults and $5.50 children is charged, ✆6278 1269.

Penitentiary Chapel and Criminal Courts, cnr Brisbane and Campbell Streets, were built in the early 1830s. Inspection is daily 10am-2pm, except Good Friday and Christmas Day. An admission fee of ✆$7.70 adults and $5.50 children is charged, ✆6231 0911.

Hobart's main shopping area is around the **Cat & Fiddle Arcade**, which has an animated clock that is activated every hour on the hour. You will see the cat, fiddle, dog, dish, cow and spoon!

The **Tasman Bridge** is one of the main landmarks of the city, and spans the Derwent Estuary just to the north of the city centre. In 1975 it was struck by a ship, causing part of the roadway of the bridge to collapse, killing 12 people. The bridge was closed for over a year, effectively creating two population centres. The only way over the Estuary was through a winding temporary bridge floated on pontoons.

The **Royal Tasmanian Botanical Gardens**, ✆6234 6299, and Queen's Domain, where you can relax after a hectic morning or afternoon sightseeing, are near Government House. If you are hungry, there is a pleasant restaurant in the Garden grounds, ✆6234 4849.

The **Wrest Point Casino**, ✆6225 0112, is Hobart's other landmark. It was Australia's first legal casino, and is as well known as a convention centre.

Anglesea Barracks is the nation's oldest military establishment. Some of the buildings date back to the early 1800s and the guns outside the gate were cast before 1774. It is ✆open daily, and guided tours are held on Tuesday morning at 11am.

Hobart's city centre is very close to the **harbour**. From certain vantage points, it often appears that boats are moored in the streets. Most of the waterfront is recreational area which is frequented by locals and visitors alike. The annual blue water classic, The Sydney to Hobart Yacht Race begins on Boxing Day, and finishes at Constitution Dock right in the heart of the city.

There are quite a few interesting museums in Hobart.

The **Tasmanian Museum and Art Gallery** is housed at 5 Argyle

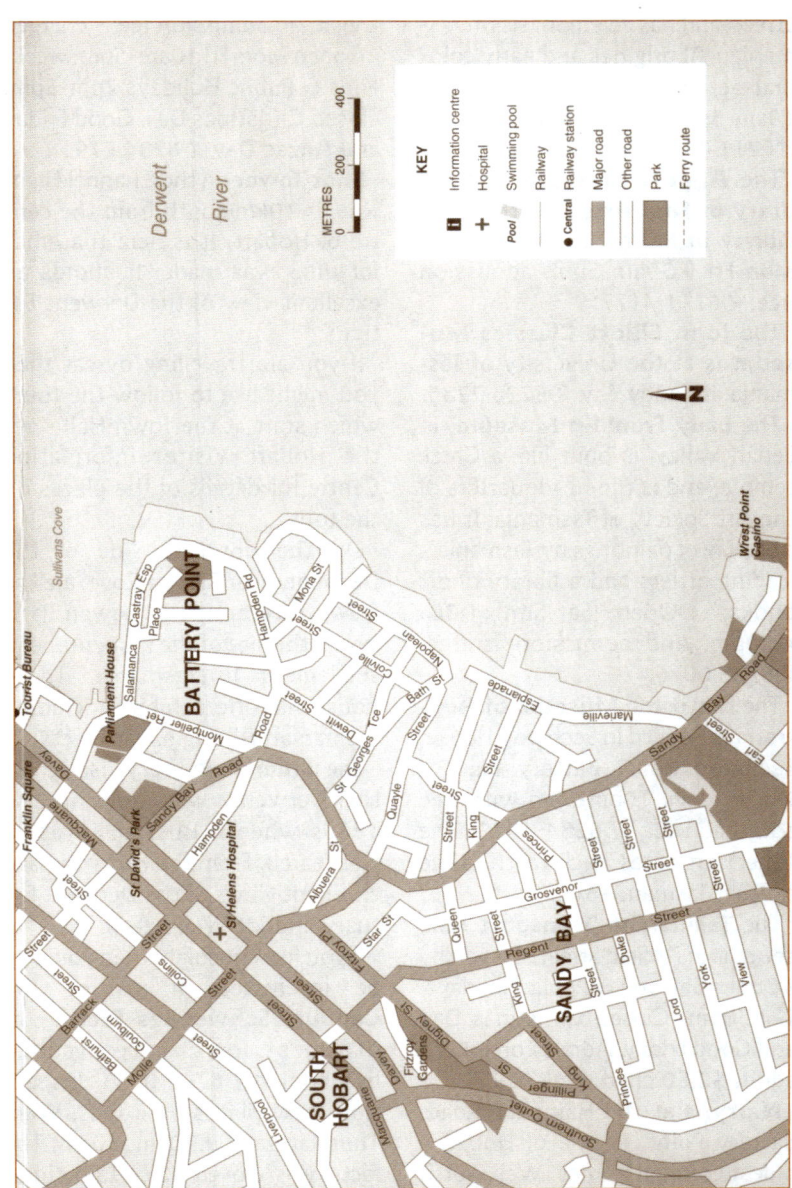

KEY

ℹ Information centre
✚ Hospital
Pool Swimming pool
⊶ Railway
● Central Railway station
Major road
Other road
Park
Ferry route

METRES
0   200   400

N

Derwent River

Sullivans Cove

Tourist Bureau

Franklin Square

Parliament House

BATTERY POINT

Castray Esp

Salamanca Place

Montpelier Ret

Hampden Rd

Mona St

Cromwell Street

De Witt Street

Napoleon Street

Bath St

Esplanade

Colville Street

St Georges Tce

Quayle Street

King Street

Marieville Esplanade

Wrest Point Casino

Sandy Bay Road

Macquarie Street

Davey Street

St David's Park

St Helens Hospital

Hampden Road

Sandy Bay Road

Albuera St

Star St

Fitzroy St

Kelvin St

Queen Street

Regent Street

Grosvenor Street

Princes Street

King Street

Duke Street

Lord Street

York Street

View Street

SANDY BAY

SOUTH HOBART

Bathurst Street

Goulburn Street

Molle Street

Barrack Street

Collins Street

Liverpool Street

Murray Street

Harrington St

Fitzroy Gardens

Macquarie St

Pillinger Drive

King Street

Southern Outlet

Princes Street

Street, and has an emphasis on Tasmanian Aborigines and early colonial activities. It is ☉open daily 10am-5pm and admission is free, ✆6211 4177.

The **Allport Museum and Library of Fine Arts** is in the State Library in Murray Street - ☉open Mon-Fri 9.30am-5pm, admission free, ✆6211 4177.

The **John Elliott Classics Museum** is at the University of Tasmania at Sandy Bay, ✆6226 2235.

The **Lady Franklin Museum**, in Lenah Valley, is built like a Greek temple, and is the headquarters of the Art Society of Tasmania. It has a display of paintings by Tasmania's leading artists and a library of art books. ☉Open Sat-Sun 1.30-4.30pm, and admission is free, ✆6228 0076.

The **Maritime Museum of Australia** is housed in Secheron House, Secheron Road, Battery Point - ☉open daily 10pm-5pm with free admission fee, ✆6234 1427. The collection dates back to the time of Abel Tasman, 1642.

The **Tasmanian Transport Museum** is in Anfield Street, Glenorchy - ☉open Sat-Sun & Public Holidays, 1-4.30pm. Closed Christmas Day and Good Friday. Admission is ✪$5 adult, $2.50 child, ✆6272 7721.

Narryna at 103 Hampden Road, Battery Point, is one of Hobart's oldest colonial homes. Well worth a visit, an admission fee is charged - ☉open Mon-Fri 10am-5pm, weekends & Public Holidays 2pm-5pm, closed Christmas Day, Good Friday and Anzac Day, ✆6234 2791.

Shot Tower on the Channel Highway, is 10km south from the centre of Hobart. It is here that shot for rifles was made. It affords an excellent view of the Derwent Estuary.

If you are travelling by car then you might like to follow the tours which start at the Town Hall - see the Hobart Visitor Information Centre for details of the places on the tour.

On the opposite side of the Derwent, near Risdon Cove, are the **Bowen pyramids** in Bowen Park. It was the site of the first european settlement in Tasmania. These house historic exhibits including Tasmanian Aboriginal artefacts.

The **Bellerive Battery** also across the Derwent, was built in the 1880s when a Russian invasion was feared. From the Fort you have excellent views of the Derwent Estuary and Mt Wellington.

If you like chocolate then you may be interested in visiting the **Cadbury/Schweppes Factory** at Claremont. Tours can be organised by phoning ✆6249 0333. Inspections take places on ☉Tues, Wed, Thurs at 9am, 9.30am, 10am. The factory is closed at certain times during the year because of annual leave by employees, so check before you visit. Children must be accompanied by an adult.

The old **Cascade Brewery** is a striking relic of colonial times, and is set picturesquely beside a stream in the shadow of Mt Wellington. Guided tours are available, ✆6221 8300.

Mt Wellington, 1270m (4,167 feet), has many walking tracks and offers a superb view of Hobart, but it can get cold up there even in summer. In winter it is often dusted with snow.

Festivals

The Salamanca Arts Festival, featuring performing arts and craft displays, is held in September.

Facilities

Hobart has all the facilities you would expect of a capital city - horse racing, car racing, lawn bowls, golf courses, squash and tennis courts, swimming pools, cricket and football ovals, convention facilities etc.

Outlying Attractions

The Derwent Valley

Head north along the Brooker Highway past Claremont and the Cadbury factory, and then take the Lyell Highway at Granton.

Granton is where you can see the Bridgewater Causeway which was built by convict labour.

Boyer is 32km (20 miles) from Hobart. The news-print mills here supply about half of Australia's news-print.

New Norfolk, which is a few kilometres further on, could almost be a village of England with its quaint old buildings. It is classified by the National Trust as a historic town. It is possible to get to New Norfolk by launch from Hobart. Hops are grown in the surrounding countryside.

Plenty, where brown and rainbow trout are raised at the 'Salmon Ponds', is 11km (7 miles) from New Norfolk.

Mt Field West National Park is 73km (45 miles) from Hobart and well worth a visit. It consists of a high plateau dotted with high peaks and tarns (lakes). The National Parks and Wildlife have huts for hire up in the Park, ✆6288 1526. They are rudimentary but are a great to use as a base for day long hiking excursions to various tarns and outcrops. The paths are well marked, but I would only advise this sort of activity during the summer months. For winter, there are a number of ski lodges up here and a number of tow bars. Nearer to the

entrance, and easily accessible, are the attractive Russell Falls whose rock formation is in a series of levels over which the water tumbles.

South of Hobart

Kingston-Blackmans Bay is south along the coast and one of Hobart's fastest growing outer suburban areas. It has attractive beaches (little surf) and picnic areas. Blackmans Bay has a small blowhole, and lookouts at Doughty Point and Piersons Point offer superb views of Bruny Island and Storm Bay.

Margate, which is 19km (12 miles) from Hobart, has a motor museum and an unusual market. The market has its headquarters in Tasma-

nia's last passenger train. The converted carriages house toy-makers, glass blowers, woodworkers, artists and other creative pursuits.

Snug, a few kilometres further south on the Channel Highway, is an aptly named village, and a little further on some 34km (21 miles) south of Hobart is Kettering. The terminal for the Bruny Island vehicular ferry is here.

Bruny Island is a popular holiday destination for campers, although I would not be too keen camping here during winter. The main township is Adventure Bay on the east coast of South Bruny Island. The island has a narrow neck, and on North Bruny there is an aero club and airstrip with a memorial to some of the country's early navigators. At Fluted Cape at the southern end of Adventure Bay on South Bruny Island is the spot where Captain Cook landed in his voyage down the east coast of Tasmania. There is also a Museum of that cruel and talented British seaman, Captain Bligh, on this part of the island. For more information, contact Bruny D'Entrecasteaux Visitor Centre, Ferry Road, Kettering, ✆(03) 6267 4494.

Huonville is south and inland from the areas mentioned above. It is 37km (23 miles) south of Hobart and is the commercial centre of the area. It is a pretty area which has

Above: The Derwent River, Tasmania   Below: Coles bay in Freycinet National Park, Tasmania

Above: Victoria Dock on Hobart Harbour, Tasmania   Below: Mt Field National Park, Tasmani

pleasant rural and seascape scenery. The Huon Valley was a large apple exporter before Britain joined the EEC. There is an apple industry museum here, as well as a motor museum and a couple of hotels. The population is a little over 1300 people. A cruise on the 'Huon Pride' is a good way to see the area. Information is available at the centre on the Esplanade, ✆(03) 6264 1838.

Greevston is a further 31km (19 miles) south of Huonville on Port Huon. It is the administrative centre of the Esperance Municipality which includes Macquarie Island some 1000 (621 miles) further south. Timber is an important industry in this area. There are stands of softwood, which is used in shipbuilding. Cruises are available on the D'Entrecasteaux Channel and South Coast. The Visitor Information Centre is in Church Street, ✆(03) 6297 1836.

Hartz Mountains National Park is reached through Greevston. It has some of the wildest and most spectacular scenery in the world, and is said to resemble the Canadian Rockies. For information on fees and road access, contact the Parks & Wildlife Service in nearby Dover on ✆6298 1577.

Dover is a further 21km (13 miles) south of Greevston on the coast. It is the last petrol stop for motorists heading into the lonely and rugged country towards South-East Cape. There are two fish processing factories there.

Southport is another 21km (13 miles) further south from Dover. Nearby is the Hastings Thermal Pool, which is 27C (80F) all year round, and Fairy Caves - ✆6298 3209. There are daily tours of the caves and a restaurant nearby, although there is no accommodation available.

Lune River is a popular place with gem collectors. A tramway still operates taking tourists for a 6km trip through bushland from the township to The Deep Hole across the bay from Southport.

North of Hobart

Richmond is as elegant today as it was in the 1820s when it was an important military post and convict station linking Hobart with Port Arthur. Situated only 27km (17 miles) north of Hobart on the Coal River, its village green is shaded by leafy green trees, and its old stone buildings house galleries, tea shops, craft boutiques and museums. Old Hobart Town, cnr Henry & Bridge Streets, is a stunning model re-creation of the convict-built town of the 1820s, which you can stroll through at your leisure. The Maze and Tea Rooms, 13 Bridge Street, are ✆open daily 10am-5pm, ✆6260 2451. The Richmond Gaol

is ☉open daily 9am-5pm except Christmas Day and Good Friday, ©6260 2127. The bridge spanning the Coal River is convict built, as are most sandstone buildings in this town. St John's Catholic Church, just up from the bridge, was built in 1836. It is the oldest Catholic Church in Australia, as up until the 1830s public worship in the Catholic faith was outlawed.

If you wish to stay overnight there are a number of hotels in the town. (The telephone area code is the same as Hobart - 03.) *Prospect House*, 1384 Richmond Road, ©6260 2207 - ✪$135; *Hatchers Richmond Manor*, 73 Prossers Road, ©6260 2622 - ✪$85-95 (both have restaurants); and *Richmond Cabin & Tourist Park*, 48 Middle Tree Road, ©6260 2192 - powered sites ✪$16-18 for two, on-site vans $35-45, cabins $45-55.

Tasmania's Holiday coast extends from St. Helens, with the Bay of Fires slightly to the north where many trekkers camp, through to Orford in the south off which is Maria Island, now a National Park. The island is serviced by a ferry in the summer. In winter, check before you leave, ©6257 1589. The coast has sheltered beaches, rocky coastline, terrific surf and great fishing. For those used to balmy water temperature, such as most 'mainlanders' (a term used by Tasmanians to describe the rest of Australia) then you will be surprised to find that even in summer the water temperature is cold. You cannot stay in for too long. Cramps are common.

Continuing north, Sorell has charming B&Bs, Orford boasts at least 8 decent motels, villas and guest houses.

Swansea

Situated 137km (85 miles) from Hobart and 51km (32 miles) north of Triabunna, Swansea is a pretty seaside town with has 2 caravan parks, more than 10 home host accommodation outlets, and 3 motels (around ✪$60-90 double).

To get to Coles Bay, a very popular tourist spot inundated with Tasmanians camping during the summer, you have to travel 32km (20 miles) north before turning south along 32km (20 miles) of partly dirt road. Coles Bay is in the vicinity of Freycinet Peninsula which is a very scenic spot.

Bicheno

The town of Bicheno is 43km (27 miles) north of Swansea, and is a very attractive spot. The beaches are covered in an incredibly soft silver sand that is unique to the area. Off the main beach is Diamond Island, home to the fairy penguin, which can be reached at low tide. Keep an eye on the time and tide because the behaviour of the penguins can be very absorbing, and you may find that you have to swim back to the beach. Bicheno was a whaling station, and is now a popular fishing and boating spot. There is a sealife centre, and East Coast

Natureworld (✆6375 1311, admission ✪$11 adult, $5.50 child) nearby. The surfing off Cape Lodt is usually very good.

Accommodation here is no problem with 3 caravan parks - *Bicheno Caravan Park*, 52 Burgess Street, ✆6375 1280, powered sites, $14 for two. There are over 20 hotels, motels and guest houses, such as *Silver Sands Resort*, Burgess Street, ✆6375 1266 - 35 rooms - ✪$50-85. There is a couple of restaurants in Burgess Street - *Cyrano* and *Mary Harvey's*.

St Marys is 46km (29 miles) north of Bicheno and slightly inland. It has a hotel with 14 rooms available. It is at the junction of the Esk Main Road and the Tasman Highway.

St Helens

This bayside town is on Georges Bay, a further 37km (23 miles) north. It is a popular holiday and commercial fishing centre, and the most northern town on the east coast. From here the road swings westwards towards Scottsdale through some beautiful mountainous country. The permanent population of St Helens is 2000 people, but this swells during the summer. It has a variety of clubs - bowling, sailing, and golf with facilities for boating, water skiing, and surfing, although you get good surf further to the north on the Bay of Fires around Binalong Bay. If you are staying overnight many backpackers camp here on the beach.

We found that if you want to swim every day and go to see a few sights and not rush yourself, but take in the feel of the east coast-seeing the fairy penguins, having a delightful lunch in one of the pubs in the towns along the coast - the trip takes two days. You can leave Hobart in the morning, go to Port Arthur for the day and then head north stopping overnight in either Swansea or Bicheno. Next day you can take your time until you get to St Helens, and stay there for the next night. The following day you can head towards Launceston, a pleasant day-long drive.

Prices of accommodation vary considerably depending on the standard and the season. Here we have a selection, with prices for a double room per night, which should be used as a guide only. The telephone area code for St Helens is 03.

Bayside Inn, 2 Cecilia Street, ©6376 1466. 27 units, licensed restaurant, indoor heated pool - ✪$50-115.

Anchor Wheel, 61 Tully Street, ©6376 1358. 7 units, licensed restaurant (closed Sun), barbecue - ✪$50-70

Cecilia House, 78 Cecilia Street, ©6376 1723. 3 rooms, unlicensed restaurant - ✪$95 including breakfast.

Artnor Lodge, 71 Cecilia Street, ©6376 1234. 6 rooms, barbecue, playground - B&B, ✪$50-75 including breakfast.

St Helens Youth Hostel, 5 Cameron Street, ©6376 1661. 32 guests in 4 dorms, dining room - from ✪$15 each.

Warrawee Guest House, Tasman Highway, ©6376 1987. 7 rooms, dining room, barbecue - ✪$130-160 including breakfast.

Hillcrest Caravan Park, Chimney Heights Road, ©6376 3298. (No pets) 80 sites, playground, barbecue - powered sites ✪$15 for two, cabins $50-70 for two.

St Helens Caravan Park, 2 Penelope Street, ©6376 1290. (No pets) 100 sites, excellent facilities - powered sites ✪$17-22, on-site vans $25-40 for two, cabins $40-80 for two.

Port Arthur & the Tasman Peninsula

Population 1,500

Port Arthur is 95km (60 miles) south-east of Hobart on the Tasman Peninsula. The Settlement is joined to the main island by Eaglehawk Neck, a narrow strip of land only 200m across, thus making it an ideal location for a penal colony.

Climate

The average annual rainfall is 1031mm (40.6ins). The wettest six months are from May to October. It has 8 sunshine hours per day in summer, 7 in spring, 5 in autumn, and 4 in winter.

Characteristics

This old penal settlement was home to 12,500 convicts who served in a rehabilitation/punishment station and lived under the threat of the lash, and an experimental isolation system that often drove them to madness. Escape was rare and many remained to be buried in mass graves on the Isle of the Dead. Today, Port Arthur rests in peace amidst English oaks and expansive green lawns that roll down to the water's edge.

How to Get There

By Bus

You can take one of the organised tours from Hobart (enquire at the Visitor Information Centre) or you can catch Hobart Coaches' service which leave Hobart Mon-Fri at 4pm, and leave Port Arthur at 7.45am, ©6233 4232.

By Car

From Hobart, take the Tasman Highway to Sorell and then the Arthur Highway.

Tourist Information

There is an information centre at the Port Arthur Historic Site, ✆6251 2371, and the staff are happy to provide you with any information you need.

Accommodation

There are quite a few motels and hotels on the road to Port Arthur, and as it can be visited in a day from Hobart there is no problem ensuring you have a bed for the night. The accommodation varies depending on price. Here we have a selection, with prices for a double room per night, which should be used as a guide only. The telephone area code is 03.

Port Arthur Motor Inn, Safety Cove Road, just past Port Arthur proper on the way to the Remarkable Cave, ✆6250 2101. 35 rooms, licensed restaurant - ✪$110.

Fox and Hounds Motor Inn, Arthur Highway, about 2km (1.5miles) north, ✆6250 2217. 28 rooms, licensed restaurant, playground, swimming pool, tennis court, games room, - ✪$95-125.

Port Arthur Villas, Safety Cove Road, ✆6550 2239. 6 units (holiday flats) - ✪$90-115.

Port Arthur Holiday World, Arthur Highway, Stewarts Bay, ✆6250 2262. 18 cottages (holiday flats), barbecue - ✪$90-115.

Youth Hostel, 27 Champ Street, ✆6550 2311. ✪$17-60 per person/night.

Eating Out

There are four restaurants where you are sure to have a pleasant meal: *Bush Mill Grill*, ✆6250 2221, *Commandant's Table Restaurant*, ✆6250 2101, *Red Fox Restaurant*, ✆6250 2217 and *Felons Restaurant*, ✆1800 659 101.

Points of Interest

The whole of the Tasman Peninsula can be seen as "convict country" although, like most country areas, it also has farms, orchards and small industry, with State Reserves and holiday homes near the beaches.

Port Arthur is the pre-eminent symbol of Australia's 19th century convict system. One which we would regard today as being anything but enlightened. Some believe that out of such a system there emerged many national characteristics especially the Aussie attitude to freedom and authority. Some

claim mateship as well, but the author prefers to ascribe this theory to life and survival in the bush, and its further forging in the hell of wars.

The settlement operated from 1830 to 1877, as a timber producing "sawing station", and later as an industrial prison. Many of the convicts were recidivists, others were political prisoners, and they were therefore treated harshly. Towards 1877, with fewer convicts in Tasmania being sent for secondary punishment, life in the prison became less austere.

After closure, most of the land and buildings were auctioned off, with new residents renaming it Carnarvon township. Bushfires virtually destroyed Carnarvon in 1895

and 1897 - only two out of perhaps 300 wooden buildings are left, together with brick and stone ruins and officer's houses.

What is left of the old penal settlement is atmospheric and following recent restoration, Port Arthur today is Tasmania's premier historic site.

The whole township area is maintained by the National Parks and Wildlife Service.

The $4.5 million Visitor Centre at the **Port Arthur Historic Site** opened in 1999. The Interpretation Centre has an imaginative and interactive method of imparting information on the site's convict heritage. In the complex is a restaurant, gift shop and cafe.

The **Museum** in the old Lunatic

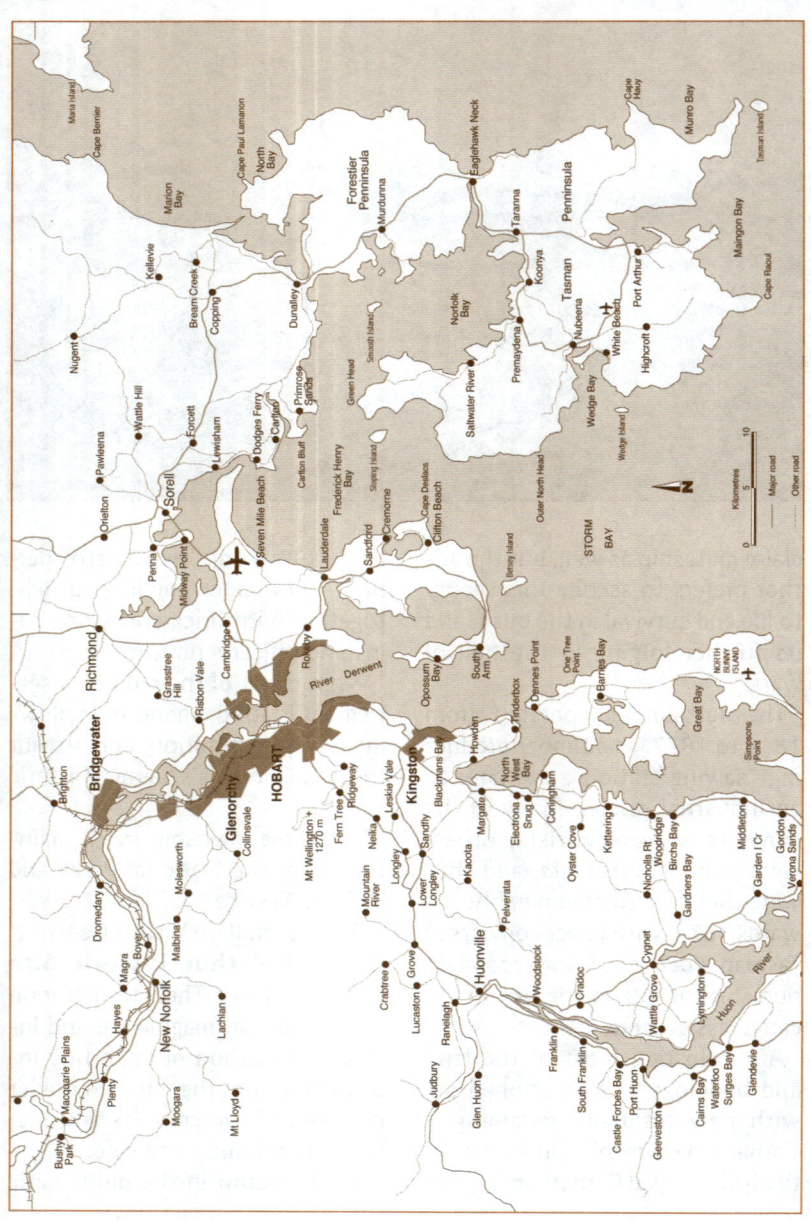

Asylum contains displays, an audio-visual theatre, a scale model of Port Arthur up to the 1870s, and a shop.

Officers' houses, newly restored, are open for inspection. The Commandant's residence shows details of 1800s construction practices, and furniture and furnishings from the period. Smith O'Brien's cottage gives an insight into the history of Irish and political prisoners. The Medical Officer's house reflects 1850s living. In 1985 this house was awarded - The Museum of the Year.

In the **Model Prison**, the solitary confinement cells can still be seen, and anyone who has experienced, even for a few minutes, the claustrophobic darkness of the cells, can well understand why one of the larger buildings in the prison complex was the Lunatic Asylum.

Other ruins include the **Penitentiary**, the **Church** (which is perhaps the most famous of the buildings as it is featured in most tourist literature), the **Guard Tower** and the **Paupers Mess**. These are perhaps the most evocative of convict life at the settlement.

Point Puer, the boys' prison, is across the bay. Here lads between the ages of 8-18 served after being convicted of crimes in Ireland or England. The ruins of the bakers' ovens and the old school are all that remain today.

The Isle of the Dead, the Port Arthur cemetery, is just off Point Puer. It can be reached by regular ferry. Here, in 0.7ha (1.7 acres), lie 2,000 convicts and free, an indication of the harshness of this convict prison.

The **Museum of Records** has actual records of the transportees sent to Tasmania (a long list of prisoner names, their crimes and punishment). The minimum term of transportation was seven years, which was imposed for such offences as stealing a lamb, a sheep, a pig. One prisoner, Joseph Parker, was transported for life for stealing a silk handkerchief. On another list, several men and women were sentenced to transportation for life for theft of articles of little value. In one case, the sentence of death for stealing 24/- was commuted to transportation for life. Even children received long gaol sentences.

Guided tours leave all day on the half hour, or you may wish to hire a tape recorder for an individual tour and ramble around Port Arthur. Entry fee to the site is ✪$20 for adults and $9 for children.

Facilities

You can swim in the beautiful bays, fish, go canoeing, boating and bushwalking.

Outlying Attractions

There were several subsidiary establishments on the peninsula, the Coal Mines, the Saltwater Agricultural Station, timber mills at Premaydena and Koonya together with the guard posts at Eaglehawk Neck and Dunalley. Semaphore stations were located on line-of-sight around the Peninsula and up to Hobart.

Cascades Cottage, Koonya, is privately owned, as are many of these outstations now. Accommodation is offered at the here in 4-star comfort.

Coal Mines Historic Site is an interesting place to explore, and is near a camping area in the northwestern part of the peninsula. The Mines in the convict days served a dual purpose. They provided fuel for use in the colony, and were used as a punishment centre. In producing 80 tons daily the convicts were basically worked to death here. Cells were even built into the mine galleries. After 1848 the Coal Mines were privately operated, and were abandoned in 1877 after an underground fire.

Eaglehawk Neck is the narrow strip of land joining the Tasman and Forestier Peninsulas. During convict times, several dogs were chained close to each other along the Neck making escape virtually impossible. Nearby are several coastal formations - the Devil's Kitchen, Tasman's Arch and Blowhole as well as the Tessellated Pavement which looks like well-laid large pavers. These natural formations are well worth a visit. They are unique in Australia. Just keep your kids away from the edge; some have been known to try to find a way down into the Devil's Kitchen.

Dootown is nearby. It is a picturesque group of holiday homes, and almost all the houses have names incorporating Doo, e.g. Much-a-Doo, Didgeri-Doo, Doo Little. I suppose that is one approach to life.

Remarkable Cave is another blowhole which, unlike the Devil's Kitchen formation, is accessible at low tide. This is 7km (4.4 miles) south of Port Arthur, and an after-dinner walk there reveals spectacular coastal scenery and 300m high sea cliffs. Large binoculars have been placed at the car turning circle. The scenery at Cape Raul is quite spectacular as years of weathering have caused the rock to split vertically, creating an organ pipe effect.

Nubeena, on the shore of Parson Bay, is the largest town on the Tasman Peninsula, and is a popular resort. In convict days, timber cut from the hinterland was shipped to England from nearby Wedge Bay.

Launceston

Population 86,000

Launceston is Australia's largest inland port, and Tasmania's second largest city. It is situated at the head of the Tamar River at the junction of the north and south Esk, in the central northern region of Tasmania.

Climate

Average temperatures: January max 21C (70F) - min 13C (55F); July max 13C (55F) - 5C (41F). The average rainfall is approximately 750mm (29.5 ins) with the wettest period being from May to October. The Sunshine hours are Summer 7, Autumn (Fall) 4, Winter 3, Spring 6.

Characteristics

Known as the 'garden city' because of its abundance of well established beautiful public and private gardens, Launceston nestles in a wide river valley amid lush green countryside. It has given rise to the description of Tasmania as 'this other England'.

How to Get There

By Sea

Spirit of Tasmania passenger/car ferry operates between Melbourne and Devonport, ©9206 6211. Tasmania's Own Redline coaches operate a service from Devonport to Launceston, ©(03) 6336 1446.

The DevilCat Express catamaran passenger/car ferry operates Port Welshpool, Gippsland, Victoria to George Town with a coach to Launceston daily return during peak season (summer) and 5 times a week during off season (not Tues & Thurs).

By Bus

Tasmania's Own Redline coaches operate a Hobart/Launceston and Launceston/Devonport, Burnie, Wynyard and Smithton service.

By Car

The trip from Hobart 199km (124 miles), via the Midlands Highway, takes approximately 2.5 hours. From Burnie 143km (89 miles) it takes about the same time. From the east coast (St. Helens) via Scottsdale, the trip is again about 2.5 hours, however via St. Marys it can take about 2 hours 45 minutes.

Tourist Information

The Gateway Tasmania Visitor Information Centre is on the corner of St John and Paterson Streets, ©(03) 6336 3133. It is ©open Mon-Fri 9am-5pm, Sat 9am-3pm, Sun & Public Holidays 9am-12pm.

Accommodation

Launceston, with many hotels/motels, boasts of first class accommodation, and also caters for moderate budgets. Prices vary considerably depending on the standard of accommodation and the season.

Here we have a selection, with prices for a double room per night, which should be used as a guide only. The telephone area code is 03.
Novotel Launceston, 29 Cameron Street, ©6334 3434. 162 rooms, licensed restaurant - ✿$164.
Country Club Casino, Country Club Ave, Prospect Vale, ©6335 5777. 104 rooms, licensed restaurant, bistro, heated indoor pool, spa, sauna, tennis, squash, golf - ✿$255-275.
Hotel Tasmania, 191 Charles Street, ©6331 4966. 25 rooms, licensed restaurant - ✿$45.
Abel Tasman Airport Motor Inn, 303 Hobart Road, Kings Meadow, ©6344 5244. 42 units, licensed restaurant - ✿$90.
Batman Fawkner Inn, 35 Cameron Street, ©6331 7222. 38 rooms, licensed restaurant - ✿$71-85.
Launceston Backpackers, 103 Canning St, ©6334 9779. Room only, ✿$16pp; 25 rooms available.

Caravan Parks

Treasure Island Caravan Park, 94 Glen Dhu Street, ©6344 2600. Powered sites ✿$17 for two, on-site vans $38-40 for two.

Eating Out

Launceston has over 40 restaurants and many additional takeaway outlets. Below we have listed some

restaurants that cater specifically for certain dishes. Most restaurants are BYO and those that are licensed have a corkage charge if you bring your own.

Quigleys, 96 Balfour Street, ✆6331 6971 - game, seafood & French, licensed - open daily.

Restaurant Synergy, 135 George Street, ✆6331 0110 - licensed - open Tues-Sat.

Calabrisella Pizza Restaurant, 56 Wellington Street, ✆6331 1958 - Italian, BYO - open Wed-Mon.

Plate of the Art, 185 Wellington Street, ✆6334 3220 - modern Australian - open for dinner Tue-Sun, lunch Fri - good selection of wines.

Terrace Restaurant, at the Country Club Casino, ✆6335 5775 - refined setting, excellent service - dinner Tue-Sat.

Waterfront Restaurant, 13 Park Street, ✆6334 0554 - take-away also available.

Snappers Seafood Restaurant, 3 Earl Street, ✆6331 9999.

Franco's Italian Restaurant, 42 George Street, ✆6331 8648.

Fu Wah Chinese Restaurant, 63 York Street, ✆6331 6368.

Arpar's Thai Restaurant, cnr Paterson & Charles Streets, ✆6331 2786.

Points of Interest

There are many quaint malls and shopping centres in the city such as the Quadrant Mall and Yorktown Square.

The **Queen Victoria Museum and Art Gallery** in Wellington Street has a unique collection of Tasmanian fauna and Aboriginal artifacts, a Planetarium and a reconstructed joss-house. ⏰Open Mon-Sat 10am-5pm, Sun 2pm-5pm, ✆6331 6777.

The **Umbrella Shop**, in George Street, is built entirely of Tasmanian Blackwood and is preserved by the National Trust, ✆6331 9248.

The **City Park**, ✆6323 3610, is spacious with well laid-out gardens amid old elm and oak trees. It contains a small zoo and houses the John Hart Conservatory which is noted for its displays of begonias, cyclamen and many other hot house blooms.

The **Design Centre of Tasmania**, cnr Brisbane & Tamar Streets, ✆6331 5506, is ⏰open Mon-Fri 10am-6pm, Sat 10am-1pm, Sun 2pm-5pm. It has displays by Tasmania's best designers and craftsmen, some available for purchase.

The **Penny Royal World**, in Paterson Street, is an imaginative man-made development. It depicts early nineteenth century gun-powder mills, cannon foundry and arsenal in a landscaped setting with streams and waterfalls. Within the complex there is a canal system and

lake complete with a fleet of vessels, two of which fire and proof their guns daily. A scale model railway system runs the 700m (766 yards) from the Gunpowder Mill to the Penny Royal Watermill complex. The Penny Royal Watermill is a motel, ✆6331 6699 - 33 units, ✪$130 for two. Besides visits to the various Mills, and a ride on the train, cruises operate from here. ⏰Open daily 9am-5pm.

The **Country Club Casino**, at Prospect Vale besides accommodation mentioned above, has various gaming tables and offers live entertainment.

Franklin House, 7km (4.3 miles) south, is an early settler's home furnished in the colonial style. It is owned by the National Trust - ⏰open for inspection daily 9am-5pm, ✆6344 7824.

Tamar Knitting Mills, Hobart Road, are ⏰open daily 9am-4pm, ✆6344 8255. The mills have been operating since 1926, and you can purchase woollen garments there after touring the operation.

The **Cataract Gorge** is quite a place, and it is only a few minutes by bus from the city. A 1.6km (1 mile) walk along the face of the cliff ends in the Cataract Cliff Grounds Reserve from where a chairlift crosses the gorge. Manicured gardens, complete with strutting peacocks, merge with native flora on the upper bank, whereas on the city side, gardens surrounding a swimming pool extend to the lake over which you pass in the chairlift.

National Automobile Museum of Tasmania, cnr Cimitiere and Willis Streets, ✆6334 8888. Showcasing a selection of international cars, some in pristine condition and others undergoing restoration, this museum is ⏰open 9am-5pm seven days.

Cruises on the Tamar River can be taken on either the Tamar Odyssey, a 14.9 metre Cougar Cat (✆6334 9900) or the Lady Stelfox, a paddlesteamer operating every hour between ⏰10am and 3pm daily (✆6331 6699).

Festivals

There are a number of local food, wine, racing and agricultural shows scheduled throughout the year, and the Visitor Centre can provide details of specific events.

Facilities

As with all cities of a reasonable size, all sports such as lawn bowls, golf, squash, water sports, horse and greyhound racing, cycling and the various football codes are catered for.

Outlying Attractions

In Launceston many tours - half day and full day - and a variety of travel packages, are offered to see the sights of the Tamar Valley and the area surrounding Launceston. Contact the Visitor Centre in Paterson Street, ✆(03) 6336 3133, for information.

South
Hadspen

Located some 13km (8 miles) south-west, the village of Hadspen is often referred to as being very much like England. Here Entally House, which is built like an English farmhouse, is ☼open daily 10am-12.10pm, 1pm-5pm, ✆6393 6201.

Liffey Valley

Around 60km (37 miles) south-west via Carrick and Bracknell, are the Liffey Falls. It is a popular destination for bushwalkers and fishermen. There is a large fernery located here which sells a large variety of ferns. The Falls are in the Reserve and drop into a beautiful rainforest.

Ross

The town of Ross on the Midland Highway, is famous for its elaborately carved convict-built bridge of 1836. 75km (47 miles) south of Launceston and on the banks of the Macquarie River, Ross is classified by the National Trust. It is well worth a stop on your way to or from Hobart. There are many interesting buildings in the village - 1836 War Memorial, Sherwood Castle Inn, Macquarie Store, Old Barracks Building (now a wool craft centre) - and information can be obtained at the Tourist Information Centre. They are located in the tea-rooms, which were originally St John's Anglican Church.

North
Exeter

24km (15 miles) north-west along the Tamar River, Exeter is the centre of a fruit growing area, and even the local school has its own farm. At the mouth of the Supply River are the remains of Tasmania's first water driven flour mill. The Visitor Information Centre is on Main Road, ✆(03) 6394 4454.

Batman Bridge

The bridge spans the Tamar River

another 30km (19 miles) down-stream at Whirlpool Reach. It was one of the world's first cable-stayed bridges. Dominated by a 100m (328 ft) high steel A-frame inclined 20 degrees from the vertical, it leans out 30m (98 ft) across the river and carries almost the entire weight of the 206m (676 ft) main span. The bridge was opened in 1968.

Bell Bay

Further downstream and very close to the coast, Bell Bay has become an important inland port mainly nourished by Comalco's aluminium smelter.

George Town

The town is the residential and commercial centre for Bell Bay, but offers little in the way of accommodation. It has a beautiful Georgian mansion, The Grove, 25 Cimitiere Street, that has been re-stored and is ☺open for inspection daily 10am-5pm, ✆6382 1336. It is the port for the Catamaran ferry service to Port Welshpool in Victoria. There is an information centre on Main Road, ✆(03) 6382 1700.

West
Scottsdale

Scottsdale, with a population around 2000, is 70km (43 miles) north-east of Launceston, and is the centre of a large market garden area. A food processing factory specialising in deep freezing and dehydrating vegetables is located here. Oil poppies are grown in the area, and when they bloom in January and February the countryside is a blaze of colour. Lavender is grown around Nabowla, 13km west of Scottsdale. It blooms in late December through January pervading the air with its perfume. The Bridestow Estate Lavender Farm is at 296 Gillespies Road, Nabowla, ✆6352 8182.

Ben Lomond National Park

The Park is 48km (30 miles) south-east of Launceston, and reached via White Hills. It boasts of spectacular mountain scenery, as do all national parks in Tasmania. It is Tasmania's leading ski resort. Access is by a very steep and winding mountain road through precipitous

gorge and across the mountain plateau. In winter it is often covered
with heavy snow. Contact the Visitor Information Centre in Launceston about bus timetables and
departure points.

Devonport

Population 25,000
Devonport is situated on the north coast of Tasmania, where the Mersey River enters Bass Strait.

Climate

Average temperatures: January max 21C (70F) - min 13C (55F); July max 13C (55F) - min 5C (41F). Average annual rainfall: approximately 800mm (31 ins). The wettest six months are May-October. Hours of sunshine are: Summer 7; Autumn 4; Winter 3; and Spring 6.

Characteristics

Devonport, the fourth largest city in Tasmania, is the gateway for the car and passenger ferries from the mainland. It was originally two towns that voted to amalgamate in 1893 - Formby on the west bank of the river, and Torquay on the east bank.

Devonport had its beginnings as the centre of a rich agricultural and orchard area. Today, the Mersey Valley remains one of Tasmania's main orchard districts, but is now also famous for its mushrooms.

How to Get There

By Bus
Tasmania's Own Redline coaches connect Devonport to Launceston, Burnie and Hobart, with a connection to Queenstown from Burnie.

By Road
From Hobart, either along the Midland Highway via Launceston, or

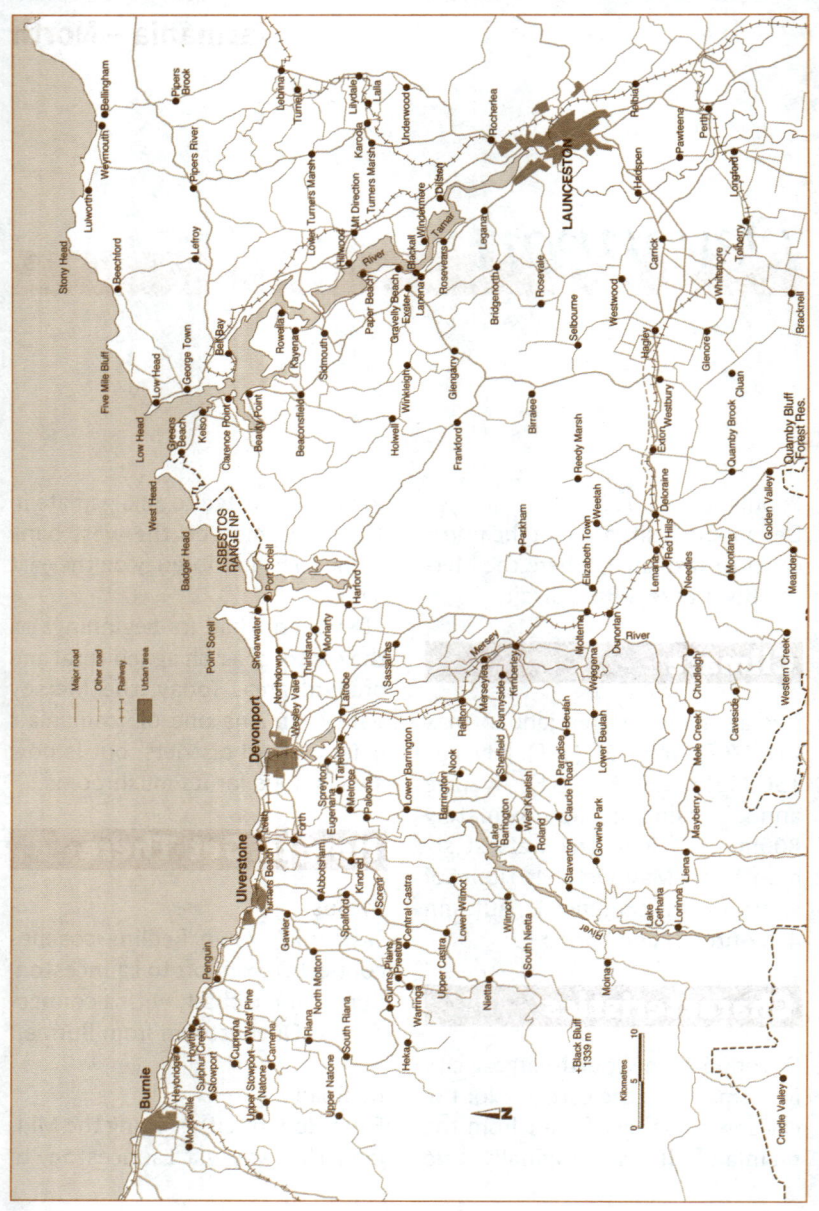

the Lakes Highway through the midlands and central highlands with 60km (37 miles) of unsealed road which may be covered with snow in winter.

By Sea

Spirit of Tasmania passenger/car ferry operates between Melbourne and Devonport, ☎9206 6211.

Tourist Information

Devonport Visitor Information Centre is at 92 Formby Road, ☎(03) 6424 8176.

Showcase Info, Best Street, ☎(03) 6424 8176, apart from being a tourist attraction in itself, has complete information about all the things to see and do in Devonport and the North West Coast. It is open seven days a week.

Accommodation

Following is a selection of accommodation with prices for a double room per night, which should be used as a guide only. The telephone area code is 03.

Gateway Inn (Innkeepers), 16 Fenton Street, ☎6424 4922. 64 rooms, licensed restaurant - ✪$108-148.

Sunrise Motor Inn, 140 North Fenton Street, ☎6424 8411. 33 units, licensed restaurant (Monday to Thursday) - ✪$120-164.

Argosy Motor Inn, 221 Tarleton Street, East Devonport, ☎6427 8872. 37 units, licensed restaurant - ✪$85-116.

Edgewater Motor Inn, 2 Thomas Street, East Devonport, ☎6427 8441. 29 units, licensed restaurant - ✪$59-69.

Hotel Formby, 82 Formby Road, ☎6424 1601. 23 rooms (some with private facilities), licensed restaurant - B&B ✪$40-75.

Barclay Lodge Motel (serviced apartments), 112 North Fenton Street, ☎6424 4722. 19 one & two bedroom units, heated swimming pool, half-court tennis, bbq - ✪$86-140.

Caravan Parks

Devonport Vacation Village, 20 North Caroline Street, East Devonport, ☎6427 8886. (No pets allowed) - powered sites $17 for two, cabin section ✪$45-70 for two.

Abel Tasman Caravan Park, 6 Wright Street, East Devonport, ☎6427 8794. (No pets allowed) - powered sites ✪$16 for two, on-site vans $33-40 for two.

Lakeside Caravan Park, Lakeside Road, Eugenana, ☎6427 2343. (Pets on application) - powered sites ✪$16 for two, cabin section $55 for two.

Mersey Bluff Caravan Park, Mersey Bluff, ☎6424 8655. (No pets allowed) - powered sites ✪$18 for two, on-site vans $44 for two, cabin section $50-65.

Eating Out

Devonport has a good selection of restaurants, and several hotels have counter meals. Coffee shops abound, as do takeaway outlets. Here are a few you might like to try.
Golden Panda Restaurant, 38 Formby Road, ✆6424 9066 - open Sun and Tues-Fri noon-2pm, Sun-Thurs 5-9pm, Fri 5-10.30pm, Sat 5-11pm.
The Cove Waterfront, 17 Devonport Road, ✆6424 6200.
Autographs on the Beach, Mersey Bluff Road, ✆6424 2204.
Tooska Restaurant, 19 Steele Street, ✆6423 5456.
China Garden, 33 King Street, ✆6424 4148.
El Mecciko, 24 King Street, ✆6423 5455.
Renusha's, 153 Rooke Street, ✆6424 2293 - Indian cuisine.
Rendevous, 142a William Street, ✆6424 7157 - restaurant and coffee lounge.
KFC, 26 William Street, Devonport, ✆6424 2285.
Pizza Hut, 132 William Street, ✆6424 9344.
McDonalds, 1 Best Street, ✆6424 9400.

Points of Interest

The **Victoria Bridge** connects East Devonport to Devonport, and it is 2km downstream from the Abel Tasman Terminal. To get to the bridge follow Formby Road along the river bank.

Walking and bicycle tracks circle the city and are found along the eastern shore. Bicycles can be hired at Mersey Bluff during the season, and the Showcase can advise of places at other times.

Mersey Bluff is one of only thirteen major sites where rock carvings by the Tasmanian Aboriginals can be viewed.

Tiagarra Tasmanian Aboriginal Culture and Art Centre at the Bluff headland has dramatic dioramas of the way of life of these people. It is ☺open daily, except for July when it is closed for renovations, ✆6424 8250. The Tasmanian Aboriginals were physically different from their mainland counterparts. Some scientists believe they were originally an African or Polynesian people who drifted to Tasmania on primitive rafts, but a more plausible explanation is that their ancestors crossed over from the mainland when Tasmania was still joined to it. An unfortunate part of Australian history began when the first European settlers reached the Derwent in 1803. They

began wiping out the Aboriginals, and by 1876 the entire race of full-blooded Tasmanian Aborigines had disappeared.

The **Devonport Maritime Museum**, Gloucester Avenue, was formerly the Harbour Master's residence and Pilot Station, built early 1920. It now has exhibits of Devonport and North West Coastal Maritime History, with fine detailed models from the days of sail and steam to the modern passenger ferries, ©6424 7100.

Devonport Gallery and Arts Centre is in the middle of the city at 45-47 Stewart Street. The lovely old converted church has the latest exhibitions, and is ©open Tues-Fri 10.30am-4.30pm, Sat 9.30am-noon, Sun 2.30-4.30pm, ©6424 8296.

Victoria Parade is a scenic garden walk which follows the river and sea to Mersey Bluff. There is a good swimming beach, children's playground, kiosk and public toilets.

Taswegia, 57 Formby Road, ©6424 8300, is an Historic Printery and Craft Gallery, and is ©open daily 10am-5pm. It has one of Australasia's largest heritage collection of print technology dating from 1852, and all in working condition. Taswegia specialises in the production of early colonial charts, convict documents, paintings, maps and paraphernalia. It also has an exclusive range of gift ware including printed linen, fabrics, woodcrafts, ceramics, pottery, posters, books and many other interesting and decorative items.

Home Hill, 77 Middle Road, was the family home of Prime Minister Joseph Lyons and Dame Enid Lyons, Australia's first woman member of the House of Representatives, and the author of several books. Dame Enid passed away in 1981, and the home is now operated by the City Council in conjunction with the National Trust. Home Hill is as Dame Enid left it and contains many interesting and historic mementoes. Phone ©6424 8055 for opening times.

The Don River Railway, ©6424 6335, off Bass Highway (road to Ulverstone) is an operating railway museum, and is ©open daily throughout the year with steam trains running hourly every Sunday and public holiday afternoons. The museum has the largest collection of steam locomotives in Tasmania, dating from 1879 to 1951, and the largest collection of passenger carriages dating from 1869 to 1961. There are many other interesting exhibits, a souvenir shops, and a refreshment outlet.

Festivals

January - Devonport Cup Carnival.
February - Food and Wine Frolic. Dahlia Show.
March - Mersey Valley Festival of Music.
October - Annual Show of the Devonport Orchid Society.
November - Agricultural & Pastoral Society Show.

Facilities

There is ample scope for skin diving and sea, river and lake fishing. Angling for trout is popular in the Mersey, Forth and Leven Rivers.

A tennis centre is situated near Mersey Bluff, and there are also courts at Wright Street, East Devonport.

At the western end of Steele Street there is an aquatic recreation centre with an olympic pool and water slide set in natural parklands.

Other sports catered for are lawn bowls, golf, greyhound racing, trotting, horse-racing and squash.

Outlying Attractions

Ulverstone

Situated in the centre of Tasmania's Holiday Coast, Ulverstone is a seaside town on the Leven River, 18km (11 miles) west of Devonport. It is in rich agricultural country reaching south from the sea to the mountains. Safe and extensive beaches and river, woodlands, parks and mountain resorts provide ideal conditions for people to stay a while.

The town is the Woodchopping Centre of Australia, and the sport had it beginnings here in 1870 when two bushmen got into an argument in a local pub about who was the best man with an axe. With a wager of $50 at stake, they adjourned to a nearby paddock to settle the matter and the sport was born. In 1974, the world championship was held in Ulverstone.

In the main street there is a large unusual War Memorial, which consists of 17m pillars joined by bronze chains.

Caves and Gunns Plains and the spectacular Leven Canyon at Nietta are some of the chief attractions of the Ulverstone district. A round trip to Gunns Plains, which is the site of a new hop industry, also traverses magnificent rural, mountain and river scenery.

Your first stop should be the Ulverstone Visitor Centre, Car Park Lane, ℰ(03) 6425 2839.

Penguin

The town of Penguin, 12km (7 miles) further west, is situated on three bays which provide safe beaches for bathing and picnicking. It is best to take the Scenic Drive (old Bass Highway) between Penguin and Ulverstone for the superb views of rugged coastal scenery, including the off-shore islets which are bird sanctuaries.

A feature of the Penguin Municipality is the ambitious Penguin Sports Club Dial Regional, ℰ6437 2767, catering for most sports, plus bushwalking. Visitors are most welcome.

Latrobe

Situated 10km (6 miles) east of the Bass Strait ferry terminal, and 5km (3 miles) south of Pardoe Airport, Latrobe was one of the first towns established on the North-West Coast. The Mersey River with its willow-lined banks flows through the town.

Sheffield

The town is the gateway to the Mersey-Forth Hydro-Electric Power Development with seven power stations and seven man-made lakes, including Lake Barrington, a venue for rowing events.

The lake is accessible by bitumen road which goes through some of Tasmania's most rugged mountain scenery. If you have your own equipment, Lake Barrington is ideal for a range of water sports including rowing, water skiing, power boating, canoeing and model yachting. There are launching ramps on both sides of the lake. It is necessary to book the rowing course with the ranger. The recreation area of the park is open daily from 8am until dusk, and facilities include a large day visitor shelter with wood barbecues, seats and tables, and a kiosk which is only open on weekends throughout the summer season.

Standing guard over Sheffield and dominating the skyline is 1231m (4039 ft) Mt Roland.

Cradle Mountain/ Lake St Clair National Park

The northern end of this 1280 sq km (494 sq miles) park can be reached from Sheffield via the Claude Road, or from Forth via Wilmot. Both roads join a 30km (19 miles) stretch that leads to Cradle Valley. The last 10km (6 miles) are unsealed. If coming from the west coast, take the Cradle Mountain Link Road from the Murchison Highway north of Que River.

The Visitor Information Centre is just inside the northern boundary of the Park, and is ☼open daily 9am-5pm, and after hours for special events, ✆(03) 6492 1133. The Centre has a model of the Cradle Mountain, children's exhibits, maps, books, posters, registration for day walks and Overland Track, toilets, electric barbecues and picnic shelters. Other day visitor facilities are a day-use hut and toilets near Waldheim, firesites by Ronny Creek, and toilets at Lake Dove. Walkers are requested to enter details of any walk in the walker registration book, and to de-register at the end of their walk, which is just as important.

Accommodation is available at the Cradle Mountain Tourist Park, ✆6492 1395, 2km outside the park boundary, and a daily transport service operates from there to Lake Dove. Camping is not permitted in Cradle Valley. The Cradle Mountain Lodge, situated on the park boundary, also provides accommodation, meals, bar, petrol and basic food supplies, ✆(03) 6492 1303.

Visitors should not forget that this beautiful area is a mountain wilderness where the weather can change abruptly and without warning. For people without experience and the right equipment, it can be a dangerous place in which getting lost is all too easy. Hiking clubs throughout Australia arrange parties to walk through the National Park to Lake St Clair, along the 85km (53 miles) Overland Track from Waldheim, and unless you are a very experienced hiker, you should go with one of these parties. For those who haven't the time or the inclination to hike, charter flights are available from Devonport, and you should enquire at the Information Centre.

Deloraine

The township of Deloraine is on the Bass Highway, 45km (28 miles) from both Devonport and Laun-ceston. It is nestled in a valley surrounded by Quamby Bluff (1226m - 4022 ft) and the Western Tiers. Historical and natural features mingled with rich farmlands make Deloraine a worthwhile stopping place.

Among the many attractions in the district are the King Solomon and Marakoopa Caves near Mole Creek. These world renowned limestone caves are ☼open every day, but you will need to be book with the Mole Creek Guest House, Pioneer Drive, Mole Creek, ✆(03) 6363 1399. Inspection times are -

King Solomon Cave - 10.30am, 11.30am, 12.30pm, 2pm, 3pm and 4pm.

Marakoopa Cave - 10am, 11.15am, 1pm, 2.30pm and 4pm.

There are several walking tracks in the area catering for both the well equipped and experienced walker, as well as those desiring more relaxed yet equally scenic walks.

For further information, contact the Deloraine Museum and Visitor Information Centre, 98 Emu Bay Road, ✆(03) 6362 3471.

Port Sorell

The port is 19km (12 miles) east of Devonport on the picturesque Rubicon River estuary. It is a popular holiday resort with prolific native flora and fauna, and good swimming and boating are available at nearby Hawley Beach.

Burnie

Population 20,000
Burnie is on the north-west coast of Tasmania on the shores of Emu Bay.

Climate

Average Temperatures: January max 21C (70F) - min 13C (55F); July max. 13C (55F) - min 5C (41F). Average annual rainfall approximately: 900mm (354 in); wettest six months - May - October. Sunshine hours: Summer 7, Autumn 4, Winter 3 and Spring 6.

Characteristics

A thriving industrial centre and deep water port which handles more than 2 million tons of cargo each year. It is the terminal for ANL sea road vessels, and trades directly with more than 40 overseas ports. Burnie is in the centre of lush dairying area and is surrounded by a wide forest belt that runs parallel with the coastline, about 50km (31 miles) inland. About 22 million super feet of quality timber is produced each year from this area.

How to Get There

By Road

The distance from Launceston along the Bass Highway is 150 km (93 miles) which takes about 2 and a half hours. From Queenstown the distance is 176km (109 miles) which again takes around 2 and a half hours. The drive from Smithton 86km (53 miles) away takes an hour and a half.

By Bus

Redline offer a service from Hobart connecting Oatlands, Launceston, Abel Tasman, Devonport, Burnie, Wynyard to Smithton four times a day, with special services between Wynyard and Burnie another 4 times a day.

Tourist Information

The Visitor Information Centre is in the Burnie Civic Centre Precinct (Museum), Little Alexander Street, ©(03) 6434 6111.

Accommodation

Burnie has about 12 hotels and motels and a number of holiday flats plus two caravan parks in the area. Prices do vary depending on the standard of accommodation and the season. In the selection below we give prices for a double room per night which should be used as a guide only. The telephone area code is 03.

Beachfront Voyager Motor Inn, 9 North Terrace, ©6431 4866. 40 units, licensed restaurant - ✪$110.
Ocean View Motel, 253 Bass Hwy, Cooee, ©6431 1925. 30 units, licensed restaurant, sauna - ✪$70.
Wellers Inn, 36 Queen Street, ©6431 1088. 24 units, licensed restaurant - ✪$104.
Burnie Town House, 139 Wilson Street, ©6431 4455. 55 rooms (private facilities), licensed restaurant - ✪$115.
Glen Osborne House, 9 Airleen Cres (off Mount St.), ©6431 9866. 6 rooms - ✪$121-132.
Baird's, 22 Cunningham St, ©6431 9212. 3 rooms, unlicensed restaurant - ✪$121.
Burnie Motor Lodge, 12-16 Bass Hwy, ©6431 1933. 30 rooms, licensed restaurant - ✪$88.
Apartments Down Town, 52 Alexander St, ©6432 3219. 9 units - ✪$110.

Caravan Parks

Treasure Island Caravan Park, 253 Bass Highway, Cooee, ©6431 1925. Powered sites ✪$16 for two, on-site vans $42.

Eating Out

You can have a decent night out at one of Burnie's restaurants. Listed below are a few with their specialities.

Mandarin Palace, 63 Wilson Street, ©6431 7878 - Chinese, licensed, open daily.
Hodgy's Restaurant & Wine Bar, 8 Alexander Street, ©6431 3947 - a la carte, licensed, open Mon-Sat.
Renusha's Indian Restaurant, 28 Ladbrooke Street, ©6431 2293.
*Fortuna Garden Chinese Restau-

rant, 68 Wilson Street, ©6431 9035.

Rialto Gallery Restaurant, 46 Wilmot Street, ©6431 7718 - Venetian, BYO, open Tues-Sat.

Wellers Seafood Restaurant, 36 Queen Street, ©6431 1088.

Gianni's Restaurant & Wine Bar, 104 Wilson Street, ©6431 9393.

Points of Interest

The **Pioneer Village Museum** in High Street, Civic Centre Plaza, is Burnie's premier attraction. It is close to the centre of the city, and the entire village is under one roof. It has more than 30,000 individual items on display. There is an inn, newspaper office, general store, blacksmith shop, and many authentic replicas of a commercial centre of the 1890-1910 period - ☉open Mon-Fri 10am-5pm, and Sat-Sun 1.30pm-5pm. Admission ✪$4.50 adult, $1.50 child, ©6430 5746.

Burnie Park is only a few minutes walk away. It has shady trees, a rose garden and the old Burnie Inn which was first licensed in 1847. It is the oldest building in the city, and is open daily for inspection during the summer. They only sell light refreshments and Devonshire Teas - a little different from days of yore. There is also an animal sanctuary.

The **Civic Centre and Regional Art Gallery** in Wilmot Street, open Tues-Fri 10.30am-5pm, Sat-Sun 2.30pm-4.30pm, are also worth a visit. Admission is free, ©6431 5918.

The **Australian Paper**, Marine Terrace, ©6430 7777, has free guided tours at 2pm Tues-Fri of the processing of wood into paper. Children under the age of 12 are not admitted, and women are asked to wear slacks and low heeled shoes. Booking is essential.

The **Lactos Factory**, Old Surry Road, has chese tastings ☉Mon-Fri 9am-5pm, Sat-Sun 10am-4pm. Admission is free, ©6433 9255.

Round Hill Lookout, 6.5km on the Stowport/Natone Road, and Fern Glade are only 3km from town and well worth a visit.

Festivals

In late July there is the Burnie Two Day Cycling Tour, and in early September the Burnie 10 Kilometre Fun Run is held. The Agricultural Show is held early in October, and the famous Athletic Carnival including the Burnie Gift, is staged every New Year's Day.

Facilities

The city and district caters for lawn bowls, boating, fishing, sailing, swimming (pool or sea), golf, bike and horse riding, as well as squash, the various football codes and cricket.

Outlying Attractions

Helleyer Gorge

The Gorge is 52km (32 miles) from Burnie on the Waratah Highway, which links the north-west with the west coast. The gorge itself is older than time, and is a scenic reserve. Nearby are glorious white sandy beaches, tidal inlets, freshwater streams and pools where campers can pitch their tents in near solitude, and enjoy nature in an undisturbed and timeless area.

Wynyard

16km (10 miles) from Burnie with a population of around 4500 people, Wynyard is a pretty town, and is almost more English than England. The town is located on the Inglis River, and the airport for Burnie is found here.

It is a major gateway to the north-west coast and offers superb panoramic views, while Fossil Buff (just beyond the Wynyard Golf Course) is a unique area rich in rare and ancient fossils. Among the important finds made here is that of a whale bone some 2 million years old.

The waters around the town are popular with divers and underwater photographers because of their clarity. Equipment for scuba diving can be hired in town, ✆6442 2247.

7km (4 miles) south is the Oldina Forest Reserve which contains a virtual museum of superb trees. At the Reserve are spacious lawns and picnic facilities.

30km (18.6 miles) east from Wynyard is Rocky Cape National Park. Some of its geological formations are 700 million years old, and some Aboriginal remains found there indicate that the area was occupied at least 9000 years ago, before Bass Strait was formed. There are also some interesting caves, and several bushwalks in the park. The walk from Sisters Beach to Rocky Cape is noted for its spring displays of wildflowers.

Tasmanian Scenic Flights, ✆6442 1111, out of Wynyard Airport, offer daily scenic flights to Cradle Mountain in the south over incredible gorges, farmland and various peaks, and shorter duration flights along the north coastline.

You can find good accommodation in Wynyard -

Waterfront Wynyard Motor Inn, 1 Goldie Street, ✆6442 2351, licensed restaurant - ✪$85.

Inglis River, 10 Goldie Street, ✆6442 2344, licensed rstaurant - ✪$50.

Alexandria Guest House, 1 Table

Cape Road, ©6442 4411, unlicensed restaurant - ✪$110-120.
Leisure Ville Holiday Units, 145 Old Bass Highway, ©6442 2291, tennis, indoor heated pool,spa - $90-115, powered sites ✪$19 for two, cabins $70-75.
Wynyard Caravan Park, Old Bass Highway, ©6442 1998 - powered sites ✪$16 for two, on-site vans $45 for two, cabins $65 for two.

Boat Harbour

On the way to Boat Harbour from Wynyard is the Shannondoah Cottage, ©6445 1141, that is essentially a craft centre, but also has tea rooms. Built in an old family homestead, it stocks Tasmanian craft items - patchwork, applique wall hangings, etc.

Boat Harbour's permanent inhabitants number about 300, but that number swells during the summer.

Only 16km (10 miles) from Wynyard, it is a popular holiday resort with beautiful beaches, facilities for boating, fishing, water skiing and is close to a number of national parks.

Boat Harbour Beach Caravan Park, ©6445 1253, on the beachfront has powered sites ✪$18 for two. There are various flats and guest houses which can be booked through Tasbureau in Burnie.

Stanley

Only a one hour drive from Wynyard Airport, Stanley is an historic town as it was the site of the first settlement in north-west Tasmania. It has changed very little since its early days.

Its most distinctive feature is 'The Nut' which rises 152m (500 ft) sheer on three sides, and is on the end of a 7km (4.3 miles) long isthmus. This landform has a 35ha (80 acres) summit that dominates the landscape, and affords a superb view of the countryside. If you wish to climb it, there is an easy walking track which begins opposite the post office and ends at the summit cairn. Alternatively, you can take the chairlift that operates from the rear of the Nut Shop Tea Rooms, ©6458 1286

There is good fishing in the bay and along the coast around Stanley.

Above and Overleaf: Freycinet National Park (Wineglass Bay overleaf)   Below: Mount Roland, Tasmania

Smithton

The administration of the Circular Head Municipality of the far north-west is based at Smithton. It has a large modern butter factory as well as a bacon factory, a large piggery and several saw mills. The district has an ideal climate for growing peas, and the town boasts of a pea freezing factory.

Lacrum Dairy Farm, ✆6452 2653, is 6km (4 miles) west of Smithton. Visitors are welcome to this 275ha (679 acres) property, where they have a Wombat Tarn, picnic and barbecue facilities, bush walks, and milking between 3pm-5.30pm every day from October to the end of June. There is an admission fee, and groups of 10 or more should book.

Driving directly south, you can visit Allendale Gardens at Edith Creek (botanical gardens in miniature), Balfour Track Reserve, Julius River Reserve, Lake Chisholm, West Beckett Reserve and Milkshake Hill Forest Reserve. You would have to do this independently, though, as there are no guided tours to these parts.

Montagu is some 20km (12 miles) north-west of Smithton, and is the site of the Van Diemen's Land Co which was founded in 1825 by Royal Charter of King George IV. This historic cattle and sheep property provides access for visitors

seven days during summer months and 10am-2pm on weekends in winter. They have a multitude of displays, activities, walks, and refreshments are available.

Marrawah

Situated at the western end of the Bass Highway, 48km (30 miles) from Smithton, and very close to Green Point on the west coast, the settlement of Marrawah is well worth a visit, as wildflowers and native fauna are plentiful. There are several important Aboriginal rock carvings at Mt Cameron a little to the north. The carvings of circles and bird tracks are similar to ones found in the deserts of the Australian mainland.

King Island

The island is a region on its own. 64km (40 miles) long and 27km (17 miles) wide at its widest point, it has 145km (90 miles) of coastline. In addition to its wildlife, the island is very famous on the mainland for its cream, which causes queues in some Sydney shops when it becomes available.

There are two main towns on the island - Currie on the west coast and Grassy in the south-east. Currie (population 700 approx.) is the administrative centre, and has almost all the available accommodation, among which are the ***Boo-***

merang by the Sea, ℰ6462 1288 -
16 suites, ✪$100-135 for two; the
guest house, *Parers*, ℰ6462 1633
- ✪$90-110 for two; holiday units
at *Naracoopa*, ℰ6461 1326 -
✪$90 for two; and the *Bass Cara-
van Park*, ℰ6462 1260 - on-site
vans ✪$45 for two.

Grassy (population 600) is a
deepwater port, and the site of the
scheelite mine. The island would appeal to travellers and those who enjoy skin diving, surfing and shooting.
The pheasant shooting season is in
June; the duck shooting season in
March and April; and mutton-birding
takes place in the autumn.

For more information about King
Island, visit ☞www.kingisland.net
.au

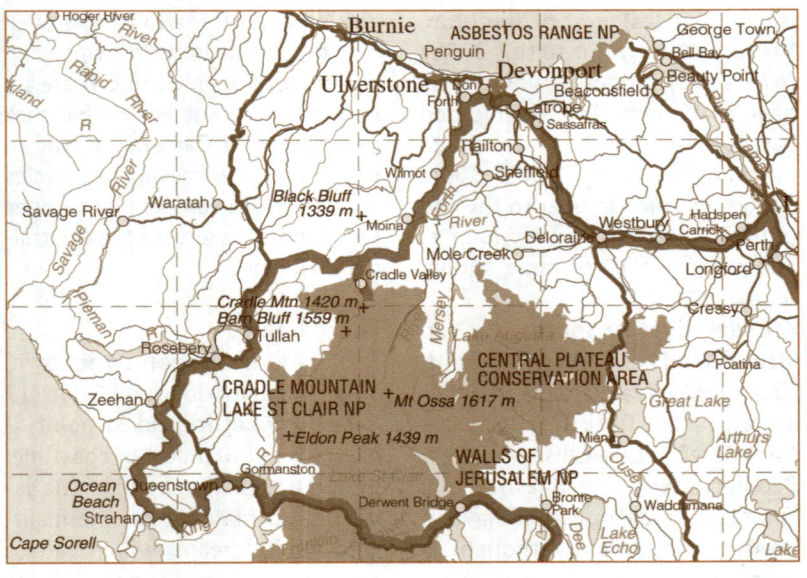

Queenstown

Population 3,715
Queenstown is located on the rugged west coast of Tasmania, in the midst of a wilderness area.

Characteristics

Queenstown is firstly and lastly a mining town. After seeing so many trees, your first glimpse of Queenstown may come as a shock because the hills around the town are denuded of greenery. This has been caused by a combination of tree felling, sulphur, fire and rainfall.

As the Lyell Highway descends steeply into Queenstown via the Linda Valley, there is a panoramic view of naked hills strewn with multi-coloured boulders which reflect the sun's rays. In the evening, the setting sun causes the mountains and hills to change from shades of brilliant gold to hues of deep pink. It is an unforgettable sight.

Climate

The area averages only 1750 hours of sunshine in a year, while it rains on an average of 320 days per year. The annual rainfall is over 3000mm (118 ins).

How to Get There

By Bus
Tasmania's Own Redline Coaches have services between Hobart, Burnie, Strahan and Queenstown.

By Road
Queenstown is 254km (158 miles)

north-west of Hobart along the Lyell Highway, and 175km (109 miles) south-west of Burnie along the Waratah and Zeehan Highways.

Tourist Information

Visitor information can be obtained from the hotels and motels in the area. There is a City Guide map in Driffield Street at the end of Orr Street.

Accommodation

Following is a selection of accommodation with prices for a double room per night, which should be used as a guide only. The telephone area code is 03.

The Gold Rush Motor Inn, Batchelor Streets, ✆6471 1005. 26 units, licensed restaurant - ✪$75-100.

Westcoaster Motor Inn, Batchelor Street, ✆6471 1033. 60 units, licensed restaurant - ✪$95.

Silver Hills Motel, Penghana Road, ✆6471 1755. 56 units, licensed restaurant - ✪$88.

Mt Lyell Motor Inn, 1 Orr St., ✆6471 1888. 40 units, licensed restaurant - ✪$50.

Commercial, Driffield Street, ✆6471 1511. 12 rooms (no private facilities), licensed restaurant - ✪$66.

Caravan Park

Queenstown Cabin & Tourist Park, 17 Grafton Street, ✆6471 1332. Powered sites ✪$20 for two, on-site vans $40 for two.

Eating Out

Most of the hotels have restaurants or counter meals. You may want to try one of the restaurants below.

Maloneys, Orr Street, ✆6471 1866.

Smelters Licensed Restaurant, Penghana Road, ✆6471 1755.

Miners' Crib Room, 10 Orr Street, ✆6471 1152.

Gerry's Bistro Restaurant, 1 Penghana Road, ✆6471 1163.

Points of Interest

In November 1883, Steve Karlson and Mick McDonough, who had only arrived in the Linda Valley the day before, discovered a strange iron outcrop which rose about 25 ft above the surface. This was the famous Iron Blow, where mining of the riches of Mt Lyell began. About two weeks later, the diggers pegged out a fifty acre lease, in the centre of which was the Blow. They suspected that the Blow was the source of the gold they washed in the creek below the outcrop. The Blow was worked as a gold mine for ten years, with everybody ig-

noring the millions of pounds of copper in it.

The Mount Lyell gold mine was bought by Bowes Kelly in 1891, and he formed the Mt Lyell Mining Company in Melbourne. But in that year gold mining at Mt Lyell came to an end, although it has always remained a welcome by-product. The directors of the company brought Edward Dyer Peters, a world authority on copper smelting, from the USA, and he conducted a successful smelting trial at the Argenton smelter, four miles south of Zeehan.

The present Mt Lyell Mining and Railway Company, one of the old- est mining companies in Australia, was formed in 1893, after the previous company had been dissolved for financial reasons. The new company failed to raise enough money for an extensive development programme, and mining at the Blow nearly came to a stop. Then an incredulously rich silver seam with an average of over a thousand ounces of silver to the ton was discovered by Dr Peters. This lucky discovery helped the young company out of its financial difficulties.

In 1895, Robert Carl Sticht, another American, but this time a metallurgist, was given a free hand by the directors of the company to design the first Mt Lyell smelters. His pyritic smelting process, which represented an important advance in the technology of copper smelting, became famous and was copied in many countries.

By 1891, the little shanty town of Penghana had sprung up around the smelters, but in 1896 it was wiped out by fire. The refugees set up home in a newly planned town on the banks of the Queen River, and called it, appropriately enough, Queenstown. In the same year the Queenstown Hotel was built.

An historic tour walk has been mapped out around the town, and information plaques have been erected at places of interest.

No stay in Queenstown would be

complete without a visit to the **Mt Lyell Mine**. Guided tours are available and depart from Farmer's Store in Driffield Street, ℄6471 2388. Tours are of approximately two hours' duration, and include viewing the mine workings and the Mining Museum.

The **Eric Thomas Galley Museum**, cnr Driffield & Sticht Streets, features displays of old photographs dealing with the West Coast, as well as items of household equipment and personal effects in use during the early days. The museum is open daily, except Saturday mornings, and a small admission fee is charged, ℄6471 1483.

Miners Siding in Driffield Street is a Queenstown Centenary Park Development, and incorporates the Miners Sunday Sculpture by Stephen Walker. The sculpture is made of bronze and Huon Pine, and depicts an early miner and his family on the day of rest, and the changes that transformed a rough miners' camp to a town and community. Part of the Miners Siding Park has been developed as a rainforest, with many species that occur mainly in Western Tasmania. Also in the Park is a restored ABT Locomotive, which was part of the system that was the only transport link between Queenstown and the outside world until 1932.

Iron Blow, the original gold mine, is situated north of the town at Gormanston, 2km off the Lyell Highway. The site has been developed as an area of historic and scenic interest, and offers excellent panoramic views over the mountains and Linda Valley.

The **Crotty and South West Access Road** turns off the Lyell Highway 10km (6 miles) north of the town, and was once the railway line for the North Lyell Copper Co. It provides access to the Darwin Meteorite Crater, the Franklin River, Fincham Park, Kelly Basin, the King Power Development and Crotty Camp.

Lake Margaret, north of Queenstown, was one of Tasmania's first hydro electric schemes and was built and owned by the Mt Lyell Co in 1914. The station and village remain as they were in the 1900s, with the original machines still working. A 2134m (7000 ft) wooden stave pipeline still delivers water from the lake to the Penstock, and a walk up the hill provides unparalleled views of the rugged West Coast.

On the Zeehan Highway, 14km (9 miles) from Queenstown, there is a **balancing rock** which gives an insight into the unique geology of the area. The parking area here offers views over the glacial valleys of the Henty and Yolande Rivers.

There are information plaques, and sign-post to the rock.

Facilities

Swimming pool, golf course, gem fossicking and gold panning.

Outlying Attractions

Zeehan

Zeehan is 33km (21 miles) north of Queenstown, and the town boomed when rich silver-lead deposits were discovered in 1882. By the turn of the century it was a town of 5000, and an entertainment 'capital' - Dame Nellie Melba and Enrico Caruso performed here. But, the ore ran out and the town declined before the beginning of World War I. A number of buildings have survived from its boom time including the Gaiety Theatre, St Luke's Church and the Post Office.

The West Coast Pioneers' Memorial Museum is housed in the old School of Mines, and is divided into five main categories of exhibits - a mineral collection; historical items relating to the West Coast; modern mining on the West Coast; locomotives and tracked mining equipment; and exhibits of Tasmanian animals and birds, with artefacts of the extinct Tasmanian Aborigines.

Places to visit around Zeehan include Trial Harbour (20km - 12 miles), Heemskirk Falls (19km - 12 miles), Granville Harbour (40km - 25 miles), and the Lower Pieman Dam (50km - 31 miles). Both harbours are popular with fishermen seeking crayfish and abalone.

Strahan

Situated on Macquarie Harbour, 36km (22 miles) south-west of Queenstown, Strahan dates back to the convict days when it was a dreaded place. Many of the convicts who were sent to Sarah Island in Macquarie Harbour found life there was hell on earth, and death was seldom from natural causes.

The closure of many mines on the West Coast, and the building of the railway line from Zeehan to Burnie led to the decline of Strahan, and today it is a fishing port, holiday village, and a base for trips into the wilderness area around the Gordon River.   From Strahan you can take a flight on a sea plane over the peaks of Frenchmans Cap National Park, majestic Lake Peddar, the rapids and gorges of the Franklin River, and then land on the tranquil Gordon River. For further information contact Wilderness Air, ©6471 7280.

Another adventure is a half-day scenic cruise on a motor launch which will take you from Macquarie

Harbour to the Gordon River, pull into Heritage Landing to walk through a rainforest on an elevated walkway to view a 2000-year-old Huon Pine, and return to Strahan via the infamous Sarah Island and Hell's Gates, the notorious entrance of Macquarie Harbour. For further information contact Gordon River Cruises, ✆6471 4300.

The interesting Strahan Visitors Centre is on the Esplanade, ✆6471 7622, and in addition to local tourist information they have details of the history and heritage of the region.

Frenchman's Cap

The mountain is part of the Wild Rivers National Park, and the Lyell Highway passes close to the northern edge of the park. There are several bushwalks in the area. You can take a short walk to view the white quartz dome of the Cap and look out over the Franklin River, or if you have more time, you can walk right into the rainforest.

For more information, contact the Parks & Wildlife Service in Queenstown, ✆(03) 6471 2511.

South Australia

Adelaide

Population 1,003,802

Adelaide, the Capital City of South Australia, is situated on a narrow plain bounded on the west by the waters of St Vincent Gulf, and on the east by the rising slopes of the picturesque Mount Lofty Ranges. It is 660km (410 miles) from Melbourne, 988km (614 miles) from Canberra, 1,196km (743 miles) from Sydney, 1967km (1222 miles) from Brisbane, and 2216km (1377 miles) from Perth. The River Torrens flows through the city.

Climate

Adelaide has a mediterranean type climate with warm dry summers and cool winters. Average annual rainfall is 530mm (21 ins), and it generally falls between May and August. Average temperatures: January max 30C (86F) - min 16C (61F); July max 15C (59F) - min 7C (45F). Water temperature: January 19C (66F); July 14C (57F).

Characteristics

Colonel Light planned Adelaide to be a city of broad streets and handsome terraces. He dotted it with spacious squares, and bounded it on all sides with a broad band of natural parkland. Today it is a vibrant, sophisticated city enjoying the fruits of Colonel Light's planning.

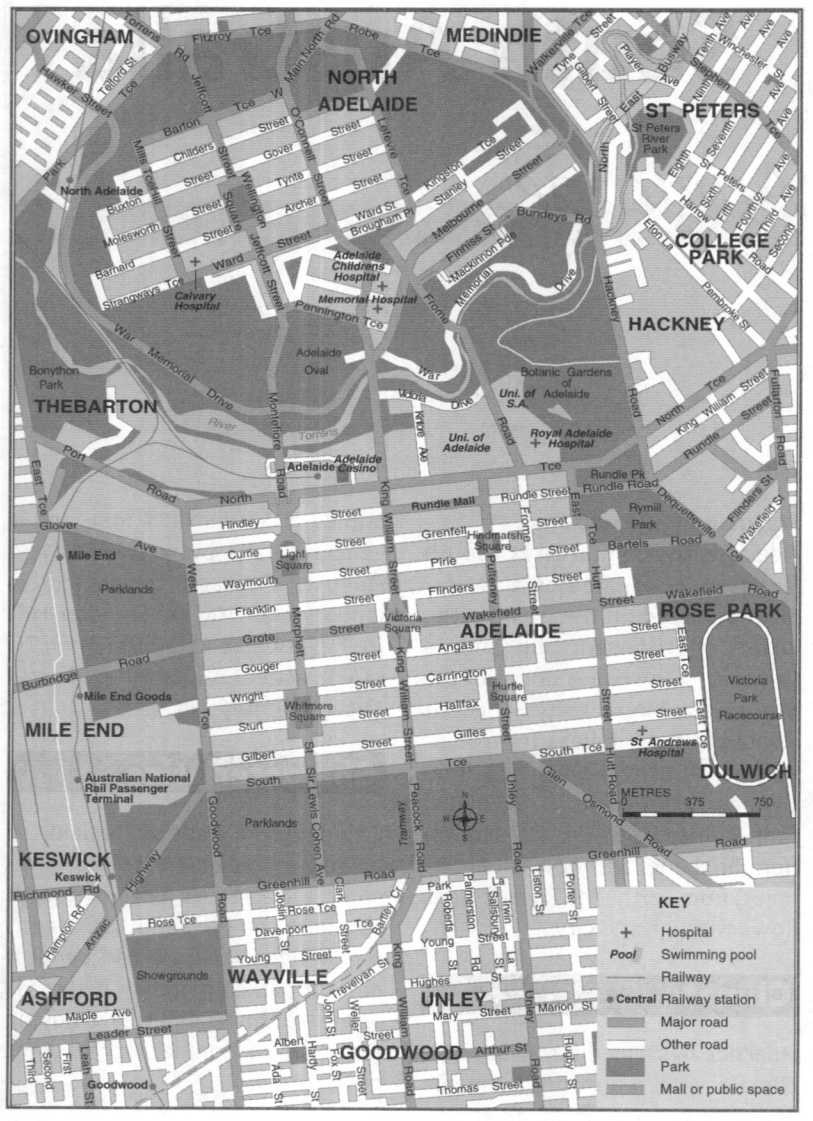

KEY

+ Hospital
Pool Swimming pool
Railway
● Central Railway station
Major road
Other road
Park
Mall or public space

METRES
375 750

How to Get There

By Air

Adelaide International Airport, ©8308 9211, is served by Air New Zealand, British Airlines, Cathay Pacific Airways, Japan Air Lines, Lufthansa Airlines, Malaysian Airlines, Philippine Airlines, Qantas, Singapore Airlines, Thai International and United Airlines. The Airport is about 6.5km (4 miles) out of the city centre, and a Transit Airport City Bus operates 7 days a week between the international and domestic airport terminals and the major accommodation houses in Adelaide City.

Qantas has services to Adelaide from the other capital cities in Australia.

By Bus

Greyhound Pioneer and McCafferty's have services from the other capital cities.

By Rail

The Indian Pacific stops at Adelaide on its Sydney to Perth run. The Overland has an overnight service from Melbourne to Adelaide.

By Car

National highways converge on Adelaide from the east, west and north. From the eastern states there are numerous possible routes. The coastal road from Melbourne enters South Australia through the forest and lakeland of the south-eastern part of the state, and provides the chance to explore the wilderness of the Coorong and its prolific birdlife, as well as winding through some old-world fishing villages on the way. The main overland route from Sydney crosses into Victoria at Mildura, and runs through the citrus and wine-producing area of South Australia. From the west, the completely sealed Eyre Highway provides safe motoring from Perth across the Nullabor Plain. An alternate route follows the Great Australian Bight, where cliffs drop to the sea below. They are the largest stretch of unbroken cliffs in the world. From the north, the Stuart Highway is the main thoroughfare, but there are still some sections which are unsealed and subject to flood damage. If you are planning to drive along this highway, *Australian Road Trips*, by Ian Read, details the route thoroughly.

Tourist Information

The South Australian Visitor & Travel Centre, 18 King William Street, Adelaide, is ⊙open Mon-Fri 8.30am-5pm. Contact them by phone on ©1300 655 276 or by email at ✎informationandbookings@south australia.com The website to explore is ☞www.southaustralia.com

Accommodation

Adelaide has a large range of accommodation to suit every budget, and for full details it is best to enquire at the Travel Centre. Here is a selection of accommodation in the city, with prices for a double room per night, which should be used as a guide only. The suburbs of Adelaide also offer good accommodation, and as with any city, the further from the city centre, the lower the rates. © The telephone area code is 08.

5-star

Hyatt Regency, North Terrace, ©08 8231 1234. 369 rooms (private facilities), licensed restaurant, bistro, swimming pool, spa, sauna, gym ✪$300-360.

Hilton International Adelaide, 233 Victoria Square, ©8217 2000. 380 rooms (private facilities), licensed restaurant, bistro, heated swimming pool, spa, sauna, gym, bbq ✪$230-360.

4-star

Adelaide Riviera Motel & Function Centre, 31 North Terrace, ©8231 8000. 84 units, licensed restaurant ✪$120 - 170.

Central Adelaide - Tower Wing, 208 South Terrace, ©8223 2744. 134 units, licensed restaurant, swimming pool ✪$121.

3 star

Festival Lodge Motel, Entrance from Bank St, 140 North Terrace, ©8212 7877. 44 units, unlicensed restaurant ✪$110.

Grosvenor Vista Hotel, 125 North Terrace, ©8407 8888. 290 rooms (private facilities), licensed restaurant, bistro, sauna, gym ✪$105-135.

Adelaide Paringa Motel, 15 Hindley St, ©8231 1000. 45 units ✪$107-120.

2-star

Clarice Motel, 220 Hutt, ©8223 3560. 6 units ✪$70.

Ambassadors Hotel, 107 King William St, ©8231 4331. 30 rooms, licensed restaurant ✪$72.

1 star

Kings Head Hotel, 357 King William Street, ©8212 6657. 8 rooms ✪$45.

Caravan Parks

Adelaide Caravan Park, Cnr Richmond & Bruton St, Hackney (3km east of city), ©8363 1566. (No pets allowed)✪ powered sites $23-26 for two, on-site vans $39-46 for two.

Levi Park Caravan Park, 69 Landsowne Terrace, Walkerville (5km north-east of city), ©8344 2209. (No pets allowed) powered sites ✪ $21-23 for two, park cabins $68-83 for two.

Woodcroft Park Caravan Park, Lot 1 Bains Rd, ✆8325 1233. (No pets allowed) - powered sites ✪$17 for two, park cabins $50-85 for two.

Adelaide Shores Caravan Resort, 1 Military Road, West Beach (8km west of city), ✆8356 7654. (No pets allowed) - powered sites ✪$26-29 for two, on-site vans $45-60 for two.

Local Transport

Bus

All metropolitan buses (STA) leave from the main city shopping areas: King William Street, Grenfell Street, North Terrace, etc. For all enquiries about timetables, destinations, and fare-saver deals, ✆8210 1000 or go online to 👁www.adelaide metro.com.au. A free inner city bus service is run by the STA called the BeeLine Bus. The bus number is 99B, and every five minutes buses travel along a set route and make ten stops for passengers to get on and off. The route is from Victoria Square along King William Street, left into North Street, left into George Street, right into Hindley Street, right into West Terrace, right into North Terrace, right into King William Street, back to Victoria Square. 🕐The service operates Mon-Thurs 8am-6pm, Fri 8am-9pm, Sat 8am-12.15pm.

Rail

All suburban trains depart from the Adelaide Railway Station, North Terrace, ✆8410 1488.

Tram

The Glenelg Tram Service operates from Victoria Square and terminates at Mosely Square, Glenelg. The trams are of 1929 vintage and the trip takes about 30 minutes.

Taxi

Taxis are available in the city and metropolitan area 24 hours a day, seven days a week. They can be hailed in the street, or booked by telephone: AAA, ✆13 1008; Taxi About Town, ✆13 2227; Taxi Adelaide, ✆13 2211; Access Cabs (wheelchair taxis), ✆1300 360 940.

Car

Most major car rental firms can be found in Adelaide. They offer a wide selection of vehicles. Car rental firms require a current driver's licence and a deposit. International credit cards are acceptable. If you are under 25 years of age, check minimum age requirements.

The Royal Automobile Association of SA, Hindmarsh Square, offers a complete service to its members and also to members of all automobile associations within Australia, ✆8202 4600; Emergency Road Service, ✆13 1111. Petrol stations are usually ☺open 7am-6pm, but some are open 24 hours. Most stations are self service, but some do offer driveway service.

O-Bahn Busway

A unique Adelaide experience is a ride on the O-Bahn busway system, ✆8210 1000. At 12km (7 miles) in length, the O-Bahn guideway is the longest in the world. You can board a bus and travel through the city onto the O-Bahn track for a smooth 100kph cruise to Paradise Interchange or Tea Tree Plaza shopping centre. The trip crosses the River Torrens ten times, passing parklands and reservoirs.

Eating Out

Adelaide has an abundance of fine restaurants, and due to its cosmopolitan population, there are many different cuisines from which to choose. If you are looking for takeaway to eat in one of the parks, start around Hindmarsh Square. If you prefer to eat in a reasonably priced restaurant, then try Hindley Street, such as **Hindley Pasta Palace** at no 100, ✆8231 9500. It's ☺open for lunch Mon-Fri and dinner Mon-Sun, is fully licensed, and has authentic Italian cuisine.

Also in Hindley Street, at 131B, is **Jerusalem Sheshkabab House**, which is licensed and BYO, and has inexpensive Lebanese and Middle Eastern food, ☺open daily noon-midnight, ✆8212 6185.

Zapata's Mexican Restaurant, at the northern end of Melbourne Street (no 42), North Adelaide, ✆8267 4653, is one of the most charming of Adelaide's restaurants and is fully licensed.

Bangkok Restaurant, on the first floor of 217 Rundle Street, ✆8223 5406, is a popular Thai restaurant with good service and prices that won't strain your travel budget.

Red Ochre Grill is a licensed restaurant specialising in native Australian flavours. It is open seven days, accepts all major credit cards and is located in Ebeneser Place, ✆8212 7266.

Stanleys The Great Aussie Fish Cafe, 76 Gouger Street, ✆8410 0909, attracts locals and visitors alike to its central location in the CBD. The main cuisine here is, you guessed it, seafood, but meat-lovers are also considered.

Entertainment

Most of the nightspots in Adelaide focus around Hindley Street and North Adelaide. You'll find nightclubs, discos, restaurants, strip clubs and coffee lounges, many of which are open until the wee small hours. Then there is the casino.

Skycity Adelaide, North Terrace, ©8212 2811, is in a classic sandstone railway station building that blends elegance, history and tradition. You're unlikely to find any of these three attributes *inside* the casino, but it does offer the usual entertainment. It features 98 gaming tables on two floors, five bars and a restaurant and carvery, and is open Mon-Thurs 11am-4am, and on the weekends it is ☺open Fri 11am and closes Mon 4am.

Many hotels, motels and restaurants have regular dinner dances or discos. Some also feature floor shows by local and international artists. Details are available in the local press.

Adelaide takes its arts seriously and is proud of its many fine theatres. Programmes cater for a multitude of cultural tastes, ranging from children's and experimental theatre to full scale national and international productions. We suggest you check for details in the entertainment pages of the daily press.

Shopping

Adelaide is a shopper's paradise, and here are the most popular shopping venues.

Rundle Mall is the city's central shopping district, with large department stores, chain stores, boutiques, specialty shops and eateries.

Rundle Arcade, is beneath the Gawler Place Car Park, and is accessed from between Stephens Place and Gawler Place, behind David Jones.

The Gallerie Australis, off Gawler Place has three floors with over 55 individual shops.

The *Renaissance Centre*, off Rundle Mall, is a patchwork of arcades, walk-throughs, flyovers and multi levels.

City Cross, accessed from Rundle Mall, James Place, Grenfell Street and Gawler Place, has over 60 well appointed specialty shops.

Southern Cross Arcade, between James Place and King William

Street, is on the site of the former Southern Cross Hotel, and has two levels of specialty shops.

Regent Arcade runs from Rundle Mall through to Grenfell Streets and houses the Hoyts Cinema complex. It also has over 30 specialty shops.

Adelaide Arcade, between Rundle Mall and Grenfell Street, was built in 1885, and has over 100 shops and two levels.

City Centre Arcade, cnr Rundle Mall & Pulteney Street, has fashion shops, an international food hall, and a licensed restaurant.

John Martin's Plaza, was built in 1983, and is situated between The Link and John Martin's Store, and linked to the latter's ground and first floors. The arcade has 18 specialty shops.

Suburbs

Unley - Metro shopping complex on Unley Road, has some of the city's top designer shops, and antiques.

Hyde Park - King William Road has many specialty shops and boutiques.

North Adelaide - Melbourne Street has boutiques, specialty shops and restaurants.

Glenelg - the main shopping area is in Jetty Road.

St Peters - Jam Factory and Craft Centre, 169 Payneham Road, ☎8362 4542, was once a jam factory but it is now a large shop featuring the best in SA contemporary craft.

Modbury - Tea Tree Plaza, North East Road, has 150 retail outlets including large department stores. It is connected to the city by the O-Bahn Busway.

Markets

The Central Market, Grote Street, Adelaide, has been the culinary inspiration of Adelaide for 120 years and still provides a dazzling array of fresh foodstuffs. ☺Open Tues 7am-5.30pm, Thurs 11am-5.30pm, Fri 7am-9pm, Sat 7am-3pm, ☎8203 7494.

Brickworks Leisure Markets, 36 South Road, Thebarton, is a 6ha (15 acres) site with a permanent variety of leisure activities and an air-conditioned main market area. ☺Open Fri-Mon 9am-5pm, and right through school holidays, ☎8352 4822.

Junction Market, Prospect Road, Kilburn, has about 150 stalls including an international food hall, a produce section and a full range of variety and specialty stalls. ☺Open Sat-Mon 9am-5pm, ☎8349 5866.

Reynella Markets, 255 Old South Road, Reynella, has over 200 variety stalls under the main roof, plus an international food hall. ☺Open Fri-Mon, 9am-5pm.

Adelaide Sunday Market, East Terrace, between Rundle and Grenfell

Streets, is based on the famous Paddy's Market in Sydney, and has around 300 stalls all under cover. ⏰Open 9am-4.30pm.

Points of Interest

City
A walk along Adelaide's wide and gracious streets allows you to see much more than you do when driving. The following walks are suggested to allow the chance to see many facets of the city.

North Terrace
Adelaide Gaol, Gaol Road, western end North Terrace, is more than 147 years old and marks the transformation of early Adelaide into a permanent settlement. The gaol complex is an example of 19th century gaol architecture although it was used as a place of confinement as recently as February 1988. Special features include the Hanging Tower, the original bell and honeycomb brickwork. ⏰Open the first and third Sunday of each month with guided tours between 10am and 3.30pm.

Newmarket Hotel, 1 North Terrace, ☎8216 5216, was erected in 1884 and has a magnificent freestanding spiral staircase.

Lion Arts Centre, cnr Morphett Street & North Terrace, is the home of the biennial Fringe Festival. The centre occupies the site of old factories, and incorporates the Lion Factory building, ⏰open Mon-Fri 9am-5.30pm.

Holy Trinity Church, cnr Morphett Street & North Terrace, on the other side of Morphett Street Bridge underpass, is the State's oldest Anglican Church. The tower houses the original, now restored clock, made in 1836 and shipped from London. ⏰Open Mon-Fri 9am-4.30pm, Sat-Sun from 8am, Sunday services from 8am.

Adelaide Plaza Complex comprises the Adelaide Convention Centre, Exhibition Hall, Hyatt Regency Adelaide, Adelaide Casino and the adjacent Festival Theatre.

The **Adelaide Convention Centre**, North Terrace, ☎8212 4099, is Australia's first multi-purpose convention centre, and can be transformed to accommodate sporting events, conventions of up to 3,500, or as an entertainment venue.

Festival Centre, King William Road, is the home of the biennial Adelaide Festival. The centre comprises a multi-purpose concert hall and lyric theatre, a drama theatre, experimental theatre and an open air amphitheatre. An interesting feature is the 1.2ha (5 acres) of open plaza and terrace surrounding the complex. There is also a Bistro overlooking the river. ⏰Open daily from 9.30am (excluding Public Holidays) and guided tours are available, ©8212 7849.

Old Parliament House, North Terrace, was built in 1855 as South Australia's original Legislative Council Chamber. It is now a museum of political history and has displays and audio-visual programmes, and a courtyard restaurant. ☺Open Mon-Fri 10am-5pm, Sat-Sun noon-5pm.

Parliament House, cnr King William Road & North Terrace, is constructed of Kapunda marble on a foundation of granite. It was commenced in 1883 and completed in 1939. When Parliament is sitting there are public viewings from 2pm.

Government House, cnr North Terrace & King William Road, ©8203 9800, is the Governor's residence, and is the oldest surviving Regency building in Adelaide. Tours of the garden are advertised in daily newspapers. Continue your walk past the Prince Henry Gardens and note the commemorative plaques laid in the footpath naming outstanding contributors to South Australia's first 150 years.

National Soldiers' War Memorial, cnr Kintore Avenue & North Terrace, features a student, a farmer and a young girl, watched over by an armed angel representing the Spirit of Duty. The memorial was unveiled in 1931, and commemorates those who died in World War I.

Royal South Australian Society of Arts, 59 King William Street, houses many interesting and historic paintings in its permanent collection. ☺Open Mon-Fri 11am-5pm, Sat-Sun 2-5pm.

Migration Museum, 82 Kintore Avenue, ©8207 7580. South Australia's living history is here to explore at the Migration Museum. The building was the old Destitute Asylum. ☺Open Mon-Fri 10am-5pm, Sat-Sun 1-5pm.

State Library of South Australia, cnr Kintore Avenue & North Terrace, ©8207 7250, is an Angaston white marble building. ☺Open daily from 9.30am, closed public holidays.

South Australian Museum, North Terrace, ©8207 7500, is a treasure-trove of objects. Collections include Ngurunder, an Aboriginal Dreaming, and the Egyptian Room. The Museum has its own shop and information centre. It is ☺open daily 10am-5pm, except Anzac Day 1-5pm.

Art Gallery of South Australia, North Terrace, ©8207 7000, has a comprehensive collection of Australian, European and Asian Art. ☺Open daily 10am-5pm.

Museum of Classical Archaeology, first floor, Mitchell Building, in the grounds of Adelaide University, North Terrace, ©8303 5638. The museum has some 500 objects, many dating back to the 3rd millennium BC. ☺Open Mon-Fri noon-3pm, closed school holidays.

Scots Church Adelaide, 237 North Terrace, ✆8223 1505, was opened in 1851, the second oldest church in the city. Extensive renovations to the building and church organ place this National Heritage Building on everyone's sightseeing agenda. Special features include the 19th century stained glass windows, the original organ, the pulpit and the font.

Elder Hall, North Terrace, was built in 1900, and is one of Australia's finest concert venues. It has a spectacular pipe organ built by Casauant Feres of Quebec in 1979. Concerts are often held and a calendar is available free at the hall.

Ayers House, 288 North Terrace, was designed by Sir George Kingston and took nearly 30 years to build. The central one-storey section was built in 1846. Sir Henry Ayers, seven times elected Premier of South Australia, later added the bow window, dining and drawing rooms. The building has been restored and houses two restaurants. It is also headquarters for the State Branch of the National Trust. ☺Open Tues-Fri 10am-4pm, Sat-Sun 2-4pm, ✆8223 1234.

Tandanya Aboriginal Cultural Institute, 253 Grenfell Street, is the first major cultural facility of its kind and scale in Australia. Some facilities within the institute are a performing arts area, a museum gallery, a visual gallery and art/craft workshops. Tandanya is the only Aboriginal multi-arts complex in Australia and is owned and managed by Aboriginals. It is ☺open Mon-Fri 10.30am-5pm, Sat-Sun noon-5pm, ✆8224 3200.

King William Street

King William Street starts at the corner of North Terrace. One of the city's widest boulevards, it is the main street of Adelaide.

Edmund Wright House, 59 King William Street, is an elaborate renaissance-style building designed by Edmund Wright in 1876 for the Anglican Bishop of South Australia. The building is now the office of the Registry of Births, Deaths and Marriages. There is a lunchtime musical performance to be seen here every Wednesday, 12.10-1.10pm.

General Post Office, cnr King William & Franklin Streets. The foundation for the present GPO was laid in November 1867, and the building completed in 1872. ☺Open Mon-Fri 7.15am-6.15pm, Sat 8.30am noon, Sun 12.30-5pm, public holidays 9am-noon for stamps and postal parcels only.

Adelaide Town Hall, cnr King William & Pirie Streets, was built from designs by Edmund Wright,

Mayor of the City, in 1859. The foundation stone was laid on May 4, 1863, by the then Governor of South Australia, Sir Dominic Daly, and the opening ceremony took place on June 20, 1866. The entire front of the building and Albert Tower is constructed of freestone.

Old Treasury Building Museum, cnr King William & Flinders Streets, parts of which date back to 1839, has a collection of exploration, surveying, drafting and computing instruments and artifacts. The major theme of the display is the history of land settlement and development of South

Australia since 1836. ⊕Open Mon-Fri 10.30am 3.30pm.

Victoria Square has some noted examples of early Adelaide architecture. The fountain was designed by Adelaide sculptor John Dowie, and has as its theme three of the rivers of South Australia - Torrens, Onkaparinga and Murray.

Supreme Court, cnr Gouger Street & Victoria Square, was built in 1869 of Tea Tree Gully sandstone, and features a three arched entrance, cast-iron gates and ionic columns.

Cathedral Church of St Francis Xavier, cnr Wakefield Street & Victoria Square, was built in three sections, the central part in 1858, with additions in 1886 and 1926. The cathedral is the centre of Roman Catholic life and worship in Adelaide, and celebrates five masses a day. ⊕Open every day.

North Adelaide

A short distance from the heart of the city, north of the River Torrens, is North Adelaide, one of the oldest parts of the city. Away from the shopping districts of O'Connell Street and Melbourne Street, North Adelaide abounds in gracious and grand old homes.

Popeye Motor Launch, Elder Park, River Torrens, leaves from near the Festival Theatre and cruises along 6km of winding waterways, stopping at the Zoo landing. Departure times vary, phone ©8295 4747 for information.

Light's Vision, Montiefiore Hill on Montiefiore Road, is a tribute to Colonel Light who planned the city of Adelaide. The statue of him points the way to a spectacular view of the city and hills.

St Peter's Cathedral, King William Road, took seven years to build and was completed in 1876. The towers and spires were built and consecrated in 1902. The Cathedral has the heaviest and finest bells in the southern hemisphere. ⊕Open daily 7.30am-5.45pm, and conducted tours are available on the second Sunday of each month at 3pm.

Carclew, 11 Jeffcott Street. 'The Home on the Hill' dates back to the late 1890s, and has a tower in the style of the German Rhine castles. Since the early 1970s, Carclew has been a centre for the arts for young people, from which the Youth Festival "Come Out" emanates biennially in May, ©8267 5111.

Parklands

Adelaide and North Adelaide are completely surrounded by extensive parklands. In many there are barbecue and picnic facilities.

Adelaide Botanic Garden, State Herbarium and Conservatory,

North Terrace, ©8222 9311, has numerous heritage buildings and subtropical and Mediterranean plant displays. The Bicentennial Conservatory is the largest in the southern hemisphere and features between 3000 and 4000 plants from Australasia and Malaysia, including 15 to 20 medium sized rainforest trees with associated understorey and ground vegetation. Free guided tours are available Tues and Fri at 10.30am from the kiosk. The garden is ©open Mon-Fri from 7am, Sat-Sun from 9am. The Conservatory is ©open daily 10am-4pm, and there is a small admission charge, ©8232 2745.

Adelaide Zoo, Frome Road, is beautifully landscaped with grassy-moated enclosures, walk-through aviaries, a new reptile house, and a licensed restaurant. ©Open daily 9.30am-5pm, admission is ©$13 adults, $8 children. ©Feeding times: seals 11.45am and 3.45pm daily; big cats 3.15pm Tues, Thurs, Sat and Sun; penguins 2.45pm daily; pelicans 2.30pm daily.

The **North Parklands** are on either side of the River Torrens, and they also surround North Adelaide. Bonython Park (Port Road entrance) has miniature lakes, children's adventure playground and a round pond for model-boat sailors. The Municipal Golf Links has two 18-hole courses, a fine club house and public restaurant. There is also a Par 3 (pitch and putt) Golf Course of 18 holes.

Elder Park, King William Road, is on the slopes of the south bank of Torrens, and is the site of the Festival Centre. The Rotunda in Elder Park was erected in 1882.

The **Eastern Parklands** combine natural and planned landscaping. To the east of Rundle and Grenfell Streets is Rymill Park, which has a boating lake, a rose garden, barbecue and picnic areas. Nearby are children's playgrounds, a wading pool and the Adelaide Bowling Club. The National Fitness Council's "sweat track" is in the East Parklands. The 600m course starts at the eastern end of Halifax Street, and is sign-posted.

Veale Gardens is a feature of the South Parklands and has lawns, flower beds, rose gardens, winding streams and weirs, grottoes and fountains, and a conservatory.

Adelaide Himeji Garden, cnr Hutt Road & South Terrace, was built to symbolise the bonds of friendship between the City of Adelaide and the Himeji Region of Japan. ©Open 7.30am-4pm, Sat-Sun 8am sunset.

Linear Park has evolved into a beautiful park that graces the banks of the River Torrens. It spans the length of the river from the hills to the sea, a distance of approximately

30km (19 miles). It can be accessed at any point of the river, and provides many recreation opportunities for cyclists, walkers, joggers, bird watchers, picnickers and fishing enthusiasts. For a pleasant way to view the park, contact Linear Park Mountain Bike Hire, in Elder Park, on ✆8223 6271.

Suburbs
St Kilda
St Kilda Mangrove Trail, Fooks Terrace. You can discover the marine life of a mangrove forest along a 1.7km boardwalk. Mangroves and mudflats are the remains of a sensitive coastal wetland system which is a valuable feeding and breeding area for marine life. Guided walks are available (subject to tides) ⏰Sat-Sun, public and school holidays 10am-3pm, phone ✆8280 8172 for more information.

Tramway Museum, St Kilda Road, preserves some of the vehicles which served the city from 1909 to 1959. ⏰Open Sun and public holidays 1-5pm, Wed during school holidays 1-5pm, ✆8280-8188.

Port Adelaide
Situated 25 minutes from the centre of Adelaide, Port Adelaide has undergone a renaissance in recent years, and here are some the attractions:

Port Dock Station Railway Museum, Lipson Street, has 26 locomotives on various track gauges and a re-created "break of gauge" railway platform. Two steam trains take visitors around the museum grounds. ⏰Open Sun-Fri 10am-5pm, ✆8341 1690.

Port Dock Brewery Hotel, 10 Todd Street, is an historic hotel first licensed in 1855. The building is registered with both the National Trust and State Heritage, and award winning beers and ales are brewed on the premises. ⏰Open daily, ✆8240 0187.

South Australian Maritime Museum, Lipson Street, is a living, working Maritime Museum in the Port. There are four restored historic buildings, an 1869 lighthouse, the museum wharf, and the historic vessels moored at the wharf house a large collection of maritime artifacts. ⏰Open Sat-Wed 10am-5pm, and daily during school holidays, ✆8207 6255.

Sailmaker Gallery, 117 Lipson Street, behind the Maritime Museum's shop, features Australian paintings and crafts. ⏰Open afternoons until 5pm.

The Port Waterfront Markets, at the end of Commercial Road, next to the red lighthouse, has over 100 stalls selling foodstuffs, plants and crafts. ⏰Open Sun 9am-4pm.

Falie Charters, 3 Divett Street. This 46m steel hulled twin masted ketch was built in Holland in 1919, and was used as a cargo vessel for 60 years, and as a guard boat in Sydney Harbour during the Second World War. She was the Flag Ship of the Jubilee 150 celebrations. ☺Cruises on the Falie operate from 9.30am and 5.30pm, ©8341 2004 for information and bookings.

One and All, Queens Wharf, ©8447 5144, is a centreboard brigantine built of timber. She has been built to operate a Sail Training programme in SA waters. Day trips, half day trips and twilight cruises are available.

Aviation Museum of South Australia, Ocean Steamers Road, in the historic Lion flour mill, has a collection of aircraft and artifacts from Australia's colourful civilian and military air past. ☺Open Sat-Sun and public holidays 10am-5pm, ©8240 1230.

Largs Bay/North Haven

Fort Largs was built as the northern battery of the SA coast defence about 1882, and is now a police training college. Landmarks include the Largs Pier Hotel and the old Post Office, now a coffee shop. North Haven has Australia's largest manmade harbour, with marina docks, ten lane trailer boat launching ramp and cruising yacht club, and a 9-hole golf course.

Semaphore

In its hey-day, Semaphore was a popular seaside resort, and holiday makers enjoyed huge carnivals, side-shows and picture palaces. In the early days of sail and steam it was also an important signal station and recorded information on all ships entering and leaving St Vincent's Gulf. Today, Semaphore is rich with historic landmarks, buildings, and antique shops. Fort Glanville, Military Road, Semaphore South was South Australia's first fortification, dating back to 1878. It was built to combat the Russian scare. The fort has been restored and its re-creation of colonial life of the 19th century includes cannon firings, rifle drills, parades and sentry changes. ☺Open the third Sunday of each month 1-5pm, with additional openings during December and January. Details are printed in the local press.

West Lakes

West Lakes provides facilities for water sports including sailing, canoeing, windsurfing and swimming. There are several indoor centres in the area, and West Lakes is the location of Football Park, home of the SA Football League.

MV *Foxy Lady* Scenic Cruises, 145 Brebner Drive, have cruises of the West Lakes, ☺departing Mon-Sun 1.45pm and 3pm, ©8242 3933.

West Beach

West Beach Reserve has numerous playing fields, two golf courses, a boating lake and a large modern caravan park. The nearby Adelaide Airport is the site of a memorial building to the pioneer aviators Sir Ross and Sir Keith Smith. It houses the Vickers Vimy aircraft they flew from England to Australia in 1919.

Novar Gardens

Cummins, Sheoak Avenue, ©8294 1939, is an historic property which belonged to the Morphett family. John Morphett, a surveyor, was among the party that witnessed the Proclamation establishing the government of the colony in 1836. In later years he became the Speaker and then President of the Legislative Council and was knighted in 1870. The house, Cummins, was built in 1842, and is ☼open Sun 2-4pm, with guided tours at 2.05pm and 3.05pm.

Glenelg

Known as The Bay, Glenelg is the State's Birthplace. On December 28, 1836, the Province of South Australia was first proclaimed beside the Old Gum Tree, now in MacFarlane Street, Glenelg North. Jetty Road, the shopping strip, is in the heart of the town, and, with the arcades running off it, there are over 400 outlets.

Shark Museum, Town Hall, Moseley Square, has a 30-year collection of displays, photographs and film of sharks, amassed by Rodney Fox. ☼Open Wed-Sun 11am-5pm, admission is ✪$4.50 adults, $3 children, ©8376 3373.

HMS Buffalo Nautical Museum, Adelphi Terrace, is a magnificent replica of the HMS Buffalo, built on site between 1980-82 using the original Admiralty plans, at a cost of $1.5 million. The museum houses illustrations and extracts from the old log books, original diary notes, sketches and photographs, and a host of other pieces that tell the story of the original ship's voyage from Portsmouth to Holdfast Bay (off Glenelg) in 1836. There is also a restaurant and an aquarium devoted to species of fish found in South Australia. ☼Open Mon-Sat 6.30pm-9pm, Sun 12pm-2pm. Admission is ✪$2.50 adult, $1.50 child.

Wayville

Royal Adelaide Showgrounds, Goodwood Road, host the Royal Adelaide Show in September each year. At other times the Showground hosts Expo, the Motor Show, Home Show, Caravan and Camping, Pools and Spas and the Christmas Earth Fair. Phone ©8231 6565 for event information.

Woodville

The Brocas Historical Museum, 111 Woodville Road, Woodville, is in a classified house built in 1840 for an early pioneer, John Newman. The house is furnished with period furniture and contains documents, artefacts, photographs, Services memorabilia, and a large scale model of Captain Cook's Endeavour. ◷Open Sun 2-5pm, ✆8347 3810.

Festivals

February - Adelaide Fringe Festival, a biennial festival run in conjunction with the Adelaide Festival of Arts. The Fringe maintains its position on the cutting edge of Australian cultural development in creating an environment which encourages new, innovative and experimental art forms alongside traditional art, ✆8100 2000.

March - Adelaide Festival of Arts, Australia's major cultural event. The programme includes music, drama, ballet, opera, dance, art exhibitions and light entertainment, ✆8216 4444.

May - Adelaide Cup Carnival, South Australia's major horse racing event held at Morphettville Racecourse.

August - Royal Adelaide Show, a week-long family event featuring showbags, livestock, fireworks and staged events.

Facilities

Whatever sport you are into, you'll find it in Adelaide. For information on sporting facilities, matches and associations, contact the Sports Institute, ✆8416 6677.

Adelaide Oval, King William Road, was established in the 1870s and is the premier venue for international and interstate cricket matches. It is also hosts local Australian Football in the winter months. The Oval is ◷open to visitors Mon-Fri, and organised tours can be arranged by telephoning ✆8300 3800.

Memorial Drive Tennis Club, War Memorial Drive, was established in the 1920s, and is set in parklands. The courts have played host to international players since 1929, and every year hosts tournaments attracting big names. Visitors can book courts, coaching and hire equipment, ✆8211 8706. There are grass courts (in summer only), Rebound and synthetic ace courts.

The Aquatic Centre, Jeffcott Road, North Adelaide, has a new leisure pools dimension. It is a world of warm activity pools, cascading water, fountains, bubble beaches, river rapids and other features in a tropical landscape setting. For further information and opening times, ✆8203 7203.

Mt Thebarton Snow & Ice, 23 East Terrace, Thebarton, has the world's first indoor artificial ski slope, designed for beginners but great fun for all. There is also an olympic size and beginners skating rink, and all equipment available for hire. ☺Open Mon-Fri from 9.30am, Sat-Sun from 12.30pm, ✆8352 7977.

Outlying Attractions

The Adelaide Hills

If there is one feature that characterises Adelaide's landscape it is the rim of hills along the city's eastern country. Within a half an hour of the city centre is another world - a world of tranquility and greenery. In the summer it is a refuge from the heat; in winter, a touch of Europe.

Hahndorf

The people who settled Hahndorf were emigrating from the eastern provinces of Prussia to escape the religious persecution they were suffering because of their staunch Lutheran convictions. Their ship, the *Zebra*, under the command of Captain Hahn, arrived at Holdfast Bay on December 28, 1838, and Port Adelaide on January 2, 1839. Captain Hahn had been so impressed with his passengers that he was determined to see them settled together on land they could farm. He finally decided on the spot, and the grateful people named their village after him. Founders Day is held on the Sunday of the Australia Day Long Weekend holiday in January. Hahndorf is 28km (17 miles) from Adelaide, and there is a regular bus service from/to Adelaide, phone ✆8391 2977 for further information.

The Adelaide Hills Information Centre is at 41 Main Street, ✆8388 1185, and is open seven days. Some of the town's attractions are: the Pioneer Memorial Gardens, Main Street, opened in January 1939, to mark the centenary of the town; St Michael's Lutheran Church, cnr Balhannah & Church Streets, built in 1859 (the foundation stone had been laid on September 29, St Michael's Day, hence the name of the church); Hahndorf Oval, in Pine Avenue, was established in 1936 to mark the State Centenary.

Early each year it is the venue for

the colourful Schutzenfest (Shooting Festival), which derived in the provinces of Germany. Traditional costumes, steins, German style foods and beverages, together with music and dancing, make this annual event very spectacular.

The Historic Old Mill (Wittwer's Mill) was built in 1864 by Mr F.W. Wittwer, and first used as a flour mill. Today it is a restaurant, motel and convention centre, ©8388 7888.

German Arms Hotel, ©8388 7013, was the first hotel built in Hahndorf, and its publican's licence was issued in 1839. The site of the first hotel is now a grocery store, and the present Hotel was built during the late 1860s.

Hahndorf's favourite son is Sir Hans Heysen, who was born in Germany in 1877, emigrated to Adelaide in 1883, and moved to Hahndorf in 1908. The success of various exhibitions of his water colours in Melbourne enabled him to purchase The Cedars, a property on the outskirts of Hahndorf in 1912. He lived there until his death in 1968. Many of the old barns, cottages and trees that he painted can still be seen in and around Hahndorf. Some of his original works are on display at the Hahndorf Academy Public Gallery & German Migration Museum, 68 Main Street, ©8388 7250.

Torrens Gorge

The North East Road from Adelaide leads to the semi rural setting of St Agnes, and a few minutes further on at Tea Tree Gully is the 100 year old Angoves Winery. 2km further on, turn left into Range Road North to Upper Hermitage, on the Ansteys Hill to Gawler Scenic Tourist Drive there are panoramic views of the city, northern suburbs and Adelaide Plains and across the Gulf of St Vincent to Yorke Peninsula. On the way to Gawler, you can go to Para Wirra National Park or go up over the mountains to Kersbrook.

Glenara Wines, 126 Range Road North, Upper Hermitage, ©8380 5277, has a picnic area and barbecues are available to customers at their cellar door sales in the heart of the vineyard.

The next town is Inglewood, about 30 minutes from the city, with the Historic Inglewood Inn, one of only three Historic Inns in South Australia. Old Inglewood Cottage, next to the General Store, was in 1860 the local blacksmith shop, but now it sells locally produced handcrafts and produce.

Cudlee Creek is home to Gorge Wildlife Park, which covers an area of approximately 6ha (14 acres). The park is privately owned and has a large collection of animals, including big cats, deer and plenty of koalas. Gumeracha is one of the oldest

settled areas of South Australia, dating back to 1839. Two historic buildings are the Baptist Church and Randell's Mill. The town also has the Biggest Rocking Horse in the World at the Toy Factory, open daily, ☎8389 2206 or ☎8389 2332.

Other towns in the Gorge include Birdwood, Mt Pleasant, Keyneton, Springton, Mt Torrens, Charleston, Tungkillo and Lobethal.

Onkaparinga Valley

The Heart of the Hills is a beautiful valley, and the small river which gives this valley its name meanders through orchards, rich pasture and meadow land, flanked by the Mount Lofty ranges.

Verdun is the beginning of the Onkaparinga Valley, and other towns that are in the valley include Balhannah, Oakbank, Woodside, Lenswood and Forest Range.

East Torrens

The East Torrens area is a nature wonderland with its many parks sheltering the native wildlife and birds. The winding roads, breathtaking views, cool waterfalls, bubbling creeks, pear, apple, cherry and plum orchards, make a trip here a memorable experience. The parks in the area are Black Hill Conservation Park, Morialta Conservation Park, Horsnell Gully Conservation Park, Ferguson Conservation Park, Waterfully Gully, Cleland Conservation Park and Montecute Conservation Park.

Marble Hill, located 6km beyond Norton Summit on the Ashton to Cherryville Road, was a residence built as a summer retreat for early Governors. The site commands wide views overlooking the plains and out to the sea. Built in 1878-79, it was surrounded by a large area of garden. Marble Hill was totally burnt out on Black Sunday (January 2, 1955). In 1967 it was offered to the National Trust and is being partially restored. ☺Open Sat, Sun, Wed and public holidays (closed during August).

The waterfalls of Morialta are its best known feature, but there are also walking trails and picnic areas in this park. The dark wooded contours of Black Hill are easily seen behind Adelaide's north-eastern suburbs. At the base of the hill are picnic areas and gardens. Towns in East Torrens include Norton Summit, Ashton, Basket Range and Summertown.

Mt Lofty Area

In 1802 Mt Lofty was sighted and named by Captain Matthew Flinders from Kangaroo Head on Kangaroo Island. Conservation and Recreation Parks in the area include Mt Lofty Summit Lookout, Mt Lofty Botanic Gardens, Mt George Conservation Park, Beechwood Gardens, Loftia Park, Sturt George Recreation Park, Scott Creek Conservation Park, Brownhill Creek Recreation Park, Belair Recreation Park, Mt Bold Reservoir and Cleland Conservation Park.

Mount Lofty Summit Visitor Centre & Gift Shop, Crafers Court, Summit Road, Crafers, ℰ(08) 8370 1054, ☉open 7 days.

Old Government House, in Queen Jubilee Drive, Belair, is a must for anyone with an interest in cultural history, historical architecture, antiques or cottage gardens. The house and gardens are open for viewing, and guided tours on Sunday and public holiday afternoons.

Blackwood Hills District

The Wittunga Botanic Gardens, Shepherd Hills Road, Blackwood, have two lakes and a sand-plain garden. There are dazzling displays of Australian and South African plants. ☉Open Mon-Fri 10am-4pm, Sat-Sun 10am-5pm, ℰ8370 8370.

The Coromandel Valley is located between Blackwood and Clarendon, and has stands of large trees, streams and gullies.

Mt Barker Area

Mt Barker is the largest town in this area of the Adelaide Hills, and is a service centre for the surrounding rural district. One of the town's best known landmarks is the historic steam flour mill. It has been restored and is now The Flour Mill Tea and Coffee Shop and gallery. Other towns in the area are Clarendon, Meadows, Macclesfield, Wistow and Nairne.

Fleurieu Peninsula

Follow the Main South Road until the McLaren Vale turn-off, then detour for a tour of the Southern Vales. McLaren Vale is the centre of the wine coast with 45 wineries, and the McLaren Vale & Fleurieu Visitor Centre on Main Road, McLaren Vale, has a map and opening times for all of them, phone ©(08) 8323 9944, or ✐email information@visitorcentre.com.au

Port Elliot

Situated on Horseshoe Bay, Port Elliott was originally selected as the site for the ocean port for the Murray River trade, but it was a poor choice as it was unprotected. Several shipwrecks followed and the port was transferred to the lee of Granite Island at Victor Harbour. Today Port Elliott is a popular tourist resort, and Boomer Beach on the western edge of the town is a gathering point for the surfing fraternity.

Victor Harbour

Victor Harbour is a delight coastal resort, and the largest of the resort towns on Horseshoe Bay. It was an old whaling base and much of its early history has been preserved at Whale Centre, 2 Railway Terrace, ©8552 5644.

An old horse tram runs out to Granite Island which has colonies of wallabies and fairy penguins. At night you can spot the penguins in their rookeries. One of the best known landmarks on the south coast is Rosetta Head, also called the Bluff. It is a natural rock formation which dominates the skyline just west of the town. There is a magnificent view from the top, but the climb is demanding.

Just out of town is the Urimbirra Wildlife Park, Adelaide Road, ©8554 6554, with a good collection of Australian animals, and Greenhills Adventure Park, ©8552 5999, with a giant waterslide and roller sled.

Cape Jervis

The cape, 109km (68 miles) from Adelaide, is mostly known as a jumping off place for Kangaroo Island. A car ferry takes passengers to Kangaroo Island from its moorings nearby, ©8553 1233.

The Heysen Walking Trail begins at Cape Jervis and goes all the way to the northern Flinders. You can explore the rugged coastline around Cape Jervis, or fossick around the nearby Talisker Mine which dates back to 1862.

Kangaroo Island

When Matthew Flinders discovered Kangaroo Island in 1802 it was uninhabited. However, the island had been inhabited by Aboriginal people, about whom little is known. Stone tools have been found in some areas, indicating their presence probably over 10,000 years ago. Kangaroo Island is not small, as most people expect, as it is approximately 145km (90 miles) by 60km (37 miles). To fully explore all that it has to offer takes a minimum of five days. Package tours including travel and accommodation are available, and you should enquire at your local travel agent. There are no foxes, dingoes or rabbits on the Island, but there are wild pigs, which are thought to have been released by the French explorer Nicholas Baudin, as a food source for shipwrecked sailors. The main towns on the island are American River, Kingscote and Penneshaw, and they all have hotels, motels, licensed restaurants, coffee shops and delicatessens.

The Kangaroo Island Gateway Visitor Information Centre is in Howard Drive, Penneshaw, ©(08) 8553 1185, ✎email tourki@ kin.on.net, ☺open Mon-Fri 9am-5pm, Sat-Sun 10am-4pm. The National Parks and Wildlife Service also has an office in Dauncey Street, ©8553 2381.

The island is home to many Fairy Penguins, who come ashore at night to roost or feed their young, and can be seen on the foreshore at Penneshaw and Kingscote. There is no public transport covering the island, however there is a bus service between Penneshaw, American River and Kingscote. You can fly to Kangaroo Island with Whale Air, ©8555 4075, or sail across.

Murray Bridge

Situated about 80km (50 miles) east of Adelaide, Murray Bridge is the favoured haunt of water skiers - the river between White Sands and Willow Banks provides a special paradise for them. Puzzle Park in the town has Australia's largest maze, 4.5km of passage ways, mini golf, and the Murray River Fish Aquarium, ©8532 3709. As with many South Australian towns, Murray Bridge has great parks, and the town is also the base for trips down the Murray River.

Above: The Barossa Valley   Below: Old Post and Telegraph Station, South Australia   Overleaf: Mt Lofty Ranges in South Australia

Mount Gambier

Population 23,000
Mount Gambier is located 451km (280 miles) south-east of Adelaide, on the slopes of an extinct volcano.

Climate

Average temperatures: January max 25C (77F) - min 11C (52F); July max 13C (55F) - min 5C (41F). Average annual rainfall: 708mm (28 ins).

Characteristics

Mount Gambier has two famous attractions, the Blue Lake and the Cave in the centre of the city. As a consequence the town is known as 'Blue Lake City' or the 'City Around A Cave'. The lake is famous for its change of colour from winter grey to intense blue in November each year. It remains blue until late March, and aside from its beauty, is the City's source of domestic water. The open cave is set in attractive gardens, well renowned for their roses, and was the original source of the water supply.

How to Get There

By Bus

Bonds Adelaide - Mount Gambier Coach departs daily via Coorong (Highway 1) and via Naracoorte (inland route).

By Rail

There is a regular service between Adelaide and Mt Gambier via Warrnambool or Ballarat.

By Road

From Melbourne, via the Princes Highway 438km (272 miles), and from Adelaide, via the Princes Highway 451km (280 miles).

Tourist Information

The Lady Nelson Visitor & Discovery Centre, Jubilee Highway East, ©(08) 8724 9750 or toll-free 1800 087 187 is ✆open seven days, 9am-5pm, with extended hours over school holiday periods. You can contact them by ✉email thelady nelson@mountgambier tourism. com.au or check out the comprehensive website at ☞www.mount gambiertourism. com.au

Alternatively, Limestone Coast Tourism is in the Old Town Hall Building, Commercial Street East , ©(08) 8723 1644, with email at ✉ tourism@thelimestone coast.com and a website at ☞www.thelimestonecoast.com

Accommodation

Mount Gambier has motels, hotel/ motels, hotels and caravan/camping parks. Here is a selection, with prices for a double room per night, which should be used as a guide only. ©The telephone area code is 08.

Mount Gambier International Motel, Millicent Road, ©8725 9699. 69 units, licensed restaurant, swimming pool, spa, sauna, bbq, tennis ✪$100-115.

Quality Inn Presidential, Jubilee Highway West, ©8724 9966. 53 units, licensed restaurant, indoor swimming pool, spa, sauna - $107.

Arkana Motor Inn, 201 Commercial Street East, ©8725 5823. 20 units, swimming pool, spa, bbq ✪$77-105.

Le Cavalier Court Motel, 37 Bay Road, ©8725 9077. 10 units, licensed restaurant (closed Monday) ✪$55.

Mount Gambier Motel, 115 Penola Road, ©8725 5800. 32 units, licensed restaurant, swimming pool, bbq ✪$60-90.

Blue Lake Motel, Kennedy Avenue, ©8725 5211. 24 units, licensed restaurant (closed Saturday and Sunday) ✪$50-65.

Lakes Resort Motel Mt Gambier, 17 Lake Terrace West, ©8725 5755. 32 units, licensed restaurant, swimming pool, spa ✪$85-140.

Tower Motor Inn, 140 Jubilee Highway West, ©8724 9411. 19 units, swimming pool, bbq ✪$65.

Caravan Parks

Mt Gambier Central Caravan Park, 6 Krummel Street, ©8725 4427. (No pets allowed) - powered sites ✪$15 for two, on-site vans $31 for two.

Jubilee Holiday Park, Jubilee Highway East, ✆8723 2469. (Pets allowed on leash) - powered sites with en-suite ✪$11 for two, cabins $39-49 for two.

Blue Lake City Caravan Park, Bay Road, ✆8725 9856. (Pets allowed on leash) - powered sites ✪$20 for two, on-site vans $32-47 for two.

Pine Country Caravan Park, Port MacDonnell Road, ✆1300 720 115. (Pets allowed on leash) - powered sites ✪$16 for two, cabins $33-49 for two.

Eating Out

As will be seen in the accommodation listed in this section, many of the motels have restaurants, and there are the usual number of takeaway outlets. Following are some restaurants you might like to try:

The Mt Gambier Hotel, 2 Commercial Street West, ✆8725 0611, has a reasonably priced smorgasbord, and also a la carte in the atrium.

The Barn Steakhouse, Nelson Road (8km out of town), ✆8726 8250, have very reasonable prices, and an extensive wine cellar. Children catered for.

Mandarin Restaurant, 68 Commercial Street West, ✆8723 2100, are ◷open Wed-Mon and serve Chinese a la carte.

Le Cavalier Restaurant, 37 Bay Road , ✆8725 9077, have an a la carte menu for lunch on Tue, Fri & Sun and are ◷open for dinner every night except Monday.

Golden Chopsticks Chinese Restaurant, 95 Commercial St East, ✆8725 3935, is ◷open for dinner Tues-Sun and lunch Thu-Fri.

Points of Interest

The 197m (646 ft) deep **Blue Lake** is the premier tourist attraction. In the area, an obelisk marks the spot where the poet Adam Lindsay Gordon made a famous leap on horseback over a fence on to a narrow ledge overlooking the lake.

The Cave in the centre of town is probably next in importance, and its sunken gardens are worth a visit.

Facing the Cave Gardens is the modern **Civic Centre**, which houses the offices of the City of Mount Gambier, Council Chambers, City Library and the Sir Robert Helpmann Theatre - a modern 528 seat theatre which is host to local and visiting artists.

The **Lady Nelson Visitor & Discovery Centre** on Jubilee Highway East, is a major historical and social interest Jubilee 150 Project, which commemorates the sighting and naming of Mount Gambier on December 3, 1800 by Lt James Grant, from the deck of *The Lady Nelson*, a small survey brig.

The major feature of the complex is the full scale replica of the brig, which is cut in half through the longitudinal cross-section, and forms part of the structure of the building. The complex provides displays and information on the area encompassing the south-east of South Australia and the south west of Victoria.

Adjacent to the Blue Lake is another volcanic crater with the Valley and Browne's Lakes and the former **Leg of Mutton Lake**, which no longer contains water but is a pleasant wooded area. The Valley Lake is used for aquatic sports and is dominated by the Centenary Tower on the summit of the mount.

Umpherston Sinkhole, with its terraced gardens and barbecue areas, is an ideal spot for a picnic, and the cave is floodlit at night.

Many **historic buildings** line the streets of Mt Gambier. Of particular note is Jens Hotel which was the original site of the town's first hotel, the Town Hall built in 1862, and the Post Office built in 1865. To guide visitors to the more interesting historic sites, a heritage walk has been devised, and the pamphlet is free from the Visitor Centre.

Visitors can walk through one of the huge timber mills, or a cheese factory, or tour the Blue Lake Pumping Station and view the Lake from the pontoons on the surface. There are also museums and galleries – including the Port MacDonnell & District Maritime Museum – and several parks and gardens. The Visitor Centre will be able to advise on these.

Festivals

The Blue Lake Festival is held in November each year and incorporates the Christmas Pageant and Generations in Jazz.

The Mt Gambier Gold Cup Racing Carnival is held in June.

Facilities

Tennis, flying, racing, trotting, cycling, go-kart racing, ten-pin bowling, squash, rifle range, gun club, stock car racing, pistol shooting speedboating, lawn bowls, golf and health studios.

Outlying Attractions

Port MacDonnell

Situated 28km (17 miles) south of Mt Gambier, Port MacDonnell is Australia's most southerly port. Originally it was busy with freight from the early settlers being sent to Adelaide and Melbourne, but now it is a base for a large fleet which fishes the Southern Ocean for lobster between the months of October and May.

The township has retained the atmosphere of a small fishing village, and is a peaceful place to visit.

2km from Port MacDonnell is the former home of well-known poet and horseman Adam Lindsay Gordon. The cottage dates back to the 1860s and has been restored. It contains some of Gordon's belongings.

The lighthouse at Cape Northumberland sits above one of the most rugged sections of the coast, and the scenic drive to the lighthouse passes a petrified forest. Near Cape Northumberland are the Frog, Dinosaur and Camel rocks and the Map of Australia reef.

Piccaninnie Ponds Conservation Park is 27km south-east of Mt Gambier off the Nelson Road, and its main feature is a large reed swamp. The area is well known as a popular cave diving spot.

North of Port MacDonnell is Mt Schank volcano, which was sighted and named by Lt Grant as he sailed by in the Lady Nelson in 1800. From the top of the mount there are spectacular views of the countryside, and walking tracks have been built on the outside and inside of the crater for the energetic.

Little Blue Lake, 3km on the opposite side of the road from Mt Schank, is a popular spot for experienced swimmers, and changes colour like its large cousin in Mt Gambier.

For local informaiton, stop in at the Port MacDonnell and District Council Office in Charles Street, ℂ(08) 8721 0444. They are ⏰open Tue-Thu 9am-4pm.

Penola

Centrally located, 51km (32 miles) from Mt Gambier, Penola is the South-East's oldest town, and a joy for anyone interested in history. The many remaining slab and hewn cottages erected in the 1850s depict the lifestyle of the early settlers, and Yallum Park, built in 1880 shows life on a grander scale. Many famous names are associated with Penola - poets Adam Lindsay Gordon, John Shaw Neilson and Will Ogilvie spent time here, and it was here, in 1866, that Mother Mary MacKillop established the first school in Australia which catered for all children regardless of income or social status. The Mary MacKillop Interpretive Centre, Portland Street, tells the story of the history of the district and Mary's life, and has an audio-visual show. It is ☉open seven days 10am-4pm and costs ✪$3.50 adult.

The Tourist Information Centre in 27 Arthur Street, ✆(08) 8737 2855, has details of all attractions.

Coonawarra

The Coonawarra grape growing and wine producing area now occupies a significant position in the Australian Wine Industry. It came into being when John Riddoch of Yallum Park, established a fruit colony on 2000 acres of his property. Grapes figured prominently among the fruit grown, and thrived in the rich soil, so in 1893 Riddoch built the first winery in Coonawarra.

Coonawarra is 10km (6 miles) north of Penola, and now has 22 wineries open seven days a week, with tastings and cellar door sales. Information on the various wineries can be obtained from the Tourist Information Centre in Penola, ✆(08) 8737 2855.

Naracoorte

Situated 39km (24 miles) north of Coonawarra, Naracoorte is one of the region's larger commercial centres. Its history dates back to the 1840s when the first hotel and store were built by William MacIntosh. The name Naracoorte, by the way, means 'running water'.

The town's main claim to fame now, though, is the Naracoorte Caves Conservation Park, ✆8762 3412. The park is 12km (7 miles) south-east of the town on the way to Penola. There are approximately 60 known caves along a 25km (15 miles) range, and many are within the park itself. Visitors can take guided tours to a range of underground caves, including the Alexandra, Blanche and the Victoria Fossil Cave. If you intend to take one of the Special Adventure Cave tours on offer, make sure you wear sneakers and take a change of clothes, as they involve crawling

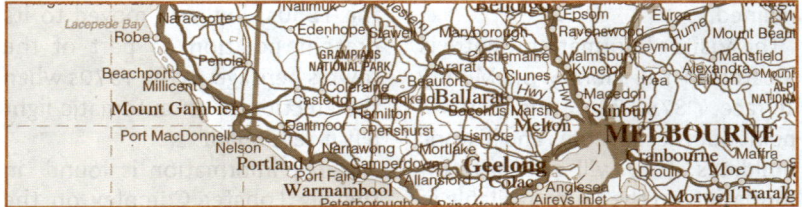

and climbing. The Park has a camping ground, picnic areas, interpretive centre and kiosk facilities.

Millicent

Millicent is 40km (25 miles) west of Mount Gambier, in the centre of the South-East. The town was named after Millicent Glen, wife of one of the early pioneers and daughter of the first Anglican Bishop of Adelaide. Millicent was a rural centre at the beginning of this century, but the development of a pine plantation and the establishment of a sawmill and two paper mills saw a change of identity, and a large increase in population.

The Tantanoola Caves are 19km (12 miles) east of Millicent, in the Tantanoola Caves Conservation Park, ✆8734 4153. They are unique in that there are no stairs in the caves, and a pathway allows wheelchair access. When you visit the caves stop off at the Tantanoola Hotel in the township, and ask about the legend of the Tantanoola Tiger, who apparently prowled the

area in the late 1800s.

Millicent Tourist Information Centre is in 1 Mount Gambier Road, Millicent, ✆(08) 8733 3205.

Beachport

35km (22 miles) west of Millicent is Beachport, which was first settled as a whaling station by the Henty Brothers in the 1830s. It is now a quiet seaside town involved in the lobster and fishing industries.

Robe

Robe is 50km (31 miles) from Beachport, and the road there passes Lakes George, St Clair and Eliza. The Port of Robe was proclaimed in 1847 and gradually grew, exporting wool and horses. An unusual import at the time was over 16,000 Chinese, heading for the Victorian goldfields, who landed in South Australia to avoid the ten pounds poll tax imposed by the Victorian Government.

By 1864 Robe had become South Australia's third most important port, then the shipping trade declined and only the fishing fleet remained.

The Visitor Information Centre is located in the Library on Mundy Terrace, ✆8768 2465, and they will point out the museums and historic buildings. They will also have information on the tours available in nearby Little Dip Conservation Park, 4km to the south. ☺Opening hours are Mon-Fri 9am-5pm and Sat-Sun 10am-1pm.

Kingston

The entrance to the town of Kingston is guarded by a 17m (56 ft) lobster named Larry, letting everyone know that this is lobster country. Situated 44km (27 miles) north of Robe, Kingston was named in 1858 after being established in 1856 by the Cooke Brothers who took up Government Land Grants near Maria Creek.

There are many fine old buildings in Kingston, including the Post Office, the Colonial Tea Rooms and Gallery, the Court House and the original Gaol and Police Station, which now houses an antique shop. The National Trust Museum, built in 1872 as a timber mill, contains general folk items including gowns and nautical items. Cape Jaffa Lighthouse was originally

erected on Margaret Brock Reef in the 1860s, but was moved to its present position as part of the town's heritage, in the 1970s when the erection of an automatic light left it redundant.

Tourist information is found in the Big Lobster Complex on the Princes Highway, ✆(08) 8767 2555.

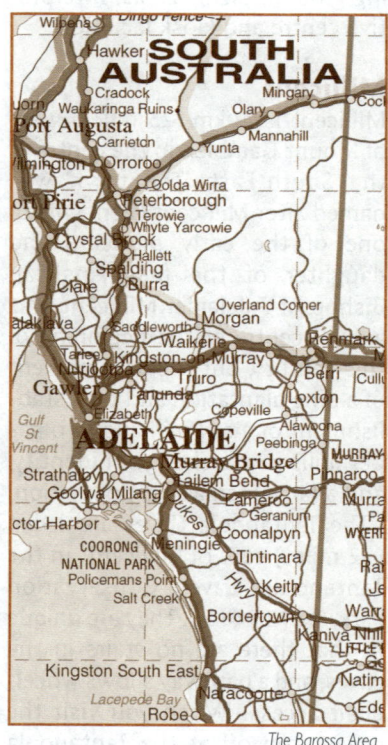

The Barossa Area

Barossa Valley

The Barossa is about 50km (31 miles) north of Adelaide.

Climate

Average temperatures: January max 29C (84F) - min 14C (57F); July max 13C (55F) - min 3C (37F). Average annual rainfall: 633mm (25 ins).

Characteristics

The Valley is the vineyard of the nation, producing nearly 60% of Australia's wine, and exporting more than 6 million litres of fine, quality wine a year. In 1842, Pastor Kavel lead a group of Lutherans to the valley, and they brought not only their vine cuttings, but also their building techniques and culture.

How to Get There

By Bus
Greyhound Pioneer stop at Nuriootpa on their Brisbane/Adelaide routes.

By Road
From Adelaide, via the Stuart Highway to Gawler, the Gateway to the Valley.

Tourist Information

The Barossa Wine and Visitor Information Centre is at 66-68 Murray Street, Tanunda. They can be contacted by phone on ✆(08) 8563 0600 or by ✎email info@ barossa-region.org. ⏰Opening hours are Mon-Fri 9am-5pm, Sat-Sun 10am-4pm. The website to explore is 👁www.barossa-region. org

Accommodation

Some of the wineries and homesteads in the valley offer accommodation, and the Information Centre has all the details. Here is a selection of hotels and motels, and of course, caravan parks. Prices are for a double room per night, and should be used as a guide only. ©The telephone area code is 08.

Gawler

Prasad's Gawler Motel, cnr Main North Road & Gawler By-Pass, ©8522 5 900. 104 units, swimming pool, tennis ✪$80.

Gawler Caravan Park, Main North Road, ©8522 3805. (No pets allowed) 82 sites, playground, barbecue, good facilities - powered sites ✪$16 for two, on-site vans $32 for two, cabins $50 for two.

Hillier Park, Hillier Road, ©8522 2511. (No pets allowed) 270 sites, barbecue, swimming pool - powered sites ✪$15 for two, cabins $50 for two.

Lyndoch

Barossa Park Motel, Barossa Valley Highway, ©8524 4268. 34 units, licensed restaurant, swimming pool, barbecue, spa ✪$90.

Barossa Caravan Park, Barossa Valley Highway, ©8524 4262. (No dogs allowed) 50 sites, good facilities, barbecue - powered sites ✪$15 for two, on-site vans $25 for two.

Tanunda

The Hermitage of Marananga Motel, Seppeltsfield Road, ©8562 2722. 11 rooms, guest house accommodation, licensed restaurant, swimming pool, spa - B&B ✪$200-250.

Barossa Motor Lodge, Murray Street, ©8563 2988. 40 units, licensed restaurant, swimming pool, spa, sauna, tennis, barbecue ✪$95-120.

Barossa Weintal Resort, Murray Street, ©8563 2303. 40 units, licensed restaurant, bistro (Fri-Sun), swimming pool, sauna, tennis, barbecue ✪$105-150.

Barossa Junction Motel, Barossa Valley Way, ©8563 3400. 33 units, licensed restaurant, indoor heated swimming pool, spa, tennis, squash, barbecue ✪$70-130.

Tanunda Caravan & Tourist Park, Barossa Valley Way, ©8563 2784. (Pets allowed on application) 276 sites, excellent facilities - powered sites ✪$17 for two, on-site vans $35 for two, cabins $75 for two.

Nuriootpa

Nooriootpa Vine Inn, 14 Murray Street, ©8562 2133. 9 units, licensed restaurant, bistro, swimming pool, spa ✪$105.

Nooriootpa Vine Court, 49 Murray Street, ©8562 2133. 17 units, heated swimming pool, spa, barbecue ✪$85.

Barossa Gateway Motel, off Sturt Highway, ℰ8562 1033. 23 units, basic facilities ✪$55-65.

Barossa Valley SA Tourist Park, Penrice Road, ℰ8562 1404. (Pets allowed on leash) 176 sites, tennis, barbecue, excellent facilities - powered sites $18 for two, cabins $35-55 for two.

Angaston

Collingrove Homestead, Eden Valley Road, ℰ8564 2061. 2 rooms, excellent facilities, spa ✪$210.

Vineyards Motel, cnr Stockwell & Nooriootpa Roads, ℰ8564 2404. 22 units, heated swimming pool, spa, undercover parking, barbecue ✪$55-90.

Barossa Brauhaus Hotel, 41 Murray Street, ℰ8564 2014. 7 rooms (no private facilities), basic accommodation, licensed restaurant ✪$55 including breakfast.

Eating Out

Most of the hotels and motels mentioned in the Accommodation Section have licensed restaurants, and each town has the usual amount of coffee lounges and takeaway outlets. The Tourist Information centres in each town have a complete list of eateries, and many are mentioned in the Points of Interest section.

Points of Interest

Gawler

Gawler was the second country town to be created in South Australia (Port Adelaide was the first), and its official birthday is January 31, 1839. Many of the buildings reflect the architectural design and influence of the late 19th and early 20th centuries, with beautiful stonework. Most were constructed of local stone, and the nearby hills show the scars of the excavation of the bluestone used for the Town Hall and churches, the Post Office and the Old Telegraph Station.

The Gawler Visitor Centre is at 2 Lyndoch Road, ℰ8522 6814, and they have information and maps for walking, cycling and driving tours of historical sites. You can email them at ✉ visitor.centre@gawler.sa.gov.au or visit the website ☞www.gawler.sa.gov.au The Centre is ⏲open 9am-5pm seven days and can organise wine tours and other activities for you.

Stroll down Murray Street for a place to dine out. Here you will find the Gawler Palace Chinese Restaurant, the Bamboo Hut Bistro, Cafe Nova. If none of these suit you, try The Wheatsheaf Inn in Sunnydale Road, ℰ8522 5762, or Zeebous in Calton Road, ℰ8522 3621.

From Gawler, the main road to the Whispering Wall Reservoir turns off to the right in Sandy Creek, passing the village of Cockatoo Valley, with its general store. Near here are the remains of the old Barossa Goldfields along Goldfields Road, and a converted miner's cottage which offers accommodation, ©8524 6213.

Further on is the Barossa Reservoir, built in 1898 and the largest in South Australia. The retaining wall has an unusual acoustic effect so that a person standing on one side can hear whispers from the other side of the dam - hence the name Whispering Wall.

Rosedale is on the western side of the Barossa Valley Highway, driving from Sandy Creek north to Lyndoch, and in the district there are many beautiful old buildings and a farm cottage that has been converted to provide accommodation.

Lyndoch

The town was named by Colonel William Light in 1838 to honour Lord Lynedoch, under whom he had served in the Napoleonic Wars. The present name came from a spelling mistake.

The first settlers arrived in 1839 and farming was the main early industry. In late 1847, a group of Germans settled at Hoffnungsthal (or Valley of Hope) in the hills behind Lyndoch. The valley basin formed a lake during wet seasons, and the village was destroyed by floods in 1853, the only remnants now being the foundations of a church and a plaque.

Vineyards were established in the early years and the first winery was set up in 1896 in a converted flour mill. Today there are ten wineries in the immediate area, all family owned, ranging in size from very small to one of the largest in the Barossa.

Tourist Information is available at Kies Family Wines, Barossa Highway, ©8524 4110, and they can provide a map pinpointing the location of the various wineries, and a pamphlet outlining a walking tour of the town.

Wineries

Wards Gateway Cellar, Barossa Highway, ©8524 4138, has a good range of interesting wines, and is ☺open for tasting and sales daily 9am-5.30pm.

Burge Family Winemakers, Wilsford, ©8524 4644, is ☺open seven days, and is a must for quality wine enthusiasts. Limited output is available ex-vineyard only.

Charles Cimicky Premium Wines, ©8524 4025, is a small winery renowned for premium boutique-style wine making. There is a Cellar Bistro offering lunch, and the winery is ☺open for tastings and sales daily 10am-4pm.

Chateau Yaldara, ☎8524 5637, is ☺open for tasting and sales 7 days a week, and has conducted tours of the winery and the Chateau Collection. There is also a Garden Bistro serving lunch and morning and afternoon teas.

Kies Estate Cellars, ☎8524 4110, have premium dry and sweet table wines, and are ☺open Mon-Fri 9am-5pm, Sat-Sun 10am-5pm. There is ample parking, and a children's playground in the grounds.

Kellermeister Wines Pty Ltd, ☎8524 4303, are ☺open every day 9am-6pm, and have award winning wines for tasting in an historic building.

Barossa Settlers, ☎8524 4017, was established by descendants of Barossa pioneers in an historic stable, and there is a collection of artefacts and implements. Award winning wines are available at the cellar door only. The winery is ☺open Wed-Sat & Mon 10am-4pm, Sun 1-4pm.

Eating places in the town include the Lyndoch Bakery and Restaurant, ☎8524 4422, fully licensed and serving home-cooked German meals, and the Lyndoch Hotel, ☎8524 4211, also with home-cooked style offerings.

Rowland Flat

Johann Gramp began commercial wine making at Jacobs Creek in 1847, and Rowland Flat was also the home of one of South Australia's earliest potters, Samuel Hoffmann. Today, the town is well known for the large winery complex, and the souvenir and craft shops in its grounds.

Driving towards Tanunda there are four wineries along Krondorf Road, running from Hallett Valley, on the western side, to the foothills of Kaiser Stuhl on the east. There are many typical valley buildings, many of which have been restored and offer farm-style accommodation. A nearby road gives access to the Heysen Trail, and the high country of the Barossa Ranges. In Hallett Valley there is a keg factory where coopers carry on their traditional craft, and ☺welcome visitors Mon-Sat 8am-4.30pm, ☎8563 3012.

Wineries

Miranda Wines, Barossa Highway, ☎8524 4537, is ☺open for tastings and sales Mon-Fri 8.30am-4.30pm, Sat-Sun 10am-4.30pm.

Orlando Wines, ☎8521 3111, have a picnic and barbecue area, and staff who are very proud of their products. The complex is ☺open daily.

Grant Burge Wines, Barossa Valley Highway, Jacobs Creek, ☎8563 3700, have excellent wines and tasting facilities, and cellar door sales ☉daily 10am-5pm.

Rockford Wines, have full bodied Australian wine styles in a restored 1850s cottage and farm buildings. ☉Tastings and sales daily 11am-5.30pm, ©8563 2720.

Charles Melton Wines, Krondorf Road, ©8563 3606, specialise in premium Barossa reds, and are highly acclaimed for quality and presentation. ☉Open daily 11am-5.30pm.

Liebuchwein, ©8524 4543, have reds, whites and fortified wines, and are ☉open daily 11am-5pm.

Bethany

Situated near Tanunda, Bethany was the first German settlement in the Barossa. In 1842, a group of Silesian families settled near the Tanunda Creek, and named their village after the biblical Bethany.

The town has many lovely old stone houses, farms and cottage gardens, and many of the old buildings have been tastefully restored. Some are still used as houses, while others have been transformed into art galleries, a restaurant and Australia's smallest motel, the Landhaus, ©8563 2191, which also has a very good restaurant.

Of interest in the town are the Pioneer Cemetery and the Lutheran Church.

Winery

Bethany Wines - Bethany Road, ©8563 2086, is ☉open Mon-Sat 10am-5pm, Sun 1-5pm. The Winery selects grapes from the Schrapel Family vineyards, and commands the best views of the Barossa Valley.

Tanunda

Tanunda was originally the village of Langmeil, the second German settlement in the Barossa in 1843. A drive through the back streets of Tanunda on the western side of the main street, takes you through Goat Square and Langmeil Road where many of the early stone buildings can still be seen. Goat Square was the site of the first town market, and many of the bordering cottages have now been classified by the National Trust. Restored buildings in the tree-lined main street include the hotel, the museum and the old institute.

Tourist Information is available at the Barossa Wine and Visitor Information Centre, at 66-68 Murray Street, ©(08) 8563 0600, and they can advise on the many attractions in the town, which include Story Book Cottage and Whacky Wood, Oak Street, ©8563 2910; and Norm's Coolie Sheep Dog Performance, ©8563 2198. They also have a pamphlet on a walking tour of the town, which visits all the important sites.

Eating places include the fully licensed, or BYO, Park Restaurant, 24 Murray Street, ℰ8563 3500, ☉open for lunch and dinner seven days, and serving German and Australian meals; Cafe Heidelberg and Art Gallery, 8 Murray Street, ℰ8563 2151, ☉open Wed-Mon 10am-10pm (children welcome); and Tanunda Hotel, 51 Murray Street, ℰ8563 2030, with an a la carte bistro and restaurant.

Wineries
Tanunda Cellars, Murray Street, ℰ8563 3544, specialise in premium and museum wines. ☉Open Mon-Sat 9am-6pm, Sun 11am-6pm.
Basedow Wines, Murray Street, ℰ8563 0333, were established in 1896, and have tastings of premium tables wines in an underground cellar. There are picnic grounds, and the winery is ☉open Mon-Fri 10am-5pm, Sat-Sun 11am-5pm.
Langmeil Winery, cnr Para & Langmeil Roads, ℰ8563 2595, is set on the river bank, and has picnic facilities and barbecues. It is ☉open for tastings and sales daily 11am-5pm.
Chateau Tanunda, Basedow Road, ℰ8563 3888, featuers an historic French-style chateau surrounded by gardens. Tastings, gourmet snacks and premium wines are available ☉daily 10am-5pm.
Peter Lehmann Wines, ℰ8563 2500, is also on the banks of the North Para River, and has a full range of premium Barossa varietals. ☉Open Mon-Fri 9.30am-5pm, Sat-Sun 10.30am-4.30pm, and there are picnic facilities and barbecues.

Barossa Valley Way

It only takes about five minutes to drive between Tanunda and Nuriootpa, through the vineyards that stretch across the valley to the Barossa Hills. There have been some new developments along the road in recent years, as well as the continuation of long established businesses.

You can wander through a fascinating private museum, or enjoy the history of Dorrien contained in murals at the old Seppelt winery building which is on the corner of Seppeltsfield Road. The village of Siegersdorf was also in this area, and the name was one of those changed during World War I (to Bultawilta) and restored in 1975. Just past the Dorrien corner on the Seppeltsfield Road there is an old cemetery, Seppelt's Mausoleum, and from the corner Siegersdorf Road takes you to Angaston.

Along Barossa Valley Way and also on Seppeltsfield Road and Research Road, are a number of wineries, some long established and others recent enterprises. Accommodation in the area is available at the travellers' hostel, a guest house, and in some imaginatively converted railway carriages. Tourist Information is available in the Rohrlach Kev Museum, ☎8563 3407, which is ⏰open daily 10am-5pm. The Museum has a kiosk, and can advise on eating establishments.

Wineries

Chateau Dorrien Winery, ☎8562 2850, has wine and mead tastings ⏰daily 10am-5pm, and don't miss the murals on the original wine tanks.

Tarchalice Schmidt Family Winery, Research Road, Vine Vale, ☎8563 0667, have picnic facilities under the vines and tastings of their complete range of wines.

Mildara Blass, ☎8562 1366, have tastings of premium red and white table wines at their Medlands winery, Seppeltsfield Road, Dorrien, ⏰on Fri and Sat 10am-5pm, and Mon-Sat during school holidays.

Marananga

Marananga, which is Aboriginal for 'my hands', was settled in the mid-1840s and originally named Gnadenfrei, meaning 'Freed by the Grace of God', by the pioneers who had gained freedom from religious persecution in Silesia.

The original Gnadenfrei Church was begun in 1857, and there are many other interesting old buildings including the old school house.

Tourist Information is available in the Gnadenfrei Estate, which is on Seppeltsfield Road, ☎8562 2522.

For good restaurants, try the The Hermitage of Marananga Restaurant on Seppeltsfield Road, ☎8562 2722, which is fully licensed, or BYO, and is ⏰open for lunch Wed-

Mon, and dinner Thurs-Sat, with bookings taken for other nights.

Wineries

Heritage Wines, a small family winery on Seppeltsfield Road, ☏8562 2880, which is ☉open daily for tastings and sales.

Gnadenfrei Estate Winery, ☏8562 2522, ☉open for tastings and sales daily 10am-5.30pm. They have picnic areas, and provide picnic baskets.

Seppeltsfield

The town was established in 1851 when Joseph Seppelt, his family and workmen arrived to run a dairy and grow tobacco and wheat in the valley. The tobacco grew too rank, so Joseph started to experiment with winemaking. Soon Seppelts became the largest winery in the colony, and the cellars and stores were described in the London Gazette 1892 as 'the most modern in the world'. They have been maintained in their original condition. Close by the winery is the old Seppelt family house, which has been restored and provides accommodation. There are also holiday units in the town.

The winery to visit here is Seppelt's, and they have tastings of their award winning wines daily, ☏8568 6200. You can explore the extensive grounds and the preserved buildings, and picnic and barbecue facilities are available. They are ☉open Mon-Fri 10am-5pm, Sat-Sun 11am-5pm and conduct daily tours.

Greenock

Situated on the western edge of the Valley en route to the mid-north, Greenock is home to one of the Barossa's famous bakeries, and the local hotel dates back to the 1870s. It is a pretty place for a picnic, or you can call into the Greenock Creek Tavern in Kapunda Road for a counter lunch Mon-Sat, or dinner Fri and Sat, ☏8562 8136.

Nuriootpa

The North Para River winds through the town of Nuriootpa, at the northern end of the Barossa Valley. The name is Aboriginal for 'a meeting place', and it was an important tribal centre for bartering. Now, Nuriootpa is the commercial and service centre of the region, with a number of government agencies' regional offices.

William Coulthard laid out the first town acre in 1854, and the town grew around his red gum slab hotel. The building is no longer there, but his home at the other end of the main street (66 Murray Street), has been preserved. The The Barossa Wine and Visitor Information Centre in Tanunda have information on a walking tour of the town, which visits about 20 sites. They can also advise on restaurants, but you might like to try the Shangri-La Thai Restaurant, at 31 Murray Street, ☎8562 3559.

Wineries

Penfolds Wines - Nuriootpa, is the largest winery complex in the Valley, and is the home of Kaiser Stuhl and Tollana wines. ☺Tours are held Mon-Fri at 10am, 11am, 1.30pm, 2.30pm, and tasting and sales are available Mon-Fri 9am-5.30pm, Sat 10am-5pm, Sun 1-5pm. The winery is on the Barossa Highway, ☎8568 9408.

Elderton Wines, on the corner of Murray Street and New Road, ☎8562 1058, is a family winery with award winning wines at reasonable prices. Available are vineyard tours, bike rental, moke rental and picnic grounds.

Wolf Blass Wines International, on the Sturt Highway, ☎8568 7311, have tastings of the full range of award winning wines in picturesque surroundings. They are ☺open Mon-Fri 9.15am-5pm, Sat-Sun 10am-5pm.

The Willows Vineyard, ☎8562 1080, has tastings of varietal wines made from fruit grown on the Scholz Family's historic property, and are ☺open daily 10.30am-4.30pm. Drive through the vineyard to Huldas Cottage for the tastings.

Stockwell

Situated at the northern approach to the Valley, the peaceful village of Stockwell is dominated by the Lutheran Church and the old flour mill group of buildings, both of which have played an important role in the town's history. The mill still produces a variety of high quality flours.

The hotel and the small winery offer a change to experience the days gone by.

The historic 1865 Gaol House was converted to a boutique winery with a fine selection of 15 year old liqueur fortifieds and Barossa table wines.

Stockwell Hotel, established in 1857, is ☺open daily for counter meals, with the dining room open Fri and Sat evenings and Sun lunch, ☎8562 2008.

Angaston

The town is named after George Fife Angas, a prominent figure in South Australia's history, who took up large land holdings in the Barossa Ranges and Valley in the 1830s. Angas himself settled Lindsay Park, near the present town, in 1851. Angaston is the centre of a rich pastoral district, with viticulture and fruit growing playing an important part in the local economy.

Tourist Information is available at Angaston Abbey, 18 Murray Street,

©8564 2648, a 125-year-old former church, now an art and craft exhibition. It is ☺open Thurs-Mon 10am-5pm. Another information place is the Collingrove Homestead on Angaston Road, a former home of the Angas family. The homestead offers casual accommodation, morning and afternoon teas, light lunches, and formal dining on Fri and Sat nights. It is ☺open daily 10.30am-5pm, ©8564 2061.

For fine food, try the Brauhaus Hotel, 41 Murray Street, ©8564 20144, home of the renowned 'Brauhaus Pepper Steak' or get takeaway from Angaston Chicken Shop, in the heart of town, ©8564 2552.

Gawler Park Fruits (Mariani Australia), 29 Valley Road, ©8564 2021, are ☺open Mon-Fri 9am-4.30pm for sales of quality glace fruit and table raisins; and Angas Park Fruit Co Pty Ltd, cnr Murray & North Streets, ©8564 2052, are ☺open Mon-Sat 9am-5pm, Sun 11am-5pm, for sales of quality nuts and dried fruit related products.

Wineries

Saltram Winery, ©8564 3355, was established in 1859, and is one of the oldest wineries in the Valley. It is ☺open for tastings and sales Mon-Fri 9am-5pm, Sat-Sun noon-5pm.

Yalumba Winery, is in an old marble building with clocktower facia, and is even older, having been established in 1849. ☺Cellar door sales are in the Old Bond Store, Mon-Fri 8.30am-5pm, Sat 10am-4pm, Sun noon-4pm, ©8561 3200.

Keyneton

Keyneton is a small village 10km (6 miles) south-east of Angaston in the Barossa Ranges. In the early 1900s, there were five wineries, all with large vineyards, located in the Keyneton area. The one remaining today, **Henschke**, is noted for the quality of its wines and old stone buildings. Henschke is owned by the fifth generation of winemakers, and was established in 1868. They are specialist makers of an exclusive range of premium quality red and white estate bottled table wines, and are ☺open Mon-Fri 9am-4.30pm, Sat 9am-noon, ©8564 8223.

Eden Valley

Situated south of Keyneton, Eden Valley is home to Eden Springs Wine Estate and the High Eden vineyard which produces classic regional wines. Tasting is available in an old Melbourne tram. There are picnic and barbecue areas, nature walks, and on Sunday a Lamp Spit Lunch. The estate is ☺open daily 10am-5pm, ©8564 1166. In the town there is also an historic hotel, which serves meals, and a general store which offers delicious Devonshire teas.

Springton

At Springton is the historic Herbig Gum Tree, where pioneers Caroline and Friedrich Herbig began their married life and had two of their sixteen children! The original old stone blacksmith shop is now a small winery and cafe, and the old store and post office has been restored and is now an art and craft gallery.

South of the town is the Merindah Mohair Farm, in Springton Road, Mt Pleasant, ✆8568 2043, where you can buy hand knits, or yarns and patterns to knit your own garments. The farm is ☼open daily 10am-4pm.

Wineries

Craneford Wine Co & Zilm's Cafe has full flavoured regional wines, and cellar door tasting and sales are available daily 11am-5pm. The restaurant provides lunches Wed-Mon 12.30pm-3pm, and dinner Fri and Sat, ✆8564 0003.

Robert Hamilton & Son - Sprinton Wine Estate, 3km east of Springton, ✆8556 2222, are 6th generation winemakers. Wine tasting and sales are in an historic bluestone building, which is ☼open daily 10am-4pm.

Festivals

The Barossa Valley Vintage Festival is a biennial event beginning on Easter Monday - April 1, 1991, April 12, 1993 - with a week of activities.

The Angaston Show is in February. The Tanunda Show is in March, as is the Essenfest (Eating Festival).

The Tanunda Christmas Parade is in December.

Facilities

Bike Hire - Barossa Valley Tourist Park, ✆8562 1404; Bunkhaus, cnr Barossa Valley Highway and Nuraip Road, Nuriootpa, ✆8562 2260; Elderton Wines, Nuriootpa, ✆8562 1058; Keil's Gift Centre, 63 Murray Street, Tanunda, ✆8563 2177.

Ten pin bowling - Barossa Bowl, Menge Road, Tanunda, ✆8563 3177.

Squash and Rollerskating - Barossa Valley Recreation & Fitness Centre, cnr Menge Road & Magnolia Street, Tanunda, ✆8563 2766.

Golf - Gawler Par Three Golf Course, ✆8522 3060.

Ballooning - Balloon Adventures, Nooriootpa, ✆8562 3111.

Helicopter Rides - Barossa Helicopters, Lyndoch, ✆8524 4209.

Renmark

Population 7,750

Situated on the Murray River in the centre of the Riverland, Renmark is the first major town in the state when entering South Australia from the Eastern States along the Sturt Highway.

Climate

Average temperatures: January max 31C (88F) - min 15C (59F); July max 15C (59F) - min 5C (41F). Average annual rainfall: 312mm (12 ins).

Characteristics

Renmark is recognised as the River Holiday Centre of Australia, offering a wide range of river holiday experiences from luxury cruising on the grandiose Paddle Steamer *Murray Princess*, self-drive house-

boats, daily river cruises, dining aboard the cruising restaurant MV *Barrangul*, relaxing in picturesque riverside caravan parks, or simply skiing, boating, canoeing or trying to catch one of the River Murray's 'tasty' fish, such as callop.

How to Get There

By Bus

Greyhound Pioneer stop at Renmark on their Sydney/Adelaide routes. Stateliner has a service from Adelaide to Renmark.

By Road

From Sydney, via the Hume and Sturt Highways, or via Wagga Wagga and Mildura.

From Adelaide, via the Sturt Highway.

Tourist Information

The Renmark Paringa Visitor Information Centre is at 84 Murray Ave, email ✎tourist@riverland.net.au, ©8586 6704. It is ⊙open Mon-Fri 9am-5pm, Sat-Sun 9am-4pm.

Accommodation

Following is a selection of available accommodation, with prices for a double room per night, which should be used as a guide only. The telephone area code is 08.

Hotels and Motels

Citrus Valley Best Western Motel, Renmark Avenue, ©8586 6717. 25 units, licensed restaurant, swimming pool, barbecue ✪$80-100.

Renmark Country Club Motel, Sturt Highway, ©8585 1401. 37 units, licensed restaurant, swimming pool, tennis, golf, undercover parking ✪$90.

Fountain Gardens Motel, Renmark Avenue, ©8586 6899. 22 units, swimming pool, barbecue ✪$60-70.

Ventura Motel, 234 Renmark Avenue, ©8586 6841. 15 units, swimming pool, barbecue ✪$75.

Renmark Hotel/Motel, Murray Avenue, ©8586 6755. 78 rooms, licensed restaurant ✪$80-130.

Caravan Parks

Renmark Riverfront Caravan Park, Riverfront, ©8586 6315. (No pets allowed) 300 sites, playground, barbecue - powered sites ✪$15-18 for two, on-site vans $30 for two, cabins $35-60 for two.

Riverbend Caravan Park, Sturt Highway, ©8595 5131. (No pets) 60 sites, kiosk, barbecue - powered sites ✪$17 for two, on-site vans $40-65 for two.

Houseboats

Renmark is now firmly established as the Houseboat Hiring Centre of Australia, and there are over 55 houseboats available for hire, ranging in size from two to ten berth, and offering from standard to luxury facilities. For information about bookings, contact the Tourist Centre, or try Liba-Liba, ©8586 6734.

Cruising

PS *Murray Princess*, ©8569 2511 or ©1800 804 843, operates 6-day cruises from Renmark, cruising both up and downstream from the town and covering 700km (435 miles) of the most beautiful scenery in the Riverland Region. The vessel is the biggest of her kind in the Southern Hemisphere, and accommodates 120 passengers in two-berth cabins with private en-suite bathrooms. The vessel has

cabins and elevators for the disabled, and facilities include 2 saunas, 2 spas and a colonial style lounge area with views back over the paddle. PS *Murray Princess* is ⊕open for inspection every Sunday 1-2pm, and the Tourist Centre has brochures and information on availability of cruises.

Eating Out

There is a good selection of restaurants, cafes and takeaway outlets, and here are some names and addresses.

Ashley's Restaurant, 210 Renmark Avenue, ©8586 6854, ⊕open 7 days from 6pm.

Riverland Golden Palace Restaurant, Renmark Avenue, ©8586 6065. Chinese cuisine, closed Monday, ☺open Tues-Thurs noon-2pm, 5-9.30pm, Fri-Sat noon-2pm, 5-10.30pm, Sunday 5-9.30pm.

Bistro in the Renmark Hotel, Murray Avenue, ©8586 6755, ☺open daily, noon-2pm, 6-8pm.

Jacaranda Room in the Renmark Country Club, off Sturt Highway, ©8595 1401, ☺open daily from 6.30pm.

Renmark Club, Murray Avenue, ©8586 6611. Thursday - family economy; Friday - smorgasbord; Saturday - a la carte, 6.30-8.30pm. Visitors welcome.

Points of Interest

Bredl's Reptile Park & Zoo, 5km from town on the Sturt Highway, has over 400 species of reptiles, birds and animals. The largest collection of live reptiles in Australia includes deadly taipans, cobras, death adders, tiger snakes, pythons, boa constrictors, crocodiles, monitor lizards. There is a kiosk with a large range of souvenirs. ☺Open daily, with the snakes being fed every Sunday 2-3pm, ©8595 1431.

Olivewood (Chaffey House), was the original home of the Chaffey brothers, who founded the original settlement here in 1887. It is a National Trust of South Australia House on the heritage list, and has a museum, ☺open Thurs-Mon 10am-4pm, Tues 2-4pm, closed Wednesday, ©8586 5745. It is located on the corne of Renmark Avenue and Twentyfirst Street, with admission ✪$4 adults.

David Ruston's Rose Garden is a 6ha (16 acres) reserve with over 30,000 rose bushes, a large collection of flowering trees and shrubs, and many varieties of iris and day lilies. A viewing tower gives a chance for some great photographs. ☺Open daily from October 1 to May 31, ©8586 6191.

The **PS Industry** was built in Goolwa, SA, and commissioned in January 1911 as a workboat for the South Australian Engineering and Water Supply Department. It played a major part in keeping the river open for traffic by removing snags. It is located on Murray Avenue, and can still be seen chugging down the river.

Harding's Folklore Gallery, Murtho Street, has a large ceiling mural depicting colonial Australian bushrangers, and a good collection of Australian art and weapons of the colonial days. The gallery is ☺open most days, ©(08) 8586 6972.

Ozone Gallery, ©8586 6368, has arts and crafts mostly by local people, with around 355 paintings on

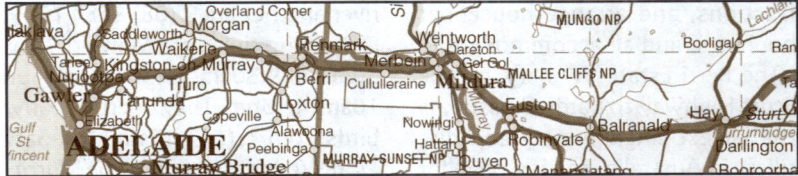

display. The gallery is run by volunteer help, and is ☺open at these hours: Mon-Thurs 9.30am-5pm, Fri 9.30am-6pm, Sat 9am-12.30pm, Sun 1-4pm. Another gallery in town is Zenith Art Gallery, ✆8586 6274.

River Cruises - 1.5 hour day cruises, luncheon, dinner and sunset cruises are available from several companies, and the Visitor Centre has all the necessary information.

Wineries

Angove's, makers of St Agnes Brandy, Marko Vermouth, Stones Ginger Wine and Angove's Varietal Table Wines, have winery tours ☺Mon-Fri 10.30am, cellar sales and tastings Mon-Fri 9am-12.30pm, 1.30-5pm (no tours over the two weeks of the Christmas-New Year period), ✆8580 3100.

Renmano Wines, , ✆8586 6771, ☺open Mon-Sat 9am-5pm for tasting and sales. Winery tours are by arrangement only.

Facilities

Three bowling clubs, lawn, all-weather and indoor tennis courts, olympic swimming pool and waterslide, football, indoor/outdoor cricket, hockey, basketball, volleyball, rollerskating, badminton, gymnasium, table tennis, golf, rifle club, horse and pony club.

Outlying Attractions

Berri

Situated on the Murray River, 18km (11 miles) from Renmark and 238km (148 miles) from Adelaide, Berri was originally settled as a pastoral area. When irrigation commenced in 1908, it became a major fruit growing area specialising in grapes for wine and drying, stone fruits and citrus. Large industries grew to process these fruits, examples being Berri Estates Winery, Berri Company Co-operative Ltd, and Berrivale Orchards Juice Plant and Food Processing Plant. Now Berri has a population of around 7000, and is a pretty town with many parks and gardens along the town riverfront.

The Berri Tourist Information Centre is in Vaughan Terrace, ✆8582 5299, and they can advise on attractions, and arrange houseboat bookings, and all accommodation.

The Berri Estates Winery, on the Sturt Highway towards Glossop, is the largest single winery and distillery in Australia, and is ☉open for sales Mon-Fri 9am-5pm, Sat 9am-4pm, closed Sunday, ☎8582 0340.

The Riverland Big Orange, Sturt Highway at the Monash/Morgan turn-off, is the largest orange in the world, and has excellent views of the River Murray. Here you can buy local produce, wines, souvenirs, or take an orchard tour. ☉Open daily 9am-5pm, ☎(08) 8582 4255.

Loxton

256km (159 miles) from Adelaide, and about 30km (19 miles) from Berri by river, Loxton was settled in 1895 as a farming community, and the Historical Village on the riverfront, ☎8584 7194, has many early buildings, and a replica of William Charles Loxton's pine and pug hut. They also have a large display of early farming equipment and machinery - ☉open daily 10am-4pm, and during holiday periods also Wed 7-9pm.

The Tourist Information office is at 45 East Terrace, ph 847 919, and has details of accommodation and attractions.

The Loxton Visitor Information and Arts Centre is in Bookpurnong Terrace, ✎email loxtour@

riverland.net.au, ☎(08) 8584 7919. ☉Opening times are Mon-Fri 9am-5pm, Sat 9.30am-12.30pm and Sun 10am-4.15pm. They open for early-birds from 7.15-7.45am Mon-Sat.

On Wednesday night, the *Murray Princess* pulls into Loxton on her cruise down the Murray, and a good time is had by all, with Village Minstrels and true riverboat celebrations.

Barmera

Barmera is situated on the shores of Lake Bonney, a freshwater lake whose source is the Murray River through Chambers Creek. Joseph Hawdon discovered the lake in 1838 whilst overlanding cattle from NSW to Adelaide, and named it after his companion Charles Bonney. The surrounding area was first taken up with pastoral leases until 1922 when they were divided into irrigation blocks for growing grapes, stone fruits, citrus and vegetables. Today, as with other Riverland towns, Barmera has been developed along community and co-operative lines.

The ideal climate, combined with the swimming, yachting, water skiing, speed boating, wind surfing and fishing that the lake provides, makes Barmera an ideal place to spend some time. The Tourist Information Centre is in Barwell Avenue, ☎8588 2289.

Waikerie

Situated on the Murray River, 175km (109 miles) from Adelaide, Waikerie was settled in 1894, and is a well-planned, pretty town with award winning gardens. Street names bear evidence of a strong German heritage. The town is acclaimed as a glider's paradise, and also has the largest citrus packing house in Australia, the Waikerie Co-op Producers Ltd.

Although the Sturt Highway bypasses the outskirts of Waikerie, it is well worth a side trip for closer examination. Apart from its natural flora and fauna, the town also has several pleasant eateries, wineries and shops specialising in locally made goods. Tourist Information is available at The Orange Tree on the Sturt Highway, ©8541 2332. It is ◷open Mon-Fri 9am-5.30pm and Sat-Sun 10am-4pm.

Morgan

The township of Morgan is on the Murray River, 166km (103 miles) from Adelaide. The site of the town was passed by Charles Sturt on his voyage down the Murray and back in 1830. Known originally as North West Bend, the Great Bend, or the Great Elbow, it became a point for overlanders, on their way to Adelaide with stock, to leave the Murray and make for Adelaide. In 1878 the town was proclaimed, and the Kapunda to Morgan railway officially opened.

Changing times forced the closure of the railway service in 1969, but relics of this era remain with the original Station, Station Master's Residence, Turntable and Rest Rooms, all in excellent condition.

Morgan Visitor Information Centre is at 11 Railway Terrace, ©(08) 8540 2354, and the local people are very friendly and will give all the advice you need to see the local attractions.

Blanchetown

Blanchetown is your first port of call in the Riverland if you are travelling the 134km (83 miles) from Adelaide, or the last if you are travelling from the eastern States. The town was laid out in 1855 and declared a port in 1863. It is the start of the River Murray lock and weir system for water quantity control. The lock was completed in 1922, and is an impressive sight from the lookout at the Blanchetown Bridge.

Blanchetown is a popular holiday resort with many holiday homes lining the river banks, and good fishing and skiing areas nearby. You can grab a hearty meal at the Blanchetown Hotel, ©8540 5017, the hub of this tiny town.

Flinders Ranges

The foothills of the Flinders Rangers begin at the northern end of St Vincent's Gulf, and stretch north for approximately 800km (497 miles) into the dry outback region.

Climate

Semi-arid climate which leads to dry-country vegetation, including saltbush and light timber. In spring the area is alive with wild flowers, making it an ideal time to visit. Winter days can also be pleasant, however the nights are very cold; summer is very hot with temperatures ranging from 30-40C (86-104F); autumn has much the same temperatures as spring.

Characteristics

Granite mountain ranges with towering peaks, razor backed quartzite ridges, slashed by precipitous gorges, and creeks with cool, deep waterholes framed by stately gums. The whole area is an artist's or photographer's delight. The colours and shadows change continually depending upon the time of day and the season of the year.

How to Get There

By Bus
Premier Stateliner service towns to Hawker and Quorn. For details of timetables phone ©(08) 8415 5555.

By Rail

Australian National operates regular air-conditioned services from Adelaide, Coonimia near Port Pirie, Port Augusta, Whyalla and Peterborough.

By Road

From Port Augusta take Highway 47 to Hawker, then a sealed road to Wilpena Pound. The road from there through Blinman and on to Arkaroola is gravel.

Tourist Information

The Flinders Ranges Visitor Information Centre is at 3 Seventh Street, ℰ(08) 8648 6419, email ✒ tourism@flindersrangescouncil. sa.gov.au

Alternatively, Wilpena Pound Visitor Information Centre is at the Wilpena Pound Resort, ℰ(08) 8648 0048. It is ☺open 8am-6pm seven days.

You might also wish to visit theuseful website ☜www.flinders .outback.on.net

Accommodation

For information and Camping Permits for the various National and Conservation Parks in this region, contact the National Parks & Wildlife SA, Hawker branch, at 60 Elder Terrace, ℰ(08) 8648 4244.

The accommodation listed here is town based, and prices are for a double room per night. They should be used as a guide only. ℰThe telephone area code is 08.

Quorn

Flinders Ranges Motel, 2 Railway Terrace, ℰ8648 6016. 12 units, licensed restaurant ✪$85.

Transcontinental Hotel, 15 Railway Terrace, ℰ8648 6076. 19 rooms, licensed restaurant, basic accommodation ✪$55-60 including breakfast.

Quorn Caravan Park, Silo Road, ℰ8648 6206. (Pets allowed on leash) 110 sites, barbecue, good facilities - powered sites ✪$18 for two, on-site vans $35 for two, cabins $55-60 for two.

Hawker

Outback Chapmanton Motor Inn, Wilpena Road, ℰ8648 4100. 14 units, licensed restaurant ✪$80.

Hawker Hotel Motel, Elder Terrace, ℰ4848 4102. 20 units, licensed restaurant, barbecue ✪$70-75.

Flinders Ranges Caravan Park, Hawker-Leigh Creek Road, ℰ8648 4266. (Pets allowed on leash) 100 sites, excellent facilities - powered sites ✪$18 for two, on-site vans $35-40 for two, cabins $50-70.

Hawker Caravan Park, Chaceview Terrace, ℰ8648 4006. (No dogs allowed) 120 sites, playground, barbecue - powered sites ✪$19 for two, cabins $65-100 for two.

Wilpena Pound

Wilpena Pound Resort, ✆8648 0004. 60 units, licensed restaurant, swimming pool, barbecue ✪$110.

Wilpena Pound Camping & Caravan Park, ✆8648 0004. (No dogs) 300 sites, basic facilities - powered sites ✪$20 for two.

Rawnsley Park Station, Wilpena Road, ✆8648 0008. (No pets) 300 sites, basic facilities - powered sites ✪$21 for two, on-site vans $42 for two, cabins $55 for two.

Blinman

North Blinman Hotel/Motel, ✆8648 4867. 9 units, basic accommodation, licensed restaurant, swimming pool, barbecue ✪$85.

Blinman Campground, Mine Road, ✆8648 4867. (Pets allowed on leash) 8 sites, barbecue, pool - powered sites ✪$10 for two.

Marree

Marree Caravan & Campers park, cnr Birdsville & Oodnadatta Tracks, ✆8675 8371. (Pets allowed on leash) 120 sites, barbecue - powered sites ✪$16 for two, cabins $30 for two.

Arkaroola

Mawson Lodge, Wilderness Sanctuary, ✆8431 7900. 20 units, licensed restaurant, swimming pool ✪$115-120.

Arkaroola-Mt Painter Sanctuary Resort, Wilderness Sanctuary, ✆8431 7900. (No pets) 150 sites, playground, pool - powered sites ✪$17 for two, bunkhouses $30-90.

Eating Out

The majority of hotels and motels in the area have restaurants, and general stores and petrol stations usually sell takeaway food.

Points of Interest

Quorn

Situated 334km (208 miles) from Adelaide, the old railway town of Quorn is an ideal holiday base. The town has many historic buildings reflecting its former importance as a railway junction. Nowadays, the only railway sounds are when the old steam trains (Afghan Express, Pichi Richi Explorer and Barwell Bull) run to through Pichi Richi Pass to Woolshed Flat and Stirling North. Trains are scheduled to run on certain days from Easter to October, and timetables are available from Information Outlets, by calling ✆8658 1109 or visiting the site 👁www.prr.org.au online. Bookings can be made at the Railway Station on the day of travel, or on the number mentioned above. There are also guided tours of the railway workshops throughout the year, and on days when the train runs.

Only a short distance from town are the Wankerie Falls, Warren, Buckaringa and Middle Gorges. About 14km (9 miles) south of the town is Mt Brown (900m - 2953 ft), the highest point in the area. Nearer town are Devil's Peak and Dutchman's Stern, both of which are richly coloured and have walking trails to the summit.

Quorn has retained much of its old world character, and the Mill, built in 1878 as a flour mill, has been restored and houses a restaurant. Other galleries with local art and craft are: Junction Art Gallery, Quandong Cafe & Art Gallery and Sue's Art Studio Gallery.

North of the town are the historic Kanyaka ruins and graveyard, all that remains of the homestead which once supported 70 families for about 20 years from the 1850s. Located near the ruins is the Death Rock waterhole.

Local 4WD tours are available from Quorn, contact Ozzies Bush Track Tours, ©8648 6016, for details.

Apart from the Flinders Ranges Visitor Information Centre, tourist information is also available at the Flinders Ranges Council at 1 Seventh Street, ©8648 6031.

Hawker

A typical outback town, Hawker is the hub of the Flinders Ranges, being the junction of roads from Port Augusta, Orroroo, Leigh Creek, Marree and Wilpena/Blinman. It is 374km (232 miles) from Adelaide, and was a thriving railway town before the line was relocated in 1956. Hawker is now an important tourist centre in the Flinders, and a Town Heritage Walk has been developed to take you through the town's pioneering history.

The Tourist Information Centre is at Hawker Motors, cnr Wilpena & Cradock Roads, ©8648 4014.

A walking trail and scenic lookout have been established at Jarvis Hill, 5km south-west of Hawker. The lookout provides a spectacular panorama of the surrounding countryside.

Easy day trips from Hawker include to Quorn and Pichi Richi Pass, Wilpena, Brachina and Parachilna Gorges, Leigh Creek coalfield and Aroona Dam.

Yourambulla Caves, south of the town, have a number of Aboriginal paintings as well as another good view.

There are many scenic drives available from Hawker, and one of the most popular is the Moralana Scenic Drive joining Wilpena and Leigh Creek Roads. It offers good scenery, particularly from the Black Gap

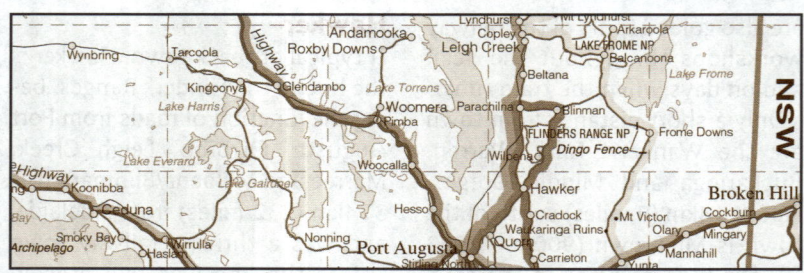

Flinders Ranges

Lookout. A more rugged drive, through Yappala and past Middle and Buckaringa Gorges to Gordon, provides a mixture of outback pastoral country, rugged hills, creeks, flora and fauna. It is advisable to check local road conditions before setting off on one of these drives.

Wilpena Pound

Situated 54km (34 miles) north of Hawker, the Pound is probably the best known feature of the Flinders Ranges. It is an oval bowl 16km (10 miles) long and 10km (6 miles) wide, surrounded by high quartzite cliffs. The only route to the Pound is over Sliding Rock along the edge of Wilpena Creek. Aboriginal legend says that the rim is formed by the bodies of two serpents. Enough rain falls on the higher walls of the range to keep the inner gorges and valleys green for at least part of the year, making it an oasis in the dry heart of Central Australia. Handsome red rivergums line the watercourses. The whole

of the Pound has been grazed at some time - some parts as recently as 1970. Sheep have removed most of the saltbush, and the plants which flower gaily each spring are generally introduced weeds. Nevertheless, in most people's eyes, this does not detract from the beauty and majesty of the oasis. There are several walking tracks from Wilpena to gorges and parks. These range from easy to difficult, taking from an hour to a day. The walk to the top of St Mary's Peak (1164m - 3819 ft), the highest point in the range, takes a whole day, but the view from the top is worth it. The walk should only be attempted after checking with the ranger, and only if you are fit. For those who haven't the time, the fitness or the inclination to attempt it, scenic flights are available (bookings at the resort, ✆8648 0004).

Rawnsley Park is 20km (12 miles) south of Wilpena on the Hawker to Wilpena Road, located in a beautiful natural setting at the foot of

Rawnsley Bluff (the southern rampart of Wilpena Pound). The area has marked walking tracks, and saddle and pack horse treks are available from Rawnsley Park Station, ✆8648 0008.

Blinman

Situated 60km (37 miles) from Wilpena, and 485km (301 miles) from Adelaide, Blinman was once a bustling copper mining town, and some of the old mine machinery can still be seen. There is one hotel and a small caravan park. Access is via the Blinman road from Wilpena and the Leigh Creek road through the scenic Parachilna Gorge, or from Parachilna through the spectacular Glass's Gorge, noted for its show of wild hops in good seasons. East of Blinman, the road winds through the scenic Eregunda Valley to Chambers Gorge, a rugged area with sparkling rock pools and Aboriginal carvings.

North of Chambers Gorge is Big Morot Gorge with numerous rock pools and cliffs, while to the south, on the Wilpena road is the extensive and prominent rocky outcrop called the Great Wall of China.

The Blinman Pools, which are near Angorichina, are fed by a permanent spring even in the heat of summer. They offer one of the most beautiful and secluded spots in the Ranges.

Leigh Creek

The new town of Leigh Creek is 13km (8 miles) south of the original township, and has excellent facilities. The town was moved when the first site was needed for further coal mining. Opened in 1981, the new town is in slightly hilly country, and has pleasant views of the Flinders Ranges.

Leigh Creek's brown coal deposits were first mined for power generation in 1943, and since 1948 it has been operated by the Electricity Trust of SA. It produces about 2.3 million tonnes of coal annually for the Port Augusta power stations. The brown coal deposits here are Triassic (200 million years old) and are the remnants of deposits laid down on a Pre-Cambrian basement. Open cut methods are used to extract the coal, and part of the workings can be viewed from the visitors viewing area, 2.7km from the turn-off to the Leigh Creek Coalfields, on the Hawker to Marree Highway.

If you need to quench your thirst or rest tired eyes, the Leigh Creek Tavern is in Black Oak Drive and has accommodation ✆(08) 8675 2025.

Marree

Once known as Hergott Springs, Marree was the staging post for the camel trains that transported supplies and heavy loads to the Outback. Marree is Aboriginal for 'possum', and the town is the beginning, or the end, of the infamous Birdsville Track.

The Birdsville Track links Marree and Birdsville in Queensland, and was developed in the 1880s as a stock route for drovers bringing cattle from the rich grazing country of south-west Queensland to the railhead at Marree. The track skirts some of the driest areas of Australia, passing between the Simpson Desert and Sturt's Stony Desert.

Since being upgraded for beef cattle transports, the track is usually in a fair condition, but as with all Outback driving, care must be taken. It is not recommended that travel by private vehicle be undertaken along the Birdsville Track during the summer months. May to October is preferable.

Allow at least two full days for the journey and carry emergency supplies for a week because rain, though infrequent, can make the track suddenly impassable.

Check with the police at Marree, or Birdsville if you are travelling from there, before departure to make sure the road conditions are favourable.

Habitation is limited to scattered and remote homesteads and not all of them are close to the Track. Fuel supplies are available at the Mungerannie Roadhouse, ©8675 8317, near Mungerannie Homestead, 204km (127 miles) north of Marree.

Arkaroola

Situated in the rugged northern Flinders, 660km (410 miles) from Adelaide, Arkaroola is a 61,000ha (150,670 acres) wildlife sanctuary. It can be reached by road from Copley, Blinman or Yunta, and all these roads are unsealed, though usually well maintained. Many tours include this resort as a focal point, and there are two airstrips, one at Arkaroola and one at Balcanoona.

The area is rich in minerals and evidence abounds of early exploration. The old Cornish-style Bolla Bollana Smelters, erected in 1861, stand as a reminder of miners of the nineteenth century.

The nearby Gammon Ranges National Park is an extensive wilderness area, and other attractions include Nooldoonooldoona, Barrarranna and Bola Bollana waterholes, Echo Camp, Dinnertime Hill, The Needles, Sitting Bull and the Pinnacles.

Paralana Hot Springs, 27km (17 miles) north of Arkaroola, are radioactive and are believed to be the last remaining evidence of volcanic activity in Australia. The area is an Aboriginal ceremonial site.

Whyalla

Population 27,500
Whyalla is situated on the western side of Spencer Gulf, 394km (245 miles) north-west of Adelaide by road, and 241km (150 miles) by air.

Climate

Average maximum temperature is 29C (84F); minimum is 7C (45F) in winter and 19C (66F) in summer. There are 301 days of sunshine every year, and the average annual rainfall is 268mm (11 ins).

Characteristics

The Gateway to the Eyre Peninsula, Whyalla is the largest regional city in South Australia, and the third largest steel producer in Australia. It is an industrial city with a difference as it is also an extremely popular venue for tourists because of its ideal, sun-drenched climate. In fact, it's booming, with top-class attractions drawing tens of thousands of annual visitors.

How to Get There

By Bus

Stateliner have six services daily from Adelaide, and connect with Greyhound Pioneer services from other states.

By Car

Whyalla is a pleasant four to five hour drive from Adelaide along National Highway One, then on to Alternative Highway One, the coastal highway to Ceduna via Port Lincoln.

For travellers from the eastern States, turn off National Highway

One 25km (16 miles) south of Port Augusta. From the west, turn off Highway One at Iron Knob, 42km (26 miles) before that recommended from the east.

Tourist Information

Whyalla Tourist Centre is on the Lincoln Highway ℰ(08) 8645 7900 or ℰ1800 088 589 and can be emailed at ⋈ tourist.centre@why alla.sa.gov.au. They are ☺open Mon-Fri 9am-5pm, Sat 9am-4pm and Sun 10am-4pm. The website ☜www.epta.com.au has further information.

Accommodation

The city has motels, hotel/motels, hotels and caravan parks. Here is a selection, with prices for a double room per night, which should be used as a guide only. ℰThe telephone area code is 08.

Alexander Motor Inn, 99 Playford Avenue, ℰ8645 9488. 40 units, licensed restaurant, swimming pool, sauna, bbq ✪$92.

Airport Whyalla, Lincoln Highway, ℰ8645 2122. 10 units ✪$65-70.

Derhams Foreshore Motor Inn, Watson Terrace, ℰ8645 8877. 40 units, licensed restaurant, swimming pool, bbq ✪$95-115.

Sundowner Hotel/Motel, Cowell Road, ℰ8645 7688. 24 units, licensed restaurant (closed Sunday), swimming pool, bbq ✪$34.

Spencer Hotel, Forsyth Street, ℰ8645 8411. 30 rooms (private facilities), licensed restaurant ✪$32.

Caravan Parks

Whyalla Foreshore Caravan Park, Broadbent Terrace, ℰ8645 7474. (Pets allowed at manager's discretion) - powered sites ✪$17 for two, on-site vans $28 for two.

Whyalla Airport Caravan Park, Malaquana Road, ℰ8645 9357. (Pets allowed on leash) - powered sites ✪$16-18 for two, cabins $52-54 for two, on-site vans $28 for two, park cabins $40 for two.

Eating Out

Most of the hotels and motels have licensed or BYO restaurants, and there are many takeaway outlets, and others which have takeaway or eat in. Here are a few restaurants you might like to try.

Oriental Inn Chinese Restaurant, 83 Essington Lewis Avenue, ℰ8645 4630.

Parkview Restaurant, 23 Essington Lewis Avenue, ℰ8644 2100.

Spagg's Mediterranean Cafe & Restaurant, 30 Patterson Street, ℰ8645 2088.

Tavern In The Town, 1 Kelly Street, ℰ8644 2255.

Points of Interest

Whyalla Maritime Museum, Port Augusta Road (Lincoln Highway), is a unique $1.3 million attraction at the northern entrance to the city. It features the 650 tonne corvette the *Whyalla*, now resting 2km from the sea. Originally named HMAS *Whyalla*, and later the *Rip*, it was the first vessel built in 1941 at the former Whyalla Shipyard. It has been restored, and there are guided tours of the ship. The nearby Tanderra building traces the city's important shipping past through models and artefacts of BHP's ship-building days (1941-1978), wartime memorabilia of the Whyalla, a scale model of the Santos plant at nearby Port Bonython, audio visual presentations, and other interesting displays. Also in the Tanderra building is the largest "00" gauge model railway in Australia. It is a model that will interest as many dads as kids. The complex is open daily 10am-4pm, with ship tours on the hour from 11am-3pm. Entry is ✪$7 for adults, $4 for children, $17 for a family of 2 adults and 2 or more children.

Tours of the **Steelworks** are operated by Whyalla's Steel City Coaches on Mon, Wed and Sat, departing from the Tourist Office at 9.30am. The costs are ✪$9 for adults, $4 children and $22 a family. For more information contact the Visitor Centre on ✆8645 7900.

The **Whyalla Art Group** has its own gallery in Darling Terrace, just a block and a half from the City Plaza. It has a display of oil paintings, watercolours, acrylic, pen and wash, covering local scenes, the Flinders Ranges and sea and landscapes. Two major exhibitions are held each year in Autumn and Spring. Opening times are weekdays noon-4pm and weekends 2pm-4pm and entry is free.

Hummock Hill Lookout was developed by BHP, and overlooks the eastern end of Whyalla, the foreshore and marina, across Spencer Gulf to the Southern Flinders Ranges, nearby Point Lowly Lighthouse, the Santos plant at Point Bonython, and westward towards the iron ore rich Middleback Ranges. Hummock Hill was the site of the first settlement at the turn of the century. During World War II it saw service as a gun battery and observation post.

Ada Ryan Gardens are located between Cudmore & Watson Terraces, and are linked to the Whyalla Foreshore. It was the first major park established in the city and named after the wife of the chairman of the original City Commission, the local government before a City Council was established. It is an ideal spot for a picnic lunch.

Whyalla Foreshore and Marina. The modern Foreshore Centre has a cafeteria, change rooms and toilets, lifesaving and rescue facilities and has had extensive landscaping, with lawns, barbecues and a playground. The beach offers safe swimming in shallow water, while a nearby fishing jetty is well used by locals after tommy ruffs, garfish, squid, blue swimmer crabs and some species of whiting. At low tide in summer, you can walk out to the blue 'line' in search of a feed of sea fresh crabs. The marina here provides boat owners with a superb four-lane launching ramp, and a small launching fee applies to assist with on-going maintenance. Access to the launching area is controlled by a boom gate which is activated by tokens available from Foreshore Cafe, ©8645 0340 (open 7 days). A new beach has resulted from the marina development, at the extreme eastern end, and it is less affected by low tides.

Mount Laura Homestead Museum in Ekblom Street, off Nicolson Avenue, behind the Westland Shopping Centre, is a National Trust Museum housed in a former sheep station homestead. It has a collection of yester-year household items, relics and many old photographs of the city. In the grounds is a fully restored and furnished cottage, originally built near Hummock Hill in 1914 and transported to the museum in the 1970s. There is also an engine shed which has a comprehensive range of more than 60 stationary engines, all fully restored and in working condition. An 80-year-old locomotive used to haul ore from Iron Knob stands next to the homestead, as does Whyalla's first lock-up. The Museum is ©open Sun, Mon and Wed, 2-4pm, and Fri 10am-noon, other times by appointment. Entry is ©$5 adults, $2 children.

The **Whyalla Health and Leisure Centre**, off Racecourse Road, near the junction of Nicolson Avenue, has a 25m indoor heated swimming pool, squash and racquetball courts, sports hall, gymnasium, weightlifting facilities and a picturesque courtyard. There is also an outdoor sweat track comprising a commando-style course, and a tennis area. Known simply in town as the Rec Centre, visitors are welcome, and if you haven't brought your sporting gear, you can hire it all on the premises. ©Open daily, except public holidays, as follows: Mon-Fri, pool 6am-8.45pm, all other areas 6am-10pm; Sat-Sun all areas 9am-5pm (pool closes at 4.45pm).

Whyalla Wildlife & Reptile Sanctuary, on the Lincoln Highway, near the airport, is one of the largest parks of its type in an arid climate. There are all kinds of Australian fauna, a reptile house, a walk-through aviary with about 200 birds, and a children's section where the favourites can be nursed and fed. The Park has barbecue and picnic facilities, and offers a bush walk through the main vegetation communities within the area. An added feature is a Nocturnal Walk Guided tour every Wednesday at 9pm in summer months, 7.30pm in winter - bookings are essential. The complex is ☺open daily 10am-6pm (Nov through March), 10am-4.30pm (other times). Entry is ✪$7 adults, $5 children, and for further information ✆8645 7044.

Information and maps for a self-guided walk, called the Historic Town Trail, and a Tourist Drive through Whyalla are available at the Visitor Centre.

Festivals

The Whyalla Show is held in August. There are many other city celebrations, and the Tourist Office has a full calendar.

Facilities

Whyalla has shopping centres in the city, and there is a theatre, cinema, etc. Check with the Visitor Centre for information on other entertainment. Sporting facilities include gliding, golf, roller skating, squash, swimming, yachting, and diving.

Outlying Attractions

Port Bonython

The Port is home to the Santos Fractionation Plant, and although tours do not operate over the plant, it can clearly be seen from the roadside and shoreline vantage points.

Liquid hydrocarbons, oil condensate and LPG, are mixed at Moomba and pumped through a 659km (409 miles) underground pipeline to Port Bonython where the liquids are split into their various components by a distillation process. Crude oil, condensate, propane and butane (LPG), and ethane are produced and held in storage tanks with capacities of between 175,000 and 250,000 barrels, before being pumped along a 2.4km jetty to waiting tankers of up to 110,000 tonnes deadweight capacity.

Generally, the crude oil and condensate is sold to Australian petroleum refineries, while the LPG is sold to both domestic and export markets. Port Bonython has been operating since 1984.

Point Lowly

The Point Lowly Lighthouse, oldest building in the Whyalla area (1883), is 2km past the Santos

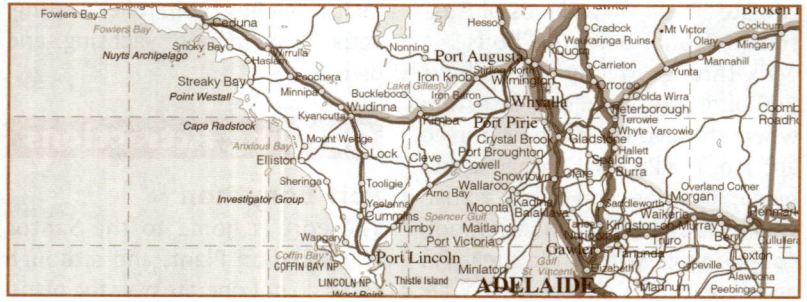

Plant, and about 34km (21 miles) from Whyalla. There are often dolphins in the area, and plenty of people fishing. Facilities include toilets, playground and picnic area.

From the Point there are good views of the gulf and the southern Flinders Ranges. The lighthouse is an unmanned station.

Scenic Drive

16km (10 miles) along the all-sealed Point Lowly/Port Bonython road is the turnoff to Fitzgerald Bay, and the start of a scenic drive to the holiday spot of Point Douglas, about 20km (12 miles) further on. The first section from the turnoff to Fitzgerald Bay is a sealed road, and the rest is a well maintained gravel surface. Along the road there are many picnic areas and opportunities for beach and bush walks.

Iron Knob

The township of Iron Knob is 52km (32 miles) north west of Whyalla on the Eyre Highway which links Port Augusta with Western Australia. Flora of the area is mainly low, stunted growth of mallee scrub and saltbush. Sheep grazing is the major local primary industry. Mining began in 1899, the ore being used as a flux in the smelters of Port Pirie. At one time the Iron Knob and Iron Baron mining operations supplied the iron ore for all BHP blast furnaces.

The Iron Knob Tourist Centre, ©8646 2129, have details of inspections of the open cut mines, which are undertaken in your own car. The Tourist Centre has been developed by BHP as a mining museum, with displays of old mining equipment, mineral specimens, photographs, and a theatre which presents the story of mining and steel making. The grounds of the centre are ideal for a picnic lunch.

Iron Knob has good facilities for a small town, and they include a nine-hole golf course, a registered race club, lawn bowls, tennis, basketball and netball, football and swimming clubs.

South of Whyalla

The coast to the south is a succession of serene villages and resorts, set on crescent-shaped bays with charming names like Tumby Bay, Arno Bay and Lucky Bay. The beaches are long and deserted, broken by low, occasional headlands, and the whole area affords good fishing.

Cowell

Situated on the sheltered Franklin Harbour, which is more like a large lagoon, is the sleepy village of Cowell. It is a safe fishing and boating resort, with night crabbing in the shallows a special attraction. Jade is mined at nearby Mt Geraghty, and is brought to the factory in Cowell where it is cut and polished. Visitors are welcome to watch the large diamond saws cutting the stone.

The Franklin Harbour Historical Museum is in the old Post Office, and preserves memorabilia from the town's past, ©8629 2032. The Cowell Area School Fauna Park is home to a range of native Australian Wildlife, ©8629 2150.

Port Lincoln

Had it not been for the lack of a permanent water supply, Colonel Light may well have selected Port Lincoln as the capital of the State of South Australia. Now it is a blue water paradise and the holiday centre of the peninsula. It is 270km (168 miles) south of Whyalla, on Boston Bay which is ideal for sailing, swimming, water skiing, fishing and skin-diving.

Port Lincoln was first settled in 1834 and has many old buildings, including the Lincoln Hotel in Tasman Terrace, which first opened for business in 1840.

The Port Lincoln Visitor Information Centre, 66 Tasman Terrace, ©(08) 8683 3544, has information on the many attractions of the town. The Centre is ☺open 9am-5pm seven days and can be emailed at ✎plvic@dove.net.au

Highlights of the town and surrounds include the Mayne and Arteyrea galleries, Mill Cottage Museum, Alex Stenross Maritime Museum, Glen-Forest Animal Park, Railway Museum, Apex Wheelhouse, Rose-Wal Shell Museum, Mikkira Station & Koala Park, and the impressive Constantia Designer Craftsman tour.

From Winter's Hill lookout, 5km from the town, there is a very good view of York Peninsula, and short trips can be made to Sleaford Bay, Lincoln National Park, Whaler's Way and Flinder's Well.

Elliston

The drive to Elliston, about 140km (87 miles) up the coast, passes Sheringa Beach, salt lakes, the Old Hamilton Eating House, and you can detour to Locks Wells, a favourite with fishermen and photographers.

The little fishing village of Elliston is nestled between some small hills and Waterloo Bay, and there are spectacular stretches of rugged cliffs rimming the coast. Flinders Island is 35km (22 miles) off the Elliston coast.

Visitor information is available from the District Council on Beach Terrace, ©8687 9177, ☉open Mon-Fri 8.30am-5pm.

Ceduna

The town is a popular overnight stop for the east-west traveller, but is gaining a reputation as a holiday destination in its own right. From here there are scenic drives to Decres Bay, Laura Bay, the Davenport Creek wilderness area and Denial Bay. Ceduna is well known for its fabulous fishing and for seafood lovers, a visit to Denial Bay Oyster Farm is a must. The Ceduna Visitor Information Centre, 58 Poynton Street, ©8625 2780, has details on this and other attractions.

Further along the coast, near Penong, is Cactus Beach, regarded as having one of the best surf breaks in the world.

Port Augusta

South Australia - North-West

Port Augusta

Population 15,300
Port Augusta lies on saltbush plains between Spencer Gulf and the Flinders Ranges, which are about 20km (12 miles) to the east.

Climate

Average temperatures: January max 32C (90F) - min 19C (66F); July max 17C (63F) - min 7C (45F). Annual rainfall: 243mm (10 ins).

Characteristics

Known as the Crossroads of Australia and Gateway to the Outback, Port Augusta was surveyed in 1852, and has a number of historical places of interest. It is an ideal base for access to the attractions of the Flinders Ranges, Eyre Peninsula and the Outback of South Australia.

How to Get There

By Bus
Stateliner and Greyhound Pioneer stop here on their Adelaide/Perth and Adelaide/Darwin routes.

By Rail
Trains arrive in Port Augusta from Perth, Alice Springs and Sydney.

By Road
Situated on the Eyre Highway, 339km (211 miles) from Adelaide, and 2,439km (1515 miles) from Perth.

Tourist Information

The Port Augusta Tourist Information Centre is in the Wadlata Outback Centre complex, 41 Flinders Terrace, ✆(08) 8641 0793. It is

☼open daily, Mon-Fri 9am-5.30pm, Sat-Sun 10am-4pm. The centre contains the Interpretive Centre, souvenirs, the Outback Tuckerbox and toilet facilities. Contact can also be made by email at ✍wadlata@portaugusta.sa.gov.au

Accommodation

Here is a selection with prices for a double room per night, which should be used as a guide only. ✆The telephone area code is 08.

Augusta Westside Motel, 3 Loudon Road, ✆8642 2488. 20 units, unlicensed restaurant, swimming pool, spa, bbq ✪$98-145.

Port Augusta East Motel, Highway One, ✆8641 1008. 15 units ✪$59.

Port Augusta Hi-Way One Motel, Highway One, ✆8642 2755. 45 units, licensed restaurant (closed Sunday), swimming pool, bbq ✪$74-112.

Standpipe Golf Motor Inn, cnr Eyre & Stuart Hwys, ✆8642 4033. 87 units, licensed restaurant ✪$92.

Acacia Ridge Motor Inn, 33 Stokes Terrace, ✆8642 3377. 50 units, licensed restaurant (closed Sunday), swimming pool, bbq ✪$65-75.

Flinders Hotel/Motel, 39 Commercial Road, ✆8642 2544. 30 units, licensed restaurant (closed Sunday) ✪$66.

Myoora Motel, Eyre Highway, ✆8642 3622. 21 units, licensed restaurant (closed Sunday), spa ✪$74-112.

Motel Pampas, Stirling Road, ✆8642 3795. 8 units, unlicensed restaurant ✪$45.

Motel Poinsettia, 24 Burgoyne Street, ✆8642 2411. 23 units, bbq ✪$61.

Caravan Parks

Port Augusta Big 4 Holiday Park, cnr Highway 1 & Stokes Terrace, ✆8642 2974. (No pets allowed) - powered sites ✪$20 for two, cabins $30-40 for two.

Shoreline Caravan Park, Gardiner Avenue, ✆8642 2965. (Dogs allowed at managers discretion) - powered sites ✪$18 for two, park cabins $50 for two, cabin $39-50 for two, on-site vans $33 for two.

Port Augusta Caravan Park at Stirling North, 9 Brooks St, Stirling North, ✆8643 6357. (Pets on leash) - powered sites ✪$17 for two, on-site vans $28 for two, park cabins $42-47 for two, cabins $38 for two.

Eating Out

Most of the motels and hotels have restaurants, and there are two clubs offering dining rooms - the *Cooinda Club, Flinders Terrace*, ✆8641 0166, and the ETSA Club, Hannagan Street, ✆8642 5853.

King Po Chinese, 88 Carlton Parade, ℂ8642 5851 is a licensed restaurant and ***Barnacle Bill Family Seafood Restaurant*** is in 78 Commercial Road, ℂ8641 0000.

For coffee shops and takeaway food outlets, there is more variety, and the Tourist Information Centre will have information.

Points of Interest

The Tourist Information Centre has organised a **Heritage Walk**, which commences, naturally enough, at the Wadlata Outback Centre where their office is located. The centre was originally St Joseph's Convent, which opened in 1927. The Walk then takes visitors to 32 other places of interest, including many classified by the National Trust or State Heritage, including the Old Railway Station, the Curdnatta Art and Pottery.

Homestead Park Pioneer Museum in Elsie Street, features the only original log station homestead in SA. It was transported from its original site to Port Augusta and rebuilt as part of the museum. The 126-year-old Yudnapinna Homestead is fully furnished in period style. For further information ℂ8642 2035.

The museum adjoins a park with large shady trees, a playground and barbecue facilities, as well as kangaroos and other animals. There is also a kiosk with cold drinks, ice creams and tea and coffee.

McLellan Lookout, Whiting Parade at the end of Edinburgh Terrace, has a stone cairn marking the spot where Matthew Flinders stepped ashore on March 10, 1802. The lookout was named after Alan McLellan, an early settler of the area, and from it there are good views of the Gulf, the Northern and Thomas Playford Stations, and the picturesque Flinders and Bluff Ranges.

Red Cliff Lookout at the very end of McSporran Crescent, off the Woomera Road on the Westside, provides an excellent view of the head of the gulf and the Flinders Ranges. The adjacent area is the site of the Australian Arid Lands Botanic Gardens, which, when completed, will be a unique attraction.

The first stage of Port Augusta's Playford **Power Station** was opened in 1954, powered by coal railed from Leigh Creek, and the second stage opened in 1960. The adjacent Northern Power Station has two generators that will each produce 259 megawatts. Ultimately the new and old power stations will consume up to 4 million tonnes of coal annually. Tours of the Northern Power Station are ⊙conducted weekdays (except public holidays) commencing 10am, 11am and 1pm. Strong footwear should be worn. Turn of Highway One at Truckers Tucker, approximately 5km each of Port Augusta. For further information, ✆8642 0666.

The **Royal Flying Doctor Service** Base at 4 Vincent Street, has tours for visitors on weekdays ⏲at 10am, 11am, 2pm and 3pm, ✆8642 2044 for large group reservations.

The **School of the Air**, at the eastern end of Commercial Road, in the grounds of the Central Primary School, has ⏲conducted tours on school days at 10am. A small entrance fee is charged.

Festivals

The Australia Day Festival is held in January, the Apex Trade Fair in March, and Race Week in June each year.

Facilities

Boating, lawn bowls, croquet, fishing, golf, greyhound racing, horse racing, horse riding, sailing, squash, swimming (beach and pool), tennis, trotting, cinemas.

Outlying Attractions

South of Port Augusta

Port Pirie

Port Pirie is 95km (59 miles) south of Port August, and 229km (142 miles) north of Adelaide, and has a population of around 14,000. In 1889 three smelters were built near Port Pirie to refine the ore being railed from Broken Hill. Today it is the largest lead smelter in the world, and produces lead, zinc, gold, cadmium, antimony and copper by-products, and sulphuric acid. Lead is South Australia's biggest single-produced export income earner. Conducted tours of the smelting works are available, and the Tourist Information Office at 3 Mary Elie Street, ✆(08) 8633 0439 (by email: ✉tourism@ppcadc.sa.gov.au), has information on times and costs.

The Railway Museum in Port Pirie has detailed pictures, documents and memorabilia of early days, and another specialist museum is Carne Brae, with a collection of over 2500 dolls, superb stained glass windows and a lifetime's collection of silverware and fine china.

The Northern Festival Centre is the cultural heart of the north and combines live theatre, art exhibitions, visiting entertainers and social happenings under the one roof.

Port Pirie has all the facilities you would expect for a city of its population, including fishing, golf, greyhound racing, horse racing, sailing, squash, swimming (beach and pool), tennis, trotting and water skiing.

Peterborough

Situated 162km (100 miles) south east of Port Augusta and 252km (156 miles) north of Adelaide, Peterborough is one of only two known towns in the world where three different rail gauges meet. Peterborough is the gateway to the Flinders Ranges for travellers from NSW, or from Adelaide via the historic mining town of Burra. The Visitor Information Centre is located in a restored 1917 Railway Car on Main Street, ☎8651 2545, and is ⏰open daily 10am-3pm. You can also email ✎cwoodman@iweb.net.au

The Steamtown Peterborough Railway Preservation Society officially commenced operations during Easter 1981, almost 100 years to the day since the first railway to reach Peterborough was opened. The Society runs steam passenger trains at specified times on the narrow gauge line from Peterborough to Orroroo, and the view enjoyed by passengers is one that shouldn't be missed. Timetables for this attraction can be obtained by phoning ☎8651 3355.

Amelia Park, 11km (7 miles) east of Peterborough, has a picnic and barbecue area, and playground. Victoria Park has a lake, an island and a large barbecue area. Tank Hill lookout gives a panoramic view of the town.

Burra

Nestling in the Bald Hills Range, 157km (98 miles) north of Adelaide, and approximately 90km (56 miles) south of Peterborough, is Burra, where copper was discovered in 1845. The mines closed down in 1877, but the era of the mining days has been preserved in the unique old buildings around Paxton Square, the nearby Bon Accord Mining Museum, the 10 metre timber junker which transported the huge boiler for the mine's engine house, the ruins of the mine buildings, and the restored Morphetts Engine House. Other interesting places to visit are the Redruth Gaol, the courthouse and the underground Unicorn Brewery. The movie *Breaker Morant* was filmed in the hills around Burra, and Redruth Gaol was used to portray Fort Edwards in the film.

The Burra Tourist Information Centre is at 2 Market Square, ☎(08) 8892 2154.

Clare

The historic township of Clare is 135km (84 miles) north of Adelaide, and approximately 43km (27 miles) south-west of Burra, and is set in a thriving agricultural district, known especially for its wines. Each of the 31 wineries in the district produce wines with a special character, and offer cellar door tastings and sales of internationally acclaimed vintages.

Special events in the valley are the Clare Valley Easter Festival, and the Gourmet Weekend in mid-May. Both events provide the opportunity to sample a range of the regions finest wines, while top restaurateurs complement the new vintages with plates of their best fare.

Full details of all wineries can be obtained from the Tourist Information Centre Clare Valley, 229 Main North Road, Clare, ℂ(08) 8842 2131 or ℂ1800 242 131. It is ☉open daily 9am-5pm (except Sun when it opens at 10am). Browse ☞www.clarevalley.com.au for more information.

Moonta

Moonta is situated on the Yorke Peninsula, 167km (104 miles) north-west of Adelaide.

Yorke Peninsula is part of a copper heritage that is uniquely South Australian. It was copper that saved the young colony and gave the place a distinctive Cornish heritage in the triangle of mining towns at the top of Yorke Peninsula. The many thousands of Cornish miners, who came to mine the precious metal during the 60 year boom, left a legacy which is now celebrated in the biennial festival of Kerneweck Lowender. It is held over the long weekend in May in every odd-numbered year, in the copper triangle towns - Moonta, Kadina and Wallaroo.

Moonta is virtually a monument to mining, its architecture belonging to a by-gone era. Of particular note is the gothic-influenced Uniting Church. Nearby at the mines site, there are mine buildings and relics to explore, and at Moonta Mines Museum, ℂ8825 1944, in what was once a school, there are exhibits of the life of the miners, and some typical cottages. The deepest shaft in the area is Taylor's Shaft at 767m (2516 ft).

The Yorke Peninsula Tourist Information Centre is in the old Moonta Railway Station, Moonta, &(08) 8825 1891 or &1800 654 991. It is ☉open 9am-5pm seven days and can be reached be email at ~tourism@yp-connect.net

Outback South Australia

There are only four main routes through the Outback, each with an individual character and history. There's the famous Birdsville Track, along which stockmen once drove herds of cattle south from Queensland. And there's the Strzelecki Track, through remote sand dune country of the Moomba Gasfields to Innamincka on the Legendary Cooper Creek. Either way crosses the famous 'dog fence' - the world's longest protective wire fence, extending more than 3000km (1864 miles) across the centre of Australia to keep wild dingoes from entering the southern pastoral zones.

Following the Stuart Highway or the Oodnadatta Track takes visitors into opal country and three of the world's most prolific opal mining areas - Coober Pedy, Andamooka and Mintabie.

Andamooka

Andamooka is 287km (178 miles) north of Port Augusta (597km [371 miles] from Adelaide), to the west of Lake Torrens. It is an opal field which although far smaller than Coober Pedy is famous for the quality of the gemstones. The opal was discovered by two drovers in 1930, but activity has been declining over recent years.

The mining is concentrated around the edge of the town on the broad flat spurs formed by Opal Creek and its tributaries, and extends about 5km to the Lunatic Hill workings north of the town.

Facilities in the town include a hotel/motel, motel, guesthouse, caravan park, camping areas, restaurant, hospital, general store, garage, post office, public phone, swimming pool and an airstrip.

The Opal Gleam dugout home may be inspected, and a local landmark is the unique Duke's Bottlehouse, built from discarded beer bottles. A petrified plesiosaur measuring 9m in length has been found in the diggings, and is on display. Historical cottages have been restored and are used as tea rooms in the cooler weather. At nearby White Dam is the late Bill McDougall's famous Ettamoggah Pub, a great place for a cooling ale. The road from Woomera to Andamooka passes the turn-off to Roxby Downs Township, which was established as a centre for the employees of the Olympic Dam Mining Project. Roxby Downs grew at a rate of 1000 persons per year, and was one of the two newly developed townships in the north of the state during the 1990s. The other was Leigh Creek.

Coober Pedy

South Australia's biggest and oldest mining town, Coober Pedy is 610km (379 miles) north-west of Port Augusta, and 850km (528 miles) north-west of Adelaide. The town was established in 1915, and the name is thought to be derived from the Aboriginal words Kupa (white man) and Piti (waterhole, or hole).

To put it mildly, Coober Pedy is very hot and very dry, and the early miners very intelligently decided the best place to live was underground. But the so-called dugouts lack nothing in comfort and furnishings, and a tour through one of those open for visitors is a must. It is also possible to stay in underground accommodation in the town, for example at the Underground Motel, ✆8672 5324. If this doesn't appeal to you, there is a hotel/motel and a camping ground above ground. Apart from the opal shops vying for your patronage, there are a few other places to visit.

The underground churches are unique, and really beautiful, and the water desalination plant interests some people. There are plenty of local companies offering tours, and for information on these contact the Tourist Information Centre, Council Offices, Hutchison Street, ph (086)725 298. The office is ☺open Mon-Fri 9am-5pm. Visit 👁www.opalcapitalofthe

world.com.au further information, ✆8672 5298 or ✆1800 637 076 (free call).

If you are feeling lucky, you can try 'noodling' for opal. This means that you must not be on a pegged claim, and must not use a pick, shovel or any digging device. It must be remembered, though, that there is a great danger of unprotected mine shafts on the opal fields, and you really have to look where you are walking. It is also especially important to keep an eye on children, and don't let them wander off the beaten track.

Oodnadatta

One of the few centres with real outback character, Oodnadatta was an important railhead between 1891 and 1929 when the rail link to Alice Springs was completed. Before then, camels were used to transport freight from Oodnadatta to Alice Springs. The railway has now been replaced by a new line 100km further to the west, but the sandstone railway station built in 1890 remains. 'Utnadata' means 'Blossom of the Mulga'.

The town has a hotel, caravan park, general stores, post office, public telephone, mechanical repairs, police station, medical services and an airstrip. There is also good swimming in some of the nearby permanent waterholes. North of Oodnadatta lies the Witjira National Park which surrounds the Dalhousie Mound Springs. However, some tracks in the Park are not maintained and their condition can change rapidly. The area is recommended for 4WD vehicles only, and visitors are advised to enquire at Oodnadatta Police Station in Oribee Avenue before setting out, ✆8670 7805.

Western Australia

Perth

Population 1,083,400
Perth, the Capital City of Western Australia, is situated on the banks of the Swan River in the south-west corner of Australia.

Climate

Perth is the sunniest of all Australian cities, averaging eight hours of sunshine a day. It boasts a superb climate with an average summer day temperature of 30C (86F), which is tempered by the arrival of an afternoon breeze called The Fremantle Doctor, and an average night temperature of 17C (63F). The average winter day temperature is a mild 18C (64F), and the night is 9C (48F). February is the hottest month, and July the coldest. The annual rainfall averages 974mm (38 ins).

The wettest months are May-August, but half the number of days during this period are sunny and clear. The driest months are November-February, when it seldom rains.

Characteristics

The city of Perth nestles by a kilometre-wide expanse of the Swan River which spreads out like a lake or harbour, edged by expensive suburbs and white sand beaches. It was known as the city of millionaires before the 1987 Stock Market crash, and still is a place of energetic growth and vigorous youth. It is a well planned city with an efficient freeway system, yet within walking distance of the city centre is Kings Park, a native bushland

KEY

i	Information centre
+	Hospital
Pool	Swimming pool
——	Railway
● Central	Railway station
	Major road
	Other road
	Park
	Mall or public space

with gum trees and wildflowers, commanding magnificent views of the city and the Swan River.

How to Get There

By Air

Perth International Airport, in Baker Road, is serviced by many airlines including Air New Zealand, British Airways, Cathay Pacific, Malaysian Airlines System, Qantas, Singapore Airlines and Thai Airways International. For information phone ©(08) 9478 8888, send an email to ✎ per@perthairport.net.au or survey the website ☜www.perth airport.com

Domestic flights from other capital cities are by Qantas. The journey from the airport to the central business district takes approximately twenty minutes, and an airport hotel bus service operates between both passenger terminals and hotels and motels.

By Bus

Greyhound Pioneer operate services from/to other State Capitals.

By Rail

The Indian Pacific operates between Sydney and Perth.

By Road

Visitors can drive across the Nullarbor Plain from the eastern States, or have their car transported across on the train.

Tourist Information

The Western Australian Tourism Commission operates the Perth Visitor Centre located in Albert Facey House, cnr Forrest Place and Wellington Street, ©1300 361 351. You can plan many aspects of your holiday using the website at ☜www.westernaustralia.net and request advice and further information by email at ✎ travel@tourism. wa.gov.au

The headquarters of the Royal Automobile Club of Western Australia are at 228 Adelaide Terrace, Perth, ©9421 4444. See the website at ☜www.rac.com.au. The RAC of WA service facilities are available to members of the RAC in other States.

There are many tours of Perth and surrounding attractions, operated by companies like Kings Tours, ©9321 2288, and Great Western Tours, ©9490 2455. The Visitor Centres have brochures and can organise bookings.

Accommodation

Perth has a range of excellent hotels, motels and other accommodation. As with most cities, accommodation is usually cheaper in the suburbs, and the Tourist Information Office has a complete list of accommodation available. Here we have a selection of city hotels and motels with prices for a double room per night, which should be used as a guide only. The caravan parks we mention are, as is usual, in the suburbs. ☎The telephone area code is 08.

Perth

Hyatt Regency Perth, 99 Adelaide Terrace, ☎9225 1234. 367 rooms (private facilities), licensed restaurant, swimming pool, sauna, tennis ✪$230.

Sheraton Perth, 207 Adelaide Terrace, ☎9224 7777. 388 rooms (private facilities), licensed restaurant, swimming pool, sauna ✪$145 - 260.

Kings Perth Hotel, 517 Hay Street, ☎9325 6555. 119 rooms, licensed restaurant, swimming pool - $95.

Emerald Hotel, 24 Mount Street, ☎9481 0866. 102 units (private facilities), licensed restaurant, sauna ✪$95 - 105.

Metro Inn Perth, 61 Canning Hwy, South Perth, ☎9367 6122. 87 rooms (private facilities), licensed restaurant, swimming pool ✪$95 - $115.

Hotel Grand Chancellor, Perth, 707 Wellington Street, ☎9327 7000. 273 rooms (private facilities), licensed restaurant, sauna ✪$100.

Murray Lodge Motel, 718 Murray Street, West Perth, ☎9321 7441. 27 units, licensed restaurant - $75.

Pacific Motel, 111 Harold Street (cnr Stirling Street), ☎9328 5599. 60 units, swimming pool, bbq ✪$80.

Park Inn International, 70 Pier St, ☎9325 2133, 96 rooms (private facilities), unlicensed restaurant ✪$85.

Miss Maud Swedish Hotel, 97 Murray Street, ☎9325 3900. 51 rooms (private facilities), licensed restaurant - B&B ✪$96.

CWA House Residential, 1174 Hay Street, West Perth, ☎9321 6081 (private facilities), unlicensed restaurant, ✪$75.

Fremantle

The Esplanade Hotel Fremantle, cnr Marine Terrace & Essex Street, ☎9432 4000. 259 rooms (private facilities), licensed restaurant, spa, sauna ✪$155 - 175.

Rosie O'Grady's, 23 William St., ☎9335 1645. 17 rooms (private facilities), licensed restaurant ✪$60 - 125

Fremantle Hotel, cnr High & Cliff Streets, ☎9430 4300. 35 rooms (some with private facilities), licensed restaurant ✪$80-90.

Tradewinds Hotel Fremantle, 59 Canning Hwy, ☎9339 8188. 83 rooms (private facilities), licensed restaurant ✪$148.

Caravan Parks

Perth Holiday Park, 91 Benara Road, Caversham, ✆9279 6700. (No pets allowed)141 sites, swimming pool, barbecue - powered sites ✪$20-23 for two, cabins $70-85 for two.

Perth International Tourist Park, 186 Hale Rd, ✆9453 6677. (No pets allowed) 82 sites, barbecue - powered sites ✪$22-27 for two, chalets $90-105 for two, ensuite cabins $75-85 for two.

Coogee Beach Holiday Park, Coogee Beach Reserve ✆9418 1810. (No dogs allowed) - 186 sites, powered sites ✪$20 for two, no on-site vans.

Fremantle Village, cnr Cockburn & Rollinson Roads, ✆9430 4866. (No pets allowed) - 142 sites, powered sites ✪$22 for two, en-suite sites $27 for two, chalets $85 for two.

Local Transport

Bus

Buses are operated by Transperth: phone ✆13 6213, look up ⊙www.transperth.wa.gov.au, or email ✉transperth@transport.wa.gov.au. The city and its surrounds are divided into 8 zones radiating out from Perth city. A standard fare within Zone 1 costs $1.80 and the journey must be completed within 2 hours of purchase. FastCards are available to save travellers money depending on their needs. For comparison, the MultiRider covers ten journeys within Zone 1 for $15.30, a DayRider allows unlimited travel for one day for $7.10, and the MaxiRider offers discounts for a family or group return journey.

Free Transit Zone/City Clippers

Within a clearly defined inner City Zone you will be able to travel on all buses free of charge, as part of the Central Area Transit System. The city CATS are a modern, efficient bus service with electronic displays at each stop and regular, satellite-updated announcements of when you can expect the next bus to roll by.

The Red CAT ⊙leaves every 5 minutes, Mon-Fri, 6.50am-6.20pm, and travels along Wellington Street, Milligan Street, and Emerald Terrace. It runs in both a clockwise and anti-clockwise direction, and includes Murray Street, Emerald Terrace, and Outram Street and a shortened circuit on weekends between 10am and 6.15pm (every 45 minutes).

The Blue CAT ⊙leaves every 8 minutes, Mon-Fri, 6.50am-6.20pm, travelling from a terminus in the Barrack St Jetty via William Street, The Esplanade, and Aberdeen Street to Northbridge Street.

A Fremantle CAT is also in operation ⊙every 10 minutes Mon-Fri from 7am–7pm.

Train

Suburban trains operate from Perth to the areas of Fremantle, Midland and Armadale. Suburban trains leave from Perth Train Station, Wellington Street; interstate trains leave from East Perth Train Station. Westrail Travel Centre is located at East Perth Station. For all information relating to buses, ferries and trains, including timetables and route maps, see the Transperth website at the address: ☞www.transperth.wa.gov.au

Taxi

Taxis operate all hours and the illuminated sign on the roof tells that they are vacant. All cabs have meters which display the fare, and there is an extra charge for baggage. There are taxi ranks through Perth Central Business District, or they can be ordered by phone. The main taxi operator is Swan Taxis, ✆13 1330.

Car

A rental car is a convenient way of sightseeing and is relatively inexpensive for a group or family. Daily rate for a late model small car is approximately $30-35 plus fuel. Here are some names and addresses:
Bayswater Car Rental, 160 Adelaide Terrace, ✆9325 1000; Geddes, 36A Geddes Street, Victoria Park, ✆361

7388; Apex, 400 William Street, Northbridge, ✆9227 9091; Ace Rent A Car, 311 Hay Street, Perth, ✆9221 1333.

Eating Out

Perth has a reputation for its remarkable variety of BYO and licensed restaurants. The eating places vary from coffee shops and bistros to luxury class restaurants. Whatever your fancy, you have a tempting range of dishes from Europe, Asia, India, Mexico and Lebanon, as well as delicious local seafood and vegetarian dishes.

There are also a number of restaurants that offer panoramic views of the city and the Swan River. Fremantle has a large variety of restaurants from side walk cafes on South Terrace to top class dining. Be sure to try the fresh seafood for which Fremantle is famous. Here are some names and addresses.

International

Picnicks Garden Restaurant, 78-82 Outram St, West Perth, ©9481 6619.

Criterion Brasserie, 560 Hay Street, ©9325 5155.

El Mambo Citadel Restaurant, 283 William Street, ©9227 5338.

Savannahs Restaurant, The Esplanade, Scarborough, ©9340 5753.

Fraser's Restaurant Kings Park, Fraser Avenue, West Perth, ©9481 7100.

Hilite 33 Restaurant, Lvl 33/ 44 St Georges Tce, ©9220 8333.

Matilda Bay Restaurant, 3 Hackett Drive, Crawley, ©9423 5000.

Gazebo Restaurant, 221 Adelaide Terrace, ©9221 1200.

Italian

Mamma Maria's, Cnr Aberdeen & Lake Sts, Northbridge, ©9227 9828.

Simon's Seafood Restaurant, 73 Francis St, Northbridge, ©9227 9055.

Gavino Restaurant, 375 Hay St, Subiaco, ©9381 1323.

Seafood

The Essex Restaurant, 20 Essex St, Fremantle, ©9335 5725.

Fremantle Mussel Bar, Fishing Boat Harbour, 42 Mews Rd Fremantle, ©9433 1800.

Jessica's Fine Seafood Restaurant & Bar, 99 Adelaide Tce, Perth, ©9325 2511.

Joy Garden Seafood Restaurant, 65 Francis St, Northbridge, ©9227 8638.

Japanese

Hayashi Japanese Restaurant, 107 Pier St, Perth, ©9325 6009.

Japanese Restaurant Kawana, 568 Hay St, Perth, ©9221 3339.

The New Shima Japanese Restaurant, 409 Murray St, Perth, ©9321 1668.

Chinese

Grand Palace Chinese Restaurant, 3rd Floor, 14 The Esplanade, Perth, ©9325 2344 .

South Sea Chinese Restaurant, 388 Fitzgerald St, North Perth, ©9227 8822.

Diamond Chinese Restaurant, 123 Murray St, Perth, ©9325 1443.

Indian

Royal India Restaurant, 1134 Hay Street, West Perth, ©9324 1368.

Burswood Casino

McDonald's is well represented, with many in the city including 572-576 Hay Street, ℂ9325 2451; and one in Fremantle, Mews Road, ℂ9430 4308.

Entertainment

Twenty years ago visitors to WA might have been forgiven for concluding that the state was somewhat lacking when it came to top-class entertainment. However, that view changed dramatically with the construction of the Perth Concert Hall and the Perth Entertainment Centre, the refurbishing of the famous old His Majesty's Theatre, the growth of taverns, restaurants, cinemas and discos, the revitalising of hotels, and the emergence of Northbridge as a centre of Perth's night life. And, of course, there is the Burswood Casino.

The Concert Hall is the home of the WA Symphony Orchestra, as well as being a venue for concerts and performances by visiting artists. Perth Entertainment Centre has a seating capacity for 8000 people, and is a venue for circuses, rock bands, musical productions, ballroom dancing championships, classical concerts and ice shows. His Majesty's Theatre is the residence of the WA Opera Company, the WA Ballet Company and the WA Arts Orchestra. Drama productions are also staged from time to time at several suburban venues and tertiary institution theatres.

The Burswood Resort Casino, Great Eastern Highway, ☎9362 7777, is set in 100ha (247 acres) of rolling parklands which include an 18-hole golf course. Burswood overlooks the Swan River and dominates the eastern approaches to the city. Apart from the glamour of the casino complex, there's the luxury of a 413 room 5-star hotel, a Las Vegas-style theatre showroom, 20,000 seat indoor stadium called the Superdome and a host of recreational facilities. ☉The action in the Casino continues non-stop 24 hours a day, except Christmas, Good Friday and Anzac Day. Covering 6968 sq m (75,000 sq ft) on a single level, Burswood has 111 gaming tables, 540 video gaming machines and a 240 seat Keno lounge.

The city is also served by many cinemas:

Hoyts, City Arcade, Hay Street Mall, ☎9325 2377.

Cinecentre 1, 2 and 3, Murray Street, east of Barrack Street, ☎9325 2844.

Piccadilly, Piccadilly Arcade, Hay Street Mall, ☎9322 3577.

Jaws Cinema, Hay Street, ☎9225 6144.

Ace Cinemas, Adelaide Terrace, ☎9425 5522.

Programmes and session times will be found in the daily newspapers. There are also a number of suburban cinemas that show first-run movies, and several drive-ins.

Shopping

☉Normal shopping hours in Perth are 8.30am-5.30pm, Mon-Fri, 8.30am-noon Sat, with many shops staying open Thursday evening until 9pm. There are many big shopping centres in the suburbs these days, but Perth city centre has retained its attraction because of the variety of shops. It is the fashion centre of the State, and has particular appeal for the young.

Department Stores

There are two main department stores in Perth -

Aherns is situated between Murray and Hay Streets, about 50m west of Barrack Street.

Myers is between Wellington and Murray Streets, with one side adjoining Forrest Place. Standing on the site where Boans Department Store once stood, the new Myer building is architecturally impressive. Overhead walkways are linked to several of Perth's arcades and to the modern Perth Train Station, which in turn is linked to the city's cultural centre.

The Malls

Hay Street, between William and Barrack Streets, has always been regarded as the very heart of Perth shopping. Before the 1970s, it was probably the most congested section of roadway in WA. Narrow, with parking allowed on both sides of the street, buses, service vehicles and general through-traffic battled for position. That all changed when Hay Street between William and Barrack Streets was made into a pedestrian mall. Murray Street, between William and Barrack Streets, was also declared a mall. The Murray Street Mall flows into Forrest Place and the Myer terraces, and is linked to the Hay Street Mall by numerous arcades. The whole effect is to create a pleasant, roomy, traffic-free shopping precinct.

The Arcades

The arcades, while still functioning as 'short cuts' and providing shelter from the rain in winter and the heat in summer, are very attractive. They are often multi-level, twist and turn along their length, interconnect with other arcades and buildings, open out on to small plazas or covered-in areas where shoppers can pause for a breather, go underground, and, in one case, lead on to an overpass that takes shoppers across the busy street below.

Shopping arcades are still frequently associated with cinemas, but many of Perth's newest office blocks and luxury hotels have incorporated their own shopping arcades.

London Court

Leading off the Mall, not far from Barrack Street, and connecting the Mall with St George's Terrace, is a piece of Olde England known as London Court. Built in Tudor style, carved woodwork, wrought ironwork, hanging signs, paved roadway and medieval towers at each end, help to create the atmosphere. The clock facing the Hay Street Mall is an exact replica of the dial of Westminster's Big Ben. Each quarter hour four knights on horseback joust above the clock face. Above the clock face in St George's Terrace, St George's and the Dragon appear each quarter hour. London Court is a photographer's delight, and is also a drawcard for tourists because of the number of shops catering especially for them.

If you are in the market for a truly Australian souvenir, or work of art, pay a visit to *Creative Native*, 32 King Street, Perth, ©9322 3398. This gallery offers Aboriginal art, in particular work from the Nyoongah people. Examples of the best artwork are on offer to the discerning collector, ranging from the tradi-

tional, carved emu eggs, boomerangs, pottery, jewellery and much more - on to the more contemporary. The gallery has an exclusive artist, Tjyllyungoo, and his work is in great demand.

Points of Interest

The first recorded sighting by Europeans of Western Australia was in October 1616, when the Dutch navigator Dirk Hartog landed at Shark Bay, near Carnarvon. Von Edels discovered land a little further south in 1618, while in 1619 Frederick Houtman sighted small rocky islands off the coast near Geraldton, and named them Abrolhos - a term meaning 'lookout'. In 1828, the British authorities decided to establish a settlement at the Swan River. On May 2, 1829, Captain Charles Fremantle, in command of the HMS Challenger, hoisted the British flag at the head of the Swan River and took possession of the territory. The following month, Captain Stirling in Parmelia, arrived with settlers, and on August 12, 1829, founded Perth at a site near the present town hall. Early difficulties in the Swan River colony included a shortage of labour, financial problems and poor communications. Acting on recommendations, the British Government sent convicts to WA from 1850 to 1868 to assist with development. It was not until the discovery of gold during the late 1880s and 1890s that real progress began. Western Australia became a state of the Commonwealth of Australia in 1901.

The Town Hall, on the corner of Hay & Barrack Streets, was built by convict labour between 1867 and 1870, in the style of an English Jacobean market hall. It seems that the convicts left their mark on the clock tower of the building, for the windows are shaped like broad arrows. Nearby in Barrack Street, a tablet set into the footpath commemorates the founding of Perth in 1829.

The alignment of Murray Street and Victoria Square appears on the earliest map of Perth, dated 1833. By the late nineteenth century, many government buildings had been located in Murray Street east of Pier Street, while buildings of the Roman Catholic Church were established in the Victoria Square vicinity. A large number of these historic buildings remain today, and though built in the late 19th and early 20th centuries, are classified by the National Trust of WA:

The **Government Printing Office** was originally the site of a home for destitute women, and was acquired for a printing office in 1870.

Government Stores Building was completed in 1911, and was originally occupied by the Treasury Department. Its style was designed to harmonise with other buildings of this period in Murray Street.

Salvation Army Fortress was officially opened in 1930.

The Health Department building was completed in 1912, and is believed to be one of the last buildings in Perth to use Donnybrook sandstone for a whole facade.

Young Australia League Building foundation stone was laid by William Morris Hughes, the Prime Minister of Australia, in 1922.

Perth No 1 City Fire Station Building was completed in 1900, and became the headquarters of the Perth City Fire Brigade after it moved from the Town Hall on January 1, 1901.

Kirkman House, constructed in 1909, was used for many years as housing for nurses of the Royal Perth Hospital. The Moreton Bay Fig Tree in front of the house was planted about 1900 and has been placed on the National Trust's Register of Significant Trees.

Royal Perth Hospital Administrative Building was built in 1894.

Colonial Hospital, behind the present Royal Perth Hospital staff canteen, east of the hospital's administrative building, was constructed with convict labour and was occupied in July 1855.

St Mary's Cathedral stands on the high ground set aside on the first town plan of Perth as 'Church Square', known now as Victoria Square. The western part of the Cathedral was built in 1963-5 with bricks made from local clay.

The Convent of Mercy, often referred to as the Mother House, was constructed in 1873, and has been used by the Sisters of Mercy ever since.

Convent of Mercy Chapel dates from 1924. The apse contains excellent painted figures copied from a medieval fresco.

Roman Catholic Presbytery,

Church Offices and Grounds. The original Bishop's Palace on this site was erected by the Benedictine Brothers in 1859.

Mercedes School House was constructed of limestone during the Gold Rush period in 1895. It was originally used as a convent school house.

Pro-Cathedral of St John the Evangelist was built between 1844 and 1846 of brick with a shingle roof.

Government House, St George's Terrace, opposite Pier Street, is the official residence of the Governor of Western Australia, and was built between 1859 and 1864. It is constructed in a romantic style with Gothic arches and turrets reminiscent of the Tower of London.

Old Court House, in the middle of Supreme Court Gardens, was erected between 1836 and 1837. It is one of the earliest surviving buildings in the city. During the 19th century it served as church, school, immigration depot, supreme court house and store. It stood close to the original river foreshore.

Old Perth Boys' School, on the south side of St George's Terrace, between Mill and William Streets, was completed in 1854. It was built of sandstone which was ferried up the Swan River from Rocky Bay by convict labour.

The Cloisters, St George's Terrace, opposite Mill Street. Bishop Hale's collegiate school for boys was opened here in 1858. The building has decorative brickwork, and the exterior was renovated in 1871-72. The Port Macquarie fig tree, on the east side of the Cloisters, is known to be over 100 years old.

Parliament House is on St George's Terrace not far along from the Cloisters. When Parliament is sitting there are ☉conducted tours of the House Mon-Fri 10am, 11am, 1pm and 2pm. Subiaco buses 2, 3, 4 and 6 ☉depart outside Newspaper House alighting Harvest Terrace. For details, ☎13 6213.

Horseshoe Bridge, in William Street, between Wellington & Roe Streets, was built in 1903, replacing a level crossing. Take note of the lamp pillars decorated with swans.

The Police Courts, Beaufort Street, between Roe and James Streets, were completed in 1905 by the Public Works Department under the direction of their Chief Architect, J.H. Grainger, father of composer Percy Grainger.

The **Art Gallery of Western Australia** in the Perth Cultural Centre, James Street Mall, displays traditional and contemporary paintings, prints, drawings, sculpture and bark paintings. ☉Open Mon-Sun 10am-5pm, public holi-

days 10am-5pm, Anzac Day 1-
5pm, ☎9492 6600.

Aboriginal Art & Craft Gallery
is a gallery specialising in the art of
Western Australia's Indigineous
people. ⏱Open 9-5.30pm daily, it
is located on Fraser Avenue, King's
Park, ☎9481 7082.

Alexander Library, 40 James
Street, ☎9427 3111, is a reference
library and also carries major interstate and overseas newspapers.

The **Battye Library of Western
Australian History** forms part of
the library. ⏱Open Mon and Fri
9am-5.30pm, Tues-Thurs 9am-
9.45pm, Sat Sun 2-5.30pm, ph
☎9427 3111.

The Old Gaol, in the museum
complex in Francis Street, is perhaps one of the best examples of
colonial architecture in the State.
Built in 1856, it served as Perth's
original prison until 1888. Many
public executions took place in the
grounds. Today it has been extensively restored, and in rooms which
once housed prisoners, there is an
old fashioned dental surgery and
pharmacy and many mementoes of
Perth's early days.

The **Western Australian Museum** (entrance in Francis Street)
possesses a Marine Gallery containing a 25m blue whale skeleton; an
Aboriginal Gallery; a superb collection of veteran and vintage cars; the
skeleton of Albert the Dinosaur;

and the 11-tonne Mundrabilla meteorite.

The Railway Station, Wellington Street, now known as the Perth
Train Station, was built between
1893 and 1894, replacing an earlier station built when the railway
was opened in 1881. The front of
the station has been renovated, and
the structure behind extensively
remodelled, with walkways connecting it to Myers and the Perth
Cultural Centre.

Other museums in and around
Perth are:

Army Museum, cnr Lord &
Bulwer Streets, East Perth, ☎9335
2077

Aviation Museum, Bull Creek
Drive, Bull Creek, ☎9311 4470 -
⏱open Thurs-Tues 11am-4pm.

World of Energy, 12 Parry Street,
Fremantle, ☎9430 5655 - ⏱open
Tues-Thurs 10.30am-4.30pm, Sat-
Sun 1-4.30pm.

Fremantle Museum, in Finnerty
Street, ☎9430 7966, is a branch of
the WA Museum. The limestone
building, constructed in the 1860s
as a lunatic asylum, has been described as one of the finest examples of Colonial Gothic architecture
in Australia - ⏱open Mon-Thurs
10.30am 5pm, Fri-Sun 1-5pm.

Museum of Childhood, Edith
Cowan University, Bay Road,
Claremont ☎9442 1373 - ⏱open
Mon-Fri 10am-3pm, Sun 2-5pm.

Rail Transport Museum, Railway Parade, Bassendean, ©9279 7189 - ☺open Sun and public holidays 1-5pm, and Wed during school holidays 1-4pm.

Rockingham Museum, Rocking -ham Road, Rockingham ©9592 3455

Telecommunications Museum, Wireless Hill, off Canning Highway, Melville, ©9364 7067 - ☺open Sat-Sun 2-5pm.

Suburban Attractions

Underwater World, in the Hillarys Boat Harbour, Sorrento, has a moving walkway through a tunnel in a large aquarium, and you can come face to face with sharks, rays, octopus and a variety of fish life. There is also a theatre, cafe and bar facilities. ☺Open daily, 9am-5pm, ©(08) 9447 5888.

The Swan Brewery, Canning Vale, offers free guided tours Mon-Wed at 10am, with beer tasting included. There is a gift shop with a range of souvenirs and clothing. Bookings are essential, ©9350 0650.

The Maze, Sequola Park, Neaves Road, Bullsbrook, has not only a maze, but also mini golf, animals and barbecue facilities. Open Wed-Sun and through the school holidays, 9.30am-5pm, ©9571 1375.

Beatty Park Leisure Centre, Vincent Street, North Perth, is open all year with the water heated to 27C (81F) in the winter. ☺Open daily 5.30am-8pm, ©9273 6080.

Cottesloe Civic Centre, 109 Broome Street, Cottesloe, is a Spanish-style mansion with probably the best gardens in Perth. The grounds are open all hours, and the centre by arrangement, ©9384 1566.

The Old Mill, at the southern end of the Narrows Bridge, was Perth's first flour mill, built in 1835. It has been faithfully restored and contains relics of pioneer days.

Parks and Gardens

Bold Park and Perry Lakes, at Floreat Park, a short drive from the city, is a large expanse of bushland for enjoyable bushwalks and barbecues. Perry Lakes adds to the scenic beauty. A marvellous view of suburban Perth and the coastline is available from Reabold Hill.

Hyde Park has superb lawns and gardens. The huge trees are at their best in autumn, and many species of wildfowl congregate on an island in the ornamental lake. The Hyde Park festival is held annually, and thousands of people come to see the arts and crafts, sample ethnic foods, and see live performances.

Kings Park, overlooks the city and is only five minutes away. It is 404ha (998 acres) of bushland, and the pride of Perth, with its scenic

drives, and displays of wildflowers. Attractions include playgrounds, a botanical garden, lookouts, nature trails, bushwalks, a restaurant and barbecue areas.

Lake Monger is a favourite picnic spot with shady trees and green lawns. Many varieties of birdlife are seen here, including black swans and wild ducks.

Queens Gardens, cnr of Hay & Plain Streets, is a peaceful park with splendid gardens incorporating small lakes and bridges. There is also a statue of Peter Pan which is very popular with the children.

The River Foreshore, between the Causeway (Herrison Island) and the old Swan Brewery building, is within easy reach of the city, and includes the Swan River ferries' jetty and the parks and miniature lakes associated with the beautification of the Narrows Interchange.

Supreme Court Gardens, cnr Barrack Street & St George's Terrace, include the Stirling Gardens, and are a very popular lunch spot

with city workers. The Perth Music Shell is in these gardens, and many outdoor concerts are held here during the summer.

Wireless Hill Park, off Canning Highway, Melville. The area was originally set aside for the use of OTC. In 1969 it was vested in the City of Melville as an A class reserve. Rich in native flora, it also has the Telecommunications Museum.

Zoos and Wildlife Parks

Perth Zoo is 5 minutes south of Perth by car or bus, or take the scenic ferry from Barrack Street Jetty. ☺Open daily 9am-5pm, ✆9367 7988, admission is ✪$13 adults, $6.50 children and $35 families.

Caversham Wildlife Park, Arthur St, West Swan, ✆9274 2202, ☺open daily 9am-5pm.

Cohunu Koala Park, Mills Road, Gosnells, 26km (16 miles) south of Perth, ✆9390 6090. ☺Open daily 10am-5.30pm.

Herdsman Lake Wildlife Centre, cnr Flynn & Selby Streets,

Wembly ☎9387 6079 - ⊙open daily 9am-4.30pm.

Beaches

Perth's beaches are within easy reach of the city by Transperth buses (enquiries ☎221 1211), and the service that runs from Fremantle Bus/Train Interchange along the coast to Warwick Bus Station.

Ocean Beaches

City Beach - bus no 84 from outside Raines Square in Wellington Street terminates at the beach. Return by bus no. 81.

Cottesloe - bus no 72 or 103 from Stand 44 in St George's Terrace.

Leighton - bus no. 103 leaves from Stand 42, on the south side of St George's Terrace, corner William Street.

NorthBeach, **Waterman**, **Mullaloo** and **Sorrento** -bus no 81 leaves from the Wellington Bus Station. Transfer to bus no 98 at Selby Street and 424 at Stirling Interchange.

Scarborough - bus no 400 depart from the Wellington Street Bus Station.

River Beaches

Crawley Beach - bus no 24 leaves from St George's Terrace.

Como Beach - bus no 33 leaves from St George's Terrace.

Diving

The coast offers very good diving from Yanchep to Fremantle, with many off shore wrecks to explore, and beautiful corals and shells to collect. There is also a wide variety of reef fish, and table fish such as breaksea cod, blue groper, kingfish, and dhufish. There are also plenty of rock lobsters, but they may only be taken in season, and you should enquire at the Tourist Information Office, or get in touch with Diving Ventures, 384 South Terrace, Fremantle, ☎9430 5130.

Festivals

The Festival of Perth is held in February/March, and has an extensive programme of music, theatre, dance, film, visual arts and outdoor activities.

The Perth Cup, Perth's Premier horse race is held each New Year's Day. West Week is held the first week in June to celebrate Foundation Day.

The Perth Royal Show is an 8 day agricultural affair with exhibitions, animals, entertainment, and is held in September. ⊙The International Festival is held in Northbridge each December.

Facilities

Cricket is a major sport in Perth, and headquarters is at the WACA Ground, Hay Street East (near the Causeway).

Australian Rules is another sport with a strong following, and the local league has eight teams. The West Coast Eagles represent WA in the Australian competition.

Greyhound racing is held at Cannington Central every Saturday night.

Horseracing has two venues - Ascot and Belmont Park, both in the suburb of Belmont.

Pacing also has two Raceways - Gloucester Park, Nelson Crescent, East Perth, and Richmond Raceway at Fremantle. Gloucester Park has meetings on Friday nights, and Richmond has about 15 meetings a year. Details are in the daily newspapers.

The Showgrounds at Claremont are the place for speedway, with meetings held on Friday nights in the spring and summer.

WA Water Ski Park, St Alban's Road, Baldivis, has four man-made lakes, with three slalom courses and a jump. Lessons are available.

The city also has many golf clubs, cycling tracks, basketball, tennis and squash facilities.

Outlying Attractions

Fremantle

Fremantle is Western Australia's chief port, and is at the mouth of the Swan River, 19km (12 miles) from Perth. It was founded in 1829 by Captain Charles Howe Fremantle, in a ceremony claiming the entire west coast of New Holland in the name of King George IV. Many of the original buildings still standing were built with convict labour, and parts of the city retain their 19th century atmosphere.

Fremantle can be reached from Perth by bus, train, ferry and taxi. One of the best ways to get acquainted with Fremantle is to take a tram tour. ☉They leave on the hour, 10am-4pm, from the Town Hall, and travel to Victoria Quay, ✆9339 8719, for more information.

The Town Hall in St John's Square, cnr Adelaide and William Streets, is an elegant and gracious building officially opened in 1887 as part of Queen Victoria's Jubilee Celebrations. The Tourist Information Office is located here, ✆9431 7878.

The Western Australian Maritime Museum, Cliff Street, has displays dating from the 1600s to the time of British Settlement. They are re-assembling parts of the 1629 Dutch wreck *Batavia*. ☉Open 10.30am-5pm daily, ✆9431 8444.

Fremantle Port Authority Building, 1 Cliff Street, ✆9430 4911, has tours to the Observation Tower ☉at 9.30am, 10.30am, 11.30am, 1.30pm, 2.30pm and 3.30pm daily.

The Round House, Arthur Head (west end of High Street) was originally a gaol, and is the State's oldest surviving building, having been built in 1831. From the site there is an excellent view of Fremantle. ☉Open daily 10am-5pm, ✆9430 7351.

Fremantle Railway Station in Phillimore Street, opposite Market Street, opened in 1907.

There are many other museums, galleries and craft shops, and of course many leftovers from the America's Cup Challenge. The Tourist Bureau has all the details.

Rottnest Island

The name means Rats' Nest, and was given to the island by Dutch mariner, William Vlamingh in 1696, as he thought the small rock wallaby (quokka) inhabitants were rats. Rottnest Island is approximately 11km x 5km (7 miles x 3 miles), and is 19km (12 miles) west of Fremantle, 45 minutes by ferry, 15 minutes by air.

Ferry services operate regular services. Rottnest Ferry Oceanic Cruises depart from the end of Barrack Street, Perth, ✆9325 1191. Another service, Rottnest Ferry Services, runs from the Hillary's Marina, north of Perth, and sails to Sorrento, ✆9246 1039.

Contrary to most people's thinking, Rottnest is not a deserted island. As well as a wide variety of accommodation, there is a restaurant, school, bakery, laundrette, tennis courts, golf course, and many other signs of habitation. Two places worth noting are, the Rottnest Museum, ✆9372 7353, and the Rottnest Rail, ✆9372 9752. Both places reflect the history of the island well, one housing convict and shipwreck relics from the past, the other taking you on a trip to see the island as it is today. The most popular pastime is swimming in the clear water with no worries about sharks or rips. Then there is diving, surfing, boating, water skiing and fishing.

Rockingham

Situated in Cockburn Sound, one of the safest stretches of water in Australia, Rockingham is 47km (29 miles) south of Perth. The two main islands in the area are Garden and Penguin Islands. The Tourist Centre is at 43 Kent Street, ©9592 3464, and is open daily. Garden Island was used as a temporary base by Captain Stirling and the first settlers of the Swan River colony, and it is now the site of the naval base, HMAS Stirling. Visitors are not allowed access by the 4km causeway, but they may visit the island by boat between sunrise and sunset, provided they stay outside the fenced naval area. Penguin Island is a part-time home for a colony of dainty fairy penguins, one of only two such colonies in Australia. A flat-bottomed ferry operates between the island and the mainland, and the Tourist Centre has details. Other places of interest are the Rockingham Museum, ©9592 3455, the old Rockingham Heritage Trail, ©9592 3464, and the Rockingham-Jarrahdale Heritage Trail, ©9592 3464.

Mandurah

Mandurah is 74km (46 miles) south of Perth, and can be reached along the Coast Road, or from the South West Highway, either way taking about 50 minutes by car. The Tourist Bureau is at 5 Pinjarra Road, ©(09) 535 1155. They have information on the accommodation available in this holiday town, built around the calm protected waters of the Peel Inlet and Harvey Estuary, one of the largest inland waterways in Australia. The area also has 40km (25 miles) of sandy Indian Ocean beaches, so boating, fishing, surfing and windsurfing fans flock to the region. Attractions include: Ferry cruises; Bavarian Castle and Adventure Playground; Marapana Deer Park; Hall's Cottage; King Carnival Amusement Park, the greyhound and horseracing tracks; and one of WA's best restaurants, Doddi's at 115 Mandurah Terrace, ©9581 3735.

Wanneroo-Yanchep

The southern boundary of this area is 16km (10 miles) north of Perth, and extends to the 63km (39 miles) peg on Wanneroo Road. The region has almost 50km (31 miles) of coastline, with some very good beaches, and a chain of lakes in the centre. Make sure you don't miss The Gumnut Factory, 30 Prindiville Drive, Wangara, ©9409 6699 (which also serves as the local information centre), or Yanchep National Park, Yanchep, ©9561 1004.

Swan Valley

The rich, alluvial soil of the valley has attracted many farmers, who have turned their attention to grapes, and the area is noted for its range of high quality wines. The smaller vineyards specialise in ports and dessert wines, however many have been replanting with new varieties to produce lighter table wines, which are winning awards, both locally and overseas. The vignerons welcome visitors to their cellars to sample the wines, and details should be obtained from the Tourist Office in Perth before setting out. Midland is the hub of the Shire of Swan, and for over 100 years it has been a busy railway centre, with all trains inland and to the Eastern States passing through the town. Guildford, at the junction of the Swan and Helena Rivers, has many historic buildings that are excellent examples of early Australian town life. Some are small townhouses, which are not open to the public, other public buildings are open for inspection. They include: Guildford Court House; Rose & Crown Inn; Guildford Gaol; St Matthew's Church; Wesley Chapel and Manse; All Saints Church; Convict Depot Commissariat; Brockman's House; and Kinsella's Hotel.

Armadale

The town of Armadale is about 30km (19 miles) south-east of Perth on the Albany Highway. Attractions include: Araluen Park; Canning Dam; Churchman's Brook Dam; Wungong Dam; History House; Elizabethan Village, an authentic period reconstruction with many fine antiques in the buildings; and Signal Box Arts & Crafts (which houses the Bert Tyler Vintage Machinery Museum).

The Armadale Tourist Information Centre can be found in Jull Street, ©(08) 9497 3543.

Mundaring

On the Great Eastern Highway, 34km (21 miles) east of Perth, Mundaring is the Gateway to the Foothills. The Mundaring Tourist Information Centre is in the Old School, 7225 Great Eastern Highway, and they will advise on the area's attractions, which include: Mundaring Weir Gallery Arts and Crafts; the Hills Forest Discovery Centre; Mundaring Weir; the Bibbulmun Track; and the C.Y. O'Connor Museum.

Kalamunda

Located in the hills area, Kalamunda is 26km (16 miles) east of Perth. Places to see are:

Kalamunda History Village Museum, Railway Road; Hills Art Gallery, Railway Road; Stirk Park and Cottage, Kalamunda Road; and Lesmurdie Falls, Falls Road, Lesmurdie, in the Lesmurdie National Park. Drop into the Visitor Information Centre at 11 Headingly Road, or phone them beforehand on ☎9293 0299. They are ⏲open 10am-3pm Fri-Sun only.

Western Australia - South

Bunbury

Population 26,000
Bunbury lies at the western end of Leschenault Inlet, 185km (115 miles) south of Perth.

Climate

Average temperatures: January max 28C (82F) - min 18C (64F); July max 17C (63F) - min 8C (46F); number of days a year with temperature over 30C (86F) - 30. Average annual rainfall: 882mm (35 ins); wettest six months - May to October.

Characteristics

Bunbury is the major seaport and administrative centre of the South-West region, and the largest centre in Western Australia outside the metropolitan area. It is an expanding regional centre with a wealth of natural and man-made resources. It is surrounded by much of WA's best agricultural land, and the area is also rich in minerals. Ilmenite, rutile and zircon have been discovered in the sands along the coast, and bauxite is found nearby.

Bunbury, however, is primarily a holiday centre, and each year thousands come here to enjoy their holidays. The city is also used as a base to visit many beauty spots of the South-West.

How to Get There

By Rail
Westrail operates a service from Perth Railway Station daily for Bunbury.

By Bus

South West Coachlines operate a Perth to Bunbury and return service daily.

By Road

Travel from Fremantle to Mandurah and along the Coast Road to Bunbury, or from Perth to Armadale, then via the South West Highway. Either way, it is about a 2 hour drive.

Tourist Information

Tourism Bunbury is in Carmody Place, ©(08) 9721 7922. They are open seven days. Go online to ☞www.tourismbunbury.com.au or send them an email at ©welcome@tourismbunbury. com.au. Alternatively, Tourism South West is located at 61 Victoria Street, ©(08) 9791 9197.

Accommodation

As mentioned, Bunbury is a popular holiday resort, so there is plenty of accommodation, but it is always a good idea to book ahead in the holiday season. Here is a selection with prices for a double room per night, which should be used as a guide only. ☏The telephone area code is 08.

The Lord Forrest Hotel, Symmons Street, ©9721 9966. 115 units, licensed restaurant (Tues-Sat), swimming pool, spa, sauna, gym - ✪$130 - 210.

The Clifton, 2 Molloy Street, ©9721 4300. 48 units, licensed restaurant, swimming pool, spa, sauna, bbq ✪$90-125.

Parade Hotel, 100 Stirling Street, ©9721 2933. 9 rooms (private facilites) ✪$88.

Welcome Inn Motel, Ocean Dve, ©9721 3100. 51 units (private facilites), licensed restaurant, swimming pool ✪$65 -130.

Bunbury Motel, 45 Forrest Avenue, ©9721 7333. 37 units (private facilities), swimming pool ✪$70-85.

Ocean Drive Motel, 121 Ocean Drive, ©9721 2033. 26 units, unlicensed restaurant, bbq - $70-80.

Rose Motel Hotel, Victoria Street, ©9721 4533. 25 units, licensed restaurant - B&B ✪$80.

Highway Hotel Motel, Cnr Forrest Ave & Spencer Street, ©9721 4966. 9 rooms (private facilities) ✪$45.

Fawlty Towers Lodge, 205 Ocean Dve, ©9721 2427. 12 units (private facilities), swimming pool - ✪$75.

Chateau La-Mer Motor Lodge, 99 Ocean Dve, ©9721 3166. 28 units (private facilities), swimming pool, bbq ✪$70 - 85.

Caravan Parks

Riverside Caravan Park, 5 Pratt Road, Eaton, ©9725 1234. (No pets allowed) 80 sites - powered sites ✪$15 - 20 for two, chalet section $60 - 80 for two.

Waterloo Village Caravan Park, Lot 9 South Western Hwy, ©9725 4434. 70 sites - powered sites ✪$18 for two, on-site vans $40 for two.

Bunbury Glade Caravan Park, Bussell Highway, ©9721 3800. (No pets allowed) 150 sites- powered sites ✪$19 for two, cabins $50 - 60 for two.

Koombana Bay Holiday Resort, Koombana Drive, ©9791 3900. (No pets allowed) 31 sites- powered sites ✪$15 - 20 for two, chalet $135 for two, cabins $55 for two.

Eating Out

There is no shortage of restaurants in all price brackets, and plenty of takeaway food outlets. For a special night out try the restaurant in the *Lord Forest Hotel*, 20 Symmons St, ©9721 9966.

Alcazars Restaurant, 64 Victoria St, ©9721 9604.

China City Garden Restaurant, 47 Victoria St, ©9721 1711.

Kokoro Japanese Restaurant, 42B Spencer St, ©9721 4474.

Mancini's Cafe Restaurant, 66 Victoria St, ©9721 9944.

Points of Interest

The French explorer Nicolas Baudin was the first to sight Leschenault Inlet in 1803, as Commander of the *Geographe*, after which Geographe Bay is named. Baudin named the inlet after his botanist Jean Batiste Leschenault, and the port was first named Port Leschenault. In 1836, seven years after the founding of the Swan River settlement, Governor Sir James Stirling accompanied an expedition in the man-of-war Sulphur to explore the Port Leschenault and Busselton regions. Lieut. Henry William St Pierre Bunbury, then in charge of a military detachment in Pinjarra, made the overland trek to meet Governor Stirling in December 1836 at Port Leschenault. For that feat Governor Stirling told the 24-year-old lieutenant that Port Leschenault would be renamed Bunbury in his honour, and records show that he was highly delighted. They also show that he was the first to note the black sand peculiar to the shoreline in the area, recognising the ilmenite and related beach sands which were to develop into a multi-million dollar industry more than a century later.

The only public building surviving from the late 19th century is the **Paisley Centre**, cnr Arthur & Stephen Streets. It was built in

1894 as a primary school, and its architectural merit lies in the massing of the various parts, the good proportions of the fenestration and the many steeply-pitched gables that give a period character. Local sandstone was used for the window facings.

An earlier school on the same site was notable for a state record - three primary school pupils went on to become State Premiers: Sir John Forrest, Sir Newton Moore and Sir James Mitchell.

The Rose Hotel, in Victoria Street on the corner of Wellington Street, was erected by Samuel Rose in 1865, and rebuilt in 1897. Internally the hotel impresses with items of period furniture and ornaments which reflect the mood of bygone days. The solid stone statue of Henry II which stands in the courtyard was once part of the British Houses of Parliament at Westminster. It was purchased by the management of the hotel and shipped to Australia in 1980.

The **War Memorial** in Anzac Park, cnr Stirling & Parkfield Streets, opposite the post office, is a fine memorial to World War I armed forces. Alongside is another memorial, to John and Helen Scott, first farmers in the Bunbury District. They began work at Eelup Farm on Sir James Stirling's property in 1838.

Boulter's Heights, Bunbury's most popular lookout is a vantage point for a panoramic view of the city, the port, the north shore and the Leschenault Estuary. The waterfall was constructed in March, 1966, and when in operation, a cascade of water tumbles down the eastern face of the heights. Boulter's Heights is in Withers Crescent, off Haig Crescent, and can also be reached on foot from the base of the waterfall at the junction of Stirling and Wittenoom Streets.

Bunbury Regional Art Galleries, Wittenoom Street, are in the old Convent of Mercy building, which was opened and blessed in December, 1897. During 1981, the convent complex was purchased by the City Council, as it was no longer being used to house the Sisters of Mercy and their pupils. The Galleries are a multiple use facility, and are available for seminars, meetings, exhibitions, lectures, discussions, etc. They also contain the City of Bunbury Art Collection, which numbers 300 works, and has grown from an initial gift of 20 paintings by Claude Hotchin in 1949.

St Patrick's Cathedral, Parkfield Street, Bunbury, is situated on the upper level of Bury Hill, and commands a fine view of the inlet, the port and the city. The building was completed in 1921, without the 18.3m (60 ft) steeple which was added 46 years later. The pews and much of the interior of the Cathedral were built of local jarrah.

St Boniface Cathedral, cnr Parkfield & Cross Streets, was consecrated on October 14, 1962, on land originally purchased in 1916. The most unusual feature of this Anglican Cathedral is the big tower at the east end crowning the sanctuary rather than at the customary west end or in the centre.

Sir John Forrest Monument, cnr Victoria & Stephen Streets, is in honour of WA's greatest son. Sir John Forrest, Baron Forrest of Bunbury, CMG, KCMG, PC, GCMG, Hon LLD, FRGS, FGS, FLS, Kt of the Order of the Crown of Italy, surveyor, explorer, politician and peer, was born in 1847 at Mill Point at the mouth of the Preston River, 7km from Bunbury. He spent 18 years in State politics, all in executive office, then 18 years in Federal politics, almost half as Cabinet Minister. First MLA for Bunbury, first Premier of WA, five times Federal Treasurer, for a time Forrest was Acting Prime Minister. In 1918, he was created Baron Forrest of Bunbury, the first Australian to be raised to the British peerage. He died that year at sea, aged 71, and is buried in Karrakatta Cemetery. In 1979, Bunbury businessmen commissioned Mark Le Buse to sculpture Forrest's head, now here in St Paul's Place.

Centenary Gardens, cnr Wittenoom & Princep Street, were built in 1936 to commemorate the town's centenary, and have a shade pavilion dedicated to Lt Bunbury, and a wishing well built by the Apex Club in 1952. Facilities include seating, drinking fountain, toilets and an infant health centre.

Bunbury Lighthouse, Ocean Drive, on the ocean side of Casuarina Point, is a striking landmark and one of a fine collection of lighthouses that are part of the state's heritage.

The Timber Jetty, off Henry Street, was commenced in 1864 and was to be 427m (467 yds) long. In 1957, after several extensions, it reached its ultimate length of 1830m (2001 yds). Due to the development of the inner harbour in the 1970s, the jetty ceased commercial shipping in October, 1982. It is now used for pedestrian traffic and is a popular fishing and crabbing spot.

The **Bunbury Basaltic Rock**, at the northern end of Ocean Beach, is formed from a volcanic lava-flow believed to have occurred 150 million years ago in the cretaceous period. Volcanic activity was quite extensive over the South-West corner for a short period of time a considerable amount of basalt can still be found west of a line from Bunbury to Windy Harbour, buried beneath sedimentary layers of sand and clay. The basalt rock formation can only be seen in Bunbury and Black Point, south-east of Augusta.

King Cottage Museum, 77 Forrest Avenue, ✆9721 7546, is a small, well kept cottage dating from 1880, and was opened as a local history museum in 1968. It houses a valuable collection of pioneer material of the area. One of Bunbury's oldest buildings, the cottage was the home of Henry King. Aided by four sons and using home-made bricks, Henry King erected the family dwelling of unique Flemish bond brick design. ⏰Open Sat-Sun 2-4pm.

The **Bunbury Recreation Centre**, in Hay Park off Parade Road, was officially opened in 1979, and is a large multi recreation centre. The enclosed area allows the presentation of major exhibitions, championships and celebrity presentations. The centre is fully utilised by sporting groups, and is equipped with a heated indoor swimming pool, spa and sauna.

Tourism Bunbury has details of an 11km (7 miles) **inland river cruise** through scenery abounding with birdlife. ⏰The cruise operates from September through May, on Saturday and Sunday.

Other attractions include: wine tasting at the Geographe Wine Region & Ferguson Valley, Koombana Bay and the Old Goldfields Orchard & Cider Factory.

Festivals

The Bunbury Racing Carnival is held in mid-March, with The Bunbury Cup, Australia's richest provincial race held on the Thursday of the Racing Round.

Facilities

Squash, tennis, cricket, croquet, bowls, golf, basketball, badminton, archery and bush walking. The Forrest Drive-In and Cinema is on the Bussell Highway, the Little Theatre is in Molloy Street, and information and show times are in the local paper.

Outlying Attractions

Busselton

Located 228km (142 miles) south of Perth, on the Bussell Highway, Busselton lies on the shores of Geographe Bay, where the Vasse River flows into the bay. The Tourist Bureau is at 38 Peel Terrace, ✆(08) 9752 1288. They have details of the available accommodation, and of the numerous scenic

drives in the area.

Attractions in the town include: The Busselton Jetty, a long wooden jetty in need of repairs due to the battering it received from cyclone Alby in 1978; St Mary's Church of England, the oldest stone church in the State; Wonnerup House, ⊕open daily 11am-noon, 1-4.30pm; Old Butter Factory, which houses the Historical Society, ⊕open Wed-Mon 2-5pm, Fri 9am-11.30am and 2-5pm; Old School and Teacher's House, classified by the National Trust; The Old Courthouse Complex; The Whistle Stop, the old Margaret River railway station, which closed in 1957, and has been relocated 11km out of Busselton on the Vasse Highway; and Ludlow Tuart Forest which holds the beauty of rare rain forests and is located just outside the town.

Margaret River

The south-west coastal town of Margaret River is 52km (32 miles) south of Busselton on the Bussell Highway. The annual concert at Leeuwin Estate lures the cultural set, while the pounding surf in Prevelly Park challenges competitors in the annual amateur and professional surf competitions. The Tourist Bureau is on the Bussell Highway in the town, ✆(08) 9757 2147, and you should visit them for information on accommodation and eating out. They have a website at ☞www.margaretriver wa.com. Send emails to ✉amrta@ netserv.net.au

Attractions in the area include: the Caves of the south-west - Mammoth Cave, 21km (13 miles) south of Margaret River, and Lake Cave, 2km further south; the vineyards (there are plenty to visit); the

Old Settlement Historical Museum; the Berry Farm; and Boranup Forest which showcases some of the State's prettiest karri forest.

Augusta

Situated 95km (59 miles) south of Busselton, on the Bussell Highway. The Augusta-Margaret River area of the State is commonly known as the South-West Corner, as it is within that anvil shaped protrusion of the land which extends into the Indian Ocean. Renowned as having some of the most picturesque scenery in WA, the district can also boast of spectacular underground attractions - there are many beautiful limestone caves, of which three are open to tourists. Modern lighting is provided and access is easy. Two are mentioned under Margaret River, the other one is The Jewel Cave, 8km from Augusta. Its attractions are the Organ Pipes and the Jewel Casket. It also has the world's largest straw - a stalactite which measures 5.9m (19 ft) in length.

The Augusta Tourist Bureau can be contacted on ©(08) 9758 0166, and they will advise on accommodation. Other attractions are Cape Leeuwin Lighthouse, Augusta Historical Museum and Hamelin Bay.

Manjimup

Manjimup is 307km (191 miles) south of Perth at the junction of South West and Muirs Highways, right in the heart of the karri and jarrah forest. The town has over 5000 residents, and the Tourist Bureau is on the corner of Rose and Edwards Streets, ©(08) 9771 1831. The town has modern shopping facilities and most sports are well catered for, including golf, lawn bowls and five squash courts.

Attractions include: Manjimup Timber Park; the King Jarrah Heritage Trail; Fonty's Pool; Glenoran Pool; the Dingup Church; and the Perup Ecology Pool.

Collie

Situated 57km (35 miles) inland from Bunbury, and 203km (126 miles) south of Perth, Collie is important as a coal mining town, and has in fact been WA's only source of coal since the 1890s, and Muja Power Station supplies the State electricity grid. The Tourist Bureau is situated at 156 Throssell Street, ©(08) 9734 2051. You can contact them by email at ✏ctb@collie.net serv.net.au or check out the website at ☞www.collieriver valley.org.au

Attractions in the town include: Muja Open Cut/Power Station Tourist Look-out; the Historical and Mining Museum; Steam Locomotion Museum; All Saints Church; Wellington Dam; and Collie Scenic Drive.

Western Australia - South

Albany

Population 24,184
Albany is situated 406km (252 miles) south of Perth on King George Sound, on the southern coast of Western Australia.

Climate

Albany has a mild Mediterranean climate with an average rainfall of 944mm (37 ins), most of which falls during the winter months. The temperatures, regulated by the ocean, vary from a summer daytime average of 25C (77F) to a winter daytime average of 17C (63F).

Characteristics

The heart of the Rainbow Coast (Great Southern) region of Western Australia, Albany is nestled by the tranquil waters of Princess Royal Harbour. As Albany was the first settlement in the State, it is steeped in history and memories. It sits amidst a relatively unspoilt area of Australia with National Parks, forests, rugged coastline, mountains, wilderness areas and tranquil rivers all within easy reach.

How to Get There

By Bus
Westrail, ©(08) 9326 2000, provides a daily service to Albany via York or Kojonup.

By Car
From Perth, via Albany Highway, approximately 4 hours, or a longer drive via the coast road.

Tourist Information

Albany Tourist Bureau, Old Railway Station, Proudlove Parade, ✆(08) 9841 1088, is ☼open seven days a week. Visit the website at ☜www.albanytourist.com.au or email them at ✎b@albanytourist.com.au

Accommodation

A wide variety of accommodation exists in and around Albany including hotels, motels, guest houses, chalets, caravan parks, farm stay and backpackers or youth hostels. Information can be obtained from the Tourist Bureau. Here is a selection with prices for a double room per night, which should be used as a guide only. ☼The telephone area code is 08.

Albany Dog Rock Motel, 303 Middleton Road, ✆9841 4422. 81 units, licensed restaurant ✪$80-105.

Ace Motor Inn, 314 Albany Highway, ✆9841 2911. 54 units, unlicensed restaurant ✪$75-85.

Frederickstown Motel, Cnr Fredericks Street & Spencer Street, ✆9841 1600. 36 units, unlicensed restaurant ✪$90-100.

Amity Motor Inn, 234 Albany Highway, ✆9841 2200. 40 units, licensed restaurant ✪$70-90.

Emu Point Motel, cnr Mermaid Avenue & Medcalf Parade, ✆9844 1001. 14 units ✪$70 - 80.

Esplanade Motor Hotel, Flinders Parade, Middleton Beach, ✆9842 1711. 48 rooms (private facilities), licensed restaurant ✪$90-105.

Caravan Parks

Mt Melville Caravan Park, 22 Wellington Street, ✆9841 4616. (Dogs allowed on bond only) - powered sites ✪$20-23 for two, on-site vans $44-48 for two.

Albany Tourist Village, 550 Albany Highway, ✆9841 3752. (No dogs allowed) - powered sites $17 for two, on-site vans ✪$37-41 for two.

Middleton Beach Holiday & Caravan Park, 28 Flinders Parade, Middleton Beach, ✆9841 3593. (No pets allowed) - powered sites ✪$19-23 for two, chalets $75 - 150 for two.

Panorama Holiday Cottages & Caravan Park, Lot 106 Frenchman Bay Road, ✆9844 4031. (Dogs allowed on leash) - powered sites ✪$20-25 for two, on-site vans $30-45 for two.

Eating Out

Albany has a very good selection of restaurants, offering every type of cuisine, cafes and takeaway outlets, and the Tourist Office has a

complete list. Here are some you might like to try:

Bangkok Rose, 112 York St, ✆9842 2366.

Al Fornetto Ristorante & Pizzeria, 132 York St, ✆9842 1060.

Goshu-ya Japanese Restaurant, 1 Mermaid Avenue, Emu Point, ✆9844 1111 - BYO, snacks and seafood - ☺open 10am-late.

The Curry Pot, 38 Stirling Terrace, ✆9842 9399.

Ristorante Leonardos, 164 Stirling Terrace, ✆9841 1732.

Dog Rock Restaurant, Middleton Road, ✆9841 1400 - Licensed, Italian - ☺open Mon-Sat, 5pm drinks, 6.30pm dinner.

Amity Restaurant, 234 Albany Hwy, ✆9841 2200.

Kooka's Restaurant, 204 Stirling Tce, ✆9841 5889.

Red Rooster, 87 Lockyer Rd, ✆9841 2033

Kentucky Fried Chicken, Lockyer Ave, ✆9841 7350.

Hungry Jacks, 13 Lockyer Ave, ✆9842 1314.

Moby Dicks Fish & Chips, 60 South Coast Highway, ✆9841 6142.

Points of Interest

The town of Albany lies on a saddle between Mt Melville and Mt Clarence overlooking Princess Royal Harbour, one of the greatest landlocked deep-water harbours in the world. It is a pretty town with lovely water vistas at every turn, and many vantage points for breathtaking views and holiday snaps.

Within the main town area there are many historic buildings, including the now refurbished Town Hall, built in 1887, the first consecrated Anglican church in WA, and the Western Australian Museum.

The **Western Australian Museum** building was built in the early 1850s, then more rooms were added and it was converted to a house for Government residents in 1873. For eighty years, it was the centre of the town's social activities. For the following twenty years, it had a variety of uses before becoming derelict. It was then rebuilt and converted to its present form. It is located in Residency Road and you can contact the museum on ©9841 4844.

Adjoining the Western Australian Museum is the Brig *Amity* replica and the Eclipse building. This building, opened back in 1989, houses the massive $5 million optic from the Old Eclipse Island Lighthouse and a Touch Gallery full of hands-on exhibits for those more tactile visitors.

The **Old Gaol** is nearby, and was built in 1851 as the convict hiring depot. In 1872 it became the district gaol, and in the early 1930s, a store house. It then stood empty for many years until 1968, when the Albany Historical Society began its restoration. The museum has an extensive collection of social and historical artefacts.

Patrick Taylor Cottage, in Duke Street, was built around 1832, of wattle and daub, and is thought to be the oldest building still standing in Albany. It now contains over 2000 items including period costumes, old clocks, silverware and kitchenware.

A short distance along Middleton Road past the famous Dog Rock, is **Old Farm Strawberry Hill**. The Old Farm has enjoyed a colourful history since it was established in 1831 as the Government Farm for the Settlement of Albany. The two-storey home was built in 1836 for the Government Resident Sir Richard Spencer. Restored to its former glory by the National Trust in 1964, it stands serene in the midst of an English garden, hidden from the view of passers-by.

One of the most unusual buildings in Albany is the **Old Post Office** building, located on historic Stirling Terrace. This building was originally used as a customs and bond store, with the middle level being a sorting area and post office. The spiral staircase in the tower is magnificent, and the building now houses restaurants, a weaver and a museum.

An admirable restoration for Albany is to be found on Mount Clarence in **Princess Royal Fortress**. This military establishment was conceived in 1878 and was operational until 1956. After an intensive restoration programme, the fortress now has an important part to play in the region. Within its boundaries are a kiosk and a restaurant with stunning views from timber decking.

For those interested in exploration in the near vicinity, **Torndirrup National Park** will provide much interest. Follow the signs to Frenchman Bay Road and only 15 minutes' drive away is some of the most dramatic and beautiful coastline in Australia. Torndirrup National Park is best known for the Gap, Natural Bridge, the Blowholes and Peak Head. Panoramic views can be obtained from the Stoney Hill Heritage Trail, and Frenchman Bay Beach is a lovely sheltered little nook in complete contrast to the coast near the open sea.

Also found in Torndirrup National Park is a museum with a difference. After being part of one of the bloodiest chapters in the history of whaling, Australia's last mainland whaling station, located in Albany, closed in 1978. This whaling station, now known as **Whaleworld**, is a museum of the whaling industry and now plays a most impor- tant part in the preservation of the magnificent creatures it once sought to slaughter.

To find out about the history of Albany it would be wise to pick up a copy of *The Amity Trail*. This bro- chure gives you a guide to the his- toric places around Albany.

There are many scenic drives you can take around Torbay which lead to places like Anvil Beach and Cosy Corner Beach.

Flora

Jarrah, marri, sheoak and pepper- mints are the principal trees, with some karris to be found. Spectacu- lar shrubs include the scarlet banksia, the bright red swamp bottlebrush, the golden showy dryandra, pink yellow and cream cone flowers and the white South- ern Cross. Orchids abound, while the yellow and red Albany catspaw is seen in sandy woodlands. Hid- ing in the dense swamps is the Albany pitcher plant, while on swamp margins the curious red and white swamp daisy may be seen. July to October are the best months for flowers, but there are blooms to be found at any time of the year.

Fauna

Many varieties of birds inhabit the area, including land and water birds both of noisy and colourful varie- ties. Small native animals such as pygmy-possums, short-nosed bandicoots and bush rats are common, as well as kangaroos, emus on occasion, and many more including a wide variety of reptiles. Whales are frequently sighted from cliffs, particularly during winter, and seals sometimes visit.

Facilities

There are good sporting facilities for most sports within the town, in addition to which there are two gyms, a large heated swimming pool with spa, horse riding and two golf courses. On a more cultural level there is an excellent town theatre for movies and stage shows, and art galleries with regular exhibitions. There are many tours available - scenic, adventure, diving and fishing - and river cruises. As Albany is a large regional centre, most needs are catered for. The Tourist Bureau has brochures detailing current events.

Outlying Attractions

The Rainbow Coast area of Western Australia, of which Albany is the heart, stretches from the hamlet of Walpole in the west to Bremer Bay in the east, and from Albany in the south to the towns of Kojonup and Katanning in the north.

A total of seven national parks can be found within the Rainbow Coast and although each has its own special characteristics, they share many common natural attractions.

Walpole/Nornalup National Park

This park covers some 18,000ha (44,460 acres) surrounding the Walpole and Nornalup Inlets at the eastern gateway to the region. It has deep rivers, majestic karri forest, waterfalls, wildflowers and unspoilt coastline. The Pioneer Cottage, in Pioneer Park, Walpole, was opened in October 1987 and was a joint venture between the Walpole Tourist Bureau and the Department of Conservation and Land Management. The Bureau provided the funds and the department carried out the construction. The cottage follows the basic design of an early pioneer home, but it is not meant to be a replica. It has been provided to commemorate the pioneers of the district who were responsible for opening up the virgin bush areas and laying the foundations of the district as it is today. The Walpole Tourist Information Centre is in the Pioneer Cottage, Walpole, ✆(08) 9840 1111.

Porongurup National Park

Nestled near Mount Barker, this park is famous for its granite rock

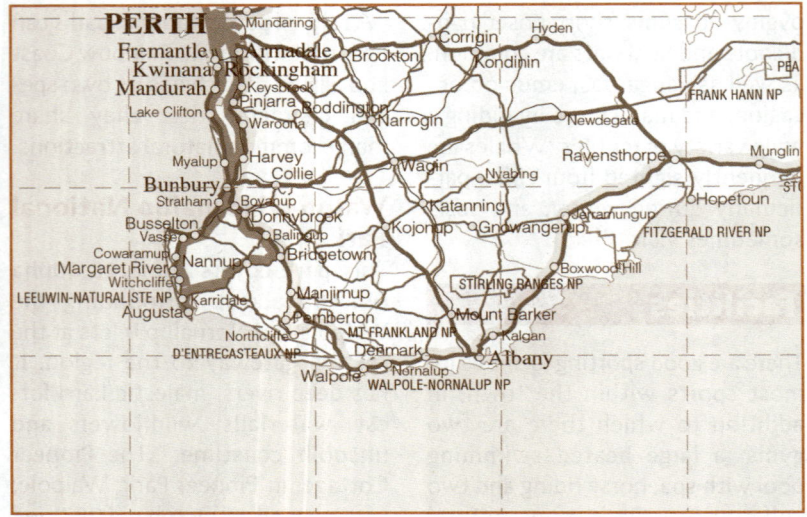

formations and luxuriant karri and marri trees. Footpaths lead to several peaks, and other paths and heritage trails cross the ranges.

Stirling Ranges

About 80km (50 miles) north of Albany the rugged peaks of the Stirling Ranges rise abruptly to more than 1000m (3281 ft) above sea level. Stark cliff faces, magnificent views and rare plants ranging from tiny orchids and heathland to flowering gums, are all part of the Stirling Range. Most peaks have paths leading from the parking areas to the top, and offer magnificent views for walkers.

Fitzgerald River National Park

In stark contract is the Fitzgerald River National Park which covers 270,000ha (666,900 acres) surrounding the inlets of the Gairdner, Fitzgerald and Hamersley Rivers between Bremer Bay and Hopetoun. In this small area of WA can be found nearly 20% of the total number of plant species found in the whole State, including 75 that are endemic to this park. The park protects magnificent scenery and is large and untouched enough to provide a habitat for many species of native plants and animals fast becoming rare elsewhere. The Fitzgerald is the only national park in WA to be gazetted as a World

Biosphere Reserve. Public use is varied with a full range from wilderness enjoyment through to coastal fishing at more accessible spots.

Wineries

The mild climate of the Rainbow Coast not only creates an ideal holiday destination, it also lends itself to wines of good quality which are beginning to come to the fore. The past couple of years have brought important recognition of the quality of grapes from this district, made up mainly of many small vineyards. Plantings in Albany, Denmark and Mount Barker all show the splendid purity of varietal fruit that vines achieve in this cool climate region. Now Mount Barker has attracted two large vineyard projects. While the boutique vineyard image won't be lost, the developments will substantiate the Rainbow Coast as a winegrowing region.

The Tourist Bureau has particulars of any winery tours and cellar door sales that are available during your visit.

Denmark

Situated 55km (34 miles) west of Albany on the South Coast Highway, Denmark has a population of around 2000. The Denmark River flows through this charming little town, and the local industries are timber milling, salmon fishing (February to April) and farming - beef cattle, dairying, sheep, pigs and potato growing.

The Tourist Bureau is in Strickland Street, ✆(08) 9848 2055, and they will be able to advise on the local attractions, which include: Wilson Head and Lions Lookout; The Aquarium and Sphinx Rock; Mount Shadford Scenic Drive, William Bay National Park; Wilson Inlet; and Parry's Inlet and Beach.

Ocean Beach, about 8km from Denmark, is one of the finest surfing beaches in the State. The town also has a golf course, bowling greens and tennis courts.

Katanning

Situated 170km (106 miles) north of Albany on the Great Southern Highway, Katanning is a bustling and progressive centre, catering for the town and farming communities. There is excellent accommodation available, and the Tourist Information Centre, 54 Austral Terrace, ✆08 9821 2634, has details.

Attractions include the Old Mill Museum, Kobeelya homestead, Katanning Mosque and the Old Winery.

Kalgoorlie/Boulder

Population 26,813
Kalgoorlie is situated in semi-desert area, 597 km (371 miles) east of Perth, at the terminus of the Great Eastern Highway.

Climate

Average temperatures: January max 34C (93F) - min 18C (64F); July max 17C (63F) - min 6C (43F). Average annual rainfall: 263mm (10 ins).

Characteristics

Situated in an area named for gold and riddled with reminders of its presence, Kalgoorlie-Boulder's association with the precious metal stands out. Not for this twin centre the boom, bust and quick extinction into a ghost town, nor any lingering on amongst remnants of former glory. The towns are as busy as ever, and stand next to what was once the richest square mile of gold-bearing earth in the world. And although nearly a century of mining has seen a thousand million dollars worth of gold removed, there is plenty left yet.

Echoes of the boisterous past can still be seen, particularly in Hannan Street, Kalgoorlie, and Burt Street, Boulder.

How to Get There

By Bus
Greyhound Pioneer operate daily services through Kalgoorlie.

By Rail
The Prospector leaves Perth Sun-Fri, and an interstate train leaves five evenings a week.

By Road
From Perth, travel straight along the Great Eastern Highway to Kalgoorlie.

Tourist Information

The Kalgoorlie-Boulder Tourist Centre is at 250 Hannan Street, Kalgoorlie, ✆(08) 9021 1966 or ✆1800 00 1880 (toll free). They are 🕐open 8.30am-5pm Mon-Fri and 9am-5pm on weekends. If you have online access, visit 👁www.kal goorlieandwagoldfields.com.au for a preliminary peek or drop them a message at ✉kbtc@emerge.net.au

Accommodation

There is quite a range of accommodation to choose from, and the Tourist Offices have a complete list. Here we have a selection, with prices for a double room per night, which should be used as a guide only. ✆The telephone area code is 08.
Hospitality Inn Kalgoorlie, 560 Hannan Street, ✆9021 2888. 56 units, licensed restaurant, swimming pool, bbq ✪$115-145.
Midas Motel, 409 Hannan Street, ✆9021 3088. 49 units, licensed restaurant, swimming pool, spa, sauna ✪$110-135.
Mercure Hotel Plaza Kalgoorlie, 45 Egan Street, ✆9021 4544. 100 units, licensed restaurant, swimming pool ✪$130-260.
Mercure Inn Overland Kalgoorlie, Hannan Street, ✆9021 1433. 87 units, licensed restaurant, swimming pool ✪$68.
Tower Hotel, cnr Bourke & Maritana Streets, ✆9021 3211. 33 units, licensed restaurant, swimming pool, spa, sauna ✪$75-105.
Star & Garter, 497 Hannan St, ✆9026 3399. 28 units, licensed restaurant, swimming pool ✪$85.
Hannan's View Motel, 430 Hannan St, ✆9091 3333. 65 units, unlicensed restaurant ✪$110-160.
Shamrock Motor Lodge, cnr Lane & Piesse Streets, Boulder, ✆9093 1399. 37 units, licensed restaurant, swimming pool, spa, sauna ✪$85.
Piccadilly Hotel, 164 Piccadilly Street, ✆9021 2109. 19 rooms (private facilities) ✪$40.

Caravan Parks
Goldminer Tourist Caravan Park, Great Eastern Highway, ✆9021 3713. (No pets allowed) - powered sites ✪$17 for two, on-site vans $44 for two.
Prospector Holiday Park, Lower Hannan Street, Great Eastern Highway, ✆9021 2524. (No pets allowed) - powered sites ✪$20-21

for two, cabins $60-90 for two.

Boulder Village Caravan Park, Lane Street, Boulder, ✆9093 1266. (No pets allowed) - powered sites ✪$20 for two, chalets $75-85 for two, cabins $75-85 for two.

Kalgoorlie Accommodation Village, Burt Street, Boulder, ✆9039 4800. (No pets allowed) - powered sites ✪$20 for two, chalets $77-83 for two, cabins $75-85 for two.

Eating Out

Most of the hotels and motels have restaurants, and there are plenty of takeaway food outlets. Here are a few restaurants you might like to try.

Amalfi, 409 Hannan Street, Kalgoorlie, ✆9021 3088.

Amy's, 1 MacDonald Street, Kalgoorlie, ✆9021 1749.

Top End Thai Restaurant, 71 Hannan Street, Kalgoorlie, ✆9021 4286.

Fu-Wah Chinese Restaurant, Shop 6, Woolworths Plaza, Wilson Street, Kalgoorlie, ✆9021 6242.

Mangia Bene Italian Restaurant & Takeaway, Lammington Square, Shop 1 Maritana Street, Kalgoorlie, ✆9021 3553.

Inland City Garden Restaurant, 93 Forrest Street, Kalgoorlie, ✆9021 2401.

Crock Pot Bar & Restaurant, Shop 10/89 Graeme Street, Kalgoorlie,

✆9021 2997.

Cornwall Historic Restaurant, 25 Hopkins Street, Boulder, ✆9093 2510.

Wah On Restaurant, 110 Burt Street, Boulder, ✆9093 108.

Points of Interest

In June, 1893, three Irishmen, Patrick Hannan, Tom Flannigan and Daniel Shea, discovered gold near Mt Charlotte. Two other prospectors soon located further large gold deposits three miles to the south - the world famous 'Golden Mile'.

The goldrush this sparked was staggering in size and speed. Men came in thousands from all over the world, ready to live in improvised shacks in a waterless near-desert. Hundreds of mining companies were floated to speculate on the rich reefs, and many of them were fraudulent.

A railway and five civic buildings sprung up in no time, but water seemed to be an insoluble problem, until C.Y. O'Connor devised the Goldfields Water Scheme. This consisted of building a 563km (350 miles) pipeline from a reservoir near Perth, which was a resounding success, but the criticism it received during the construction process caused O'Connor to shoot himself, so he never saw his dream realised.

Gold production reached a peak

in 1903, and then declined until the Depression of the 1930s, when world prices increased dramatically.

In 1931, the State's richest nugget was found and named 'The Golden Eagle'. It weighed an incredible 32,177g (1,135 ounces).

The Golden Mile is now managed as a whole for the first time in its history, which should lead to more efficient and longer-lasting exploitation of the gold reserves.

In the late 1890s, the Golden Mile Loop Line was the busiest and best paying in the colony. Over 60 passenger and goods trains passed through Boulder City Station on weekdays, 33 on Saturdays and 27 on Sundays. The locomotives used in those days were N class, and were worked extremely hard. Today the Railway is run by the Golden Mile Loopline Railway Society Inc, a voluntary group formed to make sure that the line remains open. Visitors are able to re-live some of the past events of the area while they 'Ride the Rattler', travelling over some of the Golden Mile pulled by a Wickham Track Inspection vehicle or Z1153, a jetty shunting locomotive. A full recorded commentary is played so that every feature is explained as you pass.

Regular **tours** depart from Boulder Railway Station during ⏰weekdays and Sundays at 11am, and also on Sundays and public holidays they depart at 1.30pm and 3pm. During school holidays, extra trains run, and further enquiries can be made at the Tourist Bureau, or ✆(08) 9021 1966.

Mining Hall of Fame, Goldfields Highway, ✆9091 2122, is one of Australia's most unusual tourist attractions, and provides a unique chance for the whole family to go underground in a real gold mine in safety. It is essential to wear enclosed footwear, and children under 4 are not permitted on underground tours. Children under 16 pay half the adult fee for the tours. You can pan for gold and watch some gold work. The doors ⏰open at 9am.

Underground Tours last 1.5 hours, and in the peak season run every half hour, ⏰starting at 10.30am, with the last tour at 3pm. In the non-holiday period they run at 10.30am, 1pm and 2.30pm. Gold Room Demonstrations last half an hour, and begin in peak season at 10.30am, 1pm and 3pm, in off peak, 10.30am and 1pm.

Guided Surface Tours last one hour, and begin on completion of the Gold Room Demonstrations.

Combined Tours last 3 hours, and in the peak season ⏰commence at 10.30am, 11.30am, 1pm and 1.30pm. The 1.30pm tour is not available in the off-peak season.

Western Australian Museum,

Kalgoorlie-Boulder, 17 Hannan Street, ☎9021 8533, is ☉open daily 10.30am-4.30pm. The building was formerly the British Arms Hotel, the narrowest hotel in Australia. On display are the developments in the search of gold and aspects of domestic life at the turn of the century.

Mt Charlotte Reservoir holds Kalgoorlie's permanent fresh water supply, which comes by pipeline from the weir at Mundaring in the Darling Range. In January, 1903, Sir John Forrest, explorer and Premier of WA, turned on the water at the Mt Charlotte reservoir, and the town went wild. At the official banquet that night, Sir George Reid said that he had never heard so much talk about water, and seen so little of it consumed. From the lookout at the Reservoir there is a good view of the town.

Paddy Hannan's Statue, in Hannan Street, is a replica of the original within the Town Hall. It shows a life-sized Paddy, holding his waterbag.

In a fenced area, near the head of Hannan Street, is a kurrajong tree and a plaque marking the place where Paddy Hannan first found gold.

Kalgoorlie Town Hall was built in 1908, and has a fine stamped metal ceiling and Victorian style cast seats on the balcony. On the first floor is the Art Collection, ☉open Mon-Fri 9am-5pm.

The **Royal Flying Doctor Base**, north of the main city area of Kalgoorlie, has conducted tours ☉commencing at 2.30pm each weekday. No admission fee is charged, but donations are welcome.

Lord Forrest Olympic Pool and Water Slide is on the corner of MacDonald and Cassidy Streets, and was WA's first Olympic Pool. It was built in 1938, using water from the pipeline. The park nearby has shady trees, a statue of C.Y. O'Connor, and a fountain.

The Boulder Block, back in 1905, was a thriving business centre with 6 hotels which served liquor around the clock to cater for miners on shift work. The area is only 0.5ha (1.2 acres), which makes it hard to imagine.

Boulder Town Hall in Burt Street, was built in 1908, and has a distinctive clock tower.

The Golden Mile Art Exhibition is in the upstairs gallery at the Boulder Town Hall. It is a permanent exhibition with works by local artists. Visitors are welcome, and arrangements can be made by phoning ☎9093 3283.

The Cornwall Hotel, probably the most picturesque in the area, was built in 1898 and is in vintage condition. It photographs well.

The Goldfields War Museum is in Burt Street, Boulder. It is ⊙open Mon-Fri 10am-4pm.

The Eastern Goldfields Historical Society Museum is in the Boulder City Railway Station. Its ⊙hours of opening are: Mon-Sat 10.30am-12.30pm, Sun 10am-4pm, ✆9093 3360.

Hammond Park, Lyall Street, Lamington, is a flora and fauna reserve with a lake, a rustic bridge and a miniature castle made from local stone. There is a grass picnic area with barbecue facilities, and tame emus and kangaroos roam amongst the picnickers. The park is ⊙open daily 9am-5.30pm.

Seven kilometres north of Kalgoorlie is Australia's only legalised **Bush Two-up School**, and business ⊙begins at around 1.30 each afternoon, except on the miners' pay day when the horse races are held in town. For the inexperienced, two-up is a very easy game to learn, and is an easy way to lose money very quickly. We can only suggest that you watch for a while before making a bet, and be careful what you say, as the game has a language of its own and you could find yourself called in as the spinner (person who tosses the coins). By the way, the miners get paid every second Friday - check with the Tourist Centre, ✆9021 2180.

About 18km (11 miles) north-east of Kalgoorlie-Boulder is what is left of the township of **Kanowna**. In 1905 the town had a population of 12,000 with 16 hotels, two breweries and an hourly train service to Kalgoorlie. Now there are tourist markers.

Since you are in gold territory, you might decide to try your luck at **fossicking**. It's a good idea, but make sure you have a Miner's Right first. You can pick one up at the Mines Department on Brookman Street.

Goldrush Tours offer a variety of coach tours in the area, including the Ghost Town Tour, which ⊙departs from the Palace Chambers in Maritana Street, every Thursday at 10.45am. For information and bookings phone ✆(08) 9021 2954 or ✆1800 620 440 (freecall).

Kurrawang Emu Farm, ✆9021 2845, provides you with an opportunity to come face to face with their big birds. It can be found on the Great Eastern Highway, 18km west of Kalgoorlie.

Other tours further afield are available, and the Tourist Information Centre have all the information, and can make bookings.

Festivals

The Kalgoorlie Racing Round is held in September.

The Community Fair is held each March in the Cruickshank Sports Arena.

Facilities

There are two golf clubs in the suburb of Hannan; lawn bowls at Kalgoorlie Bowling Club, cnr Maritana & Forrest Streets; swimming and water polo at the Lord Forrest Olympic Pool; motor sports at the 12ha (30 acres) complex near the airport; and gliding, tennis and other sports can be arranged through the Tourist Information Centres.

Outlying Attractions

Coolgardie

The town was built to accommodate 15,000 people, and the present population is 2000, so Coolgardie can be regarded as the best-cared-for ghost town in Australia. It is situated 45km (28 miles) west of Kalgoorlie, on the site of a reef of rich gold, found by Arthur Bayley in 1892, and called 'Bayley's Reward'. By 1900, the town had hotels, smithies, barbers, newspaper offices, stores, and 15,000 people. 'Bayley's Reward' continued to produce gold until 1963, but the town's boom time was really over by 1914 when World War I saw the prospectors volunteer for service.

The Coolgardie Tourist Bureau & Goldfields Exhibition is at 62 Bayley Street, ✆(08) 9026 6090, and is open daily. There are a series of historical markers around the township, documenting the history of Coolgardie, with photographs of what each site looked like in times gone by. It is fascinating to compare the photos with what is now in front of you.

Attractions in the town include: The Goldfields Exhibition in the same building as the Tourist Bureau, ☉open daily 8am-5pm with daily screenings of the BBC film Gold Fever.

The Railway Station Museum, in Woodwood Street, ☉open daily 8am-5pm ✆9026 6388.

Lions' Bicentennial Lookout, 2km from the main street where Bayley's South Headframe is found. Ben Prior's Open Air Museum in Bayley Street, is dedicated to WA's early explorers and the pioneers of the goldfields.

Bottle and Curio Museum, in the Exhibition Building, ☉open daily 8am-5pm.

Warden Finnerty's Residence, built in 1895 at a cost of 2,800 pounds, and now owned by the National Trust. It is ☉open Mon-

Wed, Fri-Sat 1-4pm, Sun 10am-noon, 1-4pm.

The Old Pioneer Cemetery, at the end of Forrest Street near the oval, has graves dating from 1892 to 1894.

Coolgardie Camel Farm, ✆9026 6159, is about 4km west of Coolgardie, and is ⊙open daily 9am-5pm, with rides available ranging from around the yard in the farm, to overnight camel treks. Incidentally, the reason that the streets of Coolgardie are so wide is because there had to be room to turn camel trains. You can ask at the farm why they didn't just reverse them.

If all the talk about gold, and people making their fortunes, has sparked a small case of gold fever, you can hire gold detectors and other equipment at the Railway Lodge, ✆9026 6166. Some people have been lucky! Tours of the area are available, and they include sightseeing, gold panning and detecting, and wildflowers in season. Contact the Tourist Bureau for information and bookings.

Menzies

Named after L.R. Menzies, one of the men who discovered gold in the vicinity in 1894, Menzies is another town that has declined. Within months of gold being found the population was 10,000, within thirteen years it had dropped to 1000, now it is home to 110.

The town is 132km (82 miles) north of Kalgoorlie, and many buildings from its heyday remain, including the town hall and the railway station. The Menzies State Battery for processing gold is the most modern in Australia, and visitors are welcome.

Leonora

Situated 237km (147 miles) north of Kalgoorlie, Leonora is a railhead for nearby copper and nickel mines, and the meeting point of the roads radiating north, south and east. It is the administrative town of the North Eastern Goldfields, and the centre of a wool growing area.

Attractions include:

Mt Leonora was first named by the explorer John Forrest in 1869, and rises 100m (328 ft) above the town, so is the best place to get an overall view.

The Sons of Gwalia Goldmine ran continuously for 67 years, and was the largest underground mine outside the Golden Mile. It closed in 1963, and the town of Gwalia died as a result. However, recent technological advances have resulted in lower production costs, and the mine has re-opened, as have some others in the area. A visit is worthwhile, and it is best to allow about half an hour to explore. In the mine office is the Gwalia Museum, with artefacts from the early days of mining in the areas. The ghost town of Gwalia is also worth a visit. The town was never officially gazetted, due to its tendency to flood, so it just grew like Topsy, with buildings mostly of galvanised iron. It is hard to imagine now, but the town was once so prosperous that it had the State's first electric tram service.

Situated 69km (43 miles) southeast of Leonora is the township of Kookynie which had a population of 1500 in 1905, and now has 10, many of whom work the local hotel, which in itself is worth a visit. There are many old workings and tailings dumps for you to fossick through within a kilometre of the hotel.

Niagara is about 10km (6 miles) from Kookynie, and is another ghost town, with not much to see except for the Niagara Dam, built in 1897. The cement for the 250m (820 ft) long wall was carried from Coolgardie by camels!

Laverton

Prospectors from Coolgardie found gold near the present town site in 1896, and soon there was another boom town, apparently a very wild one. It is reported that the only burial resulting from natural causes in the Burtville Cemetery, which is 25km (16 miles) from Laverton, was that of a baby six weeks old. Everyone else died with their boots on.

Laverton is 361km (224 miles) north-east of Kalgoorlie. The town died when the surface gold ran out, but has been revitalised by the Windarra Nickel Project, and it is the support base for the recently reopened Lancefield Mine. Attractions include Billy Goat Hill which gives panoramic views, Mt Windarra, from where there is a good view of the Windarra Nickel Mine, and the Old Laverton Police Station & Gaol, built in 1900.

Ghost towns in the area include Burtville, Gladiator, Heffernans and Just in Time. If you wish to explore all the ghost towns in the Gold-fields area, you would be wise to invest in a large-scale map from the Mines Department.

Leinster

This town was established in 1977 to service the nickel-mining indus-try, and is the terminus of a sealed highway north from Kalgoorlie on the way to Wiluna. It is 378km (254 miles) north-west of Kalgoorlie, and Skywest have return flights to Leinster from Perth, ©9037 0749.

The Leinster Recreation Associa-tion in Mansbridge Road, ©(08)

9037 9040, can answer all your sightseeing and accommodation enquiries.

Attractions include the old towns of Agnew, Lawlers and Poison Creek.

Kambalda

Situated 57km (35 miles) south of Kalgoorlie, Kambalda is a nickel town constructed by the Western Mining Corporation in the 1960s and 1970s. Originally, of course, it was a gold town, the precious metal having been found in 1887 by Percy Larkin, but gold mining ceased around 1907. In 1954, George Cowcill collected some specimens in the area that he thought contained uranium, but analysis proved that it was nickel. In 1962, he and John Morgan sub-mitted the samples to the West-ern Mining Corporation, who decided to drill several holes, which showed the presence of a massive deposit of nickel sulphides.

The town has approximately 5000 people, and the Kambalda Tourist Bureau is in Irish Mulga Drive, Kambalda West, ©(08) 9027 1446, ©open Mon-Fri 9am-5pm.

Attractions include: Red Hill Lookout in Gordon Adams Road; Lake Lefroy, a large salt pan that rarely contains water; Hunts Well, a remnant of the original gold town; Lion's Park, a picnic and barbecue

Great Southern Ocean

spot with an olympic swimming pool; John Hill Viewpoint, which has views over the concentrator, powerhouse, workshops and distant headframes; King Battery on Woolibar station where crushed ore was once turned into gold; and Pioneer Cemetery where pioneer William Wenzel is buried.

Norseman

Known as Western Australia's 'Eastern Gateway', Norseman is 187km (116 miles) south of Coolgardie, 724km (450 miles) south-east of Perth, and 724km (450 miles) west of the Western Australia/South Australia border. Goldfields Air Services have several flights weekly between Esperance and Kalgoorlie via Norseman, and bus services from all capital cities pass through Norseman.

Gold was discovered in the area in 1892, and many people settled in the town which had grown out of the pastoral activity in the area. Two years later, a horse named 'Norseman' stumbled over a large gold nugget, and the town got its name. The horse's owner later discovered a rich gold reef where his horse had 'turned the first sod'.

In 1905 the population was 3000, and in 1925, 300. The Central Norseman Gold Corporation still mines one of the earliest finds in the area, which is also the richest quartz reef in Australia. The population of the modern town is 2500.

The Norseman Tourist Bureau is in Robert Street, ✆(08) 9039 1071, and ⏰open Mon-Fri 8am-8pm, Sat-Sun 8am-4pm. They can advise on accommodation and sightseeing.

The Historical and Geological Museum, run by the Pensioners' League, has among other things, the largest known piece of Skylab, the US satellite that exploded over Western Australia. Beacon Hill Lookout, from where there is a good view of the old mines, the chain of salt lakes, the gypsum hills and the Jimberlana Dyke, is reputed to be one of the oldest geological areas in the world.

Lady Miller Area, was one of the area's highest producing gold deposits, but has not been worked since 1950. Many of the mines in the area are accessible by car, and can easily be explored on foot. But it is warned that no attempt should be made to venture underground, as many of the mine shafts are dangerous. Ask the Tourist Bureau for information about all the old mines in the area. The Salt Lakes are at their best at sunrise and sunset, and the gypsum crystals which grow in the lakes are worth a close look. Again, care should be taken to observe all warning signs of mining in progress, and do not drive a vehicle on to the salt lakes. The Tourist Bureau can tell you of the best location for the gypsum crystals.

Dundas Rocks are 22km (14 miles) south of Norseman off the Coolgardie-Esperance Highway, and the formations are 550 million years old. There are good picnic areas, and an old ghost town to explore. Bromus Dam is an old railway dam on the road to Esperance, about 32km (20 miles) from Norseman, and is a good spot for a picnic and a swim.

The Lone Grave, is an enigma on a spit of land on the far edge of Lake Dundas. It belongs to "Stanley Arthur Whitehead, who died April 8th, 1897, aged 7 months", and is the only sign that the area had at one time been inhabited by man. Free tours of Central Norseman Corporation Gold Mining Operations ☉leave the Tourist Bureau each weekday morning at 9.30am. They last about two hours, and enquiries should be made at the Tourist Bureau.

If you want to try your luck at fossicking for Moss Agate, Moss Opalite, Chrysophase and Jasper, obtain a permit from the Tourist Bureau. And, don't forget you need a Miner's Right from the Mines Department, if you are going to look for that piece of gold that everyone else has missed.

Esperance

Situated 369km (229 miles) south of Kalgoorlie, and 720km (447 miles) south-east of Perth, Esperance is known as 'The Bay of Isles'. Skywest have daily flights from Perth; a Westrail bus connects with the Prospector train from Perth to Kalgoorlie; and there is a Westrail bus service from East Perth three times weekly direct to Esperance.

The town's history began in 1627 when Pieter Nuyts, in command of the Dutch East India Company vessel Gulde Zeepard, charted the coast and the Recherche Archipelago, but did not land. The first to do that were men attached to a French scientific mission which was under the command of Admiral D'Entrecasteaux, whose ships sought shelter in a gale. The first ship to enter the bay was *L'Esperance*, hence the name of the bay. The second ship was the *Recherche*, hence the name of the Archipelago. The next 50 years saw visits by explorers Flinders and Eyre, and sealers and whalers, who played merry hell with the Aborigines.

In 1863, the Dempster brothers took up the first landholding in the area, and other farmer settlers followed. The discovery of gold at Coolgardie caused Esperance to become the port for the goldfields overnight, and this it remained until the completion of the Perth to Coolgardie rail link.

Now the area is a major farming region with a town population of 8000, and 11,000 people living in the Shire.

The Esperance Tourist Bureau and Travel Centre is in Dempster Street, ©(08) 9071 2330, and is ⊙open Mon-Fri 8.45am-5pm, Sat-Sun 9am-5pm. They have information on the accommodation available, where to fish, the best place to swim, or where to play golf, or any other sport.

Sightseeing attractions include:

Esperance Municipal Museum, between Dempster Street and the Esplanade, ⊙open daily 1.30-4.30pm, ©9071 1579.

The Public Library in Windich Street next to the Shire Council, ⊙open Mon 10.30am-6pm, Tues 11am-3pm, Wed-Fri 10.30am-6pm, Sat 9.30am-11.30am.

The Pink Lake, which should sometimes be called the Purple Lake.

Observatory Point & Lookout, where the two French frigates sheltered from the storm in 1792.

The Dempster Charm Cottage, ©9071 1413, built in 1867, and classified by the National Trust.

National Parks in the area include Stokes, Cape Le Grand and Cape Arid.

Scenic flights are a perfect way to see magnificent coastal scenery, islands and whales. Contact Esperance Air Service, ©9071 1467.

Geraldton

Geraldton

Population 20,000
Geraldton is located 424km (263 miles) north of Perth on the Brand Highway. It is the gateway to the Abrolhos Islands. The area is known as the Batavia Coast, named after the *Batavia* which was one of many ships wrecked off the coast.

Climate

Average temperatures: January max 32C (90F) - min 19C (66F); July max 19C (66F) - min 9C (48F). Number of days a year with temperature over 30C (86F) - 76; number of days a year with temperature over 40C (104F) - 8. Average annual rainfall: 475mm (19 ins); wettest six months - April to September.

Characteristics

Geraldton's boundary of safe beaches, its year long surf scene, the wildflowers, scenic attractions and rich historical features, give it a magnetic appeal to those who want a carefree holiday. It is known as Sun City, because it boasts of an average of 8 hours sunshine a day, all year round.

How to Get There

By Air
Skywest have daily flights from/to Perth.

By Bus
The Westrail bus departs East Perth

Terminal six times weekly, with alternate routes through Moora and Eneabba.

Geraldton is on the Greyhound Pioneer Perth/Broome/Darwin route.

By Car

From Perth, via the Brand Highway through Eneabba, or via the Midland Road through Moora and Mingenew.

Tourist Information

The Geraldton Tourist Bureau is situated on the corner of Chapman Road & Bayly Street at the Bill Sewell Community Recreation Complex, ©(08) 9921 3999. The Bureau is ⊕open Mon-Fri 8am-6pm, Sat-Sun 8am-5pm.

Accommodation

As always with holiday resorts, there is plenty of accommodation available, and bookings should be made ahead. Here is a selection with prices for a double room per night, which should be used as a guide only. ©The telephone area code is 08.

Hospitality Inn Geraldton, Cathedral Avenue, ©9921 1422. 48 units, licensed restaurant, swimming pool, bbq ✪$97-118.

Batavia Motor Inn, 54 Fitzgerald Street, ©9921 3500. 76 units, licensed restaurant, swimming pool ✪$92.

Ocean Centre Hotel, cnr Foreshore Drive & Cathedral Avenue, ©9921 7777. 51 rooms (private facilities), licensed restaurant ✪$85 - 160.

Mercure Inn Geraldton, Brand Highway, ©9921 2455. 60 units, licensed restaurant, swimming pool ✪$84-105.

Sun City Motel-Geraldton, 137 Cathedral Avenue, ©9921 6111. 20 units, licensed restaurant, swimming pool, spa, sauna, gym ✪$60-80.

Mariner Motel Hotel, 298 Chapman Road, ©9921 2544. 18 rooms (private facilities), licensed restaurant, swimming pool ✪$55-60.

Mercure Inn Wintersun Geraldton, 441 Chapman Road, Bluff Point, ©9923 1211. 36 rooms, licensed restaurant, swimming pool ✪$84.

Caravan Parks

Batavia Coast Caravan Park, Lot 3/89 Hall Rd, Waggrakine, ©9938 1222. (Pets on application) - powered sites ✪$12 for two , on-site vans $25 for two.

Separation Point Caravan Park, Separation Point, ©9921 2763. (No dogs allowed) - powered sites $16 for two, on-site vans ✪$30-35 for two.

Sunset Beach Holiday Park, Bosley Street ©9938 1655. (No pets allowed) - powered sites ✪$17 for two, on-site vans $33 for two.

Eating Out

Whatever type of food you fancy, you will find the right place in Geraldton. A stroll down Marine Terrace will take you past plenty of eateries, and then it's only a matter of choosing the one that appeals most. Here are some to consider.
Jade House, 57 Marine Terrace, ©9964 1222 - licensed - open Mon-Sat 11.30am-2.30pm, Mon-Sun 5-11pm.
Rose, 9 Forrest Street, ©9921 5645 -BYO- ☺open Tues-Sun 5.30-11pm.
China Moon, 198 Marine Terrace, ©9923 9924.
OK Corral Mexican Restaurant, 185 Marine Terrace, ©9964 5424.
The Boatshed Seafood Restaurant, 357 Marine Terrace, ©9921 5500.
Picasso's Cafe Restaurant, 20 Chapman Road, ©9965 5500.
La Famiglia, 1 Fitzgerald Street, ©9921 8655.
Tanti's, 174 Marine Terrace, ©9964 2311.
Skeetas Garden Restaurant, 9 George Road, ©9964 1619.
Raphaels, 84 Marine Terrace, ©9965 4441.
Lemon Grass, 18 Snowdon Street, ©9964 1172.

Points of Interest

The Wishing Well Lookout in Brede Street overlooks the city with its Norfolk pines lining the beach front.

St Francis Xavier Cathedral, cnr Cathedral Avenue & Maitland Street, was built in stages from 1914 until the opening in 1938. The Byzantine style architecture is one of Monsignor John Hawes' masterpieces.

Bill Sewell Community Complex, cnr Chapman Road & Bayly Street. Originally this building was the Victoria District Hospital dating from 1887 to 1966, then it was used as a Regional Prison until 1984. The building had major restoration work done, and was re-opened in 1988. The Geraldton Tourist Bureau is situated in this beautiful building and the Old Gaol Craft Centre is adjacent.

The **Western Australian Museum Geraldton** occupies two adjoining buildings in Museum Place - the Maritime Display Building and Old Railway Building, ©9921 5080. The Maritime Display Building overlooks a long sweep of coast that has witnessed some of the earliest and bloodiest events in Australia's European history. The museum contains finds from Australia's oldest shipwrecks. Three Dutch ships, *Batavia* (1629),

Zuytdorp (1712) and *Zeewijk* (1727) were wrecked on route to Holland's fabulously wealthy trading empire - present-day Indonesia. Cannon, coins, navigational instruments, pottery and personal gear have been recovered after centuries under the surf. The historic Old Railway Building was built for Western Australia's first government railway. Inside, displays depict the region's intriguing variety of plants, animals and minerals. This is interwoven with the absorbing story of man in the region. The museum is ☺open Mon-Sat 10am-5pm, Sun 1-5pm, and admission is free.

The **Lighthouse Keepers Cottage**, cnr Chapman Road & Grenville Drive, was built in 1870 and was the original lighthouse keeper's residence for the Port of Geraldton. The Historical Society is based here, and it is ☺open Thursdays only.

Geraldton Art Gallery is located in the city's original Town Hall in Chapman Road. The Town Hall was opened in 1907 and renovated in 1984. Admission to the Gallery is free, and it is ☺open Mon-Sat 10am-5pm, Sun 1.30-4.30pm, ☏9921 6811.

The **Point Moore Lighthouse** is rather difficult to overlook, due to its broad red and white stripes. It was built in 1879, and is 35m (115 ft) high and its light is visible for up to 26km (16 miles).

Flora

Wattles dominate much of the plains and coastal dunes, but among them are grevilleas, hakeas, one-sided bottlebrush, smokebush, honeymyrtles, and of course, Geraldton Wax, an evergreen shrub with pink or white waxy flowers.

Fauna

Mainly rabbits, kangaroos, foxes, some possums, emus, galahs, black and white cockatoos, crows, grey doves and many varieties of small birds.

Fishing

Rock and beach fishing in the town itself is patchy for tailor, mulloway and herring, etc. Drive south to Greenough River mouth for tailor, mulloway and bream. North of Geraldton there is Drummond Cove for the same species, and for the four wheel drivers, Buller River Mouth is great for tailor. Coronation Beach off main highway is good for tailor and mulloway.

Festivals

The Sunshine Festival is held in October each year.

Facilities

Swimming, fishing, yachting, lawn bowls, tennis, cricket, squash, pistol-shooting, go-kart racing, horse racing, golf, roller skating and ten-pin bowling.

Outlying Attractions

Greenough

Situated 25km (16 miles) south of Geraldton on the Brand Highway, Greenough features many examples of early pioneering history dating from the 1850s.

The Greenough Village complex looks very much as it did in its heyday. It was restored and is maintained by the National Trust (WA), and features Pioneer Tea Rooms and an Art Gallery, where works by significant Mid-West artists are displayed and sold. Guided tours through the buildings are highly recommended.

Adjacent to the Village in Company Road is the Hampton Arms Historic Inn (1861), and next door is the Greenough Wildlife and Bird Park, ©9926 1171, a must for the kids where all kinds of animals can be seen.

Dongara/Port Denison

The Shire of Irwin has three townships: Dongara, Port Denison and Irwin. The townsite of Dongara,

359km (223 miles) north of Perth on the Brand Highway, was surveyed in 1852, and named Dhungarra. It is a little known fact that the Brand Highway is within 2km of beautiful beaches and a rustic, almost forgotten township, that was first settled nearly 150 years ago. For years Dongara and the adjacent townsite of Port Denison have been popular retirement destinations for farmers of the surrounding rural areas. Now tourists and holiday makers are discovering the delights of this historic region. The Dongara Denison Tourist Information Centre is in the Old Police Station Building, Waldeck Street, Dongara, ©(08) 9927 1404, ⏱open Mon-Fri 9am-4pm, Sat 10am-1pm. They are able to advise on available accommodation, and attractions. The town caters for most popular sports - bowls, tennis, yachting, golf, squash, basketball, badminton and gymnastics.

Cervantes

Cervantes is a crayfishing centre, and appeals to anglers because of the wide range of fish which can be caught from the shore, or from a small boat in the local waters. The town is about 245km (152 miles) north of Perth, and the Tourist Information is in the Shell Service Station, cnr Aragon & Seville Streets, ©9652 7041. Nearby is the

Nambung National Park, whose main attraction is the Pinnacles, an area of sand of varying colours, where there are thousands of limestone pinnacles which range in size from ankle high and pencil thickness to 5m high and 2m thick at the base. Access to the park is difficult and care should be taken to avoid vehicle damage. Visitors are requested to stay on defined tracks and observe directional and warning signs.

Moora

Located on the Midlands Road, 190km (118 miles) north of Perth via New Norcia, or 175km (109 miles) via Mogumber.

Tourist Information is in the Moora Shire Office, 34 Padbury Street, ©(08) 9651 1401. Moora is recognised as the heart of the Midlands, and is on the banks of the Moore River. The town stretches across the clay flats deposited by an ancient waterway, and the area in its virgin state was a large salmon gum forest. Pioneer, Walter Padbury opened up more land in the area than anyone. He was Australia's greatest philanthropist and Western Australia's first millionaire.

Attractions include: Watheroo National Park; Jingamia Cave; the Mill Museum; Waddi Farms; and the Australian Flower Farm at Coorow.

Morawa

Morawa is the centre of a well established district. It was settled about 1905 and declared a townsite in 1912. It has a population of around 1350, and the area is based on wheat and wool growing. Prater Airport which accommodated Dove and DC3 aircraft, is now a regular port of call for light aircraft. A fully illuminated strip allows for night landing of the flying doctor and courier planes.

Tourist Information is available from the Morawa Shire Council, ©9971 1204.

Attractions include: Koolanooka Springs; Bilya Rock Reserve; old mine sites; Mingenew Coal Seam; the Historical museum; Holy Cross Church; and wildflowers. Facilities for sports include golf, football, basketball, badminton, squash, rifle shooting, tennis, bowls, swimming, gliding and flying.

Mullewa

Situated 100km (62 miles) east of Geraldton, Mullewa is the gateway to the Murchison pastoral and old goldfield area. The most direct route is along the Geraldton Highway to Mingenew, then along the Mingenew/Mullewa Road.

Tourist Information is in Mullewa Shire Council, Jose Street, ©(08) 9961 1007, email ✉admin@mull ewa.wa.gov.au, internet ☞www.

mullewa.wa.gov.au

Attractions include: Murchison Goldfields; Tenindewa Pioneer Well; Glacier Bed; St Andrew's Anglican Church; Pallottine Mission; and Tallering Peak and Gorge.

Northampton

Northampton has one of the richest histories in the State of Western Australia, and is situated 52km (32 miles) north of Geraldton.

The hills of the town, drained by creeks with permanent pools attracted game and proved a haven for Australian Aborigines. Evidence of their ancient culture can be seen in cave paintings at the Bowes River turnoff. Shepherds gradually moved into the area, and one of them, Thomas Mason, discovered copper at Wanneranooka in 1842. The copper mine which subsequently developed was the first in the State.

Lead was discovered in 1848 and the Geraldton mine was developed. The labour shortage, acute throughout the State, was relieved to some extent by the continuation of the transportation of convicts. A convict hiring station was established at Port Gregory 1853-1856.

The Northampton Tourist Bureau is on the North West Coastal Highway, ©(08) 9934 1488, and they will advise of the attractions, which include: Chiverton House Museum, Gwalla Cemetery and Church; Wanneranooka Copper Mine; Original Miner's Cottages; Alma School House; Warribano Chimney; and Port Gregory.

Kalbarri

Kalbarri is one of the fastest growing holiday resorts in WA, and is 591km (367 miles) north of Perth. The climate is suitable for all year round swimming and fishing, and the scenery is unique. The town is on the mouth of the Murchison River and it is the river gorges which provide much of the unique scenery in the area, not to mention spectacular coastal scenery south of the town. Fishing from the beach or from boats is first class, and the town's main activity, along with tourism, is the rock lobster industry. Abundant and beautiful flora is just another attraction.

The history of Kalbarri is fascinating, though violent, as its treacherous coastline has resulted in many shipwrecks. Australia's first white settlers arrived here in 1629, though probably with a degree of reluctance. Commodore Pelsaert marooned two conspirators here for their activity in the 'terrible' Batavia mutiny.

Tourist Information is available from the Kalbarri Tourist Bureau in Grey Street, ©(08) 9937 1104.

Carnarvon

Population 7,000
Carnarvon is situated 902km (560 miles) north of Perth, at the mouth of the Gascoyne River.

Climate

Average temperatures: January max 40C (104F) - min 35C (95F); July max 25C (77F) - min 16C (61F). Average annual rainfall: 127mm (5 in).

Characteristics

Carnarvon, often described as 'the sun's winter home', is the commercial centre of the Gascoyne district. It is a friendly town, with a tropical, relaxed atmosphere, and an abundance of fish and tropical fruit.

How to Get There

By Bus
Bus Australia and Greyhound have daily services to Carnarvon from Perth.

By Road
Carnarvon is 902km (560 miles) from Perth, via the Brand and North West Coastal Highways.

Tourist Information

Carnarvon District Tourist Bureau is in the Civic Centre, Robinson Street, ©(08) 9941 1146. Send emails to ✉ cvontourist@wn.com.au

Accommodation

The Tourist Bureau has a full list of the accommodation available, but here we have a selection with prices for a double room per night, which should be used as a guide only. ✆The telephone area code is 08.

Hospitality Inn Carnarvon, West Street, ✆9941 1600. 45 units, licensed restaurant, swimming pool, bbq ✪$105.

Gateway Motel, 379 Robinson Street, ✆9941 1532. 36 units, unlicensed restaurant, swimming pool ✪$99.

Fascine Lodge Motel Hotel, 1002 David Brand Drive, ✆9941 2411. 61 units, licensed restaurant, swimming pool ✪$105.

Port Hotel, Robinson Street, ✆9941 1704. 17 rooms (private facilities), swimming pool, barbecue ✪$40.

Carnarvon Hotel, Olivia Terrace, ✆9941 1412. 27 units (private facilities) ✪$65.

Caravan Parks

Wintersun Caravan Park, Robinson Street, ✆9941 8150. (No dogs allowed) - powered sites ✪$19 for two, on-site vans $50 for two.

Norwesta Caravan Park, cnr Robinson & Angelo Streets, ✆9941 1277 (No pets allowed) - powered sites ✪$14.50 for two, on-site vans $30-45 for two.

Plantation Caravan Park, Robinson Street, ✆9941 8100. (No dogs allowed) - powered sites ✪$18 -19 for two, cabins $22 for two.

Carnarvon Caravan Park, Robinson Street, ✆9941 8101. (Pets on application) - powered sites ✪$17 for two, on-site units $72 for two.

Carnarvon Tourist Centre Caravan Park, Robinson Street, ✆9941 1438 (No pets allowed) - powered sites ✪$17 for two, on-site vans $34-56 for two.

There are also several guesthouses in Carnarvon, and it is also possible to stay at farms and stations in the area. The Tourist Bureau are the people to see about these.

Eating Out

Most of the hotels and motels have restaurants, either licensed or BYO, and there are many outlets specialising in the local fish, cooked to perfection. The Tourist Bureau has a full list, and you can be guided by their recommendations. If you're in the mood for Chinese, head for the Dragon Pearl at 18 Francis St, ✆9941 1941.

Points of Interest

Plantations extend along both banks of the Gascoyne River for about 15km (9 miles), and some welcome visitors to buy their mangoes, pawpaws, bananas, oranges and grapefruit.

The **Gascoyne River** usually flows below the surface of the river bed, with irrigation channels pumping the water to the plantations along the river flats. Occasionally, after heavy rains upstream, the river can be seen, and levee banks have been built to protect low-lying areas during floods.

The most obvious landmark in Carnarvon is the **'Big Dish'**, a 26.5m (87 ft) diameter reflector which was of major importance to global communications from 1966 to 1987. It closed down in May of that year, but is open to visitors. The site also provides a magnificent view of Carnarvon and the plantations.

The building adjoining the Tourist Bureau has a **museum** with exhibits from the NASA base, a large collection of shells and some local artefacts.

Pioneer Park, in Olivia Terrace, contains a number of relics of the town's history, including the two whale bones which form the arch over the entrance. The park is a popular picnic spot, and has coin operated barbecues and swings for the kids.

Jubilee Hall, in Francis Street, was opened in 1887 and for years served as Council Chambers and Shire Offices. The first 50 pounds received for the construction of the hall was donated by Queen Victoria!

St George's Church of England, in Francis Street opposite the Shire Offices, was erected in 1907. The first Bishop of North-West Australia was enthroned here on July 4, 1910. It is the most westerly parish in Australia, and part of the largest Anglican diocese in the world.

Chinaman's Pool is a great picnic area and swimming spot in the Gascoyne River, between Marmion and Saw Streets. It was originally a watering hole for the township, and now attracts many varieties of birdlife, especially in the early morning or evening.

One Mile Jetty, on Babbage Island, actually stretches 1,493m (4,898 ft) out into the bay. It was built in 1904, and widened in 1912, and was used by ships until 1966. The jetty end was burnt by vandals in 1985, but the locals raised the funds to have it rebuilt. To get there take the main street to Babbage Island Road at the Caltex Service Station Corner, then proceed 4.5km (3 miles), then turn right at the lighthouse. In the lighthouse keeper's cottage there is a museum which is run in conjunction with the Gascoyne Historical Society.

If you turn right just before you get to the One Mile Jetty you'll come to **Dwyer's Leap**, a water ski area that is usually sheltered from the wind.

The Blowholes near the town are spectacular, as the trapped water is forced out through a hole to a height of 20m (66 ft). Nearby is a good beach where people go for oysters, fish and crayfish.

Cape Cuvier, 30km (19 miles) north of the Blowhole is a deep port where ships load salt for Japan. It is fascinating if you are there when they are loading, although not if you are too close. The port is situated beneath a 60m (197 ft) cliff and they simply bulldoze the salt over the cliff onto a conveyor below.

The *HMAS Sydney* **Memorial Cairn** was erected near High Rock, Quobba Station, to commemorate the tragic battle between the *Sydney* and the German raider *Kormoran* off Carnarvon on November 19, 1941. To get there, follow the signs from the Blowholes and the memorial is 7km to the north.

The Fascine is the bay formed by the South Arm of the Gascoyne River. The name is derived from the Latin word meaning 'bundle of sticks', because in the old days bundles of sticks were placed on the foreshore to help prevent erosion during the major river flows.

Now the waterway is lined with stately palms. The area is a favourite spot for a picnic, or an evening stroll.

Pelican Point is a popular swimming and fishing spot about 5km out of town. To get there turn left at the end of causeway on Babbage Island Road.

Bibbawarra Bore is 16km (10 miles) north of Carnarvon, and the best way to get there is via the Bibbawarra Road Crossing (when the river is dry). The Bore was originally worked for coal in 1905 to a depth of 914m (3000 ft), and now produces a continuous flow of hot water around 65C (145F). Be very careful with children and pets, as many have been scalded.

Bush Bay and **New Beach** are both excellent for swimming and fishing. They are reached from the Geraldton Road. The turn-off to Bush Bay is about 20km (12 miles) from town, that to New Beach, about 40km (24 miles).

Festivals

The Carnarvon Rodeo is held in July; Sandhurst Run, a rock concert, is held annually in August; Dry River Regatta is held between July and September, depending on the weather; and the Yachting Regatta, from Denham to Carnarvon is also held every year. The Tourist Bureau can advise the dates.

Facilities

There are sailing, surfing, fishing, windsurfing, waterskiing, snorkelling, boating, swimming, and tours, both local and further afield.

Outlying Attractions

Shark Bay

Shark Bay is an historic area. Dirk Hartog, the Dutch navigator landed on the island which now bears his name, in 1616, and nailed that famous pewter plate to a post. In 1696, another Dutch navigator, William de Vlamingh, removed Dirk's plate and took it back to Holland, and put his own plate in its place. That plate was in turn removed by a Frenchman, Captain Freycinet, in 1818. He took it back to France, and for 40 years no one knew where it was. In 1947 the plate finally turned up and was presented to the Western Australian Museum, where it has pride of place.

The French named many places in the area - Hamelin, Peron, Faure, Lesueur, Freycinet, Heirisson, for example, but Shark Bay was given its name, albeit a in a different form, by William Dampier, who visited in 1699. He called it 'The Bay of Sharks'.

The only town in Shark Bay is Denham, the westernmost town in Australia. It has a permanent population of around 400, and has excellent recreational facilities - lawn bowls, tennis courts, mini golf, trampolines, golf course, charter boats and tours.

The Shark Bay Tourist Bureau, 71 Knight Street, Denham, ©(08) 9948 1253, has accommodation details, and information on sightseeing and the Shark Bay Heritage Trail, a 130km (81 miles) self guiding drive which features sites of historical interest and the unique natural environment.

The turn-off to Shark Bay is 200km (124 miles) south-east of Carnarvon on the North West Coastal Highway. The sealed road travels west, then north a further 129km (80 miles) to Denham.

There are only two beaches in the world made completely of sea shell that has been washed up on the shore for thousands of years and compacted by nature. One of them is close to Denham, and locals have cut blocks of shell from the beach to build along the foreshore. Shell Beach is a natural wonder which still has scientists intrigued.

Hamelin Bay, on the way into Denham, has another scientific mystery. In the clear shallow waters of the Bay, stromatolites dating back millions of years, can be seen. They are one of the world's two oldest living fossils.

Shark Bay

Monkey Mia

About 25km (16 miles) from Denham across the peninsula, is Monkey Mia, where friendly bottlenose dolphins visit, apparently just to interact with people. The local Dolphin Information Centre has loads of information on these creatures ☏9948 1366.

Monkey Mia is also an excellent spot for fishing, boating, or lazing on the clean white beaches.

Gascoyne Junction

About 13km (8 miles) north of Carnarvon is the turn-off for Gascoyne Junction, which lies a further 164km (102 miles) to the east, at the junction of the Gascoyne and Lyons Rivers. It is the only town in the Shire of Upper Gascoyne, which covers an area of 57,146km2 (22,058 sq miles). There are huge sheep stations in the area which produce an annual wool clip of over 1.5 million kilograms (3,307,000 lbs). After the long drive on the gravel road, which incidentally is well formed and graded, you will welcome the site of the Gascoyne Junction Hotel, a real bush pub made of corrugated iron, which seems to have stepped out of the past. Further along the road you will pass Minnie Creek, and the Kennedy Ranges which have Aboriginal caves and rock paintings. The Ranges are known for the semi precious gem stones to be found there, so you might like to take some time out for fossicking.

Mount Augustus

The Mount is a rock. In fact it is the largest rock (monocline) in the world. It is not as famous as that other one in Central Australia, but by its geological formation it should be, and it is well worth the trip through the rugged bush country.

Mount Augustus is 289km (180 miles) from Gascoyne Junction, and accommodation is available at: Mount Augustus Outback Tourist Resort, via Carnarvon, ✆(08) 9943 0527. The Mount was of significance to the Aborigines, so there are plenty of rock paintings, and at the pools close to the rock, ornithologists catalogued more than 100 species of birds in just two days!

Coral Bay

Located 250km (155 miles) north of Carnarvon, and 150km (93 miles) south of Exmouth, Coral Bay is situated in a lagoon formed between the Ningaloo Coral Reef and the coastline. The Reef is the longest continuous and most accessible reef complex in Western Australia, extending from north of Point Murat, round North West Cape, and south to Amherst Point, a distance of about 260km (162 miles). Coral Bay is a blue-water paradise, that has yet to be commercialised. There is only one small hotel and several caravan parks, and the beach and bay area provide a perfect place for beachcombing, fishing, swimming and exploring. Offshore the occasional humpback whale, dolphin and dugong can be seen, and in summer, if you are lucky, you may see turtles lumbering up from the sea to lay their eggs.

Then, of course, there is the reef, considered one of the most beautiful in the world, with its abundance of Spanish mackerel, tuna, marlin and sailfish. Fishing tours and charter vessels can be arranged, and for diving contact Coral Dive, ✆(08) 9942 5940. Bay View Caravan Park has a glass bottom boat tour ✆(08) 9942 5932, and Sub-Sea Explorer has a semi-submersible craft for viewing the reef ✆(08) 9942 5955.

Exmouth

Located 155km (96 miles) north of Coral Bay, and 400km (249 miles) north of Carnarvon, Exmouth is one of the newest towns in Australia. It was founded in 1967 as a support town for the US Naval Communications Station, and now has a population of around 3000.

Exmouth is the home of the big fish, and draws many people eager to experience the feel of a taut line. To date, 13 world and Australian game fish records have been landed at Exmouth, as well as the largest sailfish ever caught. The town has six large charter vessels, an offshore rescue group, and a variety of accommodation houses and caravan parks. The Exmouth Tourist Bureau, cnr Murat Road and Truscott Crescent, ✆(08) 9948 1176 is ⏰open daily 9am-5pm, and they have details of all accommodation and sightseeing.

The town is situated on a peninsula surrounded by Ningaloo Marine Park, and the reef is accessible by small boat.

Surrounding Exmouth is some of Australia's best bush country with its wildlife and flora. On a scenic drive through Cape Range National Park and Ningaloo Marine Park's perimeter, there are many rugged gorges and canyons for you to explore.

For details of the many wonders of the Cape Range National Park, visit the Milyering Visitor Centre, about 52km (32 miles) from Exmouth in the heart of the Cape Range National Park.

Carnarvon and Port Hedland

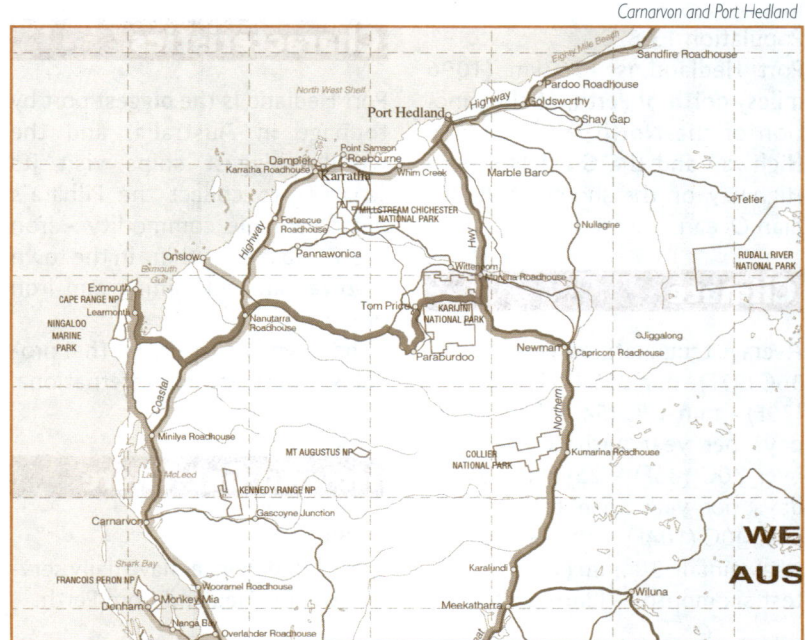

Port Hedland

Population 13,820

Port Hedland is 1763km (1096 miles) north of Perth, at the junction of the North West Coastal Highway and the Great Northern Highway, on the shores of the Indian Ocean.

Climate

Average temperatures: January max 36C (97F) - min 25C (77F); July 26C (79F) - min 12C (54F). Number of days per year with temperature over 30C (86F) - 259; number of days per year with temperature over 40C (104F) - 29. Average annual rainfall: 304mm (12 ins); wettest six months - January to June.

Characteristics

Port Hedland is the biggest port by tonnage in Australia, and the world's biggest ships visit its wharves to collect the Pilbara's most valuable commodity - iron ore. Almost everything in the town revolves around mining and iron ore.

The town has an airport that provides a gateway for international visitors.

How to Get There

By Bus

Greyhound Pioneer have daily services to Port Hedland from Perth.

By Road

From Perth, via either the North West Coastal Highway or the Great Northern Highway.

Tourist Information

Port Hedland Tourist Centre is at 13 Wedge Street, Port Hedland, ✆(08) 9173 1711. There is another outlet at South Hedland, in Leake Street, ✆(08) 9172 5177.

Accommodation

There is not a lot to choose from, but here is a selection, with prices for a double room per night, which should be used as a guide only. ✆The telephone area code is 08.

Mercure Inn Port Hedland, cnr Lukis & McGregor Streets, ✆9173 1511. 61 rooms (private facilities), licensed restaurant, swimming pool ✪$144-192.

Hospitality Inn Port Hedland, Webster Street, ✆9173 1044. 40 units, licensed restaurant, swimming pool, bbq ✪$155.

Port Hedland Walkabout Hotel, North West Coastal Highway, ✆9972 1222. 63 rooms (private facilities), licensed restaurant, swimming pool ✪$120.

The Lodge Motel & Offices, Brand Street, South Hedland, ✆9172 2188. 132 rooms, licensed restaurant, swimming pool ✪$142-160.

South Hedland Motel, Court Place, South Hedland ✆9172 2222. 54 units, licensed restaurant, swimming pool, spa, bbq ✪$110.

Caravan Parks

Port Hedland Caravan Park, Great Northern Highway, ✆9172 2525. (Dogs allowed on leash) - powered sites ✪$20 for two, on-site vans $35 for two.

South Hedland Caravan Park, Hamilton Road, ✆9721 1197. (No pets allowed) - powered sites ✪$20 for two, cabins $60-85 for two.

Cooke Point Holiday Park, Athol Street, ✆9173 1271. (No pets allowed) - powered sites ✪$20-22 for two, no on-site vans.

Eating Out

Most of the hotels and motels have licensed restaurants, and there are a few takeaway outlets. Some places you might like to try are:

Oriental Galley Chinese Restaurant, 19 Edgar Street, ✆9173 1272.

Shell Restaurant, Wilson Street, ✆9173 2551.

Bruno's Pizzeria & Ristorante, 7 Richardson Street, ✆9173 2047.

The Copper Pot, Shop 4 Keesing Street, ✆9173 1363.

Points of Interest

Port Hedland was named after Captain Peter Hedland, who discovered the entrance to the shallow bay in 1829. The first sheep station in the Pilbara was started on the nearby De Grey River in 1864.

In the 1870s, pearls were found along the coast, and Port Hedland became the home base for the pearling luggers. Inland, gold was discovered, and that brought new settlers. When the gold ran out, the town declined and in 1946 the population was 150. The 1950s saw some activity with the commencement of small tin, copper, gold and manganese outfits that used the town as a base. Then in the 1960s, the embargo on iron ore was lifted, and the modern industry was born. Port Hedland is now the major centre of Western Australia's iron ore industry, and one of the largest mineral ports in the world. The population of the town includes the two satellite towns of South Hedland and Finucane Island. Tours of the port are available and allow you to see the iron ore being loaded onto some of the biggest ore carriers in the world. The Tourist Information Centre has details.

The **Don Rhodes Mining Museum**, Wilson Street, has relics of the early mining days, and there are barbecue facilities.

Lion's Park, in Anderson Street, is a good picnic area, with lots of shade and lawn.

The tides in the area range up to 8m (26 ft), and create good **fishing** spots and chances to collect shells. Note the patterns formed on the tidal flats by the outgoing tide.

Cemetery Beach is a great fishing spot at high tides, and nearby is a children's playground. Pretty Pool is also good for fishing and picnics. Due to the dangers of stonefish, blue-ringed octopus, sea snakes and sharks, it is not recommended that you swim in the ocean or the creeks, but there is an olympic pool, with a wading and diving pool in the town, and in South Hedland there is a big aquatic centre.

There are several **Heritage Trails** in and around the town, and the Tourist Centre has full details. The Old Port Hedland Trail is a 2.25km walk retracing the development of the early port township, taking in the historical buildings and sites. It commences at the Tourist Centre. The Port Trail is a 1.8km walk combining the port's history with more recent developments. It commences at the Port Authority Offices and takes about one hour. The Sutherland Trail begins at the Tourist Centre, and its 9km route is an easy 45 minute drive. The Out and About Trail begins at Pretty Pool, covers about 85km (53 miles) exploring South Hedland's natural, Aboriginal and historic sites, and takes about half a day.

Festivals

January - The Australia Day Beach Party.

May - Beer Fest.

August - Spinifex Spree, featuring a float parade, a variety of stalls displaying local arts and crafts, and side show alley.

August - Black Rock Stakes, wheelbarrow loaded with iron ore relay or endurance race from Goldsworthy to Port Hedland, 111km (69 miles).

September - Port Hedland All Can Regatta, races among boats made from aluminium cans.

Facilities

Car Hire - Budget Rent A Car, Airport, ℰ9140 1229; Hertz Rent A Car, Airport, ℰ9140 1555; WK Motors, Anderson Street, ℰ9173 1729.

Sporting facilities include swimming pools, tennis, basketball, golf, horse racing, rifle and pistol shooting, yachting and hot rods.

Outlying Attractions

The Pilbara

Many people think of this region as one huge mine, and it is because of the mining industry that much of the Pilbara is now accessible to the visitor. Natural wonders such as Wittenoom Gorge, the Hamersley Range, and other places where 200 years of white inhabitation becomes nothing when compared with the eons it has taken to shape the landscape, are now within easy reach.

Roebourne

Situated 201km (125 miles) west of Port Hedland, Roebourne was the first capital of the North-West, and has many old stone buildings. The town is about 14km (9 miles) from the coast on the Harding River, and was established in 1864, making it the oldest town on the north-west coast of WA.

The Tourist Bureau is in the 'Old Jail', Queen Street, ph (08) 9182 1060, and they can advise on accommodation and attractions both in Roebourne, and nearby Cossack and Point Samson.

From the top of Mount Welcome, behind the town, there is a panoramic view of the coastal plains and rugged hills which surround Roebourne. You can see the railroad from Cape Lambert weaving its way through the hills to Pannawonica in the south, and the pipeline carrying water from Millstream to Wickham and Cape Lambert.

Picnic spots are found at the Harding River Dam, on the Cooya Pooya Road; Python Pool on the Wittenoom Road.

The Emma Withnell Heritage Trail begins in Roebourne and travels 52km (32 miles) tracing the development of the early settlement of the eastern corridor of the Shire of Roebourne, including Cossack and Point Samson, and the modern industrial town of Wickham.

Cossack

The first place settled on the northwest coast (1863), Cossack was a bustling seaport with a colourful multi-racial population in its heyday. Pearling was its main source of income until the industry moved to Broome. Then the wharf facilities were removed and it became a ghost town. The old graveyard and the Courthouse, which is ☉open daily 10am-3pm, are the only man-made attractions, but the ocean and river scenery make a visit worthwhile.

Karratha

The name means 'good country', and Karratha was so named because of the area's natural supply of food sources enjoyed by the local Aborigines. Today, the inhabitants enjoy the same resources along with the modern shopping centres and facilities.

Karratha is about 230km (143 miles) west of Port Hedland on the North West Coast Highway, and the Tourist Bureau is in Karratha Road, ©(08) 9144 4600. They have all the details on accommodation, tours, car hire, diving establishments, and fishing and charter vessels.

Around the town there is much evidence of early Aboriginal life, and on the Jaburara Heritage Trail, a 3.5km walk, you can see Aboriginal carvings, shellfish middens, grinding stones, artifacts and spiritual taboo sites. In the Burrup Peninsula area there are 10,000 petroglyphs (Aboriginal etchings) which are thousands of years old, showing wildlife such as turtles, fish, kangaroos, and a Tasmanian Tiger! One of the etchings is of a man in uniform, who some say is William Dampier, the English buccaneer, explorer and naturalist, who visited the coast aboard the *Cygnet* in 1688. He returned in 1699 in the *Roebuck*, and anchored in a bay in what is now known as Dampier Archipelago. He decided that the place was completely inhospitable, undoubtedly influenced by the fact that he couldn't find any water, and his disparaging reports to his superiors in England discouraged further exploration for over a century.

Dampier

Dampier is really a small satellite town of Karratha, about 17km (11 miles) to the west. It is a well-kept town, and the bay and sound area is almost picture-like with the vivid blue and earthy colourings. The town overlooks Hampton Harbour, and was built in the 1960s by Hamersley Iron to export the iron ore from the mines at Tom Price and Paraburdoo. Dampier Salt also uses the shipping facilities to export salt from the nearby pans. Fishing is a great pastime for locals and visitors alike, and the waters abound with popular game and reef fish. The Dampier Archipelago incorporates the only coral reefs found in a tropical arid setting within Australia, and they are home to more than 200 species of living coral.

Onslow

Situated on Beadon Bay, 83km (52 miles) from the turn off the North West Coastal Highway, which in turn is 456km (283 miles) southwest of Port Hedland, Onslow is said to have more potential as a tourist retreat than any other coastal spot in the north of WA.

It has a great winter climate with temperatures of up to 30C (86F)

daily, and in the waters surrounding the town you can fish for bream, whiting, catfish, mullet, reef fish, flathead, pike, kingfish, gold skipjack, whitefish and nor' west salmon. The locals say light gear is usually best, and the most successful bait is fish, crustaceans or squid, which, of course, can be bought locally. Several of these fish can be caught by spinning.

The off-shore islands are renowned throughout the world for their deep sea fishing, and there are many charter boat services waiting to take you out amongst the Spanish mackerel, skipjack, red emperor, cod, groper, coral trout, schnapper and sharks. If you are as good as you probably tell everyone, sailfish and marlin are also there for the catching.

For those who are not into fishing, the laid-back atmosphere of the town encourages just lazing around, or you can visit the site of the old township, about 45km (28 miles) out of town, which was abandoned in 1925-26. Everything that was transportable was moved to the new site, but there are still the stone and cement buildings, mostly owned by the State Government, for you to explore.

The Tourist Centre is on Second Avenue, Second Avenue, ©(08) 9184 6644.

Tom Price - Paraburdoo

The two mining towns of Tom Price and Paraburdoo, in the heart of the rocky Pilbara country and on the edge of the Hamersley Range gorge area, were built to service the iron ore industry.

Paraburdoo is 394km (245 miles) south-east of Onslow, and Tom Price is 79km (49 miles) north-east of Paraburdoo, on sealed roads. The Tom Price Tourist Information Centre is in Central Road, ✆(08) 9188 1112. Information on Paraburdoo can be obtained from the Ashburton Shire offices in Ashburton Avenue, Paraburdoo, ✆(08) 9189 5402. Mining activities and mining tours are major attractions for the traveller, and the magnificent mountain scenery is worth the long drive. This is the high country of the Pilbara. Tom Price is the highest town in WA at 747m (2450 ft) above sea level, and is accordingly called Top Town. From the summit of Mt Nameless, 1128m (3701 ft) above sea level, there are incredible views of the surrounding landscape, while on the ground the wildlife includes echidna, red kangaroo, and a variety of reptiles such as pythons, legless lizards, and the legendary bungarra. The Nameless Festival, which includes fireworks displays, a ball and mardi gras, is held every August.

Hamersley Range National Park

The Park is one of WA's largest, and within its borders are some of the most ancient parts of this planet. The slow process of erosion has carved an intriguing landscape in a complex ecology.

Within the ranges there are many gorges, and in most are permanent pools of clear fresh water. Some are exposed to the sun and are pleasant places to swim, whilst others are in deep, shaded areas and are extremely cold. Each gorge is different, and has its own attractions. Dales Gorge has sunken gardens, deep pools, ferns and waterfalls. Joffre, Red, Hancock, Weano and Knox Gorges are for those who like rock climbing.

Kalamina Gorge is easily accessible and has a clear shaded pool, ferns, tropical paperbarks and river gums. Yampire Gorge has magnificent rock formations, and the ruins of an old asbestos mine. Wittenoom Gorge, though not in the park itself, has picnic places under shady gum trees, and swimming holes.

Wittenoom

The small town of Wittenoom is in the heart of the Pilbara, and information on the town and the Range can be obtained from Auski Tourist Village Roadhouse, Great Northern Highway, ℂ(08) 9176 6988.

If you are travelling through Wittenoom, you are advised to keep in mind that there was an asbestos mine nearby, and although it closed in 1966, it still poses a health problem. It is considered that, while the risk of cancer from inhaling asbestos fibres to short term visitors and tourists is minimal, the following precautions should be taken:

Keep to main roads in the town and gorge areas.

When driving in windy or dusty conditions keep car windows closed.

Avoid parking on or adjacent to asbestos tailings.

Make sure children don't play in asbestos tailings in the town or at the mine site.

Camp only in areas set aside for that purpose. Camping is not allowed in the Wittenoom Gorge.

Newman

Newman is often described as an 'oasis in the wilderness' and was built in recent times for workers at the world's largest open cut mine, Mt Whaleback. It is 416km (258 miles) south of Port Hedland and 238km (148 miles) south-east of Wittenoom.

Tours are conducted of the world's largest open cut mining operation. For more information ℂ9175 3502. The Newman Tourist Information Centre & Museum Gallery can be found in Fortescue Avenue ℂ(08) 9175 2888 or ✎ email newmantb@norcom.net.au

Marble Bar

Marble Bar has the reputation of being Australia's hottest spot, earned in 1923-24 when the town experienced 160 consecutive days of temperatures over 38C (100F). In those days it was said that a beer at the town's hotel, The Iron Clad, was worth more than its weight in gold, as there was more gold in the town than beer.

With this in mind, if you intend to visit Marble Bar, wait until the winter (July-August), when the temperature is around a pleasant 25C (77F). Then you will have the energy to fossick for alluvial gold, or explore the natural geology of the town. The town gets its name from the bar of jasper marble across the Coongan River, and all visitors are directed to the spot. Other places to visit are Chinaman's Pool, Miles House and the State Government Offices, which were completed in 1895.

Western Australia - North

Derby

Population 4,000
Derby is situated at the southern end of King Sound, 2354km (1463 miles) north of Perth, and is the Gateway to the Kimberley Gorges.

Climate

Average temperatures: January max 33C (91F) – min 26C (79F); July max 29C (84F) – min 14C (57F). Number of days per year with temperature above 30C (86F) – 279; number of days per year with temperature above 40C (104F) – 44. Average annual rainfall: 627mm (25 ins); wettest six months – December to May.

Characteristics

Derby is one of the best known towns in the Kimberley region. The narrow channels between the islands off Derby have strong rips and currents, as well as an 11.6m (38 ft) variation between high and low tides.

How to Get There

By Bus

Greyhound Pioneer have daily services between Derby and all major centres in WA and the Northern Territory.

By Car

Derby is on the Great Northern Highway, 2354km (1463 miles) north of Perth, and 1786km (1110 miles) from Darwin.

Tourist Information

The Derby Tourist Bureau is located at 2 Clarendon Street, Derby, ©(08) 9191 1426. They have a website at ☞www.derbytourism. com and can be emailed at ✎ derbytb@comswest.net.au

Accommodation

Here is a selection of the accommodation available in Derby, with prices for a double room per night, which should be used as a guide only. ©The telephone area code is 08.

King Sound Resort Hotel, Lock Street, ©9193 1044. 82 units (private facilities), licensed restaurant, swimming pool ✪$126.

Derby Boab Inn, Loch Street, ©9191 1044. 35 rooms (private facilities), licensed restaurant, swimming pool, bbq ✪$90.

Spinifex Hotel, Clarendon Street, ©9191 1233. 20 rooms (private facilities), licensed restaurant ✪$50-80.

Caravan Parks

Kimberley Entrance Caravan Park, Rowan Street, ©9193 1055. (Dogs allowed on leash) - powered sites ✪$21 for two, no on-site vans.

Eating Out

Derby is not the gourmet capital of the world, but the motels have restaurants. A couple of places you might like to try are:

Lwoy Chinese Restaurant, Lot 269 Loch Street, ©9191 1554; and *Wharf Restaurant & Take Away*, Main Jetty, ©9191 1195.

Points of Interest

Derby is half surrounded by tidal marsh, and boab trees line the main street. Boab trees are ridiculously shaped trees resembling a bottle, and one, about 7km south of the town, is hollow with a girth of 14m (46 ft). According to legend, policemen bringing in prisoners used the tree as an overnight cell before the final trek into Derby.

Nearby is Myalls Bore with one of the largest cattle troughs in the southern hemisphere. It is 120m (131 yds) long and 1.2m wide.

The Cultural Centre in Derby houses a regional museum, library and art gallery. It is built of Kimberley colourstone from Mt Jowlaenga, south-west of Derby.

Other attractions include: the Wharfinger Museum, Derby Library, Botanic Gardens and King Sound.

Outlying Windjana Gorge and Tunnel Creek can be seen with Kimberley West Tours ✆(08) 9193 1442, operating out of Derby. Tours cost $90 per person.

Scenic and charter flights are available over the spectacular Kimberley coastline, the Napier and Leopold Ranges, and Horizontal Fall. Contact Scenic Air Tours on ✆1800 066 132 for bookings. They are located at Hangar 3, Derby Airport.

Festivals

The Country Music Festival is held in July, as is the Boab Festival.

Facilities

Almost all popular Australian sport is played in Derby – cricket, football, golf, tennis, basketball, squash, horse and car racing – and shooting clubs have been organised. Darts, lawn bowls and swimming are also very popular. The swimming pool is open all year round. The outdoor cinema screens films on Friday and Saturday nights.

Fishing

The Fitzroy River is the best major barramundi water in the Kimber-ley. Barramundi live in both rivers and salt water. Live bait or a slow spinner is needed to catch them. The town jetty is a popular place for anglers. A fishing licence is required.

Watch out for the hazards of the Kimberley coast: big tides, stone fish, sea snakes, sharks and crocodiles. Always wear sandshoes or sneakers when wading.

Tours

There are many half and full day tours and longer safaris available in Derby, and the Tourist Bureau has full information. Here we have listed some, to give an idea of what is available.

West Kimberley Tours, ✆9193 1442, have a Town Tour. It visits the Prison Tree, longest trough, crafts, art gallery and the town jetty. They also have a full day tour to Windjana Gorge/Tunnel Creek National Parks – features include the best exposed fossil reef in the world, Cave of Bats and the story of the outlaw Pigeon. Their day visit to Cockatoo Island ☉departs on request daily from May through September, and includes a 35 minute flight over the Buccaneer Archipelago, luncheon and a short island tour.

Bushtrack Safaris, ✆9191 4644, ☉depart from Mt Elizabeth Station, 360km (224 miles) from Derby

Point Leveque, Broome, Kimberley Region, Western Australia

Kimberley waterhole, a lush oasis in northern Austral

along the Gibb River Road.

Kimberley Getaway Safaris, ©9192 7436, offer: a 5 day King Leopold Safari, featuring tours of the Mornington and Bell Gorges, swimming, fishing and photography; a 6 day Bungle Bungle Safari, featuring Geikie Gorge cruise, Wolfe Creek Crater and Bungle Bungle mountain area; a 10 day Mitchell Plateau Safari, featuring gorges of the Gibb River Road, Mitchell Falls, Windjana Gorge and Tunnel Creek.

Buccaneer Sea Safaris, ©9191 1991, offer: a 4 day Cone Bay/ Strickland Bay Safari; Walcott Inlet/Yampi Sound; Walcott Inlet Sea and Land Safari, with 6 days at sea then travel by 4WD.

Outlying Attractions

Broome

Broome is 223km (138 miles) south-west of Derby, on a peninsula bounded by Roebuck Bay, stunning Cable Beach and the Indian Ocean. It is a colourful old pearling port, and its cosmopolitan population adds to the atmosphere of the town. Many of the old pearl divers were Japanese, Malays, Koepangers and Filipinos, and each year their descendants remember their ancestors in the Shinju Festival, which is held in August. Broome Tourist Bureau is on the corner of Bagot Road and Broome Road, and is ⊙open Easter to October, Mon-Fri 8am-5pm, Sat 9am-

1pm, Sun 9am-5pm, ©(08) 9192 2222. They have excellent local brochures, and information on attractions in the town, such as the Historical Museum, Captain Gregory's House, Streeters Jetty, the Court House, the half submerged flying boats, and the Japanese Cemetery. Two popular drawcards are the Broome Crocodile Park, Cable Beach Road, ©9192 1489, and the Willie Creek Pearl Farm, ©9192 6500.

Broome is not short of natural attractions either, and a must is a visit to Gantheaume Point to see the dinosaur's footprint, estimated to be 130 million years old. Cable Beach, with its 24km (15 miles) of clean, white sand, is 6km from Broome, and opposite the beach is the Cable Beach Club, a multi-million dollar development. Nearby are the Pearl Coast Zoological Gardens and the Broome Crocodile Farm.

On the web, go to ☞ebroome. com/tourism or email the Bureau at ✉ tourism@broome.wt.com.au

The Gorges

There is a loop road from Derby via Kimberley Downs, Windjana Gorge on the Lennard River, and Tunnel Creek National Park on Tunnel Creek. The road then rejoins the great Northern Highway west of Fitzroy Crossing.

The Windjana Gorge, about 140km (87 miles) east of Derby, is also called Devils Pass. It is about 5km long, and the limestone cliffs vary between 30m and 90m (98 ft and 295 ft) in height. During the wet season the Lennard River becomes a ranging torrent through the gorge, but it dries out in the dry season to form a string of picturesque pools in a spectacular setting. On the north-western cliff face, near the carpark, is Pigeon's Cave, which was the hideout of the Aboriginal outlaw of the Leopolds who terrorised police and settlers from 1894 to 1897.

Tunnel Creek is 30km (19 miles) east of Windjana Gorge, and has eroded a tunnel through the limestone 750m (820 yds) long and up to 12m (39 ft) high, and 10m (6 yds) wide in places. It is possible to walk right along the tunnel, but care should be taken and a strong torch should be used. Don't wear your best shoes as some of the floor is under water. Cave paintings can be seen near the north entrance to the tunnel, and the black dolorite and basalt rocks at the other end were used by the aborigines to make stone axes.

Geikie Gorge was formed by the Fitzroy River cutting through the limestone formations of the Geike and Oscar Ranges, and is about 19km (12 miles) north of Fitzroy Crossing. The ranges are part of a

fossilised coral reef which is thought to be one of the best preserved fossil reefs in the world. There is a 3km walk along the west bank of the river to the west wall of the gorge.

Most of the park is suitable for experienced bushwalkers only, as the terrain is rugged and inhospitable. Walkers must contact the Ranger before commencing their walks, and walking is not permitted on the east bank. The distinctive change in colour on the rock face of the gorge marks the high water level during the wet season. ☺Between November and April there are twice daily cruises on the River.

An Inland Fishing Licence is required if you intend to do any fishing, but you can swim in the rock pools. There are toilets, showers and barbecues in the gorge, and hotel accommodation at Fitzroy Crossing.

The Gibb River Road to Wyndham passes many of the West Kimber-

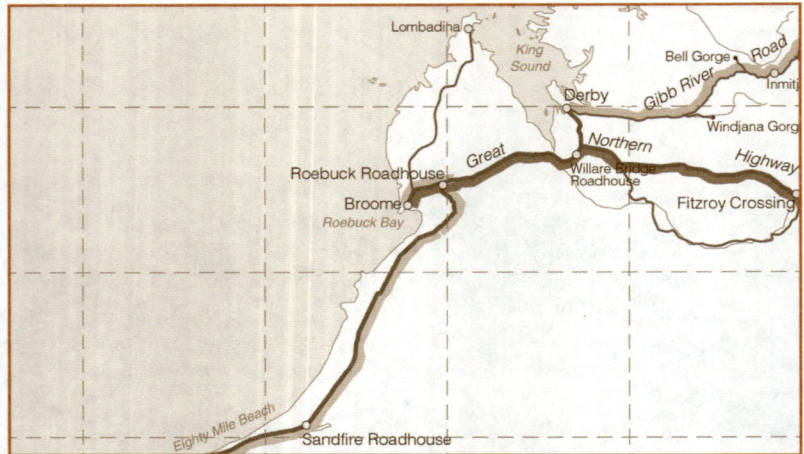

ley gorges, and many are accessible without 4WD.

Garnett Gorge, Galvan's Gorge, Adcock Gorge and Manning Gorge should satisfy most travellers' desire to hike and explore the rugged rocks. At Mt Barnett Station you can camp or stay in a caravan, and visit the nearby Manning Gorge. There are some beautiful waterfalls about 10km (6 miles) upstream.

Lennard Gorge is only accessible by 4WD.

Halls Creek

Situated on the Great Northern Highway, 555km (344 miles) east of Derby, is near the old town of Halls Creek, the site of Western Australia's first gold rush. Today it is a cattle centre, but remnants of the old town remain. Near here an almost vertical quartz vein projects above the surrounding rocks to form a startling white stone wall, which is known as the Great Wall of China.   A major attraction in the area is 133km (83 miles) north near Carranya Station, the Wolf Creek Meteorite Crater, which is 835m (913 yds) wide and 50m (164 ft) deep.

The Bungle Bungle National Park is within Halls Creek Shire and scenic flights can be taken from Halls Creek to view this incredible sight from the air.

Kununurra

A rich green oasis amid the rugged land of the Kimberleys, Kununurra is in the centre of the Ord River Irrigation Scheme, about 1057km (657 miles) east of Broome. As a result of the Ord River Scheme, a wide variety of crops are now grown, eg rice, sugar cane, peanuts, sorghum, fodder crops, sunflower and high protein beans, as well as fruit and vegetables.

Lake Argyle, which was formed as a result of damming the Ord River in the Carr Boyd Ranges, has many tranquil bays, inlets and islands, and the irrigation canals are a fascinating feature of the district. A panoramic view of the Ord Valley can be obtained from Kelly's Knob, 2.5km from town.

Hidden Valley, 3km away, has some interesting rock formations and birdlife. Among unusual rock formations on the way are some Aboriginal rock paintings.

South of Kununurra is the huge Argyle Diamond Mine with a visitors' centre at the site.

Kununurra has all the facilities you would expect and it is also on the Perth/Darwin Greyhound Pioneer route.

The Tourist Bureau is in Coolibah Drive, ©(08) 9168 1177 or ✎email kununurratb@bigpond.com

Wyndham

In the old days, crocodiles were attracted to Wyndham because of the meatworks, which were kept busy by the thousands of cattle on the vast Kimberley stations. They scented blood and used to come up to the aptly-named Blood Drain. Now that a Crocodile Lookout has been built, crocodile-sighting is not such a blood-curdling exercise.

Wyndham, a port established originally to land hopeful prospectors heading for the goldfields of Halls Creek, is now used for produce grown in the irrigated areas around Kununurra. The town stands on Cambridge Gulf, with its fast running tides, and the best views of both the town and the Gulf beyond are to be had from the Bastion, which is higher than Uluru.

The Grotto, near Wyndham, is a pleasant pool surrounded by rocks and boulders, with plenty of trees providing shade.

The Tourist Information Centre is at Kimberley Motors, Great Northern Highway, ©08 9161 1281.

NB Many roads in this area become impassible during the wet season (December to March). Even during the dry season it is best to first check with the Tourist Information or the Police, about the condition of the roads, before venturing off on your own.

Also, keep a watchful eye out for salt water crocodiles in the north of the Kimberley region, and don't forget box jellyfish are prevalent in the ocean north of the Tropic of Capricorn during the summer months (October to March).

Northern Territory

Darwin

Population 72,900
Darwin, the capital of the Northern Territory and Australia's most northerly city, is situated on the tropical north coast by the Arafura Sea. Darwin is actually closer to South East Asia than to some Australian capitals. For example, Denpasar in Indonesia is 1900km (1181 miles) from Darwin, while Sydney is 3200km (1988 miles) away.

Climate

Average temperatures: January max 32C (90F) - min 25C(77F); July max 30C (86F) - min 19C (66F). The average annual rainfall is 1525mm (60 in), and mostly falls between November and April.

Characteristics

Through the decades, Darwin town gained a reputation as a frontier of prawn trawlers, buffalo-catchers, croc shooters and wild waterfront bars. It was the boozing capital of a thirsty nation. Records show the first European explorers arrived in 1623 aboard the Dutch ship, *Arnhem*. In the early 1820s, the British began establishing military outposts in northern Australia, hoping to establish a stronger claim to the region than their Dutch and French rivals. Darwin Harbour was discovered in 1839 by the first officer of the HMS *Beagle*, and was named in honour of Charles Darwin, who had sailed on an earlier expedition on the ship. It was a strategic outpost for the British

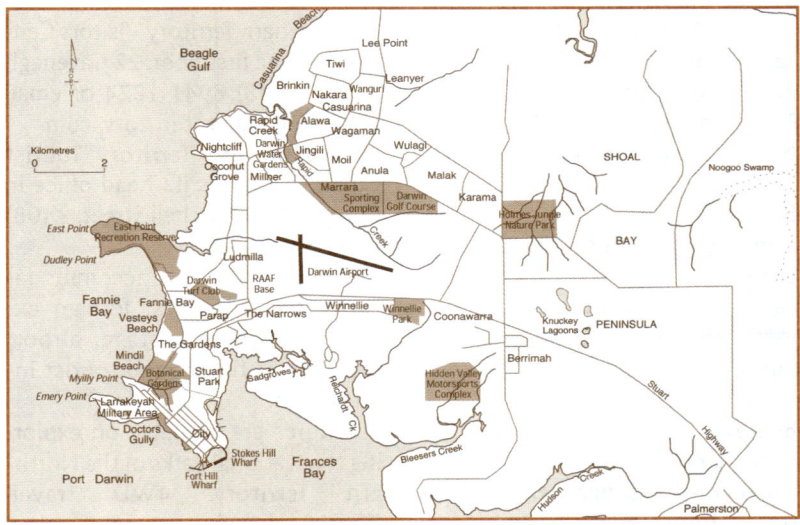

during World War II, and suffered tremendous damage during 64 air raids, with the loss of 243 lives. The Tiwi people on Bathurst Island, who were the first to see the Japanese bombers, perform a corroboree that tells the story. On December 24, 1974, Darwin was struck by one of the greatest natural disasters in Australian history, Cyclone Tracy, which left only about 500 of the city's then 8000 homes habitable. Today Darwin is considered a relaxed tropical city with a relatively young population numbering above 70,000.

How to Get There

By Air
Darwin Airport caters for international and domestic flights. International services include Qantas, Royal Brunei, Garuda, Singapore and Merpati. Frequent interstate services to all capital cities and many major centres are provided by Qantas. The airport is approximately 8km (5 miles) from the city centre.

The Darwin Airport Bus Service departs regularly for the city from the airport, and services all city accommodation. There is a taxi rank at the airport, and the trip takes about 10 minutes. Darwin Radio Taxis, ✆13 1008, has a direct telephone link for airport bookings. Taxis can be multi-hired and minibus taxis are available on request.

By Sea

International cruise ships call at Darwin throughout the year, and cargo ships, naval vessels and private cruising yachts also use the port.

By Rail

There is no rail link to Darwin. The Ghan, runs through central Australia from Adelaide to Alice Springs, connecting with express coach services to Darwin along the Stuart Highway.

By Bus

Greyhound Pioneer have services to Darwin from Adelaide via Alice Springs; Brisbane via Mt Isa; and Perth via the Kimberleys.

By Road

From Adelaide, via the Stuart Highway.
From Queensland, via the Barkly Highway.
From Western Australia, via the Victoria Highway.

Tourist Information

The Northern Territory Visitors Centre is on the first floor, 22 Cavenagh Street, ✆(08) 8941 1824 or email ✐info@northernterritory. com

The Northern Territory Tourist Commission has its head office in Darwin at 43 Mitchell Street, ✆(08) 8999 3900.

Both can organise accommodation, tour bookings, foreign exchange, luggage storage, airport shuttle bus tickets and tourist information.

Brochures are available on exploring the National Parks of the Northern Territory, 4WD travel, Aboriginal tours, fishing, boating, and many other interests.

A couple of websites to visit are ◉www.tourismtopend.com.au and ◉www.ntholidays.com.au

Accommodation

Accommodation in Darwin can be found to suit all price ranges and preferences. There are 5-star luxury through to medium priced and budget priced accommodation. There are also serviced apartments and 'self-catered' rooms with kitchen facilities, as well as caravan parks and camping areas. Backpackers and youth hostellers are well catered for in the city centre. Here is a selection, with prices

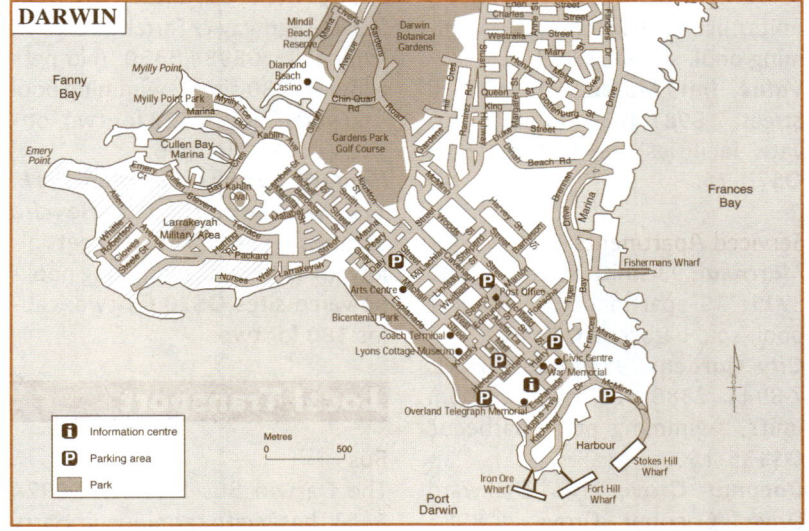

for a double room per night, which should be used as a guide only. ©The telephone area code is 08.

All Seasons Premier Darwin Central Hotel, cnr Smith & Knuckey Streets, ©8944 9000. 132 rooms, licensed restaurant, bistro, swimming pool ✪$175-195.

Rydges Plaza Hotel Darwin, 32 Mitchell Street, ©8982 0000. 233 rooms, licensed restaurant, undercover parking, swimming pool, gym, spa ✪$160-260.

Holiday Inn Darwin, 122 Esplanade, ©8981 5388. 183 rooms, licensed restaurant, swimming pool, barbecue ✪$125-200.

All Seasons Frontier Darwin, 3 Buffalo Court, ©8981 5333. 84 rooms, licensed restaurant, swimming pool, barbecue ✪$105-165.

Darwin Phoenix Motel, 63 Progress Drive, Nightcliff, ©8985 4144. 57 units, licensed restaurant, swimming pool, barbecue ✪$80-90.

Don Hotel Motel, 12 Cavenagh Street, ©8981 5311. 38 units (private facilities), licensed restaurant (closed Sun-Mon), swimming pool ✪$70-80.

Poinciana Inn, cnr McLachlan & Mitchell Streets, ©8981 8111. 51 units, licensed restaurant, swimming pool ✪$95-130.

Asti Motel, cnr Smith Street & Packard Place, ©8981 8200. 86 units, licensed restaurant, swimming pool, spa ✪$105-120.

Value Inn Motel, 50 Mitchell Street, ©8981 4733. 93 units (private facilities), swimming pool ✪$70-75.

Serviced Apartments

Marrakai, 93 Smith Street, ©8982 3711. 30 apartments, swimming pool, spa, barbecue ✪$190.

City Gardens, 93 Woods Street, ©8941 2888. 16 two-bedroom units, swimming pool, barbecue ✪$135-150.

Coconut Grove, 146 Dickward Drive, Coconut Grove, ©8985 0500. 35 suites, swimming pool ✪$100-160.

Peninsular Apartments, 115 Smith Street, ©8981 1922. 36 studio units, swimming pool, licensed bar ✪$105-125.

Caravan Parks

Coolalinga Caravan Park, Stuart Highway, Howard Springs, ©8983 1026. (Dogs allowed on leash) 101 sites, good facilities, swimming pool - powered sites ✪$18 for two, cabins $60 for two.

Palms Village Resort, 907 Stuart Highway, Berrimah, ©8935 0888. (Pets allowed by arrangement) 400 sites, excellent facilities, barbecue, pool - powered sites ✪$24 for two,

cabins $90 for two.

Shady Glen Caravan Park, cnr Stuart Highway & Farrell Crescent, Winnellie, ©8984 3330. (No pets allowed) 280 sites, swimming pool - powered sites ✪$22 for two, on-site vans $50 for two.

Howard Springs Caravan Park, 170 Whitewood Road, Howard Springs, ©8983 1169. (No pets allowed) 170 sites, swimming pool - powered sites ✪$20 for two, cabins $80 for two.

Local Transport

Bus

The Darwin Bus Service, ©8924 5463, has a city terminus in Harry Chan Avenue, and from there services the city area as well as the suburbs of Casuarina and Palmerston. ☺Buses run every day except Sunday, and there are extended services during special events and festivals. The Tour Tub, an open air bus, has a set route around the city, inner suburbs and most tourist attractions. ☺The bus runs on the hour, and day tickets can be purchased allowing you to stop anywhere and reboard when another bus comes, ©8981 5233.

Taxi

Darwin taxis operate around the clock and can be found at taxi ranks, hotels and transport terminals, or you can hail them in the street. The city rank is outside Woolworths in Knuckey Street, and there are also ranks in the suburbs. Following are a few numbers for taxi services ✆8981 3777, ✆8981 2222, ✆13 1008, ✆8947 3333.

Car

Most of the major car rental companies have offices in Darwin, and they require a current driver's licence and a deposit. Most also offer 4WD vehicles.

Avis, ✆8981 9922; Budget Campervans, ✆8981 0148; Budget Rent A Car, ✆13 2727; Hertz Rent A Car NT, ✆1800 891 112; Territory Thrifty Car Rental, ✆8924 0000.

The Automobile Association of the Northern Territory has an office in Darwin at 81 Smith Street, ✆8981 3837, and reciprocal membership is offered to members of affiliated international and interstate auto clubs. AANT has emergency road service and carries a comprehensive list of road maps. Leaded, unleaded, LPG and diesel are available at almost all filling stations. Most stations are ☼open 7am-6pm, while a few are open 24 hours-a-day.

Ferries

The MV *Darwin Duchess* leaves Stokes Hill Wharf on weekdays for cruises to Mandorah. For timetables and bookings contact Mondaorah Ferry Service, ✆8978 5015.

Eating Out

Darwin is a melting pot of people and cultures, so it is not surprising that this is reflected in the restaurants of the city. Whether you want Creole, Italian, Thai, Greek, French, Chinese, Mexican, Indian or Malaysian, you will not be disappointed. Or, you can be adventurous and go for kangaroo, buffalo, crocodile or camel, maybe for the first time. Whatever your fancy, the Visitor Information Centre has a complete list of eateries. Here are a few names and addresses:

Charlie's, cnr Knuckey Street & Austin Lane, ✆8981 3298 - licensed, Mediterranean food - ☼open daily 11am-2pm, Mon-Sat 6pm-midnight, Sun 6-10pm.

Guiseppe's Italian Restaurant, 64 Smith Street, ✆8941 3110.

Alchemy Restaurant, 130 Smith Street, ✆8941 2126.

Castaways BBQ Restaurant, cnr The Esplanade & Peel St r eet, ✆8941 0755.

Sizzler Steak Seafood Salad Restaurant, Cinema Centre, Mitchell Street, ✆8941 2225.

Rooftop Restaurant, 3 Buffalo Court, ✆8981 5333.

Magic Wok Restaurant, 48

Cavenagh Street, ☏8981 3332.

Hanuman Thai Restaurant, 28 Mitchell Street, ☏8941 3500.

Waterhole Restaurant, cnr Knuckey St & Smith Street, ☏8944 9120.

La Chaumiere Restaurant, 13 Shepherd Street, ☏8981 2879.

Sakura Japanese Restaurant, Unit 1/ 52, Marina Boulevard, ☏8981 4949.

Swiss Cafe & Restaurant, 60 Smith Street, ☏8981 5079.

Dragon Palace Restaurant, 7 Finniss Street, ☏8981 1233.

Passage To India Restaurant, 50 Smith Street, ☏8981 4340.

Entertainment

In Darwin it is illegal to consume alcohol in a public place within two kilometres of a licensed premises without a permit. That covers just about everywhere in the city. However, a few foreshore places are exempt, and the Visitor Information Centre can advise. There is no doubt that Darwin is the beer drinking capital of Australia, after all the Darwin stubby holds 2 litres (3.5 pints)! But there are rules and regulations regarding the selling and imbibing of alcohol, and they are as follows: As a general rule, hotels trade ⊕between 10am to 10pm Mon-Fri, with extended weekend hours. Nightclubs are ⊕open until 6am, but some do not open till 10pm. Roadhouses can operate 24 hours, depending on their licence. The trading hours for takeaway alcohol are ⊕10am-10pm Mon-Fri and Sun. Trading hours for Saturday and public holidays are 9am-10pm.

The legal age for drinking in a licensed establishment is 18 years. In-house hotel guests can usually order liquor 24 hours a day. The **MGM Grand Darwin Hotel & Casino**, on Gilruth Avenue, ☏8943 8888, is the city's top entertainment venue. Apart from keno, roulette and every game of chance you can think of, there are European and Asian restaurants, bars, and a disco from 11pm-6am on Friday and Saturday nights.

Shopping

Darwin has all the shops, stores and facilities a city should have for residents and tourists alike. Shops trade ⊕seven days a week, 9am-5pm, with late trading to 9pm on Thursday and Friday. Many items are for sale that are typical of the Northern Territory, such as handcrafted leather goods, local fashion items, and the bushmen's famous Akubra hats. There is also a wide selection of Aboriginal arts and crafts, including bark paintings, carvings, fish nets and hooks, didgeridoos and hand-painted fabrics such as those made by the Tiwi people on Melville Island, as well as the works of many very talented local artists, potters and weavers. The Smith Street Mall is the main shopping area, and there are shopping centres at Casuarina and Palmerston. The large hotels, of course, have the usual range of boutiques and souvenir shops.

Mindil Beach

Galleries

For a small city, Darwin has a large selection of galleries and shops catering for the collector of arts and crafts. Featured are works from both prominent local and interstate artists, and styles range from contemporary art to traditional Aboriginal. The Visitor Information Centre has a complete list, but here is one you should inspect.

Raintree Aboriginal Art Gallery, 14 Knuckey Street, ☎8981 2732, which is also the only outlet for the Raintree Collection of fashion day wear and casual mix and match.

Markets

The Big Flea Market, Darwin's oldest market, is held every Sunday, 8am-2pm, at Rapid Creek Shopping Centre on Tower Road.

The *Parap Market* is held ☼every Saturday, 8am-2pm, and many people visit in search of breakfast or brunch. There are fresh fruit drinks and ices,

plus stalls offering South-East Asian soups and satays. There are also second-hand books and knick-knacks.

At *Banyan Junction*, next to the Transit Centre in Mitchell Street, an international food market is held every day from 6pm, against a backdrop of Melbourne trams.

☼Every Friday 5pm-10pm during the Dry season, the *Palmerston Night Market* is held in Goyder Square. There are arts and crafts stalls, a wide choice of culinary delights and local musicians. Buses ☼depart Darwin terminal (route 8) at 5.15pm and return 8.30 or 9.40pm. Buses leave Casuarina (route 9) at 5.30pm, return times as above.

Mindil Beach Sunset Market is held ☼each Thursday from about 5pm-10pm, May to October. It offers a variety of taste treats from such lands as Indonesia, Laos, Sri Lanka, Thailand, The Philippines, South America, as well as some fair dinkum Aussie tucker. There are also arts and crafts stalls.

Points of Interest

A stroll around the city will take you to most of the important historical sites.

The **Tree of Knowledge**, behind the Civic Centre on Harry Chan Avenue, has been a locally-famous landmark through the town's history. It is a banyan tree (Ficus virens), a species revered by Buddhists worldwide as the 'tree of knowledge' under which Buddha gained enlightenment.

Christchurch Cathedral was built in 1975 using some of the ruins of the original cathedral which was devastated by Cyclone Tracy.

Brown's Mart, cnr Harry Chan Avenue & Smith Street, ©8981 5522, was intended as a mining exchange when it was built in the 1882. It has served many purposes through the years, despite the roof being blown off by two cyclones. In recent years, the exposed roof framing was extended to increase its lateral stability, and the building was converted to a community theatre.

The **Old Town Hall** is in Smith Street, and when it was erected in 1883 during a mining boom, it created, along with Brown's Mart and Christchurch, a streetscape of stone. In World War II it was used for naval administration, and after

that was an art gallery. Now, the ruined walls make a dramatic backdrop for outdoor theatre.

The **Old Courthouse and Police Station**, cnr Smith Street and The Esplanade, was built in 1884 for the South Australian government, in early South Australian style. Cornerstones connected the courthouse to the police station with a cellblock in the back. The navy used these buildings from World War II until Cyclone Tracy. The interior was then reconstructed, while retaining the facade, and the building now houses the offices of the Administrator of the Northern Territory.

Government House has been known as The Residency and also as The House of Seven Gables, and is an 1883 replacement in stone of a timber structure built 13 years earlier, which suffered a white ant attack. Verandahs with louvres, providing the main living area, encircle the building. The gardens and gables certainly give it a colonial look.

Hotel Darwin, in The Esplanade, is one of Darwin's oldest hotel sites. The original pub, *The Palmerston*, was proud of its 'accommodation suitable for ladies' when it opened in 1883. It was severely damaged by Cyclone Tracy and forced to close for 18 months. A convention and function centre was added to the rebuilt hotel in 1983. It is now the Carlton Hotel Darwin.

Admiralty House, The Esplanade, is one of the few tropical-style houses still surviving from the 1920s, and is now used as an arts and crafts gallery and tearooms.

Lyons Cottage, cnr Knuckey Street & The Esplanade, was built in 1924-25 to house the manager of the British Australia Telegraph Company (BAT). The Georgian Revival-style bungalow was later occupied by one-time Darwin mayor John Lyons. Among its innovations is a separate kitchen in the rear, linked to the residence by a covered walkway for protection against the tropical climate. The house is now the BAT Museum, and admission is free, ℰ8981 1750. It is ☉open daily 10am-4.30pm.

Victoria Hotel (The Vic), ℰ8981 4011, in the centre of the Mall, has survived everything thrown at it, including bombs and a cyclone. When it was built in 1894, it was called the North Australian Hotel, and has since undergone a name change and four major reconstructions, although always maintaining its architectural integrity.

The **Star Village**, opposite The Vic, is a shopping arcade, built before the war and housed one of Darwin's early cinemas. The original entrance and projection bridge

is still the modern day entrance.

The **Commercial Bank**, cnr The Mall & Bennett Street, retains the colonnade from the original 1893 'Stone Bank'. The bank was so nicknamed because the Commercial Bank of Australia had chosen to build in local stone to counter the Tin Bank erected by a nearby competitor.

The **Chinese Temple**, in Wood Street, was heavily hit by the cyclone, which left only the floor, masonry block for the altars and the stone lions, all of which are incorporated in the current temple, built in steel and concrete. The simple yet elegant curved roof is new, and the entire 1978 structure received approval from Singapore-based religious leaders. The temple is ☉open Mon-Fri 8am-4pm, Sat-Sun 8am 3pm.

The **National Trust** headquarters are housed in Myilly Point Heritage Precinct, at 2 Khalin Avenue, on the outskirts of the city centre. It is composed of four pre-World War II houses, built originally for high-ranking government employees. The Trust has an information centre and a gift shop, and is ☉open Mon-Fri 8.30am-4.30pm, ℰ8981 2848.

The **Botanic Gardens**, in Gardens Road off Gilruth Avenue, were first planted by Dr Maurice Holtze more than a century ago. They have the

Southern Hemisphere's largest array of tropical palms, an orchid farm, nursery, rainforest, waterfall and wetlands flora, as well as an amphitheatre where there are often live concerts. Admission is free and the gardens are ☉open Mon-Fri 7.30am-5pm, Sat-Sun 8.30am-5pm.

Aquascene, 28 Doctors Gully Road at the end of The Esplanade, ©8981 7837, has become Darwin's most popular attraction. Every day, at high tide, hundreds of fish come in from the sea to be fed, and you can be there to serve them. ☺Opening times depend on the tides, so it is best to enquire at your hotel reception, or ring Aquascene direct. Prices are $5.50 adult, $3.30 child.

The **Museum & Art Gallery of the Northern Territory**, in Conacher Street, Fannie Bay, ©8999 8211, features galleries of Aboriginal Man and of Oceania, full of art, artifacts, maps, photos, flora and fauna - including the legendary Sweetheart, a huge crocodile which used to terrorise trolling fishermen. The museum is also a research and scientific institute, categorising new species of plants and animals each year. In the Art Gallery, there are works by Lloyd Rees, Sidney Nolan, Clifton Pugh, Russell Drysdale, Donald Friend and Arthur Streeton, among others. It is open Mon-Fri 9am-5pm, Sat-Sun 10am-5pm and admission is free.

Wishart Siding is housed in the original buildings of the Northern Territory's now-defunct railway, where the Arnhem Highway branches off from the Stuart Highway, south of Darwin.

The **Australian Aviation Heritage Centre**, on the Stuart Highway, Winnellie, is open daily 9am-5pm, ©8947 2145. Its major exhibit is a B52 bomber on permanent loan from the US Air Force, one of only two displayed outside the USA. Also of interest is the wreckage of a Zero Fighter shot down on February 19, 1942, during the first air raid on Darwin. There are many other exhibits from World War II, as well as displays documenting the history of aviation in the Northern Territory. Admission is $11 adult, $6 child and $28 family.

The **East Point Military Museum**, at East Point Reserve, has many exhibits, including a 15 minute movie with actual footage of the 1942 bombing of Darwin. It is open daily 9.30am-4.30pm, ©8981 9702.

Fannie Bay Gaol Museum, on East Point Road, ©8999 8290, is open daily 10am-4.30pm, and admission is free. The gaol closed in 1979 after 84 years of service, and opened as a museum in 1983. The gaol was emptied in 1942, after Japan bombed Darwin, and again in 1974, after Cyclone Tracy damaged the complex. Fourteen men were hanged in the gaol, the last two in 1952.

Indo Pacific Marine in Lambell Terrace, Larrakeyah, ©8981 1294, is not really a museum, but rather a marine display. It features living coral reef eco-systems which have been isolated from the sea, and is one of four such exhibitions in the world. It is open 10am-5pm daily, and as it takes at least an hour to see everything, the management closes the doors one hour before closing time. Price of admission is ✪$16.40 adult, $6 child.

Crocodylus Park, in McMillans Road, Berrimah, ©8922 4500, is Darwin's newest attraction. It feaures crocodiles, of course, as well as other interesting wildlife, including lions and tigers. The park is open 9am-5pm daily, and prices are ✪$19.50 adult, $10 child and $49 family.

Festivals

The Northern Territory is renowned for its bizarre festivals and carnivals. One of the oddest is the Beer Can Regatta in which vessels made almost completely of beer cans race on Darwin Harbour in August. One of the major Aboriginal festivals is the Barunga Festival held over the long weekend in June. Aborigines from all over the Territory gather at Barunga, 80km (50 miles) southeast of Katherine, for four days of traditional events such as dancing, fire lighting, and boomerang and spear throwing contests. The Darwin Cup Carnival in July/August is held over six weeks of fashion, food, frivolity, and yes, there is also a horse race.

Facilities

Cricket - indoor and outdoor games have a large following.

Cycling - pushbikes, tandems and mountain bikes are available. For information, contact the Darwin Amateur Cycling Club, ©8953 4360.

Football - Australian Rules and Rugby Union are popular, with some support for Rugby League. Both indoor and outdoor soccer are played.

Horse Racing - regular meetings are held at the Fannie Bay Racecourse.

Swimming - it is inadvisable to swim in the ocean between October and May due to the presence of the box jellyfish. During this time the locals tend to use the inland waterways such as Berry Springs and Howard Springs, or municipal pools in Darwin, Casuarina, Nightcliff, and Palmerston. Swimmers should check carefully for any signs warning of crocodiles.

Sailing - ocean and harbour sailing are available. Contact the Darwin Sailing Club, ℂ8981 1700, or the Darwin Trailer Boat Club, ℂ8981 6749.

Ten pin bowling - Darwin Ten Pin Bowling, ℂ8985 4416.

Squash - courts can be found at a number of locations including the Darwin Squash and Aerobics Centre,
ℂ8948 4889; Howard Springs Squash Courts, ℂ8983 2907.

Water skiing - contact the Northern Territory Ski Association, ℂ8981 6630.

Tennis - contact the Darwin Tennis Centre, ℂ8985 2844, or Tennis Association, ℂ8981 2181. Night tennis is popular.

Driving Through The Territory

Many people decide to drive independently through the Northern Territory and Central Australia, and enjoy the experience. You are, of course, free to spend as much, or as little, time at any one place, and there is no lost time waiting for other people who are interested in something that leaves you cold. To visit some places, such as Arnhem Land and Bathurst and Melville Islands, a tour is the only way to go, but to others you are free to come and go as you please. There are a few things to remember when travelling independently, and by following a few simple rules your holiday can be a thing to remember, not something you would rather forget.

Make sure your vehicle is suitable for the roads you will encounter, and that you have a basic tool kit, plus spare fan belt, radiator hoses and tyre. Many of the locals carry two spare tyres.

Always carry ample supplies of petrol and water. Plan your trip using a reputable map, and before leaving check on road conditions.

Always tell someone where you are going, and when you expect to return.

If your car breaks down, stay with it. It is much easier for rescuers to find a car than people wandering on their own.

Keep a sharp lookout for wandering animals, especially at night.

Remember that crocodiles are active in Northern Territory waters, so observe the signs, and swim only in designated safe areas.

If you are leaving your car in the sun, make sure the windows are down a little to avoid the windscreen being blown out by expanding air.

Never leave pets or children in a parked car, even in the shade.

Outlying Attractions

South of Darwin

Palmerston

Palmerston is a new town, 20km (12 miles) south of Darwin, which was designed to become a self-sufficient city. The present population is around 8000, and four suburbs have been developed, but it is envisaged that it will grow very quickly. The town has many tourist attractions, and foremost among them is Marlow Lagoon, noted for its year-round swimming, playground, barbecue and other facilities. The town also has a nine-hole golf course and a sport and leisure centre with an olympic-sized pool and a gymnasium.

Howard Springs

Situated 34km (21 miles) south of Darwin, on and around the Stuart Highway, Howard Springs is the centre for Howard Springs Nature Park. The Park has the closest and most attractive public fresh water swimming pool to Darwin. Next to the Park is the Territory's only duck and goose hunting reserve. There is also a road leading off nearby to the Gunn Point fishing paradise. Shooters need a permit, and there is an official shooting season, so enquiries should be made at a police station, or a branch of the Parks & Wildlife Commission, ©8983 1001. Hunters and fishermen should also be aware that this is saltwater crocodile country, and they love fish and birds.

Noonamah

The town of Noonamah is 40km (25 miles) south of Darwin on the Stuart Highway, and its main attraction, the Crocodile Farm, is 2km before the town itself. The Farm is the first and largest in Australia and has more than 7000 residents, including giant crocs, baby crocs,

pygmy crocs, an albino croc and American alligators. The reptiles are bred here for their skin and meat. The Farm is open daily 9am-4pm, and feeding time is 2pm daily, with an extra feeding on Sunday at 11am. Entry is ✪$10 adult, $5.50 children, ✆8988 1450.

Berry Springs

Territory Wildlife Park is 10km (6 miles) west of the Stuart Highway turnoff, which is 48km (30 miles) south of Darwin. The park is a world-class wildlife sanctuary set in more than 400ha (988 acres) of bushland, and exhibits native and feral animals of the North Territory. It is designed on an open range plan, without bars or cages. The park is ☺open daily 8.30am-6pm, with last visitors admitted at 4pm. Fees are ✪$18 for adults, $9 children, $40 per family, ✆8988 7200.

Next door to the wildlife park is the Berry Springs Nature Park. The springs create natural swimming pools fringed with rainforest. They are ☺open year-round, 8.30am-6.30pm, although they are temporarily closed after very heavy rains. There are grassed picnic grounds and barbecue facilities, ✆8988 6310.

Batchelor

Batchelor is 13km (8 miles) west of the Stuart Highway, from the turnoff 87km (53 miles) south of Darwin. It was established as a town for miners working the Rum Jungle Uranium Mine in 1954. The mine closed in 1963 as the remaining ore was uneconomic to treat. The treatment plant closed in 1971 when the stockpiled ore had been processed. The site, which has been rehabilitated, can be visited, but only on tours organised by Batchelor Caravillage, Rum Jungle Road, ✆8976 0166.

Batchelor also has some relics from World War II, when it was the site of an air base, bombed by the Japanese in 1942. Its main function now, though, is as the gateway to Litchfield Park, one of the Territory's newest parks.

Accommodation is available at the Caravillage mentioned above, powered sites ✪$23 for two, cabins $85-90 for two; and The Rum Jungle Motor Inn, ✆8976 0123 - 22 units, licensed restaurant, bistro, swimming pool, barbecue - ✪$110 a double.

Tourist information can be obtained from the above two establishments.

Litchfield National Park

The 65,700ha (162,279 acres) park features permanent water and changing terrain that makes it one of the better bush walking areas in the Top End. There are monsoonal rainforests, hot springs, the Tabletop range escarpment with its imposing sandstone outcrops, spring fed creeks, huge groves of cycads and historic tin mines. For the more adventurous there is the Lost City. This limestone rock formation appears to be a huge petrified city of castles, statues, people and animals. It is quite a find, hiding deep in the Park, and is only accessible by 4WD, horseback or to the hardy bushwalker. The rest of the area is accessible by conventional and 4WD vehicles, and is a photographer's delight. Camping facilities are available. Before venturing into the Park it is advisable to obtain a map of the area from any of the businesses in Batchelor, and to call Road Report, ✆1800 246 199, for up to date information on the Park's road conditions, and the Parks & Wildlife Commission, ✆8976 0282, for further information on the park.

Adelaide River

The town of Adelaide River is 110km (68 miles) south of Darwin on the Stuart Highway. It is situated on a river of the same name, and was a major military centre during World War II. Attractions include the War Cemetery, Snake Creek Arsenal and Robin Falls. The pub is worth a visit, and the owners also offer some good value tours of the local region, ✆8976 7047.

East of Darwin

Humpty Doo

Humpty Doo is situated on the Arnhem Highway, 11km (7 miles) east of the Stuart Highway, and 45km (28 miles) from Darwin. A very large crocodile on the roadside, complete with boxing gloves, tells you that you are entering 'croc country', which is a good thing to keep in mind. The town is mainly a service centre for the rural belt, and has basic facilities and services. It was the site of the Humpty Doo Rice Growing Project, which began in 1956 using water stored in the nearby Fogg Dam, but was abandoned in the early 1960s.

Attractions in the town include: Graeme Gow's Reptile World, a display of some of the most deadly reptiles in the world. It is ☺open daily 8.30am-5pm, ✆8988 1661; the Humpty Doo Hotel, ✆8988 1372, which hosts the annual Darwin Stubby Drinking Competition in July; and the Adelaide River Queen, a flat-bottomed river boat that departs Adelaide River Bridge for cruises along the river, ✆8988 8144. There are regular departures for the two and a half hour cruises along a stretch of river which is home to about 60 crocs and prolific bird and animal life. The croc feeding sessions enable visitors to see the speed and power of these reptiles as they actually jump out of the water to catch the food.

Kakadu National Park

Kakadu National Park is a natural wonderland - 20,000sq km (7,720 sq miles) of magnificent sights, sounds and experiences. It has a World Heritage listing, and is owned by the Aborigines under the Gagudju Association. Kakadu begins about 250km (155 miles) east of Darwin on the Arnhem Highway, and is made up of three regions: the almost inaccessible Arnhem plateau; the rolling lowlands; and the flood plains. There are 120 known rock galleries of Aboriginal art along the escarpment, with those at Obiri Rock and Nourlangi Rock being the most easily accessible. It is extremely important to remember that the galleries are very old and they are still important and significant to the Aboriginal people today. PLEASE KEEP TO THE MARKED PATHWAYS, AND DO NOT TOUCH ANY PAINTED SURFACE. Although almost one-third of Kakadu is bare rock, the rest is lush lowlands which support 960 identified species of plants. There is also

Gagudju Crocodile Hotel

an incredible variety of animal life, with 51 species of native mammals. Other creatures include crocodiles and frill-necked lizards. A cruise on the Yellow Waters Billabong or South Alligator River offers one of the best opportunities to see the water flowers and wildlife. There are excellent bushwalks throughout the park, and drives into the bush lead to spectacular sights such as Twin Falls and Jim Jim Falls. Probably the best way to see Kakadu is with a tour operator who knows all the history and can show you the special and unique places, and many are available in Darwin. If you decide to travel on your own, you should call into the Bowali Visitor Information Centre near Jabiru,

©8938 1120, for advice, brochures and to pay your ✪$16.25 park fee. There is also a Tourist Centre in Tasman Plaza, Jabiru, ©8979 2548.

Accommodation in Kakadu ranges from the luxury of a four-star crocodile shaped hotel in Jabiru (Gagudju Crocodile Hotel), ©8979 2800, to the peace and tranquility of the Kakadu Resort, ©8979 0166, or the Gagudju Cooinda, ©8979 0145, through to caravan sites and camping grounds.

Arnhem Land

Arnhem Land is the area east of Kakadu National Park, and is traditionally inhabited by the Aborigines. A restricted number of tours take visitors through tropical bush abundant with wildlife and on to the coastal dunes from which the seascapes are truly magnificent. A permit is required for entry into this area, and can be obtained from the Tiwi Lands Council, Highway House, Bishop Street, Stuart Park, ©8981 4898. The rock galleries of Aboriginal Art in Arnhem Land are generally regarded as even more impressive than those in Kakadu, but they can only by visited whilst on an organised tour.

North of Darwin

Bathurst and Melville Islands

The islands are 80km (50 miles) off the coast of Darwin, and are owned by the Tiwi Aborigines. Until recently, the islands had received almost no visitors from the mainland for thousands of years, but there are now day and half-day tours to Bathurst Island, or you can stay overnight at Putjimirra camp on Melville Island. The tours are offered by Tiwi Tours, ©8924 1115, and are ex Darwin.

Cobourg Peninsula/Victoria Settlement

The peninsula north-east of Darwin is in Arnhem Land, and was where a brave but futile attempt was made to first settle the area. The ruins of the Victoria Settlement at Port

Essington can still be seen, but a permit is required. In the early1990s an environmentally sensitive wilderness habitat called Seven Spirit Wilderness, opened on the Cobourg Peninsula, ©8979 0277.

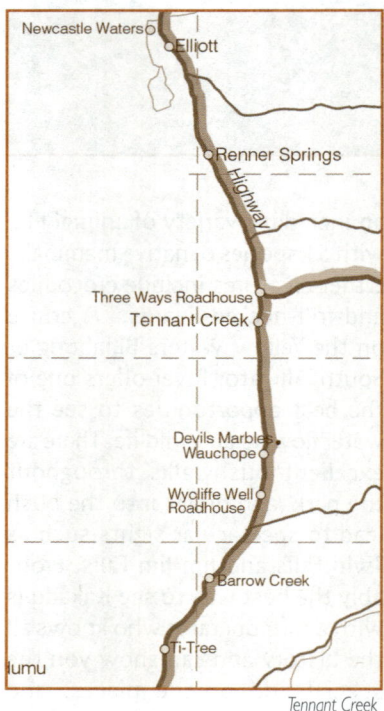

Tennant Creek

Tennant Creek

Population 3,500

Tennant Creek is on the Stuart Highway, 24km (15 miles) south of the junction of the Barkly Highway. It is 507km (314 miles) north of Alice Springs, and 675km (419 miles) south of Katherine.

Climate

As with most outback towns, Tennant Creek has two seasons, the Wet (November-March) and the Dry (April-October). Average temperatures: Dry Season max 35C (95F) - min 10C (50F); Wet Season max 43C (109F) - min 26C (79F).

Characteristics

The country of the Warumungu People centres on Jurnkurakurr, the focus of many dreaming tracks and a place of spiritual significance for several tribes. In 1860, John McDouall Stuart passed by the same spot, and named the creek there Tennant Creek, after John Tennant of Port Lincoln, South Australia. In 1872, an Overland Telegraph Line repeater station was built at Tennant Creek.

From hard beginnings, the town has steadily developed. Townsfolk worked hard to get facilities that people 'down south' took for granted. In the last 50 years, people from all over the world have settled at Tennant, and today it is a multi-cultural and harmonious township, where everyone is encouraged to participate fully in community affairs.

Tennant Creek has grown from a

small and dusty outback settlement, to a busy community and a vital part of the Northern Territory.

How to Get There

By Bus

Greyhound Pioneer stop at Tennant Creek on their Darwin/Alice Springs routes.

By Road

From Adelaide and Darwin, via the Stuart Highway.

From Mt Isa, via the Barkly Highway.

Tourist Information

Tennant Creek Visitor Information Centre, Battery Hill, Peko Road, can be contacted on ©(08) 8962 3388 or emailed at ✐info@tennant creektourism.com.au. The website is ☜www.tennantcreektourism. com.au

Accommodation

Here is a selection of the available accommodation, with prices for a double room per night, which should be used as a guide only. The telephone area code is 08.

Bluestone Motor Inn, Paterson Street, ©8962 2617. 65 units, licensed restaurant, swimming pool, barbecue ✪$85-115.

Eldorado Motor Lodge, Paterson Street, ©8962 2402. 80 units, licensed restaurant, swimming pool, barbecue ✪$75-95.

Goldfields Hotel/Motel, 603 Paterson Street, ©8962 2030. 30 units, licensed restaurant ✪$65-70.

Safari Lodge (Motel), Davidson Street, ©8962 2207. 19 units, spa, barbecue ✪$85.

Caravan Parks

Outback Caravan Park, Peko Road, ©8962 2459. (No dogs allowed) 150 sites, spa, pool, barbecue, good facilities - powered sites ✪$20 for two, on-site vans $50 for two.

Tennant Creek Caravan Park, 208 Paterson Street, ©8962 2325. (Pets allowed on leash) 90 sites, barbecue, pool - unpowered sites ✪$18 for two, cabins $40-65 for two.

Eating Out

Fernanda's Restaurant, 1 Noble Street, ©8962 3999.

Tennant Creek Chinese Restaurant, 63 Patterson Street, ©8962 3347.

Points of Interest

Near the Visitor Information Centre, there is a **Celebrity Walk**, where famous people who have passed through the town have left behind prints of their hands and feet.

From **Anzac Hill**, in Davidson Street, there is a good view over the town, and on the top there is a War Memorial, and seats.

The **Church of Christ The King**, in Windley Street, was built at Pine Creek in 1904, and trucked to Tennant in 1936 to serve the growing town. Major restoration work was done in 1986, and the church is classified as an Historic Building by the National Trust.

The **National Trust Museum** building was constructed by the army in 1942, then used as the Outpatients Clinic until taken over by the National Trust in 1978. Items of interest include: the old gaolhouse; reconstruction of a miner's camp; archive collection; and early photographs. The Museum is ☉open during the Dry season from 4-6pm daily, and during the Wet Season by appointment only, ☎8962 4257.

The **Old Australian Inland Mission** was built in 1934, and is the oldest building constructed here. It is a good example of the early corrugated iron buildings, most of which have not stood the test of time. The Mission is next to the Uniting Church in Paterson Street.

The **Aboriginal Mural**, in Paterson Street, was a community project, and it encompasses Aboriginal mythology and contemporary life. Many local Aboriginal artists participated in its planning and painting.

The **Civic Centre** and **Public Library** are in Peko Road. The Civic Centre has a gem collection and an art display, as well as the Council Chambers, and is ☉open Mon-Fri 9am-4.15pm. The Library houses the Tennant Creek Collection, written material about the region, and is ☉open Mon-Fri 10am-4.15pm, Sat 9am-12.15pm.

The **Government Stamp Battery** is further along Peko Road. Number 3 Battery is the last of the Government batteries still operating in the Territory. It is used to crush and treat free milling or easily freed gold ores. Interesting things to see include an operating 10 head 575.6kg stamper, various displays of historic artifacts, and the former battery site and buildings. Guided tours are available, and the Visitor Information Centre can advise on times and costs.

Continuing along Peko Road you come to **One Tank Hill**, Tennant's main lookout point. There are plaques set into a semi-circular wall that provide distance and direction markers for 11 significant sites.

Nobles Nob, on Peko Road 16km (10 miles) east of the town, was the richest gold mine in Australia. It was discovered in 1933, and produced $64,975,256.00 worth of ore by the time it closed in 1985. It was an underground mine, but the crown pillar collapsed in 1967, and the mine was converted to a huge open cut. The pit is 283m (930ft) long, 146m (480 ft) wide, and 82m (270 ft) deep. Work continues at Nobles Nob with gold from the White Devil Mine being processed there. There is a tourist lookout, from which visitors can see the crushing and mill buildings, and tailings dam, as well as good views of the eastern region.

Mary Ann Dam is 3km (2 miles) north of Tennant Creek, and was built in 1980 as a recreation lake. It provides excellent swimming and boating (non-power boats only), and has covered picnic tables and seats, barbecues, boat ramp, toilets, showers and playground equipment. There is also plenty of bushwalking available in the Honeymoon Ranges, and a bike track connects the dam to the town for people with that form of transport.

Camping is not allowed at the dam.

The **Old Telegraph Station**, 10km (6 miles) north of town, was completed in 1876 as part of a network stretching from Adelaide to Darwin. Only 4 of the original 11 buildings still remain, and they are the oldest in the Territory. They were used by linesmen and telegraph station operators until the transfer of communications to the Tennant Creek Post Office in 1937. Between then and 1986, the area was leased to various pastoralists, but it now forms part of a conservation area and is being restored as a museum. The old buildings in their pastoral setting provide an insight into the lives of early pioneers.

There are two interesting isolated **graves** to the west of the station. The northernmost one is that of Tom Nugent, who established Banka Banka Station, and who had apparently in his younger days been a member of the Ragged Thirteen, a gang of cattle duffers (rustlers) who roamed the Territory at the turn of the century. Another member of the Ragged Thirteen was Harry Redwood, who built Brunette Downs, and was immortalised in Boldrewood's novel Robbery Under Arms as Captain Starlight. The other grave is not his, though, it belongs to Archibald Cameron, an OTS linesman who died around 1918.

The **Devils Pebbles** are an interesting granite rock formation scattered over a large area. To see them drive 11km (7 miles) north of Tennant Creek on the Stuart Highway, then turn left on a dirt road for a further 6km (4 miles). The best time to visit is at sunset when the rocks seem to come alive as the sun's rays strike them. The area is inhabited by various wildlife species including rock wallabies. There are barbecue facilities.

Festivals

May - Goldrush Festival with street pageants, gold nugget finds, bogout competitions, music and more.
October - Desert Harmony Festival, a week of arts activities. There are theatre productions, bands, cabaret, arts and crafts displays, fashion parades, Aboriginal dancing and cultural displays.

Facilities

Olympic swimming pool, golf course, lawn bowls, squash, tennis and fossicking.
Car Hire: Budget Rent A Car, ✆8962 2402; Herz Rent A Car, ✆8962 2459; Rocky's Taxi Service, ✆8962 2522.

Outlying Attractions

South of Tennant Creek

Devils Marbles

Located 108km (67 miles) south of Tennant Creek on Stuart Highway, the Marbles are huge rounded boulders, incredibly balanced on each other. Some of the boulders seem to have been cleanly sliced in half, but in fact, their shape comes from millions of years of erosion. Sizes of the boulders vary from half a metre to six metres, and some weight thousands of tons. Aboriginal people say that these formations are the fossilized eggs of the Rainbow Serpent, and the site is sacred to them.

Facilities include wood barbecues, picnic area and basic toilet facilities. Camping is allowed, but there is no water.

Devils Marbles Tours operate out of Tennant Creek and can be contacted on ✆8962 2718 or by email ✉ info@devilsmarbles.com.au

Wauchope

Wauchope, which incidentally is pronounced 'walk up' is 113km (70 miles) south of Tennant Creek on the Stuart Highway.

The settlement is actually a pub, offering accommodation, fuel, food, ice and souvenirs, etc. It is good base for exploring the Chinese dig-

The Devils Marbles

gings in the Murchison Ranges. Each July visitors come from miles around to attend the 'Wauchope versus the World' cricket match!

Wycliffe Well

A well stocked store and recently modernised pre-war roadhouse, Wycliffe Well is 136km (84 miles) south of Tennant Creek. The Well was worked by a lady called Doreen Crookes in the 1920s. She married a man named Bill and founded the well-known property, Mt Doreen Station, in Central Australia. She then became interested in heritage and founded the NT National Trust.

There is a licensed restaurant, shop, motel units, swimming pool (guests only), takeaway food and tourist information. Shaded picnic and barbecue areas are available.

Barrow Creek

The tiny township of Barrow Creek, population 12, is 224km (139 miles) south of Tennant Creek. It consists of the historic Barrow Creek Telegraph Station, and the oldest roadhouse on 'The Track', 'The Barrow'.

The Telegraph Station was built in 1872, and is preserved as a memorial to Johns Franks, a linesman, and James Stapleton, the station master, who were killed in a surprise attack by Kaytej tribesmen in 1874. It is open to the public. The Barrow is the ultimate in outback pubs, in that it is exactly as those portrayed in movies of the outback, with real outback characters as patrons. The pub in itself is worth the long drive, and offers accommodation, a bar, dining room, shop, swimming pool (guests only), 6-hole golf course, showers for travellers, takeaway food, ice and fuel, ☏8956 9753.

North of Tennant Creek

Three Ways

Situated at the junction of the Stuart and Barkly Highways, 25km (16 miles) north of Tennant Creek, Three Ways is the major intersection in the heart of scrub country. There is a roadhouse, and a motel, tourist information, licensed restaurant, swimming pool (guests only), takeaway food, souvenirs, fuel, and usually, lots of people. The roadtrains pull in here, and hitchhikers wait here for a lift in one of the three possible directions.

Nearby is a large stone cairn commemorating the Reverend John Flynn.

Attack Creek Historical Reserve

The reserve is 70km (43 miles) north of Tennant Creek, and there is a monument to John McDouall Stuart, whose first attempt at crossing the continent from the south ended here in 1894 when the

party was attacked by Aborigines. An inscribed plaque tells the story.

Churchill's Head is 10km (6 miles) further north, and is a rocky outcrop on the Old Stuart Highway, whose shape closely resembles the head of the British statesman. During the war some American soldiers stuck a log in the 'mouth' of the rock to act as a cigar.

Camping in the area is allowed, and there are picnic tables and wood barbecues.

Renner Springs

Renner Springs, 94km (58 miles) north of Tennant Creek, is a wayside inn that is completely surrounded by the Helen Springs Cattle Station. The roadhouse offers accommodation, and good homestyle food, ☏8964 4505. The building is an old army hut, and it has a small museum of historical objects.

Nearby, at Lubra's Lookout, there is a marker peg for the change from arid to sub-tropical zone.

Elliott

The town of Elliot is 187km (116 miles) north of Tennant Creek, and approximately half way between Alice Springs and Darwin. It has a population of around 600, and is the second largest settlement in the Barkly. The town had its origins in World War II when it was a staging camp for troops on the move between Darwin and Alice Springs, and it is named after Captain Elliot from Adelaide, the officer in charge of the wartime camp.

There is a hotel/motel, and camping areas, and the hotel has a licensed dining room, ©8969 206.

North of Elliot, and 3km (2 miles) west of the Stuart Highway, is the old droving township of Newcastle Waters. The small town is situated at the intersection of the Murranji and Barkly stock routes and near the intermittent waters of Newcastle Creek. If features historic buildings, and a Drovers' Memorial Park. During the Bicentennial year 1988, the Last Great Cattle Drive began here.

Uluru and Alice Springs

Above: Mount Conner in Central Australia   Below: Kata Tjuta (The Olgas)

Left and Above:
Australia's
Kangaroos

Opposite and Below:
Crocodiles in the
Northern Territory

Above and Below: Uluru (Ayers Rock) in Central Austral

Uluru (Ayers Rock) and Kata Tjuta (The Olgas)

Uluru National Park is 465km (289 miles) south-west of Alice Springs, and has an area of 1325 square km (511 sq miles), measuring 72km (45 miles) east-west and 16.5km (10 miles) north-south.

The Yulara Resort, which can accommodate over 5,000 people a day in the various establishments, is 20km (12 miles) from Ayers Rock.

Climate

Average temperatures: January max 37C (99F) - min 22C (72F); July max 19C (66F) - min 5C (41F). Average annual rainfall - 200-250mm (8-10 ins).

Characteristics

The National Park is Australia's first Aboriginal Park, and has the Territory's greatest attraction, Ayers Rock. The Mutitjulu Community are permanent residents in the Park, and 'Uluru' is the Aboriginal name for Ayers Rock.

Uluru is one of the world's greatest monoliths and undergoes amazing colour changes at sunrise and sunset.

The Olgas, 32km (20 miles) to the west, consist of a series of large domes whose colouring and shape are impressive. The Aboriginal name for the Olgas is 'Kata Tjuta' (sometimes written as one word).

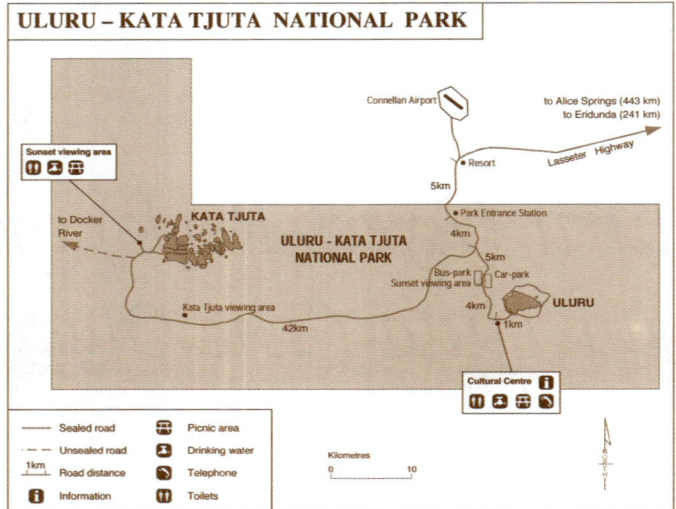

ULURU – KATA TJUTA NATIONAL PARK

Connellan Airport
to Alice Springs (443 km)
to Eridunda (241 km)
Resort
Lasseter Highway
5km
Sunset viewing area
to Docker River
KATA TJUTA
Park Entrance Station
4km
ULURU - KATA TJUTA NATIONAL PARK
5km
Bus-park
Car-park
Sunset viewing area
4km
ULURU
Kata Tjuta viewing area
1km
42km
Cultural Centre

Sealed road
Picnic area
Unsealed road
Drinking water
1km　Road distance
Telephone
Information
Toilets
Kilometres
0　　10

How to Get There

By Bus

Greyhound Pioneer have daily services to Yulara.

By Road

Alice Springs to Uluru is 465km (289 miles).

Alice Springs to Yulara is 445km (277 miles).

Yulara to Uluru is 20km (12 miles).

Yulara to Kata Tjuta is 28km (17 miles).

Yulara to Connellan Airport is 6km (4 miles).

Uluru to Kata Tjuta is 36km (22 miles).

Tourist Information

Visitors Centre is in Yulara Drive, Yulara, ✆(08) 8957 7377, and is ◷open daily 8.30am-5pm.

The Uluru-Kata Tjuta Cultural Centre, Uluru-Kata Tjuta National Park, Yulara, ✆(08) 8956 3138, has displays with a wealth of information on Aboriginal culture, wildlife, landscape and geology of Ayers Rock and the Olgas. It is ◷open 8am-5pm.

There is a Ranger Station at Uluru, with toilets, a kiosk, and information on tours and walks around Ulruru and Kata Tjuta.

The websites to explore are ◉www.centralaustraliantourism.com or ◉www.voyages.com.au

Accommodation

The accommodation prices listed here are for a double room per night, which should be used as a guide only. ✆The telephone area code is 08. You might wish to browse through the websites at 🖰www.ayersrockresort.com.au or 🖰www.voyages.com.au

Sails in the Desert Hotel, Yulara Drive, ✆9399 1040. 228 rooms, licensed restaurant, swimming pool, spa ✪$400-710.

Desert Gardens Hotel, Yulara Drive, ✆9339 1040. 160 units (private facilities), licensed restaurant, swimming pool ✪$320-350.

Outback Pioneer Hotel, Yulara, ✆9339 1040. 125 rooms, pool, licensed restaurant ✪$290-320.

Ayers Rock Campground, Yulara Drive, ✆8956 2055. (Pets allowed on leash) 500 sites, basic facilties, pool barbecue - powered sites ✪$30 for two, cabins $135 for two.

Points of Interest

There is an entrance fee to the National Park of ✪$16.25 per adult, which is valid for 3 consecutive days. If this seems a bit steep, it may help to know that the funds go straight back into the maintenance of the park, and to helping the traditional Anangu owners in their community.

Uluru (Ayers Rock)

The first European to climb Uluru was Englishman William Christie Gosse, and it had taken him about three months to reach the Rock, travelling from Alice Springs with a camel train. The year before, the Rock had been sighted by Ernest Giles, but he never actually reached it, being forced to turn back to Alice Springs because of the salty marshes of Lake Amadeus, 50km (31miles) north of Ayers Rock.

Gosse named the Rock after Sir Henry Ayers, then Chief Secretary and later Premier of South Australia. Giles had previously named the Olgas after Queen Olga of Wurtemberg in Germany.

The first plane landed at the Rock in 1930, piloted by journalist Errol Coote, a member of the support party which accompanied Lasseter in an unsuccessful attempt to locate a reef of gold in the south-west corner of the Northern Territory.

The same year, the first rough track was carved by pastoralist Sid Stanes of Erldunda Station, to Ayers Rock from the Station.

In the early 1940s the first graded road linked the Alice and the Rock, but it was usually impassable after heavy rains. At this time, Ayers Rock and the Olgas formed part of the Petermann Aboriginal Reserve, which covered almost 45,000 sq km (17,370 sq miles) of the south-western part of the Territory. In 1958, both rock formations and about 1325 sq km (511 sq miles) were excised from the reserve to become the Uluru (Ayers Rock/Mt Olga) National Park. The first ranger, Bill Harney, was appointed the same year on a part-time basis, only spending the winter at the Rock.

It was around this time that Alice Springs resident Len Tuit established a base camp to the west of the Ayers Rock climb and started the first tourist operations. The first official record of visitor numbers showed that in 1958, 2296 people made the arduous twelve hour journey from the Alice to gaze in wonder at the giant monolith. The next year leases were granted to two tour companies for the operation of a hotel, four motels, a store, and a service station and fuel depot at the airstrip.

Improvements were made to the road from Alice Springs during the 1960s, and the number of visitors in 1968 was 23,000.

It had been decided in 1965 that there was a need for a resort such as Yulara, but establishing a virtual town in an isolated area with extreme temperatures and no power, water or sewerage was a monumental task. There were many feasibility surveys carried out by both private and government authorities, and finally the Yulara Resort was completed in 1984, one year after the Alice Springs-Ayers Rock

Uluru (Ayers Rock)

road became an all-weather sealed highway.

Now to 'The Rock' itself. The maximum height above ground is 348m (1142 ft); the area is 3.33 sq km (1.28 sq miles); the circumference is 9.4km (5.8 miles); and the height above sea level is 862.5m (2829.7 ft).

Many visitors want to climb Uluru. The traditional owners advise against it – not only because of spiritual beliefs, as is widely thought, but also because of the dangers involved. Far fewer people make the climb now than a decade ago. It is not as easy at it looks, and those with high blood pressure, asthma, angina, fear of heights, or vertigo, should not even contemplate it. There are plaques near the designated climbing spot, dedicated to people who have died trying. For the fit and healthy, the climb up and back takes about two hours, and there is a hand chain to aid climbers on the way up, and steady them on the way down. It is much steeper than it looks, but the view from the summit is worth the effort. Remember to take plenty of water, and a few oranges. If you want to experience at least part of the climb, many people manage to get to 'Chicken Rock', where the chain begins, without much trouble. For those who would prefer to stay at ground level, the Austral-ian National Parks and Wildlife Service have some interesting guided walks, which are free. They either leave from the Ranger Station, or from the Climb Car Park, and ⏱begin about 9.30am. For information, times, and bookings ☏8956 2299.

One walk is around the caves at the base of the Rock with their ancient Aboriginal paintings, and another, with an Aboriginal female guide, introduces visitors to the 'bush tucker' which abounds in the seemingly barren landscape. Both tours include talks on the history and geology of the area, the Aboriginal perception of Uluru, and the flora and fauna.

Then there is the round-the-rock walk, which is on flat land all the way, and takes about 3 to 4 hours. All you need are strong shoes, a sun hat, plenty of cool drinks, and a nice added touch is a picnic hamper from one of the hotels at Yulara. The track is well marked, and passes caves with Aboriginal paintings, little Ayers Rock (known to the Aboriginal people as Taputji), and the beautiful Maggie Springs. When you are walking around the Ayers Rock area you will see signs denoting Aboriginal sacred sites, which are off-limits to visitors. These signs must be obeyed, and that will in no way effect your enjoyment of the walk.

Kata Tjuta (The Olgas), inset: Mt Conner

If you want to take the almost obligatory photograph of the Rock at sunset, you'll have no trouble finding the best spot to take it from, just follow the crowds.

Kata Tjuta (The Olgas)

The 36 domes of Kata Tjuta, together with Uluru and the lesser-known flat-topped monolith called Mount Conner, are all that is left of a mountain chain formed some 600 million years ago. There is no doubt that Uluru is the most famous of the trio, but many visitors judge Kata Tjuta to be more spectacular, and like the Rock, they also change colours at sunrise and sunset.

The Mount Olga Gorge walk is fine for all the family for the first part, then the trail enters a narrow track and becomes more difficult. The Mount Olga Lookout walk is about 3km long, and takes about 90 minutes there and back. It is suitable for all, but only those with some experience should continue along the top of the dome and down to the car park.

The Valley of the Winds walk follows the creek around the base of the dome to the lookout and takes about 2 hours. It is best to check with the Ranger Station at Uluru about details of the walks, and make sure you have plenty of water.

The only facilities at Kata Tjuta are walking trails, car parking areas, and pit toilets.

Yulara

The completion of Yulara (which is an Aboriginal word meaning 'howling' as dingoes do) in late 1984 meant that not only could around 5000 people a day be accommodated near Uluru, but also that the fragile and endangered ecology of the sand-dune lands immediately surrounding the Rock could be restored and protected from further damage.

Yulara

Prior to the development of Yulara, a collection of old and substandard motels and camping areas had grown haphazardly in the shadow of the Rock, and vehicles and visitors had gradually caused damage to the flora. This prevented the sand-dunes from drifting, and caused the animal life to retreat to safer and more peaceful areas.

Uluru was a national park which had been included in a world network organised by UNESCO, and it was obvious that a far-reaching plan was needed to protect the park, and provide better facilities for a growing number of visitors. When you first see the national park, with its red sand-dunes reaching up to 13m, it appears that there could not be much in the way of flora and fauna, but this is not the case. It is home to more than 566 species of flora, approximately 24 species of native mammals, several species of introduced Feral animals (including rabbit, fox, cat, house mouse, camel and dog), around 72 reptiles, and a number of amphibians and aquatic crustaceans. Approximately 161 species of birds have been sighted in the park, many of them being migratory. It was decided to construct Yulara outside the park boundaries, about 20km (12 miles) from Uluru and 30km (19 miles) from Kata Tjuta. This site was selected for a number of reasons - its acceptability to the Aboriginal people who have inhabited Central Australia for around 10,000 years; its proximity to underground water sources; and the views of Uluru and Kata Tjuta which could be afforded visitors. The old accommodation places were closed down and the landscape returned to its natural state. Yulara was designed by Australian architect Philip Cox, and caused quite a sensation when the artist's impressions were first released in 1981.

The reality is no less sensational, with the many characteristic 'sails', used to create shade, making up the main feature. In the complex are shopping, entertainment, information, convention centres and accommodation from five-star downwards.

Separated from the main resort complex by sand-dunes are the campgrounds, staff accommodation, a school, police station, fire station, service station and essential service operations.

Yulara has a resident community of around 2,400 people, and is the fourth largest population centre in the Northern Territory when fully booked.

Tours

There are many National Park and Resort Tours available, and the Visitors' Centre at Yulara has all the details. There are trips to the major attractions of Central Australia, camel rides, cattle station visits, scenic flights, cultural tours, dinner & champagne tours, and more. A selection of operators to contact are Austour ©1800 335 009, Australian Pacific Touring ©1800 891 121, Anangu Tours ©8956 2123, Frontier Camel Tours ©8956 2444, Uluru Experience ©1800 803 174, VIP ©1800 806 142 and Sahara Outback Tours ©1800 806 240.

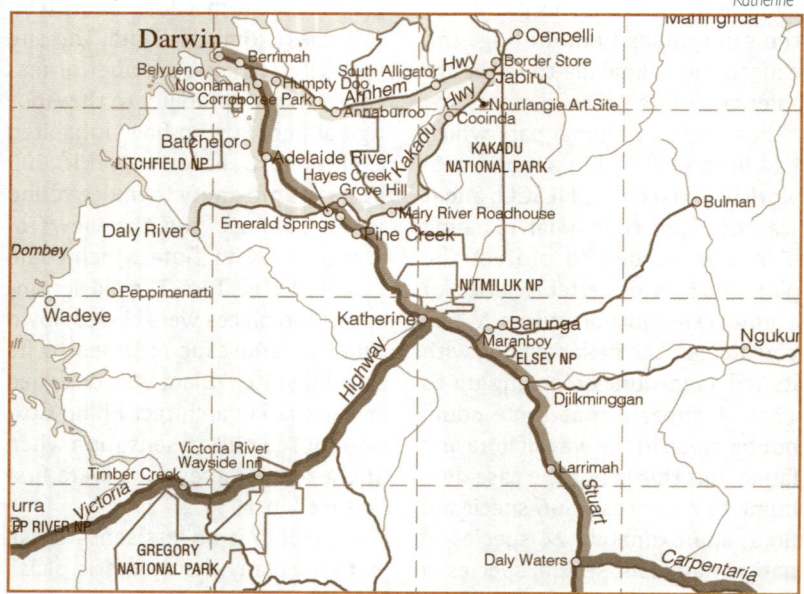

Katherine

Population 10,500
Katherine is situated on the Stuart Highway, 317km (197 miles) south of Darwin and 1182km (734 miles) north of Alice Springs.

Characteristics

Katherine is the heart of the real Outback, and is attracting an increasing number of visitors. In fact, tourism is Katherine's biggest industry, although it also has a rich horticultural and agricultural centre. The RAAF base at Tindal provides jobs for a number of local residents as well as accommodating some 700 personnel and their families. A dairy industry has been established locally, as well as chicken farms, quarries and the manufacture of building products.

The town is also a base for a growing number of gold and other mines, an educational and medical centre, and a major regional base for Commonwealth and Territory Government Departments.

Attractions in the area include places of historic interest, birds and wildlife in their natural surroundings, caves and gorges, Aboriginal lore and art, and for the adventurers, magnificent waterfalls, canyons and billabongs that are still unspoiled.

How to Get There

By Bus
Greyhound, Pioneer and Bus Australia have daily services from Darwin and Alice Springs.

By Road

From Adelaide, Alice Springs and Darwin, via the Stuart Highway.

From Western Australia, via the Great Northern Highway and the Victoria Highway.

From Mount Isa, via the Barkly Highway.

Tourist Information

The Katherine Regional Tourist Association can be contacted on ✆(08) 8972 2650 or by email at ✉krta@nt-tech.com.au

The Katherine Visitor Information Centre can be found on the Stuart Highway (cnr Lindsay Street), ✆(08) 8972 2650.

Accommodation

Here is a selection of available accommodation, with prices for a double room per night, which should be used as a guide only. ✆The telephone area code is 08.

Knotts Crossing Resort Motel, cnr Giles & Cameron Streets, ✆8972 2511. 87 units, licensed restaurant (closed Sun-Mon), bistro, swimming pool, spa ✪$120.

Mercure Inn Katherine, Stuart Highway, ✆8972 1744. 100 units, licensed restaurant, swimming pool, tennis, barbecue ✪$110-125.

Paraway Motel, cnr O'Shea Terrace & First Street, ✆8972 2644. 56 units, licensed restaurant, swimming pool, spa, barbecue ✪$80-100.

Pine Tree Motel, 129 Third Street, ✆8972 2533. 50 units, licensed restaurant, swimming pool ✪$78.

Crossways Hotel/Motel, Katherine Terrace, ✆8972 1022. 19 units, licensed restaurant, bistro, swimming pool ✪$75-90.

Katherine Hotel/Motel, cnr Katherine Terrace & Giles Street, ✆8972 1622. 40 units, licensed restaurant, swimming pool ✪$95.

Riverview Motel, 440 Victoria Highway, ✆8972 1011. 9 units, swimming pool, spa ✪$75.

Springvale Homestead (Motel), Shadforth Road, ✆8972 1355. 60 units, bistro, swimming pool, barbecue ✪$45-50.

Caravan Parks

Katherine Low Level Caravan Park, Shadforth Road, ✆8972 3962. (Pets allowed at owner's discretion) 163 sites, excellent facilities, licensed restaurant, spa, pool, barbecue - powered sites ✪$21 for two, no on-site vans, cabins $75-80 for two.

Nitmiluk (Katherine) Gorge Caravan Park, Nitmiluk Gorge National Park, ✆8972 1253 (No pets allowed) 100 sites, licensed restaurant - powered sites ✪$20 for two, no on-site vans.

Riverview Caravan Park, 440 Victoria Highway, ©8972 1011. (No pets allowed) 116 sites, spa, barbecue, pool - powered sites ✪$19 for two, cabins $65-80 for two.

Eating Out

As mentioned above, most of the motels have licensed or unlicensed restaurants. A couple of other you might like to try are:

Annies Family Restaurant, Hendry Road, ©8972 3637.

Regent Court Restaurant, 25 Warburton St, ©8971 1555.

Points of Interest

Katherine Historical Museum, Gorge Road opposite Katherine Hospital, is housed in the old airport terminal, and has many exhibits of Katherine's colourful past including the Gypsy Moth flown by Dr Clyde Fenton in 1934. The museum is managed by the Katherine Historical Society, and you can buy souvenirs and books on the history of the town. ☺Opening hours are Mon-Fri 10am-4pm, Sat 10am-2pm, Sun 2-5pm, ©8972 3945.

Knott's Crossing, 5km (3 miles) from Katherine via Gorge Road (turn off just past the hospital) is the original river crossing for the young settlement of Katherine. It was made famous by Mrs Aeneas Gunn's book *We of the Never Never*, and is a pleasant picnic and swimming spot.

The **Railway Station Museum**, Railway Terrace, is the National Trust headquarters. The present township grew around the railway after the railbridge was built in 1926. It provided a vital link to Darwin and the southern capitals for the small town. The museum has interesting displays of railway memorabilia, information on the historic sites of Katherine, and has maps, books and other items of interest for sale. It is open Mon-Fri 11am-1pm.

Katherine School of the Air, Gorge Street, ©8972 1833, has ☺guided tours Mon-Fri at 11am, except during school and public holidays.

Hot Springs are found 3km (2 miles) along Victoria Highway, on the banks of the Katherine River. It is a popular swimming spot, with a caravan park and motel adjacent, and a youth hostel nearby.

Katherine Low Level Nature Park, 5km (3 miles) from Katherine via the Victoria Highway, is open shady parkland on the banks of the Katherine River with easy access for swimming and fishing. The river here flows over the weir into a series of shallow rapids. Between November and March, visitors should check the river level on the bridge markers before entering the water. The current can be very strong and dangerous after rain. Facilities include picnic and barbecue areas, but camping is not allowed. There is a privately owned caravan and camping ground nearby.

Springvale Homestead, 8km (5 miles) from Katherine via Zimin Drive and Shadforth Road, ©8972 1355, was the destination on one of the Territory's most epic droving treks. Alfred Giles, well known explorer and pastoralist of the time took 19 months to drive stock from Adelaide. The original homestead is the oldest extant in the Territory. It is shaded by huge Indian raintrees planted by Giles' wife, one for each of her children. The privately operated tourist park runs free tours daily - ☺April to October 10.30am and 2pm; November to March 2pm.

Facilities

A wide range of sports are played in the area. Weekly competitions may be in progress when you visit. Check in the local newspapers for fixtures.

Tours

There are many tours available from Katherine, some to the Gorge, others further afield. The Visitor Centre has details of current prices and times of all tours, and here are some you might like to enquire about.

Barramundi Fish Feeding, Territory Manor, Mataranka, ©8975 4516.

Borroloola Scenic River Cruises, McArthur River Caravan Park, ©8975 8734.

Brolga Tours (Roper River cruises), Mataranka Homestead, ©8975 4544.

Crocodile Spotting Cruise Katherine River, Travel North, ©8971 9999.

Cutta Cutta Caves, Travel North, ©8971 9999.

Fishing Safaris, Rod & Rifle, ©8972 1020.

Kakadu Camping Safari ex Katherine, Travel North, ©8971 9999.

Kakadu Scenic Flights ex Katherine, Kakadu Air, ©8979 2411.

Katherine Day Tours, Travel North, ©8971 9999.

Katherine Extended Tours, Travel

North, ℂ8971 9999.
Katherine Gorge Cruises, Travel North, ℂ8971 9999.
Katherine Gorge Scenic Flights ex Katherine, Travel North, ℂ8971 9999.
Mataranka Day Tours ex Katherine, Travel North, ℂ8971 9999.

Outlying Attractions

Nitmiluk Katherine Gorge National Park

The main entrance to the park is 32km (20 miles) from Katherine on a sealed road. A second park entrance leads to Edith Falls, northwest of the Gorge.

The 180,000ha (444,600 acres) National Park was created to preserve one of the Northern Territory's greatest natural wonders. Over millions of years, torrential summer rains in Arnhem Land during the west season, have caused the waters of the Katherine River to cut thirteen spectacular serpentine gorges. During the dry season, the gorges are placid and calm, but in the wet season they can change into turbulent floodwaters with whirlpools and waves over 2m high.

Cut into ancient rock, the canyon walls climb steeply above cool blue water, and there is abundant bird, fish and animal life, including the fresh water crocodile. The rocks also have excellent examples of ancient Aboriginal art. Privately operated guided boat tours are available to the fifth gorge, or it is possible to hire canoes. A boat tour in the gorges is a highlight of any trip to the Northern Territory, and even if you have seen photographs or films of the scenery, you are still not prepared for the outstanding beauty nor the atmosphere that prevails. Facilities in the Park include a Visitor Centre, picnic and barbecue areas, toilets and a public boat ramp, where boats up to 4m with motors up to 10hp may be launched. No cats or dogs are permitted in the privately owned caravan and camping ground, and dogs are only permitted in the National Park on controlled leads.

There are over 100km (62 miles) of marked walking tracks maintained for easy access to interesting features in the Park. If you intend to do the longer hikes, you must notify the Park Rangers first, and all walkers should collect a guide pamphlet available from the Visitor Centre.

It also should be noted that when taking one of the boat tours, there is some walking involved between gorges. Between the first and second - approximately 500m of well formed pathway and rocks; between second and third - approximately 20m of unformed pathway and rocks; between third and fourth - approximately 1km of unformed pathway, rocks and some climbing;

between fourth and fifth - approximately 600m of unformed pathway, rocks and some climbing. The distances vary for canoeists. It is strongly recommended that you wear comfortable, flat, walking shoes.

Cutta Cutta Caves Nature Park

Situated 27km (17 miles) south of Katherine on the Stuart Highway, the caves were formed millions of years ago, and are still developing today. They are about 15m (49 ft) below the earth's surface, and spread for almost a kilometre. The landscape surrounding the caves is unique and provides a short and interesting walk. Ranger guided tours are available daily April to October, usually on the hour,

©8972 1940. Entrance underground is available only at these times.

Local tour operators in Katherine also have tours available to the caves.

Edith Falls Nature Park

The second entrance to Katherine Gorge National Park is 74km (46 miles) north of Katherine, via the Stuart Highway, and a sealed access road that turns off 47km (29 miles) from the town.

Edith Falls is a series of waterfalls on the edge of the Arnhem Land escarpment. The main waterfall runs all year into a huge natural billabong surrounded by pandanus palms. There are walking tracks, swimming, barbecue and picnic areas, and a camping ground with simple amenities.

Mataranka

Mataranka is 110km (68 miles) south of Katherine on the Stuart Highway, in the heart of Never-Never country. The Mataranka Pool Nature Park was dedicated as a reserve in 1967 to ensure the preservation of the thermal spring in its environs. The pool is a constant 34C (93F) and flows at an amazing 22.5 million litres (4,949,406 gallons) each day. A swim in the pool is an experience that should not be missed. The surrounding rainforest

survives from an earlier age, and feeds from the thermal spring's deep source. Combined with the thermal pool, it creates a very welcome oasis that is a popular spot for visitors.

Mataranka Homestead was established in 1916 by Dr Gilruth, the Administrator of the Northern Territory as an experimental cattle station. It has since become a major tourist resort, and among its attractions is the Elsey Homestead Replica, a faithful copy of the original hand-hewn timber homestead, which contains many interesting displays, and is open to the public.

Elsey Station was established in 1881 and the lease encompassed Mataranka, then known as Bitter Springs. Aeneas Gunn was appointed manager of the Station in 1901, and assumed the position in 1902. The following year he contracted malaria and died. His wife, Jeannie, managed the station for a short time, then returned to Melbourne and wrote her story *We of the Never Never*. The Homestead Replica was used for the set of the film of the book.

Near the homestead are Aboriginal gunyahs, constructed by the 'Duck Creek' people. A free homestead tour is conducted daily ☉May-October, departing from the kiosk at the Mataranka Homestead Tourist Resort, ✆8975 4544.

The Elsey Cemetery, containing the graves of the Station pioneers, including Aeneas Gunn, Muluka, and Henry Peckham (Fizzer) the mailman is 8km (5 miles) east of the Stuart Highway, 13km (8 miles) south of the town.

Larrimah

Gateway to the tropics, Larrimah is 72km (45 miles) south of Mataranka. The township originated in World War II when over 3,000 servicemen were based in and around Larrimah, then the largest army base in Australia. The Gorrie airstrip and railsiding still remain, but are no longer in use. One of the pubs was originally an officers' mess. Larrimah Green Tourist Complex on the Stuart Highway, ✆8975 9937, have live Johnson River crocodiles on display.

Daly Waters

The small township of Daly Waters is 72km (45 miles) south of Larrimah on the Stuart Highway, and is home to the oldest pub in the Territory - the Daly Waters Pub, ✆8975 9927. The pub is virtually an institution, and you really can't say you have seen the Territory if you haven't spent some time in the bar.

Victoria River

On the Victoria Highway, 190km (118 miles) west of Katherine, is the township of Victoria River. The river itself was discovered in 1839 by Lt John Lort Stokes aboard the British Navy sloop Beagle. The town now has a privately owned motel and camping ground servicing the nearby Gregory National Park.

Timber Creek

Continuing along the Victoria Highway, 290km (180 miles) west of Katherine, is Timber Creek, with a population of around 100. The town lies on the Victoria River and gained its name when Augustus

Charles Gregory travelled to the spot and used timber from the banks of the creek to repair a hole in his vessel.

He believed that the river led to the fabled inland sea, and he made two further trips, looking for its source some 800km (497 miles) inland.

Pine Creek

Pine Creek is situated 92km (57 miles) north of Katherine on the Stuart Highway. It was the scene of extensive mining in the 1880s, and is now experiencing a renewal of interest with the reopening of mining activities. In fact, it now hosts one of the biggest gold mines in the Territory. The population of the town is around 600, and there are numerous historical buildings still standing, including the Old Playford Club Hotel, the Repeater Station, the Bakery and the Railway Siding Complex. Private tour operators conduct tours of the surrounding area. For more information contact the Pine Creek Hotel on ✆8976 1288.

Umbrawarra Gorge Nature Park

The Park is 122km (76 miles) from Katherine, and 22km (13 miles) south-west of Pine Creek. The gorge is very rugged, but has pools quite close to the car park. There is a camping ground, picnic facilities, wood barbecues and toilets.

Alice Springs & Uluru

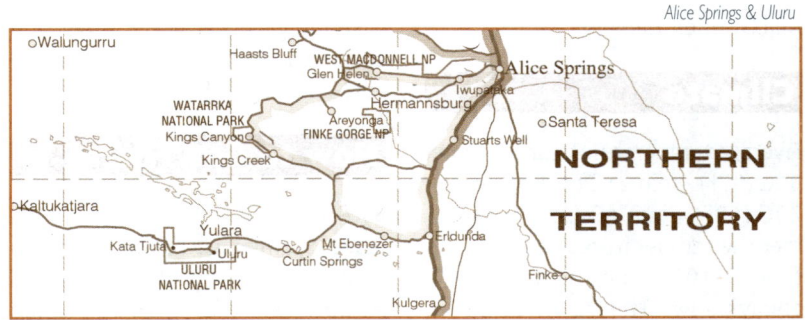

Alice Springs

Population 23,600
Alice Springs is situated in the geographic centre of the Australian continent, 23km (14 miles) south of the Tropic of Capricorn, and at the foot of the picturesque MacDonnell Ranges.

Climate

Average temperatures: January max 36C (97F) - min 21C (70F); July max 20C (68F) - min 4C (39F). In summer the temperatures can reach up to 42C (107F), but the humidity is always low. The town is 610m (2001 ft) above sea level.

Characteristics

The Northern Territory's most famous, and second largest town,

The Alice is a place to visit in its own right, but equally, it is a good base from which to explore the wonders of The Centre. The spectacular MacDonnell Ranges stretch for 150km (93 miles) to both the east and west of Alice Springs, and contain many beautiful and unusual chasms and gorges.

How to Get There

By Air

Alice Springs is 15km (9 miles) south of the airport. There is an Airport Shuttle Service which meets every incoming and outgoing flight, and picks up and drops off from all city accommodation places.

ALICE SPRINGS

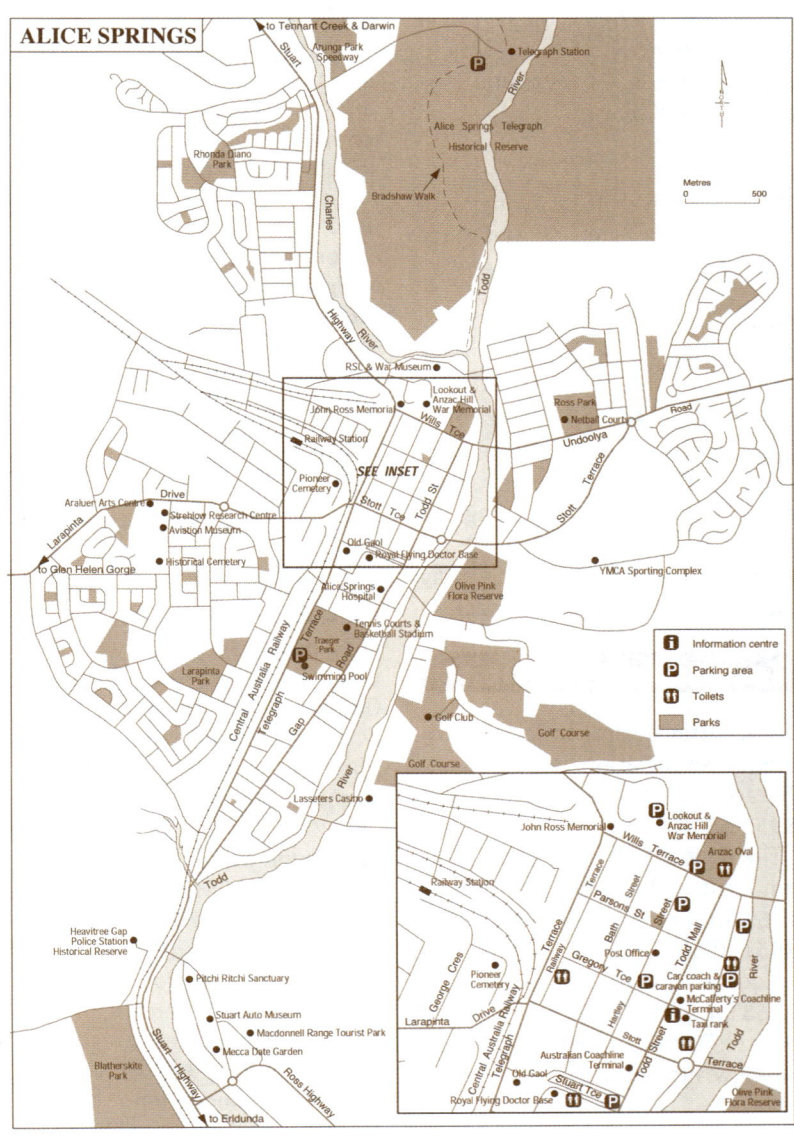

to Tennant Creek & Darwin

Arunga Park Speedway

Stuart

Highway

Charles

River

Telegraph Station

River

Todd

P

Alice Springs Telegraph
Historical Reserve

Rhonda Diano Park

Bradshaw Walk

Metres
0   500

RSL & War Museum

John Ross Memorial

Railway Station

Pioneer Cemetery

SEE INSET

Araluen Arts Centre

Drive

Strehlow Research Centre

Aviation Museum

Larapinta

to Glen Helen Gorge

Historical Cemetery

Lookout &
Anzac Hill
War Memorial

Wills Tce

Stott Tce

Todd St

Old Gaol

Royal Flying Doctor Base

Ross Park

Netball Courts

Undoolya

Road

Stott

Terrace

YMCA Sporting Complex

Alice Springs Hospital

Tennis Courts &
Basketball Stadium

Traeger
Park

Terrace

Gap

Road

Olive Pink
Flora Reserve

Central Australia Railway

Telegraph

P

Swimming Pool

Larapinta
Park

Gap

River

Golf Club

Golf Course

Golf Course

Lasseters Casino

Todd

Heavitree Gap
Police Station
Historical Reserve

Pitchi Ritchi Sanctuary

Stuart Auto Museum

Macdonnell Range Tourist Park

Mecca Date Garden

Blatherskite
Park

Stuart   Highway

Ross Highway

to Erldunda

Information centre

Parking area

Toilets

Parks

Inset

John Ross Memorial

Lookout &
Anzac Hill
War Memorial

P

Anzac Oval

P

Railway Station

Terrace

Wills   Terrace

Parsons   St

Bath   Street

Street

P

George   Cres

Pioneer
Cemetery

Terrace

Railway

Gregory   Tce

Post Office

Car coach &
caravan parking

P

McCafferty's Coachline
Terminal

Taxi rank

Larapinta

Drive

Central Australia Railway

Hartley

Stott

Todd Street

Australian Coachline
Terminal

Old Gaol

Stuart Tce

Royal Flying Doctor Base

P

Todd   (Mall)

River

Terrace

Olive Pink
Flora Reserve

By Bus

Coach companies which travel Australia wide and have depots in Alice Springs are Greyhound Pioneer and McCaffertys.

By Rail

The Ghan travels from Sydney and Melbourne to Adelaide and Alice Springs, ©13 21 47.

By Road

Alice Springs is a long way from everywhere. The Stuart Highway is sealed from Adelaide to Darwin, and the distance from Adelaide to Alice Springs is 1540km (957 miles), and from Alice Springs to Darwin is 1480km (920 miles). Mt Isa to Alice via the Barkly Highway (sealed) is 1180km (733 miles).

Tourist Information

The Central Australian Tourism Industry Association is in Gregory Terrace, ©(08) 8952 5199 or ©(08) 8952 5800.

The regional office of the Northern Territory Tourist Commission is at 67 Stuart Highway North, ©(08) 8951 8555.

Additionally, you can phone ©13 3068 for general information, email ✐ nttc@nttc.com.au or visit ☞www.alice.com.au

Accommodation

A wide variety of accommodation is available, from luxury hotels to youth hostels, and the Tourist Centre has a complete list. Here is a selection with prices for a double room per night, which should be used as a guide only. ©The telephone area code is 08.

Rydges Plaza resort, Barrett Drive, ©8952 8000. 235 rooms (private facilities), licensed restaurant, bistro, swimming pool, spa, sauna, gym, tennis ✪$210.

Alice Springs Vista Hotel, Stephens Road, ©8952 6100. 140 units, licensed restaurant, swimming pool, spa, tennis, barbecue ✪$145.

Alice Motor Inn, 27 Undoolya Road, 8952 2322. 20 units, swimming pool ✪$85-110.

Gapview Resort Hotel Motel, 115 Gap Road, ©8952 6611. 52 units, licensed restaurant, swimming pool, spa, barbecue ✪$85.

Outback Motor Lodge, South Terrace, ©8952 3888. 42 units, swimming pool, barbecue ✪$85-95.

Mount Nancy Motel, Stuart Highway, 8952 9488. 50 units, swimming pool, barbecue ✪$75.

Melanka Lodge Motel, cnr Todd Street & Stott Terrace, ©8952 2233. 55 units, licensed restaurant, barbecue, pool ✪$80-90; backpacker accommodation, 110 rooms ✪$15 per person per night.

Caravan Parks

MacDonnell Range Holiday Park, Palm Place, ✆8952 6111. (No pets allowed) 273 sites, excellent facilities, barbecue, pool playground - powered sites ✪$23 for two, cabins $55-80 for two.

G'Day Mate Tourist Park, Palm Circuit, ✆8952 9589. (No dogs allowed) 86 sites, excellent facilities, pool - powered sites ✪$20-22 for two, on-site vans $50-55 for two, cabins $55-65 for two.

Stuart Caravan Park, Larapinta Drive, ✆8952 2547. (No dogs allowed)150 sites, barbecue, pool - powered sites ✪$21 for two, cabins $50-70 for two.

Wintersun Cabin & Caravan Park, Stuart Highway, ✆8952 4080. (No pets allowed) 105 sites, pool - powered sites ✪$20 for two, cabins $45-90 for two.

Camping

There are quite a few overnight camping sites in the Centre, and for information and pamphlets contact the Parks and Wildlife Commission of the Northern Territory, South Stuart Highway, ✆8951 8211.

The sites are: Henbury Meteorite Craters, Kings Canyon, Chambers Pillar, Trephina Gorge, Ellery Creek Big Hole, Ormiston Gorge, Finke Gorge, Corroboree Rock, N'Dhala Gorge, Ruby Gap, Serpentine Gorge, Redbank Nature Park and Rainbow Valley.

Camping in the Centre is not your ordinary overnight campout, and several precautions have to be taken as regards water, petrol, tyres, clothing, and the risks of fire. The Commission can advise on all these aspects, and their advice should not be ignored.

Local Transport

All major car rental companies are represented in Alice, and there are plenty of taxis.

Bicycles can be hired from Melanka Lodge, ✆8952 2233, and mopeds from Shell Todd, cnr Todd Mall & Wills Terrace, ✆8952 2279.

The Alice Wanderer operates on an hourly circuit visiting the major attractions, and is an explorer-type service. For bookings and enquiries ✆8952 2111.

Eating Out

As with accommodation, Alice has a wide variety of eating places, ranging from takeaways and coffee shops along Todd Mall and in the Yeperenye Shopping Complex on Hartley Street.

KFC, Red Rooster, Hungry Jacks, Long John Silvers have all found their way to the Alice, and counter lunches can be obtained at the Stuart Arms Bistro in Todd Mall.

Following are some restaurants

you might like to try:

The Palms Restaurant at Alice Springs Pacific Resort, 34 Stott Terrace, ☏8951 4545 - licensed, a la carte menu, ☼open nightly from 6.30pm.

Golden Inn Chinese Restaurant, 9 Undoolya Road, ☏8952 6910 - licensed, Cantonese, Szechuan, Malaysian - ☼open Mon-Fri noon-2pm, 5-10.30pm, Sat-Sun 5-10.30pm.

The Overlanders Steakhouse, 72 Hartley Street, ☏8952 2159 - licensed, Australian food including buffalo, camel and kangaroo steaks - ☼open seven nights from 6pm, and weekdays for lunch.

La Casalinga, 105 Gregory Terrace, ☏8952 4508 - licensed, Italian and pizza bar - ☼open seven days, restaurant 6-10pm, pizza bar 5pm-1am.

Keller's, Diplomat Hotel, Shop 1, Gregory Terrace, ☏8952 3188 - Swiss and Indian cuisine - take away available.

Bojangles Saloon & Restaurant, 80 Todd Street, ☏(08) 8952 2873.

Entertainment

The famous **Ted Egan Outback Show**, with tall tales and outback songs, is presented ☼Tues, Thurs, Sat & Sun at 8pm at the Chateau Hornsby Winery, Petrick Road. Bookings are essential, ☏8952 9952. Ted is almost an Alice Springs legend, and his show is top entertainment. If you notice that many people are singing along with him, it is because they are part of coach tours that have been listening to tapes of his songs all the way to the Alice. Dinner is available from 6pm.

Lasseters Hotel Casino, 93 Barrett Drive, ☏8950 7777, has poker machines and keno from 1pm and gaming tables from 7pm, and is ☼open till very late. Dress regulations apply - no cords or jeans for men or women, and men must wear dress shoes.

Rio's Nitespot, at the Casino, has a disco from 9.30pm on Thurs-Sat. Simpsons Gap Bar in the Sheraton Hotel has live entertainment from 8.30pm, Mon-Sat.

Heavitree Gap Tavern, at the Heavitree Gap Tourist Resort, off Ross Highway, ☏8950 4413, has a disco Fri-Sat 9pm-2am, and live entertainment from 4pm Sun.

Alice Springs Gapview Resort, 115 Gap Road, ☏8952 6611, has a disco Wed-Sun 9.30pm-2am.

Araluen Arts Centre, Larapinta Drive, ☏8951 1120, has live theatre and films, and on the first Saturday of every month there is a cabaret in the Bistro.

Points of Interest

Your first stop should be **Anzac Hill** which offers a good view of the town and the surrounding ranges. Sunset and sunrise are the best times for photographers, as the hills glow with colour. To get there by car turn off the Stuart Highway just past the Shell depot, or you can walk up via the Lions walk, opposite the Catholic Church on Wills Terrace.

Adelaide House Museum, Todd Mall, was built by the Australian Inland Mission 1920-1926 as the first Alice Springs Hospital, and was designed by Rev John Flynn. It is ⏱open to the public Mon-Fri 10am-4pm, Sat 10am-noon (closed December to February). Admission is ✪$3.30 adult and $2.20 child.

Flynn Memorial Church, Todd Mall, was built in memory of the late Reverend John Flynn, founder of the Royal Flying Doctor Service and Australian Inland Missions.

Museum of Central Australia is in the Alice Springs Cultural Precinct on Larapinta Drive. Displays include the Fine Art and Natural History of this arid region. ⏱Open daily 9am-5pm, ✆8951 1122. Admission is ✪$7 adult and $4 concession for the Cultural Precinct, which includes the Aviation Museum.

The **Central Australian Aviation Museum** is housed in the Connellan Hangar on Alice Springs' original airport in Memorial Drive.

It is ☼open Mon-Fri 9am-4pm, Sat-Sun 10am-2pm, ✆8951 1122.

The **Old Court House**, cnr Parsons & Hartley Streets, was built originally as the Administrator's Council Rooms and as the Mining Wardens Court. It can only be viewed from the outside.

The Residency, on the corner of Parsons and Hartley Streets, was built in 1926-27 for John Charles Cawood, the first Government Resident in Alice Springs. It is now owned and operated by the Museums and Art Galleries Board of the Northern Territory, and is ☼open daily 9am-5pm, ✆8951 5688. Admission is free.

Old Stuart Town Gaol, Parsons Street, was built in 1907-8, and is the oldest building remaining in the Alice Springs town area. The Gaol is ☼open Mon-Fri 10am-12.30pm, Sat 9.30-noon.

Old Hartley Street School was opened at the end of 1929, and the octagonal room was added in 1946. The School is now the office and shop of the National Trust Australia (NT). It is ☼open daily from 10.30am-2.30pm.

The Panorama Guth, in 65 Hartley Street, is a 360 degree painted landscape, and should not be missed. It is ☼open Mon-Sat 9am-5pm, Sun 12-5pm, ✆8952 2013. Admission is ✪$5.50 adult, $3.30 child.

Old Tunk's Store, cnr Hartley Street & Stott Terrace, was built as a grocery and general store about 1940, and was used as such until 1980. It is now the town office of Hertz NT.

The **Old Government Homes**, further along Hartley Street, were designed for senior Government officers in the 1930s.

Royal Flying Doctor Base was funded by the women of South Australia as a centenary memorial to the pioneer women of the State. The late Harry Rolland, a government architect, designed the radio building and operators' quarters. The base is ☼open Mon-Sat 9am-4pm, Sun 1-4pm, ✆8952 1129. Admission is ✪$5.50 adult, $2.20 child.

Gnoilya (Wild Dog) Tmerga is a registered sacred site in a chained-off enclosure in the Stuart Transit Plaza. Known as Wild Dog Rock, it tells the story of an Aboriginal Legend.

The above attractions, and more, are included in a Heritage Walk that has been organised, and the Tourist Offices have all the details.

The **Telegraph Station**, the original Alice Springs communication post, is 3km north on the Stuart Highway. It features the original building and equipment in an historic reserve, and is a pleasant picnic spot. ☼Open daily 8am-5pm, with entry ⊙$6 adult and $3 child.

School of The Air, Head Street next to Braitling School, is ⊙open for visitors Mon-Fri 1.30-3.30pm. It is closed weekends, public holidays, for school activities and during the Christmas vacation. Admission is ⊙$3.50 adult, $2.50 child and it is ⊙open Mon-Sat 8.30am-4.30pm, Sun 1.30pm-4.30pm.

Olive Pink Flora Reserve, Tunks Road Golf Course Causeway, has a large variety of native shrubs and trees from a 300km (186 miles) radius of Alice Springs, and an excellent information centre. ⊙Open daily 10am-4pm, ©8952 2154.

The **Kookaburra Memorial**, next to the Aviation Museum is open during the same hours.

Alice Springs Memorial Cemetery is the final resting place of many pioneers and famous personalities, including Albert Namatjira, Harold Lasseter of the elusive 'Lasseter's Reef', and E.J. Connellan, founder of Connellan Airways, the Territory's first airline.

Diarama Village, on Larapinta Drive, depicts myths and legends of the Australian Aborigines, and also has a good selection of arts and crafts. ⊙Open daily 10am-5pm, ©8952 1884.

The Date Gardens, Palm Circuit, is Australia's first commercial date garden. It is ⊙open Mon-Sat 9am-

5pm, Sun 10am-4pm, ©8952 8493.

Frontier Camel Tours, Ross Highway, ©8953 0444, is a camel museum, and offers camel rides. It is ⊙open daily 9am-5pm, and is one of the most popular attractions in Alice.

Alice Springs Reptile Centre, 9 Stuart Terrace, has a large collection of Central Australian reptiles. It is ⊙open daily 9am-5pm, ©8952 8900. Admission is ⊙$7 adult, $4 child, and the centre is ⊙open daily 9am-5pm.

Alice Springs Desert Park, Larapinta Drive, ©8951 8788, showcases a selection of the flora and fauna which are part of the desert landscape. The Nocturnal House is excellent. The award-winning attraction is ⊙open 7.30am-6pm daily and admission is ⊙$18 adult, $9 child and $40 family.

The **Old Timers' Folk Museum**, south on the Stuart Highway, has exhibits dating back to the 1890s. It is ⊙open daily 2-4pm, ©8952 2844, with admission prices at ⊙$2 adult, children free.

The **Ghan Preservation Society**, 5km south of Alice in Norris Bell Avenue, is ☉open daily, but train rides are only available Wed, Thurs, Fri and Sun, ✆8955 5047. The museum charges admission at ✪$5.50 adult, $3.30 child.

Chateau Hornsby, Petrick Road, off South Stuart Highway, ✆8955 5133, is 15km (9 miles) from the heart of Alice Springs, and is Central Australia's first and only winery. Tours are available, as are barbecue lunches, and there is a restaurant. It is ☉open daily 10am-5pm between March and December.

Festivals

The Bangtail Muster is held on the first Monday in May, which is a public holiday in the Northern Territory. There is a parade of floats and a sort of Mini-Moomba. It is a great day for the kids.

The Camel Cup is held on the second Saturday in May, and is organised by the local Lions Club. This camel race has been held every year since 1971.

The Food and Wine Festival is held the day after the Camel Cup on the Lawns of the Verdi Club, Undoolya Road, beginning at 11am. There is a great deal of entertainment, with live music throughout the day. Wynn's Finke Desert Race - Alice-Finke-Alice, is held over the Queen's Birthday weekend in June. Finke is 240km (149 miles) south of Alice Springs, and the competitors and pit crews camp out in cold temperatures overnight at Finke, then the race recommences next morning for the trip back to Alice.

Alice Springs Rodeo is held in August/September, and cowboys and cowgirls from all over Australia compete for top prize money.

Henley-On-Todd is held in September, and is an incredible event. The ingredients for its success are: a dry river bed, bottomless boats, and plenty of human horse-power. The regatta begins with a parade of the different craft down Todd Mall, then the races start at 9.30am in the Todd River next to the Anzac Oval.

Beerfest is held the day after Henley-On-Todd at the Verdi Club. It begins at 11.30am, with entertainment throughout the day, 40 different varieties of beer, and lots of food of different nationalities.

Facilities

Lawn bowls, golf, squash, swimming, tennis, indoor cricket and horse racing.

Tours

There are many tour companies in Alice Springs offering tours in and around the town by coach, plane, helicopter, camel or horse. The Tourist Centre has a complete list, and can advise on the best tour to suit your requirements.

Outlying Attractions

The Parks and Wildlife Commission of the Northern Territory offer Ranger guided tours and talks available at the parks around Alice Springs. For information on these very interesting tours contact the Commission, ©8951 8788, or the Alice Springs Regional Tourist Association.

West of Alice

John Flynn's Grave Historical Reserve

7km (4 miles) west of Alice Springs on Larapinta Drive, there is a stone cairn which contains the ashes of Reverend John Flynn, the founder of the Australian Inland Mission, The Royal Flying Doctor Service, the first inland medical centre, and an outback padre patrol system. The cairn is crowned by a large boulder from the Devil's Marbles. The reserve has no facilities.

Simpsons Gap National Park

The Park is located in the West MacDonnell Ranges, 18km (11 miles) from Alice Springs, and is one of the largest parks in Central Australia. Access is via Larapinta Drive, then a signposted turnoff into the Park, and is suitable for conventional vehicles. The Park actually commences only 8km (5 miles) from Alice, but the Visitor Centre is a further 10km (6 miles) into the Park, and there is always a Ranger on site. The centre has a display illustrating aspects of the natural history of the area, toilets and a parking area. 5km (3 miles) further into the park there is a developed picnic area. The Park is ©open daily 8am-8pm, and is accessible year round, with the cooler months from April to September being the most pleasant. During summer, the high temperatures make bushwalking uncomfortable. The best times to observe the native wildlife are early morning and late afternoon. There are numerous opportunities for bushwalking, and while most walks are not marked, there are natural landmarks that offer adequate guidance.

Standley Chasm

The Chasm is a steep cleft in the MacDonnell Ranges, and is about 50km (31 miles) west of Alice. The reserve is ©open daily 8.30am-

4.30pm, and has a kiosk, barbecues and toilets. The entrance fee is minimal, and the Chasm is a photographer's delight when the sun is overhead and lights up the red walls.

Ellery Creek Big Hole Nature Park

93km (58 miles) west of Alice Springs on Namitjira Drive is another gorge with high red cliffs and a large waterhole with shady River Red Gums. There are picnic facilities and toilets.

Serpentine Gorge Nature Park

This gorge is 104km (65 miles) to the west, and is narrow and winding with waterholes and bush scenery. The entry road is a bit rough, and there are barbecue and toilet facilities.

Ormiston Gorge and Pound National Park

Pound National Park is the largest park in the Western MacDonnell Ranges, and its most popular feature is Ormiston Gorge, the catchment area of the Finke River, thought to be the oldest river in the world. The Gorge has a near-permanent waterhole at its southern end.

Access to the Park is suitable for conventional vehicles, although periods of heavy rainfall can cut the roads due to flooding. Up-to-date information on road conditions are available by phoning Road Reports on ©1800 246 199.

The park has picnic facilities for day visitors, including gas barbecues and toilets. The small general campground is suitable for tents, campervans and caravans. The other campground caters for large groups and coach tours. Both campgrounds have barbecues, toilets and showers, but all visitors are advised to bring their own drinking water.

There is a Visitor Information Centre in the Park, and they can advise on all the bush walks available.

Glen Helen Gorge Nature Park

Glen Helen Gorge is 133km (83 miles) from Alice Springs, and has been formed by the Finke River cutting through the MacDonnell Ranges. There is a 30m (98 ft) deep waterhole, which the Aborigines believed was the home of the Giant Watersnake. Next door to the Park is the Glen Helen Homestead, ✆8956 7489, which offers accommodation, a caravan park and barbecue facilities.

Redbank Nature Park

Redbank Gorge is 30km (19 miles) west of Glen Helen, and there are several very deep and cold pools along its 800m (875 yds) length. As with the other gorges, the scenery is magnificent, and there are picnic facilities.

Hermannsburg

The historic buildings of Hermannsburg are 123km (76 miles) south-west of Alice Springs on Larapinta Drive. It was established as a mission by the Lutheran Church, and is now owned by the Aranda People who are restoring the old buildings with the help of the National Trust. The Kata-anga Tearooms are ☺open daily 9am-

1pm, and Aboriginal artefacts are available.

Finke Gorge National Park

The Park covers 46,000ha (113,620 acres), including the famous Palm Valley. The Park is best known for its population of the rare palm Livistona mariae or Red Cabbage Palm. These 3000 or so palms have survived here for at least 10,000 years, and are unique to the area.

The Park is 16km (10 miles) south of Hermannsburg, and 138km (86 miles) from Alice Springs. The access road requires 4WD, and there are barbecues and toilets.

South of Alice

Rainbow Valley Nature Park

The park's main attraction is seen at its best in later afternoon, when the setting sun shines directly onto a stark range of richly-coloured sandstones. There are picnic facilities, and 4WD is recommended. The Park is 101km (63 miles) south of Alice Springs, turning off the Stuart Highway at 85km (53 miles).

Henbury Meteorites Conservation Reserve

Located 145km (90 miles) southwest of Alice Springs, the Park can be reached in conventional vehicles, and is accessible year round.

The Reserve contains twelve craters which were formed when a meteor hit the earth's surface at the main crater, 4700 years ago. The meteor disintegrated before impact, and the fragments formed the twelve craters. They are of interest to scientists due to their similarity to the moon's surface.

There is no drinking water in the area, and very little firewood, so visitors should take their own. Facilities include wood barbecues, picnic furniture, a pit toilet and self guiding walking tracks.

Watarrka National Park

This park contains the western end of the George Gill Range, which includes the scenically splendid Kings Canyon, attractive rockholes and areas of lush vegetation. The Canyon features a plateau of rock domes, and sandstone walls rising up 100m, covered with rock carvings formed by the erosive action of wind and water.

The park is about 310km (193 miles) south-west of Alice Springs, and is accessible by conventional vehicles. Facilities include parking areas, toilets, showers and barbecues. Wallara Ranch, near the junction of Angus Downs and Ernest Giles Road, has accommodation, food and fuel.

Ewaninga Rock Carvings Conservation Reserve

The Reserve is 39km (24 miles) down the Old South Road from Alice Springs, and the carvings are thought to predate the Aborigines who reside in the area now, as they have no knowledge of their origin or meaning. There are barbecues, toilets and explanatory signs.

Chambers Pillar Historical Reserve

This impressive sandstone pillar was used as a landmark by early pioneers, and many tales of hardship have been carved in the base. It is 149km (93 miles) south of Alice on the Old South Road, and access is by 4WD only.

East of Alice

Emily and Jessie Gap Nature Park

These are two gaps in the MacDonnell Ranges, 13km and 18km (8 and 11 miles) respectively, east of Alice Springs. They are very scenic and have great significance to the Aborigines. There are barbecue and toilet facilities.

Corroboree Rock Conservation Reserve

Another scenic pillar of rock which is significant to Aborigines is 48km (30 miles) east of Alice Springs, and has barbecue and toilet facilities.

Trephina Gorge Nature Park

Situated in the East MacDonnell Ranges, Trephina Gorge Nature Park is noted for its sheer quartzite cliffs and River Red Gum lined watercourses. There are two gorges in the park - Trephina Gorge, with its wide views and sandy creek bed, and John Hayes Rock Hole, which attracts many animals and birds.

The Park is 85km (53 miles) east of Alice Springs, and is accessible to all vehicles, although the John Hayes Rockhole track is recommended only for vehicles with a high ground clearance, as there are a number of rough crossings.

There are three picnic areas, each with toilet facilities, wood barbecues and picnic benches. Camping areas are located at Trephina Bluff and Trephina Gorge, where water is provided.

Ross River Homestead

Originally the Love's Creek Station, this is now a ranch style resort, and is 88km (55 miles) east of Alice, and 15km (9 miles) east of Trephina Gorge. All facilities are available, including fuel.

N'Dhala Gorge Nature Park

Access to this park is 4WD recommended, and it is 98km (61 miles) east of Alice Springs. The scenery is magnificent, and there are ancient Aboriginal rock carvings. The park has barbecue and toilet facilities.

Arltunga Historical Reserve

Alluvial gold was discovered in a dry creek bed downstream from Paddy's Rockhole in 1887, and at one time the area supported 3000 people. Mining activity in the area continued for 30 years.

Now you can explore the ruins of a number of stone buildings, some of which have been largely restored.

The Reserve is 110km (68 miles) east of Alice Springs, and can be reached and explored in conventional vehicles. There is a small interpretive visitor display and toilet block near the entrance, and picnic facilities are located at the Historic Mine Walks parking area and at the Great Western Mine parking area. Toilets and a picnic area are also provided at the Police Station/Kangaroo Well parking area. There are Rangers on duty in the Park.

For more information phone ℂ8956 9661.

Ruby Gap Nature Park

Access to this park is by 4WD only, and there are no facilities, just beautiful gorges along the Hale River.

Above: The Devils Marbles   Below: Victoria River in Gregory National Park in the Northern Territory

Queensland

Brisbane

Population 1,601,416
Brisbane, the capital city of Queensland, is situated on the banks of the Brisbane River, 32km (20 miles) upstream from Moreton Bay.

Climate

Average temperatures: January max 30C (86F) - min 19C (66F); July max 18C (64F) - min 6C (43F). Average annual rainfall - 1148mm (45 ins).

Characteristics

Brisbane, the capital of the Sunshine State, is a major international and interstate gateway to an exciting hub of tourism in the Pacific.

The sub-tropical city enjoys an easy-going, relaxed lifestyle, and offers the visitor a great introduction to the holiday resort destinations of the Gold Coast, and the less developed Sunshine Coast.

Just 20 minutes from the city centre you can see (and hold) koalas in their natural habitat at Lone Park Koala Sanctuary or watch sheep shearing at the Australian Woolshed. Brisbane Forest Park, with its abundant fauna and flora, not to mention rainforest, is right on the doorstep. So too are the islands of Moreton Bay - all 300 of them.

In the last decade, Brisbane has turned to the river, and fairly recent developments like Southbank and The Riverside Centre, famous for its popular Sunday craft markets, Waterfront Place, have changed the look of the city. A sightseeing cruise on the paddlewheeler, _River Queen_, is a highlight of any visit to the city.

How to Get There

By Air
As you would expect of a capital city, the Brisbane Airport is well-serviced.

International flights arrive direct from New Zealand, Asia & Pacific, Britain and Europe. North America is linked via Sydney and Auckland.

The domestic carrier Qantas, ✆13 1313 has direct flights from/to Australian capital cities and selected major regional towns. At present, Virgin Blue, ✆13 6789, and Ansett, ✆13 1300, operate from eastern state capital cities only.

By Bus
Greyhound Pioneer, ✆13 2030, and McCaffertys, ✆13 1499, have the following return services: Brisbane/Sydney, Brisbane/Cairns with connections to Darwin and Alice Springs, and Brisbane/Melbourne.

By Rail
Queensland Rail, ✆13 2232, operates a Traveltrain service that links destinations around the state. Citytrains (✆131 230) run north from Brisbane to the Sunshine Coast and south to the Gold Coast. The Queenslander and Sunlander are two additional services connecting Brisbane to areas as far north as Cairns. The Capricornian links the capital city with Rockhampton.

From Sydney, Countrylink XPT trains run directly to Brisbane daily. Alternatively, you can take the XPT to Murwillumbah and change to a connecting coach to complete the journey.

From Melbourne, you must take a Countrylink train to Sydney and then change trains for the next leg of the trip.

By Road
From Sydney, via the Pacific Highway along the coast - 1001km (622 miles); or inland via the New England and Cunningham Highways - 1033km (642 miles).

Visitor Information

The Brisbane Visitor Information Centre is situated in the Queen Street Mall, ✆(07) 3006 6290. It is ☺open Mon-Fri 9am-5pm, Sat 9am-4pm, Sun 10am-4pm. Their email address is ✉ enquiries@brisbane tourism.com.au and the website to visit is ☞www.brisbanetourism.com.au

The Queensland Travel Centre, 30 Makerston Street, ✆13 8833, is ☺open Mon-Fri 8.30am-5pm, Sat 9am-1pm. They can be emailed at

✐ queensland@qttc.com.au or visited at the website ☞www.tq.com.au

Tourism Queensland, Level 36, Riverside Centre, 123 Eagle Street, ✆(07) 3406 5400, is ☺open Mon-Fri 9am-5pm.

Two other internet addresses worth visiting are the Brisbane section of ☞www.queensland-holidays.com.au or the local coucil website at ☞www.brisbane.qld.gov.au

For Backpacker Budget Beaters, contact the Brisbane Visitor Information Centre. They offer a number of activities with reduced prices, such as ✪$10 return ferry to nearby North Stradbroke Island, where you can go bushwalking and dolphin spotting.

The newspaper, the *Courier-Mail* publishes a travel section every Friday, which details drives, picnic and camping spots.

Emergency telephone numbers: Police, Fire Department, Ambulance - ✆000; Doctor - Travellers Medical Service - ✆3211 3611; Police Station - ✆3364 6464.

The Royal Automobile Club of Queensland has a breakdown service, ✆131 111.

Banks are ☺open 9.30am-4pm Mon-Thu, and until 5pm on Fri. Major banks are represented by branches in the city centre, chiefly on Queen and Adelaide Streets.

The Australian Foreign Affairs Department is in the Commonwealth Centre, 295 Ann Street, ✆3225 0122.

Accommodation

Brisbane has several 5-star international hotels, older style hotels, motels, guest houses, private hotels and many youth hostels. As with any large city, accommodation in the suburbs is often less expensive than in the city itself, and the Tourist Information Centres has a list of what is available.

Here we have a selection of city hotels and motels, with prices for a double room per night, which should be used as a guide only. The telephone area code is 07.

Brisbane Hilton, 190 Elizabeth Street, ✆3234 2000 - 320 rooms, 6 suites, licensed restaurant, heated swimming pool, spa, sauna, gym, tennis - ✪$255-330.

Sheraton Brisbane Hotel & Towers, 249 Turbot Street, ✆3835 3535. 410 rooms, 25 suites, licensed restaurant, bistro, swimming pool, spa, sauna, gym, squash - ✪$150-320.

Country Comfort Lennons Hotel, 66 Queen Street, ✆3222 3222. 187 rooms, licensed restaurant, heated swimming pool, spa, sauna - ✪$125-180.

Holiday Inn Brisbane, Roma Street, ✆3238 2222. 191 rooms, 27

suites, licensed restaurant, sauna, undercover carpark, spa, gym - ✪$105-150.

The Chifley on George, 103 George Street, ✆3221 6044. 99 rooms, licensed restaurant, swimming pool, putting green, spa - ✪$120-140.

Metropolitan Motor Inn, 106 Leichhardt Street (cnr Little Edward Street), ✆3831 6000. 54 units, licensed restaurant - ✪$90.

Astor Motel, 193 Wickham Terrace, ✆3831 9522. 61 units, 17 suites - ✪$65-100.

Soho Motel, 333 Wickham Terrace, ✆3831 7722. 50 units, licensed restaurant, undercover parking - ✪$80.

Ruth Fairfax House - QCWA Club (B&B), 89 Gregory Terrace, ✆3831 8188. 36 rooms, communal tea making and refrigerator - ✪$70 including breakfast and dinner.

Acacia Inner City, 413 Upper Edward Street, ✆3832 1663. 57 rooms - ✪$50-70.

The latest additions to the Brisbane skyline are:

Mercure Hotel Brisbane, 85 North Quay, ✆3236 3300. 175 rooms, 15 suites, spa, sauna, licensed restaurant, room service, swimming pool - ✪$130-180.

The Point On Shaftson, 21 Lambert Street, Kangaroo Point, ✆3240 0888. 106 rooms, gym, heated pool, tennis court, children's area - from ✪$110-180.

Caravan Parks

Colonial Village Motel, 351 Beams Road, Taigum, ✆3865 0000. Licensed restaurant, tennis, pool -

powered sites ✪$20 for two, cabins $55-65 for two.

Dress Circle Mobile Village, 10 Holmead Road, Eight Mile Plains, ©3341 6133. Pool, barbecue - powered sites ✪$30 for two, cabins $80-100 for two.

Sheldon Motel & Caravan Park, 27 Holmead Road, Eight Mile Plains, ©3341 6166. Pool, barbecue - powered sites ✪$16 for two, cabins $55 for two.

Gateway Village, 200 School Road, Rochedale, ©3341 6333. 148 sites, barbecue, pool, playground, recreation room - powered sites ✪$24 for two, villas $85-100 for two.

Durack Gardens Caravan Park, 758 Blunder Road, Durack, ©3372 7300. Tennis, pool, barbecue - powered sites ✪$17 for two, on-site vans $25 for two, cabins $45 for two.

There is a **Youth Hostel** at 392 Upper Roma Street, ©3236 1004. It has 52 rooms at ✪$22 per person twin share. **Palace Backpackers** is an alternative, located at 308 Edward Street, ©3211 2433.

Local Transport

Bus

Bus routes and timetables can be downloaded from the ◉www. transinfo.qld.gov.au webpage, or you can phone ©13 12 30 (interstate callers: ©07 3215 500).

As a basic guide, the CityCircle bus (333) is blue and white, and travels around the centre of the city frequently. The white and yellow Citybuses service the city and suburbs, with many stops in between. Buses with blue and yellow stripes are the Cityxpress buses, which have express routes every half hour from designated stops. Buses to most suburbs leave from the city terminal. Day Rover tickets are available for ✪$8, entitling you to unlimited trips on all public buses, ferries and City Cats. Fare saver cards are also available. Buses to the Redcliffe Peninsula operate daily from outside the Transit Centre.

The *City Sights* tour is designed to familiarise visitors with the city so that they have an idea about what's on offer and can decide for themselves the places where they would prefer to spend some time. The tour costs ✪$20 and includes unlimited travel on buses and CityCats on the same day. Phone ©13 12 30 for more details.

Train

The new Airtrain now operates from Brisane Airport to the Gold Coast, stopping at Brisbane Central and Roma stations. For information, ring Transinfo ©13 12 30, interstate ©07 3215 5000, or visit the website at www.transinfo.qld. gov.au

A suburban train service operates

regularly throughout the city. The main city centre stations are Roma Street at the Brisbane Transit Centre, Central (next to the Sheraton Hotel on Turbot Street), and Brunswick Street Station in Fortitude Valley. For information, visit the same website listed above or call Transinfo on ☎13 12 30.

Ferry

Regular commuter services operate daily on the Brisbane River. For details and City Cat and City Ferry timetables, explore the website mentioned above or phone ☎13 12 30.

Taxi

Taxis may be hailed in the street, engaged at taxi stands, or at the front of the big city hotels, or you can book by phone. Two companies are: Yellow Cabs, ☎13 1924 and Black & White Cabs, ☎13 1008.

Car

Car hire companies are: Avis, ☎13 6333; Budget Rent A Car, ☎13 2727; Thrifty Car Rental, ☎3252 5994; Abel Rent A Car, ☎13 14 29; Hertz, ☎13 30 39.

There are many parking stations in and around the city, and the Tourist Information Centre has a full list.

Eating Out

City centre restaurants, riverside bistros and off-the-beaten-track eateries provide a host of different menus from around the globe.

Queensland's famous mudcrabs are always a favourite with locals and visitors alike, as are the not-so-famous Moreton Bay Bugs, which are a cross between a lobster and a crab. Tropical fruits also feature prominently on most menus.

The Tourist Bureau has a full list of restaurants, both in the city and in the suburbs, but here are some you might like to try.

Summit, Sir Samuel Griffith Drive, Mt Coot-tha, ☎3369 9922. Claims the best views over Brisbane, from the Mt Coot-tha Lookout. Licensed, Modern Australian cuisine. Open for lunch and dinner, brunch on Sundays. The Kuta Cafe and Kuta Gift Shop are nearby. Open daily.

Customs House Brasserie, 399 Queen Street, ☎3365 8921. Overlooks the Story Bridge on the Brisbane River. Alfresco dining with a heritage theme. A wide international food selection, from Thai to Italian to Modern Australian influences. Open daily.

Romeo's, 216 Petrie Terrace, ☎3367 0955. Award-winning traditional Italian restaurant with a Venetian emphasis. The interesting menu includes pastas, meats and seafood.

Spanish Garden Steakhouse, at the Breakfast Creek Hotel, 2 Kingsford

Smith Drive, Breakfast Creek, ©3262 5988. Try the Steakhouse for the best steaks in town.

Wang Dynasty, Ground Level, Riverside, South Bank, ©3844 8318. Most Asian styles are represented, including Chinese, Thai, Japanese and Singaporean, but there are a couple of surprises, like crocodile and kangaroo. It is open for lunch and dinner seven days, and has views of the river and parklands nearby.

Parklands Bar & Grill, at the Rydges South Bank Hotel, Grey Street, South Bank, ©3364 0844. Live entertainment and the "Succulent Seafood and Pasta Buffet" (✪$58 adult) on Friday and Saturday nights. Family oriented, with a Kids Menu and amusement pack.

Cilantro, at the Novotel Hotel, 200 Creek Street, ©3309 3364. This new restaurant provides Australian and Mediterranean cuisine with a-la-carte dining. It is licensed and open every day for breakfast, lunch and dinner.

Blu Poles, 6a, 110 Macquarie Street, Teneriffe, ©3257 2880. Licensed restaurant offering an interesting and unusual menu, such as corn-fed duck livers. Lunch Wednesday to Sunday and dinner every day except Sunday.

Daniel's, 145 Eagle Street, ©3832 3444. Licensed, open for lunch and dinner, sitauted on the banks of the Brisbane River, steak and seafood the specialities.

Captains Cove, 44 Ferry Street, Kangaroo Point, ©3891 6644. River views, interesting menu, breakfast daily, dinner Monday to Saturday.

Picasso's, at the Carlton Crest Hotel, King George Square, ©3222 1128. Licensed restaurant with a creative menu. Lunch and dinner served seven days.

McMahons, Quay West, 132 Alice Street, ©3853 6000. Licensed, wide range of seafood, pasta and meats. Elegant dining overlooking the Botanic Gardens.

Cha Cha Char Grill, Eagle Street Pier, ©3211 9944. Licensed restaurant, open for lunch and dinner, serving beef in all its forms for steak-lovers.

Pancakes at the Manor, 18 Charlotte Street, ©3221 6433. Enjoyable family dining, inexpensive meals of a good quality. Licensed and open 24 hours.

Big Fortune, Shop 8, Merthyr Road, New Farm, ©3358 6633. Chinese restaurant also serving laksas and noodles. It is BYO and open for lunch and dinner 7 days.

Rosie's Tavern, 235 Edward Street, City, ©3229 4916. International cuisine, moderate prices, open for lunch and dinner Mon-Sat.

Gertie's, 699 Brunswick Street, Fortitude Valley, ©3358 5088. Licensed restaurant set in an area with a European atmosphere. Modern flavours are the focus.

Vroom, Shop 1, cnr James and Doggett Streets, Fortitude Valley, ©3257 4455. This original Italian cafe is perfect for a light snack or meal.

Following is a list of additional international-style restaurants.

Fujiyama, cnr Ann & Duncan Streets, Fortitude Valley, ©3252 3275. Traditional Japanese.

George's On Wickam, 256 Wickam Street, Fortitude Valley, ©3854 1198. Thai and Filipino cuisine.

Govinda's, 99 Elizabeth Street, ©3210 0255. Vegetarian fare.

Green Papaya, 898 Stanley Street, East Brisbane, ©3217 3599. North Vietnamese menu.

King Ahirim, 88 Vulture Street, West End, ©3846 1678. Lebanese selections.

Mirch Masala, 95 Turbot Street, ©3220 0377. Indian food.

Also, keep in mind **Cafe 21** at the Treasury Casino for a cheap breakfast. You can get yourself a hot-and-hearty meal for less than ten dollars, which may be all you can scrape out of your pocket after an unlucky night in the gaming rooms next door.

McDonalds have branches in Queen, Albert (2), Ann, Eagle, Edward and Roma Streets, as well as many outlets further afield. KFC is in Roma, Albert and Eagle Streets, and adjoining areas. Pizza Hut is on the corner of Queen Street Mall and Albert Street, ©3221 0199.

Entertainment

When the sun goes down over the city, Brisbane's hottest night spots begin to warm up. It may not be the city that never sleeps, but its people certainly stay out late, with some of the best music in town still going strong at 5am.

Nightclubs & Pubs

PJ O'Briens, 127 Charlotte Street, ©3210 6822. A new and dazzing addition to city-centre nightlife. The pub has an Irish theme, and the music and Guiness flow freely.

Loose Goose, in the Novotel Hotel, ©3309 3366. A two hour happy hour (5pm-7pm) every evening, live entertainment and no cover charge make this a popular destination.

Club Brazil, 79 Elizabeth Street, ©3221 4144. The club has a South American theme, a lively and upbeat atmosphere, and Happy Hour from 5pm-6.30pm Tuesday to Friday.

The Adrenalin Sports Bar, You will find in this shrine to sport a shark aquarium, a Formula One car, a hang glider and the Great Wall of Sport, among other memorabilia. Even the menu cannot escape the theme.

City Rowers, 1 Eagle Street, ©3221 2888. A famous and favourite spot, patronised by the Brisbane Broncos and other locals. It claims to be a 'Brisbane institution'.

Treasury Casino, Queen Street, at the south-western end of Queen Street Mall, ✆3306 8888. Ironically, the casino was built in the former premises of the Government Treasury. The revenue-raising continues unabated - the only differences is that there are now neon lights and cocktails to disguise the process a little better. With 5 restaurants, 7 bars, over 100 gaming tables, 1100 machines, and open hours around the clock, the Casino will keep you entertained until you are unable to afford the taxi ride back to your hotel.

Cinemas

Myer Centre Cinemas, cnr Albert & Elizabeth Streets, City, ✆3221 4199.

Village Twin Cinema, 701 Brunswick Street, New Farm, ✆3358 2021.

Hoyts Regent Entertainment Centre, 167 Queen Street, City, ✆3229 5544.

Hoyts - Southbank Cinemas, Grey Street, South Bank, ✆3844 4222.

Dendy Cinemas, 346 George Street, ✆3211 3244.

IMAX, cnr Ernest & Grey Streets, ✆3844 4222.

Theatres

Arts Theatre, 210 Petrie Terrace, City, ✆3369 2344.

Brisbane Entertainment Centre, Melaleuca Drive, Boondall, ✆3265 8111.

Festival Hall, 65 Charlotte Street, City, ✆3229 4250.

Cremorne Theatre, at the Performing Arts Complex, ✆13 62 46.

Princess Theatre, 8 Annerley Road, Woolloongabba, ✆3891 3800.

Queensland Cultural Centre, South Bank, ✆3840 7100.

Metro Arts Theatre, 109 Edward Street, ✆221 1527.

Queensland Theatre Company, Stanley Street, South Brisbane, ✆3840 7000.

Opera Queensland, 114 Grey Street, South Bank, ✆3875 3030. Programmes for the above can be found in the entertainment pages of the daily newspapers, *The Courier-Mail* and *The Sun*.

Shopping

Whether you're after a souvenir, a gift for someone special, or just feel like shopping for yourself, Brisbane's malls, markets and arcades offer a cornucopia of good buys. There are nine city centre shopping arcades housing national department stores, specialty stores, Australiana and all sorts of welcome refreshment stops.

Shopping hours are:

City - ☉Mon-Thurs 9am-5.30pm, Fri 9am-9pm, Sat 9am-5pm, Sun 10.30am-4pm.

Suburbs - ☉Mon-Fri 8.30am-5.30pm, Sat 8.30am-4.30pm, Thurs 8.30am-9pm.

City Shopping

If you feel that a shopping tour might best overcome your unfamiliarity with the city's commercial centres, *The Brisbane Shopping Spree Company*, 2 Sheppard Street, ©3289 3367, offer a service that stops at bargain factory and warehouse outlets in the Brisbane area. They have included a buffet lunch at the Mt Coot-tha lookout.

Queen Street Mall.

This colourful, lavish, modern and entertaining pedestrian mall contains more than 500 specialty shops, and is the premier shopping venue in Brisbane city. The department stores on the mall are David Jones and Myer, and there are a number of banks, fast cash services, buskers, flower sellers, and plenty of chances for alfresco eating. The mall stretches between George & Edward Streets.

Wintergarden on the Mall. A three-storey complex housing a number of specialty shops, a food fair and five levels of parking. The emphasis here is on fashion. It extends from Queen Street to Elizabeth Street under the Hilton Hotel.

Myer Centre. The vast Myer Centre joins Queen, Elizabeth and Albert Streets, and has been designed to reflect the Victorian age. It has six shopping levels with 200 stores, and houses the national department store, Myer, as well as numerous specialty shops, restaurants, delicatessens and cinemas.

Rowes Arcade. The arcade is a mixture of old and new, with the restored cedar panelling of the Edward Street end and the contemporary Adelaide Street entrance, though it seems to have fallen on hard times in recent years. Two shopping levels contain up-market boutiques and designer wear outlets, and a very good coffee shop. The arcade runs towards Post Office Square.

Post Office Square. Located opposite Anzac Square, and joining Adelaide and Queen Streets with an entrance to Rowes Arcade, Post Office Square has specialty shops, bookshops, coffee shops, delicatessens and a restaurant. Underground parking is available.

Riverside Centre. Situated on Eagle Street, in the centre of Brisbane's financial district, Riverside is set back from the Brisbane River and has up-market restaurants and designer boutiques.

Brisbane Arcade. This turn-of-the-century, heritage-listed arcade is full of up-market clothing and gift shops. It runs from Queen Street Mall to Adelaide Street.

T & G Arcade. Halfway up Queen Street Mall is the T & G Arcade, whose shops specialise in designer fashions, shoes and accessories, jewellery, fine silver, ceramics, glassware and antiques.

Other Shopping Centres in the City

Chopstix. Located in the heart of Brisbane's Chinatown, Fortitude Valley, this food and retail emporium is for lovers of the Orient, with specialty shops, kitchens and restaurants.

Paddington. Only 3km from the city centre, Latrobe and Given Terraces are home to a collection of restored colonial buildings housing boutiques, cottage crafts centres, galleries, Australiana specialists and restaurants.

Savoir Faire. An up-market shopping and eating experience on Park Road, Milton, ten minutes from the city centre. The shopping area features boutiques, open air restaurants, coffee shops and underground parking.

Suburban Shopping

Out of town there is even more shopping, with eight major everything-under-one-roof shopping centres, each featuring large department stores and a variety of specialty shops. The Brisbane City Council operated 'Great Circle Line' is the easiest way of getting to these centres.

Markets

Riverside Markets, Riverside Centre, Eagle Street, City, ✆3833 2400 - ◷open every Sunday 8.15am-3pm.

"McWhirters" Marketplace, cnr Wickham & Brunswick Streets, City - ◷open daily.

Southbank Markets, Friday nights, Saturday and Sunday.

Points of Interest

The city centre is best seen on a walking tour, and the **Brisbane Transit Centre**, slightly to the northwest of your city, or your hotel are good places to start. It was opened in mid-1986 and is an integrated coach and railway terminal in Roma Street. The train service from Sydney comes right to the city centre at Roma Street Station, from where all the long distance coun-

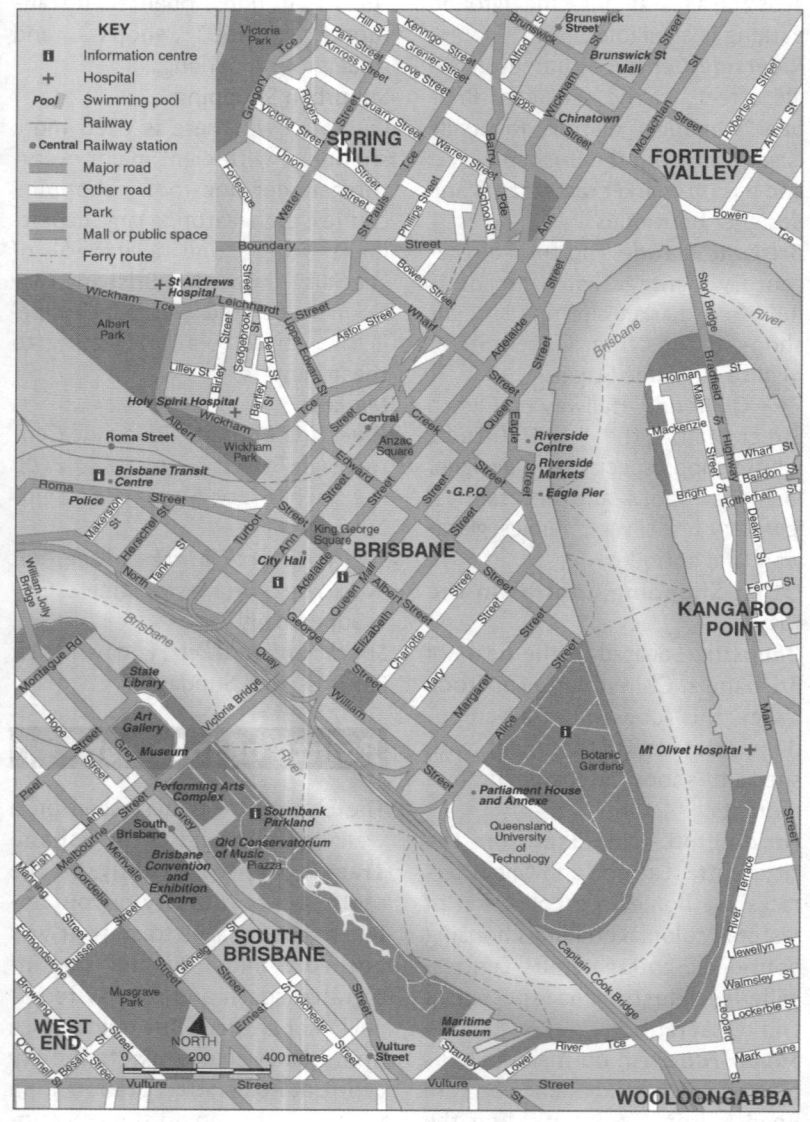

try trains leave. The suburban electric trains also leave from here, as well as interstate, intrastate and local buses. There are also long and short term car parks, taxi ranks, a hotel, commercial offices, shops and a tourist information office (☏3236 2020). Queensland has an electric train service from Brisbane through Gladstone, Rockhampton, and inland to its central Queensland Coal Fields.

The newly opened **Roma Street parklands** have been built on the site of the old railway yards. You can enjoy several self-guided walks past the lake, over bridges, through palm forests and formal gardens.

It is a leisurely stroll from the Transit Centre, of some 15 minutes, to **King George Square** and **City Hall**. This imposing building is a combined cultural and community centre. An excellent view of the city can be obtained from the clock tower, but try to avoid being up there at noon, as it gets very noisy. Also facing the square is the **Albert Street Uniting Church**, dwarfed by the high rise office blocks around it. The church is in the Gothic revival style in red brick and white sandstone, and was opened in 1889.

Around the corner in Ann Street is the **Ann Street Presbyterian Church** which was opened in 1872. Continue along Ann Street

and you will come to **Anzac Park** and the **Flame of Remembrance**, opposite Central Station. Walk down the stairs and through the park, across Adelaide Street, through the Post Office Square shopping complex, and you will come to the GPO in Queen Street, ☏3405 1202. There is a **Postal Museum** on the first floor which is ◷open Tues-Thurs 10am-3pm, and Mon-Fri during school holidays.

Turn right and you will find yourself in **Queen Street Mall**. At the end you come to the former **Treasury** building (now facilitating the Casino) near **Victoria Bridge**. It is built around a central courtyard in Italian Renaissance style. Turn left into William Street, and head south for just over one hundred metres. On your right you will see the **Commissariat Stores**, now the site of the Royal Historical Society. This building is one of only two that were built for the initial settlement and still stand today. Continue along William Street until you reach the French Renaissance style **Parliament House**, whose ceremonial frontage overlooks the **Botanic Gardens**. After all that walking, the gardens will provide a spot for rest and recuperation, as well as a view of the Captain Cook and Story bridges. Or you can continue your walk over the newly-built Goodwill

Bridge to Southbank Parklands and the Maritime Museum.

Following are some other sightseeing venues around the city:

The **Old Windmill Observatory**, on the hill to the north of the city in Wickham Terrace, was built as a windmill in 1829 by convict labour. Due to defects it was never operational, and has been used as a treadmill, a signal post and a meteorological station. It is the other legacy of the first settlement.

The **Queensland Sciencentre**, in 110 George Street, ©3220 0166, takes visitors through the weird world of science in a memorable, hands-on learning experience. ☺Open 10am-5pm daily and admission is ✪$9 adults, $6 children and $28 for families.

To the west of the city the area has been totally redeveloped. Cross the Victoria Bridge and head west along Stanley Street, you will first pass the **Queensland Art Gallery** and Queensland Museum, then come to the **State Library of Queensland**. South, on Grey Street, and the **Queensland Cultural Centre**. The 1982 Commonwealth Games provided Brisbane with the opportunity to upgrade and improve its public transport and sporting facilities, and the 1988 World Expo, held on the south bank of the Brisbane River, saw the completion of the Queensland Cultural Centre. The

Centre houses the Performing Arts Complex, and the annexed Art Gallery, Library and Museum. The Art Gallery, ©3840 7303, has an extensive collection of Australian art from colonial times to the present, and is ☺open daily 10am-5pm. The Performing Arts Complex, ©3840 7444, is ☺open daily 10am-5pm, and until 8pm on Wednesday. The Museum takes the visitor from the prehistoric age of dinosaurs up to Australia's colonial history, and is open daily, ©3840 7555.

Further south of the Victoria Bridge is the extremely popular **South Bank Parklands** development. Restaurants, cinemas, parklands, exclusive restaurants, markets, subtropical gardens, lagoons, park areas, sightseeing attractions and Australia's only inland city beach (Breaka Beach), sprawl over 16 hectares. Just south of the Parklands is the **Queensland Maritime Museum**, which has on display a number of impressive vessels from varying eras. Admission is adults ✪$6, children $3, ©3844 5361.

Close to the city the Brisbane River is spanned by five bridges, all of which have a unique architectural style and are worth seeing - the **Story Bridge**, the **Captain Cook Bridge**, the **Victoria Bridge**, the **William Jolly Bridge** and the **Goodwill Bridge**. East of the city at the mouth of the Brisbane River is the impressive **Gateway Bridge**, which was opened in 1986, and for a ✪$2 toll links the city with the Gold Coast and the Sunshine Coast. Travelling north from the Gold Coast, one can bypass Brisbane city by using this route.

The **Kookaburra River Queen** is one of Brisbane's most popular attractions, and a morning tea, luncheon or dinner cruise on this paddlewheeler is a delightful experience, and one of the best ways to view the city and its bridges. The main cruises are luncheon (from ✪$55 adults), city sights (from ✪$25 adults) and dinner entertainment (from ✪$75 adults). Phone ☎3221 1300 for bookings and departure times.

Brisbane City Council run **City Cat Cruises** which take you along the 19km length of the Brisbane River in 2 hours. If you are interested, information can be acquired and tickets purchased from the Council Customer Service outlets. The city branch is on the lower ground level of the Brisbane Administration Centre, 69 Ann Street, up near George Street, ☼open Mon-Fri 8.15am-4.45pm; and the Fortitude Valley branch is in the TC Beirne Centre, Brunswick Street Mall, ☼open Mon-Fri 9am-5pm. They are also at Embarkation Point on Eagle Pier.

Suburban Attractions

The Southern Cross, Sir Charles Kingsford Smith's plane, is preserved in a glass-walled building off Airport Drive at Brisbane Airport. Admission is free and the display is open daily.

New Farm Park has almost 12,000 rose bushes and a Jacaranda and Poinciana avenue. Like the Botanic Gardens, it is situated on the riverbank, and although it can be reached by bus, a more scenic way to visit is by the City Cat Ferry. For ferry times, contact Transinfo, ☎13 12 30.

The **Mt Coot-tha Botanic Gardens** are only ten minutes' drive from the city, and have a large collection of Australian native plants, tropical plants, an arid-zone area and tropical plant display dome, ☼open daily 8am-5.30pm. The Sir Thomas Brisbane Planetarium in the gardens is the largest in Australia. There is also a Japanese Garden, a Fragrant Plants and Herb Garden, and Australian rainforest. The picnic area at the top of Mt Coot-tha is a popular stop for a panoramic view of the city, day or night.

Lone Pine Koala Sanctuary, Jesmond Road, Fig Tree Pocket, ☎3278 1366, shouldn't be missed. It is situated on the banks of the river, and is best reached by boat - the Mirimar Boat Cruise departs from North Quay daily at 10am, ☎3221 0300. The Sanctuary is Australia's oldest, and also has a variety of native animals, reptiles and birds. It is ⊙open daily 7.30am-4.45pm, and admission is ✪$14 adults, $7 children.

Temple of the Holy Triad, cnr Park & Higgs Streets, Breakfast Creek, is an historic Chinese Temple built in 1885, ☎3262 5588. The pillars of the building were set crookedly as a reminder to all that nothing in life is perfect.

Miegunya, 31 Jordan Terrace, Bowen Hills, was built in 1884, and is a good example of colonial architecture. It is dedicated to the pioneering women of Queensland.

Newstead House in Newstead Park, Breakfast Creek Road, Newstead, ☎3216 1846 or ☎1800 061 846, is Brisbane's oldest surviving residence. It is on the banks of the river near its junction with Breakfast Creek, and is ⊙open Mon-Fri 10am-4pm, Sun 2-5pm.

The Queensland University at St Lucia, ☎3365 1111, is almost completely surrounded by the river, and has spacious parklands and sandstone buildings which are joined by sheltered walkways called The Cloisters. They are decorated with carvings of other universities' coats of arms, sculptures and grotesque faces and animals. Worth a

visit if you are into varsity ambience and style.

Alma Park Zoo, Alma Road, Dakabin, ☎3204 656, features Australian and exotic fauna, tropical gardens, picnic and barbecue facilities. There are regular feeding times for a variety of animals. It is ⊙open daily 9am-5pm. Admission is ✪$20 adults and $10 children. The zoo is located 28km (17 miles) north of Brisbane and takes about half an hour to reach.

Licoriceland, 21 Jijaws Street, Sumner Park, ☎3376 6945, is Queensland's only licorice factory. It is ⊙open 9.30am-3.30pm Mon-Fri, except in January when it is closed to visitors. Tours are available, and there is also a sweet shop selling samples.

The Australian Woolshed, 148 Samford Road, Ferny Hills, ☎3872 1100, is a wonderful experience for people who don't have time to visit the great Aussie Outback. You can see seven different breeds of sheep, watch one being shorn, and then see the fleece spun into yarn. Once you've had a taste of Australia's rural backbone, you might like to expand your activities. Native animals are on display, waterslides are open at selected times for ✪$5 an hour, and a nine-hole round of mini golf is available for ✪$4. Every Saturday night there is a Woolshed dance which includes dinner. The

Woolshed is about 20 minutes drive from the city centre and admission prices are ✪$18 adults and $11 children. A Park Package ticket is available, which includes a variety of these activites for ✪$20.

The **Boondall Wetlands** are a protected area maintained by Brisbane City Council, consisting of woodlands, tidal flats and swamp areas, north of Brisbane on the rim of Moreton Bay. The region can be explored on foot, bike or canoe, and birdwatching and exploration of Aboriginal culture are features. The Boondall Wetlands Visitor Centre has further details, ✆3865 5187.

Tours

Bus tours operate daily from Brisbane, taking in the very best of the city sights and venturing further afield to beautiful beaches and natural bushland. Following are some examples.

Brisbane Tours & Detours, ✆3830 4455:

Koalas & Brisbane Parklands Tours, 2.15pm-4.15pm, ✪$50 adults; Highlights of the City, 9.15am-1.15pm, ✪$40 adults; Brisbane Moonlight Tour, 6.45pm-8.45pm, ✪$40 adults; Best of Brisbane - In a Day, 9.30am-5.30pm, ✪$75 adults.

Brian Ogdens Historical Walking Tours, ✆3217 3673.

Australian Day Tours, Level 3, Transit Centre, Roma Street, ✆3236 4155 or ✆1300 363 436 (free call):

Brisbane After Dark, 6pm-10pm, ✪$70 adults; Brisbane Sights Full Day, 9.30am-6.30pm, ✪$58 adults; City Sights, Woolshed and River Cruise, 9.30am-6.30pm, ✪$75 adults; Morning Tour, City Sights & South Bank, 9.30am-1.30pm, ✪$40 adults.

Brisbane Ghost Tours, ✆3344 7264:

An historical tour with a difference! *Mr Day Tours*, Aminya Close, My Nebo, ✆3289 8364:

Afternoon Scenic Rainforest Drive, 12.30pm-4.30pm, ✪$70 adults; Brisbane and Its Outback Tour, 8am-6pm, ✪$135 adults; Morning Countryside Drive, 8am-12pm, ✪$75 adults.

Gray Line Tours, Level 3, Transit Centre, Roma Street, ✆3236 9444: Best of Brisbane Cruise & Tour, 9.30am-6.30pm, ✪$95 adults; Mt Tamborine & Aussie Country Show, 7.30am-7.30pm, ✪$105 adults.

Rob's Rainforest Explorer Day Tours, 44 Felix Street, Lutwyche, ✆0409 49 6607:

Glasshouse Mountains & Kondalilla Falls, 8am-6pm, ✪$55 adults; Lamington/Springbrook National Parks, 8am-6pm, ✪$55 adults; Mt Glorious & Samford Valley Tour, 8am-6pm, ✪$55 adults.

See More Scenic Tours, 4 Mallee

Street, Marsden, ✆3805 5588:
Glow Worm Express - Tambourine
Mountain, 6pm-10pm, ✪$50
adults; Rainforest & Winery Tour,
8.30am-5.30pm, ✪$65 adults.
Sunrover Expeditions, 1 Eversleigh
Road, Redcliffe, ✆3203 4241:
Moreton Bay Island Safari, 6.45am-
6.45pm, ✪$135 adults.
Regular tours to Dreamworld, Sea
World, Movie World, Wet'n'Wild,
Gold Coast, Noosa and Sunshine
Coast, Moreton Bay, Tamborine
Mountains, Toowoomba and Dar-
ling Downs are also conducted.

Festivals

The Valley Fiesta held at Chinatown
and Brunswick Street Malls is a
multicultural music and arts festi-
val held in July.
The Royal National Show (The
Ekka) is held in the Brisbane Exhi-
bitions Grounds, Fortitude Valley,
over ten days in August.
The Spring Hill Fair is held in Water
Street in September.
Brisbane River Festival is held from
August to September.

Facilities

The Gabba is Brisbane's main cricket
venue for International and interstate matches, and it is in Stanley
Street, Woolloongabba, across the
river to the south of the city centre,

✆3891 5464.
  Horse races are held at Eagle Farm
Racecourse, Lancaster Road, Ascot,
✆3268 2171, and Doomben Race-
course, 39 Brunswick Street, Forti-
tude Valley, ✆3268 6800.
  The trotting venue is Albion Park
Harness Racing, Amy Street, Break-
fast Creek, ✆3262 2577.
  The main football ovals are: Rugby
League - Suncorp Stadium, Castle-
maine Street, Milton, ✆3876 6511;
Rugby Union - Ballymore, Clyde
Road, Herston, ✆3352 8120; Aus-
tralian Rules - The Gabba. There are
also games of all three codes played
at suburban grounds on the week-
ends in winter.
  Baseball is also played at Suncorp
Stadium, and for Basketball, the
Brisbane Entertainment Centre,
Melaleuca Drive, Boondall, is the
home of the Brisbane Bullets.
  For names and addresses of other

sporting facilities, it is best to consult the Yellow Pages telephone directory.

Outlying Attractions

Moreton Bay and Island

The bayside suburbs of Wynnum, Lota, Manly, Wellington Point and Cleveland are great places for boating, and North Stradbroke and Moreton Islands are really worth a visit. They provide the opportunity for an island holiday without travelling far from Brisbane.

Moreton is the second largest sand island in the world (after Fraser Island), and much of it is National Park. There are unspoiled beaches, abundant birdlife, and the sand dunes are magnificent. In the centre, amongst the sand dunes where there is practically no vegetation, you can imagine that a camel train might arrive at any moment. Mount Tempest is one of the highest coastal sand dunes in the world. The **Wild Dolphin** resort at Tangalooma, the site of the old whaling station, offers standard and deluxe motel and cabin accommodation and a restaurant. Prices start from ✪$90 per person twin share in the peak season.

For those who prefer a simpler holiday, camping areas are found at **Accommodation Moreton Island**, The Strand Bulwer, ✆3408 3798.

Facilities include water, toilets and showers. Moreton Island Tourist Information Services, located at The Strand Bulwer, can provide further details, ✆(07) 3408 2661.

Access to Moreton Island is by launch or air. The Tangalooma Flyer leaves Holt Street in Brisbane, with a courtesy coach transfer from the Transit Centre in Roma Street at 9am daily. The launch transfers cost ✪$33 return for adults. Air transfers are from Brisbane Airport to Moreton Island, a trip lasting about 15 minutes. Enquire about your preferred transfer method when booking your accommodation or by contacting the Visitor Information Centre.

North Stradbroke Island

North Stradbroke Island is larger and has more varied scenery than Moreton Island. There are mangrove swamps, lakes, bushland and great surfing beaches.

Accommodation is available at Amity Point and at Point Lookout, with campsites at Point Lookout and Dunwich. Vehicular ferries operate from Cleveland and Redland Bay.

The Stradbroke Island Tourist Information Centre is at the end of Middle Street, Cleveland, ✆3821 3821. Stradbroke Island Tourism is in Junner Street, Dunwich, ✆3409 9555 or email ✎ redlands tourism @redlands.net.au

Beenleigh

If you are heading south to the Gold Coast from Brisbane, take time out to visit the Beenleigh Tavern at 124 Distillery Road, ©3287 4777. It is ☺open Mon-Fri 10.30am-10pm, Sat 11am until late, Sun 11am-6pm. For a moderate fee, tours are conducted between limited hours daily and include a tasting of Beenleigh rum (after all, that is why you came here).

Gold Coast

Population 275,000
The Gold Coast, Australia's most famous tourist destination, is situated in south-east Queensland.

Climate

Average Temperatures: January max 28C (82F) - min 20C (68F); July max 21C (70F) - min 9C (48F). Average annual rainfall: 1724mm (68 ins); driest months July-September.

Characteristics

The Gold Coast region is made up of the Gold Coast City, Albert and Beaudesert Shires. It covers 4254 sq km (1642 sq miles) and stretches 42km (26 miles) along south-east Queensland's world-famous, sun-drenched coastline and 100km (62 miles) inland into the Gold Coast Hinterland (*see separate listing*). The district has rolling surf, golden beaches, rainforest areas, non-stop entertainment, and millions of visitors every year.

How to Get There

By Air
Qantas, ©13 1313 services the Gold Coast frequently.

The closest airport is at Coolangatta, and there is no problem arranging coach transfers to your hotel anywhere in the Gold Coast area. The following regional services are available:
Coolangatta Airport Transfers, ©5588 8747;
Airporter, ©5588 8777;

SkyTrans, ☎3236 1000;
Sunbus, ☎5588 8740.
Coach Service to and from Brisbane City, ☎13 12 30;

By Coach

Greyhound Pioneer, ☎13 2030, and McCaffertys, ☎13 1499, stop at the Gold Coast on their Sydney/Brisbane routes.

Greyhound Pioneer has a Brisbane/Gold Coast service, and McCaffertys has a Gold Coast/Toowoomba service.

By Rail

From Sydney, a train to Murwillumbah then a bus to the Gold Coast, ☎13 2232.

By Car

From Sydney, via the Pacific Highway 900km (560 miles). From Brisbane, via the Pacific Highway, 79km (49 miles) to Southport, and 100km (62 miles) to Coolangatta.

Visitor Information

There is a Visitors Centre at Cavill Mall, Surfers Paradise, ☎(07) 5538 4419, ⏰open 8am-4pm Mon-Fri and 8am-3pm Sat.

You will also find the head office of the Gold Coast Tourism Bureau in Surfers Paradise on Level 2, Ferny Avenue, ☎5592 2699. They have a web site at 👁www.goldcoast tourism.com.au and an email address at ✉info@gctb.com.au

If you require a money exchange facility, Kings Currency Services, Shop G21 Shopping Plaza, Elkhorn Ave, Surfers Paradise, ☎5526 9599, places no charges on cash and is ⏰open 7 days, 8.30am-10pm.

Accommodation

Accommodation is not a problem on the Gold Coast. The motels, apartments, guest houses and camping grounds are more dense here than anywhere else in Australia. As a result of this, there is really no need to book in advance, except in school holidays.

Many airlines, bus companies, tour operators, travel bureaux and even the railways offer package holidays, which are very good value.

Here is a selection of accommodation with prices for a double room per night, which should be used as a guide only. The telephone area code is 07.

Coolongatta and Tweed Heads

See separate listing

Heads, ✆5535 1111 or ✆1800 641 153 (toll free). 68 units, licensed restaurant, security parking, room service, pool, spa - ✪$90-140.

Fifth Avenue Motel, 1953 Gold Coast Highway (cnr Fifth Avenue), ✆5535 3588. 38 units, licensed restaurant (closed Sunday), swimming pool - ✪$100-180.

Casino Motel, 1761 Gold Coast Highway, ✆5535 7133. 12 units, swimming pool, barbecue - from ✪$45-110. Natural setting adjacent to Burleigh National Park. 250m from Burleigh Point, 300m from Burleigh central shops, 15km from Sea World, 35km from Movie World.

Elite Motel, 1935 Gold Coast Highway, ✆5535 2920. 8 units, barbecue - ✪$35-80.

Burleigh Beach Tourist Park, Goodwin Terrace, Burleigh Heads, ✆5581 7755. Pool adjacent to park, centralised location close to all facilities, 200m from Burleigh Beach, powered sites ✪$20-25 for two, cabins $80-125 for two.

Broadbeach

Conrad Jupiters, Broad Beach Island, ✆5592 1133. Several bars and restaurants including *Andamino's* for fine-dining Italian cuisine. Two-level casino open 24hrs, free admission. Recently renovated showroom: *Innuevre*. Monorail link to Oasis shopping centre and the beach. Hotel offers double rooms ✪$180

Currumbin

Sand Castles, 31 Teemangun Street, ✆5598 2999. 19 self-contained units, heated swimming pool, spa, barbecue, secure parking - ✪$85-185. Close proximity to Bird Sanctuary. Fronts Currumbin Beach.

Burleigh Heads

Outrigger Resort Gold Coast, 2007 Gold Coast Highway, Burleigh

and suites $700-1100.

Grand Mercure Broadbeach, Surf Parade, ✆5592 2250. 298 rooms, licensed restaurant, swimming pool, sauna, gym, tennis, under-cover parking - ✪$260.

Portobello Beachside, 2607 Gold Coast Highway, ✆5538 7355. 46 units, heated pool, spa, secure parking - from ✪$60-130.

Hi Ho Holiday Motel Apartments, 2 Queensland Avenue, ✆5538 2777. 20 units, swimming pool (heated), spa, barbecue, secure parking - ✪$80-90.

Montego, 2671 Gold Coast High-way, ✆5539 9956. 24 units, salt water pool - ✪$55-135.

Surfers Paradise

Sheraton Mirage Gold Coast, Sea World Drive, Main Beach, ✆5591 1488. 323 rooms, 45 suites, spa, pool, tennnis court, gym - from ✪$470-700.

Sea World Nara Resort, Sea World Drive, Main Beach, ✆5591 0000. 391 rooms, heated pool, sauna, spa, gym, tennis court and jetty - ✪$200 (includes entry into theme park).

Surfers Paradise Marriott Resort, 158 Ferny Ave, Surfers Paradise, ✆5592 9800. 300 rooms, under-cover parking, gym, heated pool, tennis court, sauna and spa - ✪$200-500.

Gold Coast International Hotel, cnr Gold Coast Highway and Staghorn Avenue, Surfers Paradise, ✆5592 1200. 296 rooms, 21 suites, gym, pool, sauna, spa, tennis half-court - ✪$210-230.

Courtyard by Marriott, cnr Gold Coast Highway and Hanlan Street, Paradise Centre, Surfers Paradise, ✆5579 3499. 405 rooms, tennis, pool (heated), gym, spa, undercover parking - ✪$110-310.

ANA Hotel Gold Coast, 22 View Avenue, Surfers Paradise, ✆5579 1000. 404 rooms, secure parking, tennis, swimming pool (heated), gym, sauna and spa - ✪$290-340.

Parkroyal, 2807 Gold Coast High-way, Surfers Paradise, ✆5592 9900. Security parking, heated pool - ✪$165-240.

Chateau Beachside, cnr The Espla-nade & Elkhorn Avenue, Surfers Paradise, ✆5538 1022. 38 rooms, 58 suites, secure parking, pool, sauna, spa, gym - ✪$100-160.

Trickett Gardens Holiday Inn, 24 Trickett Street, Surfers Paradise, ✆5539 0988. 31 units, spa, heated pool secure parking, barbecue - ✪$100-135.

Bahia Beachfront Apartments (motel), 154 The Esplanade, Surf-ers Paradise, ✆5538 3322. 30 units, swimming pool, spa, sauna, barbecue - ✪$85-130.

Islander Resort, 6 Beach Road, Surfers Paradise, ✆5538 8000. 101 rooms, undercover parking, sauna, spa, tennis and squash, pool - ✪$85-105.

Iluka Beach Resort Hotel, cnr The Esplanade and Hanlan Street, Surfers Paradise, ℂ5539 9155. 71 suites, 32 units, restaurant, secure parking, heated pool - ✪$80-100.

Pink Poodle, 2903 Gold Coast Highway, Surfers Paradise, ℂ5539 9211. 21 Units, spa, pool (salt water) - ✪$80-130.

Durham Court, 21 Clifford Street, Surfers Paradise, ℂ5592 1855. 16 units, secure parking, swimming pool - ✪$50-150.

D'Arcy Arms Motel, 2923 Gold Coast Highway, Surfers Paradise, ℂ5592 0892. 17 units, 1 suite, licensed restaurant (closed Sunday), swimming pool (heated), spa, barbecue - ✪$70-110.

Main Beach Tourist Park, Main Beach Parade, Gold Coast, ℂ5581 7722. (No pets allowed) 170 sites, playground, pool - powered sites $20-23, self-contained sites $25-29.

There is a **Youth Hostel** in Mariners Cove, 70 Seaworld Drive, Main Beach, ℂ5571 1776. They have 29 rooms at ✪$24 per person twin share.

Southport

Swan Lane Apartments, cnr Queens & Swan Lane, ℂ5528 1900. 10 units, security parking, tennis pool (heated) - ✪$120.

Park Regis Hotel, 2 Barney Street, Southport, ℂ5532 7922. 79 rooms, car parking, pool - ✪$210-280.

Earls Court Motor Inn, 131 Nerang Street, Southport, ℂ5591 4144. 34 units, 3 suites, undercover parking, salt water pool - ✪$65-95 (unit), $75-120 (suite).

Southport Tourist Park, 6 Frank Street, Gold Coast Highway, Southport, ℂ5531 2281. 55 sites, powered sites ✪$20-30 for two, cabins $45-100 for two, caravans $35-80 for two.

Broadwater Tourist Park, Gold Coast Tourist Highway, Southport, ℂ5581 7733. 307 sites - powered sites ✪$30-35 for two.

Sanctuary Cove

Hyatt Regency Sanctuary Cove, Manor Circle, Casey Road, ℂ5530 1234. 247 rooms, 24 suites, golf, gym, marina, pool, sauna and spa - ✪$200-240.

Sanctuary Shores Resort, 1 Pinnaroo Street, ℂ5530 1111. 12 units, Putter's restaurant, spa, pool - ✪$80-95.

Outlying Areas

All Seasons Mermaid Waters Hotel, cnr Markeri Street & Sunshine Boulevard, Mermaid Beach, ℂ5572 2500. 102 units, 14 suites, barbecue, room service, swimming pool - ✪$110-150.

Runaway Bay Motor Inn, 429 Oxley Drive, Runaway Bay, ℂ5537 5555. 40 units, 3 suites, secure parking, swimming pool (heated, salt water) - ✪$105-170.

Coomera Motor Inn, Dreamworld

Parkway, Coomera, ©5573 2311. 31 units, heated pool, licensed restaurant, playground, room service - ✪$85-100.

Billinga Beach Resort, 281 Golden Four Drive, Billinga Beach, ©5534 1241. 23 units, 3 divided rooms, pool, undercover parking - ✪$60-150.

Limassol, 109 Frank Street, Labrador, ©5591 6766. 14 units, salt water pool - ✪$50-110.

Camden Colonial Motor Inn, 2371 Gold Coast Highway, Mermaid Beach, ©5575 1066. 15 units, undercover parking, spa, salt water pool - ✪$60-110.

El Rancho, 2125 Gold Coast Highway, Miami, ©5572 3655. 8 units, 1 suite, barbecue, pool, spa, playground - ✪$35-60.

Caravan Parks

Ocean Beach Tourist Park Miami, 2 Hythe Street, Miami, ©5581 7711. Shared facilities, barbecue. 81 sites ✪$18-22, 58 powered sites $20-25.

Runaway Bay Caravan Park, 20 Bayview Street, Runaway Bay, ©5537 1636. 83 powered sites ✪$19-21.

Miami Caravan Park, 2200 Gold Coast Highway, Miami, ©5572 7533. Kiosk, barbecue, no pets allowed, 200 sites - powered sites ✪$16-19.

Local Transport

Shuttle

There is an efficient and economical public transport system. Gold Coast Tourist Shuttle Bus Service, ©1300 655 655 provides unlimited travel day or night for the one price. It travels from one end of the coastal strip to the other. 1 day pass: adult ✪$14, child $8, family $32. Theme park transfers also available.

Car Rentals

Car rental companies that have offices on the Gold Coast, include:

Red Back Rentals, ©5592 1655. Open 7 days.

CY Rent A Car, Surfers International Arcade Shop 14, 9 Trickett Street, Surfers Paradise, ©5570 3777.

Freeway Rent-A-Car, Zircon Avenue, ©5591 1155. Open 7 days.

Network Car & Truck Rentals, cnr Gold Coast Highway & Palm Avenue, Surfers Paradise, ©5538 2344.

A.B.L., Gold Coast Airport, ©5598 3900. Open 7 days.

Tweed Auto Rentals, 4 Wharf Street, Tweed Heads, ©5536 8000. Open 7 days.

Sunny Top, cnr Gold Coast Hwy & Surfers Ave, Mermaid Beach, ©5578 6633. Open 7 days.

Suncoast, 3005 Gold Coast Hwy, ©5592 4087.

Always Affordable, ✆5593 6026. Open 7 days.

Budget, cnr Ferry Ave & Norfolk Ave, ✆1300 362 848.

East Coast, 25 Elkhorn Ave, Surfers Paradise, ✆5592 0444.

Bargain Wheels, ✆5534 4544.

Costless, 3269 Gold Coast Hwy, *Surfers Paradise*, ✆5538 8400.

Anthony's Ezy-Drive, ✆5534 6022. Open 7 days.

Can Do, 3084 Gold Coast Hwy, Surfers Paradise, ✆5592 5887. Open 7 days.

Or you can rent a Pedicab, a moped (Moped Hire, cnr Hamilton Ave & Gold Coast Hwy, Surfers Paradise, ✆5592 4087) or a bicycle. At the other end of the scale, you can splurge and hire a stretch limousine.

For full information on all these options, contact the Tourist Information Centres, or browse the Yellow Pages telephone directory.

Combined Rail, Bus and Ferry

South East Explorer, ✆13 12 30. All day travel on participating services, Explorer ticket 1 - ✪$10, Explorer ticket 2 - ✪$16, Explorer ticket 3 - ✪$24.

Bus

Surfside Bus Timetables. For information on routes phone ✆ 13 12 30.

Coach

The following services are available: Gold Coast Get Around, ✆1300 361 966;

Theme Park Transfers, ✆1800 426 224;

Coach Charter, ✆55 888 780.

Eating Out

The Gold Coast is said to have the largest collection of restaurants per square kilometre in Australia, and indeed there are more than 500 different restaurants on the coastal strip. You can eat and drink riverside, seaside, inside or outside. Almost every national cuisine is represented, and you can choose from licensed or BYO. The only problem is making up your mind which restaurant is going to get your patronage, and this is taken care of by phoning the Restaurant Infoline, ✆916 699, for information and bookings. Here is a taste of the wide selection, from low to lavish prices:

Four Winds Restaurant, in the Parkroyal, 2807 Gold Coast Highway. Surfers Paradise, ✆5592 9906.

Seafood and Asian buffet, revolving restaurant 26 floors above the city, all-you-can-eat, open 7 days for lunch and 2 dinner sittings.

Rakugaki, 2nd Floor, Centre Arcade, Surfers Paradise, ©5539 8741. BYO Japanese cuisine, lunch Mon-Fri (12pm-2pm), dinner Mon-Sat (6pm-10.30pm).

Hattie's Seafood Restaurant, ANA Hotel, 22 View Ave, Surfers Paradise, ©5579 1000.

Cafe Carinya, ANA Hotel, 22 View Ave, Surfers Paradise, ©5579 1000. Seafood buffet lunch 7 days a week - $25, huge seafood buffet nightly - $33.

Frenchy's Seafood Restaurant, Mariners Cove, Sea World Drive, Main Beach, ©5531 3030. Licensed or BYO.

The Aztec, Victoria Square, Broadbeach Mall, ©5538 8477. Mexican cuisine, licensed, open 7 days, lunch and dinner.

Montezuma's, Aloha Building, 8 Trickett Street, Surfers Paradise, ©5538 4748. Mexican, licensed.

Pancakes in Paradise, cnr Gold Coast Hwy & Clifford St, ©5592 0330. Licensed, open 7 days, lunch and dinner.

Bavarian Haus, cnr Cavill Ave & Gold Coast Hwy, Surfers Paradise, ©5531 7150. German cuisine as well as steak, seafood, chicken and pasta, authentic Bavarian theme and atmosphere, live shows. Breakfast, morning & afternoon tea, lunch and dinner.

The Crab Cooker, cnr Gold Coast Hwy & Thornton St, Surfers Paradise, ©5538 6884. Seafood and steak restaurant, licensed, indoor and outdoor dining, lunch and dinner.

Holy Mackeral, 174 Marine Pde, Labrador, ©5531 1017. Seafood, licensed, open 7 days, lunch and dinner.

Times Cafe Restaurant, cnr Elkhorn Ave & Gold Coast Hwy, Surfers Paradise, ©5538 3211. Steak, seafood and pasta, open 7 days. Breakfast, lunch and dinner

Mikado, cnr Elkhorn Ave & Gold Coast Hwy, Surfers Paradise, ©5538 2788. Japanese cuisine including traditional sushi and teppanyaki dishes, open 7 days.

Imperial Palace, cnr Elkhorn Ave & Gold Coast Hwy, Surfers Paradise, ©5538 9544, Chinese restaurant, open 7 days.

Mango's, Tiki Village, Cavill Avenue, Surfers Paradise, ©5531 6177. Modern international cuisine with an emphasis on seafood, open 7 nights, dinner.

Grumpy's Wharf, Mariners Cove, 60-70 Seaworld Drive, The Spit, Main Beach, ©5532 2900. Seafood, lunch Fri-Sun, dinner 7 days.

Rusty Pelican, cnr Orchid Ave & Elkhorn Ave, Surfers Paradise, ©5570 3073. Lunch 11.30am-

10.30pm, licensed until midnight, open 7 days.

Seashells Restaurant, at the Novotel Beachcomber, 18 Hanlan St, Surfers Paradise, ✆5570 1000. International seafood buffet.

Hard Rock Cafe, cnr Cavill Ave & Gold Coast Hwy, Surfers Paradise, ✆5539 9377. Restaurant open 7 days 12pm-late.

Cav's Steakhouse, 30 Frank St, Labrador, ✆5532 2954. Licensed, steak, seafood, pasta and salad.

McDonalds is on the corner of Cavill Mall and The Esplanade. Pizza Hut is in Raptis Plaza, Cavill Avenue, ✆13 11 66. There is an abundance of fast food eateries in the area, and the selection will guarantee that you are not left wanting.

Entertainment

For after-dinner entertainment, you can choose between cabarets, discos, live bands, top international performers, sophisticated night clubs, poker machine palaces, and the world famous Jupiter's Casino. Or you can opt for something completely different - the bizarre Dracula's Cabaret restaurant. Here are a few venues:

Dracula's Cabaret Restaurant, 1 Hooker Blvd, Broadbeach, ✆5575 1000, comedy entertainment, dinner and show, bookings essential.

Inneuvre, at Conrad Jupiters Casino, ✆1800 074 144, live theatre, comedy, dance, music, circus acts.

Crazies Comedy Box, Sunshine Blvd, Broadbeach, ✆5592 0755, dinner and live show.

Shopping

The Gold Coast is like one massive shopping centre, and in fact Surfers Paradise is known to some as 'Shoppers Paradise'. There are dozens of shopping centres, of every shape and size, and it is rumoured that some people never actually see the beach. To help you find your way through this consumers' paradise, the following list can be used as a guide:

On the Broadwater Spit is the stylish ***Marina Mirage***, which offers good shopping, an aviary, and several food outlets including a 50s rock 'n' roll cafe with its own FJ Holden.

Sanctuary Cove, 20 minutes' drive north of Surfers, has the Marine Shopping Village, ✆5577 6011, with over 80 specialty shops and its own brewery offering Bavarian style beer - Island Lager.

Australia Fair, Marine Parade, Southport, ✆5532 8811. Over 230 specialty stores, ⏰open 7 days.

Pacific Fair Shopping Centre, Hooker Blvd, Broadbeach, ✆5539 8766. Queensland's largest shopping centre with over 260 specialty stores and 12 cinemas, ☉open 7 days.

Mariora Australia, 3290 Gold Coast Highway, Surfers Paradise, ✆5538 9899. Opal retailer.

DFS Galleria, cnr Cavill Ave & Gold Coast Highway, Surfers Paradise, ✆5570 9401. Duty free and tax free, ☉open 7 days 8.30am-10pm

Nerang Disposals, 6 Spencer Rd, Nerang, ✆5596 4434. Camping and outdoor store.

Carrara Markets, Nerang-Broadbeach Rd, along the road west of Pacific Fair. 500 stalls, open all day every Saturday and Sunday.

Fashion Factory Outlet, 4107 Ferry Rd, Southport, ✆5531 1837. Ladies' fashion and lingerie, men's and children's fashion, swimwear, ☉open 7 days 9am-5pm.

Marina Mirage, Sea World Drive, Main Beach, ✆5577 0088. ☉Open 7 days 10am-6pm.

Paradise Centre, Cavill Ave, Surfers Paradise, ✆5592 0155. Over 120 shops, ☉open 7 days.

Robina Town Centre, off Robina Pkwy, Robina, ✆5575 0480. More than 200 specialty shops and 6 cinemas.

Raptis Plaza, Cavill Mall & The Esplanade, Surfers Paradise, ✆5592 2123. Home to a full-size replica of Michelangelo's David, which stands in the Food Court. Open 7 days 10am-late.

The Oasis, Victoria Ave, Broadbeach,

✆5592 3900. Over 100 specialty stores, direct link to Jupiters Casino via monorail.

Runaway Bay Shopping Village, Lae Drive, Runaway Bay, ✆5537 2566. Over 100 specialty stores, Boardwalk Foodcourt, water views, ☉open 7 days.

Sportsmans Warehouse, 32 Strathaird Rd, Bundall, ✆5531 6511. Australia's largest sporting warehouse, free bus from Surfers Paradise, open 7 days.

Niecon Plaza, Broadbeach Central Mall, Victoria Ave, Broadbeach, ✆5531 6659. Licensed bar, al fresco cafes.

Points of Interest

The main attractions are, of course, the beaches - and there are plenty of them, all offering clean, golden sand, and sparkling surf. But the Gold Coast has much more to offer, with special attractions in every town.

Southport

Situated across the Broadwater from The Spit, Southport was the first settlement in the Gold Coast, having been established in 1875. It is now the business and commercial centre for the region, along with neighbouring Labrador, Biggera Waters and Runaway Bay.

Inland from Southport, on the Pacific Highway, is the **Wet'n'Wild**

Water World, ☏5573 2255, with a giant fresh water wild wavepool that has one metre surf and its own lifeguards. The park also has Wild Billy the surfing kangaroo, white water twisters, and a breathtaking toboggan drop. The latest addition is the Super 8 Aqua Racer. The water park is ☉open daily from 10am. Adults ✪$31, children and pensioners $20.

Further north along the Pacific Highway brings you to **Koala Town**, where you can cuddle a koala and see the many animals that lived on Old MacDonald's Farm. Also featured are sheep shearing and horse shoeing demonstrations.

Continuing north, you come to **Dreamworld**, Dreamworld Parkway, ☏5588 1111. It comprises 100ha (247 acres) of landscaped gardens and Australian bushland featuring nine wonderful worlds of fantasy, including 16 rides, seven live shows, a tiger exhibit, and the Imax Theatre with a six-storey high screen that creates an experience of light and sound which makes the viewer feel part of the film. The new Giant Drop and Tower of Terror are the fastest and tallest rides in the world. Dreamworld is ☉open every day, and is an experience that should not be missed. Adults ✪$52, children and concession $32.

Almost opposite Dreamworld is

Warner Bros Movie World, ☏5573 8485, which is based on the world-famous Hollywood Movie set. Terrific theme rides such as Lethal Weapon and Batman Adventure lead the attractions. Movie World has movie-making facilities, which are used for actual productions. Entry costs adults ✪$52, children and pensioners $33. The live shows are a must-see.

Further north is the **Le Mans Kart Racing Complex**, Pacific Highway, Pimpana Tourist Area, ☏55 46 6 566. There is a 700m circuit with fast karts and timed laps. No licence is necessary, but age restrictions do apply for safety reasons. The complex is ☉open 7 days 10am-5pm. ✪$28 for 7 laps, $33 for 10 laps.

Not far away, for those who are fascinated by (maybe obsessed with) the amber liquid, the **Carlton Brewhouse**, cnr Mulles Rd & Pacific Highway, Yatala, ☏3826 5858, offers 45min brewery tours at 10am, 12pm and 2pm - adults ✪$8, concession $3, children $3.

Surfers Paradise

The heart of the Gold Coast, Surfers Paradise is the ultimate tourist resort, and its malls and avenues are crammed with a multitude of places to eat, drink, shop, see and be seen. Condominiums abound, rising skyward one after another amid lush vegetation and island upon island reclaimed from the sea. It has been described as 'a pristine Miami Beach'.

For entertainment there are performances by international stars, spectacular revues, cabaret shows, top restaurants, intimate bars, discos, and dinner cruises departing from the Nerang River on the western side of Surfers. There are several different cruises, from a two-hour 'scones and cream' tour, to a tropical luncheon feast, a night shipboard cabaret, a twilight trip, or a raging disco.

For family fun, right in the centre of town is **Grundy's Paradise Centre**, with over 300 different activities in the one complex, ranging from games of skill to the latest electronic arcade machines.

In Raptis Plaza, Cavill Mall, there is the only Odditorium in the southern hemisphere, which in true **Believe It Or Not!** tradition has six-legged calves, bearded women, Siamese twins and many more exhibits. The museum is ☉open 7 days 9am-11pm, ✆5592 0040. Entry fees: adults ✪$12, concession $8, family discounts available.

The Centre, the Gold Coast's entertainment and arts complex, is on Chevron Island, and has all types of theatrical performances from opera to pantomime. There is also an Art Gallery which has changing exhibitions.

For a cool change to the typically humid climate, **Frozen World**, cnr Ocean Avenue & Gold Coast Highway, ✆5570 3922, offers mini-golf on ice, exhibitions of ice sculptures and carvers, a snow and ice playground, and a kids' club. Warm jackets are supplied for those who forgot to pack for snowy conditions on the Gold Coast. Adults ✪$17, children $9 (under 4 years free), concession $12, family pass $42.

To the north of Surfers is **Main Beach**, fast becoming the 'best address' on the Coast, and nearby is the **Broadwater**, which offers still water swimming as an alternative to the open surf.

On Broadwater Spit is Australia's famous marine theme park, **Sea World**, ✆5588 2205, which has the country's first monorail, the Three Loop Corkscrew, and Free Fall Water Slide, performing dolphins, killerwhales, sea lions, water skiing shows, and lots more. The most recent attraction is a 3D Pirate adventure. Sea World is hopen every day from 10am, and you are advised to get there early if you want to see and do everything available. Adults ✪$52, pensioners and children $33.

Another attraction on the Spit is **Fishermans Wharf**, which has a swimming pool, children's playground, and live band performances on the weekend.

Above: The Central Business District of Brisbane on the Brisbane River   *Below: Storey Bridge, Brisbane*

South Bank, Brisban

Broadbeach

The town is internationally famous as the site of **Jupiter's Casino**, and the Gold Coast's first world-class hotel, the $185 million Hotel Conrad. A monorail links the casino with the Oasis-On-Broadbeach Shopping Resort and the Pan Pacific Hotel.

Burleigh Heads

Burleigh is the half-way point between Coolangatta and Surfers, and hosts one of the greatest week-long surfing events in Australia, held in March each year.

The town has a more relaxed atmosphere than Coolangatta or Surfers, and many people choose to stay here, and visit the other two when they want to get into the action. If you are into bushwalking, there is a 3km graded track that meanders among the habitat of koalas and bandicoots in the **Burleigh Heads National Park**.

The Gold Coast Highway then continues past the surfing beaches of Miami, Nobby's and Mermaid to Broadbeach.

Currumbin

Situated about 6km (4 miles) north of Coolangatta, past the settlements of Kirra, Bilinga and Tugun, Currumbin is home to the world-famous **Currumbin Wildlife Sanctuary**, Gold Coast Highway, Currumbin, ☏5534 1266, a 20ha (50 acres) wildlife reserve with the world's largest collection of Australian native fauna. The Sanctuary is visited every morning and afternoon by thousands of brightly coloured wild Rainbow Lorikeets, which don't need much encouragement to eat out of your hand, or sit on your head, and seem to love having their photographs taken. Also at the Sanctuary, which is ☉open daily 8am-5pm, are waterfalls, rainforest pools, and 250 individual species of birdlife, including the glossy black cockatoo. Entry fees: adults ☻$18, children $22, under 4 years old free, family pass $48.

North of Currumbin are Pacific and Palm Beaches.

Festivals

January - The Magic Millions Horse Race Meeting. The Daikyo Palm Meadows Golf Cup.
July - Gold Coast International Marathon and Half-Marathon.
August - The Jupiter's Yacht Classic between Sydney and the Gold Coast.
November - The Queensland Open Golf.

Sports and Facilities

The Gold Coast has all the facilities you could think of. You can play tennis, squash, golf, ten-pin bowling, lawn bowls or croquet, and go rollerskating or horseriding.

You can fish, swim, waterski, sailboard, sail, and more. There are also facilities for horse racing, greyhound racing, hot-air ballooning, mountain trekking, parasailing and many health and fitness centres.

Below are some of the sporting choices.

Golf

The Palms Golf Course, Sanctuary Cove, ✆5577 6031.

Palm Meadows Golf Course, Palm Meadows Resort, Gooding Drive, Palm Meadows, ✆1800 818 040.

Putt & Games, cnr Crescent Ave & Gold Coast Hwy, Mermaid Beach, ✆5575 3381. ☺Open 7 days.

Concept Golf Tours, ✆5578 8288, provide golfing packages from ✪$90 including green fees, cart hire and transfer to your desired resort course.

Shooting

Australian Shooting Academy, Lvl 1 Paradise Centre, Surfers Paradise, ✆5527 5100. ☺Open 7 days, 10am-10pm.

Southport Indoor Pistol Club, Unit 1 76 Ferry Rd, Southport, ✆5531 1153. ☺Open 7 days 10am-10pm.

Watersports

Shane's Watersports World, Harley Park, Labrador, ✆5591 5225. Paraflying, speedboat ride, jet ski ride.

Aussie Bob's Watersports, Berth 14D Marina Mirage, Sea World Drive, Main Beach, ✆5591 7577, parasailing, jet skis, speed boat rides, direct bookings only.

Fishing

Topline Sport Fishing Safaris, ✆5577 1953. Fresh and salt water fishing, tackle and refreshments provided, full day ✪$110pp, half day $60pp.

Paul Burt's Reel Action Fishing Charters, ✆5596 5546. Both deep sea reef (half day ✪$85pp, full day $125pp) and estuary (half day ✪$55pp, full day $105pp) fishing available.

Extreme Sports

Fly Coaster, Cypress Ave, Surfers Paradise, ✆5539 0474. Free-fall 11 stories on Australia's first extremist swing, ☺open daily until 10pm.

Bungee Rocket, cnr Palm Ave & Gold Coast Hwy, Surfers Paradise, ✆5570 2700. Rocket to a height of 50m in just over a second, ☺open 7 days 10am-10pm.

Tours and Cruises

If you have the time and desire to become intimate with the Gold Coast environment, the following selection of tours and cruises should cover all the aspects.

Tall Ship Sailing Cruises, Wharf D12 Marina Mirage, ✆5532 2444. Four different cruises, ship sails 9am daily.

Amphibious Aquabus Canal Cruises, Aquabus Safaris, 7A Orchid Ave, Surfers Paradise, ✆5539 0222, combined bus tour and canal cruise, bookings recommended, departs frequently throughout the day, 7 days, adults ✪$28, children $21, seniors $23.

Gold Coast Kayaking, ✆5527 5785. Offers morning tour or afternoon kayak snorkle tour, 9am-9pm, 7 days.

Aries Tours, 16 Barnett Pl, Ernest, ✆5594 9933. Focus on eco-tourism, choices include a Southern Skytour (5.30pm-10.30pm nightly), a Kingfisher Hinterland Tour (8am-2pm daily) and a Night Safari Tour (5.30pm-10.30pm nightly).

Tweed Endevour Cruises, Tweed River Cruise Terminal, River Terrace, Tweed Heads, ✆5536 8800. Offers 4hr rainforest & river cruise or 1.5hr river and lake cruise, lunch included, bookings essential.

Island Queen Showboat Cruises, Marina Mirage, Main Beach, ✆5571 0219. A number of cruises with various destinations, lengths and themes, prices on application.

Whale Watch, Moreton Island, ✆5591 5599. Luxury coach transfers, meals provided on cruise.

Day Tours, ✆3236 4165. Various coach tours.

Outlying Attractions

The Hinterland

Away from the coastal plain of the Gold Coast, the terrain climbs steadily but steeply up over 1000m (3281 ft) into some of Australia's richest highlands, passing through rolling rural landscapes along the way.

The Hinterland is easily accessible by a number of roads, and offers spectacular views and walking trails into rainforests.

One of the most popular lookouts is called **'The Best of All'** and is reached from Lyrebird Ridge Road. Good views can be also be obtained from **Purlingbrook Falls**, which cascade about 190m (623 ft) to the rocks belosw. You can walk to the base of the cliff and follow a track that leads behind the falls.

In the **Numinbah Valley**, just within the Queensland border, is the Natural Arch in the Natural Arch National Park. Here there are several walks through rainforest, one of which leads to the stone archway through which a waterfall plummets to a rock pool below. There is also a **Glow Worm Cave** for walkers to discover.

Lamington National Park, 45km (28 miles) from the Coast, near the state border, is the largest preserved natural stand of sub-tropical rainforest in Australia, and the park has 160km (100miles) of graded walking tracks leading to many of its highlights, including Mount Merino, Echo Point, Coomera Gorge, Picnic Rock, and the Aboriginal Cooking Caves. In all the park has more than 500 waterfalls, and majestic blackbutt, bloodwood, and giant cedar trees.

Mount Tamborine is a plateau on the McPherson Ranges, 35km (22miles) west of the Gold Coast, and comprises seven small National Parks totalling 375ha (926 acres) of rainforest in which there are 15,000-year-old Macrozamia palms, said to be the oldest living things in the world.

St Bernards historic hotel, one of the mountain's oldest establishments, is famous for its smorgasbord lunches and beautiful gardens, and there are many other guest houses and restaurants in the area.

Other popular spots in the Hinterland are **Rosin's Lookout**, which overlooks the Numinbah Valley, and Mount Warning, off the Nerang-Beechmont Road. **Mount Warning** is the first point in Australia to be struck by the rays of the morning sun, and is an ideal place to unwind and enjoy the natural beauty at the ***Springbrook Rainforest Cabins***, 317 Repeater Station Road, Springbrook, ✆5533 5366. They have three cottages with full facilities for ✪$80-120 per person per night.

Coolangatta and Tweed Heads

The twin towns of Coolangatta and Tweed Heads are the southern gateway to the Gold Coast, and occupy opposite headlands of the Tweed River, with Tweed Heads in New South Wales, and Coolangatta in Queensland.

A popular attraction in the Tweed Heads area is **Tropical Fruit World**, ✆(02) 6677 7222. It is a tropical fruit plantation with 50 types of tropical and jungle fruit, overlooking the Tweed River, and is an ideal place for a picnic. Safaris, fruit-tasting, boat cruises and live shows are on offer. There is also a cafe. Tropical Fruit World is ⊙open daily 10am-5pm, ✪$25 adults, $14 children, $19 pensioners.

Close to Coolangatta is the lighthouse at **Point Danger**.

Both towns have holiday resort centres, shopping, restaurants and tour facilities, and opportunities for all water sports on the river and the beaches.

There is a Visitor Information Centre in Shop 14B, Beachhouse Plaza, Coolangatta Place, cnr Griffith & Warner Streets, Coolangatta, ✆(07) 5536 7765.

For more information on Tweed Heads, contact the Visitor Information Centre at 4 Wharf Street, ✆(07) 5536 4244 or ✆1800 674 414, ⊙open 9am-5pm Mon-Fri, 9am-12pm Saturday. You can email them at ✉info@tactic.nsw.gov.au or visit the web page at ◉www.tactic.nsw.gov.au

Queensland - West

Toowoomba

Population 82,000

Toowoomba is situated at the top of the Great Dividing Range, 130km (81 miles) inland from Brisbane, and has an altitude of 606m (2000 ft). It is the commercial centre of the rich pastoral area of the Darling Downs.

Climate

Toowoomba has a temperate climate and therefore is less humid than on the coast, with frosts in winter and rare light snowfalls on the highest points of 'the Range'. Average temperatures: January max 27C (81F) - min 17C (63F); July max 16C (61F) - min 4C (39F).

Characteristics

A garden city which was first set-

tled in 1849. Originally the area was thought to be too swampy for a town, and the first settlement in the area was at Drayton, now a suburb of Toowoomba. But water was scarce at Drayton, and the town of Toowoomba was born. Many German immigrants settled around the town in the 1860s, successfully farming the fertile land. The soil on the Darling Downs is rich, deep and black. It is extremely fertile, but a quagmire after heavy rain, and forms deep cracks in dry weather. Toowoomba is often called 'The Garden City'.

How to Get There

By Bus

McCaffertys have a Brisbane/Sydney service via Toowoomba, and also a Brisbane/Roma service which

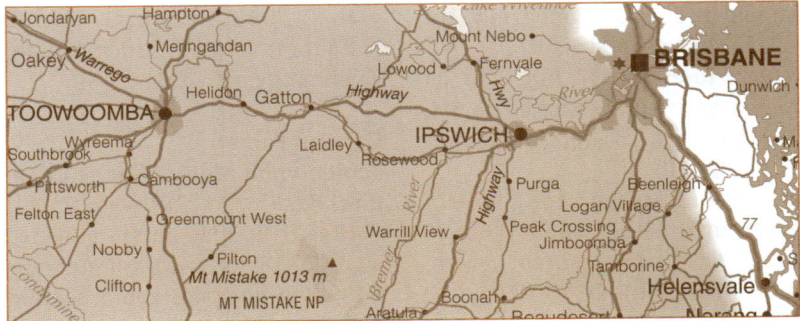

stops at Toowoomba. Skenners stop at Toowoomba on their Brisbane/Charleville service, and also on their Brisbane/Longreach Service.

By Rail

There is a daily service from Brisbane. Quite a few people get off the train at Helidon and take the McCaffertys bus to Toowoomba because it is faster than travelling the whole way by rail. A combined rail/bus ticket is available.

The Westlander stops at Toowoomba on its twice weekly run to Roma and Charleville.

By Road

From Brisbane, travel through Ipswich on the Warrego Highway, 130km (81 miles).

From Sydney, travel on the New England Highway, through Warwick.

Tourist Information

There are two Toowoomba Visitor Information Centres. One is in 86 James Street, ©(07) 4639 3797, the other is in 476 Ruthven Street, ©(07) 4638 7555. They share the email address ✉ infocentre@ toowoomba.qld.gov.au and have a website at ☜ www.toowoomba. qld.gov.au

There is also the Toowoomba & Golden West Regional Tourist Association, located at 4 Little Street, ©(07) 4632 1988 or email ✉ TGWRTA@iqnetlink.com.au.

Or you can contact the Toowoomba Local Tourist Association, on ©(07) 4635 4056.

Accommodation

Toowoomba has its fair share of motels, hotels and caravan parks. Here is a selection, with prices for a double room per night, which should be used as a guide only. The telephone area code is 07.

Blue Violet Motor Inn, Cnr 31 Margaret Street & McKenzie Sts, ℂ4638 1488. 13 units, swimming pool - ✪$70.

Glenfield Motor Lodge, 876 Ruthven Streets, ℂ4635 4466. 30 units, licensed restaurant, swimming pool, bbq - ✪$100-125.

Park Motor Inn, 88 Margaret Street, ℂ4632 1011. 47 units, licensed restaurant (closed Sunday), swimming pool - ✪$95-110.

A Tudor Lodge Motel, cnr Scott & Cohoe Streets, ℂ4638 1822. 21 units, unlicensed restaurant (closed Sat & Sun), swimming pool, bbq - ✪$75-85.

Federal Hotel Motel, Cnr James & Geddes St, ℂ4632 8686. 20 units, licensed restuarant, bbq - ✪$75-90.

Murcure Hotel Burke & Wills Toowoomba, 554 Ruthven, ℂ4632 2433. 93 rooms, licensed restaurant - ✪$132.

Garden City Motor Inn, 718 Ruthven Street, ℂ4635 5377. 15 units, swimming pool - ✪$69-75.

James Street Motor Inn, cnr James & Kitchener Streets, ℂ4639 0200. 40 units, licensed restaurants, swimming pool, bbq - ✪$75.

Leichhardt Motor Inn, 682 Ruthven St, ℂ4638 4644. 24 units, swimming pool, bbq - ✪$72-86.

Applegum Inn, 41 Margaret St,

ℂ4632 2088. 25 units, licensed restaurant (closed Sunday), bbq, swimming pool - ✪$79-100.

Caravan Parks

Toowoomba Motor Village Caravan Park, 821 Ruthven Street, ℂ4635 8186. (No pets) - powered sites ✪$18 for two, on-site vans $29 for two, park cabin section $42-55, cabin section $40.

Garden City Caravan Park, 34 Eiser Street, ℂ4635 1747. (No pets) - powered sites ✪$19 for two, on-site vans $31 for two.

Glenfield Motor Lodge Caravan Park, cnr Ruthven & Stenner Streets, ℂ4635 4466. (No pets) - powered sites ✪$18 for two.

Eating Out

Toowoomba has a good selection of restaurants, bistros, coffee shops and takeaway outlets. It even has four McDonald's - one at 277 Margaret Street, another at 827 Ruthven Street, a third on the corner of Bridge & McGregor Streets, and the fourth in the Grand Central Shopping Centre on Dent Street. Following is a selection of eateries you might like to investigate.

The Conservatory Restaurant, Mercure Hotel Burke & Wills, 554 Ruthven Street, ℂ(07) 4632 2433 - licensed, a la carte.

Carousel, 88 Margaret Street, ©(07) 4638 4727 - licensed, a la carte.

Gaby's Restaurant, 210 Herries Street, ©(07) 4632 7382 - licensed, International.

Da Vinci's, 22 Hill Street, ©4638 4606 - licensed & BYO, Italian.

Mexican Cantina Grill, 164 Margaret Street, ©4638 1888 - BYO, Mexican.

Banjo's Steakhouse, cnr Ruthven & Hanna Street, ©4636 1033 - licensed, steak/seafood.

Westlake, 127 Anzac Avenue, ©4634 7188 - licensed, Chinese/ seafood.

Crown Seafood Restaurant & Oyster Bar, 200 Ruthven Street, ©(07) 4637 6861.

Dee's Vintage Thai Restaurant, 515 Ruthven Street, ©(07) 4632 5125.

Railway's Heritage Restaurant, Station Street, ©(07) 4631 3223.

Points of Interest

Toowoomba has beautiful tree-lined streets with many parks and beautiful private gardens. The city has an active cultural and artistic life. It looks its best in September for the **Carnival of Flowers**. People come from all over the State to look at the gardens entered in the competitions. There are several categories, eg new private garden, good neighbours, factory garden, etc. The whole of the town seems to take pride in their gardens. Toowoomba's chosen the violet as its floral emblem as this small, fragrant flower flourishes here.

The view from **Picnic Point Lookout** is panoramic. On one side you have the city, and on the other side, the Lockyer Valley with Table Top and Sugar Loaf Mountains in the foreground. The range stretches off into the distance to the south. West of the city is the distinctive Gowrie Mountain and the Kingsthorpe Hills.

The scenic **Prince Henry Drive** starts and finishes at the eastern end of Bridge Street and follows the cliff top around a small spur of the Great Dividing Range. It is a one-way traffic thoroughfare from which there are breathtaking views. It goes through the suburb of Prince Henry Heights, and past Redwood Park Fauna Sanctuary.

For a view of the city lights at night, drive along Ruthven Street which becomes Crows Nest Road, to the top of **Mount Kynoch**, the site of the city reservoir. There is a 360 degree view of the town and the districts of Crows Nest, Ravensbourne, Lockyer and Gowrie Mountain.

Queen's Park and the Botanic Gardens cover more than 28ha (70 acres), and provide an attractive display all year round. Laurel Bank Park has a scented garden for blind visitors.

Toowoomba has some fine **old buildings** including the post office, court house, the White Horse Hotel, and Gabbinar and Clifford House, both built in the 1860s, as well as the more humble Tawa, a home built soon after allotments were first handed out in 1849.

The old centre of **Drayton**, now a suburb of Toowoomba, has not been completely lost to development. The Royal Bull's Head Inn, the earliest hotel on the Downs, has been restored by the National Trust. The 1850s building incorporates part of the original hostelry. St Matthew's Church was built in 1887, and contains records dating back to 1850 from an earlier building. It has a splendid hammer beam roof, and the knocker on the vestry door originally graced the Bull's Head where the settlement's first services were held. Smithfield, a stately homestead built at the end of the last century, is now a restaurant. There is also a memorial to author Arthur Hoey Davis (Steele Rudd) who made Dad and Dave famous. Davis was raised at Emu Creek, 20km (12 miles) from Drayton, where he was born in 1868.

The **Toowoomba Regional Art Gallery**, adjacent to the City Hall,

©4688 6652, has an interesting collection of paintings and antiques - ☺open 11am-3pm Mon, Wed & Fri.

The **Lionel Lindsay Art Gallery**, 27-37 Jellicoe Street, ©4688 6693, has a collection of works by great Australian artists, authors and poets. It is ☺open Tuesdays, Wednesdays and Thursdays 11am-3pm and Sundays 1pm-4pm.

The **Cobb & Co Museum**, 27 Lindsay Street, ©4639 1971, has a unique display of horse-drawn vehicles, and is ☺open Mon-Fri 10am-4pm, Sat-Sun 1-4pm. Admission is ✪$2 for adults, $1 for children under 14.

Blue Arrow Drive is a 48km (30 miles) scenic drive that is well worth following - maps are available at the Tourist Information Office.

Festivals

The Carnival of Flowers is held each year in September, and the Garden Fest in April.

Facilities

Toowoomba has all the facilities you would expect of a town with such a large population - golf, tennis, squash, horse racing, lawn bowls, ten-pin bowling, croquet, swimming pools, cinemas, theatres, and so on.

Outlying Attractions

The Darling Downs is Queensland's main wheat growing area. Neat homesteads speckle the land, and a pattern of fields stretches over the horizon. There are not only wheat fields, but other grains are grown, as well as sunflowers, other oil seeds, and cotton. Dairy and beef cattle graze on the hills, and sheep further west. No visit to Too-woomba would be complete without a drive through the surrounding countryside.

Cooby Creek Dam

The source of Toowoomba's water supply is also a popular picnic spot. Travel along the Crows Nest Road, turn left 17km (11 miles) from the post office, and the dam is a further 17km (11 miles).

Oakey

Half an hour's drive north-west of Toowoomba, on the Warrego Highway. The Museum of Australian Army Flying, ✆4691 7666, has one of the best displays of aviation memorabilia in the world. In several hangars and an outdoors area are the aircraft, which range from a fully restored replica Box Kite, and the first aeroplane in service, as well as Bristols, Cessnas, Bells, Austers and more. Admission is ✪$5 adult, $2 child, $12 family.

Jondaryan Woolshed Museum, on the Warrego Highway just past Oakey, is the oldest and largest continuously used shearing shed in Queensland. The woolshed is ⌚open daily 8.30am-5pm, and guided tours are available. There are lots of working displays and machinery, and colonial style lunches with damper and billy tea are available. For more information phone ✆4692 2229.

Dalby

Known as the Hub of the Downs, Dalby is 83km (52 miles) from Toowoomba, on the Warrego Highway, and is home to one of Queensland's principle agricultural colleges.

An oasis in the middle of town is the Thomas Jack Memorial Park, facing the Warrego Highway. The park consists of more than 3ha (7 acres) of lawns, gardens and shrubberies, with a children's playground, shelters, barbecue facilities, a lily pond and a large area suitable for social cricket. The tourist information centre is located in the north-eastern corner of the park.

In Black Street is the Pioneer Park Museum, ✆4662 4760, which is open seven days a week for visitors to catch a glimpse of the rural past, ⌚Mon-Fri 10am-3pm, Sat-Sun 10am-4pm. There is a small admission charge, and craft items are for sale.

The Dalby Tourist Information Centre can be contacted on ✆(07) 4662 1066 and are located in Thomas Jack Park, on the corner of Drayton & Condamine Streets. You can email them at ✉dalbychamber @dalby.qld.gov.au or visit 👁www. dalbytown.com.au on the web.

Bunya Mountains National Park

The Park is 60km (37 miles) northeast of Dalby and covers 11,700ha (28,900 acres). The Bunya Mountains form an isolated section of the Great Dividing Range, rising abruptly from the surrounding countryside to an average elevation of 975m (3199 ft) reaching 1100m (3609 ft) at Mount Mowbullan and Kiangarow.

The district has considerable historic significance. Once, Aborigines visited the mountains regularly for six-week tribal ceremonies of hunting, feasting, mock fighting and corroborees. These visits coincided with heavy croppings of Bunya Pine cones, usually every three years. The vegetation of the park comprises 13 types, but can be broadly grouped into rainforest, eucalypt forest and grasslands. More than 200 plant species have been identified. The Bunya Pine, with its characteristic dome-shaped top, rises in stately elegance above the other vegetation. It is unique in its abundance in the area.

The graded walking track system throughout the park provides the bushwalker with an opportunity to discover all types and varieties of vegetation for themselves. They will also come across water falls, and plenty of animal life, including the Bunya Mountains ringtail possum, found only on the mountain.

There are two camping areas - Burton's Well and Dandanbah. Burton's Well provides toilets, water and picnic facilities. Dandanbah has camping and unit facilities as well as a kiosk and restaurant. For more information contact Rosella's Restaurant in the park, ✆4668 3131.

Miles

Continuing along the Warrego Highway from Dalby to Roma, brings you to Chinchilla and further on, Miles.

Miles is well known for the Miles Historical Village & Museum in Murilla Street, ✆4627 1492. The village is open daily 8am-5pm. Another touch of history in the town is Possum Park, ✆4627 1651, where ammunition bunkers were built underground during World War II. Now the bunkers are used as visitor accommodation.

At Chinchilla, the Chinchilla Historical Museum, ✆4662 7014, has a vast collection of steam-powered traction engines. Chinchilla is one of the largest petrified wood areas of the world. The wood is from the Jurassic Age, about 140-180 million years ago. Fossicking can be done on the Hurse family's property, Eddington Stud, at a small cost per bucket. Locals Fred and Merle Newman, who live at 95 Boyd Street, Chinchilla, have a collection of rocks and petrified wood, and a large workroom where the cutting and polishing are done.

The Chinchilla Tourist Information Centre is in Chinchilla Street, ℂ(07) 4668 9564.

At Boongara, 8km east of Chinchilla, the Cactoblastis Hall is a memorial to a small insect imported from South America in the 1920s to eat out a plant that had become the curse of the west, the prickly pear.

Roma

Gas was discovered in Roma, over 400km (248 miles) north-west of Toowoomba, at the beginning of the century during a water-drilling procedure on Hospital Hill. Eight years later, Roma suffered the first petroliferous gas well fire, which took more than a month to extinguish.

The maiden oil well in Roma was discovered in 1927 but soon dried out, though more oil was discovered. Roma is also the biggest and best inland store cattle market, and has had the biggest sale yarding in Australia. It is a flourishing town of 8000 people. Crops in the district include wheat, sorghum, oats and sunflowers, and a number of fruit crops are also produced, from stone-fruit to citrus. Festival time in Roma is Easter, with street parades, goat races, more traditional horse races, dancing, open-air concerts and rodeos.

One person who spent a lot of time in Roma, mostly in the courthouse, was Henry Readford, who was the initiator of Australia's most famous cattle theft. Along with a handful of others, he stole several hundred cattle from Bowen Downs in central Queensland and drove them on a mammoth trek to Blanchewater in northern South Australia. This man's real life story is almost as amazing as the that of the book loosely based on it - Robbery Under Arms. Readford, or Captain Starlight, appeared in Roma Court on at least four occasions and was let off each time. When he was tried in Toowoomba, the result was different and he was sentenced to eight months in prison with hard labour.

The Roma & District Tourist Information Centre is at 71 Arthur Street, ℂ(07) 4622 1416.

Queensland - North

Sunshine Coast

Population 120,000
The Sunshine Coast stretches from Caloundra, 90km (56 miles) north of Brisbane, to Double Island Point in the north. It boasts 55km (34 miles) of white sandy beaches and rocky headlands.

Climate

Average Temperatures: January max 29C (84F) - min 20C (66F); July max 21C (70F) - min 7C (45F). Average annual rainfall -1776mm (70 ins). Driest months June-September. A lot of the summer rain falls in evening storms after hot sunny days.

Characteristics

The Sunshine Coast is rather like the Gold Coast was in the 1960s, but it has a friendlier, laid-back air with less razzamatazz. The beaches and surf compare favourably with the Gold Coast, and there are fewer high rise buildings that cast shadows on the beaches in the afternoons.

The high rocky headlands and areas of natural bushland divide the resorts, and afford the holiday maker the opportunity to walk along shady paths in the heat of the afternoon, or drop a fishing line into the shallow waters of the rivers and savour the peace and quiet.

There are still secluded beaches which can only be reached by narrow sandy paths meandering through sand dunes, and the mouths of the rivers are ideal places to fish, canoe, row or sail.

The Noosa River, which is navigable to near its headwaters at Tin

Can Bay, is home to thousands of birds. The river flows through several lakes on its way to the sea, and many houseboats are to be found along its reaches. The pace is more relaxed than on the Gold Coast. There is plenty to entertain, and the area boasts of excellent restaurants.

How to Get There

By Air

The major airport for the region is the Sunshine Coast Airport, centrally located at Mudjimba, and equipped for jet aircraft.

Qantas, ✆13 1313 flies directly from Sydney and Melbourne, with connections from other capital cities.

By Bus

Suncoast Pacific, ✆5443 1011, and McCafferty's, ✆13 1499, operate routes that service the Sunshine Coast frequently.

By Rail

Queensland Rail, ✆13 2232, electric trains service the area from Brisbane to the main Sunshine Coast station at Nambour.

By Road

From Brisbane, via the Bruce Highway. The four lane section puts Caloundra within an hour's drive of Brisbane, and Noosa is only another 61km (38 miles), or 45 minutes, further on.

Visitor Information

Tourism Sunshine Coast Ltd, The Wharf, Parkyn Parade, Mooloolaba, ✆(07) 5477 7311. The web site is: ☜www.sunzine.net/suncoast/tsc/index.html and the email address is ✎tourism@sunzine.net

Maroochy Tourism and Travel, Sixth Avenue, Maroochydore, ✆(07) 5479 1566, have an email facility at ✎admin@maroochytourism.com and a web page at ☜www.maroochytourism.com

Caloundra City Information Centre, 7 Caloundra Road, Caloundra, ✆(07) 5491 0202. Their web address is ☜www.caloundra.qld.gov.au and the email address is ✎c.stewart@caloundra.qld.gov.au

Tourism Noosa Information Centre, Hastings Street Roundabout, Noosa Heads, ✆(07) 5447 4988. The web site is ☜www.tourismnoosa.com.au and you can email them here at ✎info@tourismnoosa.com.au

There is another outlet in the area: Noosa Junction Tourist Information Centre, Shop 5 The Oasis Centre, 20 Sunshine Beach Road, Noosa Heads, ✆(07) 5447 3755.

Accommodation

A good variety of accommodation, ranging from caravan parks, motels, hotels, guest houses, self-contained units and five-star resorts are available throughout the coast from Noosa to Caloundra. For a copy of the *Sunshine Coast Accommodation Guide*, ✆(07) 5477 7311.

Here is a selection, with prices for a double room per night, which should be used as a guide only. The telephone area code is 07.

Caloundra

Anchorage Motor Inn and Resort, 18 Bowman Road, ✆5491 1499. 22 units, 4 suites, licensed restaurant, swimming pool, barbecue, tennis - ✪$75-125.

Altons Palm Breeze, 105 Bulcock Street, ✆5491 5566. 19 units, 1 suite, swimming pool, barbecue - ✪$55-75.

Caloundra Suncourt, 135 Bulcock Street, ✆5491 1011. 8 units, swimming pool, barbecue - ✪$65-120.

City Centre Motel, cnr Orsova Terrace & Minchinton Street, ✆5491 3301. 8 units, undercover parking, barbecue - ✪$65-80.

Caloundra Motel, 30 Bowman Road, ✆5491 1411. 14 units, swimming pool, barbecue, undercover parking - ✪$55-65.

Caravan Parks

Hibiscus & Tripcony Caravan Park, Bowman Road, ✆5491 1564. (No pets allowed) - powered sites ✪$20-26 for two, on-site vans $35-60, cabins $40-60 for two.

Danmira Tourist Park, 1 Onslow Street, Golden Beach, ✆5492 1731. 70 sites, barbecue, pool - powered sites ✪$20-25 for two, units $55-95 for two, cabins $40-85 for two.

Dicky Beach Family Holiday Park, Beerburrum Street, Dicky Beach, ✆5491 3342. 124 sites, tennis, swimming pool - powered sites ✪$18-30 for two, cabins $45-65 for two.

Maroochydore

Coachmans Courte Motor Inn, 94 Sixth Avenue, ✆5443 4099. 14 units, swimming pool, spa, undercover parking - ✪$90-95.

Heritage Motor Inn, 69 Sixth Avenue, ✆5443 7355. 18 units, swimming pool, spa - ✪$85-110.

Beach Motor Inn, cnr Sixth Avenue & Kingsford Smith Parade, ✆5443 7044. 18 units, swimming pool, barbecue - ✪$90-135.

Blue Waters, 64 Sixth Avenue, ✆5443 6700. 20 units, swimming pool, undercover parking - ✪$60-105.

Avenue Motor Inn, 106 Sixth Avenue, ✆5443 3600. 16 units, swimming pool, barbecue - ✪$85-115.

Maroochy River, 361 Bradman Avenue, ✆5443 3142. 8 units, swimming pool - ✪$55-95.

Caravan Parks

Alexandra Gardens Top Tourist Park, Okinja Road, ✆5443 2356. (No pets allowed) - powered sites ✪$19-24 for two, villas $50-100 for two, cabins $40-65 for two.

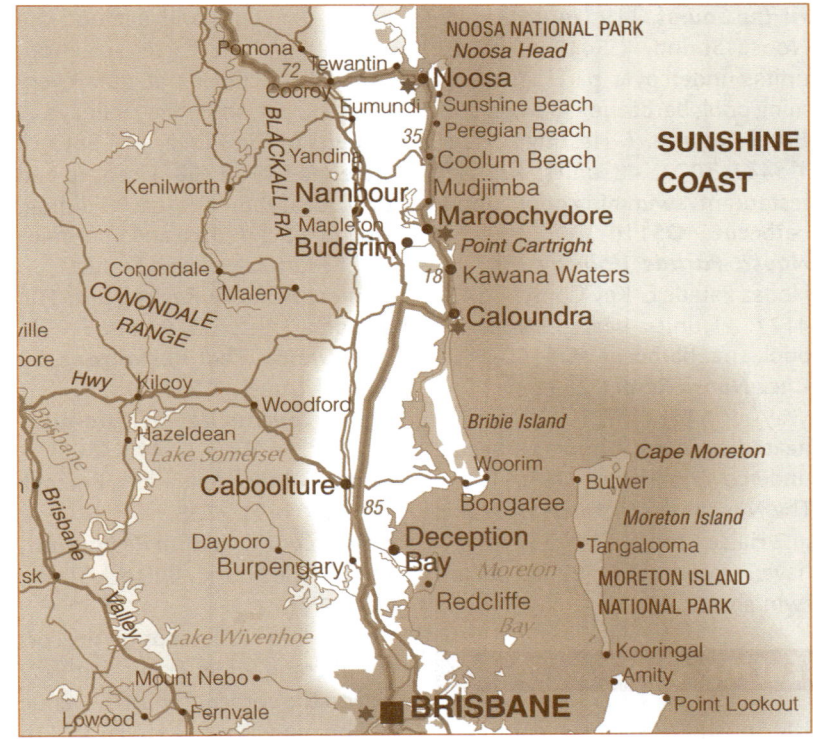

Maroochy Palms Holiday Village, 319 Bradman Avenue, ☎5443 8611. (No pets allowed) - powered sites ✪$26 for two, cabins $50-95, villas $65-125 for two.

Maroochy River Cabin Village & Caravan Park, Diura Street, ☎5443 3033. (Pets on application) - powered sites ✪$19-21 for two, on-site vans $40-55 for two, cabins $65-80 for two.

The Maroochydore **Youth Hostel** is in 24 Schirrmann Drive, ☎5443 3151. They have 9 rooms at ✪$19 per person twin share.

Noosa Heads

Netanya Noosa Motel, 75 Hastings Street, Laguna Bay, ☎5447 4722. 48 units, swimming pool, spa, sauna, gym, barbecue - ✪$200-600.

Noosa International, Edgar Bennett Avenue, ☎5447 4822. 65 suites, licensed restaurant, heated swimming pool, spas, saunas - ✪$165-210.

At the Sound, 119 Noosa Parade, Noosa Sound, ✆5449 9211. 22 units, undercover parking, swimming pool, barbecue - ✪$450-550.
Hotel Laguna, 6 Hastings Street, ✆5447 3077. 48 units, licensed restaurant, swimming pool, tennis, barbecue - ✪$110-330.
Noosa Parade Holiday Inn, cnr Noosa Parade & Key Court, ✆5447 4177. 11 units, heated swimming pool, spa, barbecue -✪$100-140.
Chez Noosa Resort, 263 David Low Way, ✆5447 2027. 28 units, heated swimming pool, barbecue, undercover parking - ✪$70-120.
The Noosa Heads **Youth Hostel** is in 2 Halse Lane, ✆5447 3377. They have 26 rooms at ✪$22 per person twin share.

Eating Out

The Sunshine Coast is a gourmet's delight. Dozens of restaurants feature fresh local seafood complemented by delicious sun-ripened tropical fruit such as avocados, pineapples and pawpaws. Beach and river fronts are dotted with picnic tables where visitors can enjoy takeaway or picnic food. Here is an idea of what is available in each district.

Caloundra

Island Restaurant, at the Anchorage Moror Inn & Resort, 18 Bowman Road, ✆5491 1499. Licensed premises, steak and seafood are specialties, a-la-carte selection, cocktail bar. Opens at 6pm every night except on Public Holidays.
Trivolis of Pia Place, 118 Bulcock Street, ✆5491 1768. Licensed and BYO, seafood, a-la-carte dining. Open 10.30am-3pm and 6pm-midnight Mon-Sat, closed Sunday.
Chinese Holiday Restaurant, 106 Bulcock Street, ✆5491 6066.
Blue Orchid Thai Restaurant, 22 Bulcock Street, ✆5491 9433.
Brunos Taverna Italian Ristorante, 725 Nicklin Way, ✆5493 1806.
Bamboo Garden, 95 Bulcock Street, ✆5491 2768.
Flower Lounge Indian Restaurant, Shop 4 The Strand, Bulcock Street, ✆5499 7677.
You will find McDonalds on the corner of Erang Street & Nicklan Way and on the corner of Fourth Avenue & Bowman Road. KFC is at 73b Bowman Road. Pizza Hut is at 69 Bowman Road, ✆5491 5100.

Maroochydore

Swells Restaurant & Bar, 6 Duporth Avenue, ✆5443 6401. Fully licensed, open 11am-11pm every day.
Sun See Chinese Restaurant, Shop 1, 50 Aerodrome Road, ✆5443 2636. BYO, wide range of cuisines with an oriental emphasis. Open 5pm-9pm every day.
Som Tam Thai Restaurant, cnr Fifth Avenue & Aerodrome Road,

©5479 1700. BYO (wine only), open 5pm-10pm 7 days and 12pm-2.30pm Fri-Sun, closed Public Holidays.

Waterfront, David Low Way, ©5448 4488.

Gauchos Mexican Restaurant, Kingsford-Smith Parade, ©5443 8877.

Jimmys Place, Shop 4, Broadmeadow Road, ©5479 2241.

Azzurro Ristorante Italiano, 93 Aerodrome Road, ©5443 3500.

Sizzler, cnr Fifth Avenue & Aerodrome Road, ©5443 4377.

Indian Hathi Restaurant, 37 Aerodrome Road, ©5443 5411.

McDonalds has two locations in Maroochydore: 14-18 Aerodrome Road and in Sunshine Plaza. Pizza Hut is on the corner of Horton Parade and First Avenue. Pizza Hut is at 153 Aerodrome Road, ©5443 4911.

Noosa Heads

Freshwater Bar & Grill, Edgar Bennett Avenue, ©5447 5900. Open 10am-midnight 7 days.

Riva Waterfront Restaurant & Bar, 10/1 Quamby Place, ©5449 2440. A-la-carte menu. Open midday-midnight 7 days.

Cocos, cnr Park Road & Mitti Street, ©5447 2440. Licensed restaurant open 8am-midnight.

Roma Pizza Restaurant, Sunshine Beach Road, ©5447 3602. Offers prawns, pizza, pasta and steak. Open 5pm-10pm.

Indian Empire, Shop 4 Noosa Wharf, Quambi Place, Noosa Sound, ©5474 5655.

Emerald House Chinese Restaurant, 11 Sunshine Beach, ©5447 3356.

Michels, 1 Hastings Street, ©5447 3880.

Lindonis Italian Ristorante, Hastings Street, ©5447 5111.

Sails, 75 Hastings Street, ©5447 4235.

Pommies, Quamby Place, Noosa Wharf Shopping Centre, ©5474 8600.

KFC is in 5 Sunshine Beach Road. Pizza Hut is on the corner of Lake

Weyba Drive and Weyba Road, ©5449 7711.

Local Transport

Sunshine Coast Coaches operate daily bus services from Caloundra to Nambour, and Noosa District Bus Lines operate a daily service from Nambour to Noosa.

Points of Interest

Visitors to the area will quickly discover why it is one of Australia's premier tourist destinations. With golden beaches, scenic hinterland, lush rainforest, breathtaking mountains views, crystal-clear lakes and waterways, the Sunshine Coast has it all. For most visitors, the main attractions are sun, surf and sand.

The beaches stretch from Caloundra in the south to Double Island Point in the north, taking in popular holiday spots like Mooloolaba, Maroochydore, Coolum and Noosa.

Everyone, though, soon discovers that the hinterland also has much to offer, with its patchwork of tropical fruit farms, rainforests, State Forests and National Parks. It is the perfect complement to the coastal resorts. You can enjoy a bushwalk, while away the hours in one of the many arts and crafts galleries, sit down to a Devonshire tea, or take in the spectacular panoramic views.

Caloundra

Population 19,700

Caloundra City, at the southern entrance to the Sunshine Coast, is an attractive and affordable holiday destination. Located just an hour north of Brisbane by four-lane highway, it is the perfect place to shake the nine-to-five blues. Apart from 30km (19 miles) of beaches, Caloundra has a special attraction which makes it the envy of other coastal resorts - the Pumicestone Passage. It is a haven for a wide variety of water sports, is famed for its fishing and harbours as well as two of the safest swimming beaches on the Sunshine Coast - Bulcock Beach and Golden Beach.

Maroochy

Population 16,600

Mooloolaba, Alexandra Headland and Maroochydore are the main coastal townships of the Maroochy Shire.

Mooloolaba Beach, with Point Cartwright on the southern side and the Mooloolaba Harbour wall, is a protected beach which is popular with families and windsurfers. Mooloolaba is home to a large fishing fleet, and fresh fish can be purchased daily from the Mooloolaba Fisheries Co-operative.

Alexandra Headland is renowned for its great surf. In summer, board riders flock to the tiny cove every day.

Underwater World at the Mooloolaba Wharf is an enjoyable experience. The moving acrylic tunnel allows glass-housed sharks, stingrays, and fish to swim over and around the visitors.

Maroochydore, at the mouth of the Maroochy River, is a thriving tourist and business centre. It has a fine surfing beach, and the river is a favourite spot for watersports and fishing alike.

Travelling north along the coast the major townships are Coolum Beach, Peregian Beach, Marcus Beach, Sunshine Beach and, finally, Noosa Heads.

Noosa

Population 6000

Noosa Heads, with its northerly facing beach, is protected from the prevailing south-easterly winds. Noosa has a cosmopolitan atmosphere, coupled with the natural beauty of the area. The headland is a National Park and there are several walks meandering through it to the various attractions, including Boiling Pot, Hell's Gates, Paradise Cave.

Noosa's boutiques and restaurants in Hastings Street are first class, and there is no shortage of entertainment.

The coloured sands at Teewah can be reached by 4WD from Noosa along the beach at low tide. Tours are available from Noosaville or Tewantin. Upstream from Tewantin, the Noosa River meanders through lakes which are surrounded by wetlands with prolific bird life. This area is the **Cooloola National Park**. In the 1870s, huge log rafts were guided down the river to Tewantin, where they were sorted before continuing their way to Brisbane. Five lakes are linked in a waterway network stretching for almost 80km (50 miles). Lake Cootharaba has a special area for learner water skiers, and many visitors spend holidays on houseboats wandering through the river system.

Inland is **Nambour**, the most southern of Queensland's sugar towns, where the old cane trolleys ramble across the main street to the Moreton Central Sugar Mill. Pineapple and other tropical fruit plantations are also found around the district.

At the Sunshine Plantation, 6km south of Nambour, you can see the **Big Pineapple**, Nambour Connection Road, Woombye, and take a tour of the plantation by train. It is ☉open daily 9am-5pm, ✆5442 1333

Bli Bli has a **Fairytale Castle**, David Low Way, ✆5448 5373, a replica 11th century Norman Castle with moat, portcullis and drawbridge. Inside, fairytales are depicted in elaborate dioramas. Popular with children, the castle is ☾open daily 9am-5pm.

Nostalgia Town, 596 David Low Way, ✆5448 7155, is another attraction, just north of Bli Bli at Pacific Paradise. Call in and have a laugh at the past.

Big Cow Antique Centre, ✆5446 8477, home of the Big Cow, is 6km north of Nambour on the Bruce Highway, and milking demonstrations and feeding of nursery animals are some of the highlights.

Another 3km north at Yandina is **Gingertown**, Pioneers Road, ✆5446 8455, the largest ginger processing factory in the southern hemisphere. The ginger processed here is grown in rich red soil between the Blackall Range and the coast.

On **Tanawha Forest Glen Tourist Drive**, visitors can visit three attractions:

Super Bee's Honey Factory near the Buderim turnoff, ✆5445 3544, has collecting demonstrations and is ☾open daily 9am-5pm. Admission is free.

At the Forest Glen **Deer Sanctuary and Wildlife Park**, ✆5445 1274, free-roaming deer can be fed from your car. Koalas, kangaroos and emus can also be seen. It is ☾open 9am-5pm, daily.

The **Moonshine Valley Winery**, Bruce Highway, ✆5445 1198, specialises in fruit wines. Free tastings are held daily.

Outlying Attractions

Gympie

Gympie is a large township situated about halfway between Maryborough and Maroochydore on the Bruce Highway. Like many towns in the north of Queensland it was once known for its abundance of gold, after its discovery by James Nash. The town sprung up during a rush in 1868 and it didn't take more than a few months for 25,000 hopeful prospectors to cram the fields nearby.

Gympie's attractions are mainly historic, including The Gold and Mining Museum, the Woodworks Forestry and Timber Museum and a number of buildings reminiscent of the town's colonial heritage.

There are two places you can contact for further information: the Gympie Tourist Information Centre, Bruce Highway, Lake Alford, ✆(07) 5482 2847 or the Coloola Regional Development Bureau, 224 Mary Street, Gympie, ✆(07) 5482 5444.

Blackall Range

The Blackall Range, on Brisbane's Sunshine Coast, is a world apart, with its art and craft galleries, Devonshire teas, comfortable pubs, green fields, hedgerows, and a feeling of Olde England. From high vantage points between Mapleton and

Maleny, the small farms and cane fields of the coastal plain stretch out to join the blue Pacific, and south from Maleny are the dramatic Glass House Mountains. Throughout the Blackall Ranges are national and forestry parks, offering superb walks through tropical rainforest, picnic spots beside waterfalls, and rock pools for swimming.

The scenic drive through the Blackall Range is one of the most popular day outings in south-east Queensland. The southern end of the range drive is little more than an hour north of Brisbane, and access is no more than half an hour from most Sunshine Coast resort towns.

The website to visit is ☞www.sunshinecoast.com/blackallranges.html

Maryborough

Including Hervey Bay and Fraser Island

Population 25,500
Maryborough is 255km (158 miles) north of Brisbane, on the Mary River.

Characteristics

Maryborough is known as Heritage City due to its magnificent homes and public buildings.

Situated on a curve of the broad Mary River, close to 150 years of history can be found in the city. The Mary River was discovered by Andrew Petrie in 1842, and not long after a member of his party returned to establish sheep farming near Tiaro. However by March 1843, the venture had failed due to disease in the sheep and attacks by natives. In June, 1847, George Furber settled in one of the deserted out-stations on the south bank and built a wharf, store and shanty. The schooner *Sisters* arrived in December to load wool from the stations and Maryborough became a wool port.

How to Get There

By Air
Sunstate Airlines, ✆13 1313, have daily flights to/from Brisbane. Sunstate and Flight West, ✆1300 130 092, both service Hervey Bay.
By Bus
McCafferty's, ✆13 1499, Greyhound Pioneer, ✆13 2030, and Suncoast Pacific, ✆5443 1011, stop at Maryborough on their Brisbane-Cairns routes.

By Road

Maryborough is on the Bruce Highway, 255km (158 miles) north of Brisbane. The journey takes about 3 hours. Hervey Bay is a further 34km (half an hour's drive) north east.

Visitor Information

The Fraser Coast - South Burnett Regional Tourism Board Ltd. is located at 388-396 Kent Street, Maryborough, ✆(07) 4122 3444. The web address is 👁www. frasercoast.org and the email address is ✐ info@frasercoast.org

The Maryborough Tourist Information Centre is at 30 Ferry Street, Maryborough, ✆4121 4111.

You will find the Hervey Bay Tourist & Information Centre at 353 The Esplanade, ✆4124 4050. There is also an Information Centre at 63 Old Maryborough Road, Pialba, ✆4124 9609.

If you wish to make bookings, the following two outlets will be able to assist you:

The Whale Booking Office, 419 The Eplanade, ✆4125 3399, and Hervey Bay Accommodation Centre, 139 Boat Harbour Drive, Hervey Bay, ✆4124 2424.

Accommodation

There is plenty of accommodation available in the South Burnett Region, and here is a selection with prices for a double room per night, which should be used as a guide only. The telephone area code is 07.

Maryborough

Susan River Homestead Ranch Resort, Fraser Coast Highway, ✆4121 6846. 16 rooms, licensed restaurant, swimming pool, spa, sauna, tennis, water skiing, barbecue - ✪$122 twin share.

McNevins Parkway, 188 John Street; ✆4122 2888. 15 units, licensed restaurant, swimming pool, spa, sauna - ✪$80.

Mineral Sands, 75 Ferry, cnr Albert Street, ✆4121 2366. 20 units, licensed restaurant, swimming pool - ✪$70-75.

Cara, 196 Walker Street, ✆4122 4288. 13 units, pool - ✪$60-75.

Arkana Inn, 46 Ferry Street, ✆4121 2261. 32 units, licensed restaurant, swimming pool - ✪$60-70.

Spanish Motor Inn Maryborough, 499 Alice Street, ✆4121 2858. 22 units, swimming pool - ✪$60-70.

Maryborough City, 138 Ferry Street, ✆4121 2568. 17 units, licensed restaurant (closed Sun), swimming pool, barbecue - ✪$60.

Royal Centre Point, 326 Kent Street, ✆4121 2241. 18 units, licensed restaurant - ✪$55-80.

Caravan Parks

Wallace Units & Caravan Park, 22 Ferry Street, ✆4121 3970. Pool, barbecue - powered sites ✪$14 for two, units $50 for two, cabins $30 for two.

Huntsville Caravan Park, 23 Gympie Road, ✆4121 4075. (Pets allowed on application) - powered sites ✪$16 for two, on-site vans $25 for two, cabins $30 for two.

Maryborough Caravan Park, 209 Gympie Road, ✆4121 6379. 50 sites, barbecue, pool - powered sites ✪$14 for two, cabins, ✪$40 for two.

Country Stopover Caravan Park, Bruce Highway, ✆4121 2764. (Pets allowed on application) - powered sites ✪$17 for two, on-site vans $25 for two.

Hervey Bay

The accommodation for the Bay is in the towns of Torquay, Urangan, Pialba and Scarness.

Playa Concha Resort, 475 Esplanade, Torquay, ✆4125 1544. 40 units, 16 suites, licensed restaurants, heated swimming pool, spa, barbecue - ✪$75.

Reef, 410 The Esplanade, Torquay, ✆4125 2744. 25 units, swimming pool, barbecue - ✪$40-67.

Kondari Resort, 49 Elizabeth Street, Urangan, ✆4128 9702. 97 units, licensed restaurant, bistro, swimming pool, spa, playground, half-court tennis, barbecue - ✪$59-99.

Shelly Beach, 509 Esplanade, Urangan, ✆4128 9888. 13 units, barbecue, undercover parking - ✪$55-80.

Hervey Bay, 518 Esplanade, Urangan, ✆4128 9277. 18 units, swimming pool, barbecue - ✪$47-72.

Urangan Motor Inn, 573 Esplanade, Urangan, ✆4128 9699. 42 units, licensed restaurant, swimming pool, spa, barbecue - ✪$42-65.

Fraser Gateway Motor Inn, 68 Main Street, Pialba, ✆4128 3666. 28 units, licensed restaurant (Mon-Thu), swimming pool - ✪$75-80.

Hervey Bay Resort, 249 Esplanade, Pialba, ✆4128 1555. 24 units, licensed restaurant, swimming pool, spa - ✪$70-80.

Sunseeker Motel, 354 The Esplanade, Scarness, ✆4128 1888. 10 units, swimming pool, playground, barbecue - ✪$62-88.

Fairway, 29 Boat Harbour Drive, Pialba, ✆4128 1911. 10 units, swimming pool, barbecue - ✪$58-78.

Golden Sands Motor Inn, 44 Main Street, Pialba, ✆4128 3977. 10 units, swimming pool, barbecue - ✪$58-75.

Caravan Parks

Happy Wanderer Village Caravan Park, 105 Truro Street, Torquay, ✆4125 1103. 92 sites, pool, spa - powered sites ✪$21 for two, on-site vans $30 for two, cabins $45-55 for two.

Fraser Lodge, Fraser Street, Torquay, ✆4124 9999. Tennis, spa, pool - powered sites ✪$24 for two, cabins $50-55 for two.

Shelly Beach Caravan Park, 61 Ocean Street, Torquay, ✆4125 1105. (No dogs allowed) - powered sites ✪$17 for two, on-site vans $25-30 for two, cabins $40-45 for two.

Lazy Acres Caravan Park, 91 Exeter Street, Torquay, ✆4125 1840. 80 sites, pool, barbecue - powered sites ✪$15 for two, on-site vans $30 for two, cabins $60-70.

Torquay Beachfront Tourist Park, Esplanade, beach frontage, ✆4125 1578. (No dogs) - powered sites ✪$18-22 for two.

The Palms Caravan Park, cnr Roberts & Truro Streets, Torquay, ✆4125 1704. Pool, barbecue - powered sites ✪$17 for two, on-site vans $25-35.

Pier Caravan Park, 571 Esplanade, Urangan, ✆4128 9866. (Pets allowed on leash) - powered sites ✪$18, on site vans $25-35 for two, cabins $50-60 for two.

Anchorage Caravan Park, Boat Harbour Drive, Urangan, ✆4128 9286. Pool, barbecue - powered sites ✪$16-19 for two, on-site vans $35-40 for two.

Windmill Caravan Park, 17 Elizabeth Street, Urangan, ✆4128 9267. 60 sites, barbecue, pool - powered sites $18-20 for two, on-site vans $30-40 for two.

Hervey Bay Caravan Park,

Margaret Street, Urangan, ✆4128 9553. Pool, barbecue - powered sites ✪$18-20 for two, cabins $6-70 for two.

Harbour View Caravan Park, Jetty Road, Boat Harbour, Urangan, ✆4128 9374. 80 sites, pool - powered sites ✪$16-18 for two, on-site vans $30 for two.

Pialba Beachfront Tourist Park, Esplanade, Pialba, ✆4128 1399. Powered sites ✪$18-22 for two.

Magnolia Caravan Park, cnr Boat Harbour Drive & Taylor Street, Pialba, ✆4128 1700. 53 sites, pool, barbecue - powered sites ✪$14 for two, on-site vans $30 for two.

Australiana Village, 295 Boat Harbour Drive, Scarness, ✆4128 2762. Pool, barbecue, excellent facilities - powered sites ✪$19-22 for two, on-site vans $35 for two, units $75-90.

Scarness Beachfront Tourist Park, Esplanade, Scarness, ✆4128 1274. (No dogs allowed) 160 sites - powered sites ✪$14 for two.

The Hervey Bay **Youth Hostel** is at Boat Harbour Drive, ✆4125 1844. They have 29 rooms ✪$18 per person twin share.

Fraser Island

Kingfisher Bay Resort and Village, North White Cliffs, ✆3032 2805. 19 units, licensed restaurant, pool, spa, tennis, fishing - ✪$280.

Fraser Island Retreat, Happy Valley, ✆4127 9144. 9 units, licensed restaurant, barbecue, pool - ✪$125-180.

Eurong Beach Resort, Eurong, ✆4127 9122. 59 units, pool - ✪$90-225.

Camping

Cathedral Beach Resort & Camping Park, Cathedral Beach, ✆4127 9177. (No pets, no permit required) 54 tourist sites, no power, hot showers, kiosk, barbecue - sites ✪$20 for two, on-site vans $50 for two, cabins $80-100 for two.

Queenslands Park & Wildlife Service, ✆4127 9128. (No pets) 250 camping sites, no power, hot showers, barbecue - ✪$16. Facilities vary, please check. 4WD vehicle access and a camping permit apply. The permit must be obtained prior to arrival, and it is available from the Department of Environment & Heritage, Rainbow Beach, ✆ (07) 5486 3160 or ✆(07) 3227 7111 (Brisbane). Permit costs are ✪$30 per vehicle if pre-paid prior to arrival, or $40 per vehicle on the island.

Eating Out

If you are having trouble deciding where to eat, here is a list of restaurants in the Maryborough area, with numbers and locations, from which you might like to make a choice. The telephone area code is 07.

Maryborough

China Dragon Restaurant, in the Central Hotel, 171 Adelaide Street, ✆4123 1399.

The Gardenia, 193 Adelaide Street, ✆4121 4967.

Muddy Water Cafe, 71 Wharf Street, ✆4121 5011.

Red Roo Hotel, 100 Adelaide Street, ✆4121 3586.

Colony Room Restaurant, cnr Ferry & Albert Streets, ✆4121 2366.

Casino Royale, 338 Kent Street, ✆4121 6225.

Lucky Chinese Restaurant, 302 Kent Street, ✆4121 3645.

McDonalds is on the corner of Quarry Road and the Bruce Highway, as well as on the corner of Alice and Ferry Streets. KFC is on the corner of Walker and Ferry Streets. Pizza Hut is on the corner of Alice and Ferry Streets, ✆13 1166.

Hervey Bay

The Deck, Hervey Bay Marina, Buccanneer Avenue, Hervey Bay, ✆4125 1155.

Don Camillo Ristorante Italiano, 486 Esplanade, Hervey Bay, ✆4125 5466.

Bay Central Chinese Kitchen, Boat Harbour Drive, Hervey Bay, ✆4124 1200.

Hervey Bay Chinese Restaurant, Shop A, 3 Fraser Street, Torquay, ©4125 6906.

Aegean Waters French Restaurant, The Esplanade, Torquay, ©4125 2232.

China Palace, 38 Torquay Road, Pialba, ©4124 8808.

Curried Away, 174 Boat Harbour Drive, Pialba, ©4124 1577.

Raphaels, 564 Esplanade, Urangan, ©4125 2183.

Fryer Tucks, Urangan Plaza, 564 Esplanade, Urangan, ©4125 5933.

Thai Diamond, 355 Esplanade, Scarness, ©4124 4855.

Marty's on the Beach, 344 Esplanade, Scarness, ©4128 1233.

KFC is on the corner of Torquay Road and Taylor Street in Hervey Bay. Pizza Hut is in Lot 2 Boat Harbour Drive, Pialba, ©13 1166.

Fraser Island

The resorts have restaurants and the camping grounds have barbecue facilities.

Points of Interest

Maryborough

The site of the original Maryborough township illustrated the real environs and features of early settlements in the then colony of New South Wales. Of particular relevance is the scale of the early settle-ment, with the landing, the inns, the sawpits, the water supply, trades and industries, and even the burial ground all within walking distance.

In the town there are two marked **Walking Routes** to see the attractions. For Route Number 1, start at the Information Centre and follow the Red Marker posts. Walk Number 2 branches from near the site of George Furber's Inn and returns past Baddow House.

Baddow House, 366 Queen Street, ©4123 1883, is one of Maryborough's most historic homes, and is fully furnished with authentic period furniture. It has exhibits of colonial and museum pieces, and is ©open daily 10am-4pm. Devonshire teas and souvenirs are available.

There are **Pioneer Graves** at the northern-most extremity of the Original Maryborough township, in Aldridge Street, Baddow. The harshness and difficulties of frontier life ensured that the early township experienced loss of life, but death from natural causes or old age was virtually unknown.

Queens Park, Sussex Street, was established more than a century ago, and many of its huge trees were planted as experiments by the Acclimatization Society. Features of the park are the fernery, waterfall and lily pond, lace-trimmed band rotunda built in 1890, and the 13cm gauge model railway built by the Model Engineers and Live Steamers Association. On the last Sunday of the month the Association meets in Queens Park to relive the steam age.

Ululah Lagoon, Lions Drive, was originally the water supply in the early days of settlement. The lagoon is now a wildlife sanctuary where tame black swans, ducks and waterfowl can be hand fed. The lagoon is surrounded by tree-studded parkland with picnic tables and barbecues.

Bottlebrush Crafts (Maitlia Potters), 320 Albert Street, ☎4122 2533, have sales and promotion of local crafts, regular exhibits and workshops. ☺Open Mon-Fri 10am-3pm, Sat 10am-1pm.

Caltex Mountain View Roadhouse, Bruce Highway, Bauple, ☎4129 2267, has an extensive range of rocks, minerals, gems and fossils, including thundereggs and petrified woods.

Macadamia Plantation, cnr Bruce Highway & Owanyilla Boundary Road, south of Maryborough, has brought the world of macadamia nuts to the public. Stage one of the complex, the processing and retail plant, is a major tourist attraction. Guided tours of the plantation aboard the Nutty Choo Choo, with running commentary, are very popular. There is also a shop selling unusual souvenirs, a kiosk with light refreshments, and barbecue lunches are available. ☺Open daily 9am-5pm.

The **MV *Duchess*** has hourly cruises on the Mary River on Wed, Thurs and Sun afternoons. Her low profile design enables her to travel un-restricted up river under all the bridges, passing past and present sites of early industry and architecture, an island bat colony and much more. There is informative and humorous commentary. For more information contact the Maryborough Tourist Information Centre, ☎4121 4111.

Hervey Bay

Situated 34km (21 miles) east of Maryborough, Hervey Bay is one of Australia's best value holiday destinations. It has a climate similar to that of Hawaii, and virtually year-round swimming in a safe and sheltered environment.

The Bay offers a variety of charter boats for fishing trips. These vary in length from a couple of hours out on the water to day/night trips. Most trips are out to the deep waters off Sandy Cape, Breaksea Spit, Rooney's and the gutters around Fraser Island. Reef fish which abound in the Bay's waters include Coral Bream, Blackall, Snapper, Coral Trout and Cod. A few companies specialising in cruises are: *Lady Elliot Island Reef Resort Day*

Tours, ☏1800 072 200 for reservations.

Splash Safaris, 6 Inman Street, Point Vernon, ☏0500 555 580.

Stefanie Yacht Charters, 7 Burum Street, Hervey Bay, ☏4125 4200.

Hervey Bay now has international recognition as one of the best vantage points for studying the **Humpback Whale**. From early August to mid-October, these gentle giants stop in at Hervey Bay on their return south to Antarctica. They frolic in the warm waters of the Bay, almost oblivious to the people watching eagerly from the safety of tour boats.

Some of the companies operating whale watch tours are:

Islander Whale Watch Cruises, Buccaneer Avenue, ☏4125 3399.

Mimi Macpherson's Whale Watch Expeditions, 449 The Esplanade, Torquay, ☏4125 1700 or 1800 683 368.

Spirit of Hervey Bay Whale Watch Cruises, 864 Boat Harbour Drive, Urangan, ☏4125 5131.

Whalesong Cruises, Torquay, Whale Watch and Dolphin Cruises, ☏4125 6222.

For further details on tours and cruises, contact the Hervey Bay Tourist & Visitors Centre, 353 The Esplanade, ☏ 4124 4050.

The **Whale Festival**, held in August, is a weekend full of activities to officially launch the whale watching season. Features include an aquatic carnival, illuminated procession of boats, the Princess of Whales competition, and the World Smiling Championships.

Hervey Bay Nature World, Maryborough Road, Pialba, on the main highway at the entrance to Hervey Bay, is an Australian theme park set in 15ha (37 acres) of bushland. Calling the place home are kangaroos, wallabies, wombats, emu, deer, buffalo, waterbirds and a large number of crocodiles. The crocodiles feed daily in summer and twice weekly in winter. Feeding time is 11.30am. Lorikeets feed daily between 3-4pm. There are free paddle boat rides, playground, barbecue and picnic areas, and toilets for the disabled. ☏Open daily 9am-5pm. You can phone them on ☏4124 1733.

Dayman Point features sweeping views of Great Sandy Strait, picnic facilities and two memorials: one to Z Force and their vessel *The Krait*; the other to Captain Matthew Flinders, who landed nearby on August 6, 1799, and Lt Joseph Dayman, RN who passed in the schooner *Asp* after making the first passage through Fraser Island (now Great Sandy) Strait in 1847.

Fraser Island

Fraser Island is the largest sand island in the world, a fishing para-

Above: Burning off in Queensland's canefields   *Below: A stockyard in Northern Queensland*

Cedar Creek Falls, Queensland

dise, and one of the world's last wilderness areas. It is 11km (7 miles) from Hervey Bay, and is composed almost entirely of siliceous sands which extend to more than 600m (1968 ft) below sea level. The only rock outcrops on the east coast are at Indian Head, Middle Rock and Waddy Point. On the west coast there is a small outcrop of hard rock at Bun Bun Rocks.

The island has an area of 184,000ha (454,480 acres), is 123km (76 miles) long, and has an average width of 14km (9 miles), ranging to 22km (14 miles) at its widest part. Dune heights reach to 240m (787 ft).

Most of the island is crown land, national park or State forest reserve. Five main tourist centres - at Eurong, Happy Valley, Orchard Beach, Cathedral Beach and Dilli Village - cater for those who like home comforts. If you prefer a real wilderness experience, you can camp in a secluded spot and explore the island by forest tracks, which are suitable for 4WD only.

All visitors to the island are required to have permits. The fee charged is used to provide facilities for visitors and to provide effective protection for the unique island environment. Permit costs are: ✪$34 per vehicle prior to arrival, ✪$45 per vehicle on the island. They are available from Department of Environment & Heritage, Rainbow Beach, ✆(07) 5486 3160 or in Brisbane, ✆(07) 3227 7111.

Fraser Island can be reached by sea and air. Cruises and vehicular barges operate from Hervey Bay, Mary River Heads and Rainbow Beach. Charter flights and tours are also available.

There are over 40 freshwater lakes on the Island. As well as the perched dune lakes, there are window lakes, formed when the shifting sand falls below the level of the island's dome-shaped water table. Remarkable is Lake Wabby, an easy walk from the ocean beach. It is the deepest of the island's lakes, and contains the greatest variety of fish, but it is dying, slowly being strangled by a sandblow that encroaches four metres each year.

Up to 72 different colours have been recorded in the sands on the island. The most famous area of coloured sand cliffs is **The Cathedrals** on the eastern side of the island midway between Happy Valley and Orchid Beach.

The island has hundreds of kilometres of white sand beaches, its own wreck (the *Maheno*, which beached during a cyclone 50 years ago) and countless freshwater streams.

Dingoes are also found on the island, not as pets or in cages, but living freely. It is generally accepted that if you leave them alone, they will leave you alone, but it is requested that you do not feed them. They find their own food, and do well without handouts.

Outlying Attractions

Burrum Heads, Toogoom, Howard, Torbanlea

Burrum Heads and Toogoom are two small coastal resorts located at the mouth of the Burrum River, both popular for their good fishing and relaxed atmosphere. In the winter months especially, fishermen come from miles around to catch whiting.

Burrum Heads is growing rapidly and is well serviced with shops. In September the area is vibrant with colourful wildflowers. Toogoom has plenty of good picnic spots, and over ninety species of birds have been identified in the area. Both of these resorts have caravan parks and holiday homes.

The Burrum River crosses the highway between Howard and Torbanlea. It is a picturesque waterway for boating, fishing and crabbing, and has a caravan park on its banks. Most houses in these two townships are the cool highset timber Queenslander homes. Howard has all the facilities of an up-and-coming small town.

Approximately 20km north of Maryborough on the Bruce Highway, there is an exit for Burrum Heads.

Bundaberg

Population 54,800
Bundaberg is situated on the Burnett River, 378km (235 miles) north of Brisbane. Strictly speaking, it is not part of the Great Barrier Reef and in fact sits on the southern side of the designated boundary. If you are travelling along the coast in either direction, there are a number of factors which may encourage you to stop here.

Climate

Average temperatures: Jan max 30C (86F) - min 21C (70F); July max 21C (70F) - min 11C (52F). Average annual rainfall: 1149mm (45 ins); heaviest rainfall falls December-March.

Characteristics

The Bundaberg district grows ap-proximately one-fifth of Australia's sugar crop, and in recent years has become a virtual salad bowl, growing large supplies of tomatoes, avocados, pineapples, beans and more. And, of course, the Famous Aussie Spirit, Bundaberg Rum, is produced here in this Sugar City.

How to Get There

By Air

Sunstate Airlines, ✆13 1313, operate several flights daily to/from Cairns, Mackay, Rockhampton, Townsville and Gladstone.
Flight West, ✆1300 130 092, operate a Brisbane to Bundaberg service 3 times a day.

By Bus

Greyhound Pioneer, ✆13 2030, and McCafferty's, ✆13 1499, stop at Bundaberg on their Brisbane/Cairns route.

By Rail

Bundaberg is on the main Brisbane/ Cairns line. The Sunlander, Queenslander and Spirit of Capricorn all stop at Bundaberg, ✆13 2235.

By Road

From Brisbane, Bundaberg is a 368km, four-and-a-half hour drive. Follow the Bruce Highway north to the turn-off at Childers.

It is 170km south of Gladstone, and the turn-off is at Gin Gin.

Visitor Information

Bundaberg District Tourism and Development Board is at the Hinkler Glider Museum, 271 Bourbong Street, next to the Base Hospital, ✆4152 2333. ☺Opening hours are Mon-Fri 8.30am-5pm, Sat-Sun 9am-5pm.

Accommodation

There are over 30 motels in Bundaberg as well as hotels, caravan parks and backpacker accommodation. Here is a selection, with prices for a double room per night, which should be used as a guide only. The telephone area code is 07.

City

Bert Hinkler Motor Inn, cnr Takalvan & Warrell Streets, ✆4152 6400. 32 units, licensed restaurant, swimming pool, spa, sauna, half-court tennis - ✪$85-130.

Sugar Country Motor Inn, 220 Bourbong Street, ✆4153 1166. 33 units, licensed restaurant, swimming pool - ✪$90-95.

Bundaberg City Motor Inn, 246 Bourbong Street, ✆4152 5011. 17 units, swimming pool, spa, barbecue - ✪$85-95.

Acacia Motor Inn, 248 Bourbong Street, ✆4152 3411. 26 units, undercover parking, swimming pool - ✪$80.

Alexandra Park Motor Inn, 66 Quay Street, ✆4152 7255. 19 units, licensed restaurant, swimming pool - ✪$50-110.

Bundaberg Spanish Motor Inn, cnr Woongarra & Mulgrave Streets, ✆4152 5444. 16 units, swimming pool, undercover parking, barbecue - ✪$75.

Butterfly Checkmate, 240 Bourbong Street, ✆4152 2700. 18 units, unlicensed restaurant (closed Sun), swimming pool, barbecue - ✪$70.

Chalet Motor Inn, 242 Bourbong Street, ✆4152 9922. 14 units, swimming pool, spa - ✪$70-100.

Bourbong Street Motel, 265 Bourbong Street, ✆4151 3089. 17 units - ✪$55.

Lyelta Lodge & Motel, 8 Maryborough Street, ✆4151 3344. 20 rooms, undercover parking - ✪$35-40.

Caravan Parks

Oakwood Caravan Park, Gin Gin Road, ✆4159 9332. 86 sites, pool, barbecue, kiosk - powered sites ✪$15 for two, on-site vans $25-30 for two, cabins $40-45 for two.

Finemore Tourist Park, 33 Quay Street, ✆4151 3663. (No pets) 66 sites, barbecue, pool - powered sites ✪$14 for two, cabins $38 for two.

Cane Village Holiday Park, Twyford Street, ✆4155 1022. 84 sites, playground, barbecue, pool - powered sites ✪$17-16 for two, cabins $35-38 for two.

Coastal

Don Pancho Beach Resort, 62 Miller Street, Bargara, ✆4159 2146. 42 units, licensed restaurant, swimming pool, spa, barbecue, half-court tennis, gym - ✪$90-160.

Nieuport 54, 54 Miller Street, Bargara, ✆4159 2164. 6 units, sauna, spa - ✪$85-105.

Dunelm House Bed & Breakfast, 540 Bargara Road, Bargara, ✆4159 0909. 3 rooms, undercover parking, pool, spa - ✪$70-80.

Bargara Beach Motor Inn, 7 Bauer Street, Bargara, ✆4159 2395. 6 units, barbecue, undercover parking - ✪$55-95.

Pacific Sun Motor Inn, 11 Bauer Street, Bargara, ✆4159 2350. 10 units - ✪$50-65.

Caravan Parks

Absolute Ocean Front Tourist Park, 117 Woongarra Scenic Drive, Bargara, ✆4159 2436. 42 sites, barbecue, kiosk, spa, pool - powered sites ✪$14 for two, on-site vans $30-38 for two, cabins $40-47 for two.

Bargara Beach Caravan Park, Nielson Park, The Esplanade, Bargara, ✆4159 2228. (Pets on application) 300 sites, barbecue, playground, 2 tennis courts, kiosk - powered sites ✪$16 for two, on-site vans $28 for two, cabins $38-46 for two.

Eating Out

Bundaberg has an abundance of licensed and BYO restaurants, licensed clubs and hotels, and plenty of coffee lounges, takeaways and snack bars. If you wish, get in touch with the Tourist Information Centre, ✆4152 2333, for a list of culinary establishments and local advice on the best places to dine. If you're not in an adventurous

mood, the major fast-food chains have branches in Bundaberg.

Beaches, at the Reef Gateway Motor Inn, 11 Takalvan Street, ©4153 2255. Licensed a-la-carte dining, large seafood selection, cocktail bar. Open 6pm-10pm every day except Sunday (closed).

Spinnaker Stonegrill & Bar, 1a Quay Street, ©4152 8033. Seafood and stonegrill selections, a-la-carte dining. Open midday to midnight 7 days, closed Public Holidays.

Rendezvous, 220 Bourbong Street, ©4153 1747. Licensed, open 24 hours.

New China Dragon Restaurant, 32 Targo Street, ©4151 1955. Seafood cuisine, BYO. Open 5am-9pm seven days and 11am-2.30pm Mon-Fri, closed Public Holidays.

The Strand, 55 Woongarra Street, ©4151 2099. Curry a speciality on Sunday nights. Open 8am-midnight every day except Public Holidays (closed).

Codiannis, 66 Woongarra Street, ©4153 0930.

Mexican Border, 27 Elliots Head Road, ©4152 1675. Licensed, Mexican dishes.

Oriental Pearl Chinese Restaurant, 69 Takalvan Street, ©4152 8655.

Zulus, 61 Targo Street, ©4152 4691.

Numero Uno, 167a Bourbong Street, ©4151 3666.

You will find KFC at 263 Bourbong Street, McDonalds on the corner of Woongarra and Targo Streets and Pizza Hut on the corner of Bourbong and Branyon Streets, ©13 6611.

Local Transport

There are weekly bus services to North Bundaberg, South Bundaberg, Norville, West Bundaberg, Sugarland Shoppingtown, Bargara and Burnett Heads, Elliott Heads, South Kolan/Bingera, Kepnock, Moore Park and Gin Gin - contact the Tourist Information Centre for details and timetables.

Points of Interest

A trip to the reef aboard the MV *Lady Musgrave* takes just over two hours from Bundaberg. The office is located in Shop 1 Moffat Street, Bundaberg Port Marina, ©4159 4519 or ©4152 9011.

Lady Musgrave Island, 49km (30 miles) from the coast, is a truly unspoiled, uninhabited coral atoll where you can stroll through the pisonia and casuarina trees and view the nesting seabirds. The launch trip includes morning and afternoon tea, smorgasbord luncheon, snorkelling gear and glass-bottomed boat rides. A fun day is assured. *(See separate listing.)*

Bundaberg has several memorials

to its most famous son, Herbert John Louis Hinkler (*Bert Hinkler*) - locally he was known as 'Hustling Hinkler'. He was the first aviator to fly solo from England to Australia, in 1928. **Hinkler House**, Mt Perry Road, was transported brick by brick from Southampton, England, to Bundaberg in 1983, by a team of dedicated workers. Hinkler designed the house and lived in it from 1926-1933. It is now an aviation museum ☉open daily 10am-4pm, ✆4152 0222.

There are memorials to Hinkler in Buss Park beside the Civic Centre, at the southern end of the traffic bridge, and on the Hummock, 10km east of the city. The **Hinkler Glider Museum** contains a replica of Hinkler's glider which he successfully flew 35m from the sand dunes of Mon Repos Beach in 1912. The historical museum is in the same complex and contains a fascinating collection of domestic items and farm equipment. The **Botanical Gardens** and steam railway are also in the **Hinkler Rose Garden Tourist Complex**, along with the *Hinkler Rose Garden Restaurant*, ✆4153 1477.

Bundaberg Rum Distillery, Whitred Street, ✆4150 8686, has five conducted tours every weekday, which run for approximately one hour. You can see the rum being processed from raw sugar through to the bottled product - the 'Famous Aussie Spirit', although you will not get to sample the end product for free!

Schmeiders Cooperage & Craft Centre, 5 Alexandra Street, East Bundaberg, ✆4151 8233 or ✆1800 222 440, sells small handcrafted American Oak Casks. You can see the coopers at work making these casks in their workshops. Also in the Craft Centre are potters, a blacksmith, woodturner, artists and many more. There is a cafe as well, where you can grab a bite to eat.

Alexandra Park Zoo, is on the banks of the Burnett River, west of the main railway line. It is ☉open Mon-Fri 6.30am-3.30pm and admission is free.

The House of Dolls, Douglas Road, ✆4159 7252, has a wonderful display of dressed dolls, in national and period costumes, and a display of the Royal Wedding.

Boyd's Antiquatorium, 295 Bourbong Street, ✆4152 2576, has a collection of classic racing motorcycles, vintage cars, early cameras, farm machinery, a coin collection, and a great musical instrument display. The display is directed at all ages.

Take a stroll through the fragrant **Pennyroyal Herb Farm** which is a delightful place to visit. The display gardens are set in native Australian bush.

Avocado Grove, Douglas Road, ©4159 7367, has something for everyone. Exotic and sociable peacocks roam the grounds whilst many native birds live happily in aviaries amid the lush, sub-tropical gardens.

What caused those strange craters just north of Bundaberg? The **Mystery Craters** are said to be 25 million years old, and their origin remains unexplained. The fascinating area has a garden setting, observation tower, kiosk, rocks, souvenirs, currency display and playground. The area, in Lines Road, South Kolan, is hopen 8am-5pm. The admission fee is ✪$5 adults and $3 children, ©4157 7291.

For an unusual treat, stop and buy some tropical fruit wine at Bundaberg's unique **Winery** at 78 Mt Perry Road, ©4151 5993. Owners, Carole and John Gianduzzo, will explain the merits of the various wines. Another unusual facet is the large range of soft drinks now produced on the premises. It is ☉open Mon-Sat 9am-5.30pm and 9am-midday on Sundays. Admission is free.

Bargara Beach is the aquatic playground for the sun and sea aficionados of Bundaberg. Just a 15 minute drive from Bundaberg, it offers safe surfing at Neilson Park. A very modern shopping centre known as 'Bargara Centrepoint'

caters for everyone's needs. The town is serviced by a modern hotel/motel, motel and unit accommodation, caravan parks, TAB, convenience store, takeaway food outlets and fine restaurants. Kelly's Beach has a natural still-water tidal swimming pool and is a patrolled beach.

Mon Repos Beach, with magnificent sand dunes, is the largest and most accessible mainland turtle rookery in Australia. It is an environmental park and contains a magnificent Kanaka stone wall. It was the site of Bert Hinkler's first flights. The conservation park ☉opens from 7pm onwards between November and March, and the Information Centre is open 8am-4pm March-October. Admission is ✪$5 for adults and $3 for children.

Burnett Heads, with **Oaks Beach**, is 18km (11 miles) from Bundaberg at the mouth of the Burnett River and has ample shops, a hotel and a couple of caravan parks. The lighthouse is located next to the hall and was taken out of service in 1972.

Moore Park, 21km (13 miles) north of Bundaberg, is an excellent seaside beach with 16km (10 miles) of firm sandy shores. Lifesavers patrol this beach throughout the surfing season. There is a motel and a caravan park.

The Town of 1770 (and Agnes Water to the south of Round Hill) was visited by Queensland's first tourist, Captain James Cook, in the *Endeavour* in May 1770. The small town takes its name from this event. Day trips to Lady Mus-grave Island depart from the Town of 1770, and a bus pick-up operates from Bundaberg.

Outlying Attractions

Eidsvold

Situated on the Burnett Highway 250km (155 miles) west of Bundaberg, via Gayndah, Eidsvold was established as a gold mining town in 1888 and is now a major producer of beef cattle. The town's past can be seen in the slab homestead 'Knockbreak' which is part of the Eidsvold Historical Museum. Eidsvold has a unique museum housing the George Schaffer bottle, rock and gemstone collection - a display of unusual items gathered over one man's lifetime. The Eidsvold Motel & General Store, 51 Moreton Street, can provide you with tourist information. ©(07) 4165 1209.

Mundubbera

Mundubbera is situated on the banks of the Burnett River, 35km south-east of Eidsvold on the Burnett Highway. The River passes through the small sub-tropical valley of the Central Burnett. One-third of Queensland's citrus is produced here and the area is surrounded by orchards, and has the Enormous Ellendale (Big Mandarin). The Golden Mile Orchard has an extensive packing facility. The Auburn Falls National Park is 35km (22 miles) west, and has beautiful rock pools and formations. Tourist Information can be obtained from the Big Mandarin complex in Durong Road, ©(07) 4165 4549.

Gayndah

Found 166km (103 miles) southwest of Bundaberg on the Burnett Highway, Gayndah is Queensland's oldest town, and was in the running with Ipswich and Brisbane for the title of State capital.

In the 1840s Gayndah was originally settled as sheep country, and it wasn't until 1892 that William Seeney planted the first orchard, for which Gayndah is now famous. Even if you weren't aware of it before, you could hardly miss the Big Orange complex.

The Golden Orange Hotel-Motel, Maltby Place, is the supplier of regional information for tourists, ©(07) 4161 1107.

Biggenden

Craggy, blue mountain ranges are the backdrop for Biggenden, 100km

(62 miles) south-west of Bundaberg. Along with agricultural pursuits - beef, grain crops, dairying, citrus, piggeries, peanuts and timber - the area is rich in minerals.

Established in the goldrush of 1889, attractions include the historic Chowey Bridge, the old Mt Shamrock Gold Mine, the operational open-cut magnetite mine, the Coalstoun Lakes, Mt Walsh National Park and Mt Woowoonga Forest Reserve.

You will find tourist information at the Biggenden Shire Council, Edward Street, ©(07) 4127 1177.

Childers

Located 50km (31 miles) south of Bundaberg, Childers has rich red soil, and is famous for its avenue of leopard trees, colonial buildings, the Olde Butcher Shoppe and the Hall of Memories. It is on the Bruce Highway.

Less than half an hour's drive away is Woodgate Beach and Woodgate National Park, which has many boardwalks allowing access to the swampy areas. There is also a special bird-watching shed. The beach is popular and stretches for about 16km (10 miles).

Rockhampton

Population 65,000
Gateway to the Capricorn Coast, Rockhampton is 660km (410 miles) north of Brisbane, on the Tropic of Capricorn. The city is situated on the Fitzroy River about 16km (10 miles) from the coast.

Climate

Average temperatures: January max 31C (88F) - min 22C (72F); July max 23C (73F) - min 9C (48F). Most rain falls between December and March - approximately 500mm (17 in).

Characteristics

'Rocky' is the heart of the beef cattle country. The main breeds are Santa Gertrudis, Hereford, Braford, Brahman, Africander and Zebu. Rockhampton also has two flour mills which process wheat from the Central Highlands around Emerald. Ever since Queensland became a separate state, there have been people politicising for the establishment of a separate North Queensland state.

How to Get There

By Air

Sunstate, ©13 1313, fly to/from Bundaberg, Gladstone, Mackay, Maryborough, Townsville and Cairns, Great Keppel Island and Toowoomba.
Eastern Airlines, ©13 1313, fly to/from the Gold Coast.
Check with your travel agent at the time of your trip.

By Bus

Greyhound Pioneer, ✆13 2030, and McCaffertys, ✆13 1499, stop at Rockhampton on their Brisbane/ North Queensland route.

McCaffertys have a daily service to/ from Longreach.

Greyhound also have a Rockhampton to Longreach service departing 3 times weekly.

By Rail

Queensland Tilt Trains, ✆13 2235, including The Spirit of Capricorn, service Rockhampton fairly frequently, with either day or overnight travel.

The Sunlander and the Queenslander both leave Brisbane in the early morning and stop at Rockhampton.

By Car

From Brisbane, via the Bruce Highway 660km (410 miles), or take the inland route via Esk and Biloela 758km (470 miles). Rockhampton is 1413km (878 miles) south of Cairns.

Visitor Information

Capricorn Tourism, is at 'The Spire' in Gladstone Road, ✆4927 2055, adjacent to the Tropic of Capricorn Spire. It is ⏱open 7 days a week.

The email address is ✎captour@ rocknet.net.au and the website is 👁www.capricorncoast.com.au

You will find the Rockhampton Tourist Information Centre in Quay Street, ✆4922 5339.

Accommodation

Rockhampton has no shortage of motels, and there are plenty of older style hotels near the city centre. There is also no shortage of camping grounds. Below we have given a selection with prices for a double room per night, which should be used as a guide only. The telephone area code is 07.

Country Comfort Rockhampton, 86 Victoria Parade, ✆4927 9933. 78 units, licensed restaurant, barbecue, swimming pool - ✪$105.

Ambassador on the Park, 161 George Street, ✆4927 5855. 70 units, 3 suites, licensed restaurant, swimming pool - ✪$100-125.

Archer Park, 39 Albert Street, ✆4927 9266. 26 units, licensed restaurant, swimming pool, undercover parking - ✪$80-85.

Sundowner Chain Motor Inns Rockhampton, 112 Gladstone Road, ✆4927 8866. 32 units, licensed restaurant, swimming pool - ✪$65-110.

Central Park, 224 Murray Street, ✆4927 2333. 26 units, licensed restaurant (closed Sun), swimming pool - ✪$70-85.

Leichardt Hotel Rockhampton, cnr Bolsover & Denham Streets, ✆4927 6733. 60 rooms, 8 suites, licensed restaurant and bistro - ✪$55-135.

Club Crocodile Motor Inn, cnr Albert & Alma Streets, ✆4927

7433. 44 units, licensed restaurant (closed Sunday), swimming pool - ✪$80-95.

Glenmore Palms, Bruce Highway, Glenmore, North Rockhampton, ☎4926 1144. 38 units, licensed restaurant, swimming pool, spa - ✪$80-100.

Centre Point Motor Inn, 131 George Street, ☎4927 8844. 48 units, licensed restaurant, heated swimming pool - ✪$100.

Golden Fountain Motel, 166 Gladstone Road, ☎4927 1055. 31 units, swimming pool - ✪$80-100.

Caravan Parks

Tropical Wanderer Resort, 394 Yaamba Road, ☎4926 3822. (No pets) 150 sites, licensed restaurants, barbecue, tennis (half court), pool - powered sites ✪$22 for two, cabins $55-65 for two.

Ramblers Motor Village, Bruce Highway, North Rockhampton, (opposite Shopping Fair), ☎4928 2084. (No pets) 60 sites, playground, pool - powered sites ✪$19 for two, units $55-60 for two, cabins $40-50 for two.

Southside Holiday Village, Lower Dawson Road, ☎4927 3013. 200 sites, heated pool, tennis (half court) - powered sites ✪$21 for two, on-site vans $30-40 for two, cabins $50-55 for two.

Riverside Tourist Park Rockhampton, Reaney Street, North Rockhampton, ☎4922 3779. (No pets allowed) 150 sites - powered sites ✪$16 for two.

Gracemere Caravan Park, Old Capricorn Highway, ☎4933 1310. 100 sites, barbecue, pool - powered sites ✪$13.

There is a **Youth Hostel** at 60 McFarlane Street, North Rockhampton, ☎4927 5288. They have 13 rooms at ✪$18 per adult per night twin share.

Eating Out

Most of the hotels serve casual counter meals, and the steaks in Rocky are particularly large, as this is the heart of the cattle country. The hotels, and several motels, also have licensed restaurants. A wide assortment of cuisine is available, from Chinese to seafood. Here are some names and numbers of establishments in the area:

Dragon Gallery, 295 Richardson Road, North Rockhampton, ☎4928 3399. Traditional Chinese cuisine.

Hogs Breath Cafe, Aquatic Place, North Rockhampton, ☎4926 3646. Hamburgers and steaks.

Hong Kong Seafood Restaurant, 98a Denham Street, Rockhampton, ☎4927 7144.

Pacinos, cnr Fitzroy & George Streets, Rockhampton, ☎4922 5833. Italian fare.

Thai Tanee Restaurant, cnr Bolsover & William Streets,

Rockhampton, ©4922 1255.

Wah Hah, 70 Denham Street, Rockhampton, ©4927 1659. Chinese selections.

Sizzler, Rockhamtpon Shopping Fair, Rockhampton, ©4926 1100. Australian steaks and salad.

Cravings Bar and Grill, cnr Water Street and Lakes Creek Road, North Rockhampton, ©4928 5666.

Le Bistro on Quay, 194 Quay Street, Rockhampton, ©4922 2019.

Cactus Jacks Restaurant, 243 Musgrave Street, North Rockhampton, ©4922 2062.

Diamonds Down by the River, Quay Street, Rockhampton, ©4921 1811.

Friends Bistro, 159 East Street, Rockhampton, ©4922 2689.

Jans Restaurant, Pilbeam Theatre, Victoria Parade, Rockhampton, ©4922 3060.

There are two McDonalds branches, one on the Bruce Highway in North Rockhampton and the other on the corner of George and Fitzroy Streets, Rockhampton. KFC also has two outlets, one at the corner of George and Arthur Streets, Rockhampton, and the other on the corner of Linnet Street and Queen Elizabeth Drive, North Rockhampton. Pizza Hut is on the corner of High Street and Bruce Highway, North Rochampton, and on the corner of Denham Street and Bruce Highway in Rockhampton, ©13 1166.

Entertainment

Rockhampton has a three cinema complex in Shopping Fair, North Rockhampton, ©4926 6977, and indoor and outdoor concert venues.

There are three nightclubs in the city:

Strutters, cnr East & Williams Streets, ©4922 2882.

The Party Shack, cnr William & Alma Streets, ©4927 2005.

William Street Nite Club, 4 William Street, ©4927 1144.

The *Pilbeam Theatre* in Victoria Parade attracts regular performances by national and international artists, ©4927 4111.

For details of current entertainment programs at hotels, clubs, and so on, ask at the Visitor Information Centre.

Shopping

Rockhampton has never been described as a shopping capital, but the *Shopping Fair*, Yaaamba Road, North Rockhampton, ©4928 9166, was refurbished a few years ago and should cater to your basic needs. It has a departent store, two supermarkets, over 100 specialty shops, a food court, and a licensed restaurant.

The *City Heart Mall*, in Bolsover Street, has local art and craft markets on Saturdays, ©4936 8481.

Points of Interest

Rockhampton was first settled in the 1850s by Charles and William Archer. Today, historic **Quay Street** contains over 20 buildings which have been classified by the National Trust.

The city is the commercial and administrative centre of central Queensland. Its wide streets are lined with trees and solid buildings, indicating a prosperity dating back to the early days. The Australian Estate Co Ltd offices were built in 1861, and the Customs House in 1901. It has a handsome copper dome and a striking semi-circular portico. Queens Wharf is all that remains of the quays of the port that was very busy until silt caused the demise of the river trade. St Joseph's Cathedral (cnr Murray and William Streets) and St Paul's Anglican Cathedral are both built in Gothic Style from local sandstone. The Royal Arcade was built in 1889 as a theatre with a special feature - the roof could be opened on hot nights.

The Botanic Gardens in Spencer Street, ✆4922 4347, are reputed to be one of the finest tropical gardens in Australia. Spreading over 4ha (10 acres), these gardens contain many native and exotic trees, ferns and shrubs, as well as a large walk-in aviary, orchid and fern house and a small Australian Zoo, which includes its own Koala Park. As part of a sister city agreement with Ibusuki City in Japan, separate Japanese Gardens were created in 1982. There are also paddle boat rides available on the lagoon. The gardens are ⏲open 6am-6pm daily and admission is free.

The Pilbeam Theatre, ✆4927 4111 and **Art Gallery**, ✆4936 8248, in Victoria Parade, form the cultural centre of Rocky. The Art Gallery has an extensive collection of Australian paintings, pottery and sculpture. The Pilbeam Theatre attracts regular performances by national and international stars.

St Aubin's Village, on Canoona Road beside the airport, consists of one of Rockhampton's oldest houses, and a number of gift shops specialising in cottage industries. It is ⏲open 9am-6pm Mon-Sat and on Sundays 9am-2pm. Admission is free.

Callaghan Park Racecourse, ✆4927 1300, is Queensland's premier provincial racetrack. Thursday night has greyhound racing, Saturday evening has harness racing, and on Saturday afternoon it's the gallopers' turn.

Fitzroy River Ski Gardens, near the Barrage bridge, beside the boat launching facilities, has picnic facilities, a children's playground and electric barbecues.

Old Glenmore Homestead, ✆4936 1033, through the Parkhurst Industrial Estate in the north of the city, is a 130-year-old complex consisting of a log cabin, slab cottage and an adobe house. Old Glenmore holds Queensland's first Historic Inn Licence, so visitors can sample some of the State's best fermented beverages in this pleasant old world setting. Bush dances and home-style cooking are also features. It is ☼open only on Sundays between 11am and 3pm. Admission is ✪$7 for adults and $2 for children. Groups are allowed by appointment.

Cammoo Caves, ✆4934 2774, and **Olsen's Capricorn Caverns**, ✆4934 2883, approximately 23km (14miles) north of Rockhampton, are two cave systems which are open to the public. Cave coral, fossils and gigantic tree roots can be inspected in these dry, limestone caves. Cammoo Caves are ☼open daily 8.30am-4.30pm and have conducted tours. Entry fees are adults ✪$8 and children $4. Olsen's, about 2km east of Cammoo, is privately owned, and 3 hour half-day tours into these caves cost ✪$33 adults, $16 children, departing from your accommodation in Rockhampton around 9am.

The Dreamtime Cultural Centre, ✆4936 1655, is a large Aboriginal Cultural Centre, and is on the Bruce Highway opposite the turn-off to Yeppoon. The centre is ☼open daily 10am-5.15pm, with guided tours between 11am and 4pm (2 hours duration). Refreshments are available (eating bush tucker is not compulsory). Adults are charged ✪$13 and children $6.

Rockhampton Heritage Village is in Boundary Road, Parkhurst, ✆4936 1026. Attractions include a blacksmith's shop, wheel wrighting, dairy, fully furnished slab cottage, pioneering tools, vintage cars, horse-drawn vehicles, Hall of Clocks and a kiosk. Tours are conducted daily, and there are working demonstrations on the last Sunday of each month. It is ☼open daily 10am-4pm and admission is ✪$12 adults and $7 children.

Koorana Crocodile Farm is in Koowonga Road, off Emu Park Road. This is a breeding farm, not a protective reserve, so don't be surprised when when you find crocodile kebabs on the menu, and crocodile skin shoes and purses for sale in the gift shop. The Crocodile Farm is ☼open daily and costs adults ✪$15, children $7, and $12 per person for groups.

Sport

Rockhampton has all the usual facilities you would expect of a town

of its size. To get to the beach, though, you have to drive 45km to the Capricorn Coast.

Diving

Capricorn Reef Diving, 189 Musgrave Street, North Rockhampton, ℂ4922 7720, offer 5-day open water certificate PADI course. Classes are taken in Rockhampton, followed by 4 dives on the Keppel Island Group.

Tours

Rothery's Coaches, 13 Power Street, North Rockhampton, ℂ4922 4320, offer tours of the city and to the Capricorn Coast, Koorana Crocodile Farm, Cooberrie Park, The Caves and the Dreamtime Culture Centre.

Duncan's Off Road 4WD Tours are in Kent Street, Rockhampton, ℂ0418 986 050 (mobile).

Outlying Attractions

Capricorn Coast

The Capricorn Coast stretches some 48km (30 miles) from Yeppoon and the Byfield area in the north to Keppel Sands in the south. The area enjoys a similar climate to that of Hawaii. The main area of the Capricorn Coast begins at the town of Joskeleigh in the south and reaches north to the forests and national parks of Byfield. The primary town on the coast is Yeppoon, and the main city is Rockhampton,

41km inland. Rockhampton airport is the departure point for flights to the nearby islands of the Reef.

If you are swimming in the tropical waters of the Capricorn Coast, remember that deadly box jellyfish can be present in the sea anywhere north of the Tropic of Capricorn in the summer months.

The web page to visit online is ☞www.capricorncoast.com.au Email for the Capricorn Coast Tourist Organisation is ✎capcoast@cqnet.com.au

Yeppoon

A modern town with a population of approximately 12,000, Yeppoon nestles beside pineapple-covered hills on the shores of Keppel Bay. Palms and pines line the main street, and shady trees continue to line the road to Rockhampton. There is a 4m difference between high and low tide, so trawlers, yachts and dinghies are left high and dry.

Yeppoon is the main town on the Capricorn Coast and is one of the largest and fastest growing coastal communities in Queensland. It is a popular holiday spot, offering access to more than 40km of safe beaches.

Cooberrie Park, 15km (9 miles) north of Yeppoon on Woodbury Road, is a bird and animal sanctuary with barbecue and picnic facili-

ties. If you want to pat a kangaroo, this is the place to do it. They also have koalas and other native animals wandering freely through the parkland. It is ⏰open daily 9am-4.30pm and costs adults ✪$12 and children $6, ☎4939 7590.

Byfield State Forest Parks are 17km (10 miles) north of Cooberrie Park, and are popular picnic areas. They include Stoney Creek, Waterpark Creek and Red Rock Forest Parks.

Nob Creek Pottery, ☎4935 1161, established in 1979, is located in the tropical Byfield Forest, and has gained a reputation as a quality cottage industry.

Wreck Point at Cooee Bay provides a spectacular view overlooking the Keppel group of islands. It is situated on the southern outskirts of Yeppoon.

Rosslyn Bay Boat Harbour is the base for a large fishing fleet, charter boats, cruise boats and catamarans. Cruises available include coral viewing, boom netting and, weather permitting, a visit to Middle Island Underwater Observatory.

Emu Park, 19km (12 miles) south of Yeppoon and linked by the Capricorn Coast Scenic Highway, has an unusual memorial to Captain Cook - a singing ship. The mast, sail and rigging contain hollow pipes, and the ship 'sings' when the wind blows. This picturesque town is worth the short and scenic drive for a visit.

The Capricorn Coast Tourist Organisation has an office at the roundabout as you drive into town (you can't miss it!) and it is ☺open daily 9am-5pm, ✆4939 4888.

Great Keppel Island

The island is a very popular tourist destination. Fringed by 17km (10 miles) of white, sandy beaches and offshore coral reefs, it provides an ideal setting for holiday makers and day trippers alike. The Keppel Island group of 30 islands is situated 55km from Rockhampton, and 15km east of Rosslyn Bay on the Capricorn Coast. Great Keppel is the only island in the group to have been developed, and this is because of its permanent water supply as well as its size (14 sq km). There are ample opportunities for fishing, cruising, boom netting, windsurfing and bushwalking.

Some islands in the group are national parks - North Keppel, Miall, Middle, Halfway, Humpy and Peak - where camping is permitted, but numbers are limited. All drinking water has to be taken to these islands, but some have water for washing, and some have toilets, but it is best to get full information from either the Naturally

Queensland Information Centre in
Brisbane, ☎3227 8187.

Although not situated on the
Reef, Great Keppel is the gateway
to the Outer Reef and North West
Island, the largest coral cay in the
Great Barrier Reef. It is a major
breeding ground for Green Turtles,
White Capped Noddy Terns,
Wedge Tailed Shearwaters and Ol-
ive Head Sea Snakes.

Day trips to Great Keppel Island
are available from *Keppel Tourist
Services*, ☎4933 6744 or ☎1800
356 744 (free call). The trip lasts 8
hours and includes a cruise transfer from Rosslyn Bay, snorkelling
and boom netting, buffet lunch and
free time. The day trip costs ✪$80
adults, $45 children and $200 for
families.

The **Middle Island Underwater
Observatory** is a popular attraction. It is surrounded by natural
coral, and the area teems with marine life of every type imaginable.
A sunken wreck nearby also provides a haven for fish, sea snakes,
turtles and a school of huge cod.
The Underwater Observatory is
☼open daily 8am-5pm, if weather
conditions are favourable, and admission charges are ✪$10 adults
and $5 children.

A glance at a map will show that
the Great Barrier Reef is a long way
from the mainland at this point, but
there is some good diving closer to
Great Keppel Island. Bald Rock and
Man & Wife Rocks are popular diving venues, and between the southern end of Halfway Island and
Middle Island Reef there is some
good coral. If the weather is calm
there is good diving at Parker's
Bombora, off the south-eastern tip
of Great Keppel. It begins in water
about 20m deep and is encircled by
sea ferns, sponges, coral and hundreds of fish. The outer islands of
the Keppel group, particularly Barren Island, have deeper and clearer
water than Great Keppel, so larger
species of sea life are encountered,
like turtles and manta rays. All diving gear can be hired from the accommodation outlets on Great
Keppel.

If you would like online details of
the Great Keppel Island Resort, the
web site is ☞www.mpx.com.au/
~adventures/gk/keppel.htm

Heron Island

The island is about 72km east of
Gladstone, roughly 100km from
Rockhampton, and has an area of
19ha. It is a true coral cay that sits
on the Tropic of Capricorn, surrounded by 24 sq km of reef. It is
possible to walk around the island
in less than half an hour, and there
is usually an organised beach and
reef walk every day. Heron's eastern end has a track system that
leads through dense pisonia forest

and open grassy shrubland, with information posts along the way. In the summer months be sure to stay on the track, or you could destroy one of the many shearwater burrows that honeycomb the island.

Unfortunately, due to its distance from the mainland, Heron Island is one of the most expensive islands to visit. Access is by helicopter for around $270 adults one-way or a choppy 2-hour catamaran trip for around $85.

At other islands on the Reef it is sometimes necessary to travel 70 or 80 km for scuba diving and snorkelling, but at Heron the Reef is at the very foot of the white sandy beaches. One of the most spectacular diving sites is the well-known Heron Bommie, a head of hard coral rising more than 18m from the seabed that is home to all kinds of fish and marine life. All equipment can be hired from the resort's dive shop.

Heron hosts a week-long Dive Festival in November each year, when divers from all over the world gather to swap knowledge and experience. There are those who think that this island rates highly among the world's premier dive locations, and given that there are twenty unique sites nearby, they are probably right.

The Resort can be phoned direct on ©132 469. There is a website at ☞www.heronisland.com and email at ✎visitors@greatbarrierreef. aus.net

Lady Musgrave Island

Lady Musgrave Island is part of the Capricorn Bunker Group, and is about 100km north-east of Bundaberg. It is a true coral cay, approximately 18ha in area, and rests on the edge of a huge coral lagoon that measures some eight kilometres in circumference and covers an area of around 1192ha. The lagoon is one of very few on the Reef that ships can enter, making the island very popular with the yachting fraternity. Lady Musgrave is a National and Marine Park, and an unspoilt section of the Great Barrier Reef.

The island is reputedly one of the finest dive sites on the Great Barrier Reef, and is home to around 1200 species of fish and 350 varieties of coral. The lagoon is reasonably shallow, allowing longer dives to be undertaken.

MV *Lady Musgrave* always has qualified diving instructors on board for the inexperienced, but they can also head certified divers in the best direction to get the most out of their trip.

If you wish to stay on Lady Musgrave Island you must camp. There are staff on-site, toilets and walking trails, and that is it. You have to first obtain a camping permit from the QNP&WS or Naturally Queensland, ✆3227 8187, and fees are ✪$3.50 per person per night.

Lady Elliot Island

The most southerly of the islands of the Great Barrier Reef, Lady Elliot has an area of 0.42 sq km and has been nicknamed Queensland's "Shipwreck Island". This name is not unwarranted, as the wrecks of many ships can be seen littered around the island's shores. The first was probably in 1851, the *Bolton Abbey* cargo ship, and the latest was the *Tenggara II* which hit the reef in April, 1989. The island is also popular with bird watchers as 57 species are known to flock here, with more than 200,000 birds nesting here during the summer. Sea turtles also nest on Lady Elliot.

It only takes about an hour to walk around the entire island, and it is one of the least commercialised.

There are ten excellent diving sites that include Lighthouse Bommie, Coral Gardens, Moiri and Shark Pool. Visibility ranges from 80 to 25 to 50 metres. This island is also paradise for those who like exploring shipwrecks. All equipment can be hired from the resort for around $60, and open water courses are available for ✪$550. Shore dives cost $30, boat dives $45 and night dives $60.

Contact the resort on ✆3348 8522 or ✆1800 072 200 (free call). You can visit the web page at 👁www.ladyelliot.com.au or send an email to ✉info@ladyelliot.com.au

Mt Hay Gemstone Tourist Park

It is 40km (25 miles) west of Rockhampton on the Capricorn Highway, Wycarbah. There you can fossick for 120 million-year-old Thundereggs. When the eggs are cut in the gemstone factory on the premises, beautiful agate patterns are exposed. Facilities here also include a swimming pool, craft and gift shop, barbecue facilities and powered caravan sites (✪$14 per night for two people), ✆4934 7183.

Mount Morgan

The historic township of Mount Morgan is 40km (25 miles) south of Rockhampton, and here you can tour through a 100-year-old mining town that is the real thing, not a reconstruction. Mt Morgan was listed as a Heritage Town by the Australian Heritage Commission in 1980, and by the National Trust of Queensland in 1981. The **Museum** on Morgan Street, ✆4938 4122, traces the history of the fabulously rich mine. Inspections of the mine are conducted by *Mt Morgan Mine*

Tours, 38 Central Street, ✆4938 1081.

Whilst in town, you can call into the **Golden Nugget Hotel** on the Central Street, for a cool ale.

Capricorn Highlands

The highlands stretch from Carnarvon to Clermont (Gregory Highway) and from Blackwater to Jericho (Capricorn Highway). The region is one of the most diverse and productive areas in the country. Coal, sapphires, cattle, sheep, wheat, sunflower, sorghum and cotton are but a few of the riches produced from around here. The Emerald Irrigation Scheme, along with the Fairbairn Dam, has increased rural productivity tenfold in the heart of the Highlands.

A visit to this area can be a re-warding experience. The **Carnarvon Gorge** offers a breathtaking view of scenery, lush vegetation and Aboriginal art.

The town of **Springsure** has the famous Virgin Rock, and from **Emerald**, the hub of the Central Highlands, you can join a conducted tour of the **Gregory Coal Mine**, ✆4982 8200.

Travelling through **Capella** brings you to the township of **Clermont**, which was almost completely destroyed by a flood in 1916, and was moved to its present location with the aid of a huge steam engine. The engine has been preserved as a memorial in the centre of the town.

A National Park at **Blackdown Tablelands** offers camping facilities and good views.

After crossing the Drummond

Range, the country opens out into Queensland's vast grazing lands, and towns like **Alpha** and **Jericho** are becoming increasingly popular stopovers for people visiting this outback area. It has become even more so since the opening in 1988 of the Stockman's Hall of Fame, ✆4658 2166, on the Landsborough Highway in **Longreach**.

The Central Queensland gemfields are a popular tourist spot in the Capricorn Region, and visitors come for a chance to 'stub their toe on a sapphire'. Towns such as **Anakie**, **Sapphire**, **Rubyvale** and the **Willows Gemfields** must be experienced to be fully appreciated. In Rubyvale you can visit a walk-in mine, called **Bobby Dazzler**, which has guided tours and is hopen daily. It is in Main Street, ✆4985 4170.

Central Highlands Tourism Queensland can be contacted on ✆4982 4942 or emailed at ✐chtour@maxspeed.net.au You will find plenty of useful information at ☜members.tripod.com/central highlands/

Gladstone

Located 107km south of Rockhampton, Gladstone is a bustling port centre, one of the busiest and largest in the country. From its modest beginnings in 1847 as a small penal colony with a population below 200, it has grown to become home to more than 42,000 people. Heron Island is only 73km off the coast of Gladstone.

The **Gladstone Art Gallery and Museum**, is in Goondoon Street and ⏲opens 10am-5pm on weekdays and 10am-4pm on weekends. The building itself is a unique mix of architectural designs, and complements the collection of Australian art and local memorabilia contained within. Admission is free.

The **Tondoon Botanic Gardens** cover 83ha and are considered the best of their type among Queensland's regional centres. The landscape is made up of lakes and forest and the fauna includes colourful birds and turtles. Access is between ⏲9am and 6pm in the summer months, and half an hour earlier (morning and evening) during winter. The Gardens can be entered through Glenlyon Road.

Just off the coast of Gladstone are the outlying **Curtis** and **Quoin Islands**.

Monto, 203km (126 miles) south west of Bundaberg, is the largest town of the North Burnett and the service centre for the surrounding dairy industry.

24km (15 miles) north-east is **Cania Gorge**, with its spectacular sandstone formations and crystal pools. Walk-ways and boardwalks extend well into the gorge. 8km further on is the massive Cania

Dam, where there are attractive picnic areas. Gold was discovered at Cania in 1891, and some flecks can be panned from the streams even today.

The Gladstone Area Promotion and Development Bureau is at Ferry Terminal, Gladstone Marina, Bryan Jordan Drive, ©4972 4000, and they will be able to assist you with enquiries. They have an online address at ☞www.gladstoneregion. com and email at ✎gapdl@ gladstoneregion.org.au

Queensland - North

Mackay

Population 58,600
Mackay is a coastal city, on the banks of the Pioneer River, 975km (606 miles) north of Brisbane.

Climate

Average temperatures: January max 31C (88F) - min 22C (72F); July max 23C (73F) - min 10C (50F). Average annual rainfall - 1672mm (66 ins), with over 1000mm (39 ins) falling January-March. The driest months are June-November.

Characteristics

Mackay is surrounded by miles and miles of sugarcane fields, which give the city its title of Sugar Capital of Australia. The district produces about one-third of Australia's total sugar crop, which is exported through the Port of Mackay.

Tram tracks meander through the fields, for the miniature engines that transport the cane to one of the seven sugar mills in the district. In some places the fields are torched between June and December, just before harvesting, and the night skies turn red with the reflections from the fires. These days this method is more frequently replaced by 'green harvesting', which involves cutting rather than burning. See under *Points of Interest* for details of a sugar farm tour.

North-east of Mackay, just off the coast from Shute Harbour, is the Whitsunday Group of Islands containing some of the most popular of the resort islands of the Great

Barrier Reef. Although these islands are not coral cays, the scenery is similar to those featuring in your dreams of lazing on a palm-fringed beach on a tropical island.

The beautiful Eungella National Park, 84km inland from Mackay, has graded tracks leading through rainforest to waterfalls and cool pools (*see separate listing*).

How to Get There

By Air
The Qantas regional airlines of Airlink and Sunstate service Mackay, ✆131 313.

By Bus
Greyhound Pioneer, ✆13 2030, stops at Mackay on its Brisbane/Cairns route.

McCaffertys, ✆13 1499, also operates a Brisbane/Mackay service which takes the inland route from Rockhampton.

By Rail
Queensland Rail Travel Trains operate The Sunlander, The Queenslander and The Spirit of Tropics from Brisbane throughout the week, contact ✆13 2235.

The number for the Mackay Railway Station is ✆4952 7418.

By Road
From Brisbane, via the Bruce Highway, 975km (606 miles).
Mackay is 1079km (670 miles) south of Cairns.

Visitor Information

Mackay Tourism and Development Bureau Ltd is in 'The Mill', 320 Nebo Road, ✆4952 2677, and they are ○open Mon-Fri 9am-5pm, Sat-Sun 9am-4pm. Their email is ✉ mtdb@mackay.net.au

Local Transport

Car Hire
The following companies operate in the area.
Avis, Mackay Airport, ✆4951 1266.
AAA Rental-U-Drive, 6 Endevour Street, ✆4957 5606.
Budget Rent-A-Car, 19B Juliet Street, ✆4951 1400
Thrifty Car Rental, 3 Mangrove Road, ✆4957 3677.
Mackay Economy Rentals, 139 Sydney Street, ✆4953 1616.
Hertz Rentals, Mackay Airport, ✆4951 4685.
Network Rentals, 196 Victoria Street, ✆4953 1022
Cut-Rate Rentals, 105 Alfred Street, ✆4953 1616

Public Transport
Buses service the Mackay area on weekdays only, not on public holidays, ✆4957 8416 for timetable information from Mackay City Buses.

Taxis
Taxi Transit, Victoria Street, ✆4951 4990.

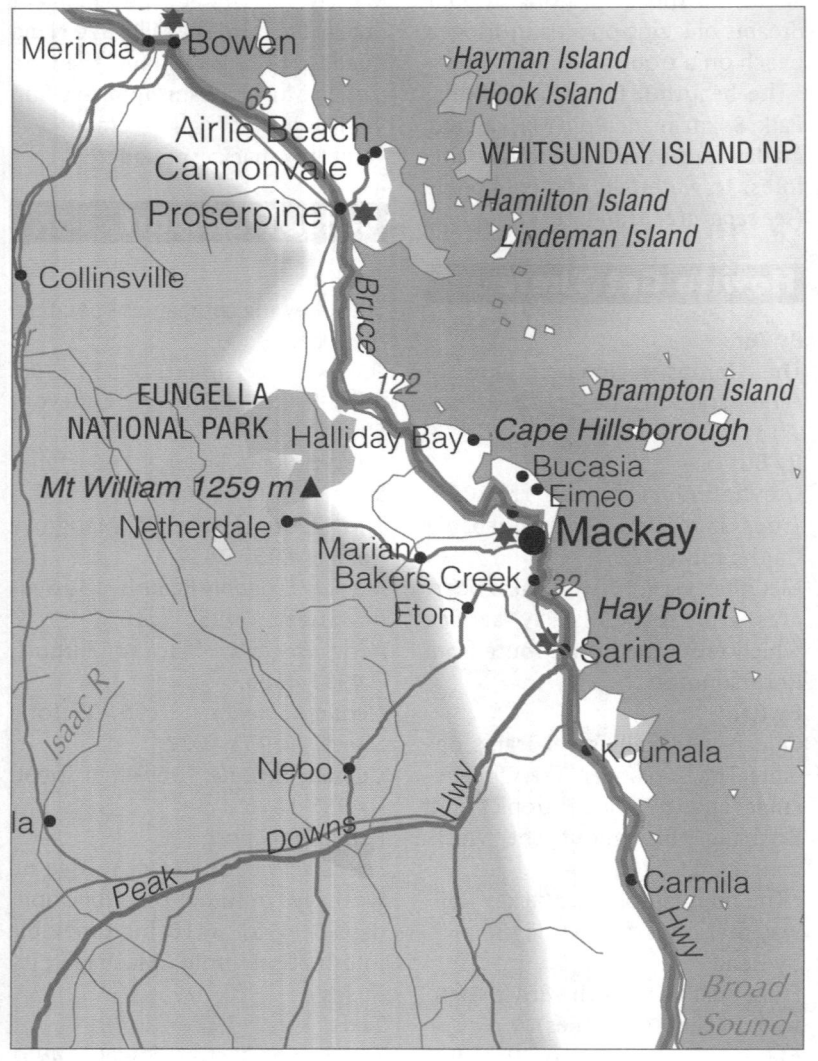

Merinda Bowen
Hayman Island
Hook Island
65
Airlie Beach
WHITSUNDAY ISLAND NP
Cannonvale
Proserpine
Hamilton Island
Lindeman Island
Bruce
Collinsville
122
Brampton Island
EUNGELLA
NATIONAL PARK
Cape Hillsborough
Halliday Bay
Bucasia
Mt William 1259 m ▲
Eimeo
Netherdale
Mackay
Marian
Bakers Creek
32
Eton
Hay Point
Sarina
Isaac R
Koumala
Nebo
Hwy
Ia
Downs
Peak
Carmila
Hwy
Broad
Sound

Mackay Taxis, Victoria Street, ☏13 1008.

Accommodation

Mackay has a wide range of accommodation, from international resort hotels and motels, to caravan parks and camping grounds. Here is a selection with prices for a double room per night, which should be used as a guide only. The telephone area code is 07.

Ocean International Hotel, 1 Bridge Street, ☏4957 2044. 46 rooms, licensed restaurant, swimming pool, spa, sauna, putting green, barbecue - ✪$165-265.

Mercure Inn Mackay, 166 Nebo Road, ☏4951 1555. 34 units, 2 suites, licensed restaurant, undercover parking, pool - ✪$130.

Marco Polo Motel, 46 Nebo Road, ☏4951 2700. 30 units, licensed restaurant, swimming pool, spa, sauna, gym - ✪$100.

Shakespeare International, 309 Shakespeare Street, ☏4953 1111. 37 units, 17 suites, licensed restaurant, swimming pool, spa, barbecue - ✪$100.

White Lace Motor Inn, 73 Nebo Road, ☏4951 4466. 36 units, licensed restaurant, swimming pool, spa - ✪$90-120.

Sugar City, 66 Nebo Road, ☏4968 4150 or 1800 645 525 (toll free). 21 units, barbecue, licensed restau-

rant, playground, room service, car parking, pool - ✪$75-90.

Alara Motor Inn, 52 Nebo Road, ☏4951 2699. 34 units, licensed restaurant, swimming pool, spa, sauna - ✪$85-100.

Ocean Resort Village, 5 Bridge Street, ☏4951 3200 or 1800 075 144 (toll free). 34 units, kiosk, tennis half-court, undercover parking, 2 pools - ✪$80.

Coral Sands Motel, 44 MacAlister Street, ☏4951 1244. 46 units, 2 suites, licensed restaurant (closed Sun), swimming pool, sauna, barbecue - ✪$70-75.

Country Plaza Motor Inn, 40 Nebo Road, ☏4957 6526. 38 units, licensed restaurant, undercover parking, pool, spa - ✪$75-80.

Paradise Lodge Motel, 19 Peel Street, ☏4951 3644. 12 units, undercover parking - ✪$60-65.

Pioneer Villa, 30 Nebo Road, ☏4951 1288. 18 units, licensed restaurant, swimming pool, barbecue - ✪$65.

Hi Way Units, Nebo Road, cnr Webberley Street, ☏4952 1800. 7 units, undercover parking, swimming pool - ✪$50.

Bona Vista Motel, cnr Malcomson Street & Norris Road, ☏4942 2211. 18 units, licensed restaurant, swimming pool, barbecue - ✪$45-55.

Boomerang, South Nebo Road, ☏4952 1755. 23 units, unlicensed restaurant, playground, pool - ✪$40-45.

Budget Accommodation

The places listed below offer double rooms at less than $50 per night:

Mackay Townhouse, 73 Victoria Street, ✆4957 6985.

International Lodge, 40 MacAlister Street, ✆4951 1022.

Austral Hotel, 189 Victoria Street, ✆4951 3288.

Taylors Hotel, cnr Wood & Alfred Streets, ✆4957 2500.

There is a **Youth Hostel** at 32 Peel Street, ✆4951 3728. 6 rooms at ✪$19 per person twin share.

Northern Beaches

Approximately 15 minutes drive north of Mackay.

Dolphin Heads Resort, Beach Road, Dolphin Heads, ✆4954 9666 or ✆1800 075 088 (free call). 2 units, licensed restaurant, swimming pool and spa, tennis court - ✪$165.

Ko Huna Beach, Homestead Bay Avenue, Bucasia, ✆5954 8555 or ✆1800 075 128 (toll free). 60 units, 2 licensed restaurants, swimming pool and spa, mini golf, tennis, watersport activities - ✪$98-130.

The Shores, 9 Pacific Drive, Blacks Beach, ✆4954 9444. 36 units, cooking facilities, undercover parking, 2 swimming pools, spa, tennis court - ✪$85-145.

Blue Pacific Village, 24 Bourke Street, Blacks Beach, ✆4954 9090.

38 units, licensed restaurant, barbecue, playground, undercover parking, cooking facilities, swimming pool, half-court tennis, heated pool, spa - ✪$83-130.

Pacific Palms Beachfront Units, Symons Avenue, Bucasia Beach, ✆4954 6277. 6 units, cooking facilities, swimming pool, undercover parking - ✪$62-69.

La Solana, 15 Pacific Drive, Blacks Beach, ✆4954 9544. 12 units, barbecue, playground, cooking facilities, swimming pool, half-court tennis - ✪$55-85.

Tropic Heart Units, 64 Waverley Street, Bucasia, ✆4954 6965. 7 units, barbecue, undercover parking, cooking facilities, swimming pool - ✪$44-65.

Hibiscus Coast

Approximately 40-45 minutes drive north of Mackay

See under *Cape Hillsborough* and *Halliday Bay*, which have separate listings.

Sarina

Approximately 30 minutes drive south of Mackay.

Sarina Motor Inn, Bruce Highway, ✆4943 1431 or ✆1800 248 087. 16 units, licensed restaurant, undercover parking, room service, pool - ✪$50-60.

Tramway, 110 Broad Street, ✆4956 2244. 12 units, cooking facilities, playground, undercover parking, pool - ✪$48-60.

Tandara, Broad Street, ☏4956 1323. 15 units, licensed restaurant, undercover parking - ❂$42-45.

Caravan Parks

Beach Tourist Park, 8 Petrie Street, Illawong Beach, ☏4957 4021 or 1800 645 111 (tollfree). (No pets allowed) 150 sites, playground, kiosk, pool - powered sites ❂$21 for two, villas $55-60, units $70 for two.

Andergrove Caravan Park, Beaconsfield Road, Andergrove, ☏4942 4922. (Pets allowed on application) 160 sites, barbecue, playground, pool - powered sites ❂$18 for two, on-site vans $35 for two, cabins $45 for two.

Tropical Caravan Park Melanesian Village, Bruce Highway, ☏4952 1211. (Pets allowed on application) 170 sites, barbecue, playground, kiosk, pool - powered sites ❂$19 for two, on-site vans $28 for two, villas $55-60 for two, units $45 for two.

Premier Van Park, 152 Nebo Road, ☏4957 6976. (No pets allowed) 42 sites, barbecue, kiosk pool - powered sites ❂$14 for two, cabins $30-35 for two.

Eating Out

Most of the motels have licensed restaurants, and many hotels serve inexpensive counter meals. Here are a few restaurants that you might like to try:

Pippi's Italian Restaurant, cnr Palmer & Grendon Streets, ☏4951 1376. BYO, Italian & Mediterranean, open Tues-Sat from 5.30pm.

Romeo & Juliet's Restaurant, 309 Shakespeare Street, ☏4953 1111. Licensed, a la carte - fresh local produce and fine Aussie wines are the specialties. Open nightly from 6.30pm.

The Beachhouse Seafood Restaurant, 2 Ocean Avenue, Slade Point, ☏4955 4733. Metres from the water's edge. Generous platters and Live Mud Crab Tank. Open for dinner seven nights, lunch Thursday, Friday and Sunday.

Valencia Restaurant, 44 MacAlister Street, at the Coral Sands Motel, ☏4951 1244. Licensed, a la carte, piano bar - open for dinner from 6.30pm, and for lunch Mon-Fri.

Toong Tong Thai Restaurant, 10 Sydney Street, Mackay, ☏4957 8051. Dinner 7 days from 5.30pm, lunch Mon-Fri 11.30am-2.30pm. McDonald's is at the corner of Hicks Road and the Bruce Highway, ☏4942 3999. Pizza Hut has a free delivery service Mon-Thurs 4-11pm, Fri-Sun noon-11pm, ☏4957 2481.

Entertainment

If you fancy seeing a **movie**, head for the cinema complex in Gordon Street, ☏4957 3515.

For some **live entertainment** contact the *Mackay Entertainment Centre*, also in Gordon Street, ©4957 1757 or ©1800 646 574, to find out about current shows.

The *Conservatorium of Music*, 418 Shakespeare Street, has regular classical and jazz concerts, often featuring overseas artists, ©4957 3727. For night owls, there are a few **night clubs** where you can dance to the wee small hours:

Whitz End, The Whitsunday Hotel, 176 Victoria Street, ©4957 2811.

The Blue Moose Nightclub, 144 Victoria Street, ©4951 2611. ©Open Wed-Sun nights.

The Balcony, 144 Victoria Street, ©4957 2241.

Katie O'Reilly's Irish Bar & Restaurant, 38 Sydney Street, ©4953 3522.

The Saloon Bar, 99 Victoria Street, ©4957 7220.

If you are in town on a Thursday night you might like to go to the greyhound racing at the *Mackay Showground* in Milton Street, ©4951 1680.

Shopping

Centrepoint Shopping Centre, ©4957 2229, is in Victoria Street, in the heart of the city, where you will also find some good street shopping.

Caneland Shoppingtown, ©4951 3311, is in Mangrove Road.

Mt Pleasant Shopping Centre, Phillip Street, North Mackay, is more convenient for those staying to the north of the city.

Weekend markets are held as follows:

The *Foundry Markets* on Harbour Road - ©Thursday, Sat-Sun 8am-4pm.

Mackay Showground Markets in Milton Road - ©Sat 8am-1pm.

Victoria Street Markets - ©Sun 8.30am-12.30pm.

On the first Sunday of every month *Paxtons Markets* are held in River Street ©9am-1pm, and on most long weekends the *Eungella Markets* are staged at Dalrymple Heights Oval.

Arts & Crafts

Pioneer Potters in Swayne Street, North Mackay, ©4957 6255, has a good selection of handmade local pottery and sculpture. It is ©open Wed and Sat 10am-4pm.

The Beach Pottery, 6 Blacks Beach Road, Blacks Beach, offers functional stoneware pottery by local potters. It is ©open Mon-Thurs 10am-5pm, and weekends by arrangement.

Bucasia Gardens and Gifts, Bucasia Road, about ten minutes drive past Mt Pleasant Shopping Centre, has a wide selection of local pottery, crafts, dried flowers and giftware. It is ©open daily 9.30am-5pm,

Above and Below: Airlie Beach near the Great Barrier Reef in Queensland

Sugar Cane Farming near Mackay

⌀4954 8134, and also has a coffee shop, plants and pots.

Homebush Store Pottery & Craft Gallery is situated 26km south-west of Mackay in an historic building, Sunnyside Road. Opening in the early 1900 as the local store for the people of Homebush and surrounding areas, it has now been restored and is operated as a pottery workshop. Also available are works of art, fibre arts, woodturned objects, hand painted T-shirts and handmade cane baskets. The Gallery is ⌀open Fri-Tues 9am-5pm, ⌀4959 7339.

Points of Interest

John Mackay discovered the Pioneer River Valley in 1860, but he named the river the Mackay. He returned with stock and registered "Greenmount" the first pastoral run in the district in 1862. Others followed and the settlement was named Mackay in his honour. The river's name, however, had to be changed to Pioneer because there was already a Mackay River.

It was only a few years before sugar became the main industry, pioneered by the efforts of John Spiller, T. Henry Fitzgerald and John Ewen Davidson. Nowadays Mackay Harbour is home to the world's largest bulk sugar terminal.

The port for Mackay was originally on the river, but because of the enormous tides (around 6.5m), a new port was built on the coast.

Tourism Mackay have put together a *City Walking Tour* that visits the historic buildings, including the Police Station (1885), Court House, Commonwealth Bank (1880), Town Hall (1912), Holy Trinity Church, Masonic Temple, National Bank, Mercury Building, Pioneer Shire Chambers, Post Office and Customs House (1901).

The closest beach to the city is **Harbour Beach**, on the southern side of the outer harbour wall. It has a children's playground, toilets and shady picnic areas, and is patrolled during summer by the Mackay Surf Club.

Queen's Park Orchid House, cnr Gordon & Goldsmith Streets, has an excellent display of native and foreign orchids.

Illawong Fauna Sanctuary, at Illawong Beach, 4km from Mackay centre, is a beachfront family recreation area amid tropical landscaping. There are kangaroos roaming free, a swimming pool, trampoline, video games and full catering facilities, as well as crocodiles (not roaming free). Feeding times are 9am, 11.30am and 3.30pm. For further information, ⌀4959 1777. The sanctuary is ⌀open 9am-6pm daily, and until 10pm on Friday night.

You can get a good panoramic view of the city and the countryside from the **Mt Oscar Lookout** in Norris Road, North Mackay.

Tours of the **Racecourse Sugar Mill**, Peak Downs Highway, are conducted during the crushing season, from June to November, ©4953 8276 for more information.

Polstone Sugar Farm Tours, Masotti's Road, Homebush, adjacent to Orchid Way, conduct a 2 hour tour covering the history, equipment and process of growing and preparing sugar cane for the mill. Costs, including refreshments, are ✪$15 adults and $8 children, ©4959 7298.

North of Mackay are several popular beach resorts.

Blacks Beach is approximately 6km in length, and is probably the best beach in the area for swimming and fishing. **Bucasia** and **Eimeo** beaches are in the semi-rural area, about a 10 minute drive north of Mackay, and are long sandy beaches that are safe for swimming and have good play areas for kids. They also offer good views of the countryside and off-shore islands.

Beaches

Illawong (Far Beach) and **Iluka** (Town Beach) offer views of Flat and Round Top Islands and Dalrymple Bay/Hay Point coal loading terminal.

Harbour Beach has a surf lifesaving patrol, toilets, adventure playground and picnic area.

Lamberts Beach has a lookout that provides island views.

Blacks Beach is a long secluded beach with picnic facilities.

Dolphin Heads has accommodation available.

Eimeo Beach has a small picnic area next to an avenue of century old mango trees.

Sunset Beach has a shaded foreshore picnic area.

Bucasia Beach has a summer swimming enclosure, picnic area and views to Dolphin Heads and islands.

Shoal Point Beach has a picnic area, toilets and lookout. The Esplanade offers views of islands, Cape Hillsborough and Hibiscus Coast, and there is a causeway to Little Green Island.

South of Mackay

Twenty-five kilometres south of Mackay, at Hay Point, is the **Dalrymple Bay Coal Terminal Complex**, the largest coal export facility in the southern hemisphere. The wharves stretch 3.8km out to sea, and coal trains up to 2km long arrive at the port daily. The Port Administration Building has recorded information and a viewing platform, ©4943 8444.

The **Big Prawn** is at Lot 1, Grasstree Beach Road, Grasstree Beach, and is the only commercial hatchery in Australia that is open to the public.

The sugar town of **Sarina** is 37km south of Mackay. It has a population of around 9,000, some picturesque scenery, and some excellent beaches. *(See also separate listing.)*

Cape Palmerston National Park is 80km south of Mackay and has 4WD only access. It offers long sandy beaches, palm forests, freshwater lagoons and large stands of melaleuca. Attractions include Ince Bay to the north, Temple Island and the volcanic plug of Mt Funnel. There is camping, but facilities are very basic.

Beaches

Campwin Beach, 8.5km from Sarina, is home to a rich fishing and prawning industry. Boat launching and mooring facilities are available and there is easy access to nearby islands.

Armstrong Beach is 9.5km from Sarina and has a picnic and camping, and an orchid nursery that is open by appointment only.

Sarina Beach, 13km from Sarina, has a picnic area, store, boat ramp, and a surf lifesaving patrol. Coral Lookout is at the southern end of the beach.

Grasstree Beach, 13km from Sarina, has a picnic area and boat ramp in a wide sheltered bay.

Salonika Beach, 24km from Sarina, is a quiet sandy beach with an inland lagoon teeming with birdlife.

Halftide Beach, 28km from Sarina, is home to the Tug Boat Harbour that services Hay Point Coal Terminal.

North of Mackay

Cape Hillsborough National Park, 45km (28 miles) north-east of Mackay, covers 830ha and features a variety of vegetation, elevated lookouts and peaceful beaches. It is not unusual to see a couple of kangaroos lazing on the beach undisturbed by humans doing the same thing.

Cathu State Forest is 70km (44 miles) north of Mackay. Drive along the Bruce Highway to 3km north of Yalboroo, turn left and continue for 12km (8 miles) along the gravel road to the Forestry Office. Within the forest is the Jaxut State Forest Park which has shaded picnic areas with friendly kangaroos, camping facilities and toilets.

Midge Point is reached by turning right off the Bruce Highway at Bloomsbury, and travelling 18km through the Condor Hill to the village of Midgetown. Named after a small survey vessel, the *Midge*, in the early 1920s, this area has been 'discovered' by developers, and has become a tourist destination.

Beaches

Roughly 25km north of Mackay, turn right onto Seaforth Road then travel 20km to the **Hibiscus Coast**. This includes the beachside settlements of Seaforth, Halliday Bay, Ball Bay and Cape Hillsborough. These beaches are all nesting sites for green and flatback turtles who lay their eggs during the three month period from October each year. The baby turtles hatch between late January and early April.

Halliday Bay has a sandy beach swimming enclosure, accommodation and a restaurant. It is reached from Cape Hillsborough Road.

Seaforth is 48km north-east of Mackay, and offers camping and picnic facilities overlooking the beach.

Belmunda Bay is reached by turning right about 5km along the Cape Hillsborough Road. The bay has secluded beaches with several fishing shacks. After rain has fallen, the nearby freshwater lakes are visited by crowds of water birds, including the brolga.

Festivals

The Sugartime Festival is held in the first week in September each year.

Sports

Golf

There are three golf courses within 40km of Mackay city:

Mackay Golf Club, Bucasia Road, Mackay, ✆4942 1362.

The Valley Golf Club, Leichhardt Street, Mirani, ✆4959 1277.

Sarina Golf Club, Golf Links Road, Sarina, ✆4956 1761.

Swimming

The *Memorial Swimming Pool*, Milton Street, is near Caneland Shopping Centre. It is ⏰open Tues, Thurs and Fri 5am-8.45pm, Wed, Sat and Sun 5am-6pm (closed June and early July).

Whitsunday Waterworld, Harbour Road, Mackay, ✆4955 6466, is a complex with waterslides, mini golf, pinball, video machines and kiosk. It is ⏰open Sat-Sun and school holidays 10am-10pm.

Indoor Sports

BG's Sports Centre on the Bruce Highway south of the City Gates, is one of the largest indoor recreational and fitness centres in Australia. It offers tenpin bowling, roller skating, squash and many other sports, ✆4952 1509. It is ⏰open daily 9am-midnight.

Diving

The Diver Training Centre, ✆4955 4228, has a dive shop by the sea next to the departure point for Roylen Cruises, where you can hire snorkel and scuba gear. They also have 5-day dive courses.

Barnes Reefdiving, 153 Victoria

Street, ✆4951 1472, offer diving trips to the Great Barrier Reef on Mon, Wed and Fri; Reef and Wreck Dive Trips on Tues; and Island Dive Trips on Thurs.

Mackay Diving, 1 Mangrove Road, ✆4951 1640, also offer gear hire and diving lessons.

Tours and Cruises

Natural North Discovery Tours, 11 Rafelo Drive, Farleigh, ✆4952 2677 or ✆4959 8360. Eungella National Park Tour - daily - 10 hours duration - ✪$80 adults, $55 children and $230 for families.

The Great Barrier Reef can be reached from Mackay by sea and air. Credlin Reef, one of the 2100 reefs that make up this coral colony, is only 2 to 3 hours from Mackay Harbour by high speed catamaran. There is a shaded pontoon, underwater viewing area and a seasub that make for excellent snorkelling, scuba diving and coral viewing.

Bushy Atoll, a half-hour seaplane flight from Mackay airport, is the only quay on the entire Reef to have an enclosed lagoon.

Elizabeth E II Coral Cruises, 102 Goldsmith Street, Mackay, ✆4957 4281, offer trips from two to 21 days aboard their specially built monohull dive and fishing boat, *Elizabeth E II*. The boat is stabilised and has the latest navigation aids,

as well as 240v throughout and a 110v charging system.

Accommodation for 12 to 28 passengers are in one double, 12 twin and two triple berths with en-suite facilities and unlimited fresh water. All meals are chef-prepared and snacks, weights, air and tanks are included in the charter costs.

Mackay Adventure Cruises, 320 Nebo Road, ✆4952 2677. High-speed catamaran transport to the Credlin Reef pontoon for coral viewing.

Whitsunday Dreamer, ✆4946 6611. Snorkelling and fishing. Stopovers to Daydream Island, Long Island and Sun Lovers coral reef.

Roylen Cruises, Harbour Road, ✆4955 3066, have daily cruises to Brampton Island; Sat, Sun & Wed cruises to Lindeman and Hamilton Islands; Mon, Wed & Fri cruises to Credlin Reef; and 5-day luxury cruises through the Whitsunday Islands and to the Great Barrier Reef, all departing from the outer harbour. The 5-day cruise departs every Monday 1pm and returns Friday 4pm.

Scenic Flights

Horizon Airways, Casey Avenue, Mackay, ✆4957 2446. Half-hour flights over Mackay.

Air Pioneer, Old Airport, Casey Avenue, Mackay, ✆4957 6661. Offers flights to a coral atoll, then onto a glass-bottomed boat for touring plus snorkelling.

Whitsunday Helicopter Group, Mackay Airport, ©4953 3061. Joy flights over the Barrier Reef.

Fredericksons Air Services, 25 Norman Drive, Yeppoon, ©4938 3404. Includes 2-hour flights to Bushy Reef.

Outlying Attractions

Sarina

The town of Sarina is 37km (23 miles) south of Mackay, and 296km (185 miles) north of Rockhampton, on the Bruce Highway. It is yet another sugar town in the area, cradled by rainforest and the Conners Range mountains. 13km (8 miles) to the north east is a charming little village by the sea, Sarina Beach. Fishing and snorkelling is popular in the tropical islands and reefs close to the mainland.

Broad Street, the main street of the town, is indeed broad with a median strip in the centre offering tables, park benches and public amenities, and best of all, shade.

There are plenty of sandy beaches and offshore islands to entice you to swim, jog, fish or go boating.

The **Dalrymple Bay Coal Exporting Facilities** at Hay Point, ©4943 8444, are the largest of their type in the Southern Hemi-

sphere.

Helpful local information is provided by the Sarina Tourist Art & Craft Centre, Lot 3 Bruce Highway, ©4956 2251.

Eungella National Park

This stunning National Park is 84km (52 miles) inland from Mackay, and the bitumen road leading to it follows the Pioneer River and its tributaries up the valley past Finch Hatton, and through Eungella township at the top of the range. Finch Hatton Gorge has attractive mountain-fed waterfalls, a natural swimming pool, plus good walking tracks.

The Broken River area provides shady pools for swimming, and well marked bush walking tracks are a feature of the Park. If you are lucky you may see a platypus near the bridge.

At the top of the range at Eungella, the fully licensed ***Historic Eungella Chalet Mountain Lodge***, ©4958 4509, has 12 rooms, a playground and pool - ✪$50-90.

A permit is required to **camp** in any of the local National Parks, and this can be obtained from the Ranger at Seaforth, ©4959 0410, the Ranger at Eungella, ©4958 4552, or from the Queensland National Parks and Wildlife Service, cnr Wood & River Street, Mackay, ©4951 8788. Typically, it costs

✪$3.50 per person per night to camp.

For information on all National Parks, the organisations to contact for information are the Environmental Protection Agency, ✆3224 5641, or the Queensland National Parks and Wildlife Service, ✆3227 8187 (Naturally Queensland).

Connect online to 👁www.env.qld.gov.au

Cape Hillsborough

Located 47km (29 miles) north of Mackay, the Cape Hillsborough National Park provides a beachfront picnic area with barbecue facilities. The park is relatively small (830ha - 2050 acres), but it is typical of the best of North Queensland, with rainforests, beaches and abundant wildlife. Walking tracks take you to billabongs, great lookouts and unusual volcanic formations. The fishing in the park is excellent.

Halliday Bay

Situated north of Mackay, near the town of Seaforth, Halliday Bay is noted for its white sandy beach and safe swimming enclosure. The bay adjoins **McBride's Point National Park**, and has a shop and boat hire facilities. The Bay is named after Captain Halliday, whose century-old stone cottage is still standing.

Proserpine

Proserpine, 127km (80 miles) north of Mackay, is mainly a sugar cane town. It serves as the centre of the Whitsunday region, in administrative terms, but most visitors bypass its scenic charm on their way to the more seductive coastline. The town has full facilities and a good range of accommodation. You may wish to stay close to the Bruce Highway on a northward/southward journey, but if you plan to be in the Whitsundays area for any significant length of time, and are not planning to stay on an island resort, the coastal settlements of Airlie Beach and Shute Harbour have all the good views. West of the town is Lake Proserpine, where waterskiing is a popular sport.

The Whitsunday Information Centre on the Bruce Highway is in Proserpine, ✆4945 3711.

Shute Harbour

Shute Harbour is the focal point for

departure of many tourist vessels cruising to the Whitsunday Islands. Not only is it the second busiest passenger port in Australia, it boasts the second largest bareboat industry in the world (a bareboat is a boat hired without a crew).

Shute Harbour is mostly a gateway for cruises out to the islands, and is one of the smaller satellite areas for Proserpine, as well as being superceded by Airlie Beach as an accommodation centre. Nevertheless, there are a couple of places to stay here.

Use the contact details for Whitsunday Tourism, listed under *Visitor Information* for Whitsunday Islands, or visit the Tourist Information Centre at Airlie Beach, 277 Shute Harbour Road, ✆4946 6665.

Airlie Beach

Airlie Beach, the main resort town on the Whitsunday coast, has a relaxed atmosphere, and is 8km (5 miles) from Shute Harbour, 24km (15 miles) from Proserpine. The town borders the 20,000ha Conway National Park, and is the mainland centre for the Whitsundays. Airlie Beach is a picturesque village and offers a lot to the holiday-maker on its own account, but when you add the close proximity of the Reef islands, it is not hard to figure out why some people choose to stay at Airlie and take day trips to the islands. It is a haven for young backpackers, which makes for interesting nightlife.

The Barefoot Bushman's Wildlife Park, Lot 2, Shute Harbour Road, Cannonvale, ✆4946 1480, has a terrific array of Australian wildlife with shows throughout the day. There are pythons, brown snakes, lizards, frogs, ducks, pelicans, owls, kookaburras, possums, wombats, fruit bats, native birds, doves, emus, dingoes and crocodiles, to name a few. Highlights include the Snake Show, where the world's deadliest snakes are put on display, and the Crocodile Feeding, where you can see these huge reptiles snapping up their lunch. The Wildlife Park is ⊙open 9am-4pm every day and admission is ✪$18 adults, $8 children and $45 for families.

The Airlie Tourist Information Centre is at 277 Shute Harbour

Road, Airlie Beach, ✆4946 6665, and can be emailed at the address ✉ abtic@whitsunday.net.au

The Whitsundays

The Whitsundays consist of 74 islands from the Cumberland and Northumberland Island groups, and they form the largest offshore island chain on Australia's east coast. The islands are the remains of a mountain range that was drowned when sea levels rose at the end of the last ice age. Most of them have National Park status, and all are situated in the marine park. The islands were named by Captain Cook when he sailed through the passage on Whitsunday, 1770. Some like to point out that it was not actually Whitsunday, since the good old captain neglected to take into account the fact that he had crossed the international date line, and so was a day out. However, because he made so few nautical and mathematical errors on his journey, Captain Cook is usually forgiven his Whitsunday oversight. Later, when European settlement began on several of the islands, there were some violent confrontations with the resident Aborigines which tarnish the history of this idyllic place.

The Whitsunday Visitors and Convention Bureau, ✆4946 6673, is found on the corner of Shute Harbour and Mandalay Roads, one kilometre from Airlie. They can be emailed at the web address ✉tw@whitsundayinformation.com.au and the website can be seen at ◉www.whitsundayinformation.com.au Alternatively, there is a website at ◉www. whitsunday.net.au

The Whitsunday Information Centre is on the Bruce Highway in Proserpine, ✆4945 3711.

There are basic camping facilities on Hook, North Molle, Whitsunday, Henning, Border, Haslewood, Shaw, Thomas and Repulse Islands. These consist of toilets and picnic tables, with a ranger patrolling. Costs are ✪$3.50 per person per night. All permits can be obtained over the phone by calling the Naturally Queensland Information Centre in Brisbane on ✆3227 8197 or emailing them at ✉nqic@env.qld. gov.au For more information on camping in the region, contact any QNP&WS branch.

Whitsunday Island

Although Whitsunday is the largest of the island in the Whitsunday Group, it does not have a resort. But it does have Whitehaven Beach, the longest and best beach in the whole group, and the destination of many cruises. There is good snorkelling off the southern end of the beach. There are several camping sites on the island.

Lindeman Island

The island has 20km (12 miles) of walking tracks that lead through 500ha (1235 acres) of National Park. There are seven secluded beaches, and at dusk from the top of Mt Oldfield, you can see the sun set over islands that stretch to the horizon in every direction. Lindeman has an area of 8 sq km, most of which is national park, and was named after George Lindeman, whose job in the Royal Navy was to chart safe passages through the Whitsunday Islands. Lindeman has six beaches and 20km of walking trails. Its highest point is Mt Oldfield, 210m. There is a resident Park Ranger who will advise and even accompany walkers.

There is not much here for scuba divers, but the Resort arranges diving trips out to the Reef. Snorkelling trips to Hardy Lagoon take place several days a week.

Contact the resort directly or follow the links to Lindeman Island at the Club Med website: ☞www.clubmed.com.au

South Molle Island

The island covers 405ha (1000 acres) and is 4km long and 2.4km wide. It is situated in the heart of Whitsunday Passage, and offers fishing, golf, tennis, water skiing, coral viewing, scuba diving, parasailing and bushwalking. South Molle has an area of 4 sq km, and is the largest of the Molle group. It is close to Mid Molle, and in fact you can walk from South Molle to Mid Molle at any time. Another island that is very close is Daydream. The oldest of the resorts in the Whitsunday Group, South Molle is mostly national park and offers some good, if short, walks. The highest point is Mt Jeffreys (198m), and from it there are great views of the surrounding islands. Balancing Rock and Spion Kop also allow you to take in breathtaking vistas. The first European settler was Henry George Lamond, who moved in with his wife and children in 1927 and stayed for ten years. There is a memorial to his son, Hal, on top of Lamond Hill.

South Molle is very much a family resort, there is even a pre-school nursery as well as activities for school-age children.

Accommodation is available at **South Molle Island Resort**, ✆4946 9433. 44 units, licensed restaurant, swimming pool, spa, sauna, tennis, squash, golf - full board ◎$310-390 a double per day. There is a Resort Dive Shop that offers short courses for beginners, and organises trips out to various parts of the reef.

The resort can be contacted on ✆4946 9433. The web site is ☞www.southmolleisland.com.au

with an email service at ✒ info@
southmolleisland.com.au

Long Island

The island is directly off the coast
of Shute Harbour, and adjoins the
Whitsunday Passage. It is deliber-
ately underdeveloped, and the un-
tamed tropical rainforest and
protected Palm Bay Lagoon make
for a very informal holiday. There
are 13km (8 miles) of well graded
bushwalking tracks, and a variety
of beaches for swimming and fishing. Long Island is separated from
the mainland by a channel that is
only 500m wide, making it the closest resort island to the Queensland
coast. It has an area of 12 sq km,
but is about 11km long, so it is

apparent that it is extremely narrow, only about 1.5km at its widest.

Long Island has 20km of bush
walks through the National Park,
and there are some nice sandy
beaches on its western side, but at
Happy Valley the tidal variations
cause the water to be so far from
the beach that it is easier to swim
in the pool. The box jellyfish makes
its appearance in the vicinity from
March to November. The beaches
on the eastern side tend to be rocky
and usually windy, but the dredg-
ing that has been undertaken at
Palm Bay makes it ideal for swimming, and for mooring yachts.

The Club Crocodile Resort can be
contacted on ©4946 9233, and for

a preliminary look at what the island has to offer, follow the links to Long Island at ☞www.club crocodile.com.au

Hayman Island

The island is a resort offering a balance between luxury living and natural beauty. Curving around the sandy shoreline of the blue lagoon on the south-western side of the island, Hayman looks out toward Langford Reef and an island called Bali Hai. All sports, both on land and water, are catered for at the resort.

Hayman Island has an area of 4 sq km, and is the most northerly of the Whitsunday resort islands. Its resort is one of the most luxurious on the Great Barrier Reef, and in fact is widely considered to be one of the top ten resorts in the world. There are several bushwalks on Hayman, including an 8km circuit and walks to Blue Pearl Bay or Dolphin Point. It is also possible to walk to nearby Arkhurst Island at low tide.

Hayman is closer to the outer Reef than other resort islands, and Hayman has a full-time dive boat to cater to every diver's desires. Thirty kilometres north-east of Hayman are the Hardy and Black Reefs.

Hayman Island Resort, ℭ4946 1234, offers luxury of the highest

quality. Antiques and treasures from around the world, as well as Australian works of art, can be found throughout the resort. Tarrifs start at $545 for a double room per night and skyrocket to over $3600. For more information, contact the resort or go to ☞www.hayman. com.au

Hamilton Island

Hamilton has an area of 6 sq km, and is home to the largest resort in the South Pacific with its own jet airport.

The resort is actually a small town with shops, restaurants and a 135-berth marina. There are a few

walking tracks on the undeveloped parts of the island, and the main one leads up to Passage Peak (230m) the highest point on the island. To get around the island, you can rent a golf buggy and drive yourself. Hamilton even has island bus tours that operate daily. There is a **Fauna Park** at the northern end of the island, with native animals, crocodiles and performing cockatoos. 4WD safari tours, go-karts and skirmish are further activities.

The Hamilton Island Resort can be contacted on ✆4946 9999 or ✆1800 075 110. An extensive website is provided at ✆www. hamiltonisland.com.au

Hook Island

Hook Island has an area of 53 sq km, some great beaches and some of the best diving sites in the Whitsundays, but it has one of the smallest resorts. The focus here is on the budget market, with a choice between camping sites, beachfront cabins and backpacker dorms. Hook Island has two long, narrow bays on its southern end - Macona Inlet and Nara Inlet. Macona has a National Park camping site, and Nara has caves with Aboriginal wall paintings. There is a variety of wildlife on the island, but one that can prove quite pesky is the large goanna. These have been known to chew through canvas to get to campers' stores.

The island is home to an underwater observatory that has an abundance of colourful corals and marine life. Though with so many trips available to the Outer Reef and the modern semi-submersible craft that tour operators use, you have to wonder why anyone would want to visit an underwater observatory. Still, it is popular with many visitors.

The northern end of Hook Island has some good diving and snorkelling sites - Pinnacle Point, Manta Ray Bay, Butterfly Bay and Alcyonaria Point. The resort can organise reef trips.

The **Wilderness Resort** can answer any further enquiries, ✆4946 9380. There is a website ✆www. hookislandresort.com.au and an email address ✉enquiries@hookis .com

Daydream Island

Daydream is a small island with an area of just 17ha. It is a little over 1km long and no more than a couple of hundred metres at its widest point, but it has one of the largest resorts. Originally known as West Molle, the island is the closest resort island to Shute Harbour. It was first settled in the 1880s by graziers, but the first resort was opened by Paddy Murray, who had purchased the island in 1933 and changed its name to Daydream after his boat. In 2001, Novotel spent $40 million refurbishing the complex.

Daydream Island Resort accommodation is divided into three categories, all of which can accommodate up to 4 people: Ocean View Room, Garden View Room and Sunlover Room. Interconnecting rooms for larger families are available on request.

Sunlover's Beach, at the north-eastern end of the island, behind the resort, has a 50m strip of sand and some good coral offshore for snorkellers. The Whitsunday tidal range does not affect Daydream as much as the other islands. The Resort dive shop offers courses, and day cruises to Hardy Reef, about 50km offshore.

Contact the resort on ✆4948 8488 or ✆1800 075 040 (reservations). The official web page is found at ☞www.daydream.net.au

Brampton Island

Brampton is not strictly in the Whitsunday region. It is part of the Cumberland Group of Islands about 32km north-east of Mackay, at the entrance to the Whitsunday Passage. The island is a National Park, with an area of 4.6 sq km, and has unspoilt bush, lush tropical foliage, swaying coconut palms and many stunning and secluded beaches. It is connected to Carlisle Island and to Pelican Island by sand bars that can be crossed at low tide.

A mountainous island with lush forests, nature trails, kangaroos and emus, Brampton also has seven sandy beaches and is surrounded by coral reefs. The walk around the island is about 7km, takes around three hours, and is best done in a clockwise direction. There is a walk up to the island's highest point, Brampton Peak, beginning near the resort golf course and the round trip takes about two hours. Both walks offer great views. The island is a 45 minute cruise from the Great Barrier Reef, but you can see underwater coral gardens and myriads of tropical fish off Brampton's East Beach.

There is nothing at Brampton itself to excite divers, but cruises from Mackay to Credlin Reef aboard the *Spirit of Roylen*, ✆4955 3066, call in at Brampton to pick up and set down. Credlin Reef is in the Hydrographers Passage area, and there is a permanent pontoon over the reef, an underwater observatory and a semi-submersible. Resort diving courses are conducted on board the *Spirit of Roylen* in transit to Credlin Reef, or at the Resort by special arrangements.

The contact number for the resort is ✆4951 4097, and the website is ☞www.bramptonislandresort.com

Townsville

Population 140,000
Townsville is situated on the eastern coast of Australia, 1443km (897 miles) north of Brisbane.

Climate

Average temperature: January max 31C (88F) - min 24C (75F) and high humidity; July max 25C (77F) - min 15C (59F). Average annual rainfall is 1194mm (47 ins) - wettest months January-March, with an average of 873mm (34 ins).

Characteristics

The second largest city in Queensland and main commercial centre of northern Queensland, Townsville sprawls along the shores of Cleveland Bay and around the foot of Castle Hill. It offers not only easy access to the attractions of the Magnetic North and the Great Barrier Reef, but also all of the facilities of a major city.

Careful zoning has ensured that the city retains much of its original architecture and character. A walk around town will show you what makes North Queensland so different. Old wooden, highset houses stand everywhere, built to allow cooling breezes under the house and to provide a refuge during the heat of the day. In the gardens, mango, paw paw and banana trees seem exotic to the visitor, but are the normal homegrown product of the Townsville backyard.

Townsville is also a busy port that services Mt Isa, southern cities and south-east Asia. It has two metal refineries and other industrial enterprises.

How to Get There

By Air

Qantas, ☎13 1313, and Ansett, ☎13 1300, have flights to/from Adelaide, Alice Springs, Brisbane, Cairns, Darwin, Gold Coast, Hobart, Launceston, Melbourne, Newcastle, Perth and Sydney.

Ansett Airlines also have flights to/from Broome, Burnie, Devonport and Orpheus Island.

Sunstate Airlines, ☎13 1313, have flights to/from Brampton Island, Lizard Island, Mackay, Proserpine, Rockhampton and Thursday Island. Flight West, ☎1300 130 092, is another airline that services Townsville.

By Coach

Greyhound Pioneer, ☎13 2030, and McCaffertys, ☎13 1499, both stop at Townsville on their Brisbane-Cairns services.

By Rail

The Queenslander and the Sunlander services connect Townsville to both Brisbane and Cairns four times weekly, ☎13 2235. Sleeping berths and motor rail facilities are available.

By Road

From Brisbane along the Bruce Highway, 1443km (897 miles); from Brisbane along the inland route, 1505km (935 miles). Townsville is 374km south of Cairns.

The Flinders Highway connects Townsville with Mt Isa and Alice Springs.

It is important to listen to a local radio station for reports on road conditions during wet weather, as roads in northern Queensland are often cut during heavy rain.

Visitor Information

The Townsville Enterprise Tourism Bureau is in Enterprise House, 6 The Strand, ☎4771 3061. There is also a Visitors Information Centre in Flinders Mall, ☎4721 3660, ⏰open 9am-5pm Mon-Fri and 9am-1pm Sat-Sun.

Accommodation

Townsville has over 30 motels, hotels, guest houses, hostels and half a dozen camping grounds. Here is a selection with prices for a double room per night, which should be used as a guide only. The telephone area code is 07.

Jupiters Townsville Hotel & Casino, Sir Leslie Theiss Drive, ☎4722 2333, jupiterstownsville. com.au. 192 rooms, 16 suites, licensed restaurant, bars, swimming pool, spa, sauna, gym, tennis courts, casino - ✪$150.

Centra Townsville, Flinders Mall,

©4772 2477. 158 rooms, licensed restaurants, bars, gym, rooftop swimming pool - ✪$220.

Aquarius on the Beach Townsville, 75 The Strand, North Ward, ©4772 4255. 100 rooms, licensed restaurant (closed Sun), bistro, swimming pool - ✪$130.

Southbank Hotel, 23 Palmer Street, South Townsville, ©4721 1474. 94 units, 4 suites, licensed restaurant, cocktail bar, swimming pool, spa, undercover parking - ✪$100-110.

Castle Lodge, cnr Warburton & McKinley Streets, North Ward, ©4721 2290. 24 units, licensed restaurant (Mon-Sat), pool - ✪$95-105.

City Oasis Inn, 143 Wills Street, ©4771 6048 or ©1800 809 515 (toll free). 42 units, 2 suites, licensed restaurant, playground, pool, 2 spas - ✪$95-170.

Historic Yongola Lodge, 11 Fryer Street, ©4772 4633. 8 units, licensed restaurant, pool, next to *National Trust* restaurant - ✪$90-110.

Shoredrive, 117 The Strand, ©4771 6851. 30 units, unlicensed restaurant, pool - ✪$70.

Bessell Lodge, 38 Bundock Street, Belgian Gardens, ©4772 5055. 50 units, licensed restaurant, cocktail bar, live entertainment, barbecue - ✪$85.

Aitkenvale, 224 Ross River Road, Aitkenvale, ©4775 2444. 26 units,

2 suites, licensed restaurant, swimming pool, playground, undercover parking - ✪$65.

Hotel Allen, cnr Eyre & Gregory Streets, ©4771 5656. 45 units, 5 suites, pool - ✪$70.

Adobi, 86 Abbott Street, ©4778 2533 or ©4778 2745. 12 units, pool - ✪$50.

Caravan Parks

Sun City Caravan Park, 119 Bowen Road, ©4775 7733. 132 sites, pool, barbecue, playground - powered sites ✪$19 for two, on-site vans $35-40 for two, cabins $55-60 for two.

Magnetic Gateway Holiday Village, Bruce Highway, South Side, adjacent to Stuart Drive-in, ©4778 2412. (No pets) 108 sites, barbecue, pool - powered sites ✪$17 for two, villas $55 for two.

Coonambelah Caravan Park, 547 Ingham Road, ©4774 5205. (Pets on application) 75 sites - powered sites ✪$17 for two, on-site vans $35-40 for two, cabins $40-50 for two.

Town & Country Caravan Park, 16 Kings Road, ©4772 1487. (No pets allowed) 72 sites, pool, barbecue, playground - powered sites ✪$18 for two, on-site vans $35 for two, cabins $55 for two.

Eating Out

Townsville has many hotels serving counter lunches and takeaways, and some good restaurants. The international hotels have at least one restaurant, and the staff where you are staying can probably recommend a restaurant on the basis of price or cuisine. Following is a broad sample for all tastes and budgets.

Scirocco Cafe Bar & Grill, 61 Palmer Street, ©4724 4508. Mediterranean and Asian cuisine, alfresco dining. Open Tues-Sat 6pm-midnight, and for lunch from midday-2pm, 10am-4pm on Sunday, closed Monday and Public Holidays.

The Pier Waterfront Restaurant & Bar, Sir Leslie Thiess Drive, ©4721 2567. Licensed restaurant with waterfront views. Seafood and steak, light lunches served. Open midday-2pm for lunch and 6pm-midnight for dinner 7 days.

Covers Restaurant, 209 Flinders Street, ©4721 4630. Open 6pm-midnight Mon-Sat and for lunch Wed-Fri, closed Sunday and Public Holidays.

Flutes Restaurant, 63 The Strand, ©4721 1777. Operates 24 hours a day, 7 days, in the Best Western Motel.

Hong Kong Restaurant, 455 Flinders Street, West Townsville, ©4771 5818. A-la-carte menu with home-style cooking a specialty. Open 5pm-8pm Mon-Sat and for lunch Mon-Fri, closed Sun-

day and Public Holidays.

Wayne and Adeles Garden of Eating, 11 Allen Street, South Townsville, ©4772 2984. Open 6.30-11pm Mon, Wed-Sat and Public Holidays, Sun 11am-3pm, closed Tuesday.

Metropole Hotel, 81 Palmer Street, South Townsville, ©4771 4285. Seafood restaurant with gaming facilities and a beer garden in the complex. Open 24 hours, 7 days.

Taiping Chinese Restaurant, 350 Sturt Street, City, ©4772 3619. A-la-carte, yum cha and buffet selections. Open midday-2pm and 5.30-midnight 7 days, closed Public Holidays.

Seagulls Resort, 74 The Esplanade, Belgian Gardens, ©4721 3111. Open 6.30am-midnight every day.

Centra Townsville, Flinders Mall, ©4772 2477. A-la-carte buffet menu and a cocktail bar. Open 7am-10pm every day.

Hogs Breath Cafe, 247 Flinders Street, ©4771 5747. Open for lunch 11.30am-2.30pm and dinner 5.30pm-2.30am every day.

Pepperleaf at the Seaview, 56 The Strand, Townsville, ©4771 5900.

McDonalds is on the corner of Flinders Mall and Denham Street.

KFC is in the Nathan Plaza Stockland Shopping Centre.

Pizza Hut is at 260 Ross River Road and on the corner of Charters Towers and Bayswater Roads, ©13 1166.

Entertainment

First and foremost in this category would have to be the:

Sheraton Townsville Hotel & Casino, Sir Leslie Theiss Drive, ✆4722 2333. It was North Queensland's first licensed casino. Here you can try blackjack, the Sheraton wheels, two-up, roulette, keno, mini-dice, craps and mini baccarat. They also have video games and Sky Channel. To get the tourists in they offer a free courtesy bus service to most hotels and motels. The casino is ○open from noon to the early hours of the morning.

Townsville Civic Theatre is in 41 Boundary Street, South Townsville, ✆4727 9013 or ✆4727 9797 (box office), and can seat 1066 people. It offers culturally diverse programs.

The **Entertainment & Convention Centre**, ✆4771 4000, on Entertainment Drive, is primarily for indoor sport, such as basketball, but if a big-name performer or band hits town, this is where the concert will be.

Fisherman's Wharf in Ogden Street has live entertainment seven nights a week, a restaurant, coffee shop and a bar.

If you are in the mood for dancing, head for Flinders Street where there is a night club, *Bullwinkles*, ✆4771 5647.

For a pub night out try the *Great Northern Hotel* in 496 Flinders Street, ✆4771 6191.

Shopping

Flinders Street Mall has several boutiques and specialty shops and *Northtown on the Mall*, ✆4772 1566, but the big shopping centres are out of town.

At Aitkenville, 20 minutes from the city centre is *Stockland*, 310 Ross River Road, ✆4779 6033, which has David Jones department stores as well as specialty shops. Nearby is *K-Mart Plaza*, Nathan Street, ✆4779 9277, which has food shops and, of course, K-Mart.

The suburb of Pimlico has *Castletown*, 35 Kings Road, ✆4772 1699, which has a variety of chain stores, including Target. The suburb of Kirwan has *The Willows*, Thuringowa Drive, ✆4773 6333.

North Queensland's largest arts and crafts market is held in Flinders Mall every ○Sunday 9am-1pm. Called *Cotters Market* it has pottery, jewellery, paintings, leadlighting, leatherwork, woodwork, crocheting and knitwear, original handicrafts, wooden toys, hats, homemade goodies, plants and preserves, islander crafts, timber, fishing lures, homemade chocolates, Devonshire teas, orchids, souvenirs, and seasonal fruit and vegies. What more could you want?

Points of Interest

Castle Hill (286m - 938 ft) offers a panoramic view of Townsville. It is topped by an octagonal restaurant which commands a 260 degree view of the town and the bay. Nearby **Mount Stuart** is also an excellent vantage point.

Flinders Mall is virtually the heart of the city. It is a landscaped pedestrian mall with a relaxed atmosphere.

The **Perc Tucker Regional Gallery** is in the mall, ℘4727 9011, and it houses an extensive collection of national and regional art in an impressive building that was originally a bank. It is ℗open Mon-Thurs 10am-5pm, Fri 10-6pm, Sat-Sun 10am-2pm, and admission is free. Nearby **St Joseph's Cathedral** in Fryer Street, North Ward, ℘4772 1973, is a reflection of the architecture of the past.

The Strand, Townsville's sea promenade, has many parks including the Sister Kenny Park, and the Anzac Memorial Park with its Centenary Fountains, waterfall and bougainvillea gardens. Also along The Strand is the Tobruk Memorial Swimming Pool.

Queen's Gardens next to Queen's Park, encompasses Kissing Point and Jezzine Army Barracks. An all-tide rock swimming pool, a restaurant and a kiosk are also in the gardens.

The Town Common Environmental Park is a flora and fauna sanctuary where visitors may see some rare water fowl, including the primitive magpie goose. In the winter months, at the height of the dry season, as many as 3000 brolgas, along with up to 180 other species of bird, flock to the Common's saltmarsh lagoons and waterholes. The brolga is famous for its courting ritual, and the park provides visitors with an excellent opportunity to see this dance at close quarters. The park is hopen daily 6.30am-6.30pm and barbecue facilities are available.

Great Barrier Reef Wonderland in Flinders Street East, is one of the most popular attractions in Townsville. It features the **Great Barrier Reef Aquarium**, ℘4750 0891 - the world's largest living coral reef aquarium. Conceived and operated by the Great Barrier Reef Marine Park Authority, the aquarium includes a huge main tank containing a living coral reef, a smaller tank displaying sharks and other reef predators and an extensive area containing numerous display tanks, educational exhibits, a theatrette and a large touch-tank. You actually walk beneath the water through a transparent tunnel surrounded by hundreds of coral reef animals. Admission costs are ✪$16 for adults, $8 children and $40 for families. This very popular attraction is ☉open 9am-5pm.

Wonderland also houses: the operational headquarters of the Great Barrier Reef Marine Park Authority, the federal government agency responsible for safeguarding the Great Barrier Reef Marine Park (Reef HQ); a licensed restaurant featuring tropical cuisine; a shop with a variety of souvenirs and educational material; a post office; and an information centre with all you need to know about national parks, marine national parks, camping permits and locations, walking trails, and wildlife.

An **Imax Theatre**, ✆4721 1481 is close to the aquarium, at 86 Flinders Street. The theatre is dome-shaped and uses a special type of projection so that the image is projected above and around the audience - a fascinating experience. The theatre seats 200 people, including facilities for the handicapped.

The **Museum of Tropical Queensland**, 78-102 Flinders Street, ✆4726 0600, has recently undergone a complete transformation. The former museum has been expanded and modernised into a new and improved complex,

opened in June 2000. It has an extensive array of exhibits, from the life-cycle of the world's largest moth to various Aboriginal crafts, and is worth a visit.

From the Wonderland ferry terminal there are cruises leaving for Magnetic Island and the Great Barrier Reef throughout the day. And while you are waiting to pick up your cruise, or the next show at the theatre, you can spend some time in the specialty shops in the complex.

Pangola Park, Spring Creek, ✆4782 9252, between Giru and Woodstock, is about 40 minutes' drive from Townsville. It has ideal swimming spots and adjoins a National Park with mountain streams and waterfalls. There is good bushwalking, picnic areas, barbecues, caravan and camping sites, a licensed kiosk, fishing spots, minibikes, and conducted horse and pony rides on weekends and public holidays. The park is ☉open daily and an admission fee is charged. Camping and powered sites are available.

South of Townsville, in fact much closer to the town of Ayr, the wreck of the *Yongala* lies off Cape Bowling Green. A coastal steamer, she was bound for Cairns when a cyclone struck on March 14, 1911, and she went down with all hands - 121 people including officers and crew. The wreck was discovered in 1958, but has only been dived regularly since the 1980s.

Diving the *Yongala* is rated as one of the best wreck-dive experiences in the world.

The wreck is 110m long, and supports a system of hard and soft corals and many different marine animals including pelagics, stingrays, gropers, turtles and sea snakes. She lies in 30m of water with her funnel only 15m below the surface. The *Yongala* is protected by the Historic Shipwreck Act as a memorial to all who went down with her, so nothing may be taken from the ship. This is a temptation as there are dinner plates, knives, forks, and some evidence of human remains, but where they are they must stay. See the Diving section under *Sport* for operators who will take divers to the wreck.

Sport

Swimming

There are three salt water mesh swimming enclosures, one at Rowes Bay, one at Pallarenda, and one next to the rock pool in Queen's Gardens. They provide safe sea swimming free from sharks, sea-stingers and other marine hazards.

Golf

Townsville Golf Club, Benson Street, Rosslea, ✆4779 0133. 27-hole championship course - equipment hire - ☼open 6.30am-6pm, clubhouse open 10am-8pm.

Rowes Bay Golf Club, Cape Pallarenda Road, Pallarenda, ✆4774 1288. 18-hole par 72 course - equipment hire - ☼open seven days.

Willows Golf Club, Nineteenth Avenue, Kirwan, ✆4773 4352 - 18-hole course - ☼open daily.

Horse Riding

Ranchlands Equestrian School, 83 Hammond Way, Kelso, ✆4774 0124 - ☼open week days and nights.

Saddle Sense Riding School, 95 Haynes Road, Jensen, ✆4751 6372 - trail rides and camping - ☼open Wed-Sun.

Fishing/Yacht Charters

Tangaroa Cruises, 19 Crowle Street, Hyde Park ✆4772 2127. 50ft motor cruiser available for extended cruises, social outings, fishing and diving trips - support vessel.

True Blue Charters, 65 Gilbert Crescent, North Ward, ✆4771 5474. Charter boat for reef and game fishing, diving, snorkelling, island cruising - maximum 8 passengers - full boat charter - half day and other charters on request.

Farr Better Yacht Charters, 76 Allen Street, South Townsville, ✆4771 6294. Yacht and boat charter - bare boat or with sail guide -

Hood 23ft yacht and *Farr Star* 40ft yacht - sailing training (AF) - 7 days. Special weekend trips to Palm and Dunk Islands.

Diving

Diving courses are not cheap, and you should expect to pay at least ✪$400 for a comprehensive open water instruction program. If you are already a qualified diver, the cost for a guided dive is considerably less, and depends on the location and duration of the dive. Following are a few examples of companies operating in the area.

Mike Ball Dive Expeditions, 252 Walker Street, ✆4772 3022 - internationally acclaimed 5 star PADI dive centre providing PADI instruction from entry level to Dive career programs - expeditions to Yongala wreck and Coral Sea, also Cod Hole - ☉open Mon-Fri 8.45am-5pm, Sat 8.45am-noon.

The Dive Bell, 16 Dean Street, South Townsville, ✆4721 1155 - sport diving and dive shop - commercial diving school - diving trips to Yongala wreck and the reef - ☉open Mon-Fri 8.30am-5pm, Sat 9am-noon.

Pro-Dive Townsville, Great Barrier Reef Wonderland, Flinders Street, ✆4721 1760. PADI scuba diving school - 5 star Gold dive shop - charter boats, hire equipment, learn to dive - Yongala wreck dives (up to 3 days) - ☉open daily 9am-5pm.

Skydiving

Coral Sea Skydivers, Shop 3, 14 Plume Street, Townsville, ✆4772 4889. Tandem and accelerated free fall dives for beginners and experienced jumpers - souvenir videos, photos and certificates - Tandem Dives: 8,000 feet ✪$245; 12,000 feet $350 - Accelerated Free Fall Course: $500 - Complete Free Fall Course, including training and 12 jumps: $2400.

Tours

Detours, Shop 5, Great Barrier Reef Wonderland Complex, ✆4721 5977, offer the following trips.

Tropical Rainforest and Waterfalls - Mt Specs National Park, Balgal Beach, Little Crystal Creek rainforest walk, Frosty Mango fruit farm - 8 hours - ✪$80 adults, $35 children - 9am Tues, Thurs, Sat.

The Real Outback - Charters Towers and outback country - 8 hours - ✪$80 adults, $35 children - 9am Wed & Sat.

Billabong Sanctuary - wildlife sanctuary - 4 hours - ✪$38 adult, $18 child (includes entrance fee) - 10am daily.

Tropical City Tour - more than 9 points of interest visited - 2 hours - ✪$26 adult, $10 child - 11am weekdays.

Night Tour - Castle Hill, Casino, Entertainment Centre - 1 hour - ✪$20 adults, $7 children - 6pm-7pm Mon-Thu May-Oct.

Hinchinbrook Island - coach to Cardwell, cruise to Hinchinbrook, self-guided walk - 12 hours - ✪$115 adults, $50 children - 6am Tues, Thu & Sun.

Dunk & Bedarra Islands - Mission Beach to Dunk Island to Bedarra Island, lunch, boom netting, tropical fruit tasting - ✪$110 adult, $50 child - 6am Thurs & Sun.

Raging Thunder, 52 Fearnlet Street, Cairns, ©4030 7990. Although based in Cairns, this company has a 5-day tour that departs Towns-ville and takes in the best of the Tropical North. The highlight of day one is 5 hours of Tully River rafting then transfer to Cairns. Day two comprises a 5 hour reef cruise. Day three begins with a Hot Air Balloon flight above the Atherton Tablelands, a visit to Kuranda Markets, then a return trip to Cairns on the Skyrail. Day four is an exploration of Cape Tribulation and Daintree, including a Crocodile Cruise on the river. On day five you are taken to Fitzroy Island to relax or take the optional tour, then return later to Cairns.

The cost of the tour is ✪$520 per person, but you must arrange your own accommodation for the duration of the tour.

Cruises

Coral Princess Cruises, Breakwater Terminal, Sir Leslie Thiess Drive, ©4721 1673 or ©1800 079 545 (free call), offer these trips.

Townsville/Barrier Reef/Islands - 4 days/3 nights Barrier Reef and Island cruise - departs Townsville 1pm - calls at resorts, uninhabited islands and reef - from ✪$1350 per person twin share. 8 day/7 night cruise - combines 3 night

Townsville with 3 night Cairns cruise - $2200 per person twin share.

Magnetic Island Ferry, Ross Street, South Townsville, ©4772 5422, offer:

Cruise to Magnetic Island - open return ticket, free pick up from accommodation - bus or mokes available - ✪$16 adult, $8 child.

Magnetic Island Cruise/Bus - open duration, pick up from accommodation, cruise and bus tour of island with commentary, exploring and swimming - ✪$28 adult, $14 child.

Cruise/Moke Hire - return ferry fare with moke hire on the island - includes insurance and island map - ✪$32 per person.

Pure Pleasure Cruises, Great Barrier Reef Wonderland, 4 The Strand, Townsville, ©4721 3555 or ©1800 079 797 (freecall), offer a:

Kelso Outer Reef Tour - 50 nautical miles north to Kelso reef on the Wave Piercer 2000 - includes swimming, snorkelling, fishing, glass bottom boat, buffet lunch, morning/afternoon tea all inclusive, bar and diving extra - ✪$135 adult, $68 child - departs 9am daily.

Scenic Flights
Townsville Aero Club, Townsville Aerodrome, Garbutt, ©4779 2069. Aircraft charter, joy flights, aerial tours.

Inland Pacific Air, Townsville Aerodrome, Garbutt, ©4775 3866 - twin engine aircraft charter 4 to 11 seats - 7 aircraft available including pressurised executive Cessna - available all hours to any destination.

Also at Townsville Airport are *Nautilus Aviation*, ©4725 6056, *Bluewater Aviation* ©4725 1888, and *Magnetic North Aviation*, ©4725 6227.

Festivals
Pacific Festival is held each September/October, and lasts for 10 days.

The Visitor Information Centre will advise on all current events at the time of your trip.

Outlying Attractions

Fitzroy Island
Fitzroy has an area of 4 sq km, and is situated 26km south-east of Cairns. It is only 6km from the mainland and was named by Captain Cook after the Duke of Grafton, a politician of the time. In 1819 Phillip King reported that Welcome Bay, where the resort is, was a good anchorage for passing ships because of its fresh water and supplies of timber.

Fitzroy Island is not a great place for swimming as the beaches tend to be corally rather than sandy, although Nudey Beach has some sand. There are a few walking trails

- the round trip to the lighthouse; a short rainforest walk to the Secret Garden; and the walk to Nudey Beach. Canoes and catamarans are available for use, and sailing is popular. There is good diving water right off-shore, and the Reef is not far away. The resort dive shop hires out all gear for snorkelling and diving, runs courses, and provides daily trips to Moore Reef.

Contact the Fitzroy Island Resort on ✆4051 9588 or ✆1800 079 080 (toll free) or visit the website at 👁www.fitzroyislandresort.com.au

Mission Beach

At Mission Beach, about halfway between Townsville and Cairns, a chain of Mountains runs down to the sea, and surrounds the small coastal settlements. Offshore lie the North and South Barnard, Dunk and Bedarra Islands, and beyond them, the Great Barrier Reef. Mission Beach is set on a stretch of 14km of coastline that includes Garners Beach, Bingil Bay, Narragon Beach, Clump Point and Wongaling Beach. There is a daily water taxi service from Mission Beach to nearby Dunk Island, and many visitors choose to stay on the mainland and visit the islands, rather than pay resort prices. The town is named after the Aboriginal Mission that was set up in 1912 at South Mission Beach, but the first settlers were the Cutten brothers who landed to the north at Bingil Bay in 1882 and founded a farming dynasty. They introduced pineapple growing to this part of Queensland and founded tea and coffee plantations. In 1918 the 'cyclone of the century' levelled the settlements and farms in the district. Nowadays the main industries are banana and sugar-cane growing, and tourism.

Four villages comprise the Mission Beach area: South Mission Beach, Bingil Bay, Wongaling Beach and Mission Beach. The region's attractions include 14km of pristine beaches, Dunk Island, the offshore Reef, rainforests, and rafting on the Tully River.

The main activities in Mission Beach involve water sports and reef viewing, so if you wish to view land-based attractions, you will have to travel a little further afield. Here are a few suggestions, and the Visitor Centre can provide you with detailed directions to each.

The **Australian Insect Farm**, Davis Road, Gurradunga, ✆4063 3860, offers regular tours daily Tues-Sun, adults ✪$10, children $8.

Paronella Park, Japoonvale Road, Mena Creek, ✆4065 3225, comprises historic rainforest gardens. It is ⏰open 9am-5pm and costs adults ✪$14, pensioners $10 and children $7.

The Australian Sugar Industry Museum, Bruce Highway, Mourilyan, ℗4063 2656, has a wealth of memorabilia from old harvesters to historical photographs.

Johnstone River Crocodile Farm, Flying Fish Point Road, Innisfail, ℗4061 1121, facilitates crocodile breeding and displays wildlife. It is ⏰open 7 days 8.30am-4.30pm, adults ☻$15, children $8, family pass $35.

In addition, trips can be taken to these popular environmental destinations: Tully Gorge, Hinchinbrook Island, Murray Falls and the Atherton Tablelands.

The Mission Beach Visitor Information Centre, Porter Promenade, ℗4068 7066, can be found 100 metres from the post office. The Centre has a wealth of information on every part of the area. They can be contacted by email at ✎ visitors @znet.net.au

Tully

With a population of around 3000, Tully is set at the foot of Mt Tyson, and is the centre of a large sugar cane and banana growing region. The Tully River rapids provide some very fine whitewater rafting and canoeing, and there is plenty of fishing for enthusiasts.

It should be noted that Tully has the highest annual rainfall in Australia (along with Innisfail) of around 3700mm. There is a definite Wet Season which begins in December and peaks in March. During this period it can rain every day, and sometimes all day. People intending to spend their holiday on either Dunk or Bedarra Islands should keep this in mind, since the paradise appeal of tropical islands is somewhat diminished when the rain just doesn't stop.

The **Kareeya State Forest** is accessible via a spectacular drive up the Tully River gorge.

The Tully Information Centre, is on the Bruce Highway in Tully, ℗4068 2288.

Cardwell

Cardwell is a fishing village situated between the mountains and the sea. It is in the middle of a natural wonderland, with world heritage rainforests, waterfalls, swimming holes, wilderness tracks, whitewater rafting, canoeing, crabbing, fishing and prawning. The Cardwell lookout offers panoramic coastal views and there are very scenic drives to Murray Falls, Blencoe Falls, the Edmund Kennedy National Park, Dalrymple's Gap Track and Cardwell Forest.

Cardwell is also the gateway to Hinchinbrook Island, the world's largest Island National Park.

Edmund Kennedy National Park, nestles into the coastline about 4km north of the township. Its features a range from mangrove swamps to open woodland to pristine rainforest. There is a 3km walking track, with wooden boards and bridges for an easy stroll, which serves as the best and safest way to view the region.

The **Cardwell Forest Drive**, is a 9km route that takes in outstanding coastal views, Attie Creek, safe swimming holes, Dead Horse Creek, Spa Pool, and barbecue picnic areas. Allow a full day to appreciate the sights and leisure opportunities along the way.

Nearby natural wonders include **Tully Gorge** and **Dalrymple's Gap**, as well as the **Falls**: Murray, Blencoe and Wallaman (Australia's highest single-drop falls at 305m).

For tourist information, contact the Development Bureau of Hinchinbrook & Cardwell Shires, 77 Townsville Road, Ingham, ©4776 5381.

Paluma

61km (38 miles) north of Townsville, and 40km (25 miles) south of Ingham on the Bruce Highway, the Mount Spec Road turns towards the mountains of the Paluma Range, following the southern boundary of Mount Spec National Park. The road was built mainly by hand during the Great Depression.

7km along the road lies **Little Crystal Creek**, with picnic, barbecue and toilet facilities, and deep pools for swimming.

18km (11 miles) from the highway, at about 900m (2953 ft) is **McClellands Lookout**, also with picnic, barbecue and toilet facilities. Near the lookout is **Paluma Village**, with its Ivy Cottage Tearooms, ©4770 8533.

Also worth a visit is **Paluma Rainforest House** in Lennox Crescent, ©4770 8560.

Dunk Island

Dunk Island, across the bay from Mission Beach, is mostly National Park land, but there is one luxury resort. The island is shaped by rolling hills and deep valleys. It is home to the famous Ulysses butterfly. Dunk Island is also part of the Family group of islands, and its Aboriginal name is Coonanglebah which means "isle of peace and plenty". Captain Cook named it Dunk after Lord Montague Dunk, the Earl of Sandwich, who was the First Lord of the Admiralty at the time. It is the largest island in the group and is sometimes called the Father of the Family Group (Bedarra is the Mother). The island's area is 10 sq km, but 7.3 sq km is national park. The Wet Season, when it is best not to visit, lasts from December to the end of March.

Dunk is very much a family resort

and it has some good high tide beaches, but at low tide they are too shallow and have a lot of weeds. The island doesn't seem to have a significant problem with box jellyfish, but it is wise to keep an eye out during the November-March period.

There are 13km of walking tracks, and the 10km walk around the island rates among the best of any on the Barrier Reef islands.

Bruce Arthur's Artists' Colony is situated just beyond the Resort garden. The colony's longest term resident is former Olympic wrestler Bruce Arthur, who produces large and beautiful tapestries. He and his cohorts lease the land, and have an open house ⊙10am-1pm between Thursday and Sunday (small entry fee) when they chat about the island and their projects, and present their work for sale.

The Great Barrier Reef is an hour away by *Quickcat*, the high-speed catamaran, and there are four reefs to dive: Beaver, Farquharson, Yamacutta and Potter. They have some of the best coral and marine life on the Reef, and feature feeding stations, coral walls, caves, caverns and gardens. Trips to Beaver Reef include glass bottom boat, semi-submersible rides, lunch and onboard dive instruction.

Contact the Dunk Island Resort directly on ©4068 8199, visit the website at ☜www.dunkislandresort. com or email an information request at ✎ visitors@greatbarrier reef.aus.net

Bedarra Island

Part of the Family Group of Islands, Bedarra lies about 6km south of Dunk Island and about 5km offshore. It is privately-owned and is shown on marine charts as Richards Island. Bedarra has an area of one square kilometre, and is a rain-forest with natural springs and plenty of water. It has some very good sandy beaches. Note that it has a very definite Wet Season from December to the end of March, when it can rain every day and sometimes all day. There is a walking track from Bedarra Bay to the resort, which is in fact the only walking track.

Activities which are not included in the resort tariff are: Great Barrier Reef trips, boutique/shop, float plains, game fishing charters, hair salon (available on Dunk Island), private boat charters, sailing charters.

The Bedarra Island Resort can be contacted on, ©4068 8233. There is a web page at ☜www.bedarra island-australia.com with an email address at ✎ visitors@greatbarrier reef.aus.net

Hinchinbrook Island

Hinchinbrook is the world's largest island national park, with over

45,000ha (393 sq km) of tropical rainforests, mountains, gorges, valleys, waterfalls and sandy beaches. It is one of the most beautiful tropical islands in the world and offers some of the best bushwalking in Australia. A magnificent jagged mountain range drops to warm seas and coral reefs, dominating the skyline. The rainforests offer spectacular views.

The island is separated from the mainland by Hinchinbrook Channel, a narrow mangrove-fringed strip of water that is very deep. From further out at sea, the channel cannot be seen, and in fact, when Captain Cook sailed past he did not record the presence of an island.

The best walk on any of the Great Barrier Reef islands is the three to four day walk along the eastern side of Hinchinbrook, but it is strongly recommended that information be obtained from the National Parks and Wildlife Service in Cardwell (near the jetty), ℂ4066 8601, before setting out. They can advise you on facilities on the island, give tips for climbing the mountains and protecting your supplies from the local wildlife, and issue permits for camping.

Remember that marine stingers may be around in the October-May period, and that crocodiles may be found in channel waters and estuaries.

Apart from the resort, the island has limited camping at ✪$3.50 per person per night (permit required, ℂ4066 8601). **Macushla Camping Area** - patrols, picnic tables, shelter shed, toilets, fires prohibited. Walking tracks, ocean swimming beaches, fishing spots, rainforest areas. **Goold Island** - patrols, picnic tables, shelter shed, toilets, fires prohibited. Fishing and swimming.

For further information, contact the Development Bureau of Hinchinbrook & Cardwell Shires, 77 Townsville Road, Ingham, ℂ4776 5381. Alternatively, call the Island Resort on ℂ4066 8585. Updated information is provided at ☞www.hinchinbrookresort.com.au

Orpheus Island

This island is mostly national park, but has a secluded resort at one end. Orpheus Island is encircled by wide beaches and a warm shallow sea. A fringe reef possesses a rich variety of marine life and provides excellent diving.

Orpheus Island has an area of 14 sq km and is the second largest in the Palm Island group. There are ten main islands in the group, but eight of them are Aboriginal reservations and permission must be obtained to visit. Orpheus is National Park while Pelorus, the other island not part of the reserve, is Crown Land.

The island is 80km north of

Townsville and roughly 20km off Lucinda Point near Ingham. It was named in 1887, after the HMS *Orpheus* - the largest warship in Australia, which sank off New Zealand in 1863 with the loss of 188 lives. Orpheus is long and narrow and its fringing reef is probably the best of all the resort islands. It is heavily wooded and is home to a large population of wild goats. The goats were introduced many years ago as food for people who might be shipwrecked on the island, but they have obviously not been needed and have multiplied to the point where they are causing some problems.

There are a few beaches on the island, although some, such as Hazard Bay and Pioneer Bay, are only suitable for swimming at high tide. When the tide is out they become wading pools. Mangrove Bay and Yankee Bay are good places to swim at low tide. Good reefs are found off Pelorus Island to the north and Fantome Island to the south. The Resort dive shop offers local dives and diving courses, but remember that these activities are not included in the Resort tariff. There are many opportunities for bush walking and rainforest study, and snorkelling, as always, remains popular.

As far as bushwalks are concerned, there is a shortage of them on this island. One traverses up to Fig Tree Hill, and the other winds from Hazard Bay through a forest to Picnic Bay.

The zoning for most of the water around Orpheus is Marine National Park B, although part of the southwest coast is zoned 'A'. So limited line fishing is allowed in the 'A' part, but collecting shells or coral is strictly forbidden.

The **Orpheus Island Resort**, ©4777 7377, has 31 rooms that are rated 4-star.

Camp sites are found at Pioneer Bay and Yankee Bay. They are patrolled, and have picnic tables, toilets and drinking water. For further information and booking, get in touch with the Rainforest and Reef Centre, Bruce Highway, Cardwell, ©4066 8601, or call Naturally Queensland on ©3227 8187. Campers cannot buy meals at the Resort, and fires are not permitted on the island, so if you are intending to camp bring all your provisions, including water and a fuel stove.

Magnetic Island

Magnetic lies 8km across Cleveland Bay from Townsville, fifteen minutes by catamaran. It is roughly triangular in shape and has an area of 52 sq km. With 16 beaches, plenty of reasonably-priced places to stay, and an ideal climate, this is one of the most popular islands on the Reef. The island's first visitor was Captain Cook in 1770, and he declared it Magnetic Island, believing that it had interfered with his compass. The island now has a permanent population of more than 2200 people, and draws millions of holiday-makers.

It is one of the largest islands on the Great Barrier Reef, and 70 percent of it is National Park. A high spine of mountains covered by forests of eucalypts and wattles, and strewn with granite boulders, runs across the island. Below the peaks lie sheltered white beaches, rocky coves and coral reefs.

More than 22km (14 miles) of walking tracks lead over and around hills to secluded coves and quiet bays. The four small settlements of Picnic Bay, Nelly Bay, Arcadia and Horseshoe Bay offer a plentiful range of services for the visitor. You will also find an aquarium and a koala sanctuary.

Box jellyfish are present around Magnetic between October and April, so during this time it is wise to swim only in the netted areas at Picnic Bay and Alma Bay. The north coast of Magnetic is zoned Marine Park B, so fishing is not permitted. There are quite a few good diving locations on the island's southern and eastern shores.

For details about other attractions on the island, contact either the Magnetic Island Tourist Information

Above: Islands in the Great Barrier Reef   Below: Coral on the Reef

Shute Harbour in Queensland's far nort

Bureau and Central Booking Office, 26 The Grove, Nelly Bay, ℰ4778 5596, or the Magnetic Island Holiday and Information Centre in Picnic Bay Mall, ℰ4778 5155. They can advise on your tour bookings, accommodation, vehicle hire, travel arrangements and the best way to climb Mt Cook (497m).

Home Hill and Ayr

The twin towns of Home Hill and Ayr are 90km (56 miles) south of Townsville on the Bruce Highway, and sit either side of the delta of the Burdekin River, slightly inland from the coast. The Burdekin is the main waterway of the Magnetic North, and its catchment area includes the mountains to the north and the goldfields to the west.

The **Ayr Nature Display**, 119 Wilmington Street, Ayr, ℰ4783 2189, has stunning displays ranging from reptiles to butterflies, birds to insects and fossils to shells. Admission is ✪$3 adults and $1.50 children, and the Nature display is ◔open 8am-5pm daily.

The river and its tributaries offer some of the best **freshwater fishing** for barramundi, grunter and bream in Australia, while the river delta and Alva Beach tempt the salt water fisherman with whiting, flathead and salmon. The Burdekin River is also the hub of other river-based activities from water skiing to picnicking.

The wreck of the SS *Yongala* lies 20km (12 miles) out to sea and is a fine diving site.

Cape Upstart National Park, some 70km (43 miles) from town, is an imposing granite headland rising from the sea.

The Burdekin Tourist Information Centre is in Plantation Park, on the Bruce Highway, Ayr, ℰ4783 5988.

Charters Towers

The Outback is just on the other side of the mountains. If you wish to divert from your coastal holiday for a while, the old gold rush town of Charters Towers can be reached 135km (84 miles) south-west of Townsville on the Flinders Highway. Now a town of 12,000 people, Charter Towers was once home to more than twice this number.

Three itinerant prospectors discovered gold in 1871, and between then and 1911, some seven million ounces of gold were taken from the region. The memories may be growing dim, but the town looks much the same as it did a century ago. Historic buildings line the streets and remnants of the gold mining era dot the surrounding countryside. In recent years a few small scale operations recommenced, and some gold was extracted from the area.

The **Venus Gold Battery**, in

Milchester Road, contains a restored gold crushing mill which operated for a century. It is ☺open from 9am-5pm daily with guided tours available. Admission prices are ✪$4 adults and $2 for children.

The **Zara Clark Museum and Military Display** is at 36 Mosman Street. The aim of the complex is to enshrine the history of Charters Towers, particularly the nostalgia of its gold rush era. There is a range of memorabilia, and some interesting period photographs. It is ☺open from 10am-3pm daily and costs adults ✪$4 and children $2.

Ravenswood is about 60km east of Charters Towers. It is also a heritage town and another centre of the gold rush. Although it once had no fewer than 55 pubs, it now has a population of less than one hundred. The town seems largely untouched by time.

Burdekin Falls Dam is a large catchment area that now provides the once dry cities of the coast with a plentiful water supply. Nearby, *Burdekin Dam Holiday Park Motel*, ✆4770 3178, offers accommodation and activities for patrons, $45-55 for two.

For more information contact the Charters Towers Dalrymple Tourist Information Centre, 74 Mosman Street, Charters Towers, ✆4752 0314. You can email them at ✍ tourinfocentre@httech.com.au

The Hinterland

The Hinterland is to the north, sweeping towards the Gulf. Volcanoes once peppered the area, and the vast underground **Undara Lava Tubes** have become a notable attraction. The trip from Charters Towers to Undara covers a distance of about 380km (238 miles). From Charters Towers, take the Gregory Development Road north to Greenvale, then on to Lynd Junction, then a further 93km (58 miles) along the same road. Turn left onto the Gulf Development Road and travel towards Mt Surprise before taking another left turn at the signposted Undara turn-off. From there it is 15km (9 miles) to the *Undara Lava Lodge*, which has bed & breakfast for ✪$109 per person per night, ✆4097 1411. They offer several different tours of the Undara Experience, starting from ✪$33 adults, $16.50 children for two hours, up to a full day tour for $93 adults, ✆1800 990 992 for reservations.

There is a website at ☞www.undara-experience.com.au, which you can check out beforehand to see if you think the attraction is worth the long drive.

Bowen

Situated just north of the Whitsunday Islands, Bowen is a town where the ocean laps the edges of the main street. It is 210km (130 miles) south of Townsville on the Bruce Highway, and has one of the best climates in Australia. The surrounding coast is indented with innumerable small headlands and quiet coral beaches. Inland, the Don River Plain is a fruit growing region.

The Bowen Historical Society Museum, 22 Gordon Street, ©4786 2035. In it you will find shipwreck relics, information on early pioneers and indigenous artefacts. It is ⏱open 10.30am-4pm Mon-Fri and 10.30am-12pm Sunday and costs ✪$3 adults and $1 for children.

Bowen's stunning coastline encapsulates its attraction for visitors. Of particular note are idyllic **Horseshoe Bay** and **Murray Bay**. **Queens Beach** is also a popular haven.

In the southern area of Bowen, swimming, fishing, diving and snorkelling are year-round activities, and for those who prefer to stay on terra firma, there is fossiking for sapphires, amethysts, crystals and opalised woods.

The Bowen Visitor Information Centre is on the Bruce Highway, Bowen, ©4786 4222.

Queensland - North

Cairns

Population 130,000
The Far North Queensland region extends from Cardwell in the south to the Torres Strait in the north, and west across the Gulf of Carpentaria to the Northern Territory border, an area of 377,796 sq km (145,829 sq miles) which is almost twice the size of the state of Victoria. Cairns, its major city and service, administration, distribution and manufacturing centre, has recorded the second highest percentage of population growth of any Australian city since 1979. In fact, it was named Australia's most livable regional centre back in 1995.

Climate

Average temperature: January max 32C (90F) - min 24C (75F); July max 25C (77F) - min 16C (61F). The humidity is high in summer, and the best time to visit is from May to October.

Characteristics

Cairns, in the heart of the tropical wonderland, is an international tourist mecca. It is a modern, colourful city situated on the shores of a natural harbour, Trinity Inlet, with a magnificent backdrop of rugged mountains covered with thick tropical rainforest.

The major glamour activity in Cairns is Big Game Fishing, and numerous fish over 450kg (992 lb) are caught each year. The game fishing season starts in early September and continues through to late November, however light game can be caught all year round.

As well as being a major city for tourism, Cairns is an important centre for the export of sugar and the agricultural products of the Atherton Tablelands.

The city was named after William Wellington Cairns, the third Governor of Queensland.

How to Get There

By Air

Ansett, ✆13 1300, and Qantas, ✆13 1313 have frequent daily flights to Cairns from major southern ports.

Sunstate Airlines, ✆13 1313, operate daily flights to/from Cairns, Cooktown and Thursday Island, along with scheduled services to other centres.

Flight West, ✆1300 130 092, is another option when travelling internally around northern Queensland. Cairns International Airport accepts many international airlines including Qantas, Thai International, Air Nuigini, Continental, Air New Zealand and Japan Airlines.

Cairns' Domestic and International airports, ✆4052 9703, are approximately 6km from the centre of the city. Regular coach services depart from the domestic terminals for the city and the northern beaches, and there is also an inter-terminal coach service.

By Rail

The Queenslander and The Sunlander operate regular services from Brisbane to Cairns. Both services provide sleeping berths, sitting cars, dining and club cars, and a lounge car. Single economy fares for The Queenslander are ✪$142 adults and $71 concession, and passengers have the option of taking their private vehicles on this service. Single economy fares for The Sunlander are ✪$177 adults and $106 concession. The Brisbane to Cairns trip takes about 32 hours on these fast and luxurious trains. For more information, ✆132 235.

By Bus

Greyhound Pioneer, ✆13 2030, and McCafferty's, ✆13 1499, operate regular daily express coach services from major southern cities.

By Road

From Brisbane, via the Bruce Highway, it is a four day trip covering 1,720km (1,070 miles).

From the north, access is via the Captain Cook Highway.

Visitor Information

The Visitors Information Centre is on the Cairns Esplanade (near the pier complex). ☉Open 7 days, 9.30am-5.30pm.

For information relating to all areas in North Queensland, contact Tourism Tropical North Queensland on ✆ 4051 3588 or at ✒ttnq@tnq.org.au. If you wish, visit the website at ⊕www.tnq.org.au

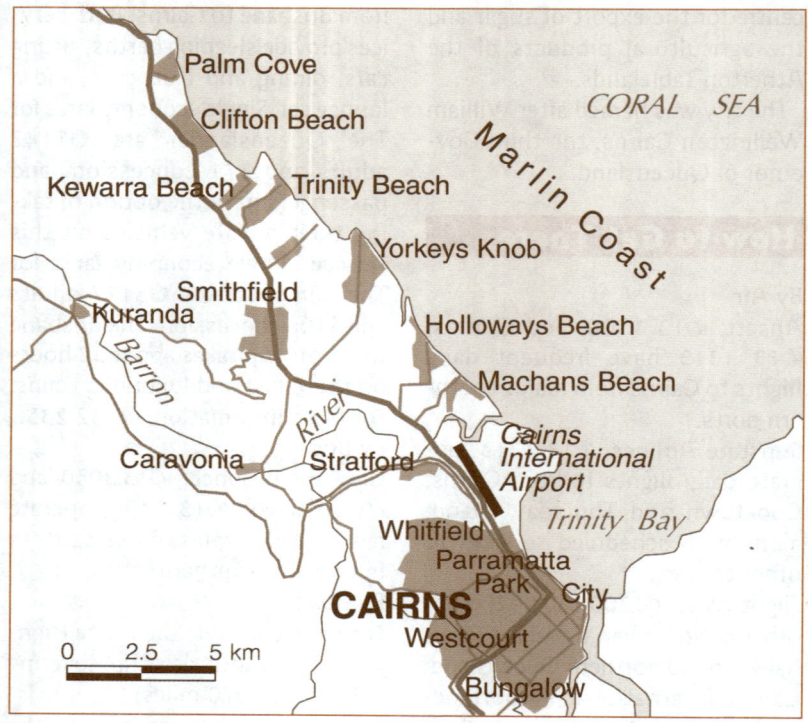

The Great Barrier Reef Visitors Bureau has developed a web site encompassing the entire region, with detailed and up-to-date information on accommodation, sightseeing, tours and more for every major locality. The address is ☞www.greatbarrierreef.aus.net with email at ✐visitors@greatbarrierreef.aus.net

Accommodation

The Cairns area has over 40 motels, as well as hotels, guest houses, holiday apartments and over 20 caravan parks. Prices vary considerably depending on the standard of accommodation and the season. Here we have a selection, with prices for a double room per night, which should be used as a guide only. The telephone area code is 07.

Radisson Plaza, Pierpoint Road, ✆4031 1411. 219 rooms, 22 suites, licensed restaurants, swimming pool, spa, sauna, gym - ✪$370-405.

Hilton Cairns, Wharf Street, ©4050 2000 or ©1800 222 255 (toll free). 260 rooms, 5 suites, licensed restaurant, 3 cocktail bars, coffee shop, barbecue area, swimming pool, fitness centre, spa, sauna, beauty salon, shopping, tour desk, garage parking - ✪$230-320.

Holiday Inn Cairns, cnr Esplanade & Florence Street, ©4050 6070. 232 rooms, 6 suites, licensed restaurant, bars, swimming pool - ✪$260-290.

Cairns International Hotel, 17 Abbot Street, ©4031 1300 or ©1800 079 100 (toll free). 339 rooms, 18 suites, licensed restaurant (closed Sunday), cocktail bars, coffee shop, entertainment, barbecue area, swimming pool, fitness centre, spa, 2 saunas, beauty salon, shopping, tour desk - ✪$320-430.

Righa Colonial Club Resort, 18 Cannon Street, Manunda, ©4053 5111. 145 units, licensed restaurants, 3 swimming pools, tennis court, courtesy coach transfers and shuttle to and from the city - ✪$220.

Bay Village Tropical Retreat, 227 Lake Street, ©4051 4622. 63 rooms, licensed restaurant, room service, bar, swimming pool, courtesy coach to airport - ✪$125.

Club Crocodile Hides Hotel, cnr Lake & Shields Streets, ©4051 1266. 70 rooms with private facilities, some with shared facilities, swimming pool, spa, bistro, bars, 24 hour security - ✪$85-120 per person (including light breakfast).

Ocean Blue Resort Cairns, 702 Bruce Highway, ©4054 7383. 36 units, licensed restaurant, bar, swimming pool - ✪$110

Country Comfort Outrigger, cnr Abbott & Florence Streets, ©4051 6188. 90 units, licensed restaurant, bar, coffee shop, swimming pool, spa - ✪$110-130.

Acacia Court, 223 The Esplanade, ©4051 5011. 150 hotel style rooms, 16 motel units, licensed restaurant, lounge, bar, swimming pool - ✪$99-110.

Flying Horseshoe, 281 Sheridan Street, ©4051 3022. 51 units, licensed restaurant, swimming pool, spa, games room - ✪$90-105.

Cairns Holiday Lodge, 259 Sheridan Street, cnr Thomas Street, ©4051 4611. 35 units, licensed restaurant, swimming pool, courtesy bus - ✪$85-95.

G'Day Tropical Village Resort, 7 McLachlan Street, Manunda, ©4053 7555. 68 studio units, licensed restaurant, swimming pool - ✪$90.

Great Northern, 69 Abbott Street, ©4051 5966. 33 rooms, air conditioning, cooking facilities - ✪$90-120.

Cairns Tropical Gardens, 314 Mulgrave Road, ©4031 1777. 55

units, licensed restaurant open Mon-Sat, pool, spa, sauna - ✪$65-85.

A1 Motel, 211 Sheridan Street, ✆4051 4499. 31 units, 1 suite, licensed restaurant and bar, swimming pool - ✪$70.

Adobe, 191 Sheridan Street, ✆4051 5511. 15 units, licensed restaurant, room service, swimming pool - ✪$55-85.

Caravan Parks

Cairns Coconut Caravan Resort, cnr Bruce Highway & Anderson Road, ✆4054 6644. (No pets) 279 sites, recreation room, barbecue, playground, cafe, transfers, tennis, pool, mini golf, basketball - powered sites ✪$28 for two, cabins $50-85 for two, units $80-95 for two.

First City Caravilla Caravan Park, Little Street, ✆4054 1403. (No pets) 100 sites, barbecue, playground, kiosk, mini golf, pool - powered sites ✪$22 for two, cabins $50-75 for two.

Cairns Villa & Leisure Park, 28 Pease Street, Manunda, ✆4053 7133. (No pets) 163 sites, recreation room, lounge, barbecue, playground, shop, pool - powered sites ✪$17-25 for two, units $55-70 for two, cabins $50-65 for two.

Crystal Cascades Holiday Park, Intake Road, Redlynch, ✆4039 1036. 92 sites, recreation room, barbecue area, salt water pool, spa - powered sites ✪$21 for two; villas $65-80 for two.

There are two **Youth Hostels** in the area: **Cairns Esplanade**, 93 The Esplanade, ✆4031 1919. 18 rooms, ✪$22 per person twin share; and **Cairns-McLeod Street**, 20-24 McCleod Street, ✆4051 0772. 30 rooms - ✪$21 per person twin share.

Local Transport

There are public transport services to all Cairns city areas, suburbs and beaches. Timetables and routes are available at hotels and bus depots.

Cairns City Airporter, ✆4031 3555, have an airport/city/airport service, and bookings are essential for trips to the airport. They also have vehicles available for charter.

Coral Coaches, ✆4031 7577, have daily services between: Cairns, Hartley Creek, Port Douglas, Mossman, Daintree, Cape Tribulation, Bloomfield, Cooktown - Inland and Coast Road. They also have airport transfers to/from: Northern Beaches, Port Douglas, Mossman and Cape Tribulation.

Whitecar Coaches, ✆4051 9533, service the Atherton Tabelands and Chillagoe.

Car Hire

Avis, 135 Lake Street, ✆4051 5911, and Cairns International Airport, ✆4035 9100.

All Car Rentals, 30 Grafton Street, ✆4031 6322.

Cairns Tropical Rent-A-Car, 141 Lake Street, Cairns, ✆4031 3995.

Hertz, 436 Sheridan Street, Cairns, ✆4053 6701.

Mini Car Rentals, 150 Sheridan Street, Cairns, ✆4051 6288.

Peter's Economy Rent-A-Car, 36 Water Street, Cairns, ✆4051 4106.

Cairns Leisure Wheels, 314 Sheridan Street, Cairns, ✆4051 8988.

National Car Rental, 135 Abbott Street, Cairns, ✆1800 350 536.

Honeycombs Cars & 4WD's, 303-307 Mulgrave Road, Cairns, ✆4051 9211.

Entertainment

Cairns has nightclubs, discos, karaoke bars, theatre restaurants, live theatre and cinemas. There are street musicians and all types of performing artists in and around the shopping areas, taverns and bars.

Club International & My Karaoke Bar, 40 Lake Street, ✆4052 1480.

Sports Bar, 33 Spence Street, ✆4041 2533.

The Beach Nite Club, 78 Abbott Street, ✆4031 3944.

The Cat House Night Club, 78 Abbott Street, ✆4051 6322.

Because the weather is quite warm at night there are always lots of people to be found along the Esplanade, eating at pavement tables, or picnicking on the lawns.

Cairns also has a couple of clubs

who welcome visitors and offer free temporary membership for those who live more than 40km from the club.

Brothers Leagues Club (Cairns), 99 Anderson Street, Manunda, ©4053 1053.

The Yacht Club, 4 The Esplanade (between Hilton Hotel and Great Adventures), ©4031 2750.

roam around the markets, creating a really festive atmosphere.

The Pier Marketplace is ©open daily 9am-9pm, but most of the shops in the city centre are open Mon-Thurs 8.30am-8pm, Fri 8.30am-9pm, Sat 8.30am-5.30pm, Sun 3-8pm. Those in the suburbs have shorter hours with night shopping on one night only.

Shopping

There are plenty of shopping opportunities in Cairns. The large hotels have boutiques offering imported fashion items and jewellery, and then there is *The Pier Marketplace*, ©4051 7244, in Pierpoint Road. The Pier is a landmark in Cairns. The building contains the Radisson Plaza Hotel and a specialty retail leisure centre.

It has separate theme walkways, the most glamorous of which is the Governor's Way, where Cairns' best fashion stores and boutiques are found. The main entrance leads to Trader's Row, which has a colonial air and some appealing shops that are not the usual 'high fashion'.

The *Mud Markets* are held on Saturday and Sunday in the main amphitheatre of the specialty retail centre, and local artisans and artists set up stalls selling all sorts of interesting objects from handcrafts to glassware. Live entertainers

Eating Out

Cairns has some of the best eating places in Queensland. Most of the international standard hotels and motels have at least one restaurant as well as a bistro, or the like. There is also a good selection of restaurants, some of which can be found along the Cairns Esplanade, where you can enjoy both the meal and views of the natural harbour inlet. Here is a selection of restaurants in the area:

Tawny's Seafood Restaurant, Marlin Parade, ©4051 1722. Seafood specialists with an a-la-carte menu. Open 5.30pm-midnight 7 days, closed on Public Holidays.

Golden Sun Inn, 313 Kamerunga Road, Freshwater, ©4055 1177. Chinese cuisine, BYO and licensed. Open 5pm-10pm every day except Tuesday and Public Holidays.

Tandoori Oven, 62 Shields Street, ©4031 0043. Open 6.30pm-10.30pm daily, closed Sunday and

Public Holidays.

Thai Pan Restaurant, 43-45 Grafton Street, ✆4052 1708. Licensed and BYO, take-away and free home delivery available. Open 6pm-8pm every day.

Cosmo On The Bay, The Esplanade Centre, ✆4031 5400. Cosmopolitan dining, seafood is a speciality. Open 5.30pm-11.30pm daily, and for lunch and extended hour on Thursdays, Fridays and Sundays.

Jango Jango Club Restaurant, Level 1 Palm Court, 34 Lake Street, ✆4031 2411. Asian influenced fare and karaoke. Open 6pm-2am daily.

Brothers Leagues Club (Cairns), 99 Anderson Street Cairns, ✆4053 1053. Betting and gambling facilities. Open 9am-11pm daily except on Public Holidays.

The Sorrento, 70 Grafton Street, ✆4051 7841. Italian cuisine, pizza, seafood and steak.

Red Ochre Grill, 43 Shields St, ✆4051 0100. Modern Australian cuisine with seafood and outdoor dining facilities. Open 10am-11pm Mon-Sat, 3pm-11pm Sunday and Public Holidays.

Aphrodisias Restaurant, 82 Sheridan Street, ✆4051 5871.

McDonalds is in both the Cairns Central Shopping Centre and on the Esplande. KFC is at Shop 5, 71-75 The Esplanade and at the corner of Mulgrave and Florence Streets. Pizza Hut is on the corner of Aurnullar Street & Mulgrave Road, ✆13 1166.

Points of Interest

There are no sandy beaches in Cairns itself, only mudflats, but prolific birdlife gathers here. Palms line many streets, with parks and gardens displaying a riot of colour from bougainvillaea, hibiscus, poinciana and other tropical blooms. The old part of town is to be found around Wharf Street and The Esplanade. The National Trust has put out a walking tour brochure about this part of town.

The Esplanade is 5km (3 miles) long and runs along the side of the bay. This park-like area is a very pleasant place to relax in the cooler part of the day.

The Flecker Botanic Gardens, Collins Avenue, Edge Hill, are ◷open daily and feature graded walking tracks through natural rainforest to Mount Whitfield. From here there are excellent views of the city and coastline.

The **Centenary Lakes**, Greenslopes Street, Cairns North, are an extension of Flecker Botanic Gardens and were created to mark the city's centenary in 1976. There are two lakes - one fresh water, the other salt. Bird life abounds and barbecue facilities have been provided. Mount Mooroobool (610m

- 2000 ft) in the background is the city's highest peak.

The Pier Marketplace hosts live entertainment daily, and is the departure point for most reef cruises and fishing boat charters. Sit on the verandah for a quick snack or a delicious meal from one of the many food outlets, while checking out the magnificent views over Trinity Inlet.

The Royal Flying Doctor Base, 1 Junction Street, Edge Hill, ©4053 5687, has fully guided tours, film shows, and displays of the history and present operations of this legendary service. ⊙Open seven days.

Sugarworld Waterslides, Mill Road, Edmonton, ©4055 5477, is 14km south of Cairns City centre, and has tropical horticulture, a licensed restaurant, tours, rides and waterslides.

The Reef Hotel Casino, 35-41 Wharf Street, ©4030 8888, offers what all casinos offer: a glitzy way to part with your money.

The **Cairns Convention Centre**, cnr Wharf & Sheridan Streets, ©4042 4200, may have a function on at the time of your visit.

Festivals

The festival season begins with the Mareeba Rodeo in early July and then onto the Cairns Show for three days of entertainment.

The Cairns Amateur Horserace Meeting is held in September, and the week-long Fun in the Sun Festival is in October.

Sports

All types of water sports are catered for, as well as the usual sporting activities.

Diving
The following companies in Cairns offer diving trips and lessons.

Pro Dive, 116 Spence Street, ©4031 5255. 5 day learn to dive courses are held 4 times weekly. 3 day/2 night liveaboard cruises 4 times weekly - PADI 5-Star facility.

Deep Sea Divers Den, Wharf Street, ©4031 5622. Dive and snorkel trips, dive courses (beginner to instructor level), diving/fishing charters on the Outer Barrier Reef.

Taka 2 Dive Adventures, 131 Lake Street, ©4051 8722. Offer dives in Cod Hole, Ribbon Reefs, Coral Sea - liveaboard, departs bi-weekly.

Great Diving Adventures Cairns, Wharf Street, ©4051 4444. PADI open water dive courses available on tropical Fitzroy Island, including accommodation, meals, transfers and certification - other great dive locations include Norman Reef and Michaelmas Cay, both on the Outer Barrier Reef.

Tours

Cairns is a staging place for tours to the Great Barrier Reef, the Islands, the Atherton Tablelands, the Barron Gorge, Cooktown and Cape Tribulation. Here are a few.

The *Cairns Explorer* bus leaves from Lake Street Transit Mall every hour 9am-4pm Mon-Sat. It visits Wescourt shopping, Earlville shopping, Freshwater swimming hole, Freshwater Connection, Mangrove Boardwalk, Botanical Gardens, Flying Doctor and Centenary Lakes. For bookings and enquiries, ✆4033 5344.

Wait A-While Environmental Wildlife Tours, 5 Alkoo Close, Bayview Heights, ✆4033 1153. Day/night wildlife tours - the best way to see the rainforest, birds and animals of North Queensland - small groups, 4WD, experienced guides - departs 2pm daily and costs adults ✪$145.

Tropic Wings Luxury Coach Tours, 278 Hartley Street, ✆4035 3555. Specialise in day tours around Cairns and The Tropical North - Atherton Tablelands, Port Douglas & Daintree, Cape Tribulation, Chillagoe, 3 day Outback and Gulf.

Down Under Tours, Cairns, ✆ 4035 5566. Offer tours to Kuranda, Daintree/Port Douglas, The Tablelands, Cairns and Orchid Valley, Weatherby Station (outback).

Australian Pacific Tours, 278 Hartley Street, Cairns, ✆4041 9419 or ✆1300 655 965 (reservations). They have an extensive range of half and full days tours, as well as extended tours from 2 to 12 days.

Wilderness Challenge, 15 Tranguna Street, Trinity Beach, ✆4055 6504. 4WD adventure safaris from 1 to 14 days or charters - travel to Cape York, Hinchinbrook, Cooktown, Daintree, Kakadu, Lava Tubes, and more.

Billy Tea Bush Safaris, 94 Upper Richardson Street, Whitfield, ✆4032 0077. 1 day to 14 day safaris available to Cape York, Alice Springs, Ayers Rock, and more.

Oz Tours Safaris, Captain Cook Highway, Smithfield, ✆4055 9535. 7, 9, 10 and 12 day overland/air or 16 day all overland Cape York safaris. Both camping and accommodated options available - also Cairns-Cape York-Thursday Island.

Barrier Reef Cybertours, Shop 9, 7 Shields Street, ✆4041 0666.

Cairns Eco-Tours, 85 Lake Street, ✆4031 0334.

Cairns Harley Tours, ✆0417 45 4962 (mobile).

Cruises

Sunlover Cruises, cnr Tingara & Aumuller Streets, ✆4050 1333. Luxurious travel aboard Super-Cats to Moore or Arlington Reef - most innovative reef pontoons afloat, underwater theatre and marine touch tanks, free guided snorkelling tours, delicious buffet lunch - free semi-sub (Moore Reef), Supa Viewer (Arlington Reef), and glass bottom boat rides - all levels of diving catered for - optional helicopter and sea plane joyflights (Moore Reef only) - free guided rainforest walk on Fitzroy Island.

Ocean Spirit Cruises, 33 Lake Street, Cairns, ©4031 2920. Daily departures aboard the *Ocean Spirit I* or *Ocean Spirit II* sailing vessels, to either Michaelmas or Upolu Cay - delicious tropical seafood buffet available.

Big Cat, Pier Marketplace, ©4051 0444. Has cruises that depart daily from The Pier at 9am and travel to Green Island - snorkelling, glass bottom boat tours, lunch served on board, submersible reef coral viewer, guided snorkel tours - return Cairns 5pm - from ✪$70 adults.

Captain Cook Cruises, Trinity Wharf, © 4031 4433. Offer 3, 4 and 7 day Reef Escape cruises every week - cruise to Hinchinbrook and Dunk Islands, or Cooktown and Lizard Island.

Coral Princess Barrier Reef and Island Cruises, Shop 5, 149 Spence Street, ©4031 1041. Sails between Cairns and Townsville, calling at island resorts and uninhabited islands for beachcombing, swimming and a tropical barbecue.

Clipper Sailaway Cruises, 287 Draper Street, Cairns, ©4052 8300. Sail on SV *Atlantic Clipper* - a 140' sailing ship catering for 34 passengers - cruises from Cairns to Lizard Island, Great Barrier Reef, Cape York.

Seahorse Sail & Dive, B16 Marlin Marina, © 4041 1919. Snorkelling, diving, lunch included.

Auspray Seafaris, 125 Aumuller Street, ©4035 3931.

Sport n Game Fishing Charters, 23 Bolton Street, ©4053 1828.

Barrier Reef Luxury Cruises, Marlin Marina, ©4051 3555.

Blue Whaler Charters, Marlin Marina, ©4051 1414.

Scenic Flights

Tiger Moth Scenic Flights, Hangar 8, Tom McDonald Drive, Aeroglen, ©4035 9400 or ©4055 9814 (after hours).

Outlying Attractions

Cape York

This remote mainland spur is Australia's northernmost tip, 2753km north of Brisbane. Like an outstretched finger the peninsula points towards the south coast of Papua New Guinea, just over 100km away on the other side of the Torres Strait. The Jardine National Park hugs the eastern por-

tion of the Peninsula about 50km south of the Cape.

From Cairns, the most direct route is by 4WD only via the Peninsula Development Road which cuts through the eastern side of the peninsula to Cape York. The journey is 861km on the direct route and 1062km if you weave through the National Parks. Road conditions vary with each Wet season, so it is essential that you check current road integrity with the Visitor Information Centre in Cairns, ©4031 4355, or visit the relevant web pages listed in the *Tourist Information* chapter.

Crocodile farming at the **Edward River Crocodile Farm,** ©4060 4177; pearl farming; black boar hunting; barramundi fishing, ©4031 3988; and Aboriginal Corroborees at **Bamaga Mission**, are just a few of the unique attractions Cape York has to offer.

The *Pajinka Wilderness Lodge* is only 400m south of Cape York, ©4031 3988. They have 24 units, resort facilities, a licensed restau-rant and a pool - ✪$460-500 for two, for a three night minimum stay with all meals included.

Several cruises sailing to Cape York and the Torres Strait are available, and this is probably the best way to visit this remote region if you are not the rugged, adventurous type.

For a preliminary look, the web pages to explore are ☞www.tnq.org.au and ☞www.visitcapeyork.com Additional information can be obtained from the Cooktown Tourism Association, ©4069 6100 or ©1800 001 770. Their email address is ✉info@cooktownau.com

Lizard Island

With an international reputation as the place for big game fishing, Lizard Island is 97km (60 miles) northeast of Cooktown and is basically a 1000ha National Park boasting pristine natural beauty. It has an area of 21 sq km, and is the most northerly of the Barrier Reef resort islands. It is 240km from Cairns, but close to the outer Barrier Reef, and has 23 beaches that are good for swimming and snorkelling, and a superb coral lagoon.

Captain Cook and Dr Joseph Banks landed on Lizard Island, after they had repaired the *Endeavour* at what is now Cooktown. They named it after the many large lizards they found there.

Lizard has over 1000ha of Na-

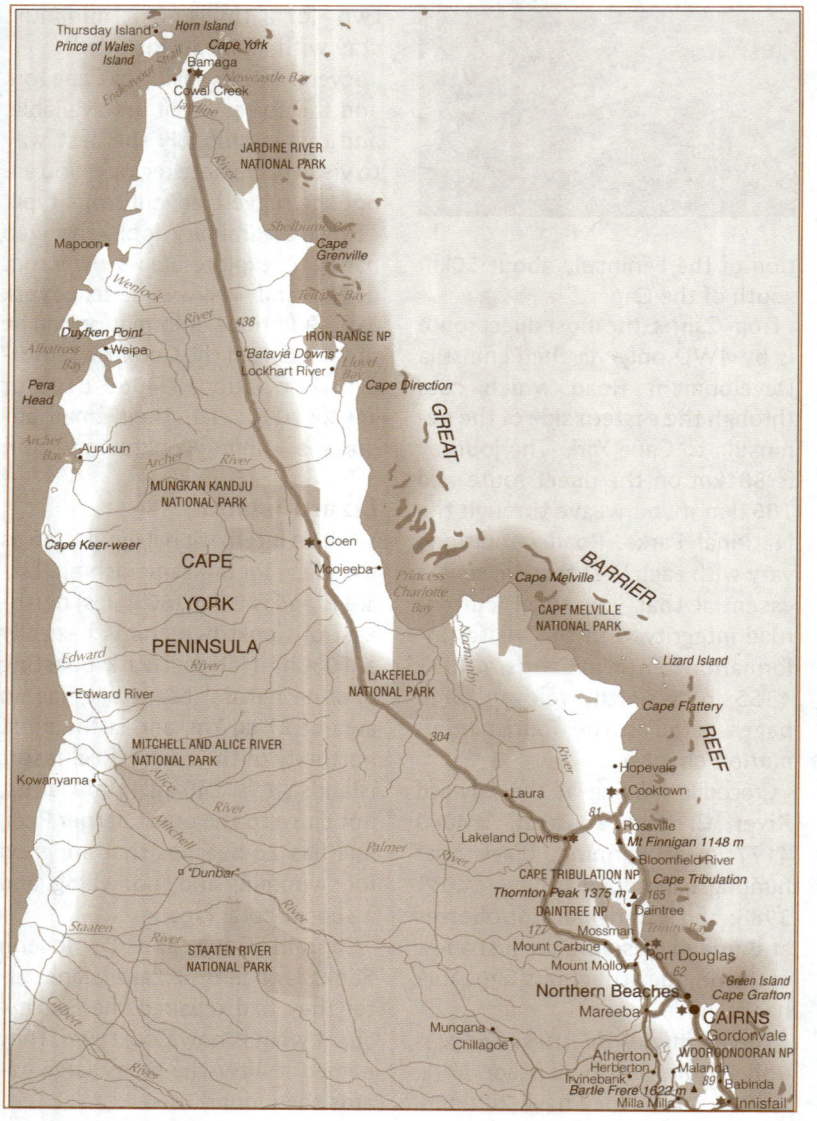

Thursday Island
Prince of Wales Island
Horn Island
Cape York
Bamaga
Cowal Creek
Newcastle Bay
Endeavour Strait
Jardine River

JARDINE RIVER
NATIONAL PARK

Shelburne Bay

Mapoon

Cape Grenville

Wenlock River

438

Temple Bay

Duyfken Point
Weipa
Albatross Bay

IRON RANGE NP
'Batavia Downs'
Lockhart River
Cape Direction

Pera Head

GREAT

Archer River

Aurukun
Archer Bay

MUNGKAN KANDJU
NATIONAL PARK

Cape Keer-weer

CAPE

YORK

PENINSULA

Coen
Moojeeba

Cape Melville

CAPE MELVILLE
NATIONAL PARK

BARRIER

Princess Charlotte Bay

Edward River

Edward River

LAKEFIELD
NATIONAL PARK

Lizard Island

Cape Flattery

Normanby River

304

REEF

Kowanyama

MITCHELL AND ALICE RIVER
NATIONAL PARK

Alice River

Mitchell River

Hopevale

Laura

Cooktown

81

Palmer River

'Dunbar'

Lakeland Downs
Rossville
Mt Finnigan 1148 m
Bloomfield River

Staaten River

STAATEN RIVER
NATIONAL PARK

CAPE TRIBULATION NP   Cape Tribulation
Thornton Peak 1375 m ▲
DAINTREE NP   Daintree
177   Mossman
Mount Carbine
Mount Molloy   Port Douglas

82

Gilbert River

Green Island
Cape Grafton

Northern Beaches
Mareeba

CAIRNS
Gordonvale

Mungana

Chillagoe

WOOROONOORAN NP
Atherton   Malanda
Herberton
Irvinebank   89   Babinda
Bartle Frere 1622 m ▲
Milla Milla   Innisfail

tional Park, and some good walks. The climb to the top of Cook's Look is the most popular, and is well signposted, and from the Resort it is a short walk to the ruins of the Watson's house. The waters around the island are home to coral reefs and countless tropical fish, including the renowned Black Marlin. From August to November it attracts fishermen worldwide.

The Island is very remote and exclusive, with access only via a scenic air one-hour flight from Cairns Airport. You can make arrangements when booking accommodation.

There are no regular ferry or boat services to Lizard Island, but it is included as a destination in some of the cruises run by Captain Cook Cruises, ©4031 4433.

Accommodation is available in 40 well-appointed units facing the beach at the *Lizard Island Resort*, ©07 4060 3999. Tariffs start from ✪$600 twin share per person per night in the Anchor Bay Rooms, to $800 for the Premium Sunset Point Villas. Enquire also about package deals on offer at the time of your trip.

Camping is also available at Watson's Bay, by application and with a permit. Facilities include toilets, drinking water, barbecues and picnic tables. Contact the National Parks and Wildlife Service in Cairns, ©4052 3096, for more information.

Some believe that Lizard Island

has the best diving along the Great Barrier Reef, and in fact it is surrounded by excellent coral reefs.

The Ribbon Reefs lie only a 20 minute boat ride from the island. These are comprised of a string of ten coral ramparts that support an immense undersea world of living coral and sea animals, and the most spectacular underwater scenery. All the Ribbon Reefs are great, but following are a few highlights:

The Code Hole is world renowned and very popular. It is at the northern tip of Reef No. 10, and divers can hand feed giant Potato Cod, some over 2.5m in length.

Pixie Pinnacle is a coral bommie on the southern end of Reef No. 10. Here divers will find species of pelagic fish, black coral, and a host of tropical fish.

Dynamite Pass is a narrow area of water just north of Ribbon Reef No. 10. the depths range is from 4m to 40m below the surface, but visibility is about 30m and there is plenty to see.

Detached Reefs are located in the Coral Sea half-way between Cooktown and Cape York. Both reefs extend from a metre or so under the surface to the seabed some 500m below. This is sheer wall diving at its best with visibility extending more than 40m. Expect to see giant sponges, sea whips, Angelfish, Clownfish, Manta Rays, sharks and varieties of coral.

You can explore the website at ☞www.lizardislandresort.com

Cooktown

Cooktown is 246km north of Cairns. Its close proximity to Aboriginal culture, diverse wildlife, rainforests, unique land formations and extensive surrounding savannah, means that it can be described as the geographical intersection of Reef and Outback. The town is clustered on the banks of the scenic Endeavour River.

Cooktown is etched in history, drawn from the early days of its Aboriginal inhabitants, to Captain Cook's forced landing, to gold rush times and the adventures of subsequent pioneers and explorers.

Apart from the picturesque surrounds, it is worth exploring the historical buildings in Cooktown, including the old Post Office, Westpac Bank and the Sovereign Hotel. The **James Cook Historical Museum** is in Helen Street, ✆4069 5386. Cook's Monument, The Cannon, Grassy Hill and the Chinese Graveyard are additonal points of interest.

Cooktown Tours, ✆4069 5125, will take you by coach on a two-hour guided historical tour of the city for ✪$18 adults, $12 children, departing at 9am.

The Cooktown Tourism Association can be contacted on ✆4069 6100 or ✆1800 001 770. They have a website at ☞www.cooktownau. com and their email address is ✉info@cooktownau.com

Daintree and Cape Tribulation

25km (16 miles) north of Mossman and about 146km (92 miles) south of Cooktown lies the township of Daintree, nestled in the heart of the Daintree River catchment basin, surrounded entirely by the rainforest-clad McDowall Ranges. The Daintree National Park lies to the west and Cape Tribulation National Park to the east; both have flourished largely unspoilt for millions of years. A World Heritage listing now ensures the continued preservation of this 17,000ha region.

Cape Tribulation, where the rainforest meets the reef, is an increasingly popular tourist area for both camping and day visits. Crystal clear creeks and forests festooned with creepers and vines, palm trees, orchids, butterflies and cassowaries, are part of the Cape Tribulation experience in one of the country's finest rainforest areas.

There are several resorts, hostels and camping grounds. The atmosphere is relaxed and 'alternative' in this tropical rainforest retreat. It is a very popular haven for backpackers.

The township has art and craft centres, and the **Daintree Timber Museum & Gallery**, 12 Stewart Drive, ✆4098 6166. The real attraction, however, is the National Park itself.

Given the majestic quality of the natural environment, the emphasis here is on eco-touring. Several cruises operate on the Daintree River offering passengers a leisurely tour observing the beauty of the river and rainforest, and enjoying morning or afternoon tea.

The Daintree Tourist Information Centre is in 5 Stewart Street, ✆4098 6120. The Great Barrier Reef website has a section on Daintree at ☞www. greatbarrierreef.aus.net as does Tourism Tropical North Queensland at ☞www.tnq.org.au

The famous **"bouncing stones"** are just north of Thornton's Beach.

Mossman

171km south of Cooktown and only 20km (12 miles) north of Port Douglas, Mossman is in the heart of the Mossman Valley. It is a sugar town surrounded by green mountains (highest is Mt Demi, 1159m-3802 ft) and fields of sugar cane. Mossman is fast becoming well-known as a centre for exotic tropical fruit growing, and a number of farms conduct tours and offer their products for sale.

The business centre of the Douglas Shire, Mossman has wide tree-lined streets, colourful gardens and a large sugar mill. Guided tours of the **Mossman Sugar Mill**, Mill Site, ©4098 1400, are conducted during the cane crushing season (June to December).

A few minutes' drive from the township, a sealed road leads to the **Mossman Gorge** in Daintree National Park. This is a wilderness area of 56,000ha (138,320 acres), with crystal clear running streams, waterfalls, walking tracks through towering rainforest, barbecue picnic sites and a unique suspension bridge over a steep ravine.

Port Douglas

The 83km (52 miles) drive north from Cairns to Port Douglas covers some of the most spectacular coastal strips and beaches in Australia. The Captain Cook Highway is wedged between towering, lush forest-covered mountains and the Coral Sea. Situated 6km east of the highway, Port Douglas is one of the closest towns to the Great Barrier Reef. It has all the charm of a fishing port tastefully combined with modern tourism facilities. This place draws visitors like a magnet, but as long as you plan ahead there is little chance of you finding yourself without a bed in Port Douglas.

The township was settled in 1877 as the main port for the Palmer River goldfields, and today it is a popular departure point for professional and amateur fishermen, for trips to the outer reef and islands, and for scuba diving and aquatic sports.

Flagstaff Hill offers a great view over Four Mile Beach.

The **Rainforest Habitat** in Port Douglas Road, ©4099 3235, has over 300m of elevated walkways with thousands of butterflies, native birds, crocodiles, koalas and wallabies set among waterways and shaded tropical gardens. They have over 1,000 animals representing more than 140 species. *Breakfast With the Birds* and *The Koala Spot* are two popular attractions. The Habitat is ☺open daily from 8am-5.30pm, with admission prices at ✪$18 adults and $7 children.

Ben Cropp's Shipwreck Treasure Trove Museum, is located on Ben Cropp's Wharf, ✆4099 5488, and houses nautical exhibits of historical significance, including Spanish galleons, a century-and-a-half-old wreck and a lost loot. It is ⊙open daily 9am-5pm and admission is ✪$6 adults, $3 children.

The Bally Hooley Steam Express travels through Mossman and its countryside to the sugar mill. For more details, contact the Information Centre in Grant Street, ✆4099 5051.

The Port Douglas Tourist Information Centre is in 23 Macrossan Street, ✆4099 5599. The relevant website is ✑www.portdouglas. com and there is an email service at ✉reserv@greatbarrierreef.aus .net

Green Island

The island has an area of 15ha and is 27km north-east of Cairns. It is a true coral cay surrounded by coral reefs, and has the only 5-star resort on a coral cay in Great Barrier Reef Marine Park. Incidentally, this island was also named by Captain Cook, after his chief astronomer.

The island grew out of debris washed from its surrounding platform of coral, and is gradually being pushed north-west by prevailing currents. The waters abound with sea life, and the beach is quite beautiful. It only takes about 20 minutes to walk around the island, passing tropical vegetation, fringing casuarinas and pandanus. Green Island is very popular with day trippers.

Green Island's Underwater Observatory is well known. From 5m below the surface, the ever-changing panorama of marine life can be seen through portholes.

Marineland Melanesia, ✆4051 4032, has been the island's main attraction for many years. It is an underwater observatory which also features Cassius, the largest salt water crocodile in captivity. It has interesting displays of Melanesian tribal art, and a collection of early Coral Sea sailing relics. Interest in the observatory draws many people out to Green Island for the day. There are shows at 10.30am and 1.45pm, daily. Marineland Melanesia is ⊙open 9.30am-4.30pm every day and costs adults ✪$8 and children $4.

For information on Green Island, either contact the Green Island Resort directly, ✆07 4031 3300, visit the web page at ✑www.green islandresort.com.au or email them at ✉res@greenislandresort.com. au

Marlin Coast - Northern Beaches

The Marlin Coast area extends from Machans Beach, at the mouth of the Barron River 13km (8 miles) north of Cairns to Ellis Beach, passing by Holloways Beach, Yorkeys Knob, Clifton Beach, Palm Cove and Kewarra Beach. Trinity Beach and Clifton Beach are popular holiday destinations, and Palm Cove and Kewarra Beach have international resorts. All beaches have picnic areas and regular bus services to and from Cairns. Palm Cove and Ellis Beach are regularly patrolled in the summer season by the local Life Saving Club members. Watersporters can hire catamarans, windsurfers and surf skis at most of the major beaches in the area. Countless cruises to the coral creefs are also available, and the Visitor Information Centre can advise.

Two attractions are located on the magnificent Cook Highway, both of which are popular with tourists and locals alike. 40km north of Cairns is **Hartley's Creek Crocodile Farm**, ℂ4055 3576, where admission rates are ✪$16 for adults, $8 children and $40 for a family pass. **Wild World**, ℂ4055 3669 at Palm Cove along the same stretch of road 20 minutes north of Cairns, is a wildlife sanctuary with a hands-on approach. It is ☺open daily 8.30am-5pm and costs ✪$22for adults and $12 for children, with family passes available.

Trinity Beach and Yorkeys Knob have their own web sites: 👁www.trinitybeach.com, email at ✒info@trinitybeach.com and 👁www.yorkeysknob.com, email at ✒hmbr@internetnorth.com.au

For other information on the Marlin Coast, use the same contact details as those listed under Tourist Information for *Cairns*.

The Atherton Tablelands

Inland from Cairns are the fertile Mareeba, Atherton and Evelyn Tablelands, rising in three gigantic steps from the coastal plains. Jungle-fringed volcanic crater lakes, waterfalls and fertile farmlands, coupled with the only temperate climate in the Australian tropics, lure many visitors to the Tablelands each year. Views from the lookouts on the Kuranda, Gillies, Rex and Palmerston Highways are spectacular.

Kuranda, a tiny mountain hamlet in the rainforest, is the first stop-off stage on the Tableland journey. The town can be reached by train from Cairns (ℂ4032 3964) and the ride passes waterfalls and stunning views to the coast before ending at picturesque Kuranda Station. Kuranda has many attractions including **Pamagirri Dancers**, an Aboriginal theatre presenting daily shows based on Dreamtime legends; **Australian Butterfly Sanctuary**, the largest butterfly farm in the world, listed in the Guinness Book of Records; and the **Kuranda Wildlife Noctarium**, which provides a close-up look at the rarely seen nocturnal inhabitants of the rainforests, and guided walks into the jungle. The town's main street is lined with galleries, shops and restaurants. The terraced *Kuranda Markets*, at 5 Therwine Street, are considered the best in the north, ©4093 8772.

The **Mareeba/Dimbulah** district, approximately 66 km (41 miles) west of Cairns, is the largest tobacco growing area in Australia.

Atherton, with its red volcanic soil, is the central town of the Atherton Tablelands. Maize silos dominate the skyline.

Malanda is situated in the heart of tropical Australia's only viable dairying district. The Malanda milk factory boasts the longest milk run in the world, which extends as far as Darwin in the Northern Territory.

Millaa Millaa is the waterfall capital of the Tablelands, taking in the Millaa Millaa, Zillie and Elinjaa Falls.

The **Millstream Falls**, south of Ravenshoe, when in flood are the widest waterfalls in Australia.

Herberton is the north's historic mining town, and tin is still produced in the area.

Irvinebank situated near Herberton, is steeped in history. Its tin crushing plant has been in operation since 1890, and it has other historic buildings.

Ravenshoe is situated on the western side of the Evelyn Tablelands, and is the gateway to the back country and gemfields of the north. It is a major timber town providing some of Australia's most beautiful woods. Close by you will find Koombooloomba Dam and Tully Falls, with many walking tracks to Eyrie Lookout.

Some of the individual Tableland attractions include Tinaroo Dam, the Crater National Park, the twin crater lakes of Eacham and Barrine, the Curtin Fig Tree and Herberton Tin Fields. Further north of the Evelyn Tablelands is the Chillagoe Caves National Park, which is accessible by road and air charter from Cairns Airport, ©4052 9703.

The Tropical Tableland Promotion Bureau has an outlet at the Old Post Office Gallery Information Centre, Herberton Road, Atherton, ©4091 4222. They have a terrific website at ☜www.athertontableland.com and can be emailed at ✎info@ athertontableland.com

Queensland - West

Mount Isa

Population 22,000

Mount Isa is situated on the Leichhardt River in the Selwyn Range, which is the only relief in the north-western flatness. It is 198km (123 miles) from the Northern Territory border, 917km (570 miles) from Townsville, and 1854km (1152 miles) from Brisbane.

Climate

Mount Isa has two distinct seasons - The Wet and The Dry. The Wet lasts from December to March, but the rainfall is not as heavy as further north, averaging 250mm (10 ins) for the four months, compared with the Burketown (about 340km - 211 miles north) average of 700mm (28 ins) for the same period. Average temperatures: January max 37C (99F) - min 24C (75F); July max 24C (75F) - min 10C (50F).

Characteristics

The Isa, as the locals call it, is a modern mining town with over 100 clubs and 70 sporting associations. Because of its isolation, the people of Mt Isa have endeavoured to make life as pleasant as possible, and like other outback towns, it exudes a 'tougher' atmosphere than the coastal cities. This is probably caused by the harshness of the surrounding countryside.

Mount Isa is listed in the Guinness Book of Records as 'The Largest City in the World in Area', and with an area of 40,977km2 (15,817 sq miles), the record will stand for a long time.

How to Get There

By Rail

There is a twice weekly service from/to Townsville, and the Inlander takes 21 hours for the journey

By Road

It is a long, hot drive from anywhere, and if travelling in wet weather, tune in to the local radio stations for the latest road reports. Extreme care should be taken when you meet road trains, which are very long, articulated trucks. It is very dangerous to overtake them, as it takes some time to get past. When possible, the road train driver will move over to let you through.

From Townsville, via the Flinders and Barkly Highways.

From Brisbane, via the Warrego and Landsborough Highways to Cloncurry, then through Mary Kathleen.

From Three Way Junction on the Alice Springs/Darwin road, via the Barkly Highway.

Tourist Information

The Riversleigh Fossil Centre & Mount Isa Tourist Information is at 19 Marian Street, ✆(07) 4749 1555. The website is 👁www. mountisa.qld.gov.au and you can email them at ✉isatourism @mountisa.qld.gov.au

Accommodation

Mount Isa has a good assortment of accommodation and the Tourist Information Centre has a complete list. Here is a selection, with prices for a double room per night, which should be used as a guide only. The telephone area code is 07.

Mercure Hotel Verona, cnr Camooweal & Marian Streets, ✆4743 3024. 32 units, licensed restaurant, swimming pool - ✪$141-150.

Mercure Inn Burke & Wills, Mt Isa, cnr Grace & Camooweal Streets, ✆4743 8000. 56 units, licensed restaurant, swimming pool, spa, gym - ✪$182.

Copper City Motel, 105 Butler Street, ✆4743 2033. 11 units, bbq - ✪$80.

The Overlander, 119 Marian Street, ✆4743 5011. 20 units, licensed restaurant, bistro - ✪$82.

Barkly Hotel, 55-65 Barkly Highway, ✆4743 2988. 40 units, licensed restaurant, swimming pool - ✪$70.

Townview, 116 Kookaburra, ✆4743 8000. 56 units, licensed restaurant - ✪$55-95.

Motel Central Point, 6 Marian St, ✆4743 0666. 19 units, swimming pool - ✪$77.

4th Avenue Motor Inn, 20 Fourth Ave, ✆4743 3477. 25 units, swimming pool - ✪$72.

Inland Oasis, 195 Barkly Hwy, ©4743 3433. 23 units, licensed restaurant (closed Sunday), swimming pool - ✪$70.

Caravan Parks

Copper City Caravan Park, 185 West Street, ©4743 4676. (Pets allowed on application) - powered sites ✪$18 for two, on-site vans $39 for two.

Riverside Tourist Caravan Park, 195 West Street, ©4743 3904. (No dogs allowed) - powered sites ✪$18 for two, park cabins $61 for two.

Sunset Caravan Park, 14 Sunset Drive, ©4743 7668. (Pets on application) - powered sites ✪$18 for two, on-site vans $35 for two.

Eating Out

The Clubs welcome visitors, and most of the pubs serve counter meals. Several of the motels have licensed restaurants, and there are restaurants and takeaway outlets in the centre of town. Below are a few options.

Mystros Restaurant, 26 Miles Street, ©(07) 4749 0388.

Red Lantern Chinese Restaurant, 1 Simpson Street, ©(07) 4743 4070.

Abyssinia Cafe Restaurant, 103 Marianne Street, ©(07) 4749 0655.

Points of Interest

The focal point of the town is the mine and the stacks. The lead smelter stack is 266m (873 ft) high, and can be seen for miles around. Mount Isa Mines employs one in five of the city's population, and most other people in the city are dependent on the mine. Mount Isa Mines Limited is Queensland's largest single industrial enterprise, and its richest.

Mount Isa dates back only to 1923, when the prospector John Campbell Miles found an ore outcrop, which is now marked by an obelisk. His ashes are buried beneath a memorial clock in Marian Street, opposite the Post Office. It was Australia's first company town, and an example of early company housing, a tent house, is on display in Fourth Avenue, and is a far cry from the company house of today. The Tent House is open from April - September, and the Tourist Centre can advise of the hours.

John Middlin Mining Centre is in Church Street, ©4749 1558, and has exhibits of mining methods, historical photographs, rock specimens, examples of ore, film of mining and smelting operations, all contained in an historic building with garden surroundings. It is ☼open daily 9am-4pm.

Surface tours of the Isa Mines

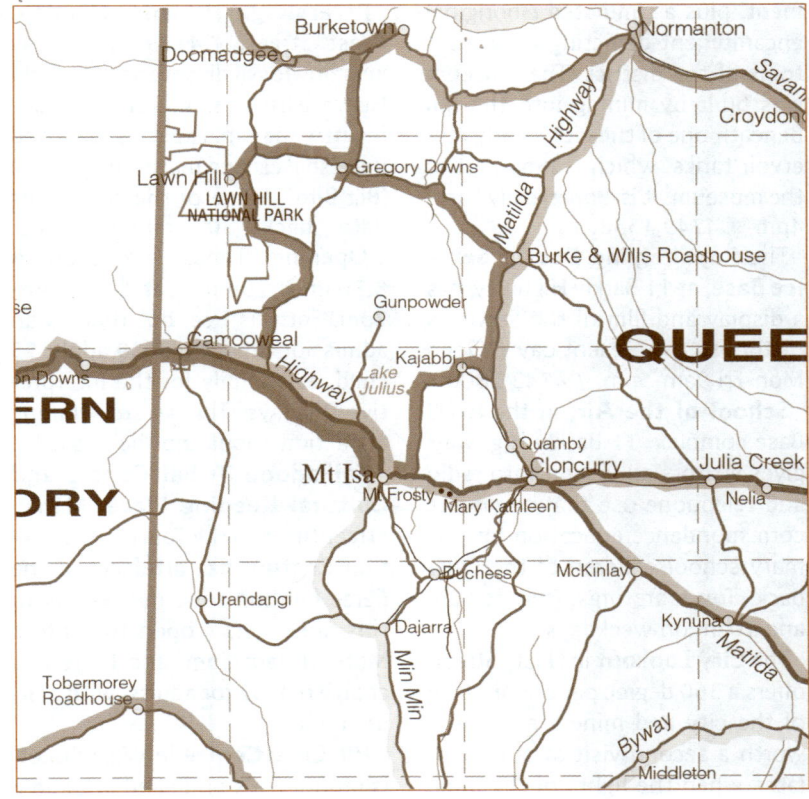

show take you through mine shafts, workshops, mills, smelters and past those huse stacks that dominate the skyline, giving you an insight into some of the processes of the industry andthe equipment used. Costs are ✪$18 adults, $9 children, ©4749 1555.

Underground tours depart early and mid morning Monday to Friday. They are designed to be a hands-on approach to learning about and experiencing life in the mines, covering ladder climbing, encountering and dealing with the dangers of working underground and navigating tricky surfaces. Age and health restrictions apply, ©4749 1555. The cost is ✪$60 per person.

Frank Aston Underground Museum, in Shackleton Street, has displays of early homestead equipment, plus a simulated Aboriginal encampment depicting tribal customs of the district. The museum was built by mining into the hill beneath one of the city's early reservoir tanks, which is now part of the museum. It is ⊙open daily 9am-4pm, ©4749 1558.

The **Royal Flying Doctor Service Base**, at 11 Barkly Highway, has a display and film of the Service's history to the present day. ⊙Open Mon-Fri 9am-5pm, ©4743 2800.

School of the Air, in the RFDS Base complex, 11 Barkly Highway, gives visitors an insight into radio and telephone use that augments correspondence education for primary school children of the Outback. Tours are organised at 9am and 10am on weekdays.

The **City Lookout** in Hilary Street, offers a 360 degree panoramic view of the city and mine area, and is worth a second visit at sunset or later, when the lights of the mine are a spectacle in themselves. The lookout has a global signpost, with distances to cities all over the world, further proof that Mount Isa is a long way from everywhere.

Lake Moondarra, 15.5km (10 miles) north of the city off the Barkly Highway, is a sanctuary and Mount Isa's regular water storage. There are barbecue facilities, children's play area, safe swimming, canoeing, sailing, water-skiing and a kiosk.

Riversleigh Fossils Display, West Street, ©4749 1555, has amazing fossil discoveries of World Heritage listing significance, including new mammal species, bats and huge snakes, and make sure you see 'Big Bird'. Some of the specimens date back 30 million years. ⊙Opening Times are Mon-Fri 8.30am-4.30pm, Sat-Sun 9am-2pm. Entry is free, but there is an admission charge of ✪$9 adult, $5 child, $24 family for the Interpretive Displays. This award-winning attraction should not be missed.

Kalkadoon Tribal Centre and Cultural Keeping Place, Marian Street (next to the Tourist Information Centre), has artefacts of the fierce fighting tribe indigenous to this area. It is ⊙open to visitors Mon-Fri 9am-5pm, and there is a charge of ✪$2 for adults, with children free.

The **Civic Centre** in West Street, is Mount Isa's pride and joy, and a showcase for local and visiting performances, presentations and conferences.

Ray Donaldson Memorial Lookout and Walking Track, at the top end of Pamela Street on the far eastern side of the city, follows the ridge of spinifex hills as far as the Overlander Hotel, and offers some great views.

The Tourist Information Centre has information on several **tours** in and around Mount Isa, including heritage tours (✪$26), tours to Aboriginal rock art sites ($55), scenic flights to the Gulf ($405), horseback trail rides ($45), fishing adventures ($314), and 3-day safari tours to rock art sites and Lawn Hill National Park ($450).

Festivals

The Mount Isa Show is held in June; The Rodeo is in August; the Festival of Arts is in September; and the Oktoberfest and Eisteddfod, are both in October.

Facilities

Mount Isa has very good sporting facilities: boating, lawn bowls, golf, sailing, swimming, tennis, water skiing. Gem fossicking is very popular in the area.

Outlying Attractions

Camooweal
Situated 188km (117 miles) west of Mount Isa, Camooweal is only a few kilometres from the Northern Territory border. It is a supply town for large cattle stations in the vast outback border area. During the 1880s, it was an important stop on the great cattle droves, and today the road trains, which transport the cattle to the coast, still stop at Camooweal.

An interesting attraction here is the Camooweal Caves National Park, featuring an extensive system of caverns and caves with some vertical shafts up to 75 metres deep. Only people with caving experience should enter. Check road conditions before visiting, and it is recommended that you make the trip during the winter. Camping is available in the National Park with a permit obtainable from the Ranger Station in Mt Isa, ©4743 2055.

Lawn Hill National Park
Also known as Boodjamulla, this fertile National Park has a spectacular gorge, scenic sandstone ranges, thriving vegetetation and freshwater springs. The main activities are conoeing and walking. A number of rewarding walking trails, from 2-7km in distance, are outlined on a detailed pamphlet by Queensland Parks & Wildlife, available from the Visitor Centre in Mt Isa. To book camp sites, ©4748 5572.

Mary Kathleen
The now deserted town of Mary Kathleen is 60km (37 miles) east of Mount Isa. It was established in the 1950s to mine the then largest known deposit of uranium in Australia. The mine was closed in 1963, reopened in 1976 and modernised, then finally closed again in 1982.

Cloncurry

Locally known as 'The Curry', Cloncurry is 124km (77 miles) east of Mount Isa. The surrounding hills hide many old ghost towns, and ruins of early copper mines. The area was a big copper producer until Mount Isa was developed. Maps of the ghost towns are available from the Court House for those who wish to explore, or to try their hand at gem fossicking. Most of these areas are only accessible by 4WD vehicles. Gold is also found in small amounts around the area.

It was here in 1928 that the Flying Doctor Service had its beginnings, and a Cloister of Plaques has been erected to commemorate its pioneers on the site where the first pedal wireless call for help was received.

The Mary Kathleen Memorial Park is situated at the eastern end of the town. The park contains a museum housing one of the best rock collections in Australia, as well as memorabilia of Mary Kathleen, and explorer Robert O'Hara Burke's water bottle. The park is ☉open daily 8am-5pm.

Beside the highway where it crosses the Corella River, 43km (27 miles) west of Cloncurry, is a cairn commemorating the ill-fated Burke and Wills expedition to cross the continent from south to north in 1860-61. At nearby Lake Corella there are picnic and barbecue facilities. The lake was formed to supply the former mining town of Mary Kathleen.

The highest official shade temperature, 53.1C (127.58F), was recorded in Cloncurry in 1889.

Cloncurry's Merry Muster is a weekend event preceding Mount Isa's Rodeo in August.

A popular swimming hole, about 9m (30 ft) deep with practically no shallows, is found at Mount Frosty, which can easily be reached in dry weather. An old limestone mine is nearby and the area is ideal for gem fossicking. On the Burke Development Road, 378km (235 miles) north of Cloncurry, is Normanton, the main centre for the Carpentaria Shire. The town was established in 1868, and has a population around 930. It is situated on the Norman River, 50km (31 miles) from the coast as the crow flies, and was once an important port. The wharf has long since rotted away, and the cattle are now transported to the eastern seaboard by cattle trains. Here is found the only rail line not linked to the main system in Queensland, and once a week there is a service between Glenore and Croydon, a distance of 132km (82 miles).

The Cloncurry Information Centre can be contacted on ✆(07) 4742 1251.

Karumba

Karumba, on the mouth of the Norman river, is 74km (46 miles) from Normanton by road, and is the centre of the $10 million prawning industry in the southern part of the Gulf of Carpenatria. The trawlers bring the prawns to Karumba, and there they are snap frozen and air freighted to the southern states and overseas.

For more information, contact the Karumba News & Trevel Centre, located in, 63 Yappar Street, on ℃(07) 4745 9187 or visit ☜www. gulf-savannah.com.au

Winton

Situated 343km (213 miles) south-east of Cloncurry on the Landsborough Highway, Winton was the birthplace of QANTAS. The Queensland and Northern Territory Air Service had its first registered office in Winton in 1920, but moved to Longreach, 180km (112 miles) south-east.

Winton is synonymous with sheep, and there is a cairn on Winton's town common commemorating the Great Shearers' Strike of 1891-4. In nearby Elderslie Street is Herb Young's wagon, the last horse drawn wagon to bring wool to Winton's railhead. Road trains now bring cattle from the Channel Country and the Northern Territory to the railway.

Banjo Paterson wrote "Waltzing Matilda" at Dagworth Station in the Winton area in 1895, and a statue of a swagman has been erected in commemoration near the swimming pool. In Elderslie Street is the Waltzing Matilda Centre, ℃4657 1466, a large complex housing Station Store, the Billabong Complex, the Home of the Legend exhibition, the Qantilda Museum, the Outback Regional Art Gallery, and the Coolibah Country Kitchen Restaurant. Contact the Centre for further information on the town.

Other attractions in town include the National Trust classified Corfield & Fitzmaurice Store, the Royal Theate, Arno's Wall and Opal Walk.

At Castle Hill, west of Winton, is Australia's hottest artesian bore, at 78.95C (174F).

Dinosaur footprints can be viewed from a suspended walkway at Lark Quarry, 5km off the Winton Jundah Road, 105km (65 miles) south of Winton.

Index

Maps Index

Photo Credits

Australian Road Trips
35 Complete Holiday Drives Around Australia

35 easy-to-follow road trips take you on some of the most scenic drives around the country.

All the information you require about where to go, what to see, what to do, what to take and how to get there, developed for the average traveller.

Many peope have thought about taking an Australian road trip, but most aren't sure where to start. Other travel guides give information on towns and national parks, but fall short of detailing how to get there, while street directories show you the way but don't tell you why to go. **Australian Road Trips** is a comprehensive combination of the two. It's aimed at the average traveller who has little or no knowledge of extended touring by car, and who doesn't necessarily have a 4WD sitting in his or her driveway. The 35 road trips have been carefully selected to ensure that traveller's experience the true Australia, and most are suitable for conventional vehicles.

Australian Road Trips takes you out of the 'comfort zone' and into the inland areas, and the less-populated places of the north, south, west and upper-east coast. Spectacular routes take you through the Barossa Valley, Margaret River, along the Great Ocean Road, up to Cape York, into Uluru-Kata Tjuta National Park, Kakadu, the Kimberley, around Tasmania, and through hundreds of towns and countless scenic landscapes.

Australian Road Trips is everything you need to explore the continent. So you don't have to put if off any longer.

By Ian Read • 190 x 220mm • 432 pages • paperback with flaps
2-colour text • 2-colour maps throughout
Little Hills Press • ISBN 1 86315 169 9 • $34.95rrp